The Fall of the Pagans
and the Origins
of Medieval Christianity

Kenneth W. Harl, Ph.D.

PUBLISHED BY:

THE GREAT COURSES
Corporate Headquarters
4840 Westfields Boulevard, Suite 500
Chantilly, Virginia 20151-2299
Phone: 1-800-832-2412
Fax: 703-378-3819
www.thegreatcourses.com

Kenneth W. Harl, Ph.D.

Professor of Classical and Byzantine History
Tulane University

Professor Kenneth W. Harl is Professor of Classical and Byzantine History at Tulane University, where he has taught since 1978. He earned his B.A. from Trinity College and his M.A. and Ph.D. from Yale University.

Professor Harl teaches courses in Greek, Roman, Byzantine, and Crusader history from the freshman to graduate levels. A recognized scholar of coins and classical Anatolia, he takes Tulane students to Turkey on excursions and as assistants on excavations of Hellenistic and Roman sites.

Professor Harl has published numerous articles and is the author of *Civic Coins and Civic Politics in the Roman East, A.D. 180–275* and *Coinage in the Roman Economy, 300 B.C. to A.D. 700*. His current work includes publishing the coins from the excavation of Gordion and a new book on Rome and its Iranian foes. Professor Harl also serves on the editorial board of the *American Journal of Archaeology*.

Professor Harl has received numerous teaching awards at Tulane, including twice receiving the coveted Sheldon Hackney Award for Excellence in Teaching (voted on by both faculty and students) and receiving the Student Body Award for Excellence in Teaching on multiple occasions. He was also the recipient of Baylor University's nationwide Robert Foster Cherry Award for Great Teaching. In 2007, he was the Lewis P. Jones Visiting Professor in History at Wofford College.

Professor Harl is also a fellow and trustee of the American Numismatic Society. ∎

Table of Contents

Table of Contents

Table of Contents

The Fall of the Pagans
and the Origins of Medieval Christianity

Scope:

T he conversion of the classical world to Christianity is one of the
fundamental changes in Western civilization that has been matched
only by the discovery of the New World and the industrial revolution.
This course will explain the reasons for the clash between the pagans and
the early Christians that ended in the Christianizing of the Roman world
between the 4th and 6th centuries A.D.

The opening lectures define paganism and explain the piety and the appeal
of the pagan cults of the Roman world. It is often assumed that these cults
were inferior to Christianity in their cosmology, spiritual values, and moral
precepts and therefore doomed to fail before the superior faith of Christianity.
Scholars writing under the influence of Franz Cumont (1868–1947) have
long argued that many pagans discarded the empty communal cults of
their ancestral gods either for the charismatic mystery cults, with their
promises of moral rejuvenation and ecstatic rites or, for the intellectuals, the
doctrines of Stoicism and Platonism. This vision of paganism has, in the past
generation, been called into question in the light of ever-growing evidence
from archaeology, inscriptions, documentary papyri, Roman legal texts, and
coins, as well as a reexamination of classical texts.

A more modern view sees mystery cults as simply cults with initiation rites
that were neither exclusive in membership nor distinct in their rituals and
sanctuaries from the civic and family cults. Instead, the major change in
pagan worship was the Hellenization or Romanization of cults. Provincials
in the eastern provinces assimilated their native cults to those of Hellenic
ones, whereas the provincials in the western provinces interpreted their gods
in Roman guises. All communities across the Roman world also linked their
ancestral gods to the veneration of the spirit (*genius*) of the emperor who, on
his death, would be enrolled among the gods.

To the Romans, the Christians presented a unique threat by their proselytizing among pagans to deny worship of the ancestral gods. In contrast, Jews were perceived by Romans as practicing a legitimate religion that posed no such threat. In turn, Christians had to come to terms with both the Roman state and the pagan cults. Therefore, the next six lectures deal with how Romans and Christians clashed, why Roman authorities singled out Christians for persecution, and what institutions Christians evolved to ensure their survival in a hostile pagan world.

Christians claimed to be the third race, distinct from Jews and pagans. In the two centuries before the conversion of Constantine, Christians were restricted in their efforts of proselytizing. Christianity had been outlawed as a superstition in A.D. 64; then the Roman governor of Bithynia-Pontus in 112–113, Pliny the Younger, created the sacrifice test and judicial proceedings to punish Christians. Persecutions were sporadic, local outbreaks; martyrs numbered at most in the dozens rather than the hundreds. Far more significant was the emergence of monarchical bishops in the apostolic churches, who also determined which texts were canonical and consistent with what would become mainline Christian doctrines.

Bishops held together their churches in times of persecution. The theologian Origen, in his *On First Principles*, expounded the Christian faith in Platonic terms so that henceforth Christianity was ever more accorded by intellectual pagans the status of a philosophy rather than superstition. These developments were far more significant than winning numbers of converts because bishops and theologians could explain to Constantine why he had converted and why he should promote the new faith.

Four lectures are devoted to the crucial turning point in the 3rd century, between 250 and 313, when emperors conducted empire-wide persecutions to compel Christians to sacrifice to the gods. While apologists claimed the blood of the martyrs was the seed of the church, pagan authors, such as Galen of Pergamum and Celsus, were unimpressed. Romans, long accustomed to the cult of blood in the arena, viewed Christian martyrs as criminals and outcasts who worshiped a weak god unable to protect them. For Christians, the persecutions defined their faith, and martyrs became examples to follow. At the same time, faith in the ancestral gods did not wane. The soldier-emperor and reformer Diocletian, who ended a military crisis, sponsored a revival of the cults. Neoplatonic thinkers, commencing with Plotinus, devised henotheistic schemes of cosmology consistent with the ancestral cults and interpreted myths and rituals in moral terms in the system known as theurgy.

Paganism was spiritually and intellectually vibrant when on October 28, 312, Constantine converted to Christianity. The emperor's conversion offers the best insight into how many pagans could be brought to consider the Christian god legitimate and powerful. His conversion proved a decisive turning point. The final lectures, comprising the last third of the course, therefore concern the Christianizing of the Roman world between the reigns of Constantine (306–337) and Justinian (527–565). Constantine effected a religious revolution. He created the imperial Christian church, giving bishops the means to claim control of the empire's cities and its high culture for the new faith. He also relocated the Roman autocracy, with its powerful bureaucracy and army, at a new Christian capital, Constantinople. At the same time, in the deserts of Egypt arose the ascetics and monks who defined holiness in a Christian society and became the missionaries who converted villages and towns across the Roman world.

Although pagans were long in the majority, they failed to reverse Constantine's revolution during the reign of the pagan emperor Julian the Apostate (360–363). With Julian's death and failure, Christian emperors ever more suppressed the pagan cults, promoted missionaries, and supported bishops in turning pagan cities into Christian ones. Later emperors, prelates, and monks not only completed the conversion of the Roman world, but created the new world of medieval Christendom. ■

Religious Conflict in the Roman World
Lecture 1

The traditional narrative of the conversion of the Roman world to Christianity is of the inevitable success of a superior religion over a corrupt and declining faith—a narrative inherited from the first scholar of Christianity, Eusebius. Our task in this course will be to take a closer look at the vision of Rome's history we have inherited from Eusebius and reexamine a host of different sources—Christian, Jewish, and pagan—to understand this great historical change.

The Conversion of Constantine

- On October 28, 312, the Roman emperor **Constantine** defeated a rival named Maxentius, who controlled the city of Rome, in an ambush at the **Milvian Bridge**, just north of the city. This battle was not particularly remarkable in its fighting, but it was significant because on the previous day there had been a miracle.

- **Eusebius**, the first historian of the Christian movement, wrote an account of this battle that he claims was given to him by Constantine himself, although he wrote it some 30 years after the event. According to to Eusebius, the day before the battle, Constantine and his entire army saw the skies part and saw an image of the **Christogram**,

Constantine's conversion revolutionized Roman culture.

©Photos.com/© Getty Images/Thinkstock.

the Greek letters chi (χ) and rho (ρ), the first two letters of "Christ" in the Greek alphabet.

- Along with this came a message in Latin: *In hoc signo victor eris*, "In this sign, you will conquer." Constantine thus put the Christogram on his labarum, or banner, and won the battle under a Christian symbol.

- Eusebius hailed Constantine's conversion as the triumph of Christianity. This report of Constantine's conversion, however, has produced a lot of controversy among scholars and popular writers. Many have questioned Constantine's motives. But there was little doubt until quite recently that his conversion was the final act of a rising powerful Christian movement.

- In some ways, accepting the interpretation that Constantine gave his approval to a successful, important Christian movement produces more problems than it solves given the existing evidence: He did not make Christianity Rome's official religion; that was Emperor Theodosius I, three generations later (391–392). He did not ban pagan worship or close pagan temples. Above all, he was a pragmatist.

- It is now clear, to scholars at least, that there were far fewer Christians in the Roman world in 312 than has previously been assumed. Christians did not occupy any significant positions in the imperial government or the army.

- Even more perplexing, Constantine's nephew, Emperor Julian, was baptized and reared as a Christian but embraced the worship of the old gods at the age of 20 and sought to restore their worship when he took the throne. Had he not died in battle after a brief reign, he might have reversed the conversion of the empire.

- Therefore, our task is to explain how the Roman world became Christian. This is a fundamental question because the Roman world at the start of the empire—more or less the time of the birth of Christ—was a traditional, hierarchical, conservative society in which the vast majority of peoples worshiped ancestral gods, bound up with rites, traditions, and social values that went back centuries.

In the Footsteps of Eusebius

- The conversion of the Roman world to Christianity between the 1st and 6th centuries A.D. was a major turning point in the Western tradition. This change would dictate the course of Western civilization thereafter.

- Eusebius is the prime source for the conversion of the empire; in fact, he is the only narrative account of the first three centuries covered in this course. He compiled many of the original documents that explained the rise of the Christian movement.

- There was never a doubt in Eusebius's mind that Christianity was the superior faith, that pagan cult statues were idols, and that Christians were the heirs

Eusebius was a Christian and a contemporary of Constantine.

The Teaching Company Collection.

to the Hebrew prophets. He also has a vision of a single Christian church. Yet Christians were by no means unified even well after Constantine's conversion.

- Eusebius drew upon the writings of earlier Christian authors, notably the **apologists**—authors who wrote early defenses of the faith. Two of the earliest apologists we know of are Justin Martyr and Tertullian.

- Justin and Tertullian agreed that the blood of the martyrs is the seed of the church. Thus the Roman imperial government, which persecuted Christians starting in A.D. 64, was actually assisting the spread of the faith. For every Christian martyr who went into the arena and died for his faith, many pagans were moved to inquire about Christianity, perhaps even to convert.

- This vision of the power of martyrdom is presented by Eusebius and has influenced modern and popular scholars down to this day. This course will question this vision.

- Eusebius continued to influence scholars into the 19th and 20th centuries. These include Adolf von Harnack, author of *The Mission and Expansion of Christianity in the First Three Centuries*. Von Harnack did a major service to all scholars by compiling an enormous array of Christian and pagan sources for others' use.

- The most brilliant exposition of Eusebius's position drawing on von Harnack's work was by British scholar W. H. C. Frend, *Martyrdom and Persecution in the Early Church*.

The Differing Perspective of Classical Scholars

- Scholars with a classical background come at the question from a different angle and look at the issue of paganism and religious change in general. One such crucial work by Arthur Darby Nock is called *Conversion*; it looks at the various forces bringing about religious change in the Roman world between the reigns of Alexander the Great and Constantine.

- Nock argues that the paganism of Rome is not the paganism of Greek mythology. Numerous pre-Roman cults—neither Greek nor Roman in origin but part of a wider Roman world, from the British Isles to North Africa—acquired a classical tinge. Thus the diversity of paganism at the time of the Roman Empire was considerable.

- Nock was also one of a number of important scholars who argues that there may already have been a spiritual crisis in the Roman world at the time of Jesus—a decline or flight from the beliefs in the traditional gods. This approach was pioneered by another leading scholar, Franz Cumont.

- Cumont studied the god Mithra, or Mithras, who was worshiped in the Roman army and by various peoples of the empire but was Persian in origin. Cumont suggested that this Mithras was the same Mithras referred to in the Avesta, the Zoroastrian text.

- Cumont also studied other cults, which he called **mystery cults**. These cults had initiation rites; members chose to join them, whereas traditional cults were a matter of birth or residence.

- Cumont built up an image that dovetails well with notions of spiritual crisis among the pagans: There was a new wave of enthusiastic, irrational cults attracting pagans away from their traditional gods and preparing them (albeit unwittingly) to accept Christianity.

- Some scholars have gone so far as to claim that Christianity was just the most successful mystery cult; this is one of the major positions this course must look at and reinterpret in light of new evidence and new scholarship.

Conversion Was about More Than Religion

- Another important trend noticed by scholars was the development of philosophies, particularly Roman Stoicism and Neoplatonism. This is not a philosophy course any more than it is a theology course, but it is important to understand these doctrines because they were embraced by the literate classes of the Roman Empire and acted as a bridge between the elite and Christianity.

- Christian faith is based on dogma, text, and universal morality and institutions, as opposed to pagan cults that varied from one city to another and from one god to another. How pagan Romans overcame this barrier to conversion will be a major question this course addresses.

- Furthermore, Christians see God as a transcendent being, beyond this world, whereas the pagans see the divine and the human as intermingled in the material world. It was very hard to convince many pagans to worship a transcendent, singular god so distant from Roman cultural and social values. One of this course's tasks is to look at how closely and deeply embedded pagan worship was in the entire fabric of Roman life.

- The modern West has inherited many assumptions from Eusebius, down to the novels of the 19th century and the books and films of the 20th and 21st centuries: *Quo Vadis?*, *Ben-Hur*, *The Passion*, and *The Last Temptation of Christ*, to name a few. This course's primary task is to examine this vision in the light of evidence from Christian, pagan, and Jewish sources and to thoroughly evaluate what we really know about this great historical change.

Important Terms

apologist: Defender; a Christian writer who penned defenses against pagan criticism. The most important of the early apologists were Justin Martyr (103–165), who wrote in Greek, and Tertullian (160–220), who wrote in Latin.

Christogram: The combined Greek letters chi and rho, the first two letters of *Christos*. Before the Battle of Milvian Bridge, Constantine applied this symbol to his military standard (vexillum) and so created a Christian labarum, or banner.

Milvian Bridge, Battle of: The victory of Constantine the Great over his rival Maxentius north of Rome on October 28, 312. Constantine credited his victory to the Christian God.

mystery cults: In older scholarship, this name was given to certain pagan sects seen as ecstatic, irrational cults that displaced traditional worship in anticipation of Christianity. Mystery cults had initiation rites and conformed to general pagan expectations of piety.

Names to Know

Constantine I (a.k.a. **Constantine the Great**; after 280–337; r. 306–337): Emperor who first legalized Christianity in the Roman Empire. Declared emperor by the Western army, Constantine reunited the empire in 324. In 312, after the Battle of Milvian Bridge, he was convinced his victory was the gift of the Christian God and converted to Christianity. The first Christian emperor, he created the imperial church. In 325, he summoned and presided over the First Ecumenical Council at Nicaea, which declared heretical the views of Arius. In his later years, Constantine was won over by the Arians, so that on his deathbed he was baptized by an Arian bishop. He built a new Christian capital at Constantinople on the site of Byzantium in 330.

Eusebius (260–340): Bishop of Caesarea (314–340) and friend of Emperor Constantine. He composed important pastoral theological works, the most important of which was his *Ecclesiastical History*, the prime source for early Christianity. Eusebius set the standard for later Christian historians. He also composed a life of Constantine, the main source for the emperor's conversion in 312, and the *Tricennial Oration* (336), praising Constantine as the ideal Christian ruler.

Suggested Reading

Augustine of Hippo.

Brown, *Body and Society in Late Antiquity*.

———, *The Making of Late Antiquity*.

Cumont, *The Mysteries of Mithra*.

Dodds, *Pagan and Christian in the Age of Anxiety*.

Frend, *Martyrdom and Persecution in the Early Church*.

MacMullen, *Paganism in the Roman Empire*.

Nock, *Conversion*.

Potter, *The Roman Empire at Bay*.

von Harnack, *The Mission and Expansion of Christianity*.

1. How has Eusebius influenced historians to this day on the nature of religious change and conflict in the Roman world? What are the virtues of Eusebius's historical vision? What are the shortcomings of his interpretation?

2. What other sources bear on the religious change and conflict of the Roman world? What are their value and their limitations?

3. Was the demise of paganism inevitable? What were the turning points in the conflict? How has each generation of scholars since the 19th century reinterpreted the conflict?

Religious Conflict in the Roman World
Lecture 1—Transcript

On October 28 in the year 312 A.D., God wrought a miracle for his chosen people, the new Israel. They may have been relatively few in numbers, but the belief is that they were rising in importance and significance in the Roman world. On that day, the 28 of October, the Roman Emperor Constantine defeated a rival emperor named Maxentius who controlled the city of Rome, and a great battle was fought at the historic Milvian Bridge just north of Rome where many important events had occurred earlier in Roman history.

From our literary accounts of the battle, we know that Constantine lured Maxentius into an ill-advised attempt to cross the Milvian Bridge. Maxentius, realizing that his army was much too large to be accommodated by that bridge, had built a second pontoon bridge parallel to it; and so his army proceeded to cross over the north bank of the Tiber and it was ambushed by Constantine's soldiers who had emerged from concealment and drove the initial columns of Maxentius's army back onto those two bridges.

Maxentius himself could do very little to rally his men; his soldiers were panicked. We are told that Maxentius, astride his horse, tried to ride through the ranks, rally his men; he was swept by the crowd of refuges onto the pontoon bridge and the bridge collapsed under the weight of all these frightened soldiers. Maxentius himself was thrown from his horse and later found drowned, and his head was cut off and paraded around Rome. This is what is known as legitimacy in the late Roman world.

This battle was not particularly remarkable in its fighting—in fact, it was pretty typical of the types of battles that were fought in the civil wars of the late Roman world—but it was significant because on the previous day there had been a miracle. Eusebius—who lived between the years 260 and 340 A.D. and is the first historian of the Christian movement—wrote of this battle and his account, he claims, was given to him by the Emperor Constantine himself, although this is some 30 years after the event.

According to Eusebius, Constantine told him that the day before, in the late afternoon, in the failing sun, Constantine and his entire army had witnessed a miracle. Apparently the skies had parted and in a flood of light there was an image of the Chi-Rho; that is, the first two letters of Christ's name in Greek, Christos, or what is often known as the Christogram, which combines the two letters. They look like the English letters X and P. Along with this was apparently an inscription in Latin; one version of it is In Hoc Signo Victor Eris. The Emperor was struck by it, as was the army; they were amazed. Not too long afterwards, the Emperor fell asleep and in that sleep Christ appeared in a dream and admonished Constantine to trust into this symbol; put it on a banner that is known as the labarum; and so Constantine went into battle under a Christian symbol and won a decisive victory. Eusebius, the church historian and bishop, hailed Constantine's conversion as the triumph of Christianity. Constantine was compared to Moses, to David; that is, the new lawgiver, the new righteous king.

The report of Constantine's conversion, particularly this report that has come down to us from Eusebius, has produced a lot of controversy among scholars and popular writers. Many have questioned the motives of Constantine's conversion; some have even questioned the genuineness of it; but there's very little doubt until quite recently that Constantine's conversion essentially was the final act of a rising powerful Christian movement. In effect, Constantine put his seal of approval on important religious changes that had been going on in the Roman world for nearly three centuries.

Eusebius's account is consistent with this vision. In fact, this vision of this interpretation of the rise of Christianity in the Roman world largely hinges on Eusebius's ecclesiastical history, and the Battle of the Milvian Bridge is essentially the climax to the entire movement. However, this vision, which has been inherited from Eusebius, has problems with it; and in some ways, accepting this interpretation that Constantine in effect gave his approval to a successful, important Christian movement produces more problems than it solves with the existing evidence.

For one, we know Constantine did not make Christianity the official religion. Contrary to what one might read in certain popular accounts, this did not come until almost three generations later in the laws of the Emperor Theodosius I in 391–392 A.D. Constantine did not even ban pagan worship or close pagan temples; many of them continued to operate long after his death. Above all, Constantine was clearly a pragmatic emperor as well as a convert. He essentially operated with a policy once attributed to the Emperor Augustus who founded the Roman Empire: He made haste slowly.

It is now clear, to scholars at least, that there were far fewer Christians in the Roman world in 312 A.D. than has previously been assumed. It is also clear that Christians did not occupy any significant positions in the imperial government or the army. What is even more perplexing is that Constantine's nephew, the Emperor Julian, who had been baptized and reared as a Christian—in fact, it was expected that he would become the Bishop of Constantinople—that this young Imperial Prince at age 20 embraced the worship of the old gods and when he became emperor sought to restore the gods.

He failed; but nonetheless, Julian's efforts are an important reminder that the triumph of Christianity was hardly inevitable. As Peter Brown noted—and Peter Brown is probably one of the most brilliant of the cultural and religious historians of the late Roman world in this generation—in a famous *Review* article, Julian, if he had lived for 30 years rather than 3 years, if he had succeeded in his war in Persia under pagan symbols and not died prematurely in a skirmish, and if had left pagan successors, Julian could well have reversed the religious developments in the Roman world. In some ways, what might've resulted—at least Brown suggests this is a possibility—was what we know happened in India, where the Brahmins and the Gupta emperors together rallied the cults of Hinduism and eventually mounted an effort to restore the worship of traditional Hinduism against the challenge of Buddhism.

Therefore, in this course, which is going to consist of 24 lectures, we are going to take as our task a way of explaining how the Roman world became Christian. This is a fundamental question of great importance because the Roman world at the start of the Roman Empire—let us take the year 1 at the time more or less of the birth of Christ; there's a dispute over the precise year of his birth, but when the Roman Empire had been established by the Emperor Augustus at the beginning of the 1ˢᵗ century A.D.—he ruled over a very, very traditional society in which the vast majority of peoples worshiped traditional gods; ancestral gods, Roman, Greek, and otherwise. These gods were all bound up with rites and traditions and social values that had gone back for centuries. Society was hierarchical, it was traditional, and many of the residents of the Roman world were very, very reluctant to give up their view of the divine, their traditional rites, and embrace a new religion, the new faith of Christianity.

The conversion of the Roman world to Christianity between the 1st and 6th centuries is a major turning point in the Western tradition. In my mind, it is one of the four great moments that come to define the Western tradition. The first of those is the emergence of self-government in the Greek city-states and in the Roman republic. The second is, of course, the conversion to Christianity and the whole change in religious and ethical perceptions from a pagan to a Christian, and those changes are going to dictate the course of Western civilization thereafter. The last two, in my opinion, are the discovery of the New World and the expansion of Western civilization overseas due to a number of changes within northwestern Europe and finally the Industrial Revolution and the advent of the modern world as we know it today. Therefore, we are looking at one of those significant moments.

I had mentioned Eusebius, and it is important to note for a moment Eusebius because he is one of our prime sources. In fact, he is the only narrative account we have for the first three centuries of this course because he sat down in the reign of Constantine, put together various documents, and explained the rise of the Christian movement. There was never a doubt in Eusebius's mind that Christianity was the superior faith, that pagan cult statues were idols, and that Christians were the new Israel and therefore the heirs to the Hebrew prophets. He also has a vision of a single Christian church. In fact, our notion of Church comes from Eusebius; and we will see in this course that the Christians themselves were by no means unified even after the time Constantine had converted and summoned the first ecumenical council in 325 A.D. to achieve a unity within the various churches of the Roman world.

In addition, Eusebius drew upon the writings of earlier Christian authors, notably apologists. Apologists are authors who wrote early defenses of the faith. It comes from the Greek word "apologia," which means "a defense," "an exposition." It is a term that is borrowed from Greek philosophy and Greek literature; the most famous apologia is, of course, Plato's rendition of the defense that Socrates gave at his trial before an Athenian jury in 399

B.C. The word has changed into an excuse in modern English, but "apology" or "apologia" in its Greek sense means a concerted defense of any kind of position.

Two of the earliest apologists that have come down to us are Justin the Martyr in Greek and Tertullian, a powerful intellect, one of the earliest Christian writers, in Latin. They both agreed that the blood of the martyrs is the seed of the church. That means that the Roman imperial government, which persecuted the Christians starting in the reign of Nero in the year 64 A.D. down to a year after the conversion of Constantine—the final persecution ends in 313 A.D., the year after the Battle of the Milvian Bridge—that these efforts by the Imperial Government to persecute Christians actually turned out to be a rather foolish policy. It backfired; that is, for every Christian martyr who went into the arena and died for his faith, many pagans were moved to inquire about Christianity; perhaps to convert to Christianity. The imperial government unwittingly gave a prominence to the Christian movement that the Christian movement itself could never have achieved. This is a position that is held by many Christian writers of the period of the Roman world, later in the medieval world; and it is a vision that is presented by Eusebius in his narrative account and one that has influenced modern and popular scholars down to this day. We will have reason to question this vision.

As comfortable and powerful as the vision is, again, we have to balance this vision, which comes from a Christian author, with other types of evidence. Nonetheless, this position that was expounded by Eusebius is absolutely important to understand if one is to turn to the issue of how the Roman world became Christian. Some of the earliest modern scholarship, which essentially starts in the late 19th century, is very much premised on this vision. The foremost important book is by Adolf von Harnack, a German scholar writing in the early 20th century. His work was first published in 1902; it was revised in 1924; it was published immediately in English, and the English translation is *The Mission and Expansion of Christianity in the First Three Centuries*.

Von Harnack did a major service to all scholars since. We all have to use his work. Von Harnack went through all the Christian sources and some of the pagan sources available to him—there were certain types of evidence he did not have access to, but all of the literary tradition; that is, all of the literature that has come down to us in antiquity—he culmed those sources and came up with the information available on the nature of the early Christian movement, their numbers, their locations, geography; and it's a real scatter of information. If you're going to start to attack the question, this is still an important work.

The most brilliant exposition of this position drawing on von Harnack's work is written by a great British scholar, W. H. C. Frend, and it is known as *Martyrdom and Persecution in the Early Church*. It was published in 1965. It has been rereleased in various editions. It is a brilliant read. It is a magisterial and well-written work that explains the rise of Christianity against the available sources. Frend does try to take into account some of the pagan sources; but fundamentally, it is a modern version of that vision of Eusebius.

In addition to these scholars who've worked through the Christian material, scholars who are of a Classical background—such as myself, who is giving this course—we have been trained in the ancient texts, the pagan texts, and we come at the question from a different angle. We are not so concerned about Christianity alone, but want to look at the whole issue of paganism and religious change in general. Again, a crucial work in this direction was written by an author Arthur Darby Nock. It was released in 1933, a rather fateful year in European history. The work is titled *Conversion* and it is looking at the various religious forces, social changes, bringing about religious change in the Roman world between the time of Alexander the Great and the time of Constantine. Nock's work was seminal. It raised a whole number of issues as to exactly what was the state of pagan worship at the time of the birth of Christ, at the time of the great persecutions, and finally, at the time of the conversion of Constantine; that is, those three vital centuries that Eusebius writes about in his ecclesiastical history, or his history of the Christian movement (which is probably a more accurate rendition of the work).

In Nock's view, you are not dealing with the paganism of Greek mythology. Instead, you're dealing with the paganism that has undergone a great deal of change, in part due to the conquest of Alexander the Great and the incorporation of the Near East into an expanded Greek world that is usually known as Hellenistic; and then a good part of this Hellenistic world is incorporated into the great Mediterranean empire of Rome. To think of paganism as essentially Greek mythology is extremely misleading. Numerous cults that were pre-Roman and that were neither Greek nor Roman in origin were part of the religions of the wider Roman world. This included the Celtic gods of northwest Europe, the gods of Syria, the ancient gods of the Nile Valley, and the numerous cults of Asia Minor, North Africa, and the Balkan provinces. Some of these cults acquired a Classical tinge; that is, the native cults were identified with Jupiter in the west or Zeus in the east—that is, they took on a Latin or Greek aspect—but again, the diversity of paganism at the time of the Roman Empire was considerable.

Furthermore, Nock was one of a number of important scholars who saw that the developments in pagan worship indicated that at the time of the birth of Jesus there may well have been some kind of spiritual crisis in the Roman world, perhaps already a decline or a flight from the beliefs of the traditional gods. This approach actually worked very well with the vision inherited from Eusebius. If Christianity is arising in an important movement, a significant movement, at the time of Constantine's conversion, it makes even more sense if the traditional gods of the Roman Empire were somehow on the wane. This approach was pioneered by another leading scholar, the fourth I must make mention of because he is so fundamental, and that is a Belgian scholar, Franz Cumont.

Franz Cumont, at the depressing age of 28, wrote a book on the *Mysteries of Mithra*. It was released in 1894 and has been reissued; it's in English translation; and what scholar can count over 100 years later that he still has four major books in print in all the major European languages? Cumont was a brilliant scholar. He understood archaeology. He understood inscriptions—that is, funerary monuments, public monuments inscribed on stone—that are a major source on the Roman world. He looked at all sorts of evidence, and in his first monograph he took as his subject the god Mithra or Mithras; a god worshiped in the Roman army and by various peoples of the Roman Empire, but a god that was Persian in origin who came from Iran.

Cumont made a brilliant suggestion that the Mithras of the Roman Empire was the Mithras referred to in the Avesta, the Zoroastrian text—that is, the ancient Persian god—and that somehow Mithras of Persia had become a Roman god. From that position, he went on to look at other cults that he called mystery cults: cults with initiation rites; cults in which membership was based on registering (choosing to join this cult over the traditional pagan cults that were a matter of birth, a matter of one's residence). Cumont built up an image that dovetails very well with these notions of spiritual demise or crisis among the pagans: There was a new wave of enthusiastic, irrational cults—somehow cults that weren't Classical—that were attracting pagans away from their traditional values and gods and actually prepared them (unwittingly, but prepared them) to accept Christianity. Some scholars have gone so far as to claim that Christianity in effect was just a version of a mystery cult and the most successful of them. This is a position that has been argued by some very serious scholars and by popular writers, and it is one of the major positions we must look at and reinterpret in light of new evidence and new scholarship.

Another important trend that has been noticed by scholars is the development of philosophy, particularly Roman Stoicism and the teaching of Plato; that is, the Neoplatonists. We will be spending time talking about the philosophical systems.

Again, we are not going to engage in a course of philosophy anymore than we're going to engage in a course of theology, but it is important to explain the doctrines of the Stoics and of the Platonists in the Roman world because these were embraced as a moral code by the literate classes of the Roman Empire; they were a way of interpreting the ancient gods morally; and therefore the argument is often made that the philosophical systems, particularly those of the Stoics and of Plato, acted as a bridge whereby the educated and intellectual classes would cross over to Christianity, and this particularly became the case in the 3rd and 4th centuries as the Christians used the same philosophical language and terms to describe their own theology. It is often argued that to some extent we're not dealing so much with a religious conflict per se among the literate classes but almost a debate among Stoics and Platonists as to who has the better interpretation of the divine, those who believe in the pagan gods or those who believe in the Christian God. There is some truth and some merit in this position; but, again, it can be overdrawn.

Our task is to look at this wider issue of religious change. How did a traditional society come to embrace a very, very different view of the divine—a Christian faith based on dogma, on text, on a sense of morality and institutions that were universal from church to church—as opposed to pagan cults that varied from one city to another, from one god to another? Furthermore, there's a major difference in the divine. Christians see a transcendent divine, a divine beyond this world, in which the godhead is beyond time, beyond definition; whereas the pagans see the divine and the human is intermingled on this world. Anyone reading Greek mythology knows that. Zeus is always intermingling with humans, particularly sweet young things of both varieties, which he bushwhacks at various springs; and the usual pickup place in Greek mythology is to go down and do your laundry at a spring, and sure enough Zeus or Ares or some such divinity is going to show up.

That notion of the interpenetration of the divine and of the human was a characteristic of all pagans, and pagans who confronted Christianity really found this transcended god rather peculiar; and to them, it was a rather sad definition of the divine because you're removing the divine from immediate contact. You can't reach him in oracles, in waking dreams, or anything and therefore the world is being emptied of the gods. It would be very, very hard to convince many pagans that a transcended god and a notion of monotheism—that is, a one and single god—really had any kind of validity. The Christians faced a very tough audience. Not only did they have to bring across a new vision of the relationship of mundane and divine, they also had to go against ancestral pagan rites and beliefs that were intimately tied with cultural and social values, particularly in the cities of the Roman world, and one of our tasks is to look at how closely and deeply embedded pagan worship was in the entire fabric of life in the Roman world.

I have raised these questions to give you some sense of what we're going to cover in this course. We're going to be looking at common assumptions of the rise of Christianity; assumptions we've inherited from Eusebius and particularly popular views that have been shaped by novels of the 19th century and movies of the 20th and 21st centuries. We have to step back for a moment and remember that the inevitable rise of a superior Christian system with values of the modern world and all, and taking it for granted that

Christians could spread their word around by preaching as you would have in modern society, has to be reconsidered.

Novels and movies like to play upon this popular image. One of my favorite movies is the movie *Quo Vadis*, based on a famous novel of the 19th century. Its title comes from the St. Jerome's translation of the Greek where Peter is going back to Rome and "Quo Vadis? Where are you going?" It stars Robert Taylor and Deborah Kerr, but it's really stolen by Peter Ustinov, who plays Nero in an absolutely wonderful sequence. It's very much premised on the images that I have been talking about—that Christians could preach; that they could persuade with the superiority of their message—and we will find that there are real liabilities of trying to preach openly to a pagan population. After 64 A.D., Christianity is outlawed; and even St. Paul, before the outlawing of Christianity, ran into major problems if he tried to deny the existence of the traditional gods. You could start riots in cities such as Ephesus with no problem at all, particularly among the craftsmen who were selling various statuettes of the goddess Artemis Ephesia, who's the patron goddess of the city.

There is another fine movie that does bring about at least some sense of how Christianity was linked to Judaism; that's the famous *Ben-Hur*. It comes from the novel of Lew Wallace. Some of you who are Civil War buffs know that Lew Wallace lost the Third Division at Shiloh and when he wasn't writing his novel *Ben-Hur*, he was going back to Shiloh to justify why he did not show up on the first day of battle. That aside, Charlton Heston plays Judah Ben-Hur; he does a great job. I always think that Jack Hawkins as the Roman Quintus Arrius probably does a better job in stealing the movie. But nonetheless, at least it gives some sense that Christianity was linked to the wider Jewish religion; and it's important to stress, and we'll do a whole lecture on Judaism to explain why Judaism played such a decisive role in the Roman world. Jews constituted a major population in the Roman Empire. They were significant in the Eastern Empire. Several times they revolted against Rome, and these were very dangerous rebellions. In addition, Christianity emerged out of Judaism; shared many of the religious assumptions of Judaism; and it is important to understand that the relationship between pagans and Jews also would influence the relationship between pagans and Christians, and particularly the imperial Government and Christians. Some of this has been attempted in more recent films such as Mel Gibson's *The Passion* or Martin Scorsese's *Last Temptation of Christ*, two films that were recently released. All of these films and novels, again, are essentially premised on that vision that goes back to Eusebius.

Our task is to look at these visions that we've inherited from Eusebius; look at a host of different sources—Christian, Jewish, and pagan—to understand this great historical change. The way this course is envisioned is the opening lectures, Lectures 2–5, are going to paint the world of paganism in all of its aspects. I will lay particular stress on Asia Minor, today Turkey, because that is where I do a lot of my work—I know the archaeology, the coinage, the inscriptions very well—and Asia Minor is one of the very well-documented sections of the Roman world. Much of what goes on in Asia Minor is paralleled in much—at least of the Mediterranean provinces—of the Roman world.

Then we need to give a lecture on the relationship of Rome and the Jews, and then follow a group of Lectures (7–11) that establishes early Christianity and its clashes with Rome. The centerpiece is going to be the great persecutions of the 3rd century; those are Lectures 12–15. There we shall test that image of "Were the blood of martyrs the seed of the church?"; that is, did martyrdoms win converts for Christianity and turn Christianity into a mass movement? That raises the significant question with the quote that I started this lecture with: Did Constantine simply give his seal of approval to an effective Christian movement that was rising in numbers and rising in importance or did Constantine, in many ways, create an imperial church and make Christianity a world religion by his act of conversion and his support for that faith? Those are two very different positions, and we will be investigating those positions through the whole course starting with Lecture 2.

Finally, the last portion of the course deals with Constantine's conversion; his efforts to build a Christian monarchy, Christian institutions; the pagan reaction under his nephew Julian; and the final efforts to Christianize the Roman world. We conclude with the reign of the Emperor Justinian in the 6th century where the Roman world has become decidedly Christian in both numbers and culture. This is our task, this is what is before us for the next 24 lectures, and it is without a doubt one of the great issues of the Western tradition.

Gods and Their Cities in the Roman Empire
Lecture 2

P agan worship in the Roman world served not only a religious function but social, economic, and political functions as well. The extraordinary expense of processions and festivals was shouldered by the Roman elite, who were rewarded for their outlay with power and prestige. The syncretic nature of Roman paganism, with its roots in Hellenistic Greece, meant that all local religious customs eventually were subsumed into the support of the state and the worship of the emperor.

The Basic Roman Temple

- We have two major types of evidence for how pagans worshiped in the Roman world from the 1st into the 4th century A.D.: literary evidence and archaeological evidence. These offer a composite idea of how pagans viewed the divine world and how they communicated with their gods.

- There were enormous differences among the cities and peoples of the Roman Empire, which comprised perhaps a fifth of the world's population and stretched from Britain to Egypt. But there were several commonalities. Foremost were their temples and sanctuaries.

- Temples in the pagan world were homes of the gods, not places for congregational worship. All a sanctuary needed was a temenos wall to block out the mundane world and an altar on which to sacrifice. The temple is an addition to a sanctuary where the god's possessions were stored, such as the *kosmos*—the robe put on the cult statue for processions—and votive offerings.

- Temples in the Roman Empire tended to look like a Greek temple in the eastern provinces or an early Roman-style temple in the western provinces. By A.D. 200, most sanctuaries presented a generally uniform look.

Greek temples were intended as places to house the cult statues, not as places for worshipers to congregate.

- The temple to Zeus and Rhea at Aezanis in Asia Minor provides a good example of a Greek-style temple. It is situated on a hill. Around it is the temenos wall and before it is the altar. The temple is the focus of the city; it is a major monument, but it does not match our modern idea of a place to pray or worship.

- The town of Thamagaudi (now Timgad), in modern Algeria, provides an example of a Roman-style temple. The city is a miniature Rome with a temple to Jupiter Capitolinus, a geometric street plan, public baths, an amphitheater complex, and all the standard features of a Roman city. All Roman cities and colonies were built on essentially the same plan.

- The cities of the empire present their temples and sanctuaries in a Roman or **Hellenistic** (Greek) style because that was high architecture—the architecture of the emperors and success. Therefore, long before the arrival of Christianity, change was already taking place in Roman paganism in the form of Hellenization and Romanization.

The Gods of the Cities

- Temples were only one part of pagan worship. Other city monuments were just as important, particularly theaters. These were assembly points for religious worship and political meetings, not just entertainment.

- Equal in importance to temples and theaters were the colonnaded streets because the real worship of the gods involved rituals and processions. These were presided over by the elite members of the society: **decurions**, **equestrians**, **senators**, and ultimately the imperial family.

- We have a description of one such procession in the city of Ephesus, in modern Turkey, from the novelist **Xenophon of Ephesus** in his romance *Ephesian Tale*, or *Anthia and Habrocomes*, written around the 2nd century A.D.

- The main sanctuary—the **Artemision**, dedicated to Artemis Ephesia—is outside the city. On the high holidays, the cult statue was dressed in its *kosmos* and paraded through the city in a sacred cart drawn by stags. It entered through the *magnesia*, or east gate, near the upper agora, or marketplace, and wound around the various districts, ending up at the theater.

- In the theater, sacrifices would be offered to the goddess, and the goddess would make an epiphany, an appearance; the statue would become the receptacle for receiving the divinity. With minor variations, this scenario characterizes all Roman pagan worship: public procession, public ritual, prayer, sacrifice, and the appearance of the deity.

The Festival Distributions

- Above all, these rituals were accompanied by distributions—gifts from the festivals' sponsors to the city's thousands or tens of thousands of residents, including meat, grain, money, and perfume.

- Inscriptions and coins (described from Stratonicea in Asia Minor) report a distribution by a husband-wife team, Tiberius Claudius Aristeas Menander and Aelia Glycinna, who held a festival in honor of the witch goddess Hecate for the entire city. The details of the inscription match the ritual at Ephesus and also describe the distribution.

- The people were summoned to the theater by means of placards placed in the deme—the residential districts. Every citizen was given two denarii, the standard silver coins of the empire. The couple also gave the city 1,000 denarii for the construction and upkeep of the public bath, and Claudius Aristeas's grandfather erected an honorary monument to the city at his own expense.

- Obviously, pagan worship was very expensive, and much of the cost fell on the landed elite, who also controlled the city government. There was no distinct clergy. One more thing Claudius Aristeas and Aelia Glycinna did: They handed out large bronze coins commemorating the festival as well as their own generosity in hosting it.

- Festivals were not always one-time affairs. The importance of these festivals and distributions is borne out by an inscription that was uncovered at the city of Oenoanda, in Asia Minor, around A.D. 125. Gaius Flavius Demosthenes set up an endowment for a four-week festival, including a tax-free market, to be held in perpetuity. Perhaps ironically, the city is abandoned today.

The Family Gods and the Pagan Afterlife

- Family and ancestor worship was widespread in the Roman world. The ancestors were known in Latin as the *maiores*, "the greater ones." There were also ancestral gods, such as the **Lares** and **penates** guarding every Roman household. The herms were the Greek protector spirits.

- Funerary monuments abounded, and a lesser Roman city had a **necropolis**—a city of the dead. Sarcophagi and funerary monuments could be quite opulent but made little comment about the afterlife; rather they were memorials to the family's wealth and position and were virtually public monuments in themselves. Many were guarded with curses against defacement.

- The purpose of these monuments was to do what in Greek is *eudoxos*, or appropriate—to perpetuate the family well-being. This included burying the ancestors appropriately and appearing each year to carry out celebrations with them. One widespread Roman practice was the Rosalia—that is, the placing of roses on a grave.

- This piety is seen in a number of ways in inscriptions. For example, many inscriptions were set up to make sure that everyone arrived on time and the appropriate dinner was arranged at the temple-tomb. Yet these family-oriented practices never developed into private devotional worship; they were always side by side with the public cults.

Faith without Dogma

- The Roman pagans revered the texts of Homer and Hesiod, who revealed the gods, as well as the early Latin texts, but they had no religious canon. They had no authoritative sacred texts. They learned the morality of the gods, as well as rituals, socially.

- Polybius, a Greek historian of the 1st century B.C., was stunned at how pious the Romans were, even compared to his fellow

Greeks. Morality and piety were taught in the home, on the street, everywhere. It was part of the fabric of society.

- Some historians have argued that the Greeks and Romans did not have a sense of right and wrong rather had a shame culture; that is probably going overboard.

Syncretism and the Cult of the Emperor

- **Syncretism** is the process of assimilating local gods into the gods of another (often dominant) culture. The Greeks made equivalents between their gods and the Egyptians', for example. Syncretism is premised on diversity; it is not an incipient monotheism.

- Syncretism in the Mediterranean world started with Alexander the Great, and the Hellenization and Romanization of temple architecture is an example of syncretism as well: Roman and Greek gods are the most powerful; therefore, we will make our local gods' versions of the Roman gods.

- In some instances, the Romans were willing to accept a god that had no equivalent. Pagans in general accepted a new god if its power and validity could be proven. This would be important during the conversion to Christianity.

- In many instances, we find the Roman emperors themselves giving approval to various local gods. The Romans had a very pragmatic view of the gods. By the 1st century A.D., all the gods in the Roman world had essentially been enrolled as Roman protectors and had assumed Roman qualities.

- The Romans had a ceremony known as the *evocatio*, the summoning out, to summon the gods of foes or rebels onto the Roman side. This is an extremely important concept in the Roman world, that all cults are legitimate if they have age and tradition behind them (that is why Judaism was legitimate to the Romans) and that all gods were able to defend the emperor. By extension, city worship and imperial worship were linked.

- Christians not only denied the pagan gods but, as we shall see, they also did not want to venerate the emperor. That meant that the Christian movement from the start was on a collision course with not only the pagan gods but the Roman emperor as well.

Important Terms

Artemision: A temple of Artemis, more specifically the one near Ephesus considered one of the Seven Wonders of the Ancient World.

decurions: The landed civic elites defined as capable of holding municipal office with wealth assessed in excess of 25,000 denarii or one-tenth the property qualification of a Roman senator.

equestrian: The landed property class of Roman citizens (assessed at 100,000 denarii) who stood below the senatorial order in the Principate. They provided the jurists, officials, and army officers of the imperial government.

evocatio: Latin for "calling out"; the Roman ceremony of winning over the gods of a foe with promises of temples and votive offerings. The ceremony was performed by a magistrate with imperium—the right to command an army.

Hellenistic: Greek-like; the period between the death of Alexander the Great and the Battle of Actium (i.e., 323–31 B.C.). It also denotes the civilization of this period, which was fusion of Hellenic and Near Eastern traditions.

Lares: The guardian spirits of Roman homes, settlements, and roads.

necropolis: Greek for "city of the dead"; cemeteries outside the walls of a Greek or Roman city. This was intended to prevent ritual pollution of the living.

penates: Roman guardian spirits of the hearth.

senator: A member of the aristocratic families of Rome of the highest property qualification (250,000 denarii) who sat in the Senate and served in the high offices of state.

syncretism: From Greek for "mixing with"; the identification of one's national gods with their counterparts of other peoples, so that Roman Jupiter was equated with Greek Zeus, Syrian Baal, and Egyptian Amon, for example. Such an outlook encouraged diversity in pagan worship rather than an incipient monotheism.

Name to Know

Xenophon of Ephesus (fl. early 2nd century A.D.): Novelist of the Second Sophistic movement who wrote the *Ephesian Tale*, a fanciful romance between Anthia and Habrocomes. The story provides details of cult practices and social mores in the Roman East.

Suggested Reading

Dodds, *The Greeks and the Irrational*.

Harl, *Civic Coins and Civic Politics in the Roman East*.

Fox, *Pagans and Christians*.

Liebschuetez, *Continuity and Change in Roman Religion*.

MacMullen, *Paganism in the Roman Empire*.

Naiden, *Ancient Supplication*.

Swain, *Hellenism and Empire*.

Vermeule, *Aspects of Death in Early Greek Art and Poetry*.

1. How did pagans define piety? Why were rituals and sacrifices so important in communication with the gods? How spiritually fulfilling were public rituals?

2. What was the nature of prayer, and what did pagans expect from their gods? How do votive offerings reveal pagan religious sensibilities?

3. What do funerary monuments and inscriptions reveal about pagan conceptions of the divine and the afterlife? How were such monuments expressions of social rank and membership in the ruling circles rather than expressions of piety?

4. How did Romans view the gods of other peoples? Did syncretism allow for enrolling all gods of the Roman world as imperial protectors? Why did Roman emperors seek to link themselves with the many gods of the empire?

Gods and Their Cities in the Roman Empire
Lecture 2—Transcript

In this lecture, I plan to introduce the worship of pagans in the Roman world from the 1st century A.D. into the 4th century A.D. We'll be looking at two different types of sources of evidence: One will be the literary evidence (well-known texts); and the other is going to be all sorts of things like archaeology, temples, coins, and inscriptions. Together, we can get a kind of composite idea of how pagans viewed the divine world and how they communicated with their gods. There are enormous amounts of differences among cities and peoples within the Roman Empire. You have to remember the Roman Empire comprised perhaps a fifth of the world's population at the time—it included very diverse populations from Britain all the way to Egypt—and so there are numerous variations in gods and types of rituals, but there are some givens, some axioms that tied all this pagan worship together. I want to look at that and give you some sort of impression of what it was like to worship as a pagan in the time of the 1st and 2nd centuries A.D.

Foremost are the temples and sanctuaries; that's what we must look at to begin this lecture. Contrary to our notion of churches, synagogues, or mosques, temples in the pagan world are homes of the gods. This is quite different from our notion of sacred buildings that are built for communal or congregational worship. Actually, all a sanctuary needs in the Roman world is a *temenos* wall—that is, a surrounding wall that blocks out the mundane world—and an altar to which you can offer sacrifice to the divinity. The temple is an addition; it is the home of the god. It's where the various objects of the god are stored; for instance, there could be what is known as the *kosmos*, the fancy dress that you put on the cult statue when you take the statue out in procession. There are various gifts; many of these are so-called votive offerings. These are thanks, offerings, given by pilgrims and worshippers. You've promised; you've made a *votum*, a promise to reward the god for some sort of prayer; the god has delivered; you leave the votive offering in the temple treasury.

The temples in the Roman world actually begin to acquire more and more of the look of either a Greek temple in the East or a Roman-style temple in the West. There is a certain convergence of these architectural styles so that by the year 200 A.D., most sanctuaries, both in cities and outside of cities, presented a generally uniform look. Let's take an example from the city Aezanis. Aezanis is a city today in northwestern Turkey. It's not visited much; it's off the beaten tourist track. It's the modern town, or really village, of Çavdarhisar. The city of Aezanis in the high imperial age may have been 30,000 strong. The current village, which is along the ancient river Penkalas, is perhaps less than 4,000; many of the younger people are emigrating to Ankara.

Aezanis provides a very, very good example of what I'm talking about. For instance, Aezanis has a magnificent temple to Zeus and to his mom, Rhea. It's situated on a hill; it's a composite Greco-Roman temple built in the time of Hadrian—that is, in the 2nd century A.D.—but around it is the *temenos* wall and before it is the altar. In some ways, Aezanis is a bit different. It doesn't have the usual features of a Greek temple because the cult was originally Anatolian; it was native. It's a weather god of the region, associated with the Hittite god Teshub, who has been identified with Zeus. What the citizens of Aezanis did is they claimed to be a Greek-style temple or sanctuary, and they claimed, actually, to be a Greek city. Several prominent citizens went to the Emperor Hadrian and petitioned that they be admitted in an outfit known as the Panhellenion; that is, the all-Greek league. If you could get your city and your major sanctuary in there, you got all sorts of benefits. For instance, you could put on games that were Olympic in scope; certain types of athletic competitions, musical contests, literary performances. It meant you attracted a much wider audience; many more pilgrims came to see these events; and above all, you got the imperial approval that you were a major sanctuary in the Greek world.

In this case, the citizens of Aezanis convinced Hadrian that Zeus, when he was rescued by his mother Rhea as a child—she substituted a stone for the child Zeus when Kronos just consumed all of his children—that Zeus was taken to a cave near Aezanis, and in that cave he grew up and eventually overthrew his father Kronos and established the rule of the Olympians. At Aezanis, the temple today—which was rebuilt in the reign of Hadrian— has a temple dedicated both to Rhea and to Zeus, who probably are simply nothing more than a Hellenized Anatolian god and goddess. There is built underneath the temple a subterranean chamber that apparently represents the original cave where Zeus was nursed; coins and inscriptions refer to the various events of the myth; and Aezanis took off. It had major building programs, not only of the temple, but also a stadium and theater, various bath complexes; all of these are going to be important for the worship.

The temple is the all-important focus. It's a major monument in the city, but it's not our idea of a place to go to pray or to worship as you would, say, in a church or in a mosque. This is also borne out in Roman temples; that is, temples that follow the Roman architectural tradition rather than the Greek. For instance, in North Africa at a town called Thamgaudi—better known by its modern name, Timgad—in Algeria (it was a Roman veteran colony), they set up a virtual mini-Rome, with a major temple to Jupiter Capitolinus, which is the Jupiter in the city of Rome today. However, that type of architecture was not confined just to the Roman colonies—that is, Roman veterans, Roman citizens who knew how to build this—but was adopted by the local population. In Africa, on the port city of Tipasa (a Punic city; there are no Romans living there), they essentially adopted the same plan. They set up Roman temples, public baths, axial streets—all of these public buildings in direct imitation of the Roman colony, which is some distance from their city—and many numerous lesser cities in Africa did the same. At Baalbek, Heliopolis, today in Lebanon, there's a construction of a whole series of baroque temples to Jupiter, Zeus, and Bacchus, which are just thinly-disguised versions of the Phoenician gods.

There is a move to present your temples and your sanctuaries either in a Roman or Greek style because that is the high architecture; that is the architecture of the emperors; that is the architecture of success; and you want to update the sanctuaries of your gods and goddesses so that they are both Roman or Greek in style. That is one of the most important points you need to make in pagan religious change in the Roman Empire: the Romanization of sacred space in the Western provinces; the Hellenization—that is, the Greek-style temples—in the Eastern provinces. Aezanis is an excellent example of the latter, the Hellenization, and for the former we have numerous examples in Africa, Spain, and Gaul.

These temples are only part of the whole package of pagan worship. As I've said, they are the home of the city gods. You are required to have other types of monuments in your city—colonnaded streets, other types of buildings; we'll get into that in a moment—and above all, theaters. Theaters are originally an assembly point for religious worship or political meetings. They are not built specifically for putting on drama—that's something the Athenians come up with in the 6th and 5th centuries B.C.—and the majority of early Greek theaters probably had no drama whatsoever; they are essentially gathering places for the faithful: the citizen body.

That gets us to the second point about paganism: You need all of these monuments—you need the home of the gods, you need the theater, you need the streets—because the real worship of the gods involves rituals and processions. These would be presided over by the elite members of the society. In cities, these would be called decurions in Roman law; that is, the so-called "local elites" who had a certain property qualification so that they could undertake the expensive festivals. Senators and equestrians—the imperial elite in Rome and in Italy—would put on many of these festivals; and, of course, the greatest patrons of all would be the imperial family.

We can get an idea of what these processions are like from the city of Ephesus, which is probably well known to many of you if you have traveled to Turkey, Asia Minor. Ephesus is one of the largest cities in the Mediterranean world; it is extremely well-preserved. We have not only the archaeology, the well-excavated site; we have a description of the procession from a novelist called Xenophon of Ephesus, writing probably in the 2nd century A.D. It's one of these fantastic romances where the most beautiful boy in the world meets the most beautiful girl in the world—Habrocomes and Anthia—and they meet at the festival, they are in the procession, they are whisked away by pirates, and they go through a series of fantastic misadventures in which the virtue of the girl is always threatened but she preserves it, and the boy, well, he succumbs (the usual double standard), and they eventually rejoin each other and are married at Ephesus and again in the festival.

If you know Ephesus, the city, very well, the main sanctuary—the Artemision, the sanctuary to Artemis Ephesia—is outside the city. What would happen on the high holidays—it's described in the novel; it's described in inscriptions; it's depicted on the city's coins—you took the cult statue all decked out in its *kosmos* (it's various ornaments or costume), and the statue would be moved along in a sacred cart drawn by stags apparently, and it would enter through the *magnesia*, or east gate, of the city at the upper agora. Then from the upper agora it would wind its way around the various districts of the city and end up at the theater where the cult statue would be placed, where sacrifices would be offered, and the goddess would make an epiphany, an appearance; that is, the statue would become the receptacle for receiving the divinity.

This is a very old concept; it's also seen in the Near East and in Ancient Egypt. It characterizes all pagan worship; that is, there is a public procession and ritual that brings the cult statue to the theater where the prayers are offered with sacrifices. You must have the proper sacrifice and prayer. Again, as I referred to this pagan writer Sallustius writing in the 4th century, his comment is: "Prayers divorced of sacrifices are only words, prayers with sacrifices are animated words, the words giving power to life and the animation to the word"; meaning that with the sacrifices, the goddess will just soak up that smoke and come and appear to her worshippers.

There are numerous inscriptions that report these sacrifices and, above all, the distributions are gifts given out at that time. In the case of Ephesus, there would be over 25,000 people packed into that theater. They would get distributions; not so much the sacred meat, but money, perfume bottles for women, grain. We have a remarkable inscription and coins issued by the city of Stratonicea in Turkey today, and that inscription reports a distribution that would have been common through the whole Roman world. Let me read that text. It comes from an inscription, and this is my own translation of it; it's in Greek. The two leading members of this festival are a husband-wife team, Tiberius Claudius Aristeas Menander and his wife Aelia Glycinna, who are obviously local worthies in the social registry of the city of Stratonicea.

They tell a great deal about how noble they are, and then they explain: They (that is, the couple) instituted a festival for the entire city, and they carefully gave to each of the citizens assembled in the theater two denarii apiece. That is, there has been the procession of the cult statue—in this case, the goddess Hecate, who is a witch goddess; she is always accompanied by two hounds or a hound, carries a torch; not the sort of goddess you want to mess around with unless you really know what you're doing—and that cult statue has been moved from the sanctuary at Lagina, which has been uncovered by a Turkish team and has now been reassembled, into the heart of the city to the theater, which is overlooking the public places. There, the citizens assembled and they got two denarii apiece (we'll get to that in a moment; that's the sum of money). Summoning by the deme—that is, by the districts where people live—by means of placards (there are apparently there are these signs that go up, "Deme, come up and get your money," and the guys march up and get it).

They also served as gymnasiarchs in the city during the two-day procession, conveying the sacred image of Hecate from her shrine at Lagina (which is known as the *kleidos* in the inscription) and then during the feast days when the cult statue is paraded around the city (the *peripolios*; that is, they paid for all of this). In addition, in the same year of the festival, which is dated to about 202 A.D., they gave 1,000 denarii (that is the Roman silver coin) for the construction and upkeep of the public bath, whereupon the grandfather of Aristeas, Flavius Aeneas, erected this honorary monument to the city at his own expense.

One of the points I must stress is that pagan worship is very expensive, and pagan worship involves a great deal of expense outlay by the elite classes, who are the landed classes, who control the local city government as well as preside over the festivals. You don't have a distinct clergy; you have magistrates, local worthies, the social elite doubling not only as the social elite but also as the magistrates, the elected officials, they sit on the council, and they serve as priest and priestess. Note: They're usually couples that do it together. The other important thing about that inscription is the amount of money. Remarkably, we have coins of this city in which the name of the magistrate, Claudius Aristeas, appears on the coins. These are large bronze coins and my guess is something like six coins—big bronze coins; they look medallions, but they're money—were handed out to each of the citizens as a way of perpetuating the memory of the festival as well as the donor; and this is a remarkably good coincidence.

The importance of these festivals, the distributions, the endowments is borne out from an inscription that was uncovered at the city of Oenoanda, dated to about 125 A.D. The benefactor is a man named Gaius Flavius Demosthenes, who set up an endowment. This endowment is remarkable. It is set up so that for a four week summer festival everything would be paid for. This would include various entertainment—horse races, chariot games, literary contests—and also tax-free days where all peddlers and merchants can come up and set up markets; there are actually three weeks of just shopping with no taxes. However, it is a religious festival. It involves a procession; it involves everything we described at both Stratonicea and Ephesus. But this donor wants to make sure that the distributions are there for the contestants, for the citizens, and everything will go in perpetuity.

What is remarkable about this inscription is Oenoanda, which is built on a high point overlooking a very rich plain, is now abandoned. It had a theater that I think, when I was up there, maybe 3,000–5,000 citizens could sit in that theater. Overlooking the plain today is the modern Turkish village. When I visited it some years ago, it was so poor and so small there wasn't even a mosque, and I had to engage a peasant there, an elderly man, to take me up to the site. You have to do this with many cases in Turkey when you are looking at sites, but when I came down, that particular man, I wanted to send him pictures—we didn't have digital cameras at the time—and he had to call over a male relative and dictate his name to write it down because he was, I suspect, illiterate. That's how poor the current village is; yet in the Roman age, in 125 A.D., it was probably a city of 20,000–25,000 at least. That drives home also the prosperity of the Roman Empire and how so much of that prosperity was put into worship, into public display, and processions.

You have the temples, you have the processions, you have the display. You worship the gods, you ask for favors. The worship and prayers are communal, the benefits are communal. However, that doesn't mean that worship was necessarily just a formality or empty; and we have two indications of this. The first indication is the widespread documentation of what we would call family or ancestor worship, which is evident throughout the Roman world. The ancestors are known in Latin as the *maiores*, the greater ones. There are ancestral gods, such as the Lares and Penates, who guard the household of every Roman house. The Herms, who are the protector spirits in the Greek world; well-known for those of you familiar with Alcibiades and the charges of mutilating the Herms in 415 B.C. Funerary monuments abound. They're outside of Athens; they're outside of Rome.

Lesser cities across the Roman world literally had what is known as a Necropolis, a city of the dead; and there would be sarcophagi and different types of funerary monuments, some of them quite opulent, showing scenes of Dionysus or Heracles, which are very heroic and triumphant. They make very little comment on the expectations of the afterlife and these monuments seem to be more memorials to the family, the wealth, and position of the family; nonetheless, you find all of these literally cities of the dead outside the walls, outside the living areas of the city, and virtually are public monuments in themselves. That is, they are private memorials to families but they are regarded as part of the public worship and part of the public monuments. They are usually guarded with curses should you mutilate them in any way; you could be fined for mutilating it. If you are in the city of New Orleans, you can appreciate this with the New Orleans cemeteries; it's the same tradition. They are private monuments but become regarded as part of the public architecture and public traditions of the city.

There are a number of spectacular cities in Asia Minor with these freestanding temple-tombs and monuments to the ancestors. One of my favorites is in Imbrogion in Turkey today, which is on a major road. There are a number of virtual temples as you're driving on the highway towards the city of Olba, which is what most people visit. When you get out there, these are simply multigenerational burials in the form of a Greek-style temple in a part of Asia Minor. One of the most remarkable ones is at Pasli where there's actually a huge phallus carved on the left side of the temple tomb to perpetuate the family productivity. Again, as I stress, most of these temple-tombs are rather disconcerting. They do not talk much about the afterlife or rewards in the next life; they are much more concerned about perpetuating the family; doing what in Greek is *eudoxos*, appropriate. We should bury the ancestors appropriately; we should appear each year to carry out celebrations to the ancestors. One of those that was a Roman practice that becomes widespread is the Rosalia; that is, the placing of roses on a grave. That goes back to the Roman age and that's very common.

This piety is seen in a number of ways in inscriptions. Often inscriptions are set up to make sure that everyone shows up on time and the appropriate dinner is arranged at the temple. One Roman worthy actually said that "All of my slaves, freedmen, and family members can come to the dinner, except for the rotten no-good-for-nothing who never was good in my lifetime, and he should be barred." What a way to be memorialized for eternity. Yet there is something peculiar about this pagan worship: It never developed into the kind of private devotional worship you see in modern Hinduism because all of this private worship was side-by-side with the public cults.

Another aspect that shows the intensity of pagan worship is fact that they revere the texts of Homer and Hesiod, who revealed the gods, or early Latin texts. But there is not any canon; there are not any authoritative sacred texts. One learns the morality of the gods, the rituals of the gods, from one's birth. It is something you learn socially; it is something that is inculcated everywhere. Polybius, writing in the 2nd century B.C., is just stunned at how pious the Romans are, and it's taught at home. You do not have a Bible, you do not have a Quran, you have a series of religious texts or texts that talk about the gods but they are not equivalent. Nonetheless, morality and piety are taught; it's just part of the fabric of society. Some historians have gone so far as to say that the Greeks and Romans did not really have a sense of right and wrong but it is more shame culture, and that is probably going overboard. The Greeks and Romans have a pretty good idea of what is right and what is wrong.

Another important point I want to bring up is the issue of syncretism. Syncretism is the idea of assimilating your gods to foreign gods. You see this with the Greeks; they make equivalents between Egyptian gods and Greeks gods. You see that with Herodotus: The animal gods of Egypt—they are not really animal gods, they are really attributes—really were the Greek gods who assumed the disguise when they had been cast out of Olympus fighting the Titans. Syncretism is really premised in many ways on diversity; it's not an incipient monotheism, as some scholars would say. What happens in the Roman world is natural: The gods of the East are assimilated to Greek gods—and this started with Alexander the Great—and the gods in the West tend to be assimilated with the Roman counterparts. You saw the same thing with temple construction: Roman and Greek gods are the most powerful; therefore, we will make our local gods' versions of the Roman gods.

In some instances, the Romans were willing to accept a god that had no equivalent. One of my best examples comes from the city of Antakya, that is in Turkey today—Antiochia ad Pisidiam, a Roman colony—where the god Men, a god who is peculiar to Turkey, Asia Minor, was accepted as a legitimate god. All the other gods of this Roman colony are typical Roman gods, but because of the importance of the sanctuary of Men, he is included as one of the city gods. He appears on the city coins; there is a magnificent sanctuary overlooking the city to the east of it, which was rebuilt in the Roman age. You will have cases of the Romans accepting a god like that because the power of Men is powerful, he is a god of the locale, we better include him. This is a very, very important concept in paganism: Pagans will accept a new god if you can prove his power and validity. We'll get to that later on with conversion and Christianity.

Besides all of these various gods in the East and West and their counterparts and the importance of piety, we should look at one other issue: how all of this worship was sustained. That is, the temples, the processions, the rituals; they cost an enormous amount of money. As I mentioned, this was sustained by the upper classes. Decurions—or decuriones, to use the Latin term—would be the members of the community who would collect the taxes and run the city for the benefit of Rome. They're local elites, and these people essentially paid for the expense of the festivals out of their own pocket. We have a number of instances of it, not only the inscription I read to you from Stratonicea, but others. In Italy and in Rome, the equestrians and the senators represent the two highest aristocratic orders. Ordo or order is a legal class, not really a social class—ordines in the plural—and the Roman world is categorized by citizenship and rank very, very carefully. The imperial aristocracy and the city aristocracy took on the expense of carrying on the festivals. Then, of course, the Roman emperor himself and members of the imperial family did the same. In many instances, we find the Roman emperors giving approval to various local gods. In the case of Hadrian, I mentioned that he set up the Panhellenion to which Aezanis had applied for membership.

The Romans had a very pragmatic view of the gods. By the time of the 1st century A.D., all the gods in the Roman world had essentially been enrolled as Roman protectors. Many of the local gods had assumed the quality of Roman gods. We see that at the city of Palmyra where Arabian gods are decked out in Roman armor. We see this in the way the Roman emperors assiduously worship at different types of sanctuaries. If they are old, they are legitimate, they should be worshiped. The Romans even have a ceremony known as the *evocatio*, the summoning out; this is a ceremony to summon the gods of foes or rebels onto the Roman side, which would then be rewarded with a temple in Rome; that is, you strip the opponents of their supernatural defender, you make them your own, and then you can take the city and the Romans always deliver. This is an extremely important concept to drive home: the importance of antiquity; the importance that all cults are legitimate if they have age and tradition behind them. That is why Judaism is legitimate to the Romans (we'll get to that). Above all, all the gods are able to defend the emperor—they are enrolled as defenders of the emperor—and that means city worship and imperial worship are linked.

This raises a question when it comes to dealing with Christians because Christians not only denied the gods but, as we shall see, they also did not want to pay veneration to the emperor. The Christian denial of both ran counter to the whole religious and social fabric of cities in the Roman world and also loyalty to the Roman emperor. That means the Christian movement from the start was on a collision course with not only the pagan gods but the Roman emperor as well.

The Roman Imperial Cult
Lecture 3

From a modern, cynical standpoint, the Roman cult of the emperor might be viewed as a top-down propaganda effort by which a tyrant imposed his rule on the populace. Nothing could be further from the truth. While the elites of the city of Rome were suspicious of the idea of a god-emperor, deified rulers were part of a long tradition in the Mediterranean world, and the imperial cult served an important purpose in fostering Roman identity and enforcing the political pecking order in the far-flung provinces of the empire.

The Pre-Roman Origins of Ruler Cults

- The Roman imperial cult was established by Augustus, the first Roman emperor. He set up an institution for the veneration of the emperor's spirit, or **genius**. On the emperor's death, if he had been a pious and good emperor, he would join the gods.

- After a formal ritual of *consecratio* and a vote of the Roman Senate, the emperor's genius would become a *divus*—a god. This was a new institution in Rome, but it drew on many older practices in the Mediterranean world and the Near East.

Emperor Augustus was not worshiped as a god during his life.

- Alexander the Great established the Hellenized version of the ruler cult in the 4th century B.C. In 324 B.C., he was proclaimed not a god but someone who would join the gods after death by virtue of his great deeds. He was considered a descendant of Achilles and Heracles, the latter of whom had his own apotheosis—Greek for "joining the gods."

- Apotheosis was a widespread tradition in what became the eastern half of the Roman Empire by the 2nd and 1st centuries B.C. These regions were ruled by the Macedonian kings—families descended from Alexander the Great's generals: the Ptolemies in Egypt, the Seleucids in Asia, and the Attalids in northwestern Asia Minor.

- Asia Minor in particular had a long-established tradition of ruler cults before Alexander. These can be seen through a succession of archaeological monuments, starting in the 13th century B.C. with Hittite kings at Yazılıkaya. In Egypt, from the Third Dynasty on, the pharaoh was believed to be a living god who became the god Osiris in death.

- All of these traditions were accommodated by the Greeks in the Hellenistic Age, from the death of Alexander the Great to the final Roman conquest in 31 B.C. It was a way of adapting their republican or democratic traditions to their Macedonian or Iranian overlords. So there were both political and religious dimensions to these ruler cults.

Augustus Initiates the Imperial Cult

- The Roman ruler cult established by Augustus was based on the veneration of Julius Caesar, his adoptive father. Caesar was believed to be taken up to join the gods shortly after his death when a comet was seen at the Latin Games in the summer of 44 B.C. Augustus took as one of his titles Filius Divi, "son of a deified one."

- Before Augustus, Rome was a republic. The Romans detested monarchy, and the Roman upper classes detested anything that smacked of ruler worship. Roman emperors had to project themselves as magistrates of the republic to the aristocracy in the city of Rome, but to the rest of the Roman world, ruler worship made sense.

- Invariably, the emperor's spirit was worshiped in tandem with other gods, usually the goddess Roma, who represents the city of Rome. The oldest example of this comes from Pergamon in 25 B.C. Augustus ensured that the provincials understood this was not a temple to a living god but to venerate a spirit.

The Imperial Cult Rituals and Temples

- The *consecratio* was carefully elaborated and formalized over the course of the 1st century. It was purported that at an emperor's funeral pyre, you would know he was deified when an eagle appeared and took him up to the heavens. In the case of empresses, it would be a peacock.

- Many of the monuments built in Rome in the imperial age had a religious dimension to them. Trajan's ashes were deposited beneath his famous column; the memorial not only celebrates his achievements but marks the fact that those achievements entitle him to join the gods.

- Emperors took pains to deify their predecessors. In some cases, these were overt political acts. Macrinus, who had ordered the assassination of his predecessor, Caracalla, promptly had Caracalla deified to throw suspicion off his involvement in the plot. Trajan Decius came to the throne by civil war; he struck coins celebrating all his deified predecessors as a way of stressing his legitimacy.

- The cult required a minimal bureaucracy, at least in Rome itself. To make the imperial cult function, the emperor depended on the same local elites who had the property, wealth, social prestige, and influence to support the other pagan cults.

- Without local initiative there probably would be no imperial cult. That fact alone vitiates arguments that the cult was imperial propaganda. The initiative for emperor worship came from below.

- Dramatic examples of imperial cult worship in the colonies are found in Ephesus. Its agora boasts temples to Augustus, Domitian, and Hadrian as well as a fountain to Trajan. These monuments made the city a showplace.

- At Pergamon, the great Attalid citadel was converted for the imperial cult, extended with a temple to Trajan and Roma that turned the Hellenistic citadel into a Roman center. Similarly, Pisidian Antioch built a Roman civic downtown with an elevated temple to Augustus made out of the rock excavated to build the city.

- Many times, an existing temple became *synnaos*; that is, cult statues of the imperial family were put into the existing temple. In Sardis, in Asia Minor, the heads of five colossal statues were dug up in the late 1990s that were given a ritual burial in the 4th or 5th century A.D. These represented Antoninus Pious and his wife, Faustina the Elder; Marcus Aurelius and his wife, Faustina the Younger; and Commodus.

Why Worship the Emperor?

- Decurions advanced their rank by their efforts to set up imperial cult temples and host processions and festivals, which were similar to those of other cults. An important inscription from a benefactor named Opramoas in Lycia, Turkey, describes giving money to imperial cult temples in the lesser cities of Lycia.

- Many moderns would take a cynical view of this behavior; writers of the time, like the historian Tacitus or the biographer Suetonius, as well as some members of the Roman senatorial upper class, would also have seen this as overt flattery of a despot, but they represent a tiny minority.

- A more common view is given by the author Seneca, who tutored the future emperor Nero. His *Apocolocyntosis*, at first glance, is a spoof on the *consecratio*. On closer inspection, however, it is a spoof of the deification of Emperor Claudius specifically, not the concept of the imperial cult itself.

- Greek intellectuals long accepted and justified the apotheosis of an emperor; in part, this is a result of the Greek language. The Greeks had a single word, *theos*, meaning "god" or "goddess." Latin has *deus*, meaning "god," and *divus*, meaning "deified one." So the Greeks were forced by the language to be hyperbolic about their patron.

- That fed into the veneration of the emperor, as for example in this loyalty oath to the emperor Caligula: "The rule of [Caligula], hoped and prayed for by all mankind, has been proclaimed, and the cosmos has found unbounded joy, and every city and people have been eager for the sight of the *theos* … the happiest age of mankind has now begun."

- The oath drives home the stereotypes about Greek hyperbole, but also the religious associations of the emperor. These oaths were taken very seriously and sanctified by sacrifices; if they did not go correctly, the gods would punish you; they were, in effect, prayers.

- It is worth noting that emperors who overtly claimed they would be gods in their lifetime—including Caligula as well as Commodus—were assassinated by the Roman elites. Other emperors, as outrageous as they were—such as Nero, Domitian, and Caracalla—never made overt claims of divinity.

- Particularly in Asia Minor, the imperial cult was assimilated with local cults. Furthermore, the ambitions of the local elites were channeled toward carrying out the activities of the imperial cult. They could not express civic loyalty by fighting their neighbors, who were also Romans, so they had to express it in other ways.

- Having an imperial cult title or the imperial title of **neokoros**, meaning "temple warden"—that is, the whole city is a protector of the temple—was a way of expressing the greatness of your city. Therefore, local elites and their cities benefited by putting on these rituals and processions to the imperial cult, and the cult was woven into the religious, social, and political fabric of cities.

Jews, Christians, and the Imperial Cult

- For the Jews, the imperial cult did not pose a problem. They were recognized in Roman law as a legitimate religion. Yahweh, his temple at Jerusalem, and the hereditary priesthood all made sense to the Romans, and the Jews would offer up prayers on behalf of Rome and the emperor, which was sufficient.

- The Christians, however, refused to participate in the imperial cult. Their refusal to participate is closely linked with their refusal to worship the pagan gods, whose statues stood side by side with the emperors'. In the Romans' eyes, therefore, the Christians were atheists, denying the gods. They were regarded as traitors, with no loyalty to Rome or the emperor.

Important Terms

consecratio: Consecration; the rite of deifying a deceased emperor.

divus/diva (m. pl. *divi*; fem. pl. *divae*): Latin for "defied one"; the spirit (*genius*) of an emperor or member of the imperial family that was, on his funeral pyre, taken to join the gods. This deification was confirmed by a decree of the Senate.

genius: Latin for "spirit"; The spirit of each man. The genius of the emperor may be defied upon his death and consecration. Juno is the spirit of each woman. *See* **divus**.

neokoros: Greek for "temple-warden"; A Greek city possessed of a temple dedicated to the Roman emperor.

synnaos: Greek for "temple sharing"; the placement of a cult statue of the Roman emperor within a temple of a city god.

Suggested Reading

Burrell, *Neokoroi*.

Fishwick, *The Imperial Cult in the Latin West*.

Harl, *Civic Coins and Civic Politics in the Roman East*.

L'Orange, *Studies on the Iconography of Cosmic Kingship in the Ancient World*.

MacCormick, *Art and Ceremony in Late Antiquity*.

MacMullen, *Enemies of the Roman Order*.

Price, *Rituals and Power*.

Taylor, *The Divinity of the Roman Emperor*.

Weinstock, *Divus Julius*.

Questions to Consider

1. What led peoples of the Roman Empire to venerate or worship the emperor? Was this an act of political loyalty or belief?

2. How did the rites, sacrifices, and temples to the imperial family conform to traditional worship? What was the impact of associating the emperor with local gods?

3. What were the practical limits emperors faced in disseminating their worship in the provinces? How did the civic elites use the imperial cult to their own advantage and to advance their cities?

4. How did Jews and Christians perceive the imperial cult? What objections would they raise against its practices? Why could Jews accommodate themselves to the imperial cult?

The Roman Imperial Cult

Lecture 3—Transcript

In this lecture, I wish to deal with the Roman Imperial Cult. This was established by the emperor Augustus, the first Roman emperor. He essentially set up an institution for the veneration of the emperor's spirit, or *genius* (where we get the word "genius"). Then, upon the emperor's death, if he had been a pious and good emperor he would join the gods and there would be a formal ritual of *consecratio* and a vote of the Roman senate that the emperor had actually joined the gods; that his genius had become what is called in Latin a *divus* (*divus* in Latin; *divus* as we anglicize it; *divi* in the plural; *diva* is the singular for the feminine). That meant the emperor, in effect—his spirit—became a god and is on Mount Olympus with the various gods of Greece and Rome. It was a new institution in many ways, but it drew on many, many older practices in the Mediterranean world and the Near East on the veneration of rulers. These practices go back quite early, but there was a decisive change in the time of Alexander the Great.

Alexander the Great essentially established the Hellenized version of ruler-cults in the 4th century B.C. In 324 B.C., he was proclaimed, essentially, not a god but someone who would join the gods by virtue of his great deeds. In the case of Alex, he was a descendant of Achilles and Heracles (the Roman Hercules), so his deeds were to be compared to these heroes of old. In the case of Heracles, Heracles himself had an apotheosis, which is the Greek word for joining the gods; that is, Heracles in myth arrived at Mount Olympus and was worshiped as a god in Alex's own time and later.

This notion of venerating the ruler who could then [join the gods] upon his death or her death—because it could extend to queens and empresses just as much—is a tradition that was widespread in the eastern half of the Roman Empire when the Romans in the republic during the 2nd and 1st centuries B.C. conquered these regions. Macedonian kings—that is, families descended from the generals of Alexander the Great—ruled as monarchs in these regions. In Egypt, there were the Ptolemies; in the Asian possessions, the Seleucids—descendants of Seleucus, one of Alexander's generals; Ptolemy, the family in Egypt, was descended from one of Alexander's generals as well—and in northwestern Turkey today at the city of Pergamon were the

Attalid kings, who were rather newcomers, parvenus, to the royal families. All of them had ruler cults. All of them projected themselves with the titles and the attributes of a divinity. The understanding was that they, too, could undergo an apotheosis upon their deaths.

In Asia Minor in particular, there was a long-established tradition of ruler cults. These can be seen through a succession of archaeological monuments that tourists may or may not see—some of them are a bit remote—but they start in the 13th century B.C. with Hittite kings at Yazılıkaya, and it runs through the great tumuli, or burials, of the kings of Lydia and Phrygia, the great tombs at Amasia to the Pontic kings. It climaxes in the sanctuary of Nemrud Dagh, which is just to the west of the Euphrates, where a tumulus was built on top of a mountain that is something like 6 or 7 thousand feet above sea level for a minor king of the kingdom of Commagene; and then huge platforms were built on the east and west end down below from the tumulus to receive the sunrise and the sunset with colossal statues of the king and the various gods. In Egypt, there was an extremely well-established tradition, at least from the 3rd Dynasty on, that the pharaoh was a living god and would become the god Osiris in death.

All of these traditions had been accommodated by the Greeks in what we call the Hellenistic Age; that is, the time from the death of Alexander the Great to the final Roman conquest in 31 B.C. For the Greeks, it was a way of accommodating the fact that they lived in city-states based on the rule of law—these were republics or democracies—and they had to accommodate the fact that their overlord was some Macedonian or Iranian dynast. The way to do that was, in effect, to venerate that ruler as if not a god, close to a god; and then you could justify the fact that the god-king had special privileges and rights, and in turn the monarch would respect the autonomy and freedom of the Greek cities. There was both a political and religious dimension to these ruler-cults.

The Roman ruler-cult established by Augustus was based on the veneration of Julius Caesar, the adoptive father of Octavian, who became the Roman Emperor Augustus in 27 B.C. Caesar, who was popular with the crowds, was believed shortly after his death to be taken up to join the gods when a comet was seen at the time of the Latin games in the summer of 44 B.C. Already,

Octavian—the future Emperor Augustus—claimed that his father had joined the gods and was *divus*; and Octavian took as one of his titles *Filius Divi*, "son of a deified one," "son of a god." The deification was not formalized until a decree of the senate on January 1, 42 B.C. From that date, many scholars would start the inception of ruler worship in the Roman world.

There had been always honors paid to great Romans, but Rome was a republic. The Romans detested monarchy and the Roman upper classes detested anything that smacked of emperor-worship or ruler-worship; and Roman emperors had to project themselves as essentially magistrates of the republic for the benefit of the aristocracy in Rome. But for the rest of the Roman world—for the numerous provinces and nations that made up the Roman Empire, especially in the eastern half of the Roman world and in Egypt; even in sections of the western provinces—ruler-worship made sense to these people. The emperor was their patron—he was, in all intents and purposes, effectively a god in many ways he operated—and so the imperial cult, as developed by Augustus (the previous revolutionary known as Octavian) was very, very much pitched to the provinces and far less pitched to Italy and Rome where there was an aversion to all of this.

Furthermore, this was not outright adulation of the emperor as a god. Invariably, the emperor's spirit was worshiped in tandem with other gods, usually the goddess Roma. There was a tradition going back to the 2nd century B.C. of many provincial cities in Asia Minor—in Spain particularly; we have a number of documented cases—where temples were set up to Roma. The goddess Roma, which represents the city of Rome, was then added to that particular provincial city among their divinities. In the case of Augustus, his *genius* was usually linked with the veneration of Roma; and again, it was his spirit—it was the potential god of Augustus—that was worshiped and not the living god.

The first example we have of this comes from a record of Pergamon in 25 B.C. where Augustus approved the erection of a temple both to Roma and to the *genius* of Augustus. It was approved by petition of the local elites who wanted to set up this temple. Augustus was very careful in supervising and making sure that the provincials understood this was not the veneration of a living god but of a spirit; plus, the goddess Roma was to be associated in the temple. That temple is still to be located in the city of Pergamon, but it's celebrated in literary sources, coins, and inscriptions so we know about it. From that point on, the honors were paid along these lines in provincial cities; that is, provinces and cities set up these types of temples.

Furthermore, the ceremony of consecration, or *consecratio* in Latin, was very carefully described and elaborated over the course of the 1ˢᵗ century and became a very, very specific and formal religious ceremony. We have reliefs of the emperor Marcus Aurelius in which the emperor is depicted as being carried off to Mount Olympus or to the gods on an eagle, which is the bird of Jupiter-Zeus. It was purported that at a funeral pyre when the emperor was deified—when his body was burned—you would know he was deified when an eagle appeared and took him up to the heavens. In the case of empresses, it would be a peacock, which was the bird of Juno (Juno, the counterpart of Jupiter). Both members of the imperial family—the emperor and the empress—and their children were all potentially deified.

Many of the monuments built in Rome in the imperial age always have this sort of religious dimension to them. The great column of Trajan—where everyone goes to see the reliefs of the Dacian War—beneath the column itself were deposited the ashes of the emperor after he had died, and his body was cremated in the forum. Of course, an eagle was seen; Trajan, Optimus Princeps—one of the best of emperors—was obviously carried up to the gods. The memorial not only celebrates his achievements but it also marks the fact that those achievements entitle Trajan to join the gods; and that's a point that's often missed when you're wandering around Rome and you see this impressive monument. Emperors took pains to deify their predecessors.

In a couple of cases, these were rather overt political acts. In 195 A.D., Septimius Severus rehabilitated the reputation of the emperor Commodus, who was the rather crazy son of Marcus Aurelius. He's the emperor in the recent movie *Gladiator* (or maybe not so recent). Commodus was condemned as an evil emperor, but Septimius Severus—who won the throne by a civil war—had himself retroactively adopted by Marcus Aurelius, and that meant Commodus was now his brother, so Commodus had to be rehabilitated and made a *divus*. The emperor Macrinus, who ordered the assassination of his predecessor Caracalla, promptly had Caracalla deified. That also threw suspicion off his involvement in the plot. In the mid-3rd century, we'll be talking about an emperor Trajan Decius who ordered the first empire-wide persecutions. He, too, was an emperor who came to the throne by civil war; he had no particular qualifications. He struck coins celebrating all the deified emperors going back to Augustus as a way of stressing his legitimacy.

This is an extremely important point to make about the imperial cult: You want to set yourself up as within the line of deified and recognized emperors who have joined the gods; that's a way to give legitimacy to yourself. That was solemnized by a formal swearing of oaths, a *sacramentum* (where we the word "sacrament"), by army and provincials to the imperial *imago* (where we get the word "image"). This institution had been set up by Augustus and is elaborated over the course of the 1st and 2nd centuries A.D.

On the other hand, to carry out this type of institution, the emperor had a minimal bureaucracy; the Roman Empire was run on very, very few officials. Most of the senior officials were members of the senatorial aristocracy who served out of loyalty to Rome rather than any kind of loyalty to the emperor. It was still in many ways supposed to be republic in trappings; true, it was a constitutional fiction, but it was an important one. In order to make the imperial cult go, the emperor had to depend on the local elites (again, those decuriones or decurions; that is, the civic ruling classes). In a large city like Athens or Ephesus, there could be 500 members on the town council; in a lesser city there might be 100 or 50. They represented the families that had the property, the wealth, the social prestige, the influence—the Latin word would be *auctoritas*—to make things go.

In this case, the imperial cult rested very much on local initiative; in fact, without local initiative there probably would be no imperial cult. That fact alone vitiates arguments that this was set up by the imperial government as some kind of PR, propaganda; comparing it to totalitarian regimes of the 20th century. These are all very, very misleading. The initiative really came from below. I mentioned earlier, it was the leading citizens of Pergamon who first petitioned Augustus—"We want a temple to you," and he said, "Yeah, you get a temple to my *genius*; and by the way, you add Roma."—but the initiative came from below.

There are several dramatic examples that illustrate this that have come to us through the archaeology. One, again, is the city of Ephesus. When you go to Ephesus today—and you usually start at the east end, the so-called Magnesia gate; the same gate through which the procession of the statue came through—you start at a public forum, or agora, which is essentially a Roman political center. There are temples to Augustus. There's a temple to Domitian celebrating his victories over the Germans off on the distant Rhine, which had a colossal statue that is now in the Ephesus museum, which is the ugliest statue of Domitian I have ever seen, marginally improved by the later Christians who put a cross on him (for some reason he was retroactively baptized). There's a temple to Hadrian; there's a fountain of Trajan. As you go down the main street to the harbor, you have all of these imperial cult temples that made the city of Ephesus a showplace, not only for civic institutions and the traditional gods, but also for the emperor.

At Pergamon, people go up to see the great Attalid citadel—that's the citadel of the 3rd and 2nd centuries B.C.—but you can only really appreciate it when you're down below, when you're looking up above, and you see these incredible vaults that extended the citadel to build a temple to the emperor Trajan and Roma that, in effect, turned the Hellenistic citadel into a Roman center with the temple of Trajan just audaciously on top of these vaults—this white marble Baroque-style temple dominating this citadel—and everywhere you stand in lower Pergamon, where the modern Turkish city is, you could still see the ruins; you couldn't miss it. Pisidian Antioch I talked about, a Roman colony set in western Asia Minor in the mountain landscape, which for the Roman colonists would have been very, very similar to Umbria or Tuscany. It's a beautiful area. They built a Roman civic downtown, and the showpiece at the end of the succession of squares is an elevated temple to Augustus made out of the rock that was excavated there. It's a sort of tuff—that is, a volcanic rock which is built up, faced with marble and brick, and dominates the whole public area. You stand up there; you have a shot all the way down to the entrance into the public regions. This is a common way of celebrating the emperor across the empire. I've drawn examples from Asia Minor, but you will find them in all provinces' imperial temples.

A more common way, which is less easy to document, is that many times an existing temple became *synnaos* in Greek; that is, cult statues of the imperial family were put into the existing temple. This was dramatically illustrated either in 1998 or 1999—my memory is a little defective, but it was one of those two years—when I visited Sardis, a city in Asia Minor well known as the city of the Lydian kings, and colossal statues had been dug up. These colossal statues had apparently been given a burial in the 4th or 5th century A.D. (They were only the heads; the statue elements have broken up.) They represent five colossal statues, which are Antoninus Pious and his wife, Faustina the elder; Marcus Aurelius and his wife, Faustina the younger; and, again, the emperor Commodus. Commodus was apparently placed in the temple of Artemis, found on the east end, and brought up in a trial trench—totally unexpected—cleaned off by a very, very well-known conservator named Kent Severson; and I arrived there when he was cleaning them up. What they are is a case of *synnaos*—that is, the imperial cult statues were put in one of the major temples of the city—and so they shared the sacred space with the city god; or, in this case, goddess. This was, again, common across the empire; we have lots of references to it.

Decurions advanced their rank by all of these efforts to set up imperial cult temples, to set up processions to the imperial cult temple; and the imperial cult had processions and festivals very, very similar to other cults. We have an important inscription I'll be talking about from a benefactor called Opramoas in Lycia, which is in southwestern Turkey, and one of the biggest items he talks about in giving money is to imperial cult temples to the lesser cities of Lycia.

It's easy to misunderstand what this is all about. Many moderns would take a cynical view of it; and if you read the historians of the time like Tacitus or the biographer Suetonius, or you go back into the literature of the Republic, the Roman senatorial upper class would see this stuff as just overt flattery of a despot and they would hate it, because they are nostalgically tied to the republic. On the other hand, they represent a very, very tiny minority and the voices of the rest of the Roman world are not articulated as well. But there are some indications that even in the literate circles this principle was accepted. One is from the author Seneca—Lucius Annaeus Seneca, the tutor to the emperor Nero—who wrote a work on clemency, which his promising student Nero never read. He penned a work known as the *Apocolocyntosis*, which is a spoof on the imperial ceremony I described. But it's not a spoof on the ceremony per se—Augustus deserved to be deified—it's a spoof on the emperor Claudius being deified. It's just a wickedly delicious piece, in which Claudius joins the gods, but then he's carried back to the underworld because Caligula comes up and claims him for a debt in some kind of gambling, and it's all nonsense parody. It's spoofing Claudius—Claudius didn't really deserve to be among the *divi*—but it's not really mocking the institution. This is from one of Nero's ministers who is of the senatorial rank.

Greek intellectuals long accepted and justified the apotheosis of an emperor; they compared it to Heracles and myth. The Greeks are prone to hyperbole, but in part it's a result of the Greek language. The Greeks had a word *theos*, meaning "god" or "goddess"—it could be either one—as opposed to *divus*. Latin has *deus*, meaning "god"—which many of you may be familiar with—and *divus*, which is a "deified one"; it makes two distinctions, Greek only has one. Sometimes when the Greeks are calling the emperor *theos*, they're meaning it in the sense of *divus*. It's easy to get confused and that's because of the difference of the languages; but they were always prone to hyperbole because the emperor was their patron.

To get an idea of how that all fed into the veneration of the emperor, I can't resist, I want to read a little snippet of what in effect is the preface of a loyalty oath to the emperor Caligula—the mad emperor Caligula—who ruled from 37–41. This inscription comes from the city of Assus on the shore of Turkey today. Let me read a selection of it, because it is the preface of an oath that all members of the town council as well as the citizen body had to swear to the emperor Caligula, and it's the type of oath expected in the imperial cult. The preface really drives home the hyperbole of the Greeks:

> Whereas the rule of Gaius Caesar Germanicus Augustus [that is, Caligula], hoped and prayed for by all mankind, has been proclaimed and the cosmos has found unbounded joy and every city and people have been eager for the sight of the god [theos, meaning the potential god] since the happiest age of mankind has now begun [wait until we get a little further on in the reign], it was decreed by the council and the Roman businessmen resident among us and the people of Assus [that would be the assembly of citizens] to appoint an embassy chosen from the foremost and most distinguished Romans

and Greeks to seek an audience and congratulate him, and beg him to remember the city with solicitude, as he personally promised when together with his father Germanicus he first set foot in our city's province [At the time, Caligula was probably about eight years old, so I'm not sure how much the emperor remembered.].

A lot of flattery and praise; it meets the stereotypes that most Romans had about Greeks. Nonetheless, the oath drives home the type of religious associations with which the emperor was linked. These oaths were very, very seriously taken. They were sanctified by sacrifices; if they didn't go right, the gods would punish you; they are, in effect, prayers the way you would offer up prayers in any kind of procession or ritual to another god or goddess.

That brings up another point, which is that I mentioned that the emperors themselves were very circumspect about this. Only those emperors who overtly claimed that they would be gods in their lifetime—someone like Caligula; apparently the emperor Commodus who had a nervous breakdown in 189 and thought he was Hercules reborn—such emperors would end up being assassinated by the Roman elites. Other emperors, as outrageous as they were—such as Nero, Domitian, Caracalla, who thought he was Alexander the Great, or Elagabalus, who thought he was the priest king of this Syrian god—none of them made overt claims of divinity. This is something that most emperors veered away from, and those sorts of claims came from below. An emperor such as Trajan was extremely circumspect. In his iconography, he was always depicted as smaller than a god whenever he was shown in association with Jupiter.

That means the initiative rests with the local elites. Particularly well-documented are the cities of the eastern Roman provinces, and among them, of course, are the cities of Asia Minor. There, the imperial cult was assimilated and tied together with local cults. Whatever the primary divinity was in the city, the imperial cult was matched with it; and so there would be processions to both. Furthermore, the ambitions of the local elites were channeled toward carrying out the activities of the imperial cult. Why? Rome locked up the swords of all the provincials; they couldn't express civic loyalty by fighting their neighbors, so they had to be expressed in other ways. Having an imperial cult title or an imperial title known as *neokoros*, meaning "temple warden"—that is, you are the protector; the whole city is a protector of that temple; it's first used in Ephesus in the time of Domitian—these were all ways of expressing the greatness of your city as well as your own greatness as a leading magistrate who's involved with the imperial cult, who's paying for the sacrifices, paying for the events that are going on; and so local elites and cities both together benefited by putting on these rituals and processions to the imperial cult that, again, are held in tandem with regular religious holidays. In many ways, the imperial cult resembled normal religion: It had sacrifices, even initiation rites or mysteries; there was a whole hierarchy of priests; the men who held these positions, and in some instances women—since military virtue was no longer important, it was a matter of money and rank we have women holding high positions in the imperial cult and civic government—all of this meant that in many, many ways the imperial cult resembled other types of worship.

It's a mistake to think that it was imposed by an imperial government; that the emperor Augustus and associates were seated around each evening figuring out: "How do we win the loyalty of the provincials? Ah, we need an imperial cult." There's nothing of the sort. That meant the imperial cult was woven into the religious, social, and political fabric of cities. This is seen in several ways: In the province of Asia—which is the western third of Turkey today, the province of 500 cities that included some of the most urbanized areas of the Roman world—the three leading cities, Ephesus, Smyrna, and Pergamon disputed the title of who was the first city of Asia, *he prote tes Asias*. Ephesus won; and you think, "Great; Smyrna's two, Pergamon's three. What's that all about?" It's at the *koinon*—that is, the religious league that's instituted to run the imperial cult—the representatives of Ephesus march first, the representatives of Smyrna second. It shows the importance of the city in the providence vis-à-vis the other cities and rivals, and also the importance of the city vis-à-vis the emperor; so it was very important that Ephesus ranked number one.

At the city of Aphrodisias, the same thing: We see all sorts of inscriptions of imperial benefits put up on the theater wall and elaborate reliefs in a great imperial entrance hall combining imperial, civic, and city mythology in a series of reliefs where apparently rituals were carried out to the imperial cult and city together. Those reliefs have now been properly assembled in the museum of Aphrodisias, and Aphrodisias's excavation team is reconstructing now the great imperial hall that, again, was probably typical in most cities of the Roman world.

Therefore, architecturally and in rituals across the Roman world you find this. To give due to the western provinces, the most famous of these is an enormous complex that used to be at the city of Lugdunum where the local league to the imperial cult—in Latin known as a *commune*, which is the equivalent of a *koinon* in Greek—had a great altar and complex there. It doesn't survive, but it is depicted on the coins of the cities of Augustus that show a great altarpiece where various rites were held by the elites of the three Gauls—the three provincial provinces that made up Gaul. With it went the arena, the amphitheater, the gladiatorial games; all of that popularization of that Roman sport was generally held in tandem with the imperial cult. You must remember: An amphitheater was the largest building in a Roman city, and it's closely linked to the imperial cult.

This raises a question as to the Jews and Christians. The Jews were not a problem; they were recognized in Roman law as a legitimate religion. The god Yahweh, his temple at Jerusalem, the hereditary priesthood; they all made sense to the Romans. The Jews were pragmatic: They would offer up prayers on behalf of Rome and the emperor, sort of a religious loyalty oath; that was sufficient. Usually the sacrifice included two goats daily in the sacrifices offered at the temple. The Christians refused to participate; and the Christian refusal to participate is closely linked with their refusal to worship the gods. As we'll see, when the Christians are questioned they are, in effect, drilled: Will you sacrifice to the gods? The imperial cult statue is right next to the gods; and so, in effect, the Christians are refusing both worship of the ancestral gods and worship of that potential spirit of the emperor. They can be nothing more than atheists denying the gods and they are regarded as traitors, having denied their loyalty to Rome and to the emperor.

The Mystery Cults
Lecture 4

In the late 19th century, the Belgian scholar Franz Cumont introduced the idea of the mystery cult: a new form of religion that emerged in the early Roman Empire out of pagan malaise. These cults focused on initiation rituals and ecstatic worship and seemed to prepare Roman culture for the coming of Christianity. But were these cults really new and nonclassical? In fact, more recent research indicates that they are a divergent set of faiths, many of which antedate Roman rule by centuries, and are no more similar to Christianity than to each other.

Mystery Cults—A Modern Concept

- The so-called **mystery cults** are cults associated with initiation rites—in fact, the word "mystery" comes from the Greek word for "initiation." Members of these cults chose to join them and to worship these particular divinities.

- Mystery cults are a very controversial subject in the history of the religion. In many ways, they are the creation of a Belgian scholar named Franz Cumont, who wrote at the end of the 19th century. The term "mystery cult" was not used by the Romans themselves.

- The mystery cult is seen as an indication of pagan spiritual malaise; it is often viewed as a bridge whereby many pagans became accustomed to an idea of the divine that drew them toward Christianity in the 3rd, 4th, and 5th centuries A.D.

- Cumont started his work on **Mithraism,** the cult of Mithras, a god of Persian origin. Mithras is seen as a creator god who fights a great cosmic bull and in dying carries out an act of creation. Cumont concluded that the cults of Mithras, Aphrodite and Adonis at Paphos, Artemis Ephesia, **Cybele** (the great mother goddess of Asia Minor), and Dionysus all had one thing in common: A creator divinity who went out of its way (usually by dying) to benefit mankind.

The Allure of the Mystery Cults

- Another feature among the mystery cults was a connection between the afterlife and redemption. The pagans had a sense of afterlife; what that notion was is still debated, and as best we can tell it was somewhat contradictory and did involve physical resurrection.

- The earliest description we have of the Greek afterlife is in the *Odyssey*, book 11, when Odysseus goes to the underworld and calls up the spirits of the deceased. He sees many ghosts, including Achilles, who says, "Would I were the slave of a landless man than lord of all the dead."

- These notions of afterlife, in Cumont's and others' opinions, meant that the mystery cults offered something new: a connection between death, redemption, and a pious life. Sin took on a much more moral connotation; it was not simply performing the proper rites to the ancestors and the gods.

- The most important rite was the **taurobolium**, associated with the myth of Cybele. A bull or pig was sacrificed while the initiate stood underneath it. One Christian writer, Prudentius, writing at the end of the 4th century A.D., said this was the pagan equivalent of baptism, which was probably a Christian misunderstanding.

- There are also references to redemption in *The Golden Ass*, the novel by Apuleius set in Tunisia in the 2nd century A.D. The protagonist, Lucius, is turned into an ass and has many misadventures. He is restored to human form and joins the cult of the Egyptian goddess Isis, the implication being Lucius has entered a new life by joining this cult.

- The mystery cults were also seen by scholars as enthusiastic, irrational, and nonclassical. E. R. Dodds argued that the communal and family cults in the Roman world were not fulfilling, whereas mystery cults had a foreign tinge to them, making them exotic and exciting.

- Members chose to join mystery cults. There were initiation rites; Cumont and others have gone so far as to say that the mystery cults proselytized, acting as models for later Christian missionaries. When you add up these features, the mystery cults were seen as prefiguring Christianity, as well as being index to something that was wrong with the traditional pagan cults.

Some Specific Mystery Cults

- The mystery cult model—foreign, nonclassical, enigmatic—has been constructed by looking at many cults. Some of them, however, were Greek and very well known in the Greek and Roman world, such as the cult of Demeter and Persephone at Eleusis (the Eleusinian Mysteries) and the rites of Dionysus preserved in the Villa of the Mysteries frescoes at Pompeii.

- Both of these Greek cults are seen as mystery cults and somehow not classical. Yet these divinities were worshiped well into the Bronze Age—between 1600 and 1225 B.C. So how long do you have to be a cult in Greece before you become Greek?

- The most famous mystery cult is that of the Persian god Mithras. Mithras is known from the Avesta, an ancient religious text of Zoroastrianism that was redacted (edited and reformed) in the 3rd and 4th centuries A.D. He was a guardian angel figure in Zoroastrianism, but he was a prime god in the Roman world.

- The cult of Mithras emerged in Rome in the Flavian Age (A.D. 69–96) and was particularly popular with Roman soldiers, customs officials, and imperial freedmen. The ruins of many Mithraea (temples) are found on Rome's borders, near old Roman army camps in Italy, the Upper Danube, and the Rhine.

- The cult involved many oaths and a hierarchy similar to the Roman military. The priestly garb of the Mithras cult was superficially Iranian; Mithras himself wore a Phrygian cap, which was the Romans' stereotype of what Persians wore. No actual Persian dressed this way. So the Mithras cult was, in structure and style, quite Roman.

The cult of the Persian god Mithras was the prototypical mystery cult.

- The cult of Cybele arrived in Rome in 204 B.C. during the Second Punic War. It came from the sanctuary of Pessinus in western Asia Minor. She is a mother goddess typical of the region. Her priests were the Galli—foreign eunuchs. The poet Catullus wrote about her lover, Attis, who castrated himself with a flint knife; that mutilation was seen by Cumont and others as another form of the dying savior god. Yet Attis was not a god, just a mortal.

- Serapis and Isis were the original divinities of Egypt. Serapis, iconographically, was an Egyptianized version of Zeus or Hades. Isis was sometimes worshiped alone, sometimes with Serapis as consort, and sometimes with her child, almost like the Madonna and child of Christianity.

Does the Mystery Cult Model Hold Up?

- Scholars have argued that this general picture demonstrates Roman pagan malaise—the flipside of Eusebius's vision. As Christianity is rising, paganism is in trouble, and the mystery cults are seen as proof of this.

- Roman authors like **Vergil** and **Horace** lamented the decline of piety during the civil war, and Augustus carried out a huge effort to rebuild temples in Rome. Many see this as part of a rearguard action—pagan cults were already on the wane at the dawn of the empire.

- In 235, there was a major political and military crisis that engulfed the empire for the next 50 years. We have very little statistical documentation for the period, but Eusebius's picture indicates that between 235 and 312, paganism, including the mystery cults, began losing out to Christianity. This included the cult of Sol Invictus, the unconquerable sun god, much of whose solar imagery came to represent the triumphant Christ.

- The cult of Sol Invictus is sometimes classified as a syncretist cult representative of all the various sun gods and therefore of an incipient monotheism. Technically, however, this is **henotheism**—a single divine power manifested in many ways. Syncretism and henotheism are premised on diversity; it is misleading to think that they lead inevitably to monotheism.

- The problems with the mystery cult idea have become ever more evident as historians have applied two points: One, they have looked at the worshipers themselves rather than the gods. Two, the way scholars have approached the cults is not how the ancients did. No ancient ever compared Christianity to a mystery cult, nor did any ancient say the mystery cults were in competition with the other cults.

The Great Diversity of Roman Religion

- The mystery cult idea operated on a modern assumption that unless religion is personal and brooded on the great questions of cosmology or questions of sin and redemption, it is not really religion. This is actually a 17th-century idea, coming mainly from Dutch theologian critics of the Thirty Years' War and an increasing sense that religion should be a matter of conscience and choice.

- Efforts to show mystery cults on the rise by the number of Mithraea or the number of inscriptions have failed; in fact, the most numerous dedications in the early empire are to the traditional gods: Jupiter, Mars, Juno, and so forth.

- Many of these mystery cults have been selectively studied to act as a parallel to Christianity rather than seen on their own terms, particularly the Mithras cult. When studied in a broader context, it becomes clear that the Mithras cult arose in Rome and relied heavily on imperial patronage, as did the cult of Cybele.

- In the case of Serapis and Isis, 85 percent of the cult's members were from Roman Alexandria; that is, expatriates worshiping their traditional divinities in their new home, not Roman converts to a foreign cult. Those non-Egyptians who did convert seemed to be suffering from general Aegyptomania—an obsession with all things Egyptian that is not unheard of in the West today.

- When you take a look at the cults themselves, they do not add up to a coherent whole. Each is quite distinct, and most importantly, wherever they go, they are assimilated to their setting. In fact, with the exception of Mithras, all of these cults long antedated Roman rule, much less the empire.

- One cult that emerges in the Roman world is described by **Lucian of Samosata**, the cult of the serpent god Glycon, set up by the charlatan prophet **Alexander of Abonoteichos**. The cult centered on a snake with a human head that delivered oracles via Alexander's ventriloquism. Alexander was clever enough to occasionally have Glycon refer a seeker's question to one of the more established oracles at Delphi or Claros and thus receive their support.

- Several Roman senators were attracted to the cult as well as Emperor Marcus Aurelius. The cult continued long after Alexander's death, reaching as far as the Bulgarian shore and northern Turkey. So even in this era of so-called pagan malaise, traditional cults were growing and thriving.

- The mystery cults, therefore, were not in competition with traditional paganism. Nor were they a measure of decline. They were simply part of the vast diversity of religious experience available to pagans of the Roman world.

Important Terms

Cybele (a.k.a. **Kubaba**): The great mother goddess of Anatolia, whose principal shrine was at Pessinus. She was known to the Romans as the Great Mother (Magna Mater).

henotheism: The religious outlook regarding traditional pagan gods as aspects of a single transcendent godhead. This was the religious vision of the Neoplatonic philosopher Plotinus and the emperor Julian II.

Mithraism: The Roman cult of the god Mithras, originally a Persian god of oaths. The cult was popular among Roman soldiers and customs officials in the 1st–4th centuries A.D.

mystery cults: In older scholarship, this name was given to certain pagan sects seen as ecstatic, irrational cults that displaced traditional worship in anticipation of Christianity. Mystery cults had initiation rites and conformed to general pagan expectations of piety.

taurobolium: A votive sacrifice of a bull or pig to the goddess Cybele; it was misrepresented by the Christian critic Prudentius, writing around A.D. 400, as distorted blood baptism.

Alexander of Abonouteichos (c. 105–c. 170): Charlatan philosopher who founded the cult of the serpent god Glycon in northern Asia Minor. He gained the patronage of Emperor Marcus Aurelius and the contempt of Lucian, who wrote a satirical critique of Alexander and the cult of Glycon.

Horace (a.k.a. **Quintus Horatius Flaccus**; 65–8 B.C.): Poet and soldier. Born at Venusia and son of a freedman, Horace fought for the Republican cause at Philippi (42 B.C.), but he was pardoned and promoted at the court of Augustus through the efforts of Maecenas. His works include *Carmen Saeculare* (chorus for the Saecular Games of 17 B.C.), *Odes*, Epodes, Epistles, Satires, and *Ars Poetica*. He is considered the master of the Roman lyric and poet laureate of the Golden Age.

Lucian of Samosata (c. 125–180): Greek satirist and brilliant prose stylist, he composed works on religious themes, including *Dialogues of the Gods*, *Banquet of Philosophers*, and a life of the false prophet Alexander of Abonouteichos.

Vergil (a.k.a. **Publius Vergilius Maro**; 70–19 B.C.): One of the most important poets of ancient Rome. Born at Mantua in Cisalpine Gaul (northern Italy), he was a friend of Horace. His patrons included Maecenas, Asinius Pollio, and Augustus. A poetic genius, Vergil composed the national Roman epic the *Aeneid* and the pastoral poems *Eclogues* (or *Bucolics*) and *Georgics*. He shares with Horace the rank of poet laureate of the Augustan court.

Suggested Reading

Apuleius, *The Golden Ass*.

Burkert, *The Ancient Mystery Cults*.

Cumont, *The Mysteries of Mithra*.

———, *Oriental Religions in the Roman Paganism*.

Dodds, *Pagan and Christian in the Age of Anxiety*.

Jones, *Culture and Society in Lucian.*

Lucian, *On the Syrian Goddess.*

————, *Works.*

MacMullen, *Paganism in the Roman Empire.*

Nock, *Conversion.*

Plutarch, *Moralia*, vol. 5.

Roller, *In Search of God the Mother.*

Wilken, *The Christians as the Romans Saw Them.*

Witt, *Isis in the Ancient World.*

Questions to Consider

1. Why was the vision about mystery cults offered by Franz Cumont so convincing? How have excavations and new sources of information transformed this vision?

2. What were the specific appeals of the cults classified as mystery cults? How did they differ from civic and family cults? Did any of these cults offer a distinctively different vision of the divine?

3. How does the cult of Glycon reflect pagan religious views? What accounted for this cult's success?

4. How did the Romans accept new gods? Did the Romans have a sense of religious conflict? Why did the Romans regulate the actions of worshipers but never rites and belief?

The Mystery Cults

Lecture 4—Transcript

In this lecture, I wish to introduce you to the so-called "mystery cults." These are cults that are associated with initiation rites—in fact, the word comes from the Greek word for "to initiate" or "initiation"—and it meant that the member of this cult chose to join that particular cult and worship that divinity.

Mystery cults are a very controversial subject in the history of the religion of the Roman world; and in many ways they are the creation of a Belgian scholar named Franz Cumont, who was a brilliant scholar writing at the end of the 19th century when he produced his first works in his late 20s. All of his works are still available in translation in both English and French, and I believe there are German translations. Cumont was the first to define what a mystery cult was; and I must stress that point: It is not a term that is used by members of the upper classes in the Roman world who wrote most of the literature we have; it's a modern invention. The mystery cult is seen as somehow an indication of pagan spiritual malaise; it's often viewed as a bridge whereby many pagans became accustomed to certain visions of the divine that instinctively drew them over to Christianity in the 3rd, 4th, and 5th centuries. That's usually been a given in most of the popular accounts that are still written today and in the scholarship, certainly before the Second World War, before 1945. First, what I'd like to do is explain what mystery cults are all about, then look at some of the specific cults, and then finally why Cumont and others have believed they were such a turning point; and then we can assess the evidence and see whether these mystery cults are really what we think they are.

Cumont started his work on the cult of Mithras. That is a god who was originally Persian in origin; he is seen as a creator-god who fights a great cosmic bull and carries out an act of creation. Therefore, Cumont concluded that not only the cult of Mithras but other cults such as Aphrodite and Adonis at Paphos on the island of Cyprus, Artemis Ephesia, and Cybele the great mother-goddess of Asia Minor all had certain features. One of the features was either a dying god or creator-god who acted on behalf of humanity. It might have been analogous to a sacrifice or the birth of Dionysus, which is told in myth; all of these involved some type of special action in which the divinity really went out of its way to benefit mankind.

Another feature among the mystery cults, and one that Cumont thought was all-important, is notions of afterlife and redemption, which go together. The pagans have a sense of afterlife. It's still debated what it was, and the best we can tell is it was contradictory. Most pagans believed there was a spiritual afterlife; they did not believe in a physical resurrection of the flesh. Earliest Greek accounts suggest a very vague notion where one puts on the feathers of a bird-like creature and flits off to Hades. The earliest description we have of the afterlife is in the *Odyssey*, Book 11, when Odysseus goes to the underworld or the gates of the underworld and sacrifices a lamb, calls up the ghosts or the spirits of the deceased—he particularly wants to question Tiresias, the famous prophet that some of you may know from the Oedipus legend—and what appears is a *nekyia*, a sort of fleeting head with an insubstantial body (the *nekyia* is a Greek word that denotes some sort of insubstantial existence). He questions Tiresias, and he also sees other ghosts including not only Agamemnon, but also Achilles, the greatest hero in the Trojan War. He questions Achilles, and Achilles says, "Would that I be the slave of a thede [that is, of a landless man] than lord of all the dead."

These notions of afterlife, in Cumont's opinion and in other scholars' opinions, meant that the mystery cults offered something new. In the mystery cults, the notion was that death and redemption were somehow connected with living a pious life; that sin took on a much more moral connotation; it wasn't just not performing the proper rites to the ancestors and the gods, but it had a moral and personal quality to it. This is seen in certain rites. The most important rite was the so-called *taurobolium*, associated with the myth of Cybele, where there was the sacrifice of a bull, sometimes a pig, and the initiate stood underneath it. One Christian writer, Prudentius, writing in the end of the 4th century A.D. said that this is the pagan equivalent of baptism (that's probably a Christian misunderstanding the rite deliberately because he then goes on to mock it). There are also references in *The Golden Asse*, the famous novel by Apuleius set in Africa in the 2nd century A.D.; that is, the Roman province of Africa, today Tunisia. The protagonist Lucius, who's turned into an ass and goes through misadventures, eventually ends up being restored to human form and joins the cult of Isis, the Egyptian goddess. He becomes one of her priests, and he undertakes the shaving of his head and putting on the garb of an Egyptian-style priest. At the end, there's some kind of promise of renewal or redemption, the implication being Lucius has now entered a new life by joining this mystery cult. Afterlife, redemption; all of that is tied up with the dying or the creating divinity.

Furthermore, these mystery cults were seen as somehow enthusiastic, irrational, and non-classical. One author, E. R. Dodds, who's written on these types of subjects in the 1950s, really drove home the point that the communal and family cults in the Roman world were just somehow not fulfilling, whereas these mystery cults, which were foreign in origin or had a foreign tinge to them, were more exciting; one chose to join them. The rites of Serapis and Isis (Serapis is the Hellenized—that is, the Greek form—of Osiris, Isis is his consort; they are the divinities of Alexandria, the great city in Egypt); Mithras, originally of Persian origin; Cybele from Asia Minor; Astarte from Syria: All of these divinities had something exciting; and we're told in particular with several of the cults—notably for Serapis and Isis and the Syrian cults—there was all sorts of jazzy music that went along, with drums and what is known as a *sistrum*, which is a musical instrument you shake to make noise. All of this was attractive; these rites would attract crowds; they would attract initiates; and somehow they're seen as more exciting and more fulfilling than the family and communal rites to which you were born.

In addition with that whole notion of [being] more spiritually and emotionally fulfilling was the fact that the initiates chose to join the cult. There were initiation rites—that is, you became a member of a specific cult—and Cumont and others have gone so far as to say that the mystery cults proselytized; that they went out of their way to find members. As a result, they acted essentially as a prototype or a model for later Christian missionaries. When you add it all up, these cults are seen as somehow prefiguring Christianity in one way or another, acting as a potential bridge to Christianity, and also as an index to something that was wrong with the other traditional pagan cults.

This composite image has been built up by looking at specific cults. Some of the cults are Greek and are very, very well known in the Greek world.

Archaeology and the study of the so-called Linear B tablet show that the cult of Demeter and Persephone—associated with the myth of the rape of Persephone; she's taken to the underworld by Hades and then released for part of the year, and that's located at the site of Eleusis near Athens where you're initiated and there's a cave, the Plutonium, where supposedly Hades went back in with Persephone—this is often classified as a mystery cult because there's initiation rites and there's a myth of redemption; along with it, it deals with rebirth and renewal, not necessarily salvation as a Christian would understand it. The rites of Dionysus are put in the same category. The Bacchantes, the Baccha; that is, the male and female devotees of Dionysus, with all the imagery and the music, and Dionysus was born in extraordinary ways. He's the god of enthusiasm, the irrational, and theater. "Ecstatic" is a word that comes out of the Dionysiac cult. It means to step out of oneself, to go into an ecstatic state and then to become *enthousiastikós*; that is, filled up with the god by some kind of ritual meal or the drinking of wine and dance. Both of these Greek cults are seen as mystery cults and somehow not Classical, although it's clear that all of those divinities were worshiped well into the Bronze Age—that would be between 1600 and 1225 B.C.—and one questions: How long do you have to be a cult in Greece before you become Greek? This classification becomes a little questionable.

Egypt and the Near East are supposed to have produced a number of mystery cults. The most famous is Mithras. The Mithras cult, in Cumont's opinion, originated from Iran. Mithras is a god known from the *Avesta*, which is the religious text of Zoroastrianism, which is redacted—that is, it's edited and reformed in the 3rd and 4th centuries A.D.—and is still the basis of the Zoroastrian religion today; and Mithras is a guardian or an angel-type figure, but he becomes the prime god in the Roman world. Cumont simply concluded that slaves and captives captured in the great wars of expansion in the eastern Mediterranean in the 1st century B.C. were taken to Rome and they popularized the cult in Rome, and that's how the cult originated. It's speculation; we don't have any documented evidence of this. What we do know is that the cult of Mithras emerges in the Flavian Age.

The Flavian Age represents the period from 69–96; it's the second dynasty of Rome associated with the emperor Vespasian and his sons, and there are a lot of important changes that occur at the end of the 1st century A.D. We have inscriptions from that date that it was Roman soldiers and customs officials, very often imperial freedmen—ex-slaves who acquired their freedom by service to the empire—who worshiped the cult. The Mithraeum is a temple of Mithras, and we have a number of Mithraea in Italy, the Upper Danube, and the Rhine.

These are associated with Roman army camps. The cult was popular in the Roman army. The priestly garb was superficially Iranian; Mithras is decked out sort of as an Eastern figure. He wears what is called a Phrygian cap, which is really the Roman equivalent of Orientalism; that is, anyone from the East wears this cap. No Persian wears this cap, but the Romans figured, "If you're from the East, you have to wear a Phrygian cap." It's actually the attire of western Asia Minor. It attracted soldiers, it attracted officials; it had a lot of support from emperors; and above all, the cult was seen as very good because it involved oaths. The initiates swore a *sacramentum* that was very similar to the type of oath taken in the imperial cult or administered to provincials at the festivals of the imperial cult. You can see the close association: Mithras was a creator-god; he killed a great cosmic bull; oaths, loyalty; a hierarchy similar to the Roman military. You could understand the appeal of this cult in the Roman army.

The cult of Cybele—or Kybele, or Kubaba as she would be known in her Anatolian name—actually arrived to Rome in 204 B.C. during the Second Punic War. It came from the sanctuary of Pessinus in what is now Western Turkey. The cult statue was brought over, and the cult was officially received at Rome. She is a mother-goddess, typical of Asia Minor and Syria. She is called in Latin *mater deum*, which is an old Latin genitive (those of you who know Latin would say *mater deorum*, but this is an archaic form of that plural of the possessive). So she's *mater deum*, mother of the gods, mother of all gods and goddesses. Her cult was never received within the *pomerium*—that is, the sacred precinct of Rome—only Roman cults could cross that limit and be in the city of Rome; but her cult was received. The priests continued to be *Galli*; that is, foreigners, eunuchs, slaves. Catullus, the brilliant lyric poet of the late republic, wrote a poem 63 talking about her lover, Atys, who self-castrated himself with a flint knife—I remember reading this poem when I was in college and we all got squeamish about it—and then serving as her priest thereafter. That's one of the cases—that mutilation; that self-mutilation—that's seen by Cumont and others as an indication of these sort of dying savior-gods that are typical of mystery cults, even though Atys is a mortal and not a divinity.

Of course, Serapis and Isis need very little introduction; they're the original divinities of Egypt. They're subject to an essay by Plutarch we'll be talking about in which they're interpreted in a Platonic guise. Above all, Serapis comes off in the iconography as essentially an Egyptianized version of Zeus or Hades in his attire. Isis is sometimes worshiped alone without her consort; most of the time she's worshiped with a consort. There are cases where she appears with her child, essentially as a Madonna and child; that appears on Roman coins, in fact. The cult was very popular with certain emperors (Domitian, Hadrian). Those of you who've been to Pergamon might have seen what is known as the Kizil Avlu, the red building, the red courtyard, which is a vast complex built by the emperor Hadrian on behalf of the Egyptian divinities worshiped in the city of Pergamon, which is today in Western Turkey, and that is very far removed from Alexandria.

The cult of Dionysus, or in his Latin form, Bacchus: We have indications of initiation rites there in the so-called Villa of Mysteries in Pompeii, a famous set of frescoes that seems to show the initiation of young girls. There's a cult to the Syrian goddess Astarte; there's a whole tract or essay written by Lucian of Samosata who is a very, very witty fellow. He's the fellow who actually puts together the tales of Aesop as we have them today, and he writes numerous entertaining works about the gods and parodies on the gods and the like. Then, of course, there's Demeter and Persephone, the cult I already discussed. These are the main cults that are usually used as the examples of mystery cults.

Cumont and others, as I say, until really down to this current generation when there's been some major revision, have again interpreted this general picture and the specific cults as a way of showing, somehow, pagan malaise, the flipside of the vision of Eusebius I mentioned earlier. That is, as Christianity is rising, paganism is in trouble, and the mystery cults are in some way a proof of the problems in paganism; they're not statistical as we would like them. Roman authors like Virgil and Horace lament the decline of piety in the civil war. August carries out a huge effort to rebuild temples in Rome. In his *Res Gestae Divi Augusti*, which is the queen of Latin inscriptions—it's on the temple of Cybele at Ankara today; it talks about all of his deeds in both Greek and Latin—one of his claims is, "I rebuilt 82 temples in Rome, I restored so many rites, I gave so much money for the restoration of the cults" and many have seen this as all part of a rearguard action; that already pagan cults were on the wane at the very beginning of the Roman Empire and this is just an effort of more moralizing rather than moral reform. That would lead to authors like Dodds and others who would see this anxiety; somehow the mystery cults are trying to fulfill it; and eventually some would argue so much as to say that Christianity was the most successful of the mystery cults, because you'll make comparisons between Christianity and the mystery cults.

In 235, we'll discuss that there's a major political and military crisis that engulfs the empire for the next 50 years. We have very little documentation, so if you take Eusebius's picture with the mystery cults and with our notions about what paganism is, it's seen that from 235–312—the conversion of Constantine—it's at this decisive point where the numbers begin to cross over significantly to the Christians and paganism loses out. The mystery cults, in effect, in some ways are subsumed into Christianity, particularly the cult of Sol Invictus, or the unconquerable sun god. Much of the solar imagery is taken over to represent the triumphant Christ. Sol Invictus is a popular god invoked in the period of crisis. He's sometimes classified as, if not a mystery cult, as a syncretist god who is representative of all the various sun gods and therefore represents an incipient monotheism. We can all agree there's a sun god and they come in different guises; and the sun god is a supreme power; and then the next step in this argument is maybe he's the only power, maybe there's only one god and everything else we look at are lesser manifestations. That's probably what they saw. That's really henotheism; that is, a single divine power but manifested in many ways. As I've said earlier, these notions of syncretism or henotheism are really premised on diversity; and it's misleading to think that this necessarily would lead inevitably to monotheism.

I've painted this picture of mystery cults. There are problems with it. These have become ever more evident as historians have applied two points: One, they've looked at the worshipers themselves rather than the gods. Two, you have to bear in mind that the way we approach mystery cults (which is a term that no ancient ever used)—no ancient ever compared Christianity to a mystery cult; no ancient author ever said that the mystery cults were in competition with the other cults; the mystery cults were just treated as one more set of cults—from the start, we're really operating on a modern assumption that unless religion is personal, it's brooding on the great questions of cosmology (that is, how the world comes into being) or questions of sin and redemption, it's not really religion. If it's just ritual, the modern conclusion could be, "That's just formulaic; that's just conforming to what everyone does. That's not real faith." Again, that comes from our notions that really come out of the 17th century with the end of the Thirty Years' war and particularly with Dutch theologians and critics of that war that we can never have a destructive war over religion again in Europe like this, and religion increasingly becomes a matter of conscience, a matter of choice, rather than of ritual, tradition, and all of that.

Furthermore, efforts to show mystery cults on the rise by the number of Mithraea or the number of inscriptions—the studying of inscriptions is known as epigraphy or epigraphic dedications; those are inscriptions with dedications to gods—yeah, they go up in the 2nd and 3rd centuries, but so do all inscriptions to all gods; and if you classify the total number of known inscriptions, and the Romans put up more inscriptions in stone and in metal than anyone in the world (we call that the epigraphic habit; this almost compulsion to record everything on stone that characterizes the early Roman Empire) the most numerous dedications are to the traditional gods: Jupiter, Mars, Juno, the usual suspects.

Furthermore, many of these mystery cults have been selectively studied to act as a parallel to Christianity rather than seen on their own terms. This is very, very true with the Mithras cult. It was a cult that was really essentially Roman with an Iranian veneer. The grades were patterned after the Roman military hierarchy. Furthermore, the cult spreads in the wrong direction. If the mystery cults are somehow out of Egypt or the Near East—that is, they're going from east to west—the cult first appears in Italy in the Flavian Age and then spreads east, and actually the Roman Mithraic cult as we know it has very little play in the eastern army; it's mostly the armies on the Rhine and the Danube. When Constantine converted to Christianity in 312 and withdrew support, the Mithraic cult essentially disappeared; it depended very heavily on the army and imperial patronage. The same thing with Cybele and her *taurobolium*: It's a votive sacrifice, it's not a baptism; that's been done by a study. In the case of Serapis and Isis, which is seen as sort of the premiere proselytizing cult—and we have cults of Serapis and Isis in other cities— when you look at the people setting up the dedications, 85 percent of them come from Roman Alexandria; that is, these are expatriates worshiping their traditional divinity in a new setting.

In some cases, a lot of this association with Serapis and Isis is nothing more than what is known as Aegyptomania. Aegyptomania is a certifiable disease that means you love everything Egyptian—I always have one or two undergraduates in my freshman class who know more about the pyramids than I'll ever know—and this was a rage that afflicted Romans. The most famous is Publius Cestius, who around 16–12 B.C. built a little pyramid that is a funerary monument in Rome. I always love traveling on the Metropolitana, the Roman subway, because there's a stop called "Pyramide" and you just get off and there's the pyramid.

When you take a look at the cults themselves, they really don't add up to a coherent body of mystery cults; they're all quite distinct; and the most important point: Wherever these cults go, they're assimilated to their setting. I can give a good example of assimilating to setting from New Orleans: We have the Saint Joseph's Day Parade, originally a Sicilian saint associated with the Sicilian community in New Orleans, and that was a very, very specific parade involving hospitals. Over time, that Italian parade has become assimilated to the rest of the city. It has the throes of Mardi Gras; all the politicians show up; and in many ways, the Saint Joseph Day Parade is now a general city-wide parade. Sure, it was originally Italian or Sicilian; sure it has a certain thrust to it; but everyone in the city participates. This would have happened to Serapis and Isis. Isis is associated with all of the divinities of the city, and therefore these mystery cults are not in competition; they're not necessarily an alternative to the existing cults.

In fact, with the exception of Mithras, all of these cults long antedated Roman rule. A way of approaching it: Again, go back to Lucian of Samosata. He wrote this work on the assembly of the gods, and it's a parody. All these new gods are being admitted, and Atlas feels the weight. But it's a parody; it still is based on belief.

There is a second cult that emerges in the Roman world, and it's very significant in a number of ways because it shows what's expected of religion by pagans. This is a cult of the god Glycon, which is a serpent divinity fitted out with a human head. Lucian, again, is our source; he writes a wickedly-satirical essay on it. It's set up by a charlatan prophet known as Alexander of Abonoteichus, who lived between 105 and about 170 A.D. I always tell my students when they read this work that it really is a handbook on how to set up a cult if you wish to buy some property in Oregon and come up with your own cult, because there are certain aspects of it that are very, very successful. First there was a miracle. That miracle was Alexander told the people of the town of Abonoteichus—which is a very small town in northern Turkey today near the Black Sea shore—that they should dig in a certain place, and they come upon a great egg and a little serpent hatched. They're all surprised; they all go away, and the next day they come back and find a fully-grown serpent with a human head (it's apparently attached with something that's papier-mâché); and Alexander just swapped out the two serpents. He picks up the serpent and proceeds to answer oracles, questions in the audience, about my love life, whatever. Apparently, he can throw his voice and it looks like the serpent is speaking; and Alexander has plants in the audience. An oracle!

It's a miracle, an oracle, sacred space; it's associated with Abonoteichus; but above all it's not a new god, it's just a god that's been rediscovered. It turns out that Glycon is the son of Asclepius, the god of healing, a god popularly worshiped in the Roman world at Pergamon, Claros, and Epidaurus, and that the oracle is equivalent to Claros and Delphi. Alexander is very, very clever here: He lays off some of the action. A question is asked to the oracle and he says, "We can't answer that. Go to Delphi. Go to Claros." The other oracles say, "Hey, that's great. This is apparently legit." Ophism, the worship of serpents, was very common in that part of Asia Minor, so it's very popular. You had your miracle, your sacred space with oracles; you've gained recognition from the other great sanctuaries; and above all: patronage. Several Roman senators are attracted to the cult, and eventually the emperor Marcus Aurelius himself. Once you get the approval of the emperor Marcus Aurelius, you've made it. He actually is briefly at the court of Marcus

Aurelius; he's on campaign on the Danube. That cult of Glycon continued long after the death of Alexander of Abonoteichus. We have coins and we actually have cult statues that have been found on the cities of the Black Sea, both on what is today the Bulgarian shore and the shore of Northern Turkey.

While perhaps a fraud set up by a charlatan, nonetheless this cult—which is a new cult in a sense—shows what is expected, and what is expected is a very traditional pagan cult. I would conclude that the mystery cults are not in competition; they're not a measure of decline; far from it. They're part of the vast diversity of religious experience available to pagans. If so, that means we have to look at the rise of Christianity from a different perspective, and that the mystery cults cannot be used as a convenient way of explaining pagan decline or Christian triumph.

Platonism and Stoicism
Lecture 5

The two most important philosophical schools of the Roman Empire were Platonism and Stoicism—related philosophies inherited from the Athenian Greeks. While not religions in themselves, the Roman ruling classes applied these philosophies to the practice of traditional paganism, which affected their views of morality, duty, piety, and cosmology. Neither Platonism nor Stoicism was inherently hostile to Christianity, and in fact both schools would influence early Christian thinkers, although those thinkers first had to learn to write in the language of Plato before Roman philosophers would take them seriously.

Greek Thought Conquers Rome

- Among the various philosophies practiced by the ruling classes in the Roman world, the two most important were Platonism—particularly middle Platonism and **Neoplatonism**—and **Stoicism**. Platonism is of course traced to **Plato**; Stoic doctrines go back to **Zeno of Citium** but were modified greatly by the 2nd century B.C., so Roman Stoicism is really a separate school of thought.

- Most people who used philosophy as a moral guide in the Roman world were among the upper, educated classes. They were eclectics, rather than strict adherents of one philosophy or another.

- Plato was the most influential philosopher to the Romans for several reasons. First, he established the philosophical language, writing in perfect, pristine Attic Greek. In the dialogue *Timaeus*, he puts forth the first scientific cosmology, one that did not resort to allegory, myth, or sexual imagery. He also tried to create a coherent body of all knowledge to that point, particularly mathematics.

The Basics of Platonism and Neoplatonism

- Within Plato's philosophical system, which is an open philosophy, are a lot of points Plato does not bother to explain. He is essentially an optimist; not everything needs to be explained. Instead, he focuses on *mythos*—that is, a plausible explanation or speculation, not hard and fast canonical truths.

- In the *Timaeus*, Plato describes three ultimate realities: a **Demiurge**, the Greek word for craftsman. This is a passive creator god who made the universe in a single act by using all available material; the ideas, or forms, eternal patterns that exist forever for the material world we experience; and finally the receptacle, which is the space that gives shape to the ideas.

- Plato's successors often replaced the ideas and the receptacle with the **nous** (intelligence), or thought in its purest form, and psyche, meaning "spirit" or "soul," respectively.

Plato's philosophies affected early Christian thinkers.

- Plato thought that evil is the absence of good, not a force as argued by some later philosophical systems, certain Christian sects, and the Gnostics, who saw the material world as innately evil. Pagan philosophers agreed with Christian thinkers that the Gnostics and others who renounce the material world are renouncing God's (or the gods') creation.

- Plato drew a strong distinction between the three realities and the physical world. The eternal world was *to einai* (the world of being), and the physical world was *gignesthai* (the world of becoming, of flux and change). What we see in this physical world is nothing but an imperfect reflection of reality. The informed individual who has *gnōmē*, "knowledge," can perceive beyond the physical world the eternal patterns and the true reality.

- One of the most important innovations on Plato's theory was made by Aristotle. Aristotle, a materialist, defined the creator god as a rational god whose thought is fully actualized—that is, the Aristotelian god is essentially a computer with eternal input going into eternal output. By the act of pure thought, he moves the universe.

- To Aristotle, the middle Platonists, and the Neoplatonists, the individual souls of humans are fragments of the world's soul imprisoned in the body. This is the beginning of a notion that will be expressed by Plotinus in the 3rd century as the Great Chain of Being. The duty of the informed person is to ascend the chain through understanding.

Plato's Ideas and Rome's Religion

- Platonic mysticism is very intellectual. It requires a great deal of discipline, learning, and training. Furthermore, Platonic philosophy in its later guises was readily adapted to the traditional cults.

- **Plutarch of Chaeronea**, who wrote biographies of the Greeks and Romans as well as moral tracts, wrote that Platonism was a way of understanding the cults and the myths. For instance, he wrote an essay on Serapis and Isis in which he reinterpreted the combat between Serapis and his brother Seth, the evil god of the desert, as a Platonic allegory in which Serapis represents the yearning to understand and Seth represents the physical world holding us back.

- Plutarch (who was also a priest of the Eleusinian Mysteries) was offering a way of using philosophy not only as a moral guide to your personal life but as a way of interpreting the cults in a higher reality—as allegorical, symbolic, and therefore worthy of perpetuation. Philosophy was not a copout; it was a way of coming to terms with and giving new moral meaning to the traditional cults and myths.

- **Philo of Alexandria** was a Jew living in the Greek city of Alexandria, Egypt, who wrote a work on the creation. He used the doctrines of Plato to understand his own Jewish faith. Philo is a pivotal figure because he shows how Platonic philosophy can be divorced from worship of the traditional gods and applied to a monotheistic creed.

- Platonic doctrines tended to prevail in the eastern half of the Roman Empire. They began to arrive in the city of Rome in the 2nd century A.D. as seats in the senate opened to provincials from the East. So the popularity of Platonism reflects the changing makeup of the Roman aristocratic class.

The Evolution of Roman Stoicism

- Roman Stoicism can be traced not only to the Stoic teacher Zeno of Citium but also to **Chrysippus**, both of whom were writing in the 3rd century B.C. and considered themselves students of Plato. Greek Stoicism had a very complicated cosmology; when the Romans first encountered it in the 2nd century B.C., they did not know what to make of it. Cato the Elder simply ran the Greek philosophers out of Rome.

- Later Stoics realized that the Romans were far more interested in morality and practical philosophy than explanations of how the world came to be. One of the most important figures behind this was **Posidonius of Apamea**, writing in the 2nd and 1st centuries B.C.

- In Roman Stoic doctrines, the creator god is the **Logos**, the word; this rational act is often identified with Jupiter. A logical order is created by the Logos; that is, what happens in the physical world matters, and each person is born into a position and should follow the divine plan. Stoicism is also an optimistic philosophy; it does not reject the physical world.

- **Epictetus of Hierapolis**, writing in the 2nd century A.D., was a slave, turned philosopher, turned Roman citizen, who summed up the earlier Stoic doctrines for the Romans. He said the divine plan was much like the Roman army: You have your rank; you might be promoted, or you might be demoted if you do not do what you are supposed to.

- Roman Stoics cultivated *apatheia*—not "apathy" in our modern sense but keeping an even keel emotionally. They believed every person contained a divine spark from the Logos; ergo, every human had a certain capacity for divinization that would be identified with the soul in the Platonic system.

The "Golden Slavery"

- It is hard to say how many Romans were really Stoics. Most of them were probably eclectics. There were probably many more Platonists because there were many more people in the eastern half of the empire. The men who were Roman Stoics were from the ruling class and ran the Roman imperial government for almost 250 years, even under the corrupt emperors, out of an obligation to family, nation, and ancestral custom, justified by Stoic doctrines.

- Roman Stoicism is best expressed in the *Meditations* of Emperor Marcus Aurelius, who was a practicing Stoic. Aurelius wrote *Meditations* while he was battling the Germans on the northern frontier of the Danube in the 160s and 170s. For him, contemplation was a luxury; this is in contrast to the Platonic view, in which contemplation was a holy attempt to reach the creator god.

- Marcus Aurelius's philosophy stresses the importance of duty, honor, and the traditional cults. This is why he persecuted Christians. He also called the emperorship "golden slavery," a duty he must perform because he was born to it.

- The Romans never believed in equality; there was always a hierarchy. The people of the upper classes had more of the divine spark than the lower classes. But each had a duty to play a part in the divine plan. You can understand why the British of the 19th century, especially those involved in the colonial government, saw in Marcus Aurelius and the Roman Stoics the models for their own governors.

The Intersection of Philosophy and Religion

- Some scholars have wondered whether philosophy was a substitute for religion for the elite or if educated Romans really believed in their gods. It seems the vast majority of them did believe. **Dio Chrysostom**, a middle Platonic scholar of the early 2nd century A.D., argued that one could not know whether the traditional rites work or whether the gods heard them, but they were ancestral and therefore it was appropriate to continue them.

- In this same period, Cynic philosophers throughout Rome rejected or renounced the world. Cynics tended to be individuals who would show up in cities and cause riots. They were unpopular with the vast majority of Roman citizens. Sometimes a Christian missionary would be compared to a Cynic, but Diogenes of Corinth, who supposedly lived in a barrel, is the classic example.

- Neither the Platonists nor the Stoics ever formed a clergy. Most of them were engaged in the wider world as teachers or as part of the ruling class. What is more, they were not necessarily hostile to Christians.

- Philosophers did not have a canon like the Christians and Jews. They had a number of important texts that were read, shared, and discussed, but no one work was considered sacred scripture, and no one teacher had a monopoly over what was taught. Instead, the philosophers shared their positions with grammarians, rhetoricians, and teachers of oratory.

- Despite this intellectual freedom, proper philosophy had to be written in proper Attic Greek, the Greek of Plato, or no one took you seriously. This was the fallout of the Second Sophistic movement of the 1st and 2nd centuries A.D.

- Mastery of all Attic Greek was part of being trained as a gentleman; it did not have a religious connotation, and eventually the Christians learned it and became learned gentlemen, just like their pagan counterparts. Until that time, however, the Romans would be hostile to the representatives of the new Christian movement.

Important Terms

Demiurge: "Craftsman"; the term used by Plato in his dialogue *Timaeus* (c. 360 B.C.) to describe the creator God.

Logos: Greek for "word"; in Stoic philosophy, the divine active intelligence of the universe. Christians (based on John 1:1) applied the term to Christ as the second person of the Trinity.

Neoplatonism: The Platonic philosophical doctrines as interpreted by Plotinus (205–270) and later philosophers.

nous: Greek for "mind": The second level of reality—rational intelligence—in middle Platonic and Neoplatonic philosophy.

Stoicism: The philosophical doctrines of Zeno of Citium (334–262 B.C.). Zeno could not afford a school, so he taught under the public stoas—hence the name of the philosophy.

Names to Know

Chrysippus (c. 280–207 B.C.): Native of Soli in Cilicia and a leading Stoic philosopher who taught at Athens, perfecting Stoic physics and logic.

Dio Chrysostom (a.k.a. **Dio the Golden Mouthed**; c. 40–120): Greek sophist and philosopher born at Prusa, Bithynia, in northwestern Asia Minor.

Dio taught at Rome until he was banished by Emperor Domitian. A convert to Stoicisim, Dio left some 80 orations on a host of subjects.

Epictetus of Hierapolis (55–135): Stoic philosopher who arrived at Rome as the slave of Epaphrodites, freedman secretary of Emperor Nero, studied Stoic philosophy with Gaius Musonius Rufus, and acquired his freedom. In 93, Epictetus, along with several other philosophers, were banished from Rome on the orders of Domitian. His writings on moral conduct gained him admirers among the senatorial class and from Emperor Hadrian.

Philo of Alexandria (c. 15 B.C.–45 A.D.): Jewish thinker and Platonist who headed the prosperous Jewish community of Alexandria and represented Jewish interests in the embassy to Emperor Caligula in protest of the laws requiring sacrifice in A.D. 39–40. A prolific writer, Philo used Platonic analysis and schemes in *On the Creation* to elucidate the Jewish faith and so set the model for Christian Platonic thinkers.

Plato (428–348 B.C.): Athenian philosopher and disciple of Socrates (470–399 B.C.) who founded the Academy and defined Western philosophy. He was from a noble family and despised the Athenian democracy. His dialogue *Timaeus*, composed around 360 B.C., defined all subsequent Greek and Roman speculation on cosmology and morality. His philosophical dialogues also set the standard of literary Attic Greek prose.

Plutarch of Chaeronea (c. 45–120): Platonic philosopher, biographer, and scholar born at Chaeronea, Boeotia, in central Greece. He studied at both Athens and Rome and was a friend of Emperor Trajan. His works include the *Moralia*, 60 essays on a wide range of topics, and *Parallel Lives of Greeks and Romans*.

Posidonius of Apamea (135–51 B.C.): Stoic philosopher, historian, and astronomer who studied under Panaetius at Athens. Favorable to Rome, he traveled the lands of the western Mediterranean, writing on geography and ethnography. In his philosophical writings, he refined Plato's doctrine on the soul (*pysche*) and Stoic cosmology.

Zeno of Citium (335–263 B.C.): A merchant turned philosopher and founder of Stoicism. From 301 B.C., he taught in the Stoa Poikile at Athens because he could not afford a proper school. His ethnical and philosophical writings survive in fragments.

Suggested Reading

Arnold, *The Physical World of the Stoics*.

Dillon, *The Middle Platonists*.

Kaster, *Guardians of Language*.

MacMullen, *Enemies of the Roman Order*.

Marcus Aurelius, *Meditations*.

Philo of Alexandria, *On Creation*.

Philostratus, *The Life of Apollonius of Tyana*.

Plato, *Timaeus and Critias*.

Plutarch, *Moralia*.

Rist, *The Stoics*.

Swain, *Hellenism and Empire*.

Questions to Consider

1. How was the cosmology of Plato in *Timaeus* adapted by later thinkers in the Hellenistic and Roman ages? What were the concerns of these so-called middle Platonists? To whom did such doctrines appeal?

2. What did Zeno of Citium teach as the primary Stoic principles? Why did Romans initially find these doctrines unappealing? How did later Stoic thinkers adapt their philosophy to Roman political and social values?

3. In the imperial age, how did senators and equestrians adapt Stoic principles to conduct a moral life as a governing class devoted to traditional worship? How did they influence the very nature of imperial government?

4. Why is it misleading to see Platonic and Stoic philosophy as a bridge to Christianity? Why would pagan philosophers reject Christianity?

Platonism and Stoicism
Lecture 5—Transcript

In this lecture, I wish to shift gears a bit and look at the various philosophies that were practiced by the ruling classes in the Roman world. The two most important were those of Plato (we call that Platonism) and particularly what we call Middle Platonists and Neoplatonists—we'll be encountering those terms in other lectures—and these would be philosophers who followed the doctrines of Plato, writing in the Classical Age. There were also many practitioners of the Stoic doctrines. The Stoic doctrines go back to Zeno of Citium, but the doctrines of Zeno of Citium were modified greatly by the 2nd century B.C., so we really refer to it as Roman Stoicism since the Romans embraced Stoic ideas much more so than the doctrines of Plato. There were also followers of the doctrines of Epicurus, of the Pythagoreans that go back to the 6th century B.C., and there were a variety of eclectic philosophical schools; and probably most people who used philosophy as a moral guide in the Roman world among the upper classes were eclectics rather than strict members of one philosophy or another. There's a great deal of exchange of ideas, concepts, and terminology among the various philosophical schools.

I mentioned that Plato was the most important, and he's the most important for several reasons. First, Plato established the philosophical language in a way. He wrote in a perfect, pristine Attic-style Greek; he's a delight, still, to read. His most influential dialog was the *Timaeus*, written very late in his career in the 4th century B.C., and there he puts out the first scientific cosmology; that is, an explanation that did not resort to allegory, to myth, to the sexual imagery that you would find in most creation myths in earlier times. He also tried to create what would be called a coherent understanding of all knowledge at that point, particularly mathematics. Large parts of the *Timaeus* deal with his mathematical calculations to justify his understanding of the physical and spiritual world. That's generally not so much of interest not only to modern readers, but to many of his successors who were Middle Platonists or Neoplatonists; they tend to put that aside and actually grab the greater concepts of Plato for devising their own philosophical systems.

Within Plato's philosophical system, which is an open philosophy, there are a lot of points Plato doesn't bother to explain. He's essentially an optimist;

he's a mystic in many ways; and he doesn't have a pedantic mind where everything has to be explained. When reading Plato, remember: All of his dialogs are what Plato would call *he mythos*; that is, a plausible explanation. Usually in his late dialogs such as the *Timaeus* they are voiced by Socrates, but they are Plato's speculation and they are not a hard and fast canonical text. Nonetheless, the great ideas that come through in the *Timaeus* would influence not only most of the intellectual classes of the Roman world, but also Christian thinkers, particularly church fathers writing in the 2nd century A.D. on and writing in the Greek language.

To Plato, in the *Timaeus*, there were three ultimate realities. These were a Demiurge, which is simply the Greek word for "craftsman." It referred to a creator-god, a rather passive figure who made the act of creation in a single act by using all available material. The second reality was the ideas, or sometimes translated as "the forms," which is the Latin equivalent of the Greek word for "ideas." These are eternal patterns that exist forever for all the material world we see. Then there's a notion known as the receptacle, which is a very difficult concept to grasp; actually, modern physicists love this. The receptacle is the third reality: the space that gives shape to the ideas; that is, it provides the means whereby the ideas can be realized. These last two concepts of ideas and receptacle were pretty hard for a lot of Plato's successors to get a hold of, and they are usually replaced by *nous*, intelligence, thought in its purest form, and the receptacle is usually replaced by the term "psyche" in English, *psykhe* in Greek, meaning "spirit" or "soul". They like the Demiurge, the creator-god, and they'll be able to grab a hold of that.

There are two other important points that come out of this. Plato fundamentally thinks that evil is the absence of good; it's not an act of force as would be the case in later philosophical systems, certain Christian sects, and the so-called Gnostics that see the physical material world as innately evil. Plato never goes down that route, nor do Middle Platonists and Neoplatonists, pagans. In that sense, pagan philosophers will be agreed with Christian thinkers that Gnostics and others who renounce the world are renouncing a physical creation ultimately created by the god or the creator-god, and that means just by the act of creation it has to be inherently good and evil has to be accounted another way; it could be human action and sin, it could be the absence of good in the Platonic system.

Furthermore, Plato draws a very strong distinction between those three realities on the one hand and the physical world on the other; and he expresses it in Greek. As I always say, Greek is an incredibly flexible language. It's the language to do philosophy in, and as I will repeatedly say, God might speak in Hebrew but he has to think in Greek; you just can't use Latin and other languages. He distinguishes between the eternal world *to einai*—that is, the world of being as opposed to the world of flux and change; the world of becoming—and he uses the Greek verb *gignesthai*, which means "to happen," "to be," "to come into being"; and the Greek parallel is very, very nice, and, of course, in Latin it's lost. There's an eternal world that's fixed, and what we see in this physical world is nothing but a reflection and an imperfect reflection of the reality. The informed individual who has *gnome*, real knowledge—"wisdom" would be an English equivalent, from where we get the word "Gnostic" and words of that sort—is able to perceive beyond the physical world to what the eternal patterns are and what the true reality is.

The image is beautiful in the *Timaeus*, and all of the educated classes of the Roman world would have read that particular tract, both for style as well as for content. Above all, the successors to Plato worked on that image. One of the most important innovations was made by Aristotle. Aristotle is a materialist in his philosophy—he had no use for the ideas or the receptacle; it didn't make any sense to him—but he did define the creator-god as a rational god in which the thought is fully actualized; that is, "thinking on thinking" is the way it's expressed. I usually give the example to my students that the Aristotelian god is essentially a computer with eternal input going into eternal output (obviously the Hal 9000 series of *2001: A Space Odyssey*) and that in Aristotle and in the Middle Platonists and Neoplatonists, the creator-god of Plato is not actively creating, he's thinking on thinking. Pure thought is pure reason is the pure good, and by the act of pure thought he moves the universe; that is, the universe moves in imitation of the creator-god and then the other realities are a hierarchy: There's thought (*nous*), there's the world's soul, there are the lesser souls of humans that are fragments of the world's soul imprisoned in the body. And you begin to get a notion that will eventually be expressed by Plotinus, the great Neoplatonist writing in the

3rd century, as a great chain of being. Therefore, all of reality is moved by this pure, thoughtful god and the effort of the informed one is to go up to the higher level and understand it: Achieve an understanding of the world's soul, that the individual soul is related to the world's soul; and then from there to the higher thought, the *nous* or the noetic realm; and eventually, to grasp the final thinking on thinking.

Platonic mysticism is very, very intellectual. It requires a great deal of discipline, learning, and training; you must understand the text to reach that higher reality. That's one aspect about Platonic philosophy. Furthermore, Platonic philosophy in its later guises was readily adapted to the traditional cults.

There are two individuals I want to stress in this. There are a lot of writings that come from the Roman world, and one could just lose themselves in a course on various Platonists in the Roman world; but the most important for our purposes is Plutarch of Chaeronea, a very nice man. He's the sort of man you'd invite to a cocktail party because he was just filled with anecdotes. He wrote biographies of the Greeks and Romans; he wrote all these moral tracts; and to him, Platonism in its later form—that is, the interpretation of Plato's doctrines—was a way of understanding the cults and the myths. For instance, he wrote an essay on Serapis and Isis in which he reinterpreted the Egyptian myth—the combat between Osiris and his brother-god Seth, the evil god of the desert (called Typhron in Plutarch) and how Seth kills Osiris and cuts him up; and Isis, the wife and sister of Osiris, assembles the parts and reassembles her husband, who then goes to the underworld as the lord of justice—he reinterprets this as a Platonic allegory in which Osiris (his Greco-Roman name is Serapis) represents the noetic realm, the yearning to understand, and Seth represents the physical world holding us back. He has all sorts of interpretations of these ancient myths.

Plutarch himself was a priest of Demeter and Kore at Eleusis. He was inducted; he was not a native of Athens, but he was inducted into the Eleusinian mysteries, as were various Roman emperors. Therefore, what you read in Plutarch is a way of using philosophy not only as a moral guide to your personal life, but interpreting the cults in a higher reality; as allegorical, as symbolic, and therefore as worthy of perpetuation. Philosophy was not essentially a copout as it's sometimes seen for the upper classes—"Oh, we can't believe in these gods and goddesses"—far from it. For most of them, it was a way of coming to terms and understanding, giving new moral interpretation, to the traditional cults and myths as they had been taught as children.

The other individual I want to mention briefly is Philo of Alexandria. He died around 45 A.D. He's responsible for writing a work on the creation. He's a Jew, writing in Alexandria—you have to remember, Alexandria is a Greek city that happens to be in Egypt; it's not really an Egyptian city, it's a great Greek intellectual center—and there, writing in Greek, he used the doctrines of Plato to understand his own Jewish faith. In many ways, Philo is a pivotal figure because he shows how Platonic philosophy can be divorced from worship of the traditional gods and applied to a monotheistic creed, and many Christian authors look to Philo as an example that way. Platonism was probably the most common philosophy in terms of numbers in the Roman world. It was practiced in the Greek-speaking half of the Roman Empire and, again, it's eclectic; it's a moral system; it's an overall discipline; there are philosophers; but all literate classes would have been familiar with Plato. They would have read Plato, if nothing else for style and grammar. Platonic doctrines tended to prevail in the eastern half of the Roman Empire.

They begin to come to Rome in the 2nd century A.D. There's a lot of speculation about it, but the simple explanation for that is that starting in the mid-2nd century A.D., many more Roman senators, as the senate is open to provincials—men of wealth and rank in the provinces who become Roman senators—many of them come from the province of Asia, Western Turkey, from Syria, and from Greece and so the popularity of Platonism in the city of Rome in the 2nd and 3rd centuries A.D. really reflects the changing makeup of the Roman aristocratic class, which becomes the imperial aristocracy. If the imperial aristocracy has more people of Greek origin, obviously they're going to prefer Plato.

The other philosophy is Roman Stoicism, as I call it. These are doctrines that go back to the Stoic teacher Zeno of Citium and Chrysippus, who were writing in the 3rd century B.C. Both Zeno and Chrysippus would say, "We're just students of Plato." They didn't see themselves as setting up an alternate philosophy; not initially, anyway. Roman Stoicism is, again, an adaptation of Greek Stoicism. The Greek version of Stoicism, going back to Zeno, had a very complicated cosmology; there's an enormous amount of physics and mathematics. This sort of stuff just went over the heads of the Romans. When the Romans first encountered it in the 2nd century B.C., they didn't know what to make of it. Cato the Elder—Marcus Porcius Cato, that marvelous conservative of the republic—just ran the Greek philosophers out of Rome. "We have no time for these eggheads," and it's typical of the Greeks. But eventually, Stoic doctrines became quite popular in Rome, and that's because later Stoics realized that the Romans were far more interested in morality and the practical side of the philosophy rather than the explanation of the world.

One of the most important figures behind this is a man named Posidonius, writing in the 2nd and 1st centuries B.C., who made Roman Stoicism popular. He's also the fellow who figures out that the tides are being affected by the moon, and I think he calculates the distance from the Earth to the Sun as 53 million miles, which is off—it's about 93 million miles—but he's on the right order of magnitude; no one got nearly that close until centuries later. In the later Roman Stoic doctrines, the creator-god is the *logos*, the word, the rational act; it's a concept that goes back to Plato and Aristotle, and very often is identified with Jupiter of Roman religion. There's a logical order created by the *logos*; that is, what happens in the physical world matters. There's an overall plan—sometimes Stoics are almost deterministic in the way they look at this—and each is born into a position and should follow the divine plan.

Furthermore, Stoicism is an optimistic philosophy in a number of ways. It doesn't reject the physical world at all; far from it. One's position in the world is part of an overall plan. The best man expounding this to the Romans, Epictetus of Hierapolis, writing in the 2nd century A.D., was originally a slave, turned philosopher; he got liberated, got Roman citizenship; taught to the leading circles of senators and equestrians at Rome; and summed up the earlier Stoic doctrines. That notion that one is born into a position— very often the image used by Stoics is it's like a soldier: you have your rank, you might be promoted, you'll be demoted if you don't do what you're supposed to do—got very easily associated (this Greek notion, this Greek philosophical concept) to Roman notions of *virtus* (virtue); *gravitas* (seriousness); the notion that there's an overall plan. The Romans liked that because Rome rules the world; that's obviously part of the rational plan. This becomes very popular in the late republic. Cicero likes this notion; he describes it in his dream of Scipio where he talks about the Stoic vision of the worlds and the morality. That's in Book 6 of the *De Re Publica*; it's one of the most beautiful passages of Latin ever to read. It's just a marvelous exposition of Roman Stoicism.

The Stoic is to cultivate *apatheia*, meaning "apathy"; meaning no emotions in either way. You don't go too emotional one way or the other, but you keep an even keel. It doesn't mean "apathy" in the modern sense. Furthermore, we all have some sort of divine spark from the *logos*, and ergo every human has what the Latin Stoics would say is *capax divinitatis*; that is, there's a certain capacity for divinization, that there's something good innately in us that the *logos* had put in and that would be identified with the soul in the Platonic system. Stoics tend to be conservative, dutiful, sometimes deterministic. Roman Stoicism appealed to the ruling classes.

In terms of numbers, it's hard to define how many Romans were really Stoics, or even card-carrying Stoics. Most of them were probably eclectics; that is, they picked from a number of philosophies. There were probably many more Platonists because there are a lot more people in the eastern half of the empire, a lot more literate classes there, but the men who were Roman Stoics were the ruling class; the men who made the republic what it was and continued to run the Roman imperial government for almost 250 years under the emperors. Or, as the historian Tacitus would say, *boni viri sub principibus malis*; that is, "good men, virtuous men under evil princes." These are the doctrines of an imperial class summed up by the figures that come out of the pages of Tacitus, where they will put up with the emperors who are obviously a test from the world's soul; Rome is the ultimate experience. Roman Stoics in the imperial age—who were essentially the ruling class in the Roman senate—served out of an obligation to family, to patriotism, to custom, *mos maiorum* ("ancestral custom") justified by these Stoic doctrines, and you get a figure like Publius Clodius Thrasea Paetus, the critic of Nero, the senator who would stand up to Nero's antics and would always run the even keel.

The most famous incident is in 59 A.D., coming out of Tacitus, when Nero has a proclamation read that his mother, whom Nero had ordered murdered—

and you can't do anything worse in Italian society than to kill mom; it's the worst thing you could ever do, it's unspeakable—that a proclamation is read that Agrippina, Nero's mother, was executed on grounds of treason. Everyone knows in the senate that this is just bogus, covering up what was a hideous murder. Thrasea Paetus listens to this, he stands up, walks out of the senate. *Quis quid fugit domnit*; what one flees, one condemns. Everyone knows what he's saying: Nero is irrational; he's out of control. Thrasea Paetus can't maintain his virtue and his *apatheia*; it's time to withdraw from public life and cast aspersions and criticisms on Nero. In effect, Thrasea Paetus himself won't carry out the assassination, but it means to the ruling classes that it's open season to get rid of this tyrant emperor and eventually Nero is done in. There's a great conspiracy in 65. Thrasea Paetus isn't involved, but he's forced to commit suicide; clearly he is the spiritual influence of that type of assassination.

Virtue is all-important; service is all-important; dutiful worship of the gods is all-important. Greeks are astonished, starting with Polybius writing in 150 B.C., how pious and how serious the Romans are about their cults; how they really maintain a close relationship; how Roman legal language and religious language are very closely related. That is, when the Roman offers a prayer, that's a legal document; the Roman intends to deliver on that contract and then expects the god to deliver in turn. Roman Stoicism becomes the doctrines of the Roman upper classes, and it's best expressed in the *Meditations* of Marcus Aurelius, who was a practicing Stoic.

Marcus Aurelius wrote his *Meditations* while he was battling the Germans on the northern frontier of the Danube in the 160s and 170s. He really brings forth some of the basics of Roman Stoicism and some of its contrast to what a Platonist would regard as important. For Marcus Aurelius, the contemplative figure is a luxury. You do that when you retire into what the Romans would call *otium*, leisure; when you've finished your public career. The Platonist sees the holy man as the contemplative figure from the start; he's trying to achieve mystical union with the creator-god or whatever. The Stoics see an active life, and Christian Stoics like Tertullian have the same attitude. He's a lawyer turned Christian, and he's a Stoic in his notions.

In Marcus Aurelius's *Meditations*, which were various letters written to his worthless son Commodus who never bothered to read it, he encapsulates the importance of duty, of honor, and the traditional cults. That's why he persecuted Christians, for instance, even though in many ways, even to Christians he would look like a very noble emperor. He called the emperorship the "golden slavery," just as Antigonus Gonatas, my favorite Macedonian king. "I was born into it; I should do it dutifully." It's emperors like Marcus Aurelius who passed legislations to modify the treatment of slaves, the corporeal punishments. The Romans never go for equality or unity of mankind; there's always a hierarchy. The people at the upper class have more of the divine spark than the lower class. But there's a definite change of tone in the 1st and 2nd century B.C. of these Roman ruling classes—both the senators and Marcus Aurelius—that it's their duty to rule properly. You can understand why the British of the 19th century, especially going out to various places such as India, saw in Marcus Aurelius and these Roman Stoics the models for their own governors and their own successful figures in running these provinces—in the 19th century; in the 18th century we have rogues like Clive running around conquering India—but Stoicism became very, very much the doctrine of the Roman upper classes, and it was closely keyed to the worship of the traditional gods and rites.

There was no contradiction here. There was no case, as some scholars wondered: All of this popularity in philosophy; is this a substitute for religion or do they really believe in the cult? The vast majority of them would believe in the cult. What comes to mind—and I'll paraphrase it—is a comment by Dio Chrysostom, writing in the early-2nd century A.D. (a Middle Platonist scholar, an orator), who put it this way: We do not know whether the sacrifices and the rites to the gods work (that the gods hear them), but they're ancestral and they're appropriate and we should continue them. The term that comes through in Greek is *eudoxos*; appropriate, worthy, the proper thing to do. You would think of the British aristocrat saying, "No, that would be un-British to do that. Of course we do it this way; that's the way things are done." Roman Stoics and even many Platonists would agree on that sort of notion: that whatever the philosophical speculation, they had still a very, very strong belief in the traditional cults; and while the Christians may use this philosophy, it doesn't mean that the pagans effectively have rejected it.

There were philosophers known as cynics who rejected the world, renounced the world. Cynics tend to be individuals. They show up in cities; they cause riots. They're usually people who have renounced the world, and they're not very popular with the vast majority of people in the Roman Empire. Sometimes a Christian missionary would probably be compared to a cynic: "Oh, it's one of those guys denouncing the world." There's immediately a riot in the theater; the governor has to close it down. Cynics, who essentially renounce the physical world, remain more individuals who made spectacular displays of their asceticism and their renunciation. Diogenes in Corinth, living supposedly in the barrel, who met Alexander the Great; that's the classic image.

Another important point about these philosophers is they never formed a clergy. That is, even those men—and women; we'll find Hypatia in Alexandria, a very important Neoplatonist philosopher, the subject of a recent movie— were still engaged in the wider world. They were members of an upper class; they had the traditional education. There would be a *scholarch*, who would run the Platonic academy; there were various appointments. Nonetheless, philosophers were part of a wider ruling class. They're not a clergy necessarily hostile to Christians. Sometimes they're compared to Buddhist monks or Jains who were teaching in classic India against the priestly caste of Brahmins; that's a very, very misleading analogy and I myself was once subject to it until I really studied Hinduism more and went to India and realized that the differences are more significant. Philosophers were very much a part of that wider world. Many of these philosophers were ascetics and mystics—we'll see that with Plotinus, the great thinker of the Neoplatonic traditions—but those were personal choices. You didn't become an ascetic in order to become a monk or a holy man; that was something that was practiced and it was usually done by the philosophers as a way of getting the material world under control in order to reach that higher level of understanding.

Second, philosophers didn't have a control over canon. I've used the word "canon" before in relationship to Christians; it's a term that means "yardstick" or "measuring stick" in Greek. Christians and Jews have written texts that are holy, innate; innately holy (the Bible is what the Christians would turn to; the Jews, the Torah; Muslims would turn to the Quran). The philosophers have lots of texts—they draw on Plato; they're very well familiar with it—but they don't have a monopoly over sacred scripture that, say, Brahmins do in India or Buddhist monks have over their own text. Instead, the philosophers shared their position with grammarians and people who taught rhetoric and oratory. Think of it this way: The ancient world was essentially divided in the humanities between the English department and the Philosophy department. That is, the written word was all-important; and particularly for the educated classes of the Roman world, it wasn't just philosophy, you had to write it properly in Attic Greek. This is very often known as a movement called the Second Sophistic in the 1st and 2nd century A.D. You had to be able to write in perfect classicizing Greek of the 5th and 4th centuries B.C. the way Plato would write or else no one took you seriously.

The importance of diction, the knowledge of the text; all of that was all part of being trained as a gentleman, and then you would move onto philosophy. This is very, very peculiar because all of that training in language didn't have necessarily any kind of religious connotation and eventually the Christians could take it and become learned gentleman just like their pagan counterparts. Then, philosophy was a higher training in order to understand morality in the higher order. So, while philosophical systems were very important, they didn't have a monopoly on the educational system, they didn't constitute a clergy, and proper language was just as important; not the *koine* or vernacular Greek of the New Testament, but the proper Atticizing Greek that would be written by the upper classes.

What you're presented with is a very conservative world of upper classes using philosophical schemes to justify the cults, very, very much wedded to the language and the literature of the past, and in some ways almost smug in their understanding of their world; and so when the Christians come along, not only do they see them having bad philosophy, but the first thing is they don't know how to write properly. Therefore, from the start, there's an innate hostility to the representatives of the new Christian movement.

Jews in the Roman Empire
Lecture 6

The Romans thought they understood the Jews, but the relationship between the two cultures was fraught with many misunderstandings. Sometimes this led to conflicts, wars, and rebellions; other times, it allowed the Jews to quietly practice their faith under a deluded but satisfied imperial patron. The chronic mismanagement of the Jewish homeland, however, would ultimately lead to tragedy, and the Romans' failure to comprehend Jewish religion would leave them further baffled when they confronted the 1st-century pacifist sect of Judaism known as the Christians.

The Jewish People at the Dawn of the Empire

- Judaism was a very important faith in the Roman Empire; some estimate perhaps as much as 10 percent of the population of the empire was Jewish in the 1st century A.D. Understanding Judaism in the Roman Empire is obviously important to this course because Christianity emerged out of Judaism during this period.

- For the Romans, contact with Judaism was the first instance in which they dealt with members of monotheistic faith, as well as a nation that defined itself overwhelmingly by religion. Unfortunately, Romans actually misunderstood Judaism in a number of ways, and some of those misunderstandings carried over into their dealings with the Christians.

- The 4th century B.C. to the 2nd century A.D. is arguably the period in which the national worship of Yahweh as the god of the Hebrews turned into Judaism as we understand it: A monotheistic faith depending on text and moral purity and—as important as the Temple of Jerusalem was—not necessarily tied to any locale.

- Judaism is a faith that is carried everywhere; it is within the heart and mind. That resulted from the redaction of Judaism's sacred texts during the Babylonian Captivity—that is, the period from 586 to 539 B.C. when the Jews were deported to Babylonia. A religion based on canon is something quite distinct from paganism.

- When the Jews were allowed to return to their homeland by the Persian king Cyrus around 539 B.C., they rebuilt their temple in Jerusalem. The **Sadducees** were the priestly caste that administered the temple sacrifices, maintained ritual purity, and interpreted the Torah.

- The Persian kings respected Judaism, in part because the Jewish homeland was not of strategic importance to them. To the Romans, the region they called Palestine was an important route for moving their armies, and thus they had an interest in controlling the region and their people. (Please note: The term "Palestine" as used in this course refers to the Roman political division, a corruption of the word "Philistine," and should not be interpreted in a modern political context.)

The Jews of the Diaspora

- By the 2nd century B.C., many Jews had emigrated and had become members of the **Diaspora**, meaning "scattering" in Greek. Many of them left as mercenary soldiers, serving in Hellenistic armies and being rewarded with land. In the Diaspora, they quickly had to come to terms with Greek language and culture.

- In Alexandria, Egypt, the Jews were a powerful intellectual community. It is estimated that a third or more of the city's population of 750,000 to 1,000,000 people were Jewish. In lesser cities scattered throughout Asia Minor and Greece, Jewish communities set up **synagogues** side by side with Greek temples and gymnasia.

- Most of these Jews spoke Greek, which is why the Septuagint was created. Many of them adhered to the Pharisee tradition, the broader and more generous interpretations of Jewish law.

The Jewish Revolt against the Syrians led by Judas Maccabaeus in the mid-2nd century B.C. added to the tradition of Jewish apocalyptic literature.

The Hasmonaean Kingdom of Israel

- Roman Palestine was an unruly place. A century and a half earlier, the Jews had been ruled by the Seleucid kings of Syria. After 190 B.C. and a defeat at the hands of the Romans, the Seleucids were in constant fiscal and military crisis. King Antiochus IV Epiphanes tried to address this problem by imposing an active Hellenizing process on his lands, including Jerusalem and its temple, by sponsoring cults to Zeus.

- The Orthodox Jews, the Hasidim, raised the call for national resistance in 167 B.C. The Jews flocked to the banner of **Judas Maccabaeus**, who was of the House of Hashmon, or the **Hasmonaeans**. In 164 B.C., the Jews won a significant victory, destroyed the mercenary army of Antiochus IV, reoccupied Jerusalem, and rededicated the temple to Yahweh. This victory is still commemorated at Hanukkah.

- The Maccabees not only liberated Jerusalem; they expanded the kingdom, brought Samaria under Judean rule, subjected the pagan towns of the coast, and colonized the northern regions of Galilee. Rome, which had no love of the Seleucids, recognized the independent Jewish state.

- This national struggle was often seen in apocalyptic terms. There is a powerful apocalyptic tradition of Jewish texts talking about final judgments and the end of days, starting with the Maccabees and ending in the early 2nd century A.D. These texts included notions of a **Messiah**, a member of the house of David who would restore the kingdom of Israel. In more cosmic terms, he was the "son of man" who would preside over the final judgment. This tradition had a powerful influence on early Christianity.

- Eventually, the Hasmonaeans failed to keep order, and in 63 B.C. the Roman general Pompey stepped in to secure the coastal highway—the *Via Maris*—from Alexandria to Antioch and Syria. Eventually the Romans placed a half-Jewish mercenary general on the Jewish throne, a man known as **Herod the Great**.

The Romans Take Control of Israel

- The Jews had many reasons to dislike Herod, but he was the only man who could keep order among the various Jewish regions. The Romans liked Herod because he spoke Greek and understood the Roman political system. Herod kept order until his death in 4 B.C.; then the Jewish kingdom was partitioned among his three sons, who were eventually deposed for incompetence.

- The religious running of the Jewish homeland was given to the Sanhedrin, a high council composed of the Sadducees and Pharisees. This is the council that, according to the Gospels, put Jesus on trial. They administered the temple and ran Jerusalem.

- For civil administration, the Romans sent in governors called procurators. These were low-level equestrians. Procurator of

Judaea was a dead-end appointment; it meant you had washed out of the Roman imperial system. **Pontius Pilate** was a perfect (and incompetent) example.

- The Roman military presence in Palestine was minimal. The soldiers were inept locals, and some of them virulent anti-Semites. Their behavior contributed to the outbreak of the great national rebellions. Overall, the Romans mismanaged the province entirely.

Roman Culture and Jewish Faith

- For all that Rome tolerated and respected (or thought they respected) Judaism, the Romans did not understand it. To the Romans, Judaism looked legitimate: It was an ancestral national religion. Although they found the idea of a single god and the lack of images peculiar, they respected the fact that the rituals had gone on for centuries and believed that they had worked.

- They also misunderstood the Sadducees. They thought of them as some variety of Stoic and believed they were loyal to Rome because they were not in open rebellion. The Sadducees were merely ignoring Rome; Rome was just one of the many trials God had given them to overcome.

- Outside the Jewish homeland, the Pharisees were able to reconcile Judaism to the wider Roman culture, including the Greek language and philosophy. The Romans misunderstood this, too, as a gesture of loyalty. They saw the historian **Flavius Josephus**, for example, who wrote in Greek, as a Pharisee who could accommodate himself to the Roman world.

- Not all Jews complied with Roman rule. The Zealots wanted to restore the House of David and, in Josephus's opinion led the Jewish nation down to the sack of Jerusalem in A.D. 70. Ascetics such as the Essenes lived apart from the wider Jewish community. Judaism was very diverse, but the Romans felt that the ruling classes were cooperating.

- The Jews offered sacrifices on behalf of the emperor at the temple, but there were certain things they could not do. A strict Jew could not serve in the Roman army because there were too many pagan cults associated with it. They also tended to give charity in local settings, rather than participate in the grand distributions and festivals of the pagan cults.

- By the time the First Jewish War of 66–73 broke out, it was driven by national outrage over the mismanagement and stupidity of the Romans, perhaps best symbolized by Emperor Caligula's attempt to have his statue placed in the Holy of Holies of the Temple of Jerusalem some 25 years before.

- The final insult was Procurator Gessius Florus raiding the sacred treasury of Jerusalem. When the rebellion broke out, Gessius Florus did what all procurators did: He made a beeline to the coast, to Caesarea Maritima, and ignored it, resulting in a major war. Two other rebellions broke out in the following century, both fueled by the same national and religious sentiments.

- The Romans treated these wars as mere rebellions in their official iconography, depicting defeated Judaea as a seated figure in mourning. They even respected the Jews for fighting for their traditions. The fact that the Romans only took actions against those Jews who rebelled and not the Diaspora Jews is a pagan outlook; their treatment of the Jews was not anti-Semitism in the modern sense.

- The Romans learned very little from their dealings with the Jews, and they were completely baffled when they met the Christians. Unlike their Jewish cousins, the Christians would defy Rome, but they would never resort to arms, and this type of resistance was something totally new to the Romans.

Diaspora: "Scattering"; the settlements of Jews living outside the homeland in the Hellenistic and Roman ages.

Hasmonaean: The royal dynasty of Judaea, founded by Simon Maccabaeus in 165 B.C. and ruling until 37 B.C. when Herod the Great seized power in the Jewish homeland.

Messiah: Hebrew for "anointed one"; in Jewish Apocalyptic literature, the Messiah is a descendant of King David who will restore Israel. The Greek equivalent is *Christos*.

Sadducees: Members of the Jewish upper classes from the mid-2nd century B.C. through the late 1st century A.D. who practiced strict ritual purity, maintenance of the sacrifices at the temple, and adherence to the Torah.

synagogue: From Greek *synagoge*, "gathering together"; a consecrated prayer space in Judaism. The synagogue did not replace the Temple of Jerusalem.

Names to Know

Herod the Great (74–4 B.C.; r. 37–4 B.C.): Second son of Antipater of Idumaea who rose in Hasmonaean service and was appointed governor of Galilee in 49 B.C. From 43 B.C., Herod adroitly exploited his friendship with leading Romans, first Marc Antony and then Octavian, so that he ousted the Hasmonaean dynasty and ruled the Jewish lands from 37 B.C. in the interests of Rome. Herod built on a grand scale, notably Caesarea Maritima and the fortress of Masada. He was despised by his Jewish subjects as a tyrant and a slack adherent to Judaism. In the Gospel of Matthew, he is charged with the Slaughter of the Innocents.

Josephus (a.k.a. **Flavius Josephus**, b. c. 37): A prominent Pharisee and historian of the first rank who composed an eyewitness account of the Jewish War of 66–73 A.D. His *Antiquities of the Jews* is invaluable for Jewish religious attitudes and customs. He also composed an apology for Judaism in two books, *Contra Apionem.*

Judas Maccabaeus (a.k.a. **Judah Maccabee**; d. 160 B.C.): Jewish priest and son of Mattathias of the Hasmonaean house who led the revolt against Seleucid king Antiochus IV Epiphanes (175–164 B.C.), who sought to Hellenize the cult of Yahweh at Jerusalem. In 167–163 B.C., Judas won spectacular victories, acquiring the nickname Maccabaeus ("hammer" in Aramaic), and he reoccupied and rededicated the Temple at Jerusalem.

Pontius Pilate (r. 26–36): Roman procurator of Judaea and fifth equestrian governor of Roman Palestine (Judaea and Samaria, notorious for his inept and venal rule. In the Synoptic Gospels, Pilate is presented as reluctant to order the crucifixion of Jesus.

Suggested Reading

Goodman, *The Ruling Classes of Judaea.*

Josephus, *Antiquities of the Jews.*

————, *The Jewish Wars.*

Nikelsburg, *Jewish Literature between the Bible and the Mishnah.*

Segal, *Rebecca's Children.*

Sherwin-White, *Racial Prejudices in Imperial Rome.*

Smallwood, *The Jews under the Roman Rule from Pompey to Diocletian.*

Vermes, *The Complete Dead Sea Scrolls in English.*

Question to Consider

1. How did Jews view the rule of Rome? How accurate is Josephus as a source in reporting the views of the Sadducees, Pharisees, Zealots, and Essenes?

Jews in the Roman Empire

Lecture 6—Transcript

In this lecture, I plan to introduce Jews and Judaism in the Roman world. I have three reasons for doing this: The first is, of course, Judaism constituted a very important faith in the Roman Empire and there were many Jews in the Roman Empire; some would estimate perhaps as high as 10 percent of the total population of the empire were Jews in the 1st century A.D. The second reason for dealing with Judaism is that it is important in order to understand the emerging of Christianity in the upcoming lectures because Christianity emerges out of Judaism; in fact, it is one of the three religions of Abraham, as I like to call them: Judaism, Christianity, and Islam. So understanding Paul of Tarsus (that is, Saint Paul) will depend very heavily on understanding what the nature of Judaism was in the 1st and 2nd centuries A.D.

Third, the Romans dealt with the Jews on various levels—legally; they also went to war with them; they tried to understand Judaism—it is for the Romans the first instance in which they deal with members of monotheistic faith, a nation that defines itself overwhelmingly by religion rather than by other ways, and it is a way of seeing how the Romans came to terms with the Jews and whether the Romans really learned anything in dealing with the Jews when it came to dealing with these Christians that represented a new religion or, as the Romans would call it, a superstition. On that regard, on that third point, the Romans didn't do as well as you would think, and the Romans actually misunderstood Judaism in a number of ways, made certain mistakes, and some of those are going to carry over in the dealings of the Imperial government with their Christian subjects.

In order to start this lecture, then, we should first look at what Judaism was like in the Hellenistic and Roman Imperial ages; that is, from the time of essentially the 4th century B.C. into the 2nd century A.D. This is a very, very important period of Judaism, and one could argue it is in this period that the national worship of Yahweh as the god of the Hebrews turned into Judaism as we understand it: A monotheistic faith depending on text and moral purity—that is, the acceptance of those texts; the position of God's plan in the world—and not tied necessarily to any locale. Jerusalem is very, very important; but nonetheless, one does not cease being a Jew when he leaves the homeland the way a pagan would take up the worship of the gods of a new homeland. You may carry your ancestral gods, but you'll accommodate the gods of the new place. Judaism is a faith that is carried everywhere; it is within the heart as well as within the mind. That is a result of the redaction of the texts in the period of the Babylonian Captivity—that is, the period from 586 B.C. to 539 B.C. that sees the deportation of the Jews to Babylonia— and the priestly editors redact (that is, they edit; they comment on; they put together) Torah as we have it today in the 6th and 5th centuries B.C. They really make the religion a religion based on canon (that is, on text), which is also going to be true of Christianity. This is something that is quite distinct from Paganism, as I've been describing: There are no such religious texts on par with Torah.

In addition, the Jews, when they were allowed to return to their homeland by the Persian King Cyrus (dated somewhere around 539 B.C.), the temple was rebuilt—this will be the temple that the Romans will destroy in the great rebellions—and there is still a priestly caste that administers the sacrifices to Yahweh; that maintains ritual purity. They will be known as the Sadducees in the Roman Imperial period and the late Hellenistic period, and they are those Jews who are devoted to the interpretation of Torah, the script interpretation of the law, the maintenance of ritual purity, the dietary laws, circumcision, all of those features that mark Jews off from the worship of idols, in effect; that is, the idolatrous world around them.

Furthermore, under the kings of Persia, then under Alexander the Great and Alexander's immediate successors, the kings who ruled in Egypt known as the Ptolemies—and you have to understand, the Ptolemies are not Egyptians, they are descendents from the Macedonian general; there are a few cases of intermarriage with Greeks, but they are essentially Macedonian dynasty down to Cleopatra the VII (the famous Cleopatra of Antony and Cleopatra)—these rulers respected Judaism. In part, it was practical. It was not a particularly strategic area, the Jewish homeland Judah—or as the Romans would call it, Judaea—and the region just to the north known as Samaria (the Samaritans one would encounter in the New Testament), and those were worshipers of Yahweh who maintained their own ritual purity and worshiped Yahweh on Mount Gerizim, which is outside the modern city of Nablus today, the ancient city of Samaria that gave its name to the area. The Samaritans were always looked upon by the Jews as not very good Jews. They were decedents of the kingdom of Israel and the various settlers brought in by the Assyrians. There is always a tension between Samaritans and Jews, and Samaritans maintained a distinct identity well into the 6th century A.D. There's a famous rebellion of them against the Emperor Justinian when he tries to tamper with their faith.

In addition, you have to keep in mind that Jews in the Roman age lived more than just in the homeland. That requires me to explain a few terms. Very often I refer to the term "of Palestine" or I will say "the Roman province of Palestine." That constituted the Jewish homeland Judaea around Jerusalem, Samaria—which would today be the West Bank, which was the original kingdom of Israel—the cities on the shore, many of them pagan, such as Gaza (never under Jewish control), and that would be a Roman provincial name. I'm not making a modern political statement by the term "Palestine." Actually, what's happened is the Roman provincial term has been taken to create a new identity in the 20th century. "Palestine" is simply a geographic term. It means this whole area between the Mediterranean and the Jordan. It actually is a Roman corruption of the word "Philistina," the land of the Philistines; and so when I refer to it, I'm referring to a Roman administrative zone, just as when I use Gaul, or Britain, or the province of Asia, or the province of Africa. So first, let's get that cleared up.

Second, is that by the 2nd century B.C., many Jews had emigrated and became members of what is known as the Diaspora. The Diaspora means "scattering" in Greek, the dispersal. Contrary to popular notions, most of the Jews left Galilee, Samaria, or the Jewish homeland in Judaea as mercenary solders. Jews had an excellent reputation as tough fighters. Many of them served in Hellenistic armies and then were rewarded with land on discharge and therefore set up settlements; that's true in Ptolemaic army, the Seleucid kings who ruled Asia. Then, later, the merchandizing, the international trade, the banking aspects sprang into action. In the Roman age, someone like Paul of Tarsus, Saint Paul, of course he was engaged in these types of activities; they naturally followed once you were settled in these cities.

In the Diaspora, Jews very quickly had to come to terms with essentially a Greek world, both in language and material culture, and they accommodated themselves very well. The Jews in Alexandria, for instance, were a powerful intellectual community. Philo was a representative of that community; he knew his Plato inside and out and he could use it to elucidate his Jewish faith. Best estimate is that the city of Alexandria was at a minimum 750,000 strong in the year 1; it may have been a million. At least 300,000 residents in the city alone were Jews; so close to a third of the city. They had a powerful intellectual position in the city of Alexandria; they were very wealthy; they were an important community.

In lesser cities scattered in Asia Minor, in Greece, communities set up synagogues and sometimes one is astonished at how they came to terms with the wider world. At Sardis, the old Lydian capital in Western Turkey today, there has been excavated and reconstructed a synagogue built between 280 and 300 A.D. It was actually a public building given over to the Jews who were resident in the city by the town council and it looks like a proto-church; and in many ways, even more astonishing despite what the rabbis say, it's right next to a gymnasium bath complex, which Jews are not supposed to frequent because it is the nude exercise of Greek athletics, it is where Greek language and literature would be trained—everything with the grammarians I talked about in the previous lecture—and there it is side by side. We find in the Diaspora, and increasingly in archeology and inscriptions, that Jews easily came to terms with the wider social world; most of these Jews spoke Greek—that's why the Septuagint, the Greek translation, was created; they don't read Hebrew anymore—and also, another important aspect about it is many of them adhered to the Pharisee traditions, which we'll talk about in a moment; that is, the broader and more generous interpretations of the law that was popular in the homeland and very popular in the synagogues of the Diaspora. The synagogues and the Diaspora functioned as essentially reading groups for men and women to learn their Judaism, often in Greek translation.

In addition, I would like to stress that what became the Roman province of Palestine was a very unruly and difficult area to control. This gets into the second issue and, in part, what the Romans learned about running the Jewish homeland, about monotheism and religious conflict; and, again, this will all feed into when we look at Christianity. It's necessary to give a little bit of background to understand the situation. The Jews had been perfectly capable of coming to terms with an overlord who worshiped idols (Ptolemaic kings, Alexander, Persian kings). The problem came in 200 B.C. when the Seleucia kings of Syria—and these, again, are Macedonians running the former Asian provinces of Alexander's empire, they are not really Syrians; they are positioned in Syrian Babylonia, but they are Macedonians—took over the Jewish homeland and kicked the Ptolemies out of that region of Palestine, Phoenicia, and southern Syria in a famous battle at Panium in 200 B.C.

Initially, the Jews continued as they had under the Ptolemies, but the Seleucids got themselves in financial and military trouble. They were decisively defeated by the Romans in 190 B.C.; the favorite king Antiochus III went down in defeat; and from there on, the Seleucid dynasty was in constant fiscal and military crisis until finally the Romans abolished the dynasty and took over the area in 63 B.C. (that's done by Pompey the Great, the famous opponent of Julius Caesar). One of those later Seleucid kings, Antiochus IV (one of them who styles himself with divine titles; Epiphanes is his title) decided that for the rump Seleucid state it was necessary to carry out active Hellenizing policies in order to win the various cities over—and these would be Syrian, Babylonian, and Jewish cities, including the city of Jerusalem—by sponsoring cults to Zeus (Zeus Ouranios, Zeus of the Heavens) who would be then tied to Yahweh worship.

This had not been done before. The Ptolemies had been scrupulous in respecting Judaism, and my suspicion is the Ptolemaic kings probably admired Judaism in a number of ways; but with Antiochus IV, there was an effort to impose a Greek cult in the temple of Jerusalem itself. That action created, in effect, the first religious conflict that we had. The Orthodox Jews raised the call for national resistance in 167 B.C. Immediately, the Jews flocked to the banner of Judas Maccabeus, who was of the house of Hashmon, and his family is sometimes known as the Hasmonean house that came to rule the Jewish homeland after they kicked out the Seleucids. In 164 B.C., the Jews won a significant victory, destroyed the mercenary army of Antiochus IV, reoccupied Jerusalem, rededicated the temple; this is the occasion of the celebration and miracle of Hanukkah, a very, very important festival in Jewish identity.

What the Maccabees did is not only revive the memories of David, Moses, and Joshua—fighting the Philistines, casting down idols—they actually rose in arms for a national struggle to make sure the purity of their faith would not be destroyed by these foreign and idolatrous overlords, and they won. They kicked out the Seleucids, they rededicated the temple; and that was a very, very important defining moment because Judas Maccabaeus and his decedents, the Maccabees, not only liberated Jerusalem but they expanded the kingdom, they brought in Samaria, they subjected the pagan towns of the coast, they colonized the northern regions of the Galilee, and the Galilee was a tough colonial area of Jews who had been brought up from Jerusalem and who didn't mess around and could be depended on to defend the strategic entrances into the homeland should any Seleucid army ever try to venture south again.

Rome, of course, recognized the Jews. The Romans had no love for the Seleucids; and already Rome under the Republic had a special tie with this Hasmonean state that emerged in the 2nd century B.C. Furthermore, in the national struggle, there were martyrs. There is a famous scribe, anonymous, a Jewish mother with her seven sons, who refused to renounce their Judaism and suffered martyrdom; that is, they were executed by the Seleucid official. Those memories were strong and, again, were carried over by the Christians. Eusebius was aware of these Jewish martyrs, and it was part of the images inherited by the Christians.

Furthermore, the national struggle was often seen in apocalyptic terms. There is a powerful apocalyptic tradition of text talking about the final judgments, the end of days starting with the Maccabees and ending in the early 2nd century A.D. In these images, there were the notions of a messiah; that is, a member of the house of David who would restore the kingdom of Israel. In more cosmic terms were the son of man who would preside over the final days and the final judgment. Again, these are images that would be inherited by the Christians in their own understanding of their faith and in their conflict with the idol worshipers of Rome. The Maccabee tradition not only defined Judaism in many ways, it also would have powerful influences in the understanding of early Christianity.

The Hasmonaeans eventually failed to keep order. The Romans were not so concerned about who ran the Jewish homeland, the whole area they would call Palestine; all they wanted was order—that is, they do not want any rebellions—and fundamentally the Roman interest in the area was strategic. There is a coastal highway—the Romans would call it the *Via Maris*, the

Highway of the Sea—that ran from Alexandria to Antioch and Syria, and the Romans needed to have access to that highway in order to move their military forces; that was their prime concern. When the Hasmonaeans failed to keep order, Pompey intervened in 63 B.C., tried to reestablish the Jewish state as a client kingdom of Rome, the Hasmonaeans failed, and eventually the Romans turned to a mercenary general—who was not a very good Jew; he was only half Jewish—known as Herod the Great who is remembered in both the Jewish and the Christian tradition as an evil tyrant. He was the king who ordered the slaughter of the innocents, for instance, in the gospel of Matthew, a favorite depiction in later Christian art.

The Jews had lots of reasons to dislike Herod as well. Herod was an Idumaean (that is, he came from the desert area); he was a mercenary general. He ruled from 37–4 B.C., and he was the only man who could keep order among the Jews, the Jews of the Galilee, the Samaritans, and the various pagan regions he ruled in southern Syria and today east of the Jordan. The Romans really liked Herod because, first, Herod spoke Greek; he understood the manipulation of patron and client in the Roman political system. I always think that the Emperor Augustus saw Herod doing in his homeland what Augustus did at Rome; that is, this incredible balancing act. The nicest thing I can say about Herod, I guess, is that he had a meeting with Cleopatra—Cleopatra the VII, associated with Mark Antony—and the story is that when they met, Herod accused Cleopatra of trying to seduce him and Cleopatra accused Herod of trying to poison her, and they were both right. In any case, Herod kept order until his death in 4 B.C. and then, essentially, that super Jewish state fell apart and was partitioned among his three sons.

No one could follow Herod. The Jewish homeland and Samaria went to a man called Archelaus; Herod Antipas, another son, got the Galilee and some areas; and then Philip got the pagan regions. This was an administrative system that didn't work too well. Eventually all the kings had to be deposed; they were incredibly incompetent.

The religious running of the Jewish homeland, the Romans in 63 B.C. turned to something known as the Sanhedrin. That is the high council in Jerusalem comprised of learned and pious men, both Sadducees and Pharisees. This is the council that apparently had some kind of trial of Jesus in 26 or 27

A.D.—whenever the crucifixion took place; the date is a little uncertain—and they were responsible for administering the temple and essentially for running Jerusalem. In 6 A.D., they got rid of that client king Archelaus and the Romans sent in governors, procurators. The procurators were low-level equestrians. In fact, if you ended up as procurator of Judaea it probably meant you washed out of the Roman imperial system. It was the equivalent of getting Yemen in the Ottoman Empire. It is so remote that whatever happens does not really matter to the overall empire. Pontius Pilate: perfect example of a procurator. We know nothing about Pontius Pilate except he was a procurator of Judaea, Galilee, and Samaria and not very good at it, and that is why he probably ended up running with what the Romans would call Palestine, that area; it is a region that is only a strategic importance.

The day to day running of the province was really in the hands of the Sanhedrin in Jerusalem. Jerusalem could expand to tens of thousands at High Holiday. The Roman military presence was minimal. They had maybe six cohorts and an *ala* of cavalry; a wing of cavalry. These were all locals recruited in the area; they were incompetent, inept. Some of them were real anti-Semites in the fact that they mocked Jewish traditions, and there were some really ugly incidents; so that the Roman presence in Judea was not very impressive and it really was a case of misrule. That contributed to the outbreak of the great national rebellions.

There were numerous incidents in which the Romans mismanaged the province. They did not understand Judaism; they did not understand monotheism. There is an amazing disconnect between Roman law in which Judaism was established as a legitimate religion by Julius Caesar, by Pompey the Great. There were all sorts of laws allowing the Sanhedrin to administer the temple, to maintain ritual purity. For instance, if a non-Jew went into these sacred holy of holies and trod on that sacred land, he was subject to the death penalty, to stoning, just as any Jew who had violated it, and the Romans were okay with this; this was fine.

To the Romans, Judaism looked legitimate. It was an ancestral national religion. They found Yahweh peculiar as the only god and they found the fact that there were no images odd, but the rituals had gone on for centuries; they had worked. There was a priestly caste, the Sadducees, who devoted themselves to text, ritual purity. The Romans actually mistook the Sadducees: "They are some kind of Stoic. Hey, you know, they are loyal to Rome because they do not cause any problems." The Sadducees just ignored Rome—it was just one of the many trials of God; Rome was going to come and go—and the Romans mistook this as some kind of residual loyalty.

The other aspect about Judaism is that it was well-established in the various cities of the Roman world, and outside of the homeland Jews came to terms with the wider world. These tended to favor the Pharisees. The Pharisees were able to reconcile speaking Greek, Greek material, culture; they expanded on Jewish doctrines (that is, the eternity of the soul; the resurrection of the flesh; the importance of angels). Some of them, such as Philo, were using Platonic thought. Pharisees, or some of them, looked to their own. "They are coming to terms with the wider world; there well maybe a loyalty there, too." Again, they misunderstood this; but nonetheless, Flavius Josephus, the man who wrote about the first Jewish war, would have been seen as a typical Pharisee who could accommodate himself to Roman rule and Greek material culture and language.

There were zealots, however; those who refused to accept Roman rule, who wanted to restore the House of David, and, in Josephus's opinion, they led the Jewish nation down to the destructive first war that led to the sack of Jerusalem in 70 A.D. There were also ascetics such as the Essenes, who at some times have been associated with the Dead Sea Scrolls, although that is a very controversial issue and there are other courses in the series of the Great Courses that handle those issues. But Judaism was very diverse; the Romans looking at it had reason to think that, "At least the ruling classes, if not coopted, at least cooperated with Rome."

The Jews very pragmatically offered sacrifices on behalf of the emperor at the temple. There were certain things they could not do: A strict Jew could not serve in the Roman army because there were too many Pagan cults associated with it. They also tended to give charity in local settings to their humble coreligionists; they did not do the grand distributions and festivals I talked about with pagan cults. Yet, in the cities of the Diaspora, we have evidence that some Jews did accommodate themselves to the wider world; but in the homeland, that would be difficult.

As a result the Romans never really understood the religious views of the Jews, and it was more than just monotheism and a transcended god. That meant the Romans failed, and those failures are represented in the great rebellions—the First Jewish War of 66–73, recorded by Josephus, brought on by zealots—but by the time the rebellion broke out, in my opinion, it was national outrage over the mismanagement and stupidity of the Romans, perhaps symbolized when the emperor Caligula, some 25 years before the rebellion, actually ordered his statue to be put in the holy of holies, following the example of Antiochus the IV, and he did it because he was annoyed at some demonstration in Caesarea Maritima and everyone knew what this meant. The governor of Syria who got the orders, Publius Patronius—who had many Jewish friends in Antioch—probably looked up and said, "Jupiter, why me?" He knew if he did this there would be a national Jewish rebellion, and it was averted because Caligula was assassinated on January 24, 41 A.D. before this idiotic thing could be carried out. But that incident probably informed most Jews who were at least tolerant of Rome that their faith depended on the whim of an emperor, and if it is a whim of an emperor like a Caligula or a Nero, that is not very reassuring.

Furthermore, the Romans had attempted different ways of running the provinces and it just got worse. It ended with this procurator Gessius Florus who raided the treasury, the sacred treasury of Jerusalem. His solders did all sorts of nasty things—one of them actually mooned the crowd; that was the final incident that caused rioting—and then when the rebellion broke out in Jerusalem, Gessius Florus did what all procurators did: He made a beeline to the coast to Caesarea Maritima and ignored it, and the result was a major war that called in the Roman imperial legions from Syria and eventually was put down. There were two other rebellions, one that broke out in Cyrenaica, today eastern Libya, from 116–117 and then the Bar-Kokhba war of 132–135 where Bar-Kokhba was actually accepted as Messiah by at least one rabbi; and all of these wars were fueled by the same national and religious sentiments that you see with the Maccabees.

The Romans, however, never understood this. They treated the wars as rebellions, as defiance, like any rebellions in the official iconography. When they defeated the Jews in these wars; the iconography—that is, a seated figure of Judaea in mourning—was the same they would show any defeated people. The Romans actually respected the Jews. They had resorted to arms; they had invoked their national god; they understood that. They respected them as fighters; they respected them as fighting for their traditions. Again, the fact that the Romans only took actions against those Jews that rebelled is very, very much a pagan outlook. They defied Rome; they will be punished. We will destroy Jerusalem to show that their god has abandoned them.

But this is not anti-Semitism in a modern sense. The regions of the Roman world in the Diaspora, for instance, where many, many Jews lived: they didn't revolt, the Romans did nothing. We know the community in Sardis flourished. We know of a community at Apamea, today the modern city of Dinar in Turkey, which was left unmolested. In the 3rd century A.D., we actually have coins struck by the city that show the legend of Noah, which had been adopted by the pagans as part of their legend because they had many Jewish residents among them, including apparently men of very high rank who actually had some connection with the imperial cult in that city. In the Galilee, for instance, Josephus, during the first war, was put in charge of commanding the cities in the Galilee, particularly the city of Sepphoris. He surrendered on terms to the future emperor Vespasian, and attached himself to Vespasian's son Titus, who would eventually become emperor. The Galilee cities were spared. They had revolted; they surrendered on terms; you cannot tax dead cities. The Romans were very practical; and it is significant, because it is in the Galilee where the great rabbinical schools would emerge in the 2nd and 3rd centuries and those were areas left unmolested.

In dealing with the Jews, the Romans still did not understand a great deal about this faith. Of course, monotheism went over their heads; a transcended god. They mistook the sectarian divisions as possible loyalty; the way they behaved vis-à-vis Rome. Rebellion was seen as an act of defiance. They really never appreciated the religious motives behind that conflict, and so the Romans learned very little from their dealings with the Jews. But they were not baffled; the Jews defied Rome, and the Romans were able to treat it as rebellion. They are going to be baffled when they turn to Christians because, unlike their Jewish cousins, Christians would defy Rome. They would obey the law, they would go to trial, but they would never resort to arms; and this type of pacific resistance was something totally new to the Romans.

Christian Challenge—First Conversions
Lecture 7

E arly Christianity was not an organized or unified faith. The religion we know today arose out of the apostolic church, led by three men: James the Righteous, who led the Jerusalem Church, which was composed of Jews and was wiped out in one of the rebellions; and Saints Paul and Peter. Paul became the Roman world's first missionary, circling the Mediterranean three times to spread his understanding of Jesus's message to Jews and gentiles. By his execution around A.D. 67, he had established what became the mainstream Christian faith.

The Original Christians

- In the immediate aftermath of the crucifixion, usually dated to around A.D. 26–27, the followers of Jesus had a debate: What was the nature of Jesus's message? Immediate leadership of the group fell to James, often known as **James the Righteous**, sometimes called James the brother of Jesus.

- James's title caused some debate in late antiquity. Saint Jerome, writing at the end of the 4th century A.D., believed James was a cousin of Jesus because he accepted the doctrine of the perpetual virginity of Mary. Others noted that a brother succeeding to his late brother's position was part of the Pharisee tradition, giving weight to James being Jesus's biological brother.

- James assumed his leadership role in what is often called the Jerusalem Church, whose members were in close association with the temple and continued to practice the Jewish dietary traditions, follow the Torah, and so forth. They were suspicious of apocalyptic traditions but accepted Jesus as the son of man and did await the impending *eschaton*.

- This group included Saint Peter, who on two occasions in the New Testament (in the letter of Paul to the Galatians and in the Acts of the Apostles) clearly defers to James's authority.

The Political Church and the Gospel of Mark

- The group's position seems to be reflected in the **Synoptic Gospel** of Mark. Mark is regarded as the oldest gospel. It was written in a simple form of Greek influenced by Aramaic grammar—Aramaic being the language that Jesus taught in. It includes appeals to an impending *eschaton*, Greek for "great reckoning," when God will reveal himself, the hypocrites will be punished, and the humble faithful will be uplifted.

- Mark also mentions the son of man, the mortal figure who will preside over the end of days; alludes to the suffering servant of the book of Isaiah; and uses the term "Messiah," which many Jews would have understood as the leader of a rebellion from Rome.

- When Jesus was crucified, it was not a Jewish punishment. Crucifixion was the Roman penalty for *seditio*—sedition, or treason. The two men crucified beside him are typically referred to as thieves; that was the Romans' euphemism for guerillas.

- The Jerusalem Church continued until around A.D. 60 or 65; then, **Hegesippus**—an early writer whose work does not survive but was used by Eusebius—tells us that the Christians at Jerusalem moved to the city of Pella, where they were destroyed in one of the great rebellions. There were tensions within the group even before this; Saint Stephen was murdered around the year A.D. 35, apparently for arguing that Jesus's message is universal.

Paul's Christianity

- A huge change in the church came with the career of **Paul of Tarsus**. Saint Paul was one of the great religious mystics and intellects of all time. He was a Pharisee Jew who, in his early life,

Saint Paul's missionary journeys created a network of churches—called the apostolic churches—throughout the empire, particularly the eastern half.

was suspicious of the Christians and took part in persecuting them. After a mystical vision on the road to Damascus, however, he took it upon himself to propagate his understanding of the message of Jesus.

- We have seven **Pauline letters**: Romans, 1 and 2 Corinthians, Galatians, Philippians, 1 Thessalonians, and Philemon. The other letters of the New Testament are called the **Deutero-Pauline letters**. They were written by his close associates, probably Timothy and some others, but reflect Paul's ideas closely. The letters were written in Greek and date from 15–35 years after the crucifixion.

- Paul asserted his authority as apostle to the gentiles—that is, to the non-Jews. He concluded that Jesus's message was universal. Yet, as a Pharisee Jew, he also accepted the resurrection of the flesh and the role of angels and believed in an incipient final reckoning. This explains the urgency of his mission to convert the gentiles.

- Paul was the ideal missionary for the Roman world. He sometimes referred to himself as a tent maker, which has misled some to think of him as a humble craftsman. In fact, given his education, social connections, and Roman citizenship, it is more likely that he came from a family with a military contract, making tents for the legions.

- Paul took it upon himself to preach in the synagogues of the Diaspora. He started in Antioch, the capital of Roman Syria (today part of Turkey). He reached many pagans called in the sources "Godfearers"—*theophobeis*. These pagans were familiar with Jewish monotheism, had gone to the synagogue, and may have intermarried with Jews and practiced some of the Jewish dietary laws.

Taking Sides in the Early Church

- To Paul, Jesus was the Messiah who fixed a new Torah. By the act of baptism, Jew and pagan both became Christians, a term that was first used in Antioch. Paul, ever pragmatic, also reasoned that gentiles did not need to obey the old Torah; the act of baptism was the new mark of the new Israel.

- James and members of the Jerusalem Church opposed Paul's views on this. Paul was not an original apostle, which also undermined his authority. Saint Peter seemed inclined to support Paul; but James exerted a great deal of authority, as evidenced by both the canonical texts and the apocryphal *Gospel of Saint Thomas*, written in the 2nd century A.D.

- Eventually a council was held around A.D. 48, as recorded in the Acts of the Apostles. Peter threw his support behind Paul, and as a result the Pauline converts did not have to follow the Torah if they had not originally been Jews. As a secondary result, the apostolic churches recognized themselves as part of a community.

Paul's Missions to the Roman World

- Paul, who in many ways is one of Christianity's first converts, was also the first missionary. We take the idea of proselytizing for granted, but it was a new concept in the Roman world. In the pagan traditions, despite scholars' efforts to find proselytizing by the mystery cults, it is not present. Missionary activities are something that belong to Paul.

- Paul's first mission, generally dated between A.D. 46 and 48, started in Antioch. He then took sea passage to key ports in Cyprus, then landed at Perge, Asia Minor, the center of a very important mother goddess cult. From there he went inland to Roman colonies, including Pisidian Antioch, Iconium, and Lystra.

- On that journey, he set up a number of successful house churches; that is, he converted families, and the leading members of the families made their houses available for services.

- A few years later, Paul took on a more ambitious mission back to a number of those churches, ending up at the port city of Alexandria Troas, a tacky Roman tourist center for the Trojan War. From there he visited the great cities of Greece—Thessalonica, Beroea, Athens, and Corinth—and set up more churches.

- His third mission in the early- to mid-50s took him back to Pisidian Antioch, then down the Maeander River Valley to Ephesus to the great churches of western Asia—many named in the book of Revelation as the Seven Churches of Asia—and back to the churches in Greece. Finally, he returned to the Jewish homeland via the city of Tyre.

- The most important result of Paul's journeys was the network of apostolic churches he established that became the cradle of the Christian movement. Except for Rome and Alexandria, the main centers of the Christian mission for the next 250 years were all cities where Paul established the first churches.

Who Were the First Christians?

- The definitive study of the earliest Christians is *The First Urban Christians* by Wayne Meeks. He found they were often Greek-speaking Jews or pagans familiar with monotheism. They were neither elites nor the lowly but ranked somewhere in between; they had money but not aristocratic bloodlines, and some may have been imperial freedmen.

- Whole families tended to convert together, which meant that early Christianity reflected the social hierarchy, prejudices, and assumptions of the wider Roman world. The leader of a Christian family played the role of a patron, just as he would in a pagan Roman family.

- As far as scholars can tell, the numbers of these communities were quite small. The earliest church we know about is a house church from the city of Dura-Europus, which had about 30 members. Bishops were more like today's parish priests.

- The apostolic church was not the only Christian church out there. Paul's letter to the Galatians warns the congregation not to accept teachers who teach another Christ. Scholars are not sure exactly who these people were; they are sometimes thought to be Docetists, from the Greek word *dokein*, "to seem" or "to appear." Certain people who witnessed the crucifixion believed that God could not be crucified; he only appeared to be crucified.

- Many Christians maintained the Torah and the dietary laws well into the 4th and 5th centuries A.D. The followers of John the Baptist maintained a separate identity—they are known as Mandaeans—and many of these heresies were condemned later by the more organized church, but the initial Christian message was quite diverse.

- Paul was conveyed to Rome around 66 or 67, where he was executed. Tradition states that Peter was martyred there as well. Christianity at this time was facing its first serious challenge: In

64 Emperor Nero had outlawed Christianity, and for the first time, the Roman imperial government persecuted people based on their religion. That was a major change, not only for Christians, but for the Roman world in general.

Important Terms

Deutero-Pauline letters: Letters attributed to Saint Paul that were likely written by his disciples. These are Colossians, Ephesians, 2 Thessalonians, Hebrews, 1 and 2 Timothy, and Titus.

eschaton: Greek for "last"; the ultimate reckoning by God.

Pauline letters: The seven letters of the New Testament written by Saint Paul in about A.D. 48–65: Romans, 1 and 2 Corinthians, Galatians, Philippians, 1 Thessalonians, and Philemon.

Synoptic Gospels: The Gospels of Mark, Luke, and Matthew, composed between A.D. 75 and 85, which offer a synopsis of the ministry and crucifixion of Jesus.

theophobeis: Greek for "God-fearers"; pagans who accepted Jewish monotheism without converting to Judaism.

Names to Know

Paul (a.k.a. **Paul of Tarsus**; c. 5–67): Saint and early Christian writer and missionary, born to a wealthy Pharisee family with Roman citizenship. After his conversion on the road to Damascus in about 35, Paul defined the universal message of Jesus as the conversion of the wider pagan world. He conducted three missions establishing churches in the Greek cities of Asia Minor and Greece in 46–48, 49–52, and 53–57. At the council of Jerusalem (c. 48), Peter and James the Righteous accepted Pauline converts in a compromise. Paul was arrested and imprisoned at Caesarea Maritima in 58–59. He was conveyed to Rome and martyred in the wake of the Great Fire. His seven Epistles (Romans, 1 and 2 Corinthians, Galatians, 1 Thessalonians, Philippians, and Philemon) are fundamental to Christian theology.

Hegesippus (c. 110–180): Reportedly a convert from Judaism and the earliest known Christian chronicler. His work was a major source for Eusebius's *Ecclesiastical History*, but it does not survive.

James the Righteous (d. 62) Called the brother of Jesus by Saint Paul (Galatians 1:19). He succeeded to the authority of the Jerusalem church after the crucifixion.

Suggested Reading

Brandon, *Jesus and the Zealots*.

Brown, *The Body and Society*.

Brown and Meier, *Antioch and Rome*.

Eusebius, *The History of the Church*.

Frend, *Martyrdom and Persecution in the Early Church*:

Louth and Saniforth, ed. and trans., *Early Christian Writings*.

Smith, *Jesus the Magician*.

Questions to Consider

1. What are the sources for the development of early Christian communities in the first century? What were the religious debates among early Christians? How did these debates produce different religious visions? What authority did Saint Paul claim over Saint Peter and James the Righteous?

2. How important were the missionary travels of Saint Paul? How did he turn Christianity into a world faith?

3. Who were the first urban Christians? Why did they convert, and how did they organize their congregations? What other types of Christian confessions emerged in the late 1st and early 2nd centuries?

Christian Challenge—First Conversions
Lecture 7—Transcript

In this lecture, I wish to bring on the earliest Christian mission, and we're going to deal with subjects such as the first conversions, the creation of the early Apostolic churches (as I prefer to call them), and also the challenge that it posed to Rome and the wider pagan world. This requires us to look somewhat at the ministry and crucifixion of Jesus; but again, as I've noted, this is a course that deals with wider religious change in the Roman world. Therefore, for those who are interested in the historical Jesus, the various texts (Gnostic and otherwise) that are the basis for our knowledge, there are other excellent courses in the series of the Great Courses that deal with that issue specifically. That's something that we'll only with dealing in passing.

Where we want to start is in the immediate aftermath of the crucifixion, which is usually dated to around 26–27 A.D., somewhere in there in the procuratorship of Pontius Pilate. From the start, the followers of Jesus had a debate: What was the nature of the message? Eventually, Saint Paul—who was martyred in Rome in either 66 or 67 A.D. along with Saint Peter—came up with a vision of Jesus's message that became the basis for the apostolic churches that in turn would eventually become the basis for the imperial church of Constantine and the traditional medieval church; and that's going to be a long development we'll look at. However, in the immediate aftermath, the followers of Jesus—the original apostles as well as other associates—were really kind of perplexed. Apparently, immediate leadership fell to James, very often known as James the Righteous; he's called James the brother of Jesus, which caused a debate already in late antiquity. Saint Jerome, writing in the end of the 4th century A.D., believed that this was probably a cousin of Jesus; couldn't be an actual brother because he accepts the doctrine of the perpetual virginity of Mary. The Greek tends to suggest that he was a brother and that he succeeded to the role of Jesus's position with the followers, very similar to what happened with other Pharisee's groups; but it's still a perplexing issue.

What's clear is James—I'll call him James the Righteous—assumed a leadership in what is often called the Jerusalem church; that is, those Christians who stayed in Jerusalem (the term is a bit misleading), who were in close association with the temple, who continued to practice the Jewish dietary traditions, they followed Torah, and were very, very suspicious of apocalyptic traditions. They did accept Jesus as the son of Man and did wait for what is often known as the impending eschaton, which we'll get to in a moment. In any event, this group of sometimes they're called Jewish Christians, Church of Jerusalem—it included Saint Peter who, on two occasions in the early Christian literature, defers to James; clearly in the letter to Galatians by Saint Paul and again a reference in Acts where there is a debate that eventually leads to the council of Jerusalem in 48 or 49 A.D.— in any event, these first Christians were closely associated with Jerusalem and their position seems to be reflected in the synoptic gospel of Mark.

I should stop for a moment and explain some terms. The Synaptic gospels refer to Mark, Luke, and Matthew as they were written in chronological order. They represent a synopsis of Jesus's teaching and the relevant parts of his life. They are seen as quite different in purpose from the gospel of John, which is the proclamation of the faith and is thought to have been written slightly later. We'll get into some of the authorship of these texts later on. Mark is regarded as the oldest gospel. It's clearly written in a simple form of Greek, and underneath it is an Aramaic grammar; that is, the author Mark is not really familiar with Greek and he's a native speaker of Aramaic, which is the language that Jesus taught in. There's every reason to believe that the parables recorded in there and the various incidents go back to the time of the ministry and crucifixion and it was written at a time where memories were beginning to fade and everyone wanted to make sure that we have exactly what Jesus taught.

In Mark, there are appeals to an impending eschaton, which is a Greek term that means a "great reckoning": that God will reveal himself in time and his plan that the hypocrites will be punished; the poor, the humble, and the faithful will be uplifted. In addition, in Luke there are mixed images, probably that were contemporary with Jesus's own teachings. There's an appeal to the Son of Man who, in Jewish apocalypse, is a figure, usually mortal, who presides over the end of days. There are images to the suffering servant of Isaiah. There's also the term "Messiah" used, which many Jews would have understood as rebellion from Rome, as in the great rebellion we talked about; the restoration of the House of David.

The images were mixed; many Jews were probably perplexed by exactly what was going on; and furthermore, Jesus was crucified, and that was a Roman punishment. He was executed for *seditio*—that is, for treason; we get the word "sedition"—and most Jews would see that as a noble death. Those who have read the New Testament accounts, they're translated in English as "thieves" on either side of him, but that's just a Roman euphemism for "guerillas." The fellows who are up there are not stealing bread in the market place; they've been killing Roman tax collectors. They're up there for what is an execution of defiance of Rome. In any case, it seems—and again, this is debated among theologians—that James took the meaning literally that the message was for Jews and perhaps Jews of the Diaspora. He and his group stayed in and around Jerusalem and that church continued until somewhere around 60 or 65 A.D., where we're told by an early source, Hegesippus— who doesn't survive but was used by Eusebius—that the Christians at Jerusalem moved to the city of Pella, which is across the Jordan; or, another speculation, they were destroyed in one of the great rebellions. In addition, there was tension even within this group. Saint Stephen was martyred around 35 A.D., stoned for apparently arguing that the message is universal; it goes beyond the Jews. But in any event, we have this Jerusalem church.

The big change came with the career of Paul of Tarsus, which is his Hebrew name, or Saint Paul. Saint Paul is clearly one of the great religious mystics and intellects of all time. Paul originally started out as a Pharisee Jew who was very suspicious of the Christians, actually took measures against some of these early Christians, and he reports his conversion in his own writings in his letter to Corinthians (the first letter) and Galatians, and we also have an extended report of his conversion in Acts. In Acts, he has a mystical vision on the road to Damascus: Christ appears to him and asks "Why do you persecute me?" As a result, Paul became convinced that Jesus was the Messiah. He reversed position on this and took it upon himself to propagate his understanding of the message of Jesus. We have from Paul seven letters. Those would be Romans, the two letters to the Corinthians, Galatians, Philippians, 1 Thessalonians, and Philemon. The other letters that have been preserved in the New Testament are usually called by scholars Deutero-Pauline Letters. They were written by his close associates, probably Timothy and others. Some may have been coauthored, but they clearly reflect Paul's ideas and these are very, very important sources; they're our earliest written testimonies about the Christian message. You have to remember, they're written in Greek; they date from 15–35 years after the crucifixion; so there's always a question of transmission here. We also believe that Paul never met Jesus and he asserted his authority as apostle to the gentiles; that is, to the pagans, the non-Jews.

Paul concluded that Jesus and—as he says in Romans, "God was in Christ"; a very important point that leads to Christian theological developments—that the message was universal. Yahweh, as the lord of all the universe, as the transcended God of all mankind, had sent his son as a universal message; it's not just to the Jews, it's to everyone. Paul, as a Pharisee Jew, accepted the resurrection of the flesh and the role of angels. He also apparently believed that there would be a final reckoning soon—there's references to that in Romans and Corinthians—and that his mission was to convert the Gentiles, the wider world of Rome, in order to bring about the impending eschaton, the final kingdom, and that he worked with frenzied activity to carry out his missionary activity that we'll get to in a moment.

Paul also was the ideal missionary from his background. He sometimes refers to himself as a tentmaker, and everyone thinks, "Oh, he's a nice, humble guy making tents." No, his Roman name Paulus indicates he had Roman citizenship, and that meant one of his ancestors proved very, very important to the Roman government, probably in the late republic—there were a number of possibilities where the citizenship came. And as for tent makers, it was more likely he was a government contractor and his ancestors said, "You want 10,000 tents for the legions? We can deliver."

Paul came from a well-to-do family. He knew Greek, he knew Plato; he had a very, very good education; and he was a Roman citizen. There were very, very few Roman citizens in the east at this point. He could move among circles in a way most people could not because he was a Roman citizen, and if he got in trouble with local authorities, all he had to say was, "I'm a Roman citizen." There's a reference to that when he's in trouble at Caesarea Maritima late in his career and he says, "I appeal unto Caesar," and that's how he ends up in his final journey to Rome. That's perfectly consistent of what we know of Roman law. As it will become clear, many of the details recorded in Acts and in the letters of Paul, I don't know if they're 100 percent historically accurate—and there might be some retelling, elaboration, embroidering—but the overall picture is very consistent and plausible with what we know of legal conditions and social conditions in these cities in the Roman east in the time of Saint Paul.

Above all, Paul took it upon himself to preach in the synagogues of the Diaspora; he didn't have to operate in the Jewish homeland. He started in the great city of Antioch, which was the capital of Roman Syria. His teachings went out to Jews of the synagogue, Pharisees; these would be people of the same background of Saint Paul himself. Furthermore, he reached many pagans who are often called in the sources "Godfearers," *theophobes*. These would be pagans who were familiar with Jewish monotheism; who had gone to the synagogue; may have intermarried; and may have even practiced some of the Jewish dietary laws, for all we know. His audience from the start was mixed. It was Greek-speaking, not Aramaic-speaking. Most of them could not read the Hebrew bible; they would have used the Septuagint, which is the Greek translation (there are several other Greek translations available).

To Paul, Jesus was the Messiah, and in this sense the Messiah who fixed a new Torah. By the act of baptism, Jew and pagan now became Christians, a term that was first used in Antioch and a very appropriate term; that is, they were going to live their life like Jesus. They had now accepted a new vision of what that Jewish monotheism meant. Paul, as I said, was a Pharisee and if you asked Paul what his identity was, he would have said, "I'm a Jew; I'm a Pharisee; and by the way, I accept Jesus (or by his Hebrew name, Joshua bar Joseph) as the Messiah who had created a new Torah." In addition, Paul, ever of the pragmatic missionary thought: We have these gentiles coming now into this new community; it's not regarded as necessary for them to obey all the dietary restrictions, be circumcised, especially men late in age. The very act of baptism was the new mark of the new Israel; the new Torah, by the act of baptism. Again, it's debated where the Christians got this notion. It goes back to John the Baptist; there's a number of ritual baptisms and purity traditions in Judaism. That becomes the new mark of the community.

From the start, Paul ran into some opposition on this. Not surprisingly, James and others in Jerusalem wondered what Paul was doing. He was not an original apostle; he claimed to have this commission due to a mystical vision from Christ; and there was some real debate about this. Peter himself, Saint Peter, was inclined, I think, to go with Paul; but James exerted a great deal of authority at this point, not only from what became the Canonical text but also from the Apocryphal text we have, particularly the gospel of Saint Thomas, written in the 2nd century A.D., that records a lot of interesting material about the early Christian tradition. It survived largely in a Coptic translation—that is, the native Egyptian translation of the 4th century—but again, it's a very early text and very plausible in some ways.

Eventually a council was held; some sort of meeting in Jerusalem, usually dated around 48 A.D. It's recorded in Acts, and there's no reason to disbelieve any of this. It's perfectly understandable that an agreement was reached. Peter threw his support behind Paul on this, I suspect, and the result was that the Pauline converts did not have to follow Torah if they not had originally been Jews. That was a major break. That meant the original converts, the apostles, the associates in Jerusalem, now recognized as members of their own community—of their own religious community, and it's a religious community; that's the definition—all of these churches in the wider Roman world that are being set up by Paul and his followers, as well as those apostles who went in and converted those early Christians in Alexandria and Egypt, which is not associated with Paul or Peter. That meant that the apostolic churches are a loosely associated federation of churches from the start, but they all recognized that they're members of the same community.

There will be other churches—there will be so-called heresies; "heresy" comes from the Greek word "to choose," as those Christians have chosen the wrong doctrines, is essentially what it means—that will be outside these apostolic churches or, as one very famous theologian would say, outside the mainstream; but the council of Jerusalem was all-important. From the start, it's clear the Pauline churches in numbers and wealth were all-important. I think James and the members of the Jerusalem church were amazed at the amount of money that was brought in for charitable purposes from the wider churches; and as a result of that council, Paul's activities were now legitimized and he could go out as the apostle to the gentiles and start preaching in those synagogues.

This meant that Paul, who in many ways is one of the first converts—there's a very fine work written by Segal on essentially Paul the convert; that is, he carries over much of his Judaism to his new Christian faith and that's one way of understanding him—but Paul is not only the first convert, he's not only a powerful intellect and a great religious thinker (and really, in order to understand a Christian you always have to go back to the letter to the Romans; that's an absolutely all-important definition of what the Christian faith is), Paul also was the first missionary; or pretty close to it, we don't know of any other.

This is something we would take for granted; we think: The way Christianity spreads itself is by missionary activity. This is a new concept in the Roman world, and I really have to drive home how different it is. Think for a moment: In the pagan traditions, despite the efforts to find proselytizing with the mystery cults, it isn't there; that's really trying to read Christian notions into pagan cults. Even with the Jews, you don't have this tradition of missionary activity; that is, going out and coming to people and saying, "I have a new faith; I have a new message to give you." This is quite different. Pagans would understand going on a pilgrimage to a specific sanctuary; to consult an oracle, to participate in a festival. That makes sense. Jews would have the same tradition: They'd all crowd into Jerusalem on the high holidays for the Passover (which is always the time that the Roman government lost control of the city, and without the temple guards the place would go crazy); that all makes sense. But going out on missionary activities; no, this is something that belongs to Paul, and it's part of his mystical religious drive: "I must convert the gentiles; I'm the apostle to the gentiles, and this is my mission from Jesus directly."

He undertakes this first mission, generally dated between 46 and 48 A.D., and he and Barnabas undertake—and this is recorded in Acts—a mission that starts in Antioch. Again, Antioch is an important city. It's the third city of the Roman world. It's today the modern city of Antakya in Turkey—which some would call Turkish Syria, in a way—and at the time it was part of the capital of the greater Roman Syria. It's a city of at least 500,000 strong. There was a large Jewish community there; there were important synagogues; and Paul and Peter both made important conversions in the city of Antioch. He left Antioch through its port at the mouth of the Orontes River and took sea passage to key ports in Cyprus (Salamis, Paphos) and then landed on the shores of Turkey today at the city of Perga—which is the center of a very important mother goddess cult—and then went inland to cities that were either Roman colonies or associated with Roman rule. That included the city of Pisidian Antioch—I talked about that earlier in regard to the god Manes and the imperial cult—the city of Iconium, which is today Konya in Turkey, and the city of Lystra.

On that travel, he preached and set up a number of successful what we would call churches. You have to think of these in a moment as "house churches"; that is, he converted families, and that the leading members of the family made the house available for services. He returned by sea through the city of Attaleia, today Antakya, not satisfied. A few years later, probably in 49, he took on a more ambitious mission that carried him back to a number of the same churches, and eventually he ended up at the port city of Alexandria Troas, a tacky Roman tourist center for the Trojan War, and took passage to the great cities of Greece—Thessalonica, Beroea, Athens, Corinth—where he again preached and then set up churches. Then, finally, his third mission in the early- to mid-50s A.D. took him back to Pisidian Antioch, then down the Maeander River Valley to Ephesus, to the great churches of western Asia—many of these churches named in Revelation as the seven churches of Asia; they probably all go back to Pauline missions—passage back to the churches in Greece, and then returning to the Jewish homeland by sea via the city of Tyre.

The journeys racked up an enormous number of miles, but what is important: Paul established a network of apostolic churches in northern Syria, in southern and western Turkey today, and in the Greek world that become the cradle of the Christian movement. Again, the exceptions are the city of Rome—which has close associations with Peter and Paul, particularly Peter, and has reasons to believe those traditions—and the city of Alexandria. These would become the main centers of the Christian mission for the next 250 years. All other churches are essentially extensions from those churches founded by Paul and the early apostles. There's is a tradition of Saint Thomas going east to India following the trade routes and establishing churches in India and Iran; there are probably reasons to believe it. There's a Latin-speaking church that emerges in North Africa by the 2nd century A.D., and that's an extension and its origins are of little debate. But fundamentally, when we're looking at the first Christians, we're looking at Christians in these regions: Greek speakers, converts from the synagogue, and located in cities.

This gets us to the next important question about these missions: Who were these first Christians? These first urban Christians have been documented and studied in a number of ways. There has been some pivotal books, the most important one by Wayne Meeks, *The First Urban Christians*, which really is now the definitive study. That set of churches that were set up by Paul won over people from the synagogue. Often, these people were Jews who spoke Greek or they were pagans familiar with monotheism. They didn't have high social rank. They weren't members of the local elite; they weren't members of the imperial aristocracy; they weren't Roman soldiers. But, then again, they weren't from the lower rungs of society. They were people who had a certain amount of money and rank, and yet at the same time had sort of a low social origin according to Meeks so that some of them found a social side to these early churches; that is, they became prominent members and donors. One thinks of Damaris of Athens who made her church available; a woman of some rank and note who supposedly heard Paul at the Areopagus and converted. Others suggest that you have cases of imperial freedman. That would be Aquila and his wife who came over and provided the early church in the city of Corinth. They came from just below the ruling ranks; they had money, they had property. Many of them were in Roman colonies or great cosmopolitan centers; they're Greek speakers. This identity—this social and linguistic identity—characterizes Christians probably up to the time of Constantine.

Another important point about these early conversions: You converted families. The families of early Christians reflected the social hierarchy, prejudices, and assumptions of the wider Roman world. Therefore, an issue such as slavery—so important to us today as a moral anathema—that wasn't such a problem; they always accepted slavery, that's just a given. In some cases, when you converted one family they would convince another family member; so you have to think of these Christian families as little social pyramids with someone like Aquila and Priscilla—that couple at Corinth who gave over their church, they're at the head of the family—Damaris at Athens, who's supposedly the wife of Dionysius the Areopagite; in some ways, they played the role of patrons that would be familiar from the wider Roman world. Damaris of Athens in particular has been compared to a pagan lady known as Julia Severa at the city of Akmonia in Turkey today. Julia Severa was a pagan who actually donated considerable money to the synagogue because the Jewish community there was very important. The world reconstructed from the letters of Paul—the Deutero-Pauline letters; that is, the later letters associated with Paul in Acts—is a very plausible world and we can get a pretty good idea of what the social and economic identity of these Christians were.

Christian cities, again: on main highways, crucial ports; churches of revelation; later churches such as this church of Sinope where the teacher Marcion was born in 85, it clearly was a church established from one of the Pauline churches from western Asia. This Christian identity, as I said, persists well into the 2nd century A.D. These early conversions by Paul created a new network of Pauline churches.

The question comes up: What about numbers? As far as we can tell, the numbers of these communities are quite small. The earliest church we know about is a house church from the city of Dura Europos from about 256 A.D. There's also an important synagogue there. The house church probably just accommodates about 30 members. When you're talking of these early Christians communities, you're talking about, really, face-to-face societies. Bishops function more in the form of a parish priest today. All of this information that we have from Paul's letters tells us that you're dealing with very, very discrete communities.

From the start, these Christian churches set up by Paul were somewhat in opposition not only to the wider pagan world and Jews, but also other Christians missions that were out there. We know from Galatians, for instance, that Paul warns that congregation not to accept teachers who teach another Christ. We're not sure exactly who these people were. They are sometimes thought to be Docetists, which comes from the Greek word *dokeo*, which means "to seem" or "appear." This was a set of teachings that goes back very early. Certain people who either witnessed or heard the crucifixion said, "God can't be crucified on the cross; he only appeared to be crucified." Any of you who may have watched that movie *The Last*

Temptation of Christ, based on the novel, actually that final sequence is essentially perfect Docetist theology when Christ supposedly comes down and lives longer; it's a whole dream sequence in the movie, which is a rather controversial and rambling movie in some ways. In any case, there clearly was this mission. Eusebius, writing in the 4th century A.D., was convinced all of these doctrines came from Simon Magus (Simon the Magician). They were out there to deceive Christians.

We know of many Christians who continued to maintain Torah and the dietary laws well into the 4th and 5th centuries A.D. To later Christians writing in the 4th and 5th centuries, these people are curiosities; they've gone back to Judaism. The likelihood is they never left it; that in many ways they accepted Jesus as Messiah, but behaved in very, very many ways as Jews do in their Torah and their dietary laws and even in their understanding of what the Christian message may have been. We do know that followers of John the Baptist maintained a separate identity—they're known as Mandaeans—and many of these heresies, which were written up only in the 4th century A.D. in a compendium by a man named Epiphanius of Salamis, these heresies were all looked upon and condemned later in retrospect when you have a much more organized church; you have a bunch of clear doctrines. Therefore, you're not quite sure in the 4th century who these people were in earlier times. What it is, is the initial Christian message was very, very diverse and it's eventually the apostolic churches that would win out—that is, the churches established by Paul; those who come out of the Jerusalem church with James—and particularly the churches at Antioch and Rome are already being given special treatment.

Paul was conveyed to Rome probably around 66–67 where he was executed. The tradition is that Peter was martyred there; there's every reason to believe it. Both Paul and Peter had close associations with the early imperial capital but, again, remember that would have been a Greek-speaking community; a community in its identity that was very, very similar to the communities in Greece, Asia Minor, and Antioch. To the apostolic churches, these alternate explanations, these sects—or maybe let's use a word from the Reformation: these other confessions—of Christianity represented a challenge; perhaps the most serious challenge, more of a challenge then the pagans or the Jews. But in 64 A.D., the position of all Christians changed abruptly; it would affect all Christians of all backgrounds and confessions: The emperor Nero had outlawed Christianity; and for the first time, the Roman imperial government persecuted people based on their religion. That was a major change, not only for Christians, but for the Roman world in general.

Pagan Response—First Persecutions
Lecture 8

W hen we think of the persecution of Christians, it is often a Hollywood-driven image of vast numbers of martyrs thrown to the lions in the Coliseum. The truth is that for the first two centuries, there were no lions, no genocides, no systematic programs to root out and destroy Christianity in the Roman world. With a few notable exceptions, the imperial government mostly regarded Christians with baffled irritation, giving them every opportunity to recant and punishing their treasonous behavior only when compelled by law.

The First Persecution

- We have limited information on how the wider world of paganism immediately received Christianity, but we do have information as to how the Roman imperial government handled it. In the year 64, **Emperor Nero** ordered the first persecution of Christians in the city of Rome. This would have a profound influence on the Christian mission and on pagan perceptions of Christianity.

- Nero targeted the Christians as scapegoats for the Great Fire of 64. His second wife, Poppaea Sabina, who had connections in Rome's Jewish community, may have made the suggestion. Nero needed a scapegoat because he was being accused of lighting the fire himself so he could rebuild the city in his own image—the origin of the (erroneous) image of Nero fiddling while Rome burned.

- In Nero's time, the persecutions were conducted in a circus that he had specially constructed, not in the Coliseum, which was built after his death and dedicated in 80. Saints Peter and Paul were, according to tradition, executed during this persecution.

- We have an account of Nero's persecution, written by the Roman historian **Tacitus**, who was born around the year 56. He was a boy during the persecutions, but he relied on eyewitness accounts. He reports that:

Nero fastened the guilt and inflicted the most exquisite tortures upon a group hated for their abominations, whom the populous call Christians. ... Those who confessed membership were arrested. Then, on their information, great numbers were convicted not so much of guilt for the conflagration as of hatred of the human race.

Tacitus, one of Rome's great historians.

- After describing in horrifying detail the punishments Nero visited on the Christians and his own outlandish behavior, Tacitus notes, "A feeling of pity arose as people felt that [the Christians] were being sacrificed not for the public good but because of the savagery of one man."

- Tacitus's report reveals that Romans of senatorial and equestrian rank had to this point very little contact with Christians; they are not quite sure who they are.

The Confusing Rebellion of Christianity

- Tacitus's account is also verified by his contemporary **Pliny the Younger**, a distinguished government official and later governor of Bithynia-Pontus in Asia Minor. Having encountered the Christians, he wrote to Emperor Trajan because he was unsure about why they were being persecuted. He asked Trajan whether it was because of their faith or because of other crimes. Trajan's answer was evasive.

- The Romans had no real means of dealing with something like Christianity. There were no precedents to assist them. Christians did not revolt nor resort to arms, yet their faith was treason. The Romans rarely outlawed gods; therefore, they labeled

Christianity as superstition and magic, which they were more comfortable outlawing.

- One of the most significant instances of the Romans taking action against a cult was in 186 B.C. A **Senatus consultum** ("decree of the senate") took measures against devotees of Bacchus (Greek Dionysus)—not against the god. The worshipers were meeting under suspicious circumstances (the same was later said of Christians); they met at night and could therefore be a conspiracy, which could lead to social disorder.

- In Gaul and in Britain, the Romans took action against the Druids because they incited rebellion. In 70, the future emperor Titus burned down the Temple of Jerusalem not as an act of anti-Semitism but as a way of punishing the Jews for rebellion. The closest the Romans came to Christian behavior before were their dealings with Cynic philosophers, but these were usually individuals.

- The **rescript** of Nero was a legal turning point. From then on, the Christians had the unique distinction of being singled out by the imperial government as illegal. That would change the whole nature and development of the Christian message. The Christians would respond by developing institutions and means of communicating their mission in very different ways; they could no longer publicly preach.

Pliny the Younger and the Sacrifice Test

- Pliny the Younger, in his correspondence with Emperor Trajan, reveals to us he devised the sacrifice test. This was the main method the Romans used to determine whether those who were accused of Christianity really were Christians.

- Pliny set up the altars of the traditional gods of Rome or of the city, as well as a statue or icon of the emperor. Then the people denounced as Christians were brought before the statues and were told to worship the gods. That is, they had to sacrifice and eat the sacrificial meats. If they did so, they were released. If not, they were punished.

- Pliny mentioned that many people admitted they had been interested in Christianity and attended some services but had reverted to the ancestral gods. He was surprised at how many people fell into this category. Later on, in the great persecutions, these people were known as *lapsi*, people who lapsed and had sacrificed.

- Pliny continued to be perplexed by the status of Christianity in the empire. He had reports of Christians holding orgies, committing cannibalism, and committing incest; these seem to be misunderstandings based on real Christian doctrines—loving all humankind, the Eucharist, calling one another brother and sister. But all of this was based on denunciation, not evidence.

The Extent of the Early Persecutions

- What is also evident in the letter is that Pliny depended heavily on the locals to tell him who were Christians. The imperial government did not have the machinery to carry out a persecution.

- What is clear is that the persecutions are nothing like the Nazi Holocaust or the kind of ethnic cleansing that fills newspapers today. In fact, the persecution was a legal proceeding. Trajan responded to Pliny's letter about the sacrifice test with a legal argument:

It is not possible to lay down any general rule to serve as a kind of fixed standard. … [The Christians] are not to be sought out. If they are denounced and proved guilty, they are to be punished. … But anonymously posted accusations ought not to have a place in any prosecution, for this is both a dangerous kind of precedent and out of keeping with the spirit of our age.

- This is an extraordinary response from an emperor: We are supposed to follow the law. Therefore, any image of the early persecution that calls to mind the Gestapo or the KGB is an inaccurate picture; there is no place for such abuse in Roman law. Even the word "martyr," attached to those Christians who died in the arena, literally means "witness," as in a legal proceeding.

- The *cognitio extra ordinem* was an extraordinary legal proceeding in which the governors could interrogate Christians, and there were many instances—even in Christian records—where the governor gave the accused every opportunity to repent and worship the Roman gods.

- Another important fact that comes out of Trajan's letter and is verified by later sources is that persecutions were local, sporadic, and short-lived. There was no concerted effort to root out Christians.

- Saint Cyprian, writing in North Africa, said there was a depressing correlation between an earthquake and a persecution. The great plague of 166–169, which swept the empire when the Roman army returned from the East, led to outbursts of persecution. So the tradition of scapegoating that began with Nero remained a part of persecutions into the 2nd century.

- But otherwise, Christians, if they avoided overt actions—if they did not proselytize or insult the gods directly—were mostly left alone. They could live inconspicuous lives and convert people through family and social networks, as long as they did not disrupt the fabric of civic life.

- The Romans never did comprehend what they were facing in Christianity. The whole idea of Christians standing in a law court, following the rules of law, and then denying the sacrifice was extraordinary. Meanwhile, the Christians themselves now had to find new ways of defining themselves, organizing their communities, and disseminating their message.

rescript: The response of a Roman emperor to a petition that had the force of law.

Senatus consultum: Decree of the Senate; a resolution by the Roman Senate that gave its backing to a proposed law.

Names to Know

Nero (a.k.a. **Lucius Domitius Ahenobarbus**; 37–68; r. 54–68): The last Julio-Claudian emperor. Nero was the son of Gnaeus Domitius Ahenobarbus and Agrippina the Younger (the great-granddaughter of Augustus). In 49, his mother married Claudius and secured Nero's adoption as Claudius's heir. Nero took the name Nero Claudius Caesar. In 54, Nero succeeded as emperor, but he craved popularity as an artist and therefore entrusted the affairs of state to his ministers down to 62, when he assumed direct control. By his amoral and outrageous conduct, he alienated the ruling classes and legions and thus precipitated his downfall and suicide in 68. In 64, Nero ordered the first persecution of Christians at Rome.

Pliny the Younger (a.k.a. **Gaius Plinius Caecilius Secundus**; 61–112): Roman senator from northern Italy and adopted son of a famous naturalist, Pliny penned letters to Emperor Trajan that reveal the workings of civic life in Asia Minor during the Roman peace.

Tacitus (a.k.a. **Publius Cornelius Tacitus**; 56–after 120): From a northern Italian or southern Gallic provincial family, Tacitus entered a senatorial career under Vespasian. In 77, he married Julia, daughter of Gnaeus Julius Agricola. In 97, he was consul, and in 112–113, he was proconsul of Asia. He is the greatest historian of imperial Rome. He wrote *Annals* and *Histories*, covering the periods 14–68 and 68–96, respectively. He also wrote *Germania*, *Agricola*, and *Dialogus de oratoribus*. In *Annals*, Tacitus reports the persecution of Christians by Nero in 64.

Suggested Reading

de Ste Crox, "Why Were the Christians Persecuted?"

Eusebius, *The History of the Church*.

Fox, *Pagans and Christians*.

Frend, *Martyrdom and Persecution in the Early Church*.

Hopkins, "Murderous Games."

MacMullen, *Enemies of the Roman Order*.

Musurillo, ed. and trans., *Acts of the Christian Martyrs*.

Pliny the Younger, *The Letters of Pliny the Younger*.

Tacitus, *The Annals of Imperial Rome*.

Wilken, *The Christians as the Romans Saw Them*.

Questions to Consider

1. What was the impact of Nero's persecution of the Christians in 64? How did Romans view Christians in the 1st and 2nd centuries A.D.? What motivated Romans, and pagans in general, to compel Christians to sacrifice?

2. What does Pliny the Younger reveal about the imperial government's aims in persecuting Christians? Was this a priority? How does Pliny's perspective differ from that of Eusebius and the acts of the martyrs?

3. Why did the Romans fail to understand Christianity? Did they see a conflict of religion?

Pagan Response—First Persecutions
Lecture 8—Transcript

In this lecture, I wish to deal with the pagan response to the Christian mission—that is, the missions of Saint Paul and of the associated apostles and Peter and others—who created this Christian heartland in the late 1st and 2nd centuries A.D. We will be looking primarily at the Roman imperial government.

We have limited information on how the wider world of paganism immediately received Christianity, but we do have information as to how the Roman imperial government handled it. In the year 64 A.D., the emperor Nero, one of the most notorious emperors of all times and probably one of the most depraved rulers of all times, ordered a persecution of Christians in the city of Rome; and I must stress that the persecution was only conducted in the city of Rome, not in the empire as a whole. That persecution in 64, the first persecution on record, had a profound influence in directing the Christian mission, in pagan perceptions of Christianity, and also, as we shall see in the upcoming lectures, the very identity of Christianity had to be defined in relationship to a government of pagan Roman emperors who had now outlawed Christianity.

Nero himself targeted the Christians as scapegoats. It is not sure where Nero got all of his information; one suggestion is that his wife—and partner in crime, really, his second wife Poppaea—was a sympathizer of Judaism; that she had connections with prominent Jews in the city (there was a very, very wealthy Jewish community in the city of Rome going back at least 150 years before Nero's reign) and that she learned from Jews the difference between Jews and these Christians who were followers of such fellows as Paul and Peter, and pointed out to her husband that they would make an ideal set of scapegoats.

The reason Nero needed a scapegoat was that in 64 A.D., the city of Rome had been ravaged by a great fire. It had raged for days. At least 10 of the 14 districts—or *regiones*, as they're known in Latin—had been reduced to ashes. The rumor went out everywhere that Nero was behind the lighting of the fire because he wanted to rebuild the city of Rome in his own image, and he was even reported to have played or performed his own epic known as the "Sack of Troy," which he would've done on a lyre. This image gave rise to the popular image of Nero fiddling while Rome burned. The charge of being an incendiary—that is, lighting fires deliberately—goes back deep in Roman history. The accusation was raised in 63 B.C. by Cicero against the conspirators of Catiline, who supposedly were going to burn the city down; and that would, of course, incense the urban plebeians, the residents of the city. This notion that the Christians may have started the fire was ideal. Nero or Poppaea had vague notions of what the Christian apocalypse was about; Christians are somehow thinking of the end of the world in fires. This would be ideal to fasten this charge on them; they were ideal scapegoats; there were not that many of them. It is extremely well-depicted in this Hollywood spectacle of the old style with Anthony Quinn playing Barabbas where he is a very, very uncertain Christian. He really doesn't really know much about Christianity, and when the city of Rome is burning, he thinks this is the end of days. He starts torching it; he is arrested and when investigated he says, "I am burning the city down to bring about the second coming." It is probably misinformation of this sort that was available to Nero and to the imperial government as a whole that the Christians were behind the burning to bring on the end of days.

I should note that in Nero's time, the persecutions were conducted in a circus that he had constructed, not in the Coliseum. Many tourists going to Rome have the notion that the Coliseum is where the Christians were destroyed, particularly in 64. That is an impossibility because the Coliseum was built after Nero's death. Its official name is the Flavian Amphitheater and in 1749, Pope Benedict XIV dedicated the Coliseum as a sacred place. Benedict's reason for doing this was to prevent the building from being a quarry. It had been used for bull fights, it was a fortress at one point. People were just carting away sections of the Coliseum to build their own homes. While Benedict got it wrong—that is, the Coliseum was built and dedicated in 80 A.D.; its official name is the Flavian Amphitheater—nonetheless, he did a very, very important service in preserving the monument. I think one Pope actually thought that the Coliseum would make a very good factory for wool and spinning. There are all sorts of ways ancient monuments get put to use in later years; sometimes it's a bit horrifying and we're surprised that almost anything comes down to us. But in any event, the persecutions did take place in 64. There were subsequent persecutions; and in those later persecutions of maybe 66, Peter and Paul were probably martyred at that point. There is no reason to disbelieve the Christian tradition that both saints were in Rome and were executed on orders of Nero.

Nero's persecution was very important also from the Roman viewpoint and shaped Roman opinions and attitudes about Christians really down to the year 313 A.D. when the Edict of Milan was issued by the Emperor Constantine that ended the illegal status of Christianity. We do have an account of that persecution, written by the Roman historian Tacitus, Cornelius Tacitus, who was born about 56 A.D. and died sometime after 120 A.D. thereabouts. I'd like to read that, or an excerpt from that passage, about the persecution of 64. These are Tacitus's words from his annals, which is his account of the Roman Empire from the time of Tiberius through the Civil War of 68–69. This is what he writes, based on eyewitness reports. Tacitus at this point was just a boy, but he did talk to people who witnessed the persecution.

> Consequently to scotch the rumor [that is, the rumor that Nero had set the fire] Nero fastened the guilt and inflicted the most exquisite tortures upon a group hated for their abominations whom the populous call Christians [and you notice by the very wording, Tacitus isn't quite sure who these guys are]. First then those who confessed membership [that is membership in Christianity] were arrested. Then on their information, great numbers were convicted not so much of guilt for the conflagration [that is, the great fire] as of hatred of the human race [which is a very peculiar wording that has caused scholars to raise debates, but what Tacitus is saying: These Christians really tend to avoid the company of other people and they must be somehow social misfits, and it's a common charge cast about by pagans for the next 200 years]. Mockery was added to their deaths. They were covered with skins of wild beasts and torn to death by dogs or they were nailed to crosses and when the day failed, were set afire and burned to provide light at night. Nero had offered his gardens for the spectacle [that is, for the execution of the Christians] and was providing circus games, mingling with the populous in the dress of a charioteer or driving a chariot. [This is a degradation of the emperor; this is something emperors should not do. Charioteers are low-lifes, like gladiators and prostitutes and

the like.] Hence though they were deserving of the most extreme punishment [Tacitus thinks that there's every reason to execute these people], a feeling of pity arose as people felt that they [that is, the Christians] were being sacrificed not for the public good but because of the savagery of one man.

The Latin is quite clear. *Savitia*, it means not only "savagery" but "cruelty," and that's one of Nero's prime vices: He's cruel; and if someone is cruel the way Nero is, he is also likely to be a coward, and turns out to be the case with Nero.

Tacitus's report, which is the earliest record we have from a Roman about the Christians, is very telling in a number of ways. It reveals several points about the Roman upper classes. One is: Romans of senatorial and equestrian rank, or emperors, really had very, very little contact with Christians; they are not quite sure who they are. This is true probably into the early 3rd century A.D. Most Romans would have no reason to come into contact with Christians given that Christians were Greek speakers; they were residents of certain cities; they were not of high rank; they were not imperial service.

Tacitus's account is also verified by a contemporary of Tacitus, a fellow called Pliny the Younger. His official name would be Gaius Plinius Caecilius Secundus. He is the adoptive son of Pliny the Elder, who is very important, writing on a whole bunch of subjects of natural history. Pliny had a distinguished senatorial career. He ended up as Governor of Bithynia-Pontus somewhere between 110 and 113 A.D. Bithynia-Pontus is, today, the shores of the Black Sea in the modern Republic of Turkey. There are a number of important Greek cities on those shores, and Pliny was moving from city to city as an imperial troubleshooter. One of his jobs was to straighten out the finances of cities as well as administer the province. In moving from city to city, close to the city of Amisus—today the city of Samsun, which is the one of the great ports on the Black Sea—Pliny was a bit perplexed because he had encountered these people known as Christians, and he wrote back to the Emperor Trajan of how he dealt with Christians.

We will deal with Pliny's letter to the Emperor Trajan and Trajan's response in later lectures dealing with the persecutions; but what's significant for us right now is the fact that Pliny was unclear why the Christians were being persecuted. They were obviously outlawed by an imperial letter—actually the official term would be a *rescript*; that would be imperial response to a petition—that is, in 64, Christians were outlawed; they were an outlawed group. He wrote to the Emperor Trajan, "Why are they outlawed? They are a *superstitio* [that is, they are a superstition, not a religion], but is it because of their faith [and he uses the Latin term *nomen Christianum*]?" "Is it simply the fact that they are Christians that they are outlawed, or is it because of other crimes [*legitia*; that is, moral crimes, depravity, perhaps treason of the Roman government]?"

Trajan does not really answer him directly on this; in fact, the Romans in general just see the Christians as "The faith is a superstition and, of course, if they are under suspicion for treason, every moral crime you can come up with is to be associated with the Christians." This terminology is used time and time again. There is a report in the reign of Domitian, who ruled from 81–96, that certain Roman aristocratic ladies were held accountable for superstition, for moral crimes. Some thought they may be early converts to Christianity; they were more likely converts to Judaism, and there were incidences of this in the Roman upper class. But in any event, it gives you some sort of sense of the language and the invective used and really the limited amount of information that Romans had about Christians.

Furthermore, the Romans had no real means of dealing with something like Christianity. There were no precedents to assist them. I mentioned that the Jews revolted; the Romans understood that. But Christians who did not revolt, did not resort to arms, and whose faith was somehow perceived as treasonable, this was new. There is a tradition in Roman law of taking actions against what we would call religions, but you have to qualify that. The Romans themselves never really outlawed gods, religion, or faith per se. They would outlaw magic, superstition, astrology—we will get to that in a moment—that was not really religion. To the Romans, there was a very, very strong distinction between magic and religion. Religion was praying to the gods asking for the god's favor according to traditional rites. Magic was bending demonic powers, dark powers, to your will. There is a long tradition of this with lead tablets, curse tablets, usually involving issues of love or, more likely, gambling; creating lead tablets and nailing them down in the arena or the circus before gladiatorial games or chariot races so the guy you want to win will win because you have cursed his opponent. That is not really religion; that is on the fringes and we shouldn't be doing that. You do not know what you are doing when you summon up these powers. But when it came to gods, when it came to cults, when it came to worship, the Romans were very, very reluctant to outlaw gods.

In Tacitus in particular, but also later Roman writers, we encounter instances where the Romans looked down upon the cults of Egypt because the gods were depicted in animal form. There was a certain amount of prejudice and stereotyping; but it was not the gods of Egypt that Tacitus found distasteful but what he found distasteful was the way in which Egyptians were worshipping them. This was a misunderstanding of the Egyptian cults; and, again, Tacitus had very, very little contact with Egypt. He probably never went there; he was just repeating stereotypes.

One of the most significant instances of the Romans taking action against a cult was in 186 B.C. We have what is known as a *senatus consultum* (that is, a "decree of the senate") in which the Roman senate—and this was in the Republic at the time the Romans were conquering the Mediterranean world—takes measures against the devotees of Bacchus (Greek Dionysus). We have the official inscription on stone; that is, the actual resolution of the senate that was passed. We also have a very detailed account from the Roman historian Livy writing in the time of Augustus; that would be in the end of the 1st century B.C. The two accounts actually supplement each other and really coincide very nicely; this doesn't always happen with our sources.

The decree is quite specific. It outlaws the devotees, not the god. That is a point that is often missed in popular writing. "Oh, the Romans have a tradition of outlawing cults they find distasteful." No. Bacchus is a god. What they were afraid of is the fact that the worshippers are meeting under suspicious circumstances; the same is later raised of Christians. First, they met at night; that immediately drew the attention of the imperial government or, in this case, the government of the republic, the Roman government. It was nocturnal; it was secret. Furthermore, the Romans defined that they were meeting at night and they could be a conspiracy, a *coniuratio*, if they were more than five members; that is, two men and three women for a total of five constituted a potential conspiracy. They were worried about orgies and crazy rites that could lead to treason, to rioting, and all sorts of disruptions; that is, social disorder.

The decree was very, very significant. At the end, it tells the officials—these would be the *praetor peregrinus* who handled foreigners in Rome and Italy—that the praetor is supposed to investigate and to tear down and demolish all unauthorized sanctuaries to Bacchus. However, he was not to touch those sanctuaries that are holy—that is, that were legitimate—and throughout the decree, there are references that this was the action unless they had authorization from the praetor and the senate, unless there was authorization. The Romans were going after people they saw as potential rioters and people who would create social discontent, not the god himself. This was also clear in the late republic when *collegia* (burial clubs) of Jews or worshippers of Serapis were expelled; it was because they were rioting.

In Gaul and in Britain, the Romans encountered the Celtic gods and a priestly caste known as the Druids. The Druids are subject to all sorts of popular misunderstanding; but those priests were perceived as anti-Roman. They carried out a revolt in 26 A.D. in northern Gaul. Druids on the island of Britain were seen as inciting the provincials. The Roman governor Gaius Suetonius Paullinus, for instance, went into the island of Mona—which is the modern island of Anglesey off the north shore of Wales—to clean out one of these sanctuaries. But all the reports were, again, against the Druids because they incited rebellion. I mentioned that this was the same aspect of the Roman punishment of the Jews; the same aim was to crush rebellion. Hence Titus (the future emperor) in 70 A.D. burned down the temple at Jerusalem not as an act of anti-Semitism, not because he didn't like the worship of the god Yahweh, but a way of showing to the Jews, "You have revolted; we have punished you; your god has abandoned you." Not that Yahweh was illegitimate as a god, but, "The god has abandoned you, and do not rebel from Rome."

These were the precedents that the Romans had in dealing with the Christians. The closest the Romans came to were dealing with certain cynic philosophers who were usually individuals, ascetics, detached from the world; they were seen as cranky critics. One of the most impressive was a fellow called

Peregrinus who ran around and carried out all sorts of criticisms and violated social conventions, and in 165 A.D., actually threw himself on his own funeral pyre thinking he was going to experience an apotheosis; that is, go up to heaven and join the gods just like Heracles (the Roman Hercules). He was seen as essentially a cranky nutcase. Lucian, that famous essayist, wrote a marvelously witty parody on this man's career. They've had certain misfits, but these were individual philosophers; cynics who had rejected the material world. They have dealt with sorcerers, with astrologers, people involved in the black arts, bringing in demonic powers, and also certain instances of punishing priests or devotees of certain cults perceived as seditious, but the Romans have never outlawed a faith or a god before.

The *rescript* of Nero in 64 A.D. was a legal turning point. From then on, the Christians had the singularly unique distinction of being singled out by the imperial government as illegal—that is, their faith is illegal; the *nomin Christianum*—and that was a distinction that no other religion had ever had in the Roman world. With the edict—or the *rescript* is the technical term; we might call it an edict or a letter—with this provision by Nero that Christians were outlawed that was going to change the whole nature and development of the Christian message. The Christians would have to respond by developing institutions; developing means of communicating their mission in a very different way; they couldn't go out and publicly preach. We will be dealing with that in the coming lectures.

However, what about the Romans and the pagans after the persecution of 64? I go back to that letter of Pliny the Younger to the Emperor Trajan, written on the northern shores of Turkey today somewhere around 110–111 A.D. when he was Governor of Bythinia-Pontus. In that letter, the exchange is very, very significant. Pliny reveals to us that he was the one who devised what we call the sacrifice test. How do you distinguish Christians from everyone else? Pliny found a very simple solution: He set up the altars of the gods—these would be the traditional gods of Rome or of the city; in this case the city of Amesis, which was a Roman colony at the time—and also a statue (or an icon as it would be called, where the Greek Christians later got the word "icon") of the emperor, and then brought the people denounced as Christians before the statues and said, "Worship the gods." That is, "Sacrifice, and eat the sacrificial meats." If they did so, they were simply released. If they did not, if they refused to sacrifice, if they refused to taste the sacrificial meats, then they were clearly Christians. That way, Pliny was able to determine who had been denounced unfairly. He also mentioned there were people who, "Yeah, I was interested in Christianity. I had gone to some of the services, but I'm not a practicing Christian now; I believe in the ancestral gods," and Pliny was surprised at how many people fell in this category; and later on, in the great persecutions, when the imperial government conducted empire-wide persecutions, these people were known as *lapsi*, people who lapsed and had sacrificed.

There is also in Pliny, even with the sacrifice, again this perplexed aspect to the letter; not only "Why are we persecuting?" but "What are they really accused of?" He has all these reports of orgies, of cannibalism; they were feasting on the bodies of the dead; there was incest. These seem to be misunderstandings. The cannibalism might have arisen out of misunderstanding the Eucharist. The address of "brother" and "sister" among Christians, again, might have been deliberately distorted as, "Oh, they are all incestuous and sleeping together." Then orgies: "If they meet at night, there has to be orgies." Actually, the Romans had a very, very vivid imagination. I am sure the Christians were living far more boring lives than any Roman governor would ever imagine; but all of this was somehow involved with moral crimes. What is also evident in the letter is that Pliny depended heavily on the locals to tell him who were Christians. The imperial government did not have the machinery to carry out a persecution. This will become very clear when we look at the empire-wide persecutions.

This might be astonishing to us, because you would think, "The imperial government has outlawed Christianity; it is obviously seen as a threat; it has the unique distinction of a faith that has been outlawed," and yet the persecutions are nothing like a Holocaust; they were not even close to the Holocaust—that is, the Nazi efforts to destroy European Jewry—or even the kind of ethnic cleansing that fill newspapers today with depressing regularity. It's nothing on that order, or the purges of Stalin; any of these. Actually, the persecution was a legal proceeding. One of the most significant points about it is made in Trajan's response to Pliny. I think always Trajan was tired of Pliny writing about it: "Pliny had one more question. This guy just is afraid to make a decision without the emperor's approval." Let me read that brief passage.

This is Trajan responding to a very long letter from Pliny about the sacrifice test, who the Christians are, why we are persecuting, them, and he approves what Pliny has done. But then he goes on to say (and this is the emperor Trajan):

> For it is not possible to lay down any general rule to serve as a kind of fixed standard [that is, you have to treat Christians individually as they come up to you; there is no hard and fast rule here]. They [that is, the Christians] are not to be sought out. If they are denounced and proved guilty, they are to be punished. With this reservation that whoever denies that he is a Christian really proves it [that is, by worshiping our gods] even though he was under suspicion in the past shall obtain pardon through repentance [that is, if you sacrifice, they let you go]. [This was in response to a direct question in Pliny's letter.] But anonymously posted accusations ought to have no place in any prosecution for this is both a dangerous kind of precedent and out of keeping with the spirit of our age [the word is *clementia*; clemency in the age is *siculum*, which is a very, very loaded Latin term with religious connotations].

It is an extraordinary response by the emperor; that is: We are supposed to follow law. We are not supposed to seek them out. Ideas of pogroms, anonymous knocking on the door late at night, anonymously dragging people off by Gestapo or the KGB; there is no place for this in Roman law. If they are denounced, yes, we will punish them according to the law. But the imperial government made no effort to go out and seek out who these people were. There was no effort to eradicate Christianity by killing them all, and the sacrifice test was set up as a way of determining, "Do you worship the gods or not?" Governors actually administered these legal proceedings; and you should think of the persecutions, first and foremost, as a legal proceeding. The word "martyr," which is attached to those Christians who died in the arena, literally means the word "witness"; and what they were, they were witness to their faith. It is, again, a legal term. The *cognitio extra ordinem* was an extraordinary legal proceeding in which the governors could interrogate Christians, and there were many instances—and we have this from records of acts of the Christian martyrs—where the governor could go quite easy on these guys; give them every opportunity to repent, to worship the gods.

The second important thing that comes out of Trajan's letter and is verified by later sources down to 250: persecutions were local, sporadic, short-lived. There was no concerted effort to root them out by the imperial government. Saint Cyprian, writing in North Africa, says there is a depressing correlation between an earthquake and a persecution. The great plague of 166–169, which swept the empire when the Roman army returned from the East and spread the plague, led to outbursts of persecutions because Christians were somehow blamed for the plague. The plague had been sent by the gods—that would be Apollo Smintheus for those who read their Homer—in punishment for the fact that Christians were not worshipping the gods, and the entire empire was deserving of a communal persecution. An immediate aspect that comes out of that letter of Trajan—and one that is perhaps quite surprising to many of you—is the fact that the imperial government is not conducting anything remotely like a persecution as we would understand it in the modern age, certainly since the French Revolution on with telecommunications. Persecutions were sporadic prior to 250 A.D.

This meant that Christians, if they avoided overt actions, if they didn't go in and proselytize, if Christians didn't insult the gods directly, were pretty much left alone. That is, Christians could simply live an inconspicuous life, go about their business, try to convert people through family and social networks, if they did not disrupt the fabric of civic life, they were left alone; and this is very, very typical of the Roman government, which is often neglect: If it is not an immediate threat, if it does not interrupt the taxes, does not destroy security, the Romans might have a law in the books outlawing Christians; enforcing it is quite another matter. There was a difference between the legal and social reality of Christians in the 1st and 2nd centuries A.D.

What is most important that comes out of this early Roman response to the challenge of Christianity are two things: First, the Romans never comprehended what they were facing. The whole idea of Christians standing in a law court, following the rules of law, and then denying the sacrifice was extraordinary. The Romans understood defiance in terms of arms; that is, fighting Rome. The Christians did not do that. The second important point that comes out of this is for the Christians themselves. They now had to find new ways of defining themselves, organizing their communities or congregations, and finding other ways of disseminating the message and speaking to the wider pagan audience. The outlawing of Christianity by Nero had the unintended consequences of initiating important developments in Christianity, which we will deal with in the coming lectures: Those will be organization, cannon, and theology. In so doing, the Christians will acquire the means of not only surviving, but ultimately of disseminating their message even though they are outlawed.

Christian Bishops and Apostolic Churches
Lecture 9

Before the Council of Nicaea in A.D. 325, one could not speak of a Christian Church with a capital *C* and a clear mission. But the apostolic churches of the 1st and 2nd centuries made two significant advances toward that goal: First, they developed the concept of an apostolic succession, the hierarchical structure that would become the basis of Constantine's church. Second, they rapidly created the New Testament canon that would become, with few changes, the dogma of Christianity for the next 1,500 years.

The Church in the Apostolic Heartland

- By A.D. 64 and Nero's outlawing of Christianity, the apostolic Christian heartland stretched from the imperial capital at Rome, across Greece and Asia Minor, to Antioch and Syria, down to Jerusalem, and to Alexandria in Egypt.

- Other confessions, which later Christians called heresies, existed elsewhere, but the developments in leadership and canon are peculiar to those apostolic churches in response to the fact that Christianity was now outlawed.

- There were different ways of organizing congregations before 64 and even shortly after. Most Christian churches were private property—house churches. Meetings of the faithful were comparable to reading groups. There was nothing comparable to the later basilicas and Gothic cathedrals.

- Missionary activity essentially ceased in this subapostolic era. As inefficient and limited as the imperial government was, if a missionary started preaching the way Paul did in Ephesus, he would inevitably cause a riot and be arrested.

- The only known exception is Gregory the Wonder Worker, who preached in Alexandria. A biography of Gregory written by **Gregory of Nyssa** (whose grandmother, Marciona, had been converted by Gregory the Wonder Worker) is now understood to be full of anachronisms, so we have little information about Gregory's actual doings.

The Language of Christianity

- Language also restricted Christian activity. Over half of the Roman population did not speak Latin or Greek, whereas Christians were essentially Greek speakers. There simply were no missionaries available who knew the necessary languages.

- We have no references to Coptic, Syriac, or other native language translations of the New Testament until the about the 4th century A.D., and many languages of the Roman world were never written down. Compounding this, only about 15–20 percent of the Roman population was literate, so most people had to be taught orally.

- Some missionaries converted pagans by charisma, exorcism, and miracle working, but once the missionary moved on, if there was no church to follow up, the message was essentially lost.

- What literature there was, was not written in the high literary style of the Second Sophistic movement—that is, Attic Greek; it was written in **Koine** (the vernacular). The Roman elite would therefore look upon Christian literature—if they encountered it at all—as unworthy of serious attention. To the Romans, expression and clarity of language went side by side with intellectual achievement.

- Latin did become a language of the Christians during the late 2nd century in what is today Tunisia. However, the city of Rome and much of the empire remained Greek-speaking well past the mid-3rd century.

A Small Community of Small Communities

- Christian communities were small and self-contained well into the mid-3rd century. They were very much restricted to cities.

- Christians had little money. Bishop **Cyprian of Carthage** (the second-wealthiest city of the Roman West), once raised 100,000 sestertii to ransom Christian prisoners, but a Roman senator would blow that amount of money throwing a gladiatorial game. Pope **Fabian** had about 1,500 people in his employ and living on papal charity; by comparison, the Roman emperor at the same time would hand out distributions of grain and money to 250,000 residents during a festival.

Early popes, like Pope Fabian, had little power or wealth.

- Some interesting information about early Christians comes from inscriptions on funerary monuments found in Turkey, the only early monuments we have besides the catacombs in Rome. They come from areas where there were also important Jewish communities, and the inscriptions are similar to Jewish inscriptions of the period. The symbols and information suggest that a number of these families were converts from Judaism several generations earlier and some of them were still following Jewish law.

- Many early churches were established by other churches, such as the church at Sinope on the shores of the Black Sea. The first church in Gaul, at Lugdunum (modern Lyon) was founded by Pauline Christians from either Smyrna, Ephesus, or Pergamon.

The First Authorities and the First Heresies

- In response to the threat of persecution and heresy, the monarchial bishops began to arise in the 2nd century. Bishop **Ignatius of Antioch** wrote seven letters to various churches in Asia Minor in 107. They asserted three sources of authority in the Christian community: the *episkopos*, or bishop; the evangelist, or preacher; and the prophet or prophetesses. Prophetesses still had significant respect in the early church, a holdover from Judaism.

- A generation later, Bishop **Polycarp of Smyrna**, who was martyred in 155, writes of monarchical bishops as the sole source of authority in the church. This is the beginning of the notion of apostolic succession. In particular, the bishops of Rome, Alexandria, and Antioch had special authority because of their connections to Saint Peter; Rome, as the imperial capital, had the highest position of all.

- Pope Clement I wrote a letter to the church in Corinth, just as Paul did, to settle issues around the year 95, so the pope (that is, the bishop of Rome) already had authority even with churches in the Roman East.

- One of the earliest heresies was **Montanism**, named after their leader, **Montanus**, who emerged in Asia Minor in the mid-2nd century A.D. offering what he called the New Prophecy. He was followed by two female associates, **Priscilla** and **Maximilla**, who claimed to speak in the name of the Paraclete—the Holy Spirit.

- Montanus, Priscilla, and Maximilla presented a particular challenge to the bishops because they were producing a new revelation. Polycarp would argue that revelation was over and God's message was fixed.

- The Montanists were received with skepticism. They were banished at a number of synods—local councils of bishops. In fact, the first reports of synods we have were assembled to respond to the Montanists, and the Montanists forced bishops to develop their positions.

- Developing doctrine thus became another challenge. Which texts belonged in the New Testament? By 180, there were several versions of the New Testament circulating. Some were regarded as spurious and others as genuine, but it was difficult to distinguish among them.

- The **Gnostics** were teachers, such as **Valentinus**, who took Christian notions, principles, and faith and reinterpreted them in pagan myth to create cosmic schemes of redemption. They used myth allegorically, much the way a Buddhist or Hindu teacher does. This was considered heresy and presented another problem to those who wished to establish a canon.

- **Marcion of Sinope** created his own version of the canon that rejected the entire Old Testament. He concluded that Yahweh of the Old Testament could not be the God of the New Testament, which only included the Gospel of Luke, Acts of the Apostles, and a few of Paul's letters.

- Pope Pius summoned the First Synod at Rome in 143–144 in response to Marcion's text. Marcion was excommunicated and expelled from the Roman church and—happily, it seems—went off to found his own church, which flourished in Syria. The apostolic church was forced to finally establish which texts belonged in the New Testament and how to arrange them.

- No one in the 2nd and 3rd centuries knew who would eventually end up a heretic and who would be part of the established church, despite the surety of hindsight found in Eusebius. Eusebius goes so far as to condemn the heretics as serpents planted in the bosom of mother church by Satan himself, but we must remember it was not as clear at the time.

- The pagan critic Celsus captured a sense of these Christian divisions, writing around 177. He said that the Christians were like frogs sitting around a small pond croaking about sin. Celsus understood that the Christians were divided and that division hindered proselytizing.

- Fortunately for the church, despite their divisions, the apostolic bishops were able to make two important strides toward healing their divisions during this period: They established a formal church organization, and they defined a canon of texts.

Important Terms

episkopos (pl. *episkopoi*): Greek for "overseer"; a bishop.

Gnostics: From Greek *gnostikos*, "knowledgeable"; mystics and teachers with a deeper esoteric knowledge of religious texts and therefore of the path to salvation. Many Gnostics premised their cosmology on dualist beliefs. *See* **dualism**.

Koine: From Greek *koinē*, "common"; the vernacular, simplified Greek spoken in the Hellenistic world and the Roman Empire. The books of the New Testament are written in Koine Greek rather than the archaizing literary Greek of the upper classes.

Montanism: The Christian heresy of Montanus, who in the mid 2nd century, proclaimed direct inspiration from the Holy Spirit. Also called the New Prophecy.

Celsus (fl. 2nd century A.D.): Pagan critic of Christianity who wrote *On the True Doctrine* in 177. His work is largely known from quotations by Origen.

Cyprian of Carthage (a.k.a. **Thasciius Caecilius Cyprianus**; d. 258): Saint and bishop (250–257) who composed in Latin numerous tracts on issues of baptism of *lapsi*, readmission of heretics into the church, and episcopal authority. He was martyred during the persecution of Valerian.

Fabian (r. 236–250): Pope respected by African and Italian bishops and credited with missions to cities in Gaul. He was martyred during the persecution of Trajan Decius on January 20, 250.

Gregory of Nyssa (335–394): Saint and bishop of Nyssa (372–394). Born at Caesarea in Cappadocia, he was the younger brother to Saint Basil of Caesarea. Gregory penned important tracts on the Trinity and the omnipotence of God, thereby rejecting the views of Origen and the pagan Neoplatonists.

Ignatius of Antioch (d. c 107): Saint and bishop. He wrote seven letters that offer the first insight into the authority and role of bishops in apostolic churches.

Marcion of Sinope (c. 85–160): Christian theologian and editor of the New Testament. In 143/4 he emigrated to Rome. He produced his own edited version of the New Testament based on the letters of Paul and the Gospel of Luke. His teachings were rejected and condemned at the first reported synod at Rome, presided over by Pope Anicetus. Marcion then founded his own church that flourished into the 5th century.

Montanus (c. 150–200): Credited with apocalyptic revelations from the Holy Spirit either in 157 or 172, Montanus and his associates, Maximilla and Priscilla, offered a so-called New Prophecy that promised redemption only to the elect. Montanus challenged the authority of bishops in apostolic churches, who condemned Montanus as a heretic and convert from paganism. Montanist churches, however, survived in Asia Minor into the 7th century.

Polycarp of Smyrna (fl. 2nd century A.D.): Saint and bishop martyred at an uncertain date during a persecution in c. 150–155. He established the role of bishops in apostolic churches and was in the forefront of fixing the Christian canon by editing the books of the New Testament.

Priscilla and **Maximilla** (fl. mid-2nd century A.D.): Prophetesses and associates of Montanus, through whom the Paraclete (Holy Spirit) was believed to have spoken.

Valentinus (c. 100–160): A noted Gnostic teacher and thinker born at Alexandria who founded school at Rome. His dualist cosmology, based on allegorical myths and middle Platonic principles, were rejected by Christians as heretical. The *Gospel of Truth*, among the texts found at Nag Hammadi, was penned by Valentinus.

Suggested Reading

Brown, *The Body and Society*.

———, *The Churches the Apostles Left Behind*.

Brown and Meier, *Antioch and Rome*.

Eusebius, *The History of the Church*.

Frend, *Martyrdom and Persecution in the Early Church*.

Grant, *Augustus to Constantine*.

———, *Formation of the New Testament*.

Harnack, *Marcion*.

Louth and Saniforth, ed. and trans., *Early Christian Writings*.

Pelikan, *The Emergence of the Catholic Tradition*.

Richardson, *The Christianity of Ignatius of Antioch*.

Richardson, ed., *Early Christian Fathers*.

Robinson, *Ignatius of Antioch and the Parting of the Ways*.

Trevett, *Montanism*.

Tyson, *Marcion and Luke-Acts*.

Questions to Consider

1. What limited the dissemination of the Christian message after the persecution of 64? What barriers did Christian missionaries face in proselytizing in the late 1st and 2nd centuries? What are the sources for determining the numbers and rank of Christians?

2. Why was the evolution of episcopal organization and canon decisive for the success of the apostolic churches? Why were alternative organization or religious authority offered?

3. What accounted for the success and long-term popularity of the confessions outside the apostolic mainstream? Were these confessions fairly condemned as heretical churches?

Christian Bishops and Apostolic Churches
Lecture 9—Transcript

In this lecture, I plan to deal with development of Christian organization. This is an organization that will involve two important topics: One is the emergence of the monarchical bishop; that is, a bishop who essentially is the soul source of authority in leadership in a church. The other will deal with canon. That comes from the Greek meaning "yardstick," and canon refers to those texts all Christians accept as the yardstick or basis for judging one's faith.

These developments are very important but again, I must remind you that they develop in the apostolic churches. These are the churches that have been established by Saint Paul and his associates. It also included churches set up by Peter. Paul and Peter both were probably responsible for the church in Rome and the church at Alexandria, which is in Egypt, which was established by usually either Luke or Matthew; there's both associations. That is that Christian heartland that stretches from the imperial capital at Rome, across Greece, Asia Minor, to Antioch and Syria, down to Jerusalem, and to Alexandria. That's where most of the Christians were located; that's where the original apostolic churches are located. There will be other confessions, which later Christians call "heresies"; we'll talk about them in the course of this lecture. But the developments in leadership and canon are peculiar to those apostolic churches and that is, again, in response to the fact that Christianity was now outlawed by the persecution of 64 A.D.

There were different ways of organizing congregations before 64 and even after 64. It's important to keep in mind that most Christian churches were really private property. They were house churches; that is, members of the congregation provided the houses for meetings, and the meetings were in informal settings. Some of these would be very comparable to reading groups that Jews and pagan philosophers had assembled in similar circumstances. Furthermore, we have what's known as a house church. This comes from the city of Dura-Europos on the Euphrates; that would be on the border of Roman Syria. The city was sacked in 256 A.D., and there's a small house church. We know it's Christian from the decorations, and it could probably only accommodate about 30 individuals. This would be typical of churches down to the time of Constantine. We believe that they were rather inconspicuous, and you can't think of these churches as magnificent Basillican cathedrals that you would have in the Gothic or the Baroque of the Reformation and Counterreformation; no, they're far from that. When we speak of bishops, you're dealing with the face-to-face community, and a bishop would function far more like a parish priest today than a grand bishop of the Renaissance that everyone would think of; say, the Medici family or the Renaissance popes starting with Leo X.

In addition to the fact that the Christians met in these informal settings, the Christians now had very limited ways of getting their message out. That meant that missionary activity essentially ceased in what we call the subapostolic era; that is, the generation after Paul and the apostles. There seems to be an exception in a figure known as Gregory the Wonderworker who lived in eastern Asia Minor between 213 and 270 A.D. He actually attended the great Christian center at Alexandria, and we have a biography of Gregory written by Gregory of Nyssa, a very, very important church father of the 4th century A.D. writing in the region known as Cappadocia. However, Gregory of Nyssa was descended from Marciona, his grandmother, who had been converted by Gregory the Wonder Worker; and it now seems pretty clear that most of the activities attributed to the Wonder Worker are really anachronistic; that is, they represent the activities of bishops and missionaries and monks of the 4th century rather than the activities of the 3rd century A.D. If you remove Gregory the Wonder Worker from our information, we really have very little information about any kind of missionary activity that we would associate with conversion today. That's because as inefficient and limited as the imperial government was, if a missionary got up and started preaching the way Paul did in Ephesus, he'd inevitably be arrested, and probably he'd be preceded by a riot. That really restricted Christian activity.

There were other reasons why Christian activity was restricted and that you don't have a widespread missionary movement, as some would think. One was the simple fact of literacy and language. I mentioned earlier that over half of the Roman world didn't speak Latin or Greek, and that many languages were never written down. Christians were essentially Greek speakers. We have no references to Coptic, Syriac, or native language translations really until the 4th century A.D. There was a Syriac. It's not really a translation; it's essentially an abridgement narrative of the four Gospels, the Diatessaron, written by Tatian in the 2nd century A.D. for those people in Syria who didn't speak Greek, and that is exceptional. But the great translations into other languages—one thinks of the Jerome translation of the Bible into Latin; that's from the late 4th century—there just wasn't available missionaries who knew all of these languages. Furthermore, at most maybe 15–20 percent of the Roman population was really literate and could read something like the New Testament and actually get the message. Most people had to be taught orally.

There are instances of missionaries who by their charismatic manner converted, but those would be incidence—you could maybe convince some pagans that by an exorcism, for instance, or a miracle that this man was holy, he had the power of a god—but then the missionary would move on and if there was no church to follow up, the message was essentially lost, and a generation later members in the village were saying, "Now who was that god that that missionary had? Was it Apollo or this Christ God?" You really couldn't convert and retain populations given the legal status of Christianity, the barriers of language and literacy; and I think of as an example of the limited amount of literacy in the Roman world and the circulation of Christian literature. One example that comes to mind is something from the Reformation, when the Anabaptists seized the city of Munster in the 16th century. They were under siege by both Protestant and Catholic armies; essentially, the Protestants and Catholics agreed—these would essentially be the Lutherans—that, "We'll fight each other afterwards, but these guys have to go first." Nonetheless, in a year and a half they smuggled out tens of thousands of pamphlets because of printing presses and distributed this literature across north Germany. There was no printing press; there was no way of distributing Christian literature like this. Most of the libraries were private; bishops had them, such as Saint Polycarp who had a personal library. You have to keep in mind while there was writing, it's only available to a limited number of people, and when we get to Christian writings, particularly the Apologies, most of this literature is circulating in very limited circles.

Furthermore, in the 2nd century A.D., the earliest Christian literature was not written in the high literary style of the Second Sophistic; that is, in that atticizing Greek, that learned language that all of the literate classes of the Greek world and educated Romans—Roman senators spoke and read both Latin and Greek; they were bilinguals in every sense of the word—they would look upon Christian literature as sort of vernacular and low-level; it's written in Koine (that is, the common Greek). They can't do alpha-contract verbs and they get confused on the third declension, so how can you take them seriously? I stressed before in earlier lectures that grammar and diction were all-important in the Greek and Roman world. Proper diction in either Greek or Latin was just as important as having mastery of philosophy and the higher learning in order to understand moral issues, religious issues; they went hand-in-hand. There was never in the Roman world, "Oh, the guy has great ideas but he just doesn't express them well." Expression, clarity of language, went side-by-side with intellectual achievement. The Christians of the late first and 2nd century A.D. were still trying to attain that kind of level of literacy and mastery of the grammar and the language. Even that literature that did get out, very few pagans would've been inclined to read it and I doubt any pagan was ever convinced by reading a Christian apology.

Latin did become a language of Christians, but not in the city of Rome. The city of Rome was still Greek-speaking until the mid 3rd century and later. Only in the Roman cities in Africa—that is, what is today Tunisia—in the 2nd century, late 2nd century, with Tertullian and Minucius Felix, we began to get Latin-speaking Christians and they wrote in Latin. In the case of Tertullian, Tertullian was very good in his Latin; he wrote in a Ciceronian Latin. Therefore, you have to think of Christian communities as small and self-contained.

This image of Christian communities as small and self-contained, which persisted into the mid-3rd century, is best expressed by the scholar Peter Brown who is without a doubt the genius who has defined religious change and the culture of late Antiquity; that is, from the Classical to the early medieval world. Peter really is an extraordinary scholar; probably you only have a scholar, one or two scholars, like this in any generation. Brown described it this way in one of his books:

> The mid 3rd century Christian community is most fruitfully imagined as an uneasy conglomeration of old Christians [I like to use the term "old believers," borrowed from czarist Russia myself, but old Christians] for whom Christianity was an ancestral religion [meaning these are people who had been converted by Saint Paul or his associates, or Saint Peter] and a wider penumbra of half-

participants, who in times of pagan persecution, were predictable *lapsi* [that is, they would sacrifice to the gods; they lapsed]. Just as a century later when the Christian church was officially established [this would be in the 4th century A.D.] they would be predictable *ficti* [that means guys rushing and saying, "We're Christians, too, now that the emperor is Christian."]. The greatest achievement of such a group in discipline, ritual, and literature was to find a voice in which to speak to the outside world.

Peter Brown is ever perceptive on these matters. He doesn't get involved in questions of numbers; we have no information for the statistical rise of Christianity. Christians had very limited money. They couldn't attract crowds; they couldn't do the kind of social networking you have at sacrifices. What charity is reported was directed by Christians to Christians. There's nothing equivalent to Rice Christians as you had in China in the 19th century. By Rice Christians I mean those Chinese who would show up when rice was distributed at a missionary church. They were Christians for getting the food and then they went home to their villages and practiced their ancestral faith. The Christians were in no position to do that and they were very much restricted to cities.

We have two bits of information about this: Saint Cyprian, the bishop of Carthage, who was a very, very important figure in the development of Latin Christian literature, claims that he raised 100,000 sestertii—a sum that's very difficult to understand in the time of inflation—to ransom Christian captors, and this was a major effort on the part of his congregation in the second wealthiest city of the Roman west, so it's not a particularly impressive sum. A Roman senator would just blow that amount of money throwing a gladiatorial game. Pope Fabian at Rome, we're told by Eusebius, had on his—for lack of a better word—payroll some 1,500 people including exorcists, priests, orphans, widows, and poor members of the Christian community living on papal charity. That's a fraction of one percent of the city's total population. The Roman emperor at the same time would hand out distributions of grain and money to 250,000 residents; would throw gladiatorial games on a colossal scale. It gives you some sense of the disparity between what Christian charity could be—or alms-giving, to use a more traditional term—

and the kind of distributions done by both the emperor and the pagan elite classes, both in the city of Rome and in the provincial cities.

Furthermore, we have some funerary inscriptions. They're often called phaneo-Christian—that is, appearing to be Christian, it's like pseudo—funerary monuments; I prefer to call them Christian funerary monuments. Again, they come from Turkey; and I keep stressing Turkey as so important as a source of our information. These funerary monuments are the only pre-Christian monuments we have outside of written text with the exception of the catacomb paintings in Rome before the time of Constantine. These are inscriptions set up in Greek in stone, usually in marble or local stone, and they celebrate the deceased. They come from five distinct regions of western Turkey today, the region of Phrygia; and in three of the regions, clearly those funerary monuments are where there were important Jewish communities. In many ways, the inscriptions are very, very close to Jewish inscriptions of the period: They have curse formulas; that is if you in any way damage the inscription, you will be cursed. There are symbols and information that suggest that a number of these families were converts from Judaism several generations earlier. They use Hebrew names. Some of them seem to be keeping kosher. Some of the men are probably even circumcised from what we can tell from the information of these inscriptions.

Another one is from a city where apparently several of the members of the town council converted to Christianity, and the last one is from a little village today known as Altıntaş, which means "gold stone" in Turkish. It's a very small village and it was probably attached to the city of Cotiaeum as a satellite town, and it's a group of Christians living there in the mid-3rd century; we don't know what their origin was but again, the funerary monuments are apparently from a very self-contained community, and Cotiaeum was still a major pagan center. Today it's the modern city of Kutahya, which is the porcelain center of Turkey. All porcelain bought by tourists is made at Kutahya.

You're dealing with very small numbers; with self-contained communities. Churches would be established by other churches. That's how a church at Sinope, which is on the shores of the Black Sea today of Turkey, it's a town that's built on a peninsula. It was later the Ottoman Naval Base actually.

It's a small Greek town, an important port, and obviously Christians from western Asia, Pauline Christians from the Pauline churches, had come there and settled as merchants and then set up their own church. Churches were established beyond that original network by the apostolic churches but again, they represent some kind of immigration pattern from the original churches. In Gaul, the first church we know of in Gaul is at Lugdunum—Lyon today, where the imperial altar is—all of those Christians were clearly Christians from either Smyrna, Ephesus, or Pergamon; they're immigrants from the East; they're essentially Pauline Christians.

In addition to the self-contained aspect of these Christian communities, there are two very important developments going on, and this is in response to the threat from the outside world; part of it persecution, the other's the challenge of heretics. The first and most important is the emergence of monarchical bishops. We have the letters of Ignatius of Antioch, a bishop who was conveyed from Antioch to Rome where he was executed for his Christianity; he was apparently a Roman citizen. He wrote seven letters to various churches in Asia Minor, which is really very bizarre because he's being conveyed to Rome to be executed and in the meantime the imperial government, or at least the soldiers, were delivering the letters to these congregations; so much for the efficiency of the imperial government. In any case, Ignatius wrote that there were three members of the community who were sources of authority: One is the *episkopos*, or bishop. The other is the evangelist, the man who proclaims the good news; and the other is the prophet. Many prophets are really prophetesses, females; there's a very important role for females to play as prophetesses. That goes back to a Jewish tradition, actually. The bishop lived in imitation of Christ and therefore had authority, but he shared the authority.

By the time we get the writings of Saint Polycarp of Smyrna, who was martyred in 155 A.D.—and that's about a generation later—we have a monarchical bishop, and we have the beginning of the notion of apostolic succession. This will only be articulated as a doctrine in the 3rd century, but it's clear that those churches that could trace their origins back to the apostles through various ways, the bishops in those churches were now the unquestioned authority; they were ordained by the congregation; they lived in imitation of Christ; and they were the successors usually of Peter and Paul (even at Rome, you would couple Peter and Paul together as late as 220, not just Peter). Already, the Christians had a sense that Rome, Alexandria, Antioch, those had special authority with Saint Peter; and Rome, as the imperial capital, had a special position from the start. Polycarp is a good example of this: He was a powerful bishop. He had a library. He was involved in editing New Testament text. He was martyred, and therefore is a martyr bishop. The bishops that followed Polycarp acquired his authority and charisma just for holding the office. We know Pope Clement I around 95 A.D. wrote a letter to the church in Corinth, just as Paul did, to settle issues. It's clear that the Pope had this particular authority, even with churches in the East. In 144 A.D., a Pope summoned a senate to kick out Marcion, who was held responsible for certain heretical teachings about the New Testament.

All of this information that we have, which we pieced together, suggests that from 100–200, or maybe by 175, bishops had emerged as the major figures running these apostolic churches; and that is a very, very significant development. You need bishops, first and foremost, to combat other confessions, which Eusebius would call heresies. One of them was the Montanists, named after their leader Montanus, who emerged in Asia Minor in the mid-2nd century A.D. offering a new prophecy. He was followed by two female associates, Priscilla and Maximilla, as they were usually called, and they claimed to speak in the name of the Paraclete, the Holy Spirit; that the Holy Spirit spoke through them. They stood in a tradition going back to revelation and Judaism, which had a tradition of prophecy. What they represented was a challenge to the bishops because they were producing new revelation. Saint Polycarp would argue, "No, no, no, revelation is now over. The message is there. I'm the source of the authority in the church of Smyrna," and these prophetesses and Motanists could potentially change the rules (although in many ways they were clearly Trinitarian Christians).

There's a marvelous way of determining the difference between a false and a true prophet. It comes out of this interesting manual of the *Didachē* from the early 2nd century A.D., probably written in Syria. It's got a lot of practical advice for Christian congregations. "A false prophet is someone who stays for more than three days and begins to smell like fish." You know that old adage; it already goes back to the *Didachē*, and I throw that in as an interesting anecdote. Above all, the Montanists believed that the second coming was about to appear, and two little towns in Turkey today, Pepuza and Tymion, were supposed to be the new Jerusalem.

The Montanists were received with skepticism. They were banished at a number of synods; that is, local councils of bishops that get together. In fact, the first reports of synods we have in Asia Minor and measures taken by bishops such as Claudius Apollinaris from Hieropolis in the late 2nd and early 3rd centuries A.D. are against the Montanists, and the Montanists forced bishops to develop their position. That meant holding synods, regional councils, to deal with heresy; to deal with the readmission of those who had fallen away. The doctrines of the Montanists were very, very attractive. We're told one congregation, it's the city of Thyatira, went over entirely to the confession of Montanists. We believe that Tertullian, the very important Latin writer and apologist in Africa, in his later days joined a version of that enthusiastic Christianity. The Montanists, while outlawed by synods, continued to flourish at least into the 8th century A.D. They represented a challenge to the authority of the bishops and the result was the development of more Episcopal institutions to counter it.

There was another challenge, and that was interpreting the doctrine. How do you do this? I mentioned at the start of this lecture, besides the organization, the other important development is canon, that yardstick. What books belong in the New Testament? By 180 A.D., there were clearly Greek New Testaments circulating. There were certain types of other literature—the Gospel of Thomas or Paul's Letter to the Laodiceans—that were regarded as somehow spurious or bogus and circulating to propagate doctrines as if they're the writings of Paul, and it was very difficult to distinguish what texts were canon and which were not.

In addition to the question of sorting out the documents, there was a challenge from the Gnostics. These were teachers, such as Valentinus at Rome and others in Alexandria, that took Christian notions, principles, and faith and reinterpreted them in myth, very often pagan and other myth, and created these cosmic schemes of redemption. They used myth allegorically; in this way, they'd be similar to a Buddhist or a Hindu teacher. They're usually mocked by Christians as actually believing the myths. The myths were probably more allegorical than literary, but it alarmed the bishops.

Irenaeus of Lugdunum—Lyon today, in Gaul—around 180 A.D. wrote a tract condemning the heresies, particularly the Gnostics. He used ridicule and invective; but what he's concerned about is the Gnostic teachers went beyond the canon and started using myths taken from paganism, taken from Persian religion, to explain their faith. This, in effect, would destroy canon if you went down this route.

Another was just the very act of editing the canonical text. Marcion of Sinope—that town on the Black Sea I mentioned earlier; a very early Christian church established by the Pauline churches—Marcion, born in 85, died around 160 A.D., edited his own version of the Bible; he actually rejected the Old Testament. He came to the conclusion that Yahweh of the Old Testament can't be the God of the New Testament—and then you'll get different types of heresies that'll actually worship Satan as a result if you follow it out to its logical conclusion—and created his own New Testament, a very abbreviated version of Luke's Gospel and the Acts plus certain letters of Paul. He's responsible for the summoning by Pope Pius of the First Synod at Rome in 143–144. He was excommunicated and expelled from the Roman church. Again, that type of challenge of figuring out canon, producing a New Testament—and Marcion came up with a New Testament probably close to a generation before the version that we more or less have today—that forced the apostolic churches, people like Polycarp and others, to come up with a clear definition of what texts belong in the New Testament, what were secondary texts, and how to arrange the New Testament as we see it today.

Marcion might've been condemned, excommunicated, and expelled, but he happily went off to found his own church, particularly in Syria. In fact, the earliest inscription we have documenting a church is a Marcionite church—that is, a church following the doctrines of Marcion—and it's found near Damascus and dated to 318 A.D., shortly after the conversion of Constantine. We know that Marcion's text and tract were circulating throughout the Christian world. We have in the year 500 A.D. the report of over 500 of these texts circulating in one diocese in Syria alone, much to the dismay of the bishop. While the Christians will debate their doctrines, their canon, their authority, their organization, and while the apostolic churches, the bishops, could impose that discipline and that canon, if they were expelled from the apostolic church—people such as Marcion, Montanus, Gnostics—they went on and formed their own confessions, and these confessions persisted well into the time of Constantine and beyond.

It's very deceptive; and you've noticed throughout this course, I've avoided the use of Church and I've stressed that you have to think of Christianity, or the Christian mission, in terms of confessions and a variety of churches in which organization and canon were going to be worked out over the course of the 2nd and 3rd centuries, and no one knew in the 2nd and 3rd centuries who's going to end up a heretic and who wasn't. That's something that comes with the perspective of Eusebius writing in the time of Constantine, looking back at this diversity and then seeing very clearly, "These groups are to be classified as heretics"—it comes from the Greek verb *hairetos*, "to choose"; that is, you've chosen the wrong faith—and then Eusebius condemns them as serpents planted in the bosom of mother church by Satan himself.

In addition, the pagan critic Celsus captured a sense of these Christian divisions. He's writing around 177 A.D., and it comes through quotations of his text by Origen; we'll talk about that later. But in any event, Celsus—who's our first pagan critic who goes out of his way to condemn the Christians— makes a note that's very significant. He says Christians sit around a small pond croaking about sin like frogs. It's not a very flattering image at all, and actually it's a play on an image used by Plato talking about the Greeks in the 4th century B.C.; but nonetheless, what Celsus does understand is that the Christians are divided and that division really hinders proselyting and converting pagans if the Christians themselves are uncertain about what the message is. Is there an Old Testament? Is there a New Testament? Is Yahweh of the old Israel the God of the New Testament? All of these issues were being debated very, very seriously; and therefore it's not until the creation of an imperial church by Constantine, the Council of Nicaea in 325, when you really had a clear imperially-sponsored church where you could speak of the church as an institution with a capital "C" and a clear mission. There were a lot of alternate churches.

But the bishops in the apostolic churches had made two significant achievements: First, the organization and the notion of apostolic succession, the monarchical bishop; and those bishops were the basis of Constantine's church. It's upon those bishops that Constantine would build his church. It's a very, very effective hierarchy, and it's unprecedented in paganism and in Judaism; it's a Christian creation. The second is the definition of canon, and the very rapid definition of canon by the end of the 2nd century; the creation of a New Testament. There were just a couple of books that came in later, like Revelation; but the Christians were agreed. They had found, what Peter Brown said in that quote I read, "They have found a voice by which they can speak to the outside world." That's more important than numbers converted or any other consideration. The Christians had the organization, the identity, and the clear message of what their faith was.

Pagan Critics and Christian Apologists
Lecture 10

The pagan critics of Christianity, such as Galen and Celsus, had doubts about the Christian god's power and the sanity of his worshipers. But as the apologists adopted the techniques and language of the best of classical rhetoric, Christians were finally able to explain their position to the wider Roman world. They presented themselves in very Roman terms as well: as a revival of an ancient faith, as loyal to Rome and the emperor, and as consistent with Platonic philosophy.

Who Were the Apologists?

- The **apologists** were Christian authors who wrote in defense of the faith. An apology—or *apologia* in Greek—was a formal, philosophical, and moral tract that had a long history going back to the 5th century B.C. The most famous is Plato's *Apology*, which recounts the trial of Socrates in 399 B.C.

- The need for Christians to adopt the apology was driven by pagan criticisms and Christianity's illegal status. This was the second classical literary genre the Christians had adapted for their own use, the first being the epistolary form, as in the letters of Saint Paul.

- Christians were not only answering legal charges; they were also addressing rumors like those recorded in Pliny the Younger's letters to Emperor Trajan. These charges were difficult to address because the public had no knowledge of Christian doctrines and practices.

- The apologists also had to assert over and over that they were loyal Romans, albeit in their own fashion, and should not be lumped together with social misfits like the Cynics.

The Pagan Response to Christian Apology

- The pagans, in turn, got better at criticizing Christians. The intellectual classes became increasingly aware of Christianity, and the charges leveled against Christians shifted over the course of the 3rd century toward more substantial criticisms of actual Christian doctrines. This, in turn, pushed Christian writers to become more sophisticated in explaining their faith and answering the charges.

- **Galen of Pergamon** is the first pagan whose opinions of Christianity we know in any detail. Galen is remembered as one of the great physicians of antiquity. He was a product of the Second Sophistic movement, a Platonist, and a very incisive scientist with professional connections to the imperial family.

- Galen made remarks about Christians in passing. Notably, he was not bewildered the way Pliny or Tacitus was. Rather, he was horrified by their behavior. Galen found it illogical and unreasonable that they should decide to die for their faith, especially that the men should let their wives and children die in the arena. He also opines, like many pagans, that if the god of the Christians allows so many of his people to die in the arena, he is not a very powerful god.

- Galen was perplexed by Christian doctrines such as the resurrection of the flesh because it contradicts Platonism and his own observations about the world. Platonists either believed in reincarnation or spiritual salvation. Galen, of course, was well aware of the mortality of the flesh.

- **Celsus**, mentioned in the previous lecture, was a contemporary of Galen. We know little about him; most of his writing survives as quotations in the work of the Christian writer Origen. Celsus's *On the True Doctrine* is a critique of Christianity that seems to be based on reports from Jewish informants.

- What is significant about Celsus is his approach, one that was not popular among other pagans, although many modern critics would return to it. Celsus reported that Jesus was the reputed illegitimate son of a carpenter whose mother had an affair with a Roman soldier named Panthera. He said that the adulterous couple fled to Egypt, where Jesus learned magic; calling others' religion magic or superstition was a stock insult.

- He said Jesus's followers were fishermen and tax collectors. He said it was Jesus's hysterical female followers who found the empty tomb and put out the story of his appearances. These stories are very early criticisms, probably made by the first Jews to reject Christianity. It seems Celsus went out of his way to refute Christianity on what we would call historical grounds.

- Origen went out of his way to refute Celsus's charges, and his refutation apparently was regarded as definitive. But Celsus writing reveals the important point that by the late 2nd century, pagans could distinguish Jews from Christians.

Redefining the Christian Church

- Some Christian authors actually saw Judaism as a rival. An early apologist, **Melito of Sardis**, wrote a critique of the Jews and was concerned about Christians going back to Judaism. As late as the A.D. 400, John Chrysostom, patriarch of Constantinople, told a Christian, "If you go into a building and you are not sure whether it is a synagogue or a church, ask."

- The Christian apologists helped frame the debate and elevate Christianity to the level of a philosophy rather than a superstition. Most of them drove home the fact that the Christians were loyal Romans. They cited the passages from the Synoptic Gospels where Jesus instructs his followers to "render unto Caesar his due."

- Christian apologists of the 2nd century A.D. were already framing Pontius Pilate not as an agent of Rome but as an agent of God. It was not the Romans per se who carried out the crucifixion; this was ordained, a fulfillment of prophecy.

- In paganism, new cults were never presented as new cults but the rediscovery of an old cult. To some extent, the Christians were following this notion. Christianity was a *Mos maiorum*, the custom of the ancestors, neither new nor dangerous to the Roman world.

Four Early Apologists

- **Justin the Martyr** wrote two important apologies, one addressed to the emperor Antoninus Pius, in which he stressed again the loyalty of the Christians to Rome and the second to the Roman senate.

- Justin's apologies are important because they elucidate the faith using Greek philosophical terms from Plato's *Timaeus*. While he claims that the Greek gods are false, he allows that Greek philosophers and thinkers had some glimpse of reality thanks to God's clemency and mercy. Justin thereby initiated the process of Christians appropriating the classical literary tradition.

- **Theophilus of Antioch**, writing a little bit earlier than Justin, addressed a fictional pagan friend of his named Autolycus in the work *Ad autolycum*. Not only does he use Platonism; he is the first author we know of to use the term "Trinity" and identify the three realities in Plato with the three persons of the Godhead defined at the Council of Nicaea in 325.

- Theophilus, unlike Justin, used a lot more invective and ridicule of pagan authors. He was also the first person to expound that "genesis" means "creation ex nihilo," out of nothing, not out of preexisting matter as in Platonism. This was important in moving Christian philosophy from apology to theology—that is, from defense to exposition.

- **Minucius Felix**, a Roman citizen of Carthage, wrote an important apology, *The Octavius*, in which he tried to use logic to win over a pagan. Octavius is a fictional Christian who debates with a fictional pagan called Cecilius Natalis. In the course of the debate, Octavius persuades his pagan friend of the superior revelation of Christianity.

- **Tertullian** was also a North African Roman, as well as a jurist and Stoic. Later in life, he joined the Montanists, but early on he wrote important apologies of apostolic Christianity. He was a stark rigorist, expected the incipient end of days, and had little good to say about pagan idols and traditions. He was uncompromising about the truth of Christianity; he called Rome "the whore of Babylon" and Nero "the beast of Revelation."

Tertullian was uncompromising in his theology.

- Tertullian was almost too narrowly focused; the future of Latin Christianity rested with later authors such as Saint Cyprian, Saint Augustine of Hippo, and Minucius Felix, who had a broader notion of the church as the church of all sinners, set up to help us. Nonetheless, he was an important ancestor of the Latin Christian authors whose work culminated with Saint Augustine in the 5th century A.D.

Important Terms

apologist: Defender; a Christian writer who penned defenses against pagan criticism. The most important of the early apologists were Justin the Martyr (103–165), who wrote in Greek, and Tertullian (160–220), who wrote in Latin.

Mos maiorum: Latin for "custom of the ancestors"; the Roman expression for the superior authority of traditional religious and social practices.

Celsus (fl. 2nd century A.D.): Pagan critic of Christianity who wrote *On the True Doctrine* in 177. His work is largely known from quotations by Origen.

Galen of Pergamon (a.k.a. Aelius Galenus; 129–205): Physician and philosopher born of a prominent family with Roman citizenship; wrote extensively on human physiology and biology. In his writings, Galen makes a number of references to Christians and martyrdoms.

Justin the Martyr (103–165): Christian apologist who wrote (in Greek) the *First* and *Second Apologies* and *Dialogue with Typhro*.

Melito of Sardis (d. c. 180): Perhaps bishop of Sardis, he wrote an apology in Greek addressed to Emperor Marcus Aurelius. He also expressed his anxiety over Judaism and so reflected the fact that Jews occupied a favored position at Sardis.

Minucius Felix (c. 150–270): This otherwise anonymous figure wrote the earliest surviving Latin apology, *Octavius*, set as a debate between Christian Octavius and pagan Caecilius Natalis.

Tertullian (a.k.a. **Quintus Septimius Florens Tertullianus**; c. 160–c. 220): Lawyer and Christian apologist at Carthage who wrote the first major Christian works in Latin. Of foremost importance was his *Apology*, defending Christianity.

Theophilus of Antioch (d. c. 183): Bishop who wrote the apology *Ad autolycum*, in which he advanced the doctrine of creation *ex nihilo* and a doctrine of the Trinity.

Barnes, *Tertullian*.

Brown, *The Body and Society*.

Celsus, *On True Doctrine*.

Eusebius, *The History of the Church.*

Grant, *Augustus to Constantine.*

————, *Formation of the New Testament.*

Justin Martyr, *Saint Justin Martyr: The First and Second Apologies.*

Irenaeus, *Irenaeus of Lyons.*

Louth and Saniforth, ed. and trans., *Early Christian Writings.*

Parvis, *Justin Martyr and His World.*

Pelikan, *The Emergence of the Catholic Tradition.*

Richardson, ed., *Early Christian Fathers.*

Rogers, *Theophilus of Antioch.*

Theophilus of Antioch, *Ad autocylum.*

Tertulllian, *Apologia and De Spectaculis.*   Minucius Felix. *Octavius.* Translated by T. R. Glover and G. H. Rendall.

Wilken, *The Christians as the Romans Saw Them.*

————, *John Chrysostom and the Jews.*

Questions to Consider

1. How did pagan criticisms of Christianity change over the course of the 2nd and 3rd centuries? What were the most popular charges raised by pagans? What were the most damaging? What does this criticism reveal about pagan acquaintance with Christians and Christian doctrine?

2. How did apologists adapt classical genres to create defenses of the faith? Why did pagan writers so often resort to polemic? How convincing were arguments drawn from Plato and Aristotle?

3. What was the impact of the apologists on Christian self-definition? Would pagans be convinced by reading these apologies?

Pagan Critics and Christian Apologists
Lecture 10—Transcript

In this lecture, I intend to deal with both pagan critics and Christian apologists. Apologists are Christian authors writing a defense of the faith. It's important to keep in mind that the apology—or apologia, as it would be in Greek—was a formal, philosophical, and moral tract that had a long history going back to 5th century B.C. The most famous, of course, is Plato's *Apology* for Socrates at his trial in 399 B.C.; and "apology" literally means "a defense." It's come to mean "an excuse" in modern English; and therefore we have to keep in mind when I'm speaking of apologists and apologies, I'm speaking about specific works defending the Christian faith and, of course, the apologists were the authors of those works.

The need for the Christians to create the apology as specific literary form was again driven by pagan criticisms and also the fact that Christianity had been outlawed. It's very significant in two ways: One, it forced the Christians to adapt yet another classical literary genre to their own use. The first was the letter (the Letters to Saint Paul); that is, writing letters to explain the faith, to settle issues in the congregation. That's the first significant innovation of taking a Classical literary form and making it Christian. This is the second one, the apology. The second is that Christians now have to answer charges. These were not only the legal charges that they were outlawed but all of those rumors I talked about in the letter of Pliny the Younger to the emperor Trajan. These included the stock rumors of cannibalism, of moral depravity. They often spoke of the feasts of Tantalus—that is, the dining on the flesh of humans—nocturnal associations; all of these various charges, which persisted among pagans. Most pagans just resorted to these charges almost down to the time of Constantine. These charges would be difficult to address in many instances because it would require you to have a fairly good knowledge of Christian doctrines and practices, and so the Christians had to take the time to answer these types of charges.

The third important point I want to make about the apologists is not only did they adapt the literature, not only were they answering the charges, but they also revealed that the Christians had become isolated by choice and by law. They were forced to live in the shadows of the Roman world because of their legal status, and repeatedly the apologists were making appeals to the wider pagan world that they really were loyal Romans in many ways; that they shouldn't be lumped together with social misfits, characters like the cynics. Yes, they were a distinct third race separate from Romans and from Jews, but there would come through many of the apologies—not all of them; some of them like Tertullian are rigorous, they didn't want to have anything to do with the Roman imperial government or the secular world—but many of the apologists were already trying to stress that, "We are loyal Romans in our own fashion." The apologists and the apologies represent a very, very important development in Christian writing, thinking, and self-identity.

The pagans, in turn, got better at criticizing Christians starting from the time of Pliny down to the time of Constantine. That means the pagans— at least the intellectual, the literate classes—became increasingly aware of this sect or this religion, and the charges shifted over the course of the 3rd century from the typical invective you saw in Pliny's day to more substantial criticisms of Christian doctrines, use of texts, and the like. That is a very, very significant development on two ends: First, not only were the pagans becoming more familiar with Christianity, but second, the Christians themselves were becoming more sophisticated in explaining their faith and answering charges. What I want to do is first look at those pagan critics so important in stimulating the Christian response, and then look at the Christian apologists and sum up with what the significance of this debate or these exchanges represented for religious change in the Roman world.

The first pagan we have significant information from about pagan perceptions of Christianity is a man named Galen of Pergamon. That might be surprising to those of you in the medical profession because Galen is remembered as one of the great physicians of antiquity. He was born in the city of Pergamon in Western Asia Minor today—Bergama is the modern Turkish name—and it was the capital of the Roman province of Asia; that is, the most densely urbanized and in many ways arguably the most sophisticated region of the Roman world. He was born in 129 A.D., he lived at least to 205 A.D.; so he lived through much of what we call the imperial peace. He's a product of the Second Sophistic; that is, that tradition of writing in Classic Greek language, grammar, and diction. He's also a Platonist by training—that is, he knew the doctrines of Plato—but above all, he was a very, very incisive scientist. He wrote numerous works on pathology, on what we would call today surgery. He, for instance, noted the circulation of blood; he understood the heart was a pumping mechanism. In 162 A.D., he's actually appointed as the physician to the future emperor Commodus by his dad, Marcus Aurelius. He also was appointed the physician to the gladiatorial schools—gladiators who fought in the arena—and carried out vivisection, and that's how we know so much about the anatomy of the human body. You're dealing with a highly sophisticated mind; a very logical man who knew his Plato; had been trained in the traditional Greek classics.

Furthermore, the city of Pergamon was a center in and of itself. After Alexandria, it boasted the second most important Greek library in the Roman world, probably more important than Athens. Furthermore, it was the center of the great sanctuary of Asclepius that I mentioned in an earlier lecture; Asclepius is the healing god. The Asclepieion that was the sanctuary there was home to very important senators who traveled there and settled in Pergamon; it was sort of a combination health spa and healing center. It was visited by emperors such as Hadrian and Caracalla who rebuilt the Asclepieion on a grand scale. The sanctuary is still a very, very important tourist attraction and gives you an idea of what these sanctuaries looked like in the high empire, particularly healing sanctuaries. It has the misfortune that it's right next to the artillery range of the Turkish army, so it's sometimes a little dicey going there. I also went there when there was a psychologists' meeting in the sanctuary itself and there were a bunch of psychologists seated in the therapeutic rooms where people would go for dream analysis. I thought that was a very nice reusing of that ancient healing sanctuary. So Galen was very, very familiar with all sorts of aspects of medicine. He had been trained at the Asclepieion, and he ended up in Rome as the physician to the imperial family.

Galen made remarks about Christians in passing. It's remarkable how many remarks Galen made. It's also remarkable that Galen was actually familiar with Christian doctrines. He's not bewildered the way Pliny was or even Tacitus—Who are these guys? Why are they illegal?—Galen, as a Greek intellectual and a member of the Greek ruling classes, was familiar with Christians; he came into contact. There's a Pauline church probably in Pergamon at this point that's quite important. He's horrified about certain aspects of Christians. One was their social behavior; their decision to die in the arena. He made the remark that it's illogical, it's unreasonable to send your wives and children *ad bestias*—that is, to be killed horribly—as if they were criminals in the arena. He doesn't say that Christians were undeserving of punishment. He's very much in line with the legal attitudes of the time, particularly the jurist Gaius writing in the reign of Hadrian who evolved a doctrine that is called the doctrine of dual penalties; that is, the upper classes were exempt from death penalties and corporal punishment whereas the lower classes, the *humiliores*—the people looking at the ground, the *humus*; as opposed to the *honestiores*, the honorable ones—could be subject to the death penalty, to torture, cruelty like that and it's a very significant development that started substituting social rank from legal status in the Roman world, which we'll get into later on. But in any event, Galen had no problem that the Christians should be punished, he just found it bizarre that the Christians would allow their families to be destroyed, and he's not impressed. In Galen's opinion, as many pagans, if the God of the Christians allowed people to die in the arena, he's not a very powerful god.

He was also perplexed by Christian doctrines such as the resurrection of the flesh, and he made comment about that: "This is illogical, this is against what Plato told us"; that is, rebirth or rejuvenation, it could be cyclical, reincarnation, or it could be a singular salvation. Many Platonists probably edged towards the reincarnation, a cycle of rebirth, but it would be spiritual; that the body simply disintegrates. Galen was well aware of this. I do know in 177 A.D. when the Christians were martyred in Lugdunum, the officials actually burned the bodies and scattered the ashes, apparently to deny this doctrine, which educated pagans found very, very irrational. If there's an afterlife, it's spiritual; there's no resurrection of the flesh as Saint Paul would say.

Galen's text is very, very telling. It reveals that members of the ruling classes in the Greek cities where the Christian communities were located, by the 2nd century were already familiar with certain Christian doctrines, with Christians and their social behavior, and on the whole they found them quite irrational and unconvincing. There's an absence of that bewilderment and perplexed comments that you would have in Pliny.

The second author I'd like to bring up is a man named Celsus who's a contemporary with Galen. We know very little about him. He's writing around the year 177 A.D. and that's because of citations in his work. The work is against the Christians and it's often entitled *On the True Doctrine.* We get these titles and the quotations from the Christian theologian Origen who, in the 240s—that is, two generations later—wrote a critique against Celsus; that is, it's a Christian critique on a pagan critique. Origen cites a number of points of information; there are quotes; there are summaries of Celsus's work; and therefore we're able to reconstruct what Celsus said.

Celsus apparently talked to Jewish informants, or he had access to Jewish sources in very early Christian texts. What is significant about Celsus is his approach. Furthermore, what is even more significant is that Celsus's approach was apparently not very popular among many pagans, although it would be the approach that many modern critics would take towards early Christianity. Instead, we'll see that pagan critics went in a different direction. Celsus reported information that Jesus was the reputed illegitimate son of a carpenter in the Galilee and he had gathered Galilean fishermen and publicans, that is tax collectors, which were even lower than any other form of life in the New Testament and probably also in Roman law. (For those of you filing taxes, you can remember that.)

In any event, Celsus charged Jesus as a magician; a very stock charge. "All of these miracles, they're just magic acts." He also said that Jesus's mother—and he doesn't name her—had an adulterous affair with a Roman soldier called Panthera and that they fled off to Egypt, and that's where Jesus may have been born and learned his magic. He also reported other outlandish explanations. For instance, it was his hysterical female members who found the empty tomb and put out the story of appearances. These stories go back very early; they're probably early criticisms, probably made by the first Jews to reject Christianity. Somehow Celsus got a hold of this information, and there's an inscription that comes from the Roman Rhineland that was uncovered I think when they were building a railway in which it's dedicated to a Roman soldier whose name is Tiberius Julius Abdas Pantera. The last name is the same in the Celsus account, and he's a soldier who died somewhere in the early 1st century A.D. He was originally from Sidon, the Phoenician city, and recruited into a Roman auxiliary unit; that is, a provincial unit of archers. What the inscription suggests is that the name that appears in Celsus is a legitimate name of many Roman soldiers; it may have been a common name. Again, it suggests that these stories go back very early and Celsus went out of his way to refute Christianity on what we would call historical grounds.

From what we have of our surviving literature, later pagan critics really didn't take this approach. There were scholars who liked Celsus's work because they used it for trying to reconstruct the historical Jesus. Origen went out of his way to refute these charges, and the refutation apparently was regarded as pretty definitive. Later pagan critics essentially dropped Celsus's approach; they had bigger issues to deal with than this historical approach. Celsus also revealed a point that's very important: Celsus could distinguish Jews and Christians in a way that probably many pagans didn't do in Pliny's time; and it also brings out very clearly that Christians and Jews were starting to part company in the 2nd century A.D.

Some Christian authors actually saw Judaism as a rival; the survival and literally the flourishing of the old Israel was seen as a threat. The synagogue at Sardis I talked about in an earlier lecture that was set up in the late 3rd century A.D.; that Jewish community was clearly far more important than the Christian community. We have an early apologist from Sardis—his name is Melito, he's apparently the bishop; he died probably around 180 A.D.— and he wrote a critique of the Jews and he's very, very concerned about many Christians going back to Judaism; and this, again, stresses the importance of Judaism in the Roman world. It's a very, very important religion; and particularly in the Diaspora, we have inscriptions, local coins, and all sorts of information that educated Jews in the Greek-speaking cities where Christian communities were located played a very, very prominent role in local society. As late as John Chrysostom, patriarch of Constantinople, at the end of the 4th century, who wrote a series of works against the Jews; he has a very telling comment. This was written around 400 A.D., and his comment to a Christian was: "If you go in a building and you're not sure it's a synagogue or a church, ask and they'll tell you," which goes to show that they're still very, very close in many, many ways. This anxiety concerned a number of these bishops so that the old Israel is seen as, in a way, a vitiation of the new Israel. In any case, Galen was aware of this.

I want to mention briefly one other critic, and that's Porphyry of Tyre; we'll be returning to him in the late 3rd century A.D. in connection with pagan spiritual developments. Porphyry actually criticized the Christians on philosophical and textual terms, and he represents the common approach taken by pagan critics starting in the late 3rd century as the Christian apologists got much better at answering charges and as Christian theologians in one of the upcoming lectures such as Origin were able to present their theology, present their faith in a clear, literate Greek. That's a significant change at the end of the 3rd century. No one follows the stock charges of Pliny, and certainly Celsus's approach was not very interesting to most pagan intellectuals. They're dealing with Christianity on a whole other level.

What about the apologists themselves? The Christian apologists themselves actually helped frame the debate and helped elevate Christianity more to the level of a philosophy rather than a superstition. They achieved that important goal, and they also achieved another important goal: Most of them—not all of them, but most of them—really drove home the fact that the Christians were loyal Romans. They constantly cited the passages from the Synoptic Gospels where Jesus tells "Render unto Caesar his due, and then render unto God his due." The apologists made references to this all the time. That's a very, very important point they had to make because the crucifixion was a Roman punishment for treason, and the Christian apologists already in the 2nd century A.D. were elevating the issue. "Pontius Pilate was simply the agent of God. It wasn't necessarily the Romans per se who carried out the crucifixion; this was ordained; and that we really are a Roman faith, we are an ancestral faith, we are the new Israel." Remember the point I made about paganism that new cults were never presented as new cults but the rediscovery of an old cult; and to some extent, the Christians were following this notion. Christianity's ancestral; it's *mos maiorum*. "We are the fulfillment of the Old Testament, therefore we are not new; we are not dangerous to the Roman world. We do not represent *res novae* (that is, new things; the Latin phrase for 'revolution')." The apologists achieved these aims, and this is very, very important.

In addition, as I mentioned, they're able to write texts that show increasing sophistication and language. They adapted the *Apology* and made it their own. This was a type of writing that appealed to pagans. One of the most famous contemporary works of the time of the apologies is called *Doctors at Dinner* by a deservedly obscure figure known as Athenaeus of Naucratis, which is a Greek city in Egypt. It's a very learned apology talking about culinary delights; this is the extent that they'd go in learnedness and erudition. Then we had more serious apologies and debates from Greek and Roman literature, but it gives you an example of this.

Two apologists writing in Greek and two writing in Latin deserve our attention for several reasons. The first Greek author that we must look at is Justin Martyr, who's from the city of Neapolis or Samaria, today the modern city of Nablus; he wrote two apologies. Neapolis, which is its Roman name, later became a Roman colony; but it was home to the Samaritans, and there were also many Jews and pagans. Justin was apparently a convert to Christianity—he may have been originally a Jew or a Samaritan—and he wrote two apologies, one addressed to the emperor Antoninus Pius, in which he stressed again the loyalty of the Christians to Rome; the second one was actually addressed to the Roman senate.

Justin made several important points in these two apologies. First, he begins to elucidate his faith and gives certain explanations based on Greek philosophical terms coming from Plato's *Timaeus*. It's his first efforts of theology, and that's a very, very important step on the part of Justin. The second point about Justin's apologies: They're charmingly naïve in a number of ways; but he explains that the Greek gods are false, but Greek philosophers and thinkers, epic writers like Homer, had some glimpse of reality thanks to God's clemency and mercy. In a peculiar way, he denies the validity of the pagan gods, but at the same time upholds the validity of the literature. This was a very, very clever reworking of the type of tracts you'd get with Lucian and the like. He avoided ridicule and invective, and he initiated a process whereby the Christians were going to appropriate the Classical literary tradition.

The second Greek apologist is a man named Theophilus of Antioch. Theophilus of Antioch, writing a little bit later than Justin—these dates, again, are a bit difficult to pin down; he was apparently a bishop of the city of Antioch from 169–183—and he wrote a work addressed to a fictional pagan friend of his named Autolycus, and the work is *Ad Autolycum* in Latin; that is, a letter or an apology addressed to his friend. The work in many ways resembles the types of debates you would find in Tacitus's *Dialogue*—you see that in both Greek and Latin traditions; debates over philosophy, oratory, all sorts of issues—and Theophilus makes several important contributions to the apology. Not only does he use Platonism, he's the first author we know who uses the term "trinity," and begins to make that identification of the three realities in Plato with what's going to be defined as the trinity at the Council of Nicaea in 325. That's a very, very significant step.

In addition, Theophilus, unlike Justin, used a lot more invective and ridicule of pagan authors—the gods are false; they're nothing more than idols—and he made again that statement that the scriptures antedates the Greek authors and therefore are superior. Those types of arguments made by Theophilus as well as by Justin are part of the way of framing the debate; that's why Celsus's criticisms go nowhere. They're saying, "Our texts are older and have more authority" and the pagans are then forced to answer, "No, no, no, our texts are better. You're misusing them." All of those historical criticisms that Celsus would bring up, those were kind of petty; those weren't really very important in the way the religious debate was being framed.

He also made another important contribution to Christian theology: He was the first to expound that "genesis" means "creation ex nihilo"; that is, not out of preexisting matter. That God is transcended; God orders the creation of the world; he is not restricted by preexisting matter, which is the image that comes out of Plato. That becomes an extremely important notion for later Christian thinkers. As I said, he made the identification of Christ with the logos of Plato and the Stoics, and the Holy Spirit as being the wisdom of Proverbs. These notions were passed on to later Christian thinkers and will be very, very important contributions in moving from apology to theology; that is, from defense to exposition. That will come up in a future lecture with the theologian Origen.

At the same time, there were Latin apologists writing in the province of Africa. They both probably came from the city of Carthage, or at least lived in the city of Carthage. One of them was named Minucius Felix; obviously a Roman citizen, Latin's his first language. We know almost nothing about him except for the apology. He lived sometime in the late 2nd or early 3rd

century. The other one we know quite a bit about, and that's a man named Tertullian, who was a Roman jurist and Stoic. We have 31 major works by him and there were probably more written that haven't come down to us.

It's important to stress that Africa and the city of Carthage, which had been refounded as a Roman colony in 46 B.C., was really the intellectual rival to Rome in the western half of the empire. Carthage was the second largest city in the Roman West. It was very much a Roman Latin-speaking city, and the province of Africa had many of these Roman or Punic Roman cities; I discussed them earlier with regard to paganism. At least 15 percent of the Roman senate at this time came from towns in North Africa; so the senators and the imperial aristocracy from Africa, including the imperial family Septimius Severus, they exercised a disproportionate influence in the Roman world. Minucius Felix and Tertullian were extremely important authors. They'e the first Latin Christian authors, and they really did define Latin Christianity, which culminated with the writings of Saint Augustine in the 5th century A.D. who was in direct line from these authors.

Minucius Felix wrote a very important apology, the *Octavius*, in which he tried to use logic to win over a pagan. Octavius is a fictional character. He has a debate with a fellow called Cecilius Natalis. In the course of the debate, Octavius persuades his pagan friend of the superior revelation of Christianity; and again, this is defining and elevating to debate. The Christian scriptures and understanding of the divine world is superior to the old pagan tradition.

Tertullian, the jurist—whose full Latin name is Quintus Septimius Serverus, so we're using an Anglicized version of it—was a Stoic in inclination, would be very much at home with the Roman Stoics in the senate, and was very much a lawyer and jurist. His Latin was excellent. He wrote in Ciceronian style; and his Latin could stand side by side with any of the best pieces of Cicero, Tacitus, or Livy in prose. As I said, he wrote at least 31 different treatises. He defended Christianity in most of these. He also criticized pagans and heretics, but he above all targeted the pagans. There are two important aspects that come out of Tertullian's work: First, he's a rigorist. He obviously was expecting the millennium—that is, the second coming—and late in life, he joined a Motanist version, or a Montanist confession, known as the Cataphrygians in North Africa and went over to this enthusiastic sect of prophecy.

The second important point about the fact that he was such a stark rigorist and really had very, very little good to say about pagan idols and traditions (he often ridiculed them), he also was uncompromising about the truth of Christianity, and he calls Rome a "whore of Babylon," Nero is the "beast of revelation"; Christianity is the "one and true faith." Tertullian's writings, while beautiful in the exposition of the faith and its language, are almost too narrowly focused; and the future of Latin Christianity rests with later authors such as Cyprian, Saint Augustine, or even with our fellow Minucius Felix who had a broader notion of the church as the church of all sinners and if it's the church of all sinners and the church is set up to help us, it's open to pagan converts as well. Tertullian's long-term role is probably more limited than we like to think despite the effectiveness of his writing.

The apologists, besides defining the Christian church as the church of all sinners and open to pagans, also stressed that this church was not new; it was not revolutionary; but it was a fulfillment of the old Israel. Therefore, Christianity was an ancestral religion. It was a *renovation*: a renewal, a revival of the old Israel's prophecy. This was consistent with Roman notions of tradition, *mos maiorum*, and very, very important if Romans were to be attracted to the new faith.

What the apologists achieved were two very important steps: First was defining Christianity as Roman and loyal to the emperor, and that was an important political position that Christians would increasingly take. The second one was to take the first steps in defining the new faith in Platonic terms, in the Greek language, and this allowed for the theologian Origen to create the first coherent explanation of theology, and Christian theology came of age with him.

First Christian Theologians
Lecture 11

The important work of the Christian apologists was soon followed by the first Christian theologians, the most important of whom was Origen. Working from a deep knowledge of both Platonic philosophy and the Hebrew Old Testament, he was in the forefront of establishing the Christian canon, as well as reconciling Christian and classical philosophy. Although many of Origen's ideas were later condemned by the church, he nonetheless made important contributions to such doctrines as the nature of the Trinity and the human soul.

Christian Alexandria

- Two of the leading figures in early Christian theology, **Saint Clement** and **Origen**, lived and worked in Alexandria, and the city of Alexandria was arguably just as important for the formation of Christian theology as they were. This Greek city in Egypt, established by Alexander the Great, was home to the great library called the Mouseion.

- Alexandria was also home to many important intellectual circles in the 2nd and 3rd centuries A.D.—Christian, Jewish, pagan, and particularly Gnostic. Saint Clement refounded the Catechetical School here around 190 or 200 (the original had been disrupted by persecutions), and it became the center for Christian thinking in the Roman world.

- Alexandria was home to a Christian church of unknown origins. There is speculation that the Gospel of Matthew was composed in Alexandria at the end of the 1st century A.D. Whatever its origins, the Christian community here was serious in taking on pagan philosophers on equal terms. In this way, the Christians were heirs to the Jewish philosophical tradition in Alexandria.

Saint Clement

- Clement contributed significantly to the development of Christian theology. He wrote *Stromata*, a set of miscellaneous interpretations and observations on Christian theology. He was also convinced that the truly enlightened philosopher—one who was inspired with real knowledge (gnosis), as opposed to just technical skill—was really a Christian.

- In arguing this, Clement changed the relationship between pagans and Christians. He is saying that Christians are heirs to classical intellectual culture as much as the pagans, moving the debate away from the polemic of Tertullian's day. Christians and pagans will instead debate who has the better interpretation of Plato's vision of reality.

Origen—His Background and the Sources

- Clement's writings, as important as they were, were dwarfed by his successor and student, Origen. This name does not resonate with moderns today, in part because his writings were condemned at the Fifth Ecumenical Council in 553 by the Emperor Justinian in an effort to carry out a religious reunion within the divided imperial church.

- Origen's writings were very controversial and survive in fragments in the records of the council and a Latin rewrite by **Rufinus of Aquileia** from around 400. Rufinus actually changes Origen's text to conform to the doctrines of the early 5th century—sometimes reversing the meaning entirely.

- We also know a fair amount about his life. Origen was born into a Christian family somewhere around 185 A.D. His father was martyred in the Severan Persecution of 202–203. The family was clearly of Greek ancestry, so Origen was a speaker of Greek, but he also mastered Hebrew, one of the few church fathers who did. In some ways, he was an ascetic, and his writings are the intellectual basis for the monastic movements of the 4th century.

- Origen went on missions and was ordained a priest in Cappadocia. Origen may have been received at court in 222 by Emperor Severus Alexander. Origen eventually moved to Caesarea Maritima, founded by King Herod as his Greek capital, because it had a major library of Greek and Hebrew texts. There he wrote most of his works.

Origen's Main Works

- Origen's writings are important for several reasons. He was at the forefront of establishing the canon through his commentaries on various books of the Old Testament. His commentary on Numbers defines in middle Platonic terms what God is and defines creation as a rational act.

- Origen's *Hexapla*, or *Six Books* contains the Hebrew text, the Hebrew text transliterated into Greek letters, and then the four main Greek translations of the Hebrew Bible—including the Septuagint translation—as well as comments about how these texts relate to the New Testament. Here he created the official biblical typology (that is, the passages in the Old Testament that prefigure the New Testament) that is used to this day.

- Origen's greatest contribution to Christian theology was a work he wrote early in his career, *On First Principles*, or *Peri Archon*. It was controversial not only because of its views but also because it only exists in fragmentary form. The first three books have been reconstructed fairly accurately. The later books are more questionable.

- In this book, Origen has refined the language of analysis, which became the hallmark of Christian exegesis—the interpretation of texts. He stressed the importance of understanding the inner meaning, not just the literal meaning of the text.

- It also contains the first clear explanation of the creation of the godhead, as well as discussions of the nature of evil that borrow heavily from Plato: Evil is the absence of good. He stresses the importance of understanding free will to achieve salvation, which is the process of moving the soul back toward God.

Origens Theology

- Origen accepted the Gospel of Saint John's identification of Christ with the Logos—"the word" but more specifically the rational word of creation. The Christ Logos was eternally generated from the father—*aei gennetos*, "always generated." He seems to believe that God the father, the Christ Logos, and the Holy Spirit represent three aspects of the godhead and have a hierarchical relationship; the image uses is an eternal torch, one lighting the other.

- In the 4th century, there will be serious debate over Origen's view of the Trinity. Did he mean a hierarchy of emanations—that is, the father generated the son generated the Holy Spirit—or are they coequal and coeternal? Origen set up the intellectual debate that would occur at the Council of Nicaea and the Council of Constantinople—literally for the next century.

- Despite his dependence on Platonic thought, Origen was very much a Christian and knew his Hebrew text very well. He had a strong sense of the transcendence of God; the Christ Logos was the bridge between divinity and the material world or, in Platonic terms, from the world of being to the world of becoming.

- Souls, the *psyche*, are eternal and good, yet at the same time they possess free will. The first three books of *On First Principles* spend a great deal of time telling how souls fell away from God. They are divine, but because they have free will, they become inattentive and fall away from God like a charioteer who falls asleep at the reins—an image from Plato's *Phaedrus*.

- Some souls fell away and became angels. Others became humans and became embodied in the material world. The soul that fell the furthest was Satan. But all souls, by knowledge, can return to God.

Origen's Surprising Ideas

- At this point, Origen got himself in trouble. He thought that, if souls could fall away from God and re-attain perfection once, perhaps they could fall away again. In the next cycle, Origen suggested, perhaps Satan will play the role of Christ and Christ the role of Satan.

- This was a move away from the strong sense of linear progressive time from the Hebrew tradition and toward a Greek philosophical sense of time. Also, in this scheme, no soul need be condemned to hell for eternity; punishment is the soul contemplating and remembering with remorse its evil acts and in so doing perceiving God and attaining divinization.

- Obviously, there was a wide range of speculation available to Origen in 215 that, 100 years later, was going to be closed when decisions were made at the great councils in the 4th and 5th centuries. Later authors, including Eusebius, had great difficulty understanding how Origen could speculate so freely.

- Origen made some important contributions toward the debate between Christians and pagans. Henceforth, critics of Christianity could not resort to the stock criticisms Celsus used in the early 2nd century. Second, Origen used the language of high philosophy that the Roman elite could not dismiss. In many ways, Christian theology had now come of age.

Origen's Legacy

- Origen had gone through the Hebrew text and determined what the best Greek version of the Old Testament was. Many of the theologians and thinkers who would follow Origen did not know Hebrew; they had to depend on his work.

• One of his most important achievements was the synthesis of Platonic reasoning and philosophy with Christian doctrine. Christians were no longer as divided as they had been. They could present themselves as the heirs of Plato and claim that they had as much claim to classical tradition as the pagans did. The Christian thinkers now had a serious religious vision.

Important Terms

aei gennetos: "Eternally generated"; term used by Origen in *On First Principles* to explain the relationship between God the father and the Christ-*logos* in the Trinity.

Hexapla: Greek for "sixfold"; a set of texts complied by Origen (185–254) to establish the canonical text of the Old Testament. It comprised the Hebrew text, the Hebrew transliterated into Greek letters, and the translations in Greek of Aquila of Sinope, Symmachus the Ebionite, the Septuagint, and Theodotian.

Names to Know

Clement (c. 150–215): Saint and theologian who refounded the Catechetical School at Alexandria in about 202 and composed the *Stromata*, in which he elucidates his doctrine of salvation that influenced his most brilliant student, Origen.

Origen (185–254): Brilliant Christian theologian. Born at Alexandria of a Christian family and studied under Saint Clement, whom he succeeded as head of the Catechetical School. He was sent on a number of diplomatic missions by Bishop Demetrius of Alexandria. In 230, Origen removed himself to Caesarea Maritima because Demetrius protested Origen's ordination. Origen wrote numerous commentaries on books of the Bible and pastoral works, establishing the discipline of exegesis and typology. In 215–217, Origen composed *On First Principles*, the first serious theological work that reconciled Christian faith and Platonic philosophy. He also produced the *Hexapla*, a study of the Hebrew and Greek texts of the Old Testament. His views on cosmology and salvation were later condemned at the Fifth Ecumenical Council in 553.

Rufinus of Aquileia (c. 350–410): Roman monk who translated Greek theological and historical writings into Latin. In 372, he traveled to Alexandria and then resettled at Jerusalem, where he disputed with Saint Jerome the doctrines of Origen. In 397, Rufinus returned to Rome and translated and adapted into Latin Origen's *On First Principles*.

Suggested Reading

Bigg, *The Christian Platonists of Alexandria.*

Brown, *The Body and Society.*

Celsus, *On True Doctrine.*

Clement of Alexandria, *Works.*

Eusebius, *The History of the Church.*

Irenaeus, *Irenaeus of Lyons.*

Layton, trans. and ed., *The Gnostic Scriptures.*

MacMullen and Lane, eds., *Paganism and Christianity.*

Origen, *On First Principles.*

Pelikan, *The Emergence of the Catholic Tradition.*

Porphyry, *Against the Christians.*

Richardson, ed., *Early Christian Fathers.*

Trigg, *Origen.*

Wilken, *The Christians as the Romans Saw Them.*

1. Why was Alexandria home to so much serious intellectual debate and theology? What issues were raised by Gnostic, pagan, and Christian teachers in the city?

2. What was the impact of the Catechetical School of Alexandria? How important was Saint Clement in evolving Christian letters and thought?

3. What was the importance of *On First Principles*? What was Origen's religious vision, and how consistent was it with scripture? Why did later Christian thinkers find Origen's views heretical?

4. Why was Origen so important for Christians in evolving their doctrine? Why was this doctrine in Platonic terms acceptable to pagans? How important was Origen to the ultimate success of Christianity in the Roman world?

First Christian Theologians
Lecture 11—Transcript

In this lecture, I plan to deal with the emergence of Christian theology. We'll be looking at two leading figures: Saint Clement and Origen. Origen is perhaps one of the most brilliant minds to work in Christian theology between Saint Paul and Saint Augustine. In addition, we'll be looking at the city of Alexandria as well—that is, the Greek city in Egypt on the westernmost branch of the Nile—and Alexandria is just as important for the formation of Christian theology as were Origen and Saint Clement. In part, that's because Alexandria was the leading intellectual capital of the Greek East; that is, the eastern half of the Roman Empire. It had been established by Alexander the Great as a Greek city. It wasn't an Egyptian city. The Romans were very specific about this; they said *Alexandria ad Aegyptum* (that is, "Alexandria in the vicinity of Egypt"), so it shouldn't be regarded as an Egyptian city, it's really a Greek city. It was home to a great library, the so-called Museion, established by King Ptolemy I, the man who ruled in Egypt after Alexander's death.

In addition, Alexandria was home to many important intellectual circles in the 2nd and 3rd centuries A.D. Some of these were Christian, but also pagan and particularly Gnostics. Gnostics were religious thinkers who used philosophical terms, they used allegory, they used myth in order to explain the great divine reality. The most famous of them is a man named Valentinus who taught initially in Alexandria and then he moved to Rome and established an important school in Rome. In addition, the Christians had their own reading circles; and Saint Clement, the first of those two intellectual giants, refounded the Catechetical School around 190 or 200 A.D.—it had been disrupted by persecutions—and that became the center for Christian thinking, Christian instruction; and the hope was to train priests and theologians who could debate with Gnostics, pagans, and Jews on equal terms, both using the philosophical language of Plato and the high Greek literary language of the Second Sophistic.

Alexandria was home to a number of important intellectual circles. It was home to a Christian church whose origins are really quite unknown to us. We're not sure how the Christians emerged there; they claimed they went back to a very early time. There's speculation that the Gospel of Matthew may have been composed in Alexandria at the end of the 1st century A.D., but we really know very little until we get the writings of Clement and Origen. When we do, we find a fully developed Christian community and a Christian community that was very, very serious in taking on pagan philosophers on equal terms and debating what the divine reality was. This means these Christians were heirs to a Jewish tradition in Alexandria—I talked about Philo of Alexandria earlier—and that is they were using the literary language of Greek, the high language of what is known as Atticizing Greek of the Second Sophistic, and the various analytical schemes of the Middle Platonists and the Stoics.

Clement himself contributed very significantly in the development of this theology, and it was more than just his refounding of this school that was used to train theologians and priests. You have to think of this school as really more of a reading circle where you met in someone's home; there's a large private library. I've made reference to a film called *Agora*—or "*Agora*" as it's usually pronounced in film circles—released about, I think, in 2009. That film had some real advantages because it recreates what those reading circles might've looked like. They weren't the kind of public-funded schools we would think of, but they were really run more as private outfits in someone's home.

Clement himself applied his intellect to defining Christian theology. He wrote a work known as the *Stromata*, which is a set of miscellaneous interpretations and observations on Christian theology; and he was convinced that the truly enlightened philosopher, the true Gnostic, as he would say—and Gnostic is a term that means "one who knows," one who's inspired with real knowledge (gnosis) as opposed to just technical skill—that the true Gnostic was really a Christian. In arguing this, Clement made a very, very important change in the whole relationship between pagans and Christians. He is, in effect, saying that Christians are heirs to the philosophical schemes, the high language, the Classical intellectual culture as much as the pagans, and he's moving the debate away from the type of polemic you would've seen in Tertullian's day where you were using crude comments against the pagan gods and much more on an intellectual level where Christians and pagans are going to debate who has the better interpretation of Plato's vision of reality, something that had been occupying pagan intellectuals, pagan ascetics, pagan thinkers for at this point nearly 500 years. Clement's writings were very important in moving the Christians along this line of debate.

Clement's writings, as important as they are, are really dwarfed by his successor and his student Origen. Origen, as I mentioned at the start of this lecture, is arguably the most important Christian intellect between Saint Paul and Saint Augustine, and it's remarkable how his name doesn't really resonate with moderns today. Part of the problem is he got condemned at the Fifth Ecumenical Council in 553—his writings were condemned, not he personally—and that was carried out by the Emperor Justinian in an effort to carry out a religious reunion within the divided imperial church. It's something I never forgave Justinian for; he really shouldn't have done that. But, in any case, that has more to do with ecclesiastical politics of the 6th century A.D.

In addition, his writings were very, very controversial. They survive in fragments. Part of the writings survived because of the canons of the Fifth Ecumenical Council—that is, the various articles of faith—and those include large passages taken from Origen's texts, particularly his work *Peri Archon*, *On First Principles*, which I'll be talking about soon, in which these passages are quoted, and then you shouldn't believe in them. In addition, we have a Latin translation—or more correctly, we have a Latin rewrite— by a fellow named Rufinus of Aquileia writing around 400 A.D. who did a Latin translation, and it's a very loose translation. He actually changes the words and meanings of Origen's text so that his writings conform with the then-existing doctrines of the late 4th, early 5th centuries. In some instances, when you have the Greek text, which has survived on papyri or from the canons of the Fifth Ecumenical Council, and you compare them to the Latin text, they're literally contradictory; Rufinus has gone very, very far in editing Origen's writings. Origen, because of his fate at the Fifth Ecumenical Council, is generally not well known outside of academic circles. Yet he's pivotal; he's one of the most important intellectual figures in all of early Christianity. I really do put him on the level of Saint Paul and Saint Augustine. In fact, in many ways, Origen is really my favorite of all the early church fathers because of his originality and because of his knowledge of scripture and his ability to argue in Platonic terms.

We also know a fair amount about his life. Origen was born into a Christian family somewhere around 185 A.D. His father had been martyred in the Severan Persecution of 202–203 A.D. His father's name, interestingly enough, is Leonidas; that's the same name of the Spartan king who died at Thermopylae. The family was clearly of Greek ancestry, it wasn't really Egyptian; and that's often a mistake that's made: The community in Alexandria were largely Greek speakers, at least those who were full citizens. Some were pagans, many of them were Jews; and the conversions came from Judaizing pagans and Jews who would've used Greek as their first language, not Egyptian. So Origen, from birth, was a speaker of Greek. He also mastered Hebrew, one of the few church fathers who really understood Hebrew and Hebrew scripture. He proved himself to be in some ways an ascetic, and his writings in a certain way are the intellectual basis for asceticism—that is, the monastic movements that we'll see in the 4th century—and he himself was credited as, following the passage in the Gospel of Matthew 19:12, for selling off his possessions and then removing temptation by castrating himself. We don't know if this is just a story circulated, but it's a very old tradition. He came to the attention of Saint Clement, Saint Clement's successor, the bishop Demetrius. He went on missions to Rome, to cities in Syria, into Cappadocia. He was ordained as a priest while he was in Cappadocia, and that got him in trouble with the Bishop of Alexandria who refused to accept it and eventually ran Origen out of Alexandria for a number of years.

In addition, we're told that he had an entrée into the imperial family. In 222 A.D., the emperor Severus Alexander—and we will encounter him again—the last of the Severan dynasty, was a very young ruler, very courteous ruler, under the control of his mother Julia Mamaea. The family, being in part of Eastern origin, had very eclectic religious tastes; and it's reported that Origen was actually received at court by Severus Alexander. Whether the story is true or not, certainly that period of Alexander's reign—that is, from 222–235 A.D.—was regarded by Christian authors, particularly Eusebius, as a particular bright spot during the time of the early church.

Origen eventually moved to the city of Caesarea Maritima. The city of Caesarea Maritima—which is today being excavated by a team from the University of Maryland as well as from Israeli schools—was a city founded by

King Herod as his Greek capital for his kingdom. It became a Roman colony, and Origen settled in this city because it had a major library, intellectual center, and he had access to both Hebrew and Greek works. At Caesarea Maritima, he wrote many of his most important works, which really dealt with commentaries on books of the Bible, on homilies, and a lot of pastoral works for teaching. That's what Origen probably saw himself first and foremost as: a Biblical scholar rather than as a philosopher and theologian.

The writings that have come down to us from antiquity for Origen are important for several reasons. First, Origen was in the forefront of establishing texts, and that's very important for the development of what I talked about earlier: canon; that is, the yardstick in Greek. The means of defining what theology is rests on "What is the scripture?" If the word is sacred, then we have to know that we have the word correct. In this case, Origen made major contributions. His commentaries on various books of the Old Testament particularly were important for establishing an understanding of what that text in the Old Testament meant for Christians because he could read the Hebrew. His commentary on Numbers, for instance, is a brilliant work in which he not only establishes the text but also defines in very nice Middle Platonic terms what God is: God is the ultimate act of the rational divinity; the act of creation is a rational act; and he marries the Old Testament vision with the Platonic tradition out of the *Timaeus* in a perfect exposition.

He also went through and published a work known as the *Hexapla* or *Six Books*. The *Hexapla* is an unusual work. It has the Hebrew text; it has the Hebrew text transliterated into Greek letters; and then the four main Greek translations of the Hebrew Bible—and one of those is the Septuagint, which is the one used most by Christians—as well as comments about how these texts relate to the New Testament. In putting this multivolume work together, in which you in effect have five major versions of what Christians call the Old Testament, Origen was able to determine what canon should be; he established the text. He did the same for a number of other early Christian writings, including the First Letter of Saint Clement and the *Didachē*, works I've referred to before. In many ways, Origen is responsible for creating the texts as we have them today.

He also did something almost as important, and that is he created what later authors called typology; that is, determining passages in the Old Testament that prefigure the New Testament: the promise of the law, the fulfillment of the law, by the teachings and crucifixion of Jesus. Those have remained down to this day. If you go through—I always use the King James Version of the Bible; I'm wedded to that because it's a beautiful translation—and you see most editions have references to the Old Testament text from the New Testament, those were all worked out by Origen.

Origen's greatest contribution, however, was a work that he wrote fairly early in his career *On First Principles*, or *Peri Archon* in the Greek. This is a seminal work that is in some ways controversial not only because of its views but also, as I noted, it's come down to us in fragmentary form. The first three books have been reconstructed fairly accurately. The later books are more questionable. Nonetheless, enough of this work survives—especially in the Greek versions—that we can tell that Origen took first serious steps to present Christianity in a coherent, philosophical Platonic explanation. He refined the language of analysis, which became the hallmark of Christian exegeses; that is, the interpretation of texts. He stressed the importance of understanding the inner meaning, not just the literal meaning or the obvious meaning of the text. This is a very Platonic way of doing things, Saint Clement was the same; there's a deeper knowledge of gnosis in the text. From *First Principles*, from that work, we get the first clear explanation of the creation of the godhead, of salvation, and in Origen's mind, salvation is open to all; that ultimately all souls will be saved (*anakatastasis* is the word he uses). Also, discussions of the nature of evil, which is very Platonic—that is, evil is the absence of good—and the importance of human free will and soul, which are essential to understand in order to achieve salvation, which is to move the souls back toward God.

The work is absolutely brilliant; it's amazing that he penned it in such a short time. There are several very important elements that come out of that work that are essential for understanding not only the development of theology, but also the success of Christianity in the 4th and 5th centuries, and why Christians in part were able to overcome their pagan critics by these intellectual arguments based on Origen's theological perceptions. That's a very, very important turning point, and the full implications of Origen's works and ideas won't become evident until the 4th and 5th centuries.

First, Origen accepted an identification that was often made going back to the Gospel of Saint John that Christ was the logos. The logos is a term that comes out of Stoic and Middle Platonic philosophy in which it means "the word," but it means "the rational word of creation." In Origen's opinion, Christ logos, the word Christ, was eternally generated from the Father. He uses a term in Greek called *aei genetos*, always generated. In Origen's opinion, God is a perfect circle; it's almost a perfect form of both intellect and good. He seems to believe that God the Father, the Christ logos, and the Holy Spirit represent three persons or three aspects of the godhead— he doesn't quite yet use the word "persons," although this is what's going to be determined at the Council of Nicaea a generation later—that these represent the godhead, and he seems to think of them as having some kind of hierarchical relationship; that is, the Father generates the Son, which generates the Holy Spirit. The image he likes to use is an eternal torch, one lighting the other.

That effort to reconcile Christian thought with the three realities in Plato— remember the *Timaeus*: there are the three realities, the three persons that become the persons of the trinity are sort of equated with those three realities in Plato—Origen seems to imply that there's some kind of hierarchy, but he didn't establish it in time. What will happen in the 4th century, there's going to be a debate over exactly what Origen meant. Did he mean a hierarchy of emanations—that is, the Father generated the Son generated the Holy Spirit and therefore those other two persons are subordinate—or are they coequal and coeternal? In effect, Origen set the debate of what the nature of the trinity would be of the 4th century A.D., and furthermore he provided the text for the debate by all of his commentaries; his typology of looking at Old Testament; prefiguring of New Testament. Origen really set up the whole intellectual debate that would occur at the Council of Nicaea, the Council of Constantinople, literally for the next century.

Despite his dependence on Platonic thought, Origen was very much a Christian, and he knew his Hebrew text very well. While his notion of what became the trinity might not be, shall we say, consistent with what was later accepted, he did have a very, very strong sense of the transcendence of God; that God was beyond time, that he was a perfect circle unto himself. He was fully rational, and therefore fully good. Creation was at a certain act of time, and the Christ logos, for Origen, represents the bridge between divinity and the material world; or, in Platonic terms, from the world of being and the world of becoming. That Christ logos is essentially equated with the *nous*, or the thought, of the Middle Platonic schemes. In addition, God not only created or eternally generated—let's use his terms, Origen's terms—Christ logos and the Holy Spirit, there were also souls that were created. The souls, the *psuche*, are eternal and good; and yet, at the same time, they possess free will.

Origen was put in a rather peculiar position. He's a Platonist—he very, very much knows his *Timaeus*—and yet he's also a Christian in the same time and he believes in free will and the individual souls. In Origen's scheme, as far as we can tell in the first three books of *On First Principles*, he spends a great deal of time telling how souls fell away from God. Souls were eternally created. They are divine; but because they have free will, souls become inattentive, they become lazy, and they fall away from God at varying rates. He uses, right out of Plato, the image from the *Phaedrus* of the charioteer driving who falls asleep and then the horses go off and there's danger with the sun; the famous myth that comes out of Greek mythology. He uses that as a way of explaining how souls fell away. Some souls fell away and became angels. Others became humans and became embodied in the material world. The lowest of them all is Satan at the far end of it. But all of them possess souls, including Satan; all of them have free will. Therefore, Origen is extremely optimistic about this. He writes that all souls, by knowledge, by gnosis, by moving themselves towards God through perfection, understanding God's scripture, can return to a state of closeness to the godhead—that is, rise from the material world; rise from angels—and even Satan can rise back to that original state of perfection, and the ones who attain that are the enlightened ones. In effect, what he's saying is humans can be divinized; that is, they are capable—*capax divinitatis* is how Rufinus would put it in the Latin—they have the capacity for divinity; that is, they have a capacity for achieving good with the godhead.

Origen got himself in trouble. He wasn't satisfied with that, and being the Platonist that he was, thought, "If we do achieve this perfection and if what

I said is correct"—and again, a lot of this is put in speculative terms by Origen—"then perhaps once everyone achieves perfection and returns to original state, including Satan, the souls could fall away again," and that you get an eternal cycle of souls falling away from God, attaining perfection. Then Origen goes really on a limb—and this is probably why Justinian and his crowd condemned him—and in the next set of cycles of falling away and regaining perfection, perhaps Satan will play the role of Christ and Christ the role of Satan. Who's to tell? That was a move away from the strong sense of linear progressive time that you have from the Hebrew tradition, and very much towards a Greek philosophical sense of time where you have a cyclical view of souls, transmigration of souls—which Plato apparently believed— and the fact that the cycle can be repeated. Finally, in this scheme—as Origen puts it—no soul needs to be condemned to a hell. Punishment, in Origen's notion, is the soul contemplating and remembering with remorse its evil acts in its lifetime, and in so doing perceiving the good, perceiving God, and attaining divinization. It's a Christian version of the whole allegory of the cave in Plato's *Republic*, where you see the true reality and you finally understand how to join the godhead.

These positions, or theories—and you have to remember, Origen was writing this at the beginning of the 3rd century—the texts were still being established, and he was, in fact, establishing the authority of the texts, and many questions about Christian theology had not been answered or determined. There was a wide range of speculation available to Origen in 215 A.D. that, 100 years later, was going to be closed when certain decisions were made at the great councils in the 4th and then later in the 5th centuries A.D. Later authors, including someone like Eusebius writing in the reign of Constantine, had great difficulty understanding how Origen could speculate so freely like this, since some of this was now obviously accepted; and that's because of the state of Christian theology at that time.

In addition, Origen made some very, very important contributions towards the debate between Christians and pagans. For one, henceforth, critics of Christianity couldn't resort to the stock criticisms you saw in the attack by Celsus writing in the early 2nd century A.D. In fact, Origen himself wrote a refutation of Celsus's work. Second, Origen used the same high language that you found in Saint Clement. It's highly-polished literary Greek and very,

very different from the *koine* or common Greek—that is, the vernacular Greek of the New Testament. That's something I've stressed repeatedly in this course: If you're to win over the pagan elite classes, you have to be able to speak to them in the same language that they write in, and that's a very, very artificial (it's often called Atticizing) Greek; that is, Greek of the 5th century B.C. You have to know your Plato; you actually should know your Homer as well; and Origen achieved this. He had a mastery of the Greek language, the technical skills, to write commentaries and expositions on the Christian faith that now moved the Christian faith up to a whole new level. If you read Origen's work and compare it to some of the earlier apologists that I'd mentioned earlier such as Justin the Martyr, you've really made a leap in the types of writing and debate among Christian thinkers. In many ways, Christian theology had now come of age. Furthermore, Origen had gone through the Hebrew text and determined what the best Greek version of the Old Testament was. Many of the theologians and thinkers that would follow Origen didn't know Hebrew; they had to depend on his work; depend on the *Hexapla*, which had determined what the text was. Origen, again, had played an extremely important role.

But for me, I think one of the most important achievements of Origen was this synthesis of Platonic reasoning and philosophy with Christian doctrine. That synthesis had created a Christian theology that was very, very Platonized, so that henceforth Christians were not so much divided as they had been earlier. They really could present themselves as heirs of Plato and claim that they had as much claim to that Classical tradition as the pagans did. This was very, very important, because it gave the Christians the ability in the 4th and 5th century to argue with pagans on a whole new level.

Above all, he defined doctrine. Most pagan critics had noticed that the Christians were hopelessly divided; that they tediously talked about sin, and Celsus's comment, "Yeah, they talk about sin like a bunch of frogs croaking around a pond." With Origen, you really couldn't say that anymore. The Christian thinkers now had a serious religious vision explained in Platonic terms; they had mastery of the language.

Maybe this theology didn't contribute to numbers—very, very few pagans read Origen's works in Origen's lifetime and decided, "This is a great

Platonic argument; I'm going to become a Christian," that didn't happen—but what it did do was it defined canon; it gave a sense of what doctrines were for the bishops of the apostolic churches; so that when the Roman emperor Constantine did convert, those bishops not only had the organization, but they also had the theology and the reasons to explain to the emperor Constantine why he converted and why he should remain a Christian. There, Origen did his greatest deed of all for the advancement of Christianity.

Imperial Crisis and Spiritual Crisis
Lecture 12

The traditional view of the so-called crisis of the 3rd century is a Roman world in complete political, economic, and spiritual breakdown, which in turn led great numbers of ordinary people to turn to Christianity. The problem with this view is that the archaeological evidence does not support it. More modern scholarship indicates that the Romans turned to Christianity for very traditional Roman reasons: because the Christian god proved himself of value to the emperor, and the emperor's faith became the faith of the elite.

The 3rd-Century Persian Wars

- The next four lectures deal with paganism in the years 235–305, which are often seen as a turning point. Roman government moved from the Principate, wherein the emperor ruled as the Princeps, or "first citizen," into the Dominate, where the emperor was an autocrat known as a *dominus noster*.

- There were several reasons for this crisis, first and foremost were military ones. The first threat came from the East: the **Sāsānid** shahs of Persia. **Ardashīr I** and **Shāpūr I** claimed the Roman eastern provinces as part of their legacy from the Persian kings of old. The Sāsānid shahs were a much more formidable foe than the Romans had fought previously.

- In 229–232 A.D., Emperor **Severus Alexander** was forced to wage the first Persian War against Ardashīr, which ended in a truce. For the first time, a Roman emperor returned from the East without a decisive victory. Severus Alexander was later assassinated by his soldiers on the Rhine.

- The next emperor to go east was **Gordian III**. He waged an expensive campaign in 242–244 and was murdered by his

Persian emperor Shāpūr I captured Emperor Valerian and subjected him to humiliations to demonstrate his power over Rome.

Praetorian prefect, Philip the Arab, who signed a treaty with the second Persian shah, Shāpūr, and promised him the equivalent of 10,000 pounds of gold.

- Two later expeditions by Emperor **Valerian** in 253–255 and 258–260 ended in an ignominious defeat. Valerian was captured and, according to Latin literary sources, used as Shāpūr's horse step.

- The frontier was stabilized by **Odenathus**, a merchant prince of Palmyra. He rallied the Roman armies to defeat Shāpūr in lower Iraq. However, he and his wife, Queen **Zenobia**, advanced their son as an emperor of the East, and Emperor **Aurelian** had to reconquer the East from its would-be protector.

- In 300, under Emperor **Galerius**, the Romans and Persians signed a treaty in which the strategic victory of Rome was recognized. But victory came at a high cost that forced the Romans to recognize the Persians as equals.

The Crisis on the German Frontier

- The humiliations suffered on the eastern frontier were matched by defeats and setbacks on the northern frontiers, particularly along the Rhine and the Danube. The East Germanic peoples who had arrived from Scandinavia in the mid-2nd century—Goths, Vandals, Herulians, and Gepidai—attacked Rome's borders and drove Rome's West Germanic allies into the Roman western provinces.

- In 251, Emperor **Trajan Decius** was defeated and slain by the Goths. They were checked not so much by the efforts of the central government in Rome but by a breakaway regime, the so-called Gallo-Roman emperors.

- In 260, General Postumus, commander of the Rhine armies, declared himself emperor and established a separatist Gallo-Roman state in Britain, Gaul, and Spain. His successors ruled down to 273, when the western provinces were reunited with Rome by Emperor Aurelian, the same emperor who would restore the East to central rule.

- In meeting the Germanic threat, the Roman emperors essentially had to admit that it was too big a job for any one emperor. Imperial unity briefly was compromised in meeting the multiple barbarian threats.

The Rise of the Soldier-Emperors

- More destructive than this split were the civil wars. In 40 years, there were five such major wars and a number of lesser ones, and when you pit two Roman armies against each other, they will hack each other to pieces.

- In the first half of the 3rd century, the traditional ruling aristocracy was so discredited that they were replaced by tough soldier-emperors from the Balkans. These emperors fought the foes of Rome and restored the frontiers, as well as imperial unity. They included such rulers as Aurelian, who restored the unity of the empire; Probus, who won significant victories over the Goths; and Diocletian, who reformed the state after a generation of civil war, rebellion, and foreign invasion.

- These soldier-emperors were traditional in many ways. They invoked the gods of Rome, particularly the gods of the army camp—Jupiter, Mars, and Venus Victrix. Many of them were of provincial origin and had received their citizenship through military service, but that only made them more conservative—more Roman than the Romans in some ways.

The Enigma of the 3rd-Century Crisis

- Scholars of the past generation have spent an enormous amount of effort trying to make sense out of the 3rd century. There were great costs for beating back these barbarians and for ending the civil wars. First and foremost was money.

- The usual argument is that the money was rapidly debased—that is, the silver money was turned from a silver coin into a copper coin with a silver coating—sparking an inflationary spiral often compared to the Great Depression. By extension, it is argued that the savings of the Roman world were wiped out and that this hardship played to the benefit of Christianity.

- This view is overdrawn. First, the actual debasement lasted only a short time, approximately 25 years. Second, during the period of debasement, the coins were still valuable. Numerous hoards from all over the Roman Empire indicate that people were still saving these coins during the period, indicating that they still had value as money.

- Finally, in 274 and in 293, then throughout the 4th century, the soldier-emperors reformed the coinage, creating fiat money that was negotiable for a fixed amount of gold. By the 270s and 280s, prices had stabilized; the borders had restabilized; and the emperors, starting with Diocletian, had imposed reforms that brought peace and order back to the Roman world.

- There is other evidence from coins, inscriptions, and relief sculpture that indicate that the 3rd century was not as dismal as previously thought. In the cities of Italy, Africa, and Asia Minor, the ruling classes survived the crisis of the 3rd century, carrying on civic government and rallying to the soldier-emperors.

- Archaeology shows a remarkable continuity in imperial patronage to the cults of the cities and to the sanctuaries of the Roman world, as well as a loyalty expressed by the ruling elites to the Roman emperor. While invasion and civil war did bring about change, it was not a spiritual crisis.

Not Crisis but Continuity

- Romans believed in powerful ancestral traditions. Changes in perception, while important, were not revolutionary. Loyalty was now centered on the Roman emperor, not necessarily on the city of Rome or all the abstract traditions of the republic, and that resulted in the creation of a new tone of government: the Dominate, in which the emperor could rule as an autocrat.

- Rather than create disorientation or flight from public service, the religious history of the 3rd century is better understood not as a failure of nerve on the part of the ruling classes but a reaffirmation of traditional values, a move back to traditional religion and invoking of the gods of Rome as their defenders against invasion.

- We have no evidence of large numbers of Romans giving up their traditional faith for mystery cults or Christianity. We have no evidence for any new cult in the Roman Empire since Alexander of Abonouteichos created the cult of Glycon in 160, and the visual evidence indicates rebuilding of traditional cult sanctuaries during this period. That calls very much into question the idea that this was one of rapid Christianization.

- Some scholars have tried to use Christian funerary monuments of the period found in Turkey as documentation of rising numbers of Christians in the 3rd century. On closer inspection, these gravestones are simply a subset of a much larger body of gravestones, most of them pagan. Most of the monuments are very difficult to identify as Christian unless you read the inscription. They do not represent a rural Christianity on the rise.

- The problem is our preconceptions about religious change in the ancient world. In many ways, we are the heirs to the fact that the Christians won the dispute. We also are heirs to the French Revolution and the notion that a mass movement is the only significant movement in history.

- We have to divorce ourselves from both of these preconceptions when looking at the evidence of the 3rd century and remember that we are dealing with a traditional hierarchical society. Romans understood the world in terms of legal categories rather than social or economic classes.

- It was far more important that Christians converted a Roman emperor and members of the ruling aristocracy who had the means and patronage to change religion and society than to convert large numbers of pagans in the countryside.

- What came out of the 3rd century, from the pagan viewpoint, was not a social upheaval but a reaffirmation of the traditional religious values. The important change was in iconography: Henceforth, the icons placed the emperor in the company of the gods. They spoke to the gods. They had battle miracles.

- At the same time, the gods gave victory. So when Emperor Constantine invoked the Christian god and won the Battle of Milvian Bridge, that was perhaps the most powerful argument of all in favor of Christianity.

Sāsānid: The dynasty of shahs who ruled the New Persian Empire (227–642).

Ardashīr I (fl. 3rd century A.D.): Shah of Persia (224–240) who overthrew the Arsacid dynasty of Parthia and founded the Neo-Persian or Sāsānid Empire. Ardashīr waged war against Rome, proclaiming his aim to conquer the Roman East.

Aurelian (a.k.a. **Lucius Domitius Aurelianus**; c. 207–275; r. 270–275): "Restorer of the Roman world." Born of a military family in Dalmatia, Aurelian distinguished himself as a cavalry commander under Gallienus and Claudius II. In 270, the Danube army saluted Aurelian emperor, and he secured Rome after a brief civil war. Aurelian restored the political unity of the Roman Empire, defeating Zenobia of Palmyra in 272 and the Gallo-Roman emperor Tetricus in 274.

Galerius (a.k.a. **Gaius Galerius Valerius Maximianus**; c. 250–311; r. 305–311): Balkan officer created Caesar of the East in 293. He married Diocletian's daughter Galeria Valeria. In 305, Galerius succeeded Diocletian as Augustus of the East, but his political arrangements denied the succession to both Constantine and Maxentius (each the son of an emperor), so that civil war erupted after 306. Galerius was credited with the initiative for the Great Persecution in 303–313.

Gordian III (a.k.a. **Marcus Antonius Gordianus**; 225–244; r. 238–244): Grandson of Gordian I, the young Gordian III was proclaimed emperor by the Praetorian Guard and Senate at Rome in opposition to Maximinus I. His father-in-law and Praetorian prefect Gaius Furius Timisitheus directed policy after 240. In 242–244, Gordian took the field against the Persian Shah Shāpūr I. The young emperor was slain in a mutiny, staged by his prefect, Philip the Arab (who had succeeded Timistheus in 243).

Odenathus (a.k.a. **Septimius Odenathus**; r. 262–267): Merchant prince of the caravan city Palmyra, Roman senator, and Roman general (*dux*). He imposed his authority over the Roman eastern frontier after the capture of Valerian I in 260. In 262, he imposed a treaty on Shah Shāpūr I. He was murdered at Emesa.

Severus Alexander (a.k.a. **Marcus Aurelius Severus Alexander**; 208–235; r. 222–235): Son of Julia Mamaea and the senator Gessius Marcianus, he was the last Severan emperor. In 221, he was promoted to Caesar by his cousin Emperor Elagabalus (r. 218–222), whose devotion to the orgiastic rites of the Syrian sun god of Emesa compromised the dynasty. In contrast, Severus Alexander ruled judiciously under the guidance of his mother Julia Mamaea. His inconclusive wars against the Persians and Germans led to his assassination by mutinous soldiers of the Rhine army.

Shāpūr I (r. 241–272): The second Sāsānid shah of Persia, who waged three successful campaigns against the Roman Empire (242–244, 253–255, and 258–260). In 260, he captured Emperor Valerian. He sacked Antioch, the third city of the Roman Empire, in either 253 or 260. Odenathus, prince of Palmyra, compelled Shāpūr to negotiate a peace.

Trajan Decius (a.k.a. **Gaius Messius Quintus Traianus Decius**; 201–251; r. 249–251): A Pannonian provincial who attained senatorial rank under Severus Alexander and legate of Upper Pannonia, he was declared emperor by the Danube legions. He defeated and slew the emperor Philip at Verona in 249. Trajan Decius was defeated and slain by the Goths at Abrittus in Lower Moesia. He initiated the first empire-wide persecution of Christians in 250–251.

Valerian I (a.k.a. **Publius Licinius Valerianus**; c. 195–260; r. 253–260): A senator of noble origins who became legate of Raetia in the civil war of 253. He was proclaimed emperor by the Rhine legions and defeated his rival Aemilian. Valerian issued the second empire-wide persecution of Christians in 258–260. Valerian faced barbarian assaults along the northern and eastern frontiers. He waged two Persian wars (253–256 and 258–260). He was treacherously captured by Shah Shāpūr in 260 and died in captivity.

Zenobia (a.k.a. **Septimia Zenobia**; r. 267–272): The wife of Odenathus of Palmyra and mother of Vaballathus. In 267, she succeeded her husband's extraordinary position in the Roman East. Styling herself as Empress Augusta, she advanced her son Vaballathus as emperor in 270. In 270–271, Palmyrene forces occupied Asia Minor, Palestine, and Egypt. In 272, she was defeated by Aurelian and allowed to retire to a Campania villa.

Suggested Reading

Dodds, *Pagan and Christian in the Age of Anxiety.*

Harl, *Civic Coins and Civic Politics in the Roman East.*

———, *Coinage in the Roman Economy.*

MacCormack, *Art and Ceremony in Late Antiquity.*

MacMullen, *Roman Government's Response to Crisis.*

Potter, *The Roman Empire at Bay.*

Watson, *Aurelian and the Third Century.*

Questions to Consider

1. How did political and military crises transform pagan perceptions of the gods and the Roman emperor? Why would they likely not reject the ancestral gods in a crisis? Why would pagans become impatient with Christian refusal to sacrifice to the gods or the genius of the Roman emperor?

2. Why did military defeats discredit an emperor of the Severan aristocracy? What were the religious beliefs of the solider-emperors between Claudius II (268–270) and Diocletian (284–305)? Why did they allow themselves to be compared to their divine protectors? Why did Romans come to accept a certain divinity in their emperors?

3. What are the sources for arguments of spiritual crisis and a loss of faith in traditional gods after 235? What are the dangers in surmising explanations based on modern analogies?

Imperial Crisis and Spiritual Crisis
Lecture 12—Transcript

In this lecture, I plan to deal with what is often called the crisis of the 3rd century. This involves not only an imperial crisis but usually a spiritual crisis as well, and it covers the years 235–305 A.D. The lecture also is important because it acts as a transition from the first to the second half of the course.

In this course, I've spent time dealing with the emergence of Christianity, the nature of paganism, the role of Judaism in the Roman world, and we ended with the development of Christian theology. The next four lectures are going to deal with what happened to paganism in this period of imperial crisis, which is often seen as a turning point. For one, we know that the Roman institutions were changed in such a way that you move from what's called the Principate into the Dominate; that is, from a government based on an emperor ruling as a *princeps* (or "first citizen") of a republic to, in effect, an autocrat known as a *dominus noster* (that is, an "absolute ruler"). In addition, the period is also thought to have seen major spiritual changes and led to a rapid development of Christianity and a time when Christians increased in numbers.

There are several reasons for this crisis, and first and foremost, they're military. I want to look at the two leading forces: One is the threat from the East from the Persians, the Sassanid Shahs of Persia, who had overthrown the rather weak Parthian rulers in the East and doubled the size of the old Parthian Empire that came to embrace what's today Iraq, Iran, most of Central Asia, and Northern India. This was a powerful Iranian state ruled by a dynasty. The first ruler was a man named Ardashir and his son Shapur. Both of these shahs, both of these kings, saw themselves as heirs to the old Persian Empire, the empire that had been overthrown by Alexander the Great. In their mind, the Roman Eastern provinces were part of that legacy, so they were bent, at least publicly, in reconquering those lost provinces.

The Sassanid Shahs of this so-called Neo-Persian Empire possessed a siege train, they possessed logistics; they were a much more formidable foe than the Romans had fought previously in the Middle East. In addition, they were propelled by a religious dimension: They saw themselves as the vice regents of Ahura Mazda. Ahura Mazda is the god of Zoroastrianism, the monotheistic and universal creed of the Persians. Zoroastrianism was really reorganized in the 3rd century along the lines of what we see today: It's a monotheistic creed, which, while universal in its doctrines—the god of Zoroastrian is the universal god of creation—nonetheless, the religion tended to be essentially Iranian in ethos and a very, very powerful support to those shahs. The Romans, in the 3rd century, found themselves confronting a very dangerous foe with heavy cavalry, with horse archers from central Asia, with a siege train; with an ability not only to win victories, but also to conquer and rule Roman cities. For the first time, the Roman army had to fight a very, very serious set of wars on that Euphrates frontier and sometimes they lost, which was something that had been unheard of in early imperial history.

In 229–232 A.D., the emperor Severus Alexander—that courteous prince who apparently received the Christian theologian Origen—was forced to wage the first Persian War against the first shah, Ardashir, and this war ended in essentially a truce. It was a negotiated settlement. For the first time, a Roman emperor returned from the East without a decisive victory, and this discredited Severus Alexander who was later assassinated by his soldiers on the Rhine. A major reason for it was that he and his mom, Julia Mamaema, had failed to deal with the Persian threat.

The next emperor to go east was a young emperor, Gordian III. He waged an expensive campaign in 242–244. He had to recapture fortresses in what is today southwestern Turkey and northern Iraq, which the Romans called Mesopotamia. These were vital fortresses for protecting the Roman Eastern frontiers. He was murdered by his praetorian prefect, Philip the Arab, who signed a treaty with the second Persian shah, Shapur, and promised to pay him what I believe was the equivalent of 10,000 pounds of gold. Two later expeditions by the emperor Valerian in 253–255, again in 258–260, ended in an ignominious defeat and the emperor Valerian was captured and, according to Latin literary sources, he was used as Shapur's horse step. Whenever the shah Shapur wanted to get on his horse, the emperor Valerian just rolled over and he stepped on top of him and kind of said, "Ex-Roman emperors; these are useful for shahs to have." It was an incredible humiliation because the then-reigning emperor Gallienus was the son of Valerian and he could do nothing about it.

In the early 3rd century, the Romans found themselves facing a major threat on the eastern frontier. The only reason why the frontier was stabilized was because a man named Odenathus, who was a merchant prince of the city of Palmyra, which is today in Syria—which was a great caravan city that had commercial connections stretching from the Red Sea to the Persian Gulf—took it upon himself to rally the Roman armies and carry the war into lower Iraq and defeat Shapur. However, Odenathus, and then his wife, Queen Zenobia, who advanced their son as an emperor of the East, eventually became a threat and it required the emperor Aurelian to reconquer the East from their would-be protector. Nonetheless, for all of the fighting, the Romans in the end—at the end of the 3rd century—had won the war over the Persians. There was a very important, successful campaign by the emperor Galerius, and the first round of fighting, which had raged for almost 50 years, went to Rome. In 300 A.D., the Romans and Persians signed a treaty in which essentially the strategic victory of Rome was recognized.

But the victory came at a very high cost; a cost that forced the Romans to recognize the Persians as equals, something they'd never done to the Parthian kings. Shapur himself commissioned a rock relief showing the submission of the emperors Philip and Valerian and a dead Gordian III. He set up a huge monumental inscription narrating his wars and victories over the Romans.

The humiliations suffered on the eastern frontier in the early 3rd century were matched by defeats and setbacks on the northern frontiers, particularly along the Rhine and the Danube, a frontier that ran almost 1,500 miles from the mouth of the Rhine to the mouth of the Danube. There, the Romans faced new threats, mostly East Germanic peoples, who'd arrived from Scandinavia in the mid-2nd century A.D., notably Goths, Vandals, Herulians, Gepidai, names replete with history in the later Middle Ages. All of these tribes learned horsemanship on the south Russian steppes from the Iranian peoples, and they began to attack the lower Danube frontiers of the Roman Empire. The East Germanic peoples also drove a hammer into the West Germanic peoples—that is, the peoples living on the upper Danube and Rhine—who had long been in association with the Romans. These West Germanic tribes were literally forced into the Roman western provinces in large part because of the pressure coming from their East Germanic kinsmen, who were pushing both south and west at the same time. Therefore, you had the

Romans facing Goths in Dacia—that is, Romania, a very important province of the Roman Empire noted for its gold mines—and in the Balkans. In 251 A.D., the emperor Trajan Decius, noted as a persecutor of Christians, was defeated and slain by the Goths who have the singular distinction of all the Germanic peoples of slaying two different emperors, Trajan Decius in 251 and later the emperor Valence at Adrianople in 378.

The Goths, too, were beaten back. Important victories were won over the Goths by the emperor Gallienus in 267, by Claudius II Gothicus in 269. The Germanic tribes on the western frontier, on the Rhine and the upper Danube too were checked; but they were checked not so much by the efforts of the central government in Rome, but by a breakaway regime, the so-called Gallo-Roman emperors. In 260 A.D., the general Postumus, who was commander of the armies on the Rhine, declared himself emperor, and with his armies established a separatist Gallo-Roman state in Britain, Gaul, and Spain, and he checked the attacks of the west Germanic peoples, and his successors ruled down to 273 A.D. when the western provinces were united by the emperor Aurelian, the same emperor who would restore the East to central rule, which had fallen away under Queen Zenobia and the Palmyrenes.

In meeting the Germanic threat on the northern frontiers, the Roman emperors essentially had to admit that it was too big a job for any one single emperor. The Western army put up its own emperor; the army of the Balkans in Italy represented the central government; and then there was that breakaway Eastern state centered on Palmyra. Imperial unity briefly was compromised in meeting the multiple barbarian threats: Germanic peoples from the north, Iranian peoples from the east, the Sassanid Shahs.

The fighting on these frontier wars was incredibly destructive; however, more destructive were the civil wars. In 40 years, there were five major civil wars and a number of lesser ones, and when you pit two Roman armies against each other, they will hack each other to pieces on the battlefield. What happened in the first half of the 3rd century A.D., foreign invasions and civil war so discredited the traditional ruling aristocracy—and these are families that had risen to distinction in the end of the 2nd, beginning of the 3rd centuries A.D., they were of the great senatorial families (that is, they were of the elite classes of Rome); they were polished aristocrats; many of them had been advanced under the so-called Severan emperors from 193–235 A.D., the last stable dynasty of Rome—they were replaced after 268 by tough soldier-emperors from the Balkans, and these emperors fought the foes of Rome and restored the frontiers; restored imperial unity. They included the emperor Aurelian in 270–275, who restored the unity of the empire; the emperor Probus, who won significant victories over the Goths; and above all, the emperor Diocletian—we'll be discussing him in the coming lectures—is the emperor who restored not only imperial unity, but also reformed the Roman state after, literally, a generation of civil war, rebellion, and foreign invasion.

These soldier-emperors invoked the gods of Rome. They were traditional emperors in many ways. They were devoted to the gods of the Roman army camp—to Jupiter, to Mars, to Venus Victrix—and above all, they were Roman to the core. Many of them were of provincial origin; they had received their citizenship through service in the Roman army. Many had been franchised under the 212 law of Caracalla, which gave citizenship to all residents of the Roman Empire. They were more Roman than the Romans in some ways. To them, the victory over the barbarian threat represented their obtaining the favor of the traditional gods of Rome (anyway, that's my opinion).

This period of imperial crisis had major social and economic consequences for the Roman world. Scholars in the last generation—myself included—have spent an enormous amount of effort trying to make sense out of what we call the period of the 3rd century; that is from 235–305 A.D. That's a period that saw the assassination of Severus Alexander, the end of political stability, and the retirement—which is amazing; the emperor Diocletian actually retired, the only emperor to do so—of the emperor Diocletian after 20 years on the throne and reforming the Roman world.

There were costs that had to be paid for beating back these barbarian attacks and for ending civil war. First and foremost was money. There's been a study on imperial coinage—that's where some of my expertise is—and the usual argument is that the money was rapidly debased; that is, the silver money was turned from a silver coin into a copper coin with a silver coating. This debasement was to produce more money, and therefore you could buy more armies, more officials, and in the process, you spark an inflationary spiral that's often been compared to the Great Depression of the 1920s and 30s.

This is a view that is commonly held in most textbooks today; it's got a long scholarship going back to the 1920s and 30s, and it's a view to which I don't subscribe. I should make that clear right now. My view is that of my own research and my own opinion. Hence, it's often argued, based on this usual view of economic chaos and fiscal instability and debasement, that the savings classes of the Roman world were wiped out; that many people, as one scholar put it, "Many more people got poorer, and very few people got richer," and that this social hardship and this dismal economic situation led to religious change, and that social and economic crisis wrought spiritual crisis, which in the end played to the benefit of Christianity, as many Romans in this period turn to Christianity as a new faith, a promise of salvation; some kind of stability in a period of social and economic chaos.

This view is overdrawn. First, the actual debasement lasted only a short time, approximately 25 years. The notion that the money was totally worthless is wrong, and that the price surges had the same impact on the Roman economy as the spiral inflation of the 1920s and 30s is really very misleading. There are a number of reasons why I don't subscribe to this theory, or more accurately, this interpretation. One of them is my own study of the coins. For one, during the periods of debasement, the coins were still valuable. They may have been copper with a silver coating, but we have numerous hoards from all over the Roman Empire. Hoards are savings people have secreted for a better day, and then we're looking at their bad luck. For instance, a hoard from Britain I have studied: It has some 535 coins of the emperor Gallienus and his Gallo-Roman rivals. It was deposited on the island of Britain and I obtained this hoard legally; I'm going to be publishing it. The coins are all coins of the period of debasement and someone put them aside and never recovered them. I think what happened is he was either killed, enslaved, or in the civil war of 273 that saw the reunification of Britain to the central government. There's a coin of Gallienus from the Roman mint that shows *Marti Pacifero* (that is, Mars, Bringer of Peace); all sorts of traditional symbols. Clearly, these coins were money. I published similar hoards from Turkey from the period of inflation (supposedly) and monetary crisis. All of these hoards indicate that the money was still worth being set aside.

Second, starting in 274 and then again in 293, and through the whole of the 4th century, soldier-emperors didn't debase coins, they reformed the coins, and they created what I would call a fiduciary coinage, very similar to the type of money we use today. That is, fiat money; money in which the state says it has value and you can negotiate it and exchange it against gold and pay taxes. The notion that this money was worthless is really incorrect. The extent of the crisis—the extent of the fiscal chaos—has been largely overdrawn, and by the 270s and 280s, the prices had been stabilized; the borders had been restabilized; and the emperors, starting with Diocletian, had imposed reforms that brought peace and order back to the Roman world. Again, it came at a high price; but nonetheless, the Pax Romana, the Roman peace, was restored by the end of the 3rd century.

There's other evidence from coins, from inscriptions, from relief sculpture that indicate that the picture we have of the 3rd century is not as dismal as we think it is. In part, it's dismal because we don't have many literary sources; but we have other sources from archaeology, from the coins, from the inscriptions. These sources have indicated that in the cities of Italy, Africa, and Asia Minor, the ruling classes—the decurions I mentioned earlier; that is, the families who had sufficient wealth to run their cities—that many of them survived the crisis of the 3rd century; many of them continued to carry on civic government; and what is more important, these elites rallied to the emperors of the 3rd century. That rallying can be documented in a number of ways. One is by the issuing of all sorts of coin types, relief sculpture that was put up in public places, which celebrated games and festivals to the traditional gods; and those gods were honored in the presence of the emperor. Many of the coins in reliefs depict the emperor arriving to the East to that particular city as they're going off to fight the Persians. The emperors were hailed as companions to the native gods, or in Latin, a *comes*; we have many coins in which the local god is shaking hands with the emperor, or the emperor is being received by the decurions calling out and presenting the cult statue. We have large numbers of coins and inscriptions, especially inscriptions from the great sanctuaries such as Didyma, the Asclepieion at Pergamon, where the emperors who were fighting the wars of the 3rd century went there and invoked the help of these gods; extended privileges; gave them dynastic games, especially games that were on the level of the Olympic games or the Pythian games, that is Pan-Hellenic.

In many ways, the coins, the inscriptions, the relief work, the archaeology shows a remarkable continuity in imperial patronage to the cults of the cities and to the sanctuaries of the Roman world, and at the same time, a loyalty expressed by the ruling elites of the numerous cities of the Roman world to the Roman emperor. While invasion and civil war did bring about change—there's no doubt there was change—it's not the kind of spiritual crisis that we would think of. First, you're dealing with a traditional society. Romans—both those of Italy; and now you have to remember, after 212 A.D., all residents of the Roman Empire were legally Romans—believed in powerful ancestral traditions. Revolution (*res novae* in Latin) was something they really didn't consider; and the changes in perception, while important, weren't revolutionary. For one, loyalty was now centered on the Roman emperor, not necessarily on the city of Rome or all the abstract traditions of the republic; and that resulted in the creation of a new tone of government we call the *dominate* in which the emperor could rule as an autocrat. He was surrounded by officials, by eunuchs at the court, which were men of high rank who had been fixed so they couldn't compete with the emperor; that is, they couldn't assassinate and take over because the emperor's position was possibly in question, he was a military man who'd risen to power so he's trying to gain the legitimacy.

All of this autocracy that has been discussed in current literature is the result of a Roman world that was expected and thankful that the emperor had the favor of the gods and restored prosperity, ended civil war, and ended invasion. Rather than create the kind of disorientation, flight from public service, yearning for something new and trendy in the way of religion, I'd argue that the religious history of the 3rd century is better understood not as a failure of nerve on the part of the ruling classes of the Roman world, but a reaffirmation of traditional values; a move back to traditional religion and invoking of the gods of Rome as their defenders against invasion.

We have no evidence of large numbers of Romans giving up their traditional faith for mystery cults, for Christianity. In fact, we have no evidence for any new cult in the Roman Empire ever since Alexander of Abonouteichus created that wild serpent cult of Glycon back in 160 A.D. Quite to the contrary: What we have is an unbroken record through most of the 3rd century, not in the literary sources but in the visual evidence, the coins, and the medallions, in the archaeology that demonstrates the rebuilding of sanctuaries, the refurbishing of sanctuaries that pagan worship continued; perhaps on a diminished level—funding wasn't as lavish as it had been—but nonetheless, it continued. That's an extremely important point to stress. That calls very much into question that the period—especially from 260, when the great persecution of Valerian ceased and 303, when the persecutions of Diocletian began; this period of some almost 45 years that Christian authors like to call the peace of the church—often seen as a period of rapid Christianization; there really is no evidence for it. It's essentially surmised from believing that there was a loss of nerve and a flight from traditional religion as a result of the 3rd century crisis. The evidence from the imperial sources, from the local coins, from the archaeology, really gives us no reason to believe that that was necessarily the case.

There's one body of evidence from the 3rd century, and these come from essentially the 220s to about the 280s A.D., and they come from five distinct regions in what is today Turkey; and these are Christian funerary monuments. I've mentioned them before. They come from a region called Phrygia in western Turkey today, and they come from four distinct cities: the ancient cities of Hierapolis, Eumenia, Acmoneia, and Cotiaeum. Cotiaeum today is Kutahya, which is the porcelain center of Turkey and actually has a mosque built out of porcelain—it's rather bizarre, but in any case—and then from a village near Cotiaeum called Altıntaş, which I've visited as well. These inscriptions are put up by Christians for Christians—they're definitely Christian funerary monuments—and some scholars have tried to use them as a documentation of rising numbers of Christians in the 3rd century. Except for the catacombs at Rome, they're the only Christian inscriptions that we have from the Roman world. I've analyzed these inscriptions—I've photographed a number of them; I've done quite a bit of study on them—and what these gravestones really reveal is that they're a subset of a much larger body of gravestones, most of them pagan; that the art on the gravestones are very conventional—they're cut by artists who work for both Christian and for pagan customers—and most of the monuments are very difficult to identify as Christian unless you really read the inscription. The one exception is the inscriptions from Altıntaş where it says *cristianoi cristianois*, Christians for Christians; but otherwise, these funerary monuments are really part of a wider funerary tradition.

When you analyze those monuments, you find out that the Christians named on these inscriptions are very similar to the Christians in the time of Saint Paul. Many of them probably had Jewish ancestors; several of them were clearly keeping kosher; some of them were using Hebrew names. They certainly were very, very close to their Jewish relatives and neighbors; and what we believe happened in four of these cities, several Christian families probably entered the town council and it wouldn't be proper to deny these people to have funerary monuments, and so in those particular towns, the Christians were able to put up funerary monuments in a rather tasteful and discreet way. What they reveal is a group of Christians who were largely urban, Greek-speaking, of Jewish ancestry, keeping kosher perhaps, certainly devoted to the Old Testament, and significantly from regions that later were the center of iconoclasm in the Byzantine Age; that is, the dispute of the 7th, 8th, and 9th centuries over the use of icons. The reason for it is these Christians were probably early converts from either Greek-speaking Jews or Judaizing pagans. The Christian congregations were probably isolated, and pretty much congregations similar to their ancestors who were converted by Paul or the early apostles. They don't represent a rural Christianity on the rise. Some have said they're equivalent to the Presbyterians in Scotland in the 16th and 17th centuries; this is just over-reading the evidence. There was no widespread rural Christianity in Asia Minor.

Otherwise, you have to step back from the evidence and then think about a question I asked at the beginning of this course, and the problem is our preconceptions and our understandings of religious change and religion in the ancient world. In many ways, we are the heirs to the fact that the Christians won the dispute; that religion is identified as the religions of Abraham in the Western tradition; they're canonical text; there has to be a coherent cosmology, a notion of salvation. We also are heirs to the French Revolution and the notion that a mass movement is the only significant movement in history. We have to divorce ourselves from both of these preconceptions when looking at the evidence of the 3rd century and remember we are dealing with a traditional hierarchical society. Romans understood the world in terms of ordines and categories; legal categories rather than social or economic classes, as we understand.

It's far more important that Christians converted a Roman emperor or members of the ruling aristocracy who had the means and patronage to change religion, to change society, rather than to convert large numbers of pagans in the countryside of Asia Minor, which I don't believe happened and we'll discuss more about the conversion at the countryside in the 4th and 5th centuries A.D. in this course. That was far more important, the conversion of the emperor, the emperor Constantine in 312, than trying to play the numbers game in the 3rd century for which we really have very little evidence, and the evidence we do have suggests to me that the way we have approached this problem is really misleading. It's warning I always give my students: The fact that the question's important to us doesn't necessarily mean it was important to them, the people of the past. Numbers weren't that significant in understanding the religious change in the Roman world; converting an emperor was.

What came out of the 3rd century, from the pagan viewpoint, was not social upheaval, not alienation, not a flight to Christianity, but a reaffirmation of the traditional religious values. But there was an important change: Henceforth, the iconography and all the visual arts place the emperor in the company of the gods. Emperors were expected to speak to the gods. They had ceremonies that were virtually divine. They had battle miracles, like Marcus Aurelius fighting the Germans on the Danube or Aurelian, the sun god, intervening and throwing back the Palmyrene cavalry. Emperors were expected to be the comrade—the *comes* is the Latin word—of the gods. Therefore, imperial loyalty, imperial integrity, are closely bound up with loyalty to the emperor and the gods. The 3rd century essentially expanded the powers of the Roman emperor as Pontifex Maximus, as chief priest of the Roman Empire.

At the same time, the gods gave victory. They vanquished the barbarian foes who were shown unsympathetically; they reestablished peace. But above all, the Roman emperors expected the gods to intervene and for divine intervention to give them victory. With the emperor Constantine, the pagans were willing to consider that the gods he invoked to win the Battle of the Milvean Bridge would be legitimate divine powers if they delivered victory. In the case of Constantine in 312, he didn't invoke the traditional gods of Rome but he invoked the Christian God, and that was perhaps the most powerful argument of all because the Christian God gave Constantine victory and many pagans now had to sit back and think maybe the Christian God was legitimate.

The Great Persecutions

Lecture 13

Until the mid-3rd century, persecution of Christians in the Roman Empire was local, brief, and sporadic. The emperors Trajan Decius and Valerian enacted the first empire-wide persecutions, in which large numbers of Christians were actively sought out and put to the sacrifice test, then punished by public execution *ad bestias* in the amphitheaters. There is little doubt that these early martyrs helped forge the identity and strengthen the resolve of their fellow Christians; whether they played any role in converting pagans to Christianity is a matter of debate.

New Emperors, New Motives

- The Great Persecution ordered by the soldier-emperors **Trajan Decius** in 250–251 and **Valerian I** in 258–260 differed from those described previously in that they were empire wide. Residents of the entire Roman world were required to appear before altars to offer sacrifice not only to the gods, but also to the genius of the Roman emperor.

- Potentially, the imperial government could have done this at any time but had not. Previous persecutions were local, sporadic, and did not last long; they depended on the attitude of the Roman governor or local decurions toward the faith.

- The reason for these empire-wide persecutions is easily linked to the civil wars and invasions of the 3rd century and the need to win the favor of the traditional gods. Scholars have argued that the persecutions were an indication that paganism was in demise and Christianity on the rise. However, it could also be argued that the persecutions were a sign of a traditional pagan revival.

- According to pagan belief, the danger of Christians was that they denied the traditional gods their due. If you do not offer sacrifice to the gods and goddesses, they become angry and then visit communal punishment. It only took a few citizens opting out of the traditional sacrifices to bring down the wrath of the gods on everyone.

The Bureaucracy of the Persecutions

- Some scholars have suggested that tax registers were used to determine who was a Christian and who was a pagan, but imperial officials did not designate people by religious affiliation until the 4th century—that is, until the Christian emperors ruled and Christians had certain civil advantages, not disadvantages, versus pagan taxpayers.

- It is more likely that the persecutions depended on local initiative as they always had. The leading members of a city would have some sense of who the Christians were by who did not show up at the sacrifices and festivals. Eusebius says that on various occasions, especially in Asia Minor, Jews helped point out who the Christians were.

- A number of certificates—in Latin, *libellus* or *libelli*, meaning "little booklet"—have been found in Egypt that indicate that individuals appeared before the magistrates and offered sacrifice to prove their loyalty. *Libelli* were issued in enormous numbers and in some ways functioned like tax receipts. Sometimes, instead of papyrus *libelli*, these receipts were written on ostracon—potsherds, the scrap paper of the Roman world.

The Progress and Process of Persecution

- On January 1, 250, Roman officials went out to investigate and interrogate all over the empire, and governors were given wide powers to hold tribunals and determine who was a Christian and who was not, then to deal with those who failed to sacrifice. Those who failed to sacrifice could be sent to the arena for execution *ad bestias*.

- The persecution took the Christians by surprise. Pope **Fabian** was arrested and beheaded. Numerous Christians in the Church of Rome and in North Africa lapsed—that is, they sacrificed to the gods, were given certificates, and were let go.

- The Eastern churches in Asia Minor seemed to hold up much better. We know of a number of acts of Christian martyrs from Eusebius's *Ecclesiastical History*.

- The persecutions lasted for about 18 months. They came to a very abrupt end when Trajan Decius was killed by the Goths and his successor, **Trebonianus Gallus**, issued an act of clemency, in effect saying, "I have more important matters to deal with." The Christians saw the end of the persecution as an act of God.

- In 258–260, persecution resumed and raged for about two and a half years under Emperor Valerian. This one, too, abruptly stopped when the emperor was captured by an enemy—this time, the Persians.

The Effect of the Persecution on Christians

- Looking back on this era, Eusebius repeated the apologists' phrase that the blood of martyrs is the seed of the church—that is, for every Christian cut down in the arena, another pagan was moved to inquire about Christianity. This position has long been the lens through which scholars have investigated and judged religious change in the 3rd century.

- During this same period, Christians were coming to the attention of the imperial government in various other ways. Paul of Samosata, the bishop of Antioch, treated the church as his private property and tried to sell it, and his congregation asked Emperor Aurelian (r. 270–275) to adjudicate the case. Aurelian sided with the congregation, showing that Roman emperors could deal with their Christian subjects as Roman citizens.

- A second important point about those persecutions was that the Christians saw them as great tests of their faith. In Eusebius's mind, these empire-wide persecutions were the final test that led to the conversion of Constantine.

- On the whole, most Christians had stood up quite well to this test. Many bishops, like Pope Fabian, had refused to sacrifice and were martyred. This resulted in the development of two important traditions: Christians remembered the martyrs by naming their children after them, so that Christians gradually evolved their own nomenclature; and a cult of the holy dead sprang up by the end of the 3rd century.

- Among the greatest beneficiaries of these developments were the bishops. Those who stood strong against the persecutions not only increased their own fame but the fame and authority of the institution of the bishop.

- To average Christians, the empire-wide persecutions seemed like the apocalypse. This accounts in part for the popularity of the book of Revelation in this period and its addition to the New Testament.

- Martyrdom was a powerful way for Christians to define themselves as the new Israel. Christians were not supposed to offer themselves up for martyrdom like suicide victims. One was not supposed to, for example, go to a pagan festival and spit on the cult statue just to be captured and martyred; that was an act of pride. Martyrdom was carefully defined by the church fathers as an act of bravery and courage when there was no other option.

- After the persecutions, the church had to decide how to treat those who had lapsed and sacrificed but now wanted to return to the church. Should they be rebaptized? Was confession alone good enough? This division between rigorists and people with a broader notion of what the sin of sacrifice represented often split churches, particularly in North Africa. It became a major issue at the opening of the 4th century when Constantine converted.

The Christian martyrs were barely noticed by a Roman audience that was used to the violent gladiatorial games.

The Effect of the Persecution on Pagans

- Did the Great Persecution lead to large numbers of pagans being impressed by acts of martyrdom, learning about Christianity, and then converting? We have no statistical evidence for any surge in Christian numbers during the 3rd-century crisis. It is an act of faith to argue that the persecutions backfired on the imperial government.

- So, what did the persecutions and martyrdoms mean to pagans? Until very recently, it was assumed that dying in the arena would be seen as a noble act. Then Keith Hopkins, a great social historian, wrote a seminal article, "Murderous Games," in which he elucidated the pagan response to martyrdom in the broader context of Roman arena entertainment.

- Hopkins cast a great deal of doubt on claims that martyrdom converted any significant number of pagans. Romans watched many bloody spectacles. The largest building in any Roman city was an amphitheater built to house gladiatorial and animal combats, games dating back to the republic in the 3rd century B.C. that grew ever-larger throughout the centuries.

- These games were a vicarious psychological experience. They reaffirmed that the Romans were masters of the world. They also bore a message: Do not oppose the Roman order or you end up in the arena.

- One questions whether the execution of 20 or 30 Christian martyrs as an intermission during these games had much impact on the audience at all, given that the largest games might last 120 days and involve 11,000 beasts and 10,000 pairs of gladiators, not to mention the distributions of food and gifts.

- Above all, certain emperors used the gladiatorial games as a way of reinforcing the Roman social order. Romans were seated in the arena based on their ranks. The lowest of all were the criminals and outcasts on the arena floor. It is difficult to argue that the pagans in the seats would have been inclined to think that the execution of some Christians in the arena was something special.

- The persecutions and the destruction in the arena undoubtedly had a powerful impact on the Christian community, but to the Romans, they represented a traditional Roman attitude that married belief in the gods with patriotism and invoked standard punishments of invaders and outcasts. If the Christians were to make any headway, they had to demonstrate that they were Romans, too.

Names to Know

Fabian (r. 236–250): Pope respected by African and Italian bishops and credited with missions to cities in Gaul. He was martyred during the persecution of Trajan Decius on January 20, 250.

Trajan Decius (a.k.a. **Gaius Messius Quintus Traianus Decius**; 201–251; r. 249–251): A Pannonian provincial who attained senatorial rank under Severus Alexander and legate of Upper Pannonia, he was declared emperor by the Danube legions. He defeated and slew the emperor Philip at Verona in 249. Trajan Decius was defeated and slain by the Goths at Abrittus in Lower Moesia. He initiated the first empire-wide persecution of Christians in 250–251.

Trebonianus Gallus (a.k.a. **Gaius Vibius Trebonianus Gallus**; r. 251–253): A legate of Trajan Decius, he was declared emperor by the Roman army after Decius's death. Gallus faced attacks by northern barbarians and Persians. In 253, he was defeated and slain by Aemilian, governor of Moesia, whom the Danube legions had declared emperor.

Valerian I (a.k.a. **Publius Licinius Valerianus**; c. 195–260; r. 253–260): A senator of noble origins who became legate of Raetia in the civil war of 253. He was proclaimed emperor by the Rhine legions and defeated his rival Aemilian. Valerian issued the second empire-wide persecution of Christians in 258–260. Valerian faced barbarian assaults along the northern and eastern frontiers. He waged two Persian wars (253–256 and 258–260). He was treacherously captured by Shah Shāpūr in 260 and died in captivity.

Suggested Reading

Dodds, *Pagan and Christian in the Age of Anxiety.*

Eusebius, *The History of the Church: From Christ to Constantine.*

Frend, *Martyrdom and Persecution in the Early Church.*

Hopkins, "Murderous Games."

MacMullen, *Paganism in the Roman Empire.*

Nock, *Conversion.*

Potter, *The Roman Empire at Bay.*

Wilken, *The Christians as the Romans Saw Them.*

1. How did pagans and Christians view the edict of persecution issued by Trajan Decius in 250? By what means could emperors enforce empire-wide compliance of sacrificing to the gods and the spirit of the emperor?

2. How did empire-wide persecutions sharpen Christian identity and shape institutions? Why did martyrdoms fail to attract large numbers of converts?

3. What were pagan motives for empire-wide persecutions? How did they sharpen the pagan sense of piety and patriotism?

The Great Persecutions
Lecture 13—Transcript

In this lecture, I'm going to deal with the great persecutions. These were the persecutions ordered by the emperor Trajan Decius in 250–251 and then by the Emperor Valerian in 258–260. These two persecutions differed from the previous ones I discussed in that they were empire wide. The imperial government issued edicts that required residents of the entire Roman world to appear before altars to offer sacrifice not only to the gods, but also to the genius of the Roman emperor; that is, the spirit, the potential spirit of the emperor that would be sanctified to join the gods. These persecutions represented a turning point. Potentially the imperial government could always have done this; but previously I noted that persecutions were local, they were sporadic, they didn't last for a very long time; and very much it depended on the attitude of the Roman governor, or more often the local officials in the cities, the so-called decurions, who were so important in rooting out Christians and dragging them in front of the altars so they had to make sacrifice to the gods..

The reason for these empire-wide persecutions can easily be linked to what I discussed in the previous lecture: the civil wars, the invasions, and the need to win the favor of the traditional gods. This is an issue that's often raised questions among scholars, some arguing that the persecutions really were an indication that paganism was on the demise; that Christians were on the rise, they had now become noticeable, and that Roman emperors and the pagan elites felt that they had to root out the Christians. On the other hand, it could also be argued that the persecutions were a traditional revival and that the main reason that Christians were being forced to appear before the altars was not because of their numbers but because they denied the gods their due.

That's a point I've stressed time and time again in dealing with traditional cults; for instance, the goddess Artemis at Ephesus, Artemis Ephesia, her great cult statue that was well known throughout the ancient world. If you did not offer sacrifice to the gods and goddesses, they would become angry and they would then visit communal punishment. Everyone suffered. Jupiter, or Artemis Ephesia, or Zeus, or whoever the divinity was would send plague, would send thunderbolts upon the entire community, and it only took a few to opt out of the traditional sacrifices to bring down the wrath of the gods.

There really are two ways of looking at what's behind these persecutions. It's remarkable that the Roman imperial government felt the need to do this, and that suggests a very powerful religious motive behind the emperors to detect Christians. Some have suggested that they'd use the tax registers in order to find out who was a Christian and who was a pagan, but we're not sure of that because imperial officials didn't designate people by their religious affiliation until the 4th century—that is, until the time that Christian emperors ruled—when it was important to designate Christians and pagans because Christians had certain civil advantages over the pagan taxpayers.

On the other hand, it's more likely that the persecutions again depended on local initiative; that is, decurions, the local elites, the leading members of a city had some sense of who were Christians, who were not showing up at the sacrifices. In addition, we're told by Eusebius, who wrote the history of the Christian church, that on various occasions, especially in cities in Asia Minor, Jews helped point out who the Christians were. There are cases where Jews actually helped pagans in finding out who was a Christian and who was a Jew and bringing it to the attention of the local officials, who then brought it to the attention of the governor. Again, that meant that so much of this empire-wide persecution really did depend on local initiative, even though the emperor had passed an edict. This is what we know about a great deal of the administration of the Roman world; that is, imperial rule very much dependent on co-opting the local ruling elites and their cooperation. Even with the empire-wide persecutions of Trajan Decius, the scope and extent of this persecution is still difficult to document.

For the Christians, however, it was frightening. For the first time, the imperial government had interfered directly in the lives of its citizens on a matter that didn't involve tax collection. As I always say, the emperors of Rome, their main interest was, "Pay your taxes and don't revolt and we'll provide the protection." For the first time, the imperial government wanted all of its citizens to indicate by the act of sacrifice to the gods and to the spirit of the Roman emperor that they were loyal citizens and that they were behind the ancient ancestral gods who were the protectors and essential in the battle against barbarian invaders, usurpers, and rebellious legions.

We do have from Egypt a number of certificates—the Latin word is *libellus* or *libelli*; it means a little booklet, in effect—written on papyri that indicate individuals appeared before the magistrates and offered sacrifice. Let me read one such document just to give you a flavor of the administrative language in the Roman world, and this one comes from the city of Arsinoe in Middle Egypt—that's in the Fayum district—and it's dated June 14, 250 A.D. It states the following:

> To the select commissions supervising sacrifices from Aurelia Demos, daughter of an unknown father and Helena and wife of Aurelius Irenaios, residing in the Helenian quarter [that's the Greek district of this particular city in Egypt]. I have always dutifully sacrificed to the gods, and now also in your presence, in accordance with the edict, I have made sacrifice and libation and tasted the offerings.

One of the important points, going back to the letter of Pliny I read: Not only do you sacrifice to the gods and you pour a libation—that might be some oil or it might be incense—you also partake of the sacrificial meat; the steaks, since the fat and the bones are generally what's burned to the gods.

> I request you to countersign my statement. Fare thee well. I, Aurelia Demos, have submitted this. I, Aurelius Irenaios [that's her husband], wrote for her, as she is illiterate. Aurelius Sabinus, head councilman [that is, head of the local boule, council], saw you sacrificing. Year one of the Emperor Gaius Messius Quintus Traianus Decius Pius Felix Augustus [that is, Trajan Decius].

These *libelli* were issued across the empire in enormous numbers, and in some ways functioned like the kind of receipts you received for paying your taxes. These survive in Egypt on *ostracon*, that's broken potshards, which was essentially the scrap paper of the Roman world.

It was a daunting effort to carry out this action. It began on January 1, 250 A.D. The order went out at the beginning of the year; officials went in to investigate, to interrogate; governors were given wide powers to hold tribunals and to determine who was a Christian and who wasn't, and then to deal with those who failed to sacrifice. Those who failed to sacrifice could be sent to the arena, *ad bestias*. The persecution took the Christians by surprise. Pope Fabian was arrested; he was beheaded. Numerous Christians in the Church of Rome essentially lapsed; that is, they broke down, they sacrificed to the gods. They were given certificates and let go. The same happened in the churches in North Africa. The Eastern churches in Asia Minor seemed to hold up much better. We have a number of acts of Christian martyrs. These are recorded in Eusebius's *Ecclesiastical History*. They referred to those Christians who refused to buckle under. They wouldn't sacrifice, and they became martyrs. As I mentioned, "martyr" is the Greek word for "witness"; it's a legal term. Instead of sacrificing to the emperor and to the gods, you in effect say, "I'm a witness to my faith in Jesus; I won't do this," and the term "martyr," meaning "witness," stuck as a term to designate Christians who refused to follow the imperial orders.

The persecutions lasted for about 18 months. They came to a very abrupt end in 250 A.D.—in the summer of 250 A.D.—when the emperor Trajan Decius was killed by the Goths and his successor, a man named Trebonianus Gallus, essentially issued an act of clemency (a *clementia*, *clementia temporum*; clemency of the age), a very common virtue stressed on Roman imperial coins and Roman documents. In this regard, Trebonianus Gallus was in effect saying, "I have more important matters to deal with, and the persecution had gone on long enough" and effectively the imperial government just halted the persecution as abruptly as it began it. The Christians themselves saw this as an act of God; they'd been delivered from the imperial government. Then, in 258–260, there was another persecution that raged for about two-and-a-half years under the emperor Valerian; and that, too, abruptly stopped when Valerian was captured by the Persians and, as I mentioned in the last lecture, he became the horse stool to the Shah of Iran. Many Christian authors later on wrote, "Trajan Decius, killed by Goths; Valerian captured and humiliated by the Persians; good indication you shouldn't persecute Christians," although at the time I'm sure most pagans didn't really pay much attention to that argument.

The second important point that comes out of this is, among the Christian authors, Eusebius repeats the long-known phrase that came out of the apologist Tertullian and Justin Martyr writing in the 2nd century A.D. that the blood of martyrs is the seed of the church; that is, for every Christian cut down in the arena, killed in the arena, more pagans were moved to inquire about Christianity; to investigate, "Why are these people dying for their faith?" Pagans weren't going into the arena and dying for their faith. This position, which was argued by the apologists in the early 2nd century A.D. and picked up by Eusebius, writing much later in the time of Constantine after the triumph of Christianity—the conversion of Constantine—has been a powerful argument by which scholars have investigated and judged religious change in the 3rd century: that martyrdoms and persecutions gave Christians a much wider publicity than they could've ever attained on their own. They were prohibited from missionary activities since 64; they had to go underground. It was only in the early 3rd century that Origen actually developed a coherent Christian theology and wrote in a language that pagan elites could understood, if they chose to read it. It's in the mid-3rd century, in the later 3rd century that these empire-wide persecutions were launched; and these persecutions, it could be argued, gave much more publicity and potential validity to the new faith. This position was argued brilliantly in W. H. D. Friend's *Martyrdom and Persecution of the Early Church*. I mentioned that work at the start of this course. It's often the basis by which many scholars approach the whole issue of religious change.

This issue is fundamental to understanding the whole conflict and debate between pagans and Christians. What did persecutions mean to Christians? What did persecutions mean to pagans? Those are two very different issues. Already, Christians were coming to the attention of the imperial government in various ways. There's a famous legal case involving a bishop in Antioch named Paul of Samosata. He had apparently treated the church as his private property and tried to alienate it; that is, to either sell or dispose of it. The congregation objected. The emperor Aurelian, who at the time was in the East in Syria to fight the Palmyrian army, actually was asked to adjudicate the case and he sided with the congregation, awarding the church to the fellow representing the congregation over Paul. That was an important legal precedent, later used by the emperor Constantine to legislate on bishops and the whole competence of ecclesiastical courts and the powers of bishops and cities. It's also a remarkable case of equity, and it shows that Roman emperors could, when called upon, deal with their Christian subjects as legal Romans, as Roman citizens, even though they were technically outlawed under imperial law for their religious beliefs. It gives you some sense of the difference between the social reality and the legal reality of Christians. Persecutions, even empire-wide persecutions, were violent and sporadic, just like the earlier ones.

Second important point about those persecutions vis-à-vis the Christians: To the Christians, these persecutions were seen as great tests; as testing the faith. In Eusebius's mind, the Decian persecution, the persecution of Valerian, and the later one I'll be discussing—the final one, the persecution of Dioclesian and the Tetrarchs from 303–313—all three of these empire-wide persecutions were seen as the final test that led to the conversion of Constantine, the miracle of God; that Christians had held up against these threats, and God relented and brought about the conversion of Constantine and the success of the new faith. Christians had reason to believe this, and we'll be discussing the conversion of Constantine and what that meant to both Christians and pagans. But before the conversion of Constantine, these persecutions were the most virulent, most widespread, and most persistent of all those that Christians had faced before.

On the whole, many of them had stood up quite well. For one, certain bishops refused to sacrifice. Pope Fabian at Rome, for instance: He was beheaded in late January, 250; the act was regarded as a great act of martyrdom, it became a Saints' Day. Christians remembered those martyrs who went into the arena, often naming their children after martyrs who had refused to sacrifice and died in the arena, usually horribly destroyed by animals or killed as essentially helpless victims to the thrill of the crowds. It resulted in two important aspects of Christianity in the 3rd century: One, the development of a whole set of names associated with saints, so that Christians gradually evolved their own nomenclature; and the children of Christians were being named after famous saints. You get the development of a cult of the holy dead, of martyred saints. Those martyred saints were already being venerated at the end of the 3rd century in what are known as *martyria*. Those are often little cases with the bones of saints or some fragments of the saint that was collected at the time of their martyrdom. Eventually, in the 4th and 5th

centuries when we get to the Christian empire, you'll actually have churches being built to remember these saints.

One of the greatest beneficiaries of this change was, again, the bishops. The bishops, I mentioned earlier, were essential in the 2nd and early 3rd centuries A.D. in creating the organization of the apostolic churches; that is, the churches that go back to Paul and Peter and the original apostles. They were also important in defining canon and collecting documents; and, increasingly, making Christianity an independent religious organization based on that monarchical bishop in a church. Bishops who refused to sacrifice, who held up against the persecutions, increased not only their own fame but also the fame and the authority of the institution of the bishop; or, as we would like to call them, Episcopal institutions. It's in the 3rd century that bishops in Italy, in North Africa, in the cities of Asia Minor in Syria begin to acquire the kind of reputation that we'd associate with the bishops of, say, the Middle Ages.

This was already true in the 2nd century A.D., and I'd like to read a very short excerpt from Eusebius talking about the martyrdom of the bishop Polycarp I talked about before. He was martyred in the city of Smyrna, today Izmir, in western Turkey on the shores of the Aegean. He was martyred in a local persecution. But the way Eusebius talks about the impact of that martyrdom is just as relevant to those bishops who suffered martyrdom in the 3rd century during the great persecutions. Eusebius goes in great detail, in excruciating detail, how the officials of the city of Smyrna order a great pyre; a funeral pyre, in effect. They're going to burn Polycarp; they want to nail him to it. They find they don't have enough nails so they tie him to it. Then Polycarp offered up a prayer, very much in the vein of Christ on the cross. Then, the fire was lit to burn Polycarp alive, and this is what Eusebius reports. Eusebius was apparently reporting from an eyewitness account of Christians who actually saw this martyrdom.

> When he [that is, Polycarp] offered up the Amen and completed his prayer, the men in charge lit the fire and a great flame shot up [that would be wood that has lots of olive oil on it in order for it to ignite]. Then we saw a marvelous sight. We, who are privileged to see it and were spared to tell others what happened, the fire took the shape of a vaulted room like a ship sail filled with wind and it

made a wall around the martyr's body, which was in the middle not like burning flesh but like gold and silver refined in the furnace. Indeed, we were conscious of the wonderful fragrance like a breath of frankincense or some other costly spice. At last, seeing that the body could not be consumed by the fire, the lawless people [by which Eusebius means the pagans] summoned a *confector* [that's an executioner] to come forward and drive home his sword. When he did so, there came out a stream of blood that quenched the fire so the whole crowd was astonished at the difference between the unbelievers and the elect. To the elected belong this man, Polycarp, the most wonderful, apostolic, and prophetic teacher of our time, the bishop of the Catholic Church in Smyrna. For every word that he uttered was and shall be fulfilled.

That's a powerful description based on an eyewitness account of what those martyrdoms of bishops meant. To Christians in the great empire-wide persecutions, that was virtually going to an apocalypse itself. The great persecutions of the 3rd century accounted for the popularity of Revelation and its inclusion in the New Testament. To sectarians like the Montanists, a persecution in the arena was virtually a mini-apocalypse, they thought it would be the end of days. To many other Christians who did sacrifice, who broke down, sometimes seeing those few brave Christians ready to march off to the arena, they became voluntary martyrs is the term; that is, they declared, "We are Christians, too; we'll join our brethren, our sisters, in the arena." That was a powerful way of the Christians defining themselves as the new race, the third race, as the new Israel; and the martyrdoms and persecutions were absolutely essential in Christian self-definition. The martyrs emerged as the new heroes.

On the other hand, many of the church fathers were often a little concerned about what martyrdom meant. You weren't supposed to offer yourself up for martyrdom like a suicide victim. You'd try to escape detection; and if you couldn't and they caught you and they brought you in front of the tribunal, then you had no choice but to declare your Christianity and to suffer martyrdom. There's a famous Council of Elvira in Spain in 300 A.D. in which the bishops agreed if you go up to a pagan festival with a cult statue and spit on it and they kill you, that's not martyrdom, that's stupidity; that's a result of the sin of pride. Martyrdom was very, very carefully defined by the Christian church fathers as an act of bravery and courage when there's no other option.

In addition, there were many Christians who did lapse and did sacrifice, and that brought on issues later on: Should they be re-baptized? Had they renounced their faith? They had to be brought back in the church; or was just confession significant? This division between rigorists and people with a broader notion of what the sin of sacrifice represented often split churches after the great persecutions and the Christians had to resolve this issue. It became a major, major issue at the opening of the 4th century when the emperor Constantine converted; the North African church was actually split on that matter. On the whole, the persecutions and martyrdoms unquestionably were of great importance for the definition of the Christian communities.

On the other hand, did it lead to large numbers of pagans being impressed by this act of martyrdom to at least find out about Christianity and then convert? As I mentioned in the last lecture, we have no statistical evidence for any kind of major surge in Christian numbers during the 3rd century crisis, the same period that saw these great persecutions. It's really an act of faith to argue that there were a large number of pagans who were stirred to investigate Christianity, and that in the generation before Constantine the great persecutions, in effect, had backfired on the imperial government and you had large numbers of pagans seeking out Christianity as a possible religion.

That view—which, again, cannot be sustained statistically; we have no pagan evidence to that effect—has problems when we compare much of what I talked about in the last lecture on the conservative religious appeals, the expectation that gods give victory to the emperors, the great battle miracles, the iconography of imperial arts and coins; but there's another important issue that's been raised by the persecutions, and that's the question I asked earlier: What did these persecutions, what did these martyrdoms, mean to pagans? Until very recently, it was simply assumed that dying in the arena was a noble act; pagans would have to be impressed. Absolutely, he really is one of the brilliant scholars of his generation—unfortunately, he died prematurely—Keith Hopkins, a great social historian, one of the great social historians of the past generation, wrote a seminal article that is known as "Murderous Games" in a collection of essays. That article really has elucidated the importance of gladiatorial games and animal combats in Roman society. It also casts a great deal of doubt, in my opinion, on claims that martyrdom converted any significant number of pagans.

Romans expected to see bloody spectacles. In fact, the largest building in a Roman city was an amphitheater—that is, an arena—built to house gladiatorial combats and animal combats; men pitted against animals, or various types of slaves, outcasts, and victims to fight each other. These games go back to funerary rites that the Romans had learned from their Etruscan neighbors in the period of the middle and late Roman republic from 264–30 B.C. when the Romans conquered the Mediterranean world. Gladiatorial games were put on with ever-greater spectacles; larger and more elaborate combats. They became a way of the Roman upper classes showing their patronage and power. With the emperor Augustus, the emperors tended to monopolize these games. They restricted the number of games the provincial elites could give, the cost and the outlay; and increasingly, provincial cities across the Roman world either built amphitheaters—as they did in the Western provinces—or in the Greek provinces, they modified Greek theaters so that animal combats and gladiatorial games could take place. For instance, in a very small Greek city such as Priene in Asia Minor near Miletus, which is essentially a perfect city of the 4th century B.C., you can see in the theater the holes where poles were put in and nets set up so you could have an animal combat in the orchestra area and more or less protect the spectators.

"The Murderous Games" were a vicarious psychological experience. It reaffirmed that the Romans were masters of the world. Roman authors repeatedly noted—Pliny the Younger says this—that the gladiatorial games "inspired a glory in wounds and a contempt for death since the love of praise and desire for victory could even be seen in the bodies of slaves and criminals." The Romans appreciated blood and gore. It was also a message: Don't get defeated and don't oppose the Roman order, or you end up in the arena being destroyed. In this type of psychological situation, where the Romans expected to see vast outlays for the destruction of men and animals, one questions whether the execution of 20 or 30 Christian martyrs as an intermission had much of an impact at all. The few authors who write about it such as Galen, the physician of Pergamon in the 2nd century A.D., he just is amazed that Christians would allow their wives and children to endure this.

The scale of gladiatorial games and animal combats are staggering. The emperor Trajan, to celebrate the Deician victories—the conquest of Dacia; that is Romania—had something like 120 days of continual celebration, and this was held in the year 109–110 A.D.; it was over 120 days for thanksgiving: 11,000 beasts and 10,000 pairs of gladiators were slain in the Flavian Amphitheater (the Coliseum) to the entertainment of the spectators. Furthermore, at gladiatorial games all sorts of certificates were handed out for free goodies, clothes, food, etc. Above all, certain emperors—particularly emperors of the more demented variety—loved to use the gladiatorial games as a way of indicating that they had control over the Roman order. Romans were seated in the arena based on their ranks: senators, equestrians had the privileged seats; the urban plebeians, the mob, lesser seats. The emperor Commodus, who performed in the arena as the god Hercules, actually reenacted the labors of Hercules. One of them was cutting off the head of an ostrich and then brandishing it towards the senators with a dagger saying gleefully, "You see, I can do this; and you better not cross me senators, I can do that to you as well." The lesson was learned by all the Romans: The arena wasn't only just a bloody spectacle but an affirmation of the Roman imperial order, and those who were put into the arena were criminals, were outcasts sometimes forced to play the role of hideous reenactments of mythological spectacles; and it's very unclear to me whether any of these combats and gladiatorial games inclined pagans to think that the execution of some Christians in the arena was something special. I think not. The few indications we have from the pagan sources is they really weren't impressed.

The result is that the persecutions and the destruction in the arena had a powerful impact on the Christian community; but to the Romans, it represented a traditional Roman attitude that married belief in the gods and patriotism to Rome and invoked both against invaders and outcasts, and any of those who were seen outside the Roman order. If the Christians were to make headway, they had to no longer go into the arena, but demonstrate that they were Romans, too.

The Spirit of Late Paganism
Lecture 14

In many ways, the middle Platonic philosopher Plotinus can be seen as the pagan equivalent to his Christian contemporary, the theologian Origen. Plotinus had a mystical, henotheistic view of the *to hen*, or the One, from whom all creation descended in a Great Chain of Being, a vision that would affect Christian theologians as well. Meanwhile, on the borders of the Roman and Persian empires, the new faith of Manichaeism was rising—neither Roman nor Persian, Christian nor pagan, but a true world religion in many senses of the phrase.

The Everyday Pagan

- The majority of the residents of the Roman world during the political and military crisis, as well as the persecutions, of the 3rd century were still traditional pagans. To understand their religious attitudes, we need to look at three related but distinct issues.

  o What was happening to public pagan worship in the 3rd century?

  o What were the philosophical trends of the 3rd century?

  o How did the new faith of Manichaeism affect pagans and Christians in the empire?

- The 3rd century period is a dark period for historians because of the paucity of contemporary narrative sources. We have only the *Scriptores historiae augustae*, written at the end of the 4th century, and the Byzantine *Epitomes*, are abridgments of earlier histories created seven centuries later for Byzantine aristocrats.

- What we do have are a rising number of civic and imperial coins that provide iconography about the gods. We have a large number of inscriptions, at least to the mid-to-late 3rd century. We have archaeology, and we have enough literary sources to be able to piece together a sense of what happened to pagan worship.

- After 235, it certainly became more and more expensive to put on pagan festivals and worship. Many cities also suffered destruction at the hands of barbarians or the Persian army. Those cities that did escape destruction had to remodel themselves, even far from the frontier, constructing new walls and abandoning areas far from the city center.

What Is Civic Honor?

- More important are changes in social attitudes in the Roman world. Peter Brown expressed these as a change in the definition of honor. In the early Roman world, honor was a matter of patriotism and piety to one's city, putting on festivals and games, holding local offices and constructing civic buildings at one's own expense.

- Starting in the early 4th century, honor becomes a matter of serving the emperor by making donations and staging public and social activities that would lead to promotion within the imperial bureaucracy or army, in turn leading to privileges and exemptions from taxation for you and your family.

- That shift in honor explains, in part, some of the shifts going on in public worship. The civic elites needed assistance from the imperial government in the form of patronage and tax relief to afford these activities. Diocletian and his colleagues, as part of their reforms, supported the civic elites in restoring the cults and the cities to the way they had been before the wars.

- On the other hand, more and more of the city elite were looking at imperial service as a better option than civic service. This became a major source of tension in the 4th and 5th centuries with implications for both the pagan cults and the emerging Christian church.

The Life of Plotinus

- The philosopher **Plotinus** was one of the intellectual giants of the 3rd century. An Alexandrian born into a Greco-Egyptian family, he was very much a product of the Greek educational system. He trained with some of the city's great thinkers, including Ammonius Saccas, who may also have trained Origen.

- Plotinus was a devotee of middle Platonic text, particularly Alexander of Aphrodisias, who had reinterpreted the realities of Plato's *Timaeus*.

- Plotinus, according to the biography penned by his student **Porphyry of Tyre**, joined Gordian III in his expedition to India, where he planned to study the wisdom of the Buddhist monks and Hindu Brahmins. However, the expedition failed, and he was forced to return to Rome.

- There, he came to the attention of the emperor Gallienus, who gave him a villa in Campania, where the ruling class would visit and listen to his lectures. Plotinus popularized certain doctrines of Plato but did not write a synthetic account of his ideas; that was put together by his student Porphyry and is known as the ***Enneads***, or the *Nine Books*.

Plotinus's Godhead

- Plotinus, at the apex of more than 500 years of Platonic thought, presented a mystical, **henotheistic** vision of the divine world. He referred to glimpsing "the *to hen*, **the One**, the ultimate godhead," a single divine power manifesting itself in many ways, including the traditional gods of the Greco-Roman world.

- Plotinus godhead is an Aristotelian god of thinking on thinking. It is pure reason and rational thought detached from the material world. That intellect, which is inherently good, orders the world around it and is so full of existence that it must bubble over in **emanations**, and therefore you have an act of creation.

- The *to hen* almost unwittingly creates the world mind, which creates the world soul, which creates souls, which then create the material world and matter. A Great Chain of Being is oriented around this world soul, and the emanation scheme settles the question in Plato: How did creation take place?

- Human souls have a divine element; they are capable of rising and merging their individual souls into the godhead. Once you achieve knowledge, you are able to extinguish the individuality of your soul into the world soul. If you fail to do so, you are reincarnated and have another opportunity.

Plotinus's Legacy

- The henotheistic vision of Plotinus gains a great deal of popularity, particularly in eastern intellectual circles, and accommodated the traditional rites and gods of the Roman world. Julian the Apostate understood Plotinus's doctrines very well and would put it this way: There are many paths to the one. All are valid.

- Christians did not like Plotinus's Platonism. Origen saw it as dividing up the godhead, imposing necessity on God, and therefore limiting God. On the other hand, Origen probably liked Plotinus's eternal cycle of creations and reincarnations.

- Porphyry not only collected Plotinus's lectures; he also wrote an incisive criticism of Christian beliefs on philosophical grounds, not the crude arguments of earlier pagan critics. Porphyry's criticism is almost a compliment to Origen's work; pagan intellectuals had to take Christianity a lot more seriously.

- **Iamblichus of Chalcis** expanded on Plotinus by defining **theurgy**, an intellectual approach to the rites and traditions of the ancient gods. In *On the Mysteries* (*De mysteriis*), he wrote that having a higher knowledge of what those traditional rites and pagan worship mean was a way to achieve union with the *to hen*. Theurgy, then, becomes in some ways almost a pagan equivalent to a doctrine of grace.

- These developments were also the intellectual underpinnings of Emperor Julian II's unsuccessful attempt to reverse Constantine's conversion of the empire to Christianity and restore the pagan cults.

Mani and Manichaeism

- The religious leader **Mani** was born in a Jewish-Christian sectarian community in what we would today call Iraq. Until recently, the **Manicheans** were regarded as Christian heretics. But an important papyrus fragment from the 5th century containing a biography of Mani was recently discovered, providing new and enlightening information about the man and his followers.

- Mani was actually an inspired prophet who established a new religion that had many similarities to Christianity but also drew on the allegory and myth of the Gnostic traditions and various religions of the Near East. He received sacred books and inspiration from the son of man and the Holy Spirit, and he claimed that he was the twin brother of Jesus.

- The surviving Manichaean text are in a bewildering array of languages. They traveled from the Atlantic to China along the Silk Road. Therefore, this was a world religion from the start, and no one had as much success as the Manichaeans in carrying out missionary activities since the time of St. Paul.

- Mani taught a fundamentally dualist vision of the world. In many ways, he seems to fall into the Gnostic tradition where the material and spiritual world are in dichotomy. But Christian authors often overplay that feature. Fundamentally, Mani was an optimist who believed humans contained a spark of light and could achieve divinization with full knowledge.

- Where Mani differs from Plotinus and Origen is that he was neither pagan nor Christian. He offered an alternate vision drawing on both traditions plus traditions farther East. There are reports that he traveled to Central Asia and Northern India, and in some ways, Manichaeism in its organization is very similar to contemporary Buddhism, with a wide body of believers and an ascetic missionary monastic elect.

- Manichaeism was seen as a challenge by both pagans and Christians. Diocletian ordered the persecution of Manichaeans because he thought they were Persians loyal to the Shah. Meanwhile, the Shah was persecuting them as well.

- For the Christians, the Manichaeans posed a real challenge. They had a remarkably successful missionary tradition and won converts from the Atlantic to the borders of the Chinese Empire. To counter Manichaeism, they had to redouble their efforts at turning themselves into a Roman religion.

Important Terms

emanation: One generation of the descending levels of reality from the One in the Great Chain of Being posited by Plotinus (205–270).

Enneads: The writings of Plotinus (205–270) as collected and edited by Porphyry.

henotheism: The religious outlook regarding traditional pagan gods as aspects of a single transcendent godhead. This was the religious vision of the Neoplatonic philosopher Plotinus and the emperor Julian II.

Manichaean: A follower of the dualist faith of the prophet Mani (216–276), who taught a universal monotheism often dismissed by Christian writers as a heresy.

One, the: In Greek, *"to hen"*; term used by Plotinus (205–270) to define the ultimate, infinite divine reality that is the source of all creation by emanation.

theurgy: The esoteric practices of the enlightened Neoplatonist who understands how traditional rites have a deeper meaning to achieve mystical union with the One.

Names to Know

Iamblichus of Chalcis (c. 250–325 A.D.): Neoplatonist theurgist from Syria who studied with Porphyry at Rome. Iamblichus composed *De mysteriis* (*On the Mysteries*), an exposition of theurgy and the efficacy of sacrifice that influenced Julian and Proclus. He also composed three treatises on mathematics and a tract on the Pythagorean life.

Mani (216–276): Prophet and founder of the dualist monotheistic religion Manichaeism. Born into a community of Elcesaites, an ascetic sect of Judaizing Christians, near Ctesiphon in Babylonia, between 218 and 228, Mani experienced mystical visions, and in 240–242 he traveled to India, where he might have conversed with Buddhist monks. He returned to Persia and gained favor at the court of Shāpūr I. His teaching, however, offended Kartir and the strict Zoroastrians, who likely contrived his arrest and crucifixion by Shah Bahrām I in 276. Mani's writings, originally written in Syriac, have survived in translations.

Plotinus (205–270): Born at Lycopolis, Egypt. Plotinus gained the favor of Emperor Gallienus. He defined Neplatonism, and his disciple Porphyry compiled Plotinus's teachings into the *Enneads*. Plotinus's vision of the Great Chain of Being and synthesis of Platonic thought provided the intellectual basis for the revival of the pagan cults by Emperor Julian (360–363).

Porphyry of Tyre (c. 232–304): Greek Neoplatonic philosopher who wrote a life of his mentor, the philosopher Plotinus, a work *Against the Christians* (15 books), and a historical chronicle from the fall of Troy to about A.D. 270.

Suggested Reading

Brown, *Body and Society in Late Antiquity*.

Cox, *Biography in Late Antiquity*.

Dodds, *Pagan and Christian in the Age of Anxiety*.

Fowden, *Empire to Commonwealth*.

Frend, *Martyrdom and Persecution in the Early Church*.

Hadot, *Plotinus or the Simplicity of Vision*.

Iamblichus of Chalcis, *De mysteriis*.

Lieu, *Manichaeism in the Later Roman Empire Medieval China*.

MacMullen, *Paganism in the Roman Empire*.

Plotinus, *The Enneads*.

Potter, *The Roman Empire at Bay*.

Shaw, *Theurgy and the Soul*.

Wallis, *Neoplatonism*.

Questions to Consider

1. What are the sources for pagan religious experiences in the 3rd century? How has the paucity of sources led to scholarly misunderstanding? Why is it misleading to take a lack of sources for a lack of belief?

2. What would explain the continuity of cults and sanctuaries during the crisis of the 3rd century? How would imperial victories after 268 have altered perceptions?

3. How did the henotheism of Plotinus and Iamblichus of Chalcis create a new moral and intellectual explanation of the cults? How satisfying were their visions of the divine? How did Porphyry alter the views of pagan intellectuals towards Christianity?

4. How did Manichaeism pose a challenge to both pagans and Christians? What accounted for the remarkable success of Manichaean missionaries?

The Spirit of Late Paganism
Lecture 14—Transcript

In this lecture, I plan to look at what I call the spirit of late paganism. In the last two lectures, we dealt with the military and political crisis that led to changes in the Roman world, the usual interpretations about it, its impact on Christianity and paganism; also, the great persecutions that flowed out of that crisis or in response to that crisis. What I want to do in this lecture is look at what else happened in the spiritual life of the majority of residents of the Roman world at the time of this crisis, this political and military crisis, and the great persecutions.

The majority of the Roman Empire was still pagan. All scholars agree on that whether they believe there's a rising number of Christians or not. This requires us to look at three issues that are somewhat related but distinct. First, I want to deal in this lecture with what happens to pagan worship, to the public worship I've described in the previous lectures, in the 3rd century. Second, I want to then turn and look at certain intellectual trends among pagan philosophers, particularly the career and writing of Plotinus, who lived from 205–278 A.D. and is roughly a contemporary with the Christian theologian Origen. He really shares with Origen the title of great intellectual of the 3rd century. Finally, I want to turn and look at Mani and what's known as Manichaeism—that is, the faith of the Manichees—a faith that emerged in the Fertile Crescent (Mesopotamia) on the Persian side of the border. Manichaeism, in a peculiar way, represented an independent religion. It was not a Christian heresy, as previously believed—that's now been proved by new texts that have come to light—and it offered a challenge both to pagans and to Christians, which was very important in rethinking and reshaping the beliefs of both pagans and Christians in the 4th and 5th centuries; that is, in the lectures that are to come with the recovery of the Roman Empire under Diocletian, and then the conversion of the Roman Empire to Christianity with the emperors of the 4th and 5th centuries.

Let's look at the first topic: What about pagan religious life in the cities and the countryside of the Roman world between, say, 235 and 305 A.D.? As I've mentioned in the previous lectures, the 3rd century period is a really dark period for us because of the paucity of sources. We don't have narrative accounts; we have very insufficient sources. The lives of the so-called SHA, the Scriptores Historiae Augustae; probably an author masquerading under six names writing at the end of the 4th century A.D. Byzantine epitomes; these are narrative accounts that are abridgments of earlier histories. Think of it as the *Reader's Digest* to Roman history, written seven centuries later for Byzantine aristocrats who want a couple of pithy phrases from Roman history. We don't have the great historical accounts of the 1st and 2nd centuries A.D. by authors such as Tacitus, or the Greek authors Cassius Dio and Herodian, or the account of Ammianus Marcellinus we'll be talking about in the 4th century. The 3rd century, we just don't have the literary record.

In addition, we do have a rising number of civic and imperial coins that provide us iconography about the gods. We have a large number of inscriptions, at least to the middle to late 3rd century, and then inscriptions become costly and they drop off for a couple of decades and resume again in the opening of the 4th century under the so-called Tetrarchs; that is, Diocletian and his colleagues from 285–305. We do have archaeology, and we have enough literary sources that aren't historical that we're able to piece together some sort of sense of what happened to pagan worship. It's undeniable that costs soared. After 235 A.D., it just became more expensive to put on pagan festivals and worship. It's also true that many cities suffered destruction at the hands of barbarians or the Persian army. Those cities that did escape destruction had to remodel themselves. For instance, the city of Athens was attacked by an East Germanic people known as the Herulians in 267. They were driven off, but the city was drastically reduced in size; the wall circuits were shortened; large parts of the Classical city were abandoned.

This happened in scores of cities across the Roman world. Even in cities that were far from the frontier—for instance, in Western Asia Minor or North Africa, or cities in Gaul—very often new walls were constructed very hurriedly. They were made out of *spolia*; that is, the debris of earlier buildings. You can see that at cities such as Side or Hierapolis, today Pamukkale, in Turkey. In some instances, public areas were given up, sometimes theaters were abandoned because they were outside the city; you see that very clearly at the city of Perga in Asia Minor. In Gaul, there's a steady move from the Roman cities built on the plains to the old Celtic hill forts, the *oppida*, the citadels, because they were better fortified. You have a phenomenon in a number of the Western provinces in Britain, the Rhineland, and Gaul, and in some of the provinces of the Danube regions, where you have Roman settlement of the 1st and 2nd century A.D. on the main highways and then the settlements move up to the high points, that is to the pre-Roman sites, in the 3rd and 4th centuries. There is a change in the physical look of cities, and that was brought about by the civil wars and invasion.

More important are also changes in social attitudes in the Roman world. Peter Brown—really, he's a genius in cultural and religious history of the late Roman world; that is, from about 150–750 A.D.—Peter Brown once expressed the social change of the Roman world as a change in the definition of honor. In the early Roman world, honor came by patriotism and piety to one's city. That is, you put on festivals and games. You held the local offices at your own expense. You put up all those marvelous buildings that tour groups trek out to see in Asia Minor, Italy, Greece, Spain, and Africa today. Stunning cities: Leptis Magna, Ephesus, the Roman monuments of Southern France today; any of a number of cities like Benevento in Italy, which have marvelous public buildings of the high empire. They're also matched with large numbers of inscriptions, benefactions, and of donations by the elites. They reveal a civic government and a civic worship that depended upon those elites. In some cities, for instance the city of Stratonicea, which is in southwestern Turkey today, there are two important shrines: one to Zeus Panamarus, the other to Hecate at Lagina. There's an unbroken record of inscriptions running through the 1st, 2nd and 3rd, into the 4th century of votive offerings to the gods; expansion of the sanctuaries; better and more elaborate games and donations to the spectators and the visitors. In the words of Peter Brown, "It's as if the 3rd century never happened in Stratonicea." We have a number of cities that continued the traditional worship; they weren't affected by all the changes.

But many cities were; and they were affected not only by the physical remains—the building of walls, the giving up of certain areas, the retrenchment that we can document so well in the archaeology—but in the social change that Peter Brown spoke of. In this case, honor, starting in the early 4th century, starting at the time of Diocletian—who came to the throne in 284; retired, abdicated in 305; and represents an important shift in the whole procession of Imperial government—honor comes by serving the emperor; by coming to the emperor's attention; by making donations and staging public and social activities that draw your attention to the imperial figures and then leads to your promotion within the imperial bureaucracy and army, and with that exemptions and privileges from taxation; you don't suffer corporal punishment; a whole number of advantages that come to you and your family.

That shift in honor explains, in part, some of the shifts going on in public worship: Cities had been hit hard by the 3rd century. Many of them survived; Stratonicea is one, Aphrodisias is another one. Around 250 A.D., the government of Aphrodisias, its council and assembly, decided to inscribe on the north *parodos* wall of the theater 16 select documents that proclaimed the importance of their cult and the unique role that Aphridisias played in the Roman world and her relationship to Rome. These were set up at the height of the 3rd century crisis as a way of making a special statement: Things in Aphrodisias are still the way they've always been, whatever the difficulties on the imperial frontiers. You have a number of cities that project those images, but on the whole, the festivals, the games; they're more costly, they're now more closely linked to the Roman emperor. The civic elites did need assistance from the imperial government in the form of patronage, in the form of tax reliefs, and in the form of support. Diocletian and his colleagues, the three emperors who ruled with him who were known as the Tetrarchs (the four rulers)—the Tetrarchy, the rule of four; I'll be explaining in an upcoming lecture—they understood this, and when they re-imposed order and prosperity in the Roman world, one of the major actions was to support the civic elites in restoring the cults and the cities to the way they had always been. We have a number of sanctuaries that show that.

On the other hand, there was this change in attitude where more and more of the elites of the cities were looking at imperial service as a better option than civic service, and this became a major conflict in the 4th and 5th centuries, a tension between cities and imperial government that had major implications for both the pagan cults and also the emerging Christian church that was established by the emperor Constantine. That's one important change in the world of late paganism.

The second change I want to talk about are the intellectual changes going on, and these intellectual changes concern one of the great giants of the 3rd century, the philosopher Plotinus. As I mentioned, he came from Roman Egypt, the city of Lycopolis. He was born into a Greco-Egyptian family, so Greek would have been his language; he was not an Egyptian by language. He was very much a product of the Greek educational system and of the Hellenic culture in Alexandria. He trained at Alexandria with some of the great thinkers. One of them was a thinker called Ammonius Saccas, a noted philosopher of the mid-3rd century, and according to one source, a philosopher who actually trained Origen. There was a later tradition that was circulated that Origen and Plotinus actually knew each other; they had been to lectures with Ammonius; and, again, that whole interplay of Christians and pagans at Alexandria is well caught, captured, in that recent film *Agora*, or *Agora*. It's centered on the late 4th, early 5th centuries A.D., but it's a very good recreation of the type of reading circles you had.

Plotinus was a devotee of Middle Platonic text. He'd read particularly the works of a fellow named Alexander of Aphrodisias, and Alexander wrote a number of important commentaries on Middle Platonic texts reinterpreting the realities of Plato's *Timaeus*; that is, the demiurge (the creator God); the ideas or forms (that is, the eternal patterns of all objects in the universe); and the receptacle (the space that it fits into). These Middle Platonists had turned those three realities into the ultimate godhead, often still using the term "demiurge" for the creator God; for the World Mind, nous; for rational thought, the logos, the nous; and the World Soul. These are variations on that Platonic scheme in the *Timaeus*.

Plotinus, according to the life penned by his student Porphyry writing at the end of the 3rd century, joined the expedition of Gordian III, the boy emperor who went off to fight the Persians and was lynched by mutinous soldiers; actually, lynched on February 25, 244 A.D.—I remember the date because it's the date of my sister's birthday, or more accurately my sister was born on the day that Gordian III got lynched—but in any case, by his Pretorian prefect, and the idea that Plotinus had is he would go with Gordian all the way to India and study the wisdom of the Buddhist monks and the Hindu Brahmins, who were all called gymnosophists; that is, the naked thinkers.

It's a catch-all phrase for the thinkers of India. He never made it, of course, because the expedition failed and returned to Rome.

He came to the attention of the emperor Gallienus, who ruled at the middle of the 3rd century from 253–268, and Gallienus gave him a villa in Campania where all sorts of senators, the ex-Roman emperors, Queen Zenobia; everyone defeated by the emperor, really and actually, ended up as members listening to the lectures of Plotinus. Plotinus popularized certain doctrines of Plato, and he gave lectures. He didn't write a synthetic account; that was put together by his student Porphyry, Porphyry of Tyre, and that collection is known as the *Enneads*, *The Nine Books*, and in it, Porphyry ordered the lectures and mystical visions that Plotinus had.

Plotinus represented the summation of over 500 years of Platonic thought and presented a beautiful, mystical vision of what the divine world was. Plotinus himself was a mystic. At least twice he had experiences in which he described it as, "Logic leaped over itself and I flew the alone to the alone." That is, "For a brief moment I glimpsed the *to hen*, the One, the ultimate godhead." It's a beautiful henotheistic vision; that is, there's a single divine power manifesting itself in many ways, including the traditional gods of the Greco-Roman world.

In Plotinus's scheme, the ultimate godhead—*to hen*, the one; "the one and only" in Greek that, in a sense, represents infinity, and actually Plotinus's *to hen* is translated in Latin as *nihilo*, meaning "infinity" rather than "zero." The *to hen* is the ultimate godhead; it's an Aristotelian god of thinking on thinking. It's pure reason and rational thought; it's detached from the material world. I always like to think of the Plotinian God as essentially a computer; eternal output going into new input; HAL-9000 series out of *2001: A Space Odyssey*. It's an eternal computer operating steadily. But as a result of that intellect, which was inherently good—being a Platonist, reason is good—the *to hen* orders the World around it, and the *to hen* is so full of existence that it must bubble over in emanations, and therefore you have an act of creation.

The *to hen* almost unwittingly creates World Mind, which creates World Soul, which creates Souls, which then create the Material World and then Matter. There's a great chain of being that's oriented around this World

Soul, and the emanation scheme settles the question in Plato: How did this whole creation take place? Plato never really explains that in the *Timaeus*; it's left open-ended. According to Plotinus, it's by necessity, by the virtue of his fullness of being, the World so bubbles over and creates this beautiful great chain of Being. As you go down the great chain of Being, there's still always a divine spark in it. Humans with souls have that divine element; they're capable of rising and joining the *to hen* and merging their individual soul into the ultimate godhead. That ultimate godhead, as he says, the flight of the alone to the alone—that is, understanding that one's individual soul is just but a fragment of the ultimate soul, the *to hen*—once you achieve that gnosis or knowledge, you're able to extinguish the individuality of your soul into the World Soul. If you fail to do so, no problem; you'll simply be reincarnated and you'll have another opportunity.

The henotheistic vision of Plotinus—which gains a great deal of popularity, particularly in the Eastern intellectual circles of the Roman world who were Greek speakers—this vision accommodated the traditional rites and gods of the Roman world. The *to hen* was manifested in many ways. A common phrase used in the 4th century, particularly by the emperor Julian the Apostate, who understood Plotinus's doctrines very well, would put it this way: There are many paths to the one. There are many rites; there are many prayers and traditions. All are valid. All can lead you to the one. All eventually will lead back to the ultimate godhead. When the British, particularly in the 18th century under the administration of Warren Hastings, the first Governor General of India (who in many ways created India), when he opened up, or ordered, the writing down of the Hindu doctrines—you know, we have Christians, Muslims; who are these Hindus?—and they began to study Sanskrit, particularly Jones, the Sanskrit linguist, they read the Hindu texts, the Sanskrit texts, and they were struck by some of the similarities between Hindu thought and the vision as proposed by Plotinus. Actually, one of the finest translations of Plotinus is done by McKenna, an Anglo-Irish fellow who had been in India and understood the Hindu traditions as well as Plotinus, and that translation is still used today.

What Plotinus offered was this beautiful vision of emanations and schemes, but the Christians didn't like it. Origen saw it as dividing up the godhead; as imposing necessity on God and therefore limiting God. Origen was a

Christian; God must be transcendent. That's one aspect of his Christianity he took from the Hebrew text. On the other hand, Origen probably really liked the eternal cycle of creations and reincarnations; that's not too far away with some of his visions. Plotinus, as a vision of the Platonic tradition for pagans, was very satisfying, but it's contrary to the kind of single act of creation and linear time that most Christians believed. The Plotinian traditions were never really available to the Christians to use; in fact, it sparked a lot of Christian criticism, and there are a number of critiques of Plotinus by later Christian writers.

In addition, I want to mention two other authors. Porphyry of Tyre, who lived from 234–305, collected the lectures of Plotinus and wrote *The Enneads* up so we have this coherent view. He also wrote a very incisive criticism of Christian beliefs, and he attacked it on philosophical grounds. He didn't attack it on the crude sort of arguments that you'd have among the earlier pagan critics. Porphyry's criticism is almost a compliment to Origen's work: that from now on, pagan intellectuals are going to have to take Christianity a lot more seriously.

The other figure I wish to stress is also from the same period, slightly later: Iamblichus of Chalcis. Iamblichus of Chalcis, more than any other thinker of the late 3rd, early 4th centuries—he died around 325 A.D. in the time of Constantine; he was supposed to be a student of Porphyry—and he defined something known as theurgy in his work *On The Mysteries* (De *mysteriis*). Theurgy is an intellectual approach to the rites and to the traditions of the ancient gods. I mentioned that Plotinus and his student Porphyry accepted the traditional worship and rites as lesser manifestations of the *to hen*, of The One. Iamblichus of Chalcis evolved a tradition that cloaked that Plotinian God in solar imagery that was very common in Syria; Iamblichus was apparently a hereditary priest from perhaps the city of Emesa (today Homs), which was home to a great solar cult. He also articulated a doctrine of theurgy, and that is having a higher knowledge of what those traditional rites and pagan worship mean to achieve union with the *to hen*. Theurgy, then, becomes in some ways almost a pagan equivalent to a doctrine of grace. By carrying out the sacrifices and rites, the truly initiated one will achieve union with The One and will extinguish his soul in the flight to the alone to the alone.

These developments by Plotinus, Porphyry, and Iamblichus of Chalcis were very important because they are the intellectual underpinnings of the reform program offered by the emperor Julian II between 360 and 363, the somewhat eccentric nephew of the emperor Constantine, who attempted to reverse the Constantinian Revolution and proclaimed a new faith, Hellenism; that is, a restoration of the pagan cults. Julian tried to rally the cults around the very Plotinian vision of a solar *to hen* and also the theurgic rites as proposed by Iamblichus of Chalcis.

Finally, I want to shift over and mention one other powerful thinker of this period, and that is the figure Mani from 216–276 A.D. He was born in a Jewish-Christian sectarian community in what we would today call Iraq and lower Mesopotamia, and up until recently Mani and his followers, known as the Manichees or the Manichaeans, were regarded as essentially quirky Christian heretics. But an important papyrus fragment had been discovered in Cologne. It comes from Egypt originally. It dates from the 5th century A.D. and it was translated and published by Ludwig Koenen, a brilliant papyrologist at the University of Michigan. This document is a life of Mani, and it provides a whole bunch of information that we didn't have before.

Several important points become clear. First, Mani was an inspired prophet who established, in effect, a new religion; a religion we call Manichaeism that had many similarities to Christianity, but also drew on the allegory and myth of the Gnostic traditions and the various religions of the Near East. Mani grew up in this Jewish-Christian community outside of the city of Cteisphon, which was one of the capitals of the old Parthian Empire and was still an important city under the Persian Shahs. He was seen as a prophet who had inspired visions, just like Plotinus, and he received sacred books and inspiration from the Son of Man and Holy Spirit, and he claimed that he was the twin brother of Jesus. Between the ages of 12 and 24, he had a series of heavenly experiences and encounters with his Holy Twin, Jesus, and revealed that his mission was to preach a new faith.

The texts that we have of Manichaeism—and many are much later after Mani's death in 276; he was actually crucified on orders of the Shah of Iran—the texts we have from Mani are in a bewildering array of languages; something like 20 different languages. They traveled from the Atlantic to China, across the great Silk Road of Central Asia; so they appear in languages such as Tocharian, Sogdian, Persian, Chinese, Pali (the spoken language of India); they're in Greek; they're in Latin; they're later in Coptic and Syriac (vernacular languages of the Roman East); finally, in Arabic. It was a world religion from the start; and no one had such success in carrying out missionary activities, really since the time of St. Paul.

Mani taught a fundamentally dualist vision of the world in which there's a constant fight between evil and darkness, and in many ways he seems to fall into that tradition of the Gnostic tradition where the material and physical world are in dichotomy. But Christian authors often overplay that clash and try to condemn Mani as someone who envisions the material world as inherently evil. Mani does have a series of creations; there's an active agent of demons working for the Lords of Darkness. But fundamentally, he's an optimist that humans have within them particles of that light and that higher divinity and they can attain divinization, again, with full knowledge. His texts are allegories to allow you to reach union with divine, and in this way Mani is very much in line with the traditions and ideas taught by Plotinus, and even in many ways with Origen.

Where he differs with Plotinus and Origen is he was neither pagan nor Christian. He offered an alternate vision drawing on both traditions plus traditions farther East. There are reports that he'd traveled to the cities of Central Asia, to the cities of Northern India, which were then under the control of the Kushans, a foreign dynasty who were inclined toward Buddhism. He developed an organization of hearers—those who were the elect, who were ready to achieve union with the divine—and a wider community who supported them. In some ways, Manichaeism in its organization is very similar to contemporary Buddhism in Northern India, with a wide body of believers and an ascetic missionary monastic elect.

This organization of Manichaeism was seen as a challenge by both pagans and Christians. The Roman emperor Diocletian ordered the persecution of the Manichees because he said they were Persians and they were loyal to the Shah. At the same time, the Shah was persecuting the Manichaeans, and the Manichaeans had the singular distinction of being persecuted by Roman emperors and Persian shahs at the same time, largely for the wrong reasons.

For the Christians, the Manichaeans posed a real challenge. They had a remarkably successful missionary tradition and they won converts from the Atlantic to the Indus in Central Asia to the borders of the Chinese Empire, and eventually obtained recognition as an imperial religion in China. Therefore, the Christians found that to counter Manichaeism they had to redouble their efforts at turning themselves into a Roman religion and once again finding out ways to reach to that wider pagan audience and succeed because they now had a challenge from the Manichees on one side and the pagan emperors on the other.

Imperial Recovery under the Tetrarchs
Lecture 15

Emperor Diocletian would revolutionize the Roman imperial military and bureaucracy through creating the tetrarchy, or "rule of four," wherein imperial authority was vested in two senior and two junior emperors. Gone was the fiction of emperor as first citizen; Diocletian's system made the emperors true autocrats, backed by an army loyal to the emperor alone. Traditional pagan worship was more important than ever to supporting this system, so empire-wide persecution of Christians returned; ironically, in about a quarter century, the first Christian emperor would use Diocletian's institutions to convert the empire to his new faith.

Diocletian Addresses the Succession

- Emperor **Diocletian** ruled from 284 to 305, a period called the **tetrarchy**, meaning "the rule of four." Diocletian chose to share his imperial power with three other colleagues and, remarkably, to step down and end a successful 20-year reign. This arrangement was a response to the military and political crisis of the 3rd century.

- The big weakness of the Roman imperial government was its lack of succession principle. The emperor did not have a real job description and was not a hereditary monarch in law, although he was in practice. When power was transferred from ruler to ruler—or dynasty to dynasty—the empire always hovered on the brink of civil war.

- It is remarkable that in the first 300 years of the empire, there were only two significant civil wars; however, between 235 and 284, there were five major civil wars and numerous invasions and usurpations; the average emperor's reign lasted about 18 months. This makes Diocletian's achievement nothing short of miraculous.

- Diocletian was a pragmatist and, contrary to opinions of earlier scholars, very much a conservative Roman. The tetrarchy made a virtue out of weakness: He had no sons and only one daughter, so he used marriage alliances and adoption to create, in effect, a new imperial family.

- Diocletian also recognized that no single emperor could meet all the threats on all the empire's frontiers as well as administer the Roman Empire at its current extent. Therefore, in 285, he elevated as his co-emperor, or Augustus, **Maximianus**, a fellow Balkan military man with a similar political outlook. Diocletian ruled the East while Maximianus ruled the West.

- In 293, Diocletian and Maximianus extended the college of rulers by creating two junior emperors, or Caesars, also from Balkan military families. The Caesar in the East was **Galerius**, who married Diocletian's daughter. The Caesar in the West was **Constantius I Chlorus**. He had a wife, Helena, and a son, Constantine; he divorced Helena and married a stepdaughter of Maximianus, so that the two Caesars were linked by marriage to the Augusti.

- Each emperor had a capital on the frontiers: Constantius at Trier, near the Rhine; Maximianus resided at Milan, the nexus of all military routes for the defense of the upper Danube; Diocletian took up residence at Nicomedia, in Asia Minor; and Galerius resided at Antioch. This provided an imperial presence at each of the four key frontiers.

- In part, the system operated so effectively because Diocletian was recognized as senior among the partners. It also allowed Diocletian and his colleagues to carry out a series of sweeping reforms.

The Failure of the Second Tetrarchy

- The arrangement worked until May 1, 305, when Diocletian, who was at that point ailing, decided to retire, and he prevailed on Maximianus to join him and make way for the Caesars. By this time,

Galerius had undue influence over Diocletian, and as a result the two new Caesars were essentially appointees of Galerius: **Severus II** in the West and **Maximinus II Daza**, Galerius's nephew, in the East.

- This second tetrarchy lasted a little over a year. It set aside the succession principles near and dear to the imperial army, cutting Maximianus's son **Maxentius** and Constantius's son Constantine out of the succession. When Constantius Chlorus was killed in York in 306, the Western army immediately declared Constantine Augustus of the West. In October, the Praetorian Guard—that is, the guard of the city of Rome—declared Maxentius Augustus of the West.

- Galerius would recognize neither of these men and elevated Caesar Severus II to Augustus of the West. Within 18 months of the abdication of Diocletian, the Roman Empire experienced a new wave of civil wars. These were significantly different from those waged in the earlier 3rd century. In effect, the empire broke up into as many as six competing states controlled by competing rulers.

Diocletian's Bureaucratic and Military Reforms

- In one way, the tetrarchy can be looked on as a failure, that it did not achieve permanent political stability. However, it gave Diocletian and his colleagues the opportunity to carry out significant reforms, among them building a new imperial army and bureaucracy beholden to the emperor alone.

- The tetrarchs dropped the fiction of ruling as a first magistrate. In the new army, the legions and cavalry bore dynastic names stressing their connection with Jupiter and Hercules. The army was reorganized on a new scale in which the cavalry was elevated to a premier military force.

- The old senatorial elite were now cut out of military commands; commands went to men who had moved up through the ranks, soldiers just like the emperors themselves. There would be further military changes under Constantine.

- The civil administration was vastly increased. Before Diocletian, Rome's civil service may have numbered 3,000 men; by our best count, the number of senior officials by Diocletian's time was 35,000. Provincial administration was divided into three levels, reflected in the later organization of the Christian church.

- These changes helped prevent civil wars and rebellion by powerful governors by dividing up the provinces and dividing the civil and military administration. That also meant the emperor no longer had to depend on the traditional elites of Rome; he was not challenged by the senators. The administration and army would follow him unquestioningly so long as they were paid.

- To play to their new servants, as well as to their subjects, the emperors created a whole new set of ceremonies to elevate themselves and enhance their divine aura. Ceremony focused power and created a barrier between the emperor and the traditional elite so they could not challenge the emperors.

- Furthermore, the emperors could now dispense with consent by the senatorial families; they did not have to mix with them as equals. They created their own civil bureaucrats, drawing heavily on the decurions of the cities, and they created a new officer corps, drawing very heavily on provincial soldiers and eventually on mercenary barbarians. This gave the tetrarchs a new position of power they could use to enforce their reforms.

- The whole tradition of honor changed. The route to advancement was now to serve one's emperor, not to serve one's city or traditional gods; not to show traditional patriotism and piety but instead to stage events in the arenas, hippodromes, or stadiums that would bring you to the attention of the emperor.

- The administration and army proved extremely expensive to fund. The emperors increased taxes, but to the credit of Diocletian and his colleagues, they also made a serious effort to roll back prices and carry out currency reforms.

The Politics of Paganism

- A keystone to this reform was winning the favor of the gods. Here, the tetrarchs took their cue from Augustus and the earlier emperors. They forged a new ideology in which the emperors were the favorites of the gods. Panegyrics—orations of praise—were delivered at imperial palaces.

- The iconography of the 3rd century culminated in a new image of the emperors and their association with the divine. Emperors were the equals or the comrades of gods. We see this with Diocletian and Jupiter, Maximianus and Hercules.

- The emperors' gods were not the gods of mystery cults nor irrational, nonclassical gods; they were the traditional gods of Rome, particularly those who had protected the armies: Sol Invictus, the Unconquerable Sun; Mars Propugnator, the conqueror; Jupiter Conservator, the preserver; and Hercules, the mortal who became a god.

- Increasingly, archaeology is revealing that in the late 3rd and early 4th centuries, there was a trend toward restoring many of the traditional shrines and sanctuaries across the Roman world. For example, the tetrarchs restored a number of temples in the city of Ephesus, including a temple to Hadrian, where four altars were added, each to one of the tetrarchs.

- All of this was part of a single policy to do homage to the traditional gods who had been the protectors of the Roman world. Diocletian's coins were stamped with the legend *GENIO POPULI ROMANI*, "to the divine spirit of the Roman people"—to all of its shrines, cults, and religious traditions. This seems a sharpened, focused, conservative revival, not the last gasp of dying paganism.

The Revival of Persecution

- These implications were not happy for the Christian community living under the tetrarchs. Back in 260 the persecutions had been halted by Gallienus. This changed abruptly in 303, when Diocletian issued the first of four edicts against the Christians. Officially, he was reacting to some Christians present at one of his public sacrifices causing ill omens.

- Additional edicts of persecution followed; these included confiscation of churches and Christian property, destruction of books, and prohibition of Christian services. One inscription from Arycanda, in Asia Minor, indicates while this was, again, an empire-wide persecution, it depended on the support of the local decurions, who call the emperors "saviors of every province and nation of mankind."

- The persecutions were not only legal; they were also in keeping with imperial policy of the tetrarchy—namely, that the spirit of the Roman people took precedence over all other religious values, and Christians and others who did not worship to the gods must be forced to conform.

- Persecutions would continue for the next 10 years, until 313. They halted because of a battle miracle, one in perfect keeping with the institutions, ceremonies, and legal positions forged by the tetrarchy in all ways but one: It was not a miracle delivered by the traditional gods of Rome but by the god of the Christians.

tetrarchy: Rule of four; the collective imperial rule established by Diocletian in 285, with two senior Augusti and two junior Caesars.

Constantius I Chlorus (a.k.a. **Flavius Valerius Constantius**; c. 250–306; r. 305–306): Born to an Illyrian military family, Constantius served under Probus and Diocletian. In 293, Maximianus adopted Constantius as his heir and appointed him Caesar. Constantius divorced his wife Helena, mother of Constantine I, and married Theodora, the stepdaughter of Maximianus. In 305, Constantius I succeeded as Augustus of the West. He died in 306, after conducting an expedition against the Picts.

Diocletian (245–316; r. 284–305): Roman emperor. A humble Dalmatian soldier declared emperor by the Eastern army, Diocletian ended the crisis of the 3rd century and retired from the throne in 305. His administrative, monetary, and fiscal reforms established the Dominate, or late Roman state. He created collegial rule, the so-called tetrarchy, whereby imperial power was shared by two senior emperors called Augusti and two junior emperors called Caesars. In 305, Diocletian retired from public life to his fortress palace of Spalato (modern Split, Croatia).

Galerius (a.k.a. **Gaius Galerius Valerius Maximianus**; c. 250–311; r. 305–311): Balkan officer created Caesar of the East in 293. He married Diocletian's daughter Galeria Valeria. In 305, Galerius succeeded Diocletian as Augustus of the East, but his political arrangements denied the succession to both Constantine and Maxentius (each the son of an emperor), so that civil war erupted after 306. Galerius was credited with the initiative for the Great Persecution in 303–313.

Maxentius (a.k.a. **Marcus Valerius Maxentius**; c. 278–312; r. 306–312): Son of Maximianus, Maxentius revolted at Rome and declared himself emperor after he had been denied the succession by Galerius. Maxentius controlled Italy and Africa. In 312, he was defeated and slain by Constantine at the Battle of Milvian Bridge.

Maximianus (a.k.a. **Marcus Aurelius Valerius Maximianus**; c. 250–310; r. 286–305): A Pannonian comrade of Diocletian, Maximianus was promoted as Augustus in the West. He abdicated in 305 but reentered politics, first as co-emperor with his son Maxentius and then with his son-in-law Constantine. He committed suicide at Massilia in 310 after he failed to raise a revolt against Constantine.

Maximinus II Daza (a.k.a. **Galerius Valerius Maximinus Daia**; c. 270–313; r. 309–313): Nephew of Galerius, he was named Caesar of the East in 305. Devoted to the old gods, Maximinus persecuted Christians. In 309, he proclaimed himself Augustus and warred against Galerius and later Licinius. In 313, defeated by Licinius, he died a refugee at Tarsus.

Severus II (a.k.a. **Flavius Valerius Severus**; c. 260–307; r. 306–307): An Illyrian officer who was created Caesar of the West by Galerius in 305. In 306, after the death of Constantius I, Galerius elevated Severus II to Augustus of the West. In 307, Severus invaded the Italian Peninsula, but his soldiers defected, and he fell into the hands of Maxentius, who executed him.

Suggested Reading

Barnes, *The New Empire of Diocletian and Constantine.*

Corcoran, *The Empire of Tetrarchs.*

Lactantius, *On the Manner in Which the Persecutors Died.*

L'Orange, *Art Forms and Civic Life in the Late Roman Empire.*

Nixon and Rodgers, *In Praise of Later Roman Emperors.*

Potter, *The Roman Empire at Bay.*

Rees, ed. and trans., *Diocletian and the Tetrarchy.*

Talbert, *Rome's World.*

1. How were Diocletian and his colleagues traditional emperors? Why did Diocletian's political solution to succession fail?

2. How did the military, administrative, and fiscal reforms of Diocletian change religious life in the Roman world? Was it possible for worship of the gods to be revived in the fashion of the Principate?

3. How conservative were tetrarchic religious policies? Why was persecution of Manichaeans and Christians part of this policy? What were the limitations of the imperial persecutors? What accounts for the acts of toleration by Galerius and Maximinus II Daza?

Imperial Recovery under the Tetrarchs
Lecture 15—Transcript

In this lecture, I plan to deal with the Roman imperial recovery under the emperor Diocletian, who ruled from 284–305. We often call the period the Tetrarchy, meaning "the rule of four"; "Tetrarch" refers to one of the four rulers. Diocletian, who restored order to the Roman world after a brief civil war, shared imperial power with three other colleagues; and so the four emperors are known as Tetrarchs, or rule of four.

The Tetrarchy represents both the period as well as an institutional change for the Roman world. Diocletian was, remarkably, the first emperor in over 50 years who reigned for some 20 years, and even more remarkable, abdicated. On May 1, 305 A.D., he stepped down from power along with his senior colleague Maximianus, and the two emperors then made way for the two junior emperors, who in turn created new Caesars (or junior emperors) to follow them.

This arrangement, whereby imperial power was shared among four rulers, was a response to the military and political crisis of the 3rd century. As I've noted before, the big weakness in the Roman imperial government was there really was no succession principle. The Empire was technically a continuation of the Republic. The emperor didn't have a real job description, as we would understand it. It wasn't a hereditary monarchy in law, although it was in practice; and as we've noted from the religious side, emperors were essentially venerated as if they were comrades of the gods or virtually divine, and were expected to become divine upon their deaths. When power was transmitted from ruler to ruler—or, even worse, from dynasty to dynasty—the Empire always hovered on the brink of civil war. It's remarkable that in the first 300 years there were only two significant civil wars; but between 235 and 284, there were five major civil wars, numerous invasions, usurpations—that is, breakaway rulers, such as in Gaul or in the East—and something on average of a reign of about 18 months if you average out all the emperors who claimed power in that 50 years. The fact that Diocletian not only ended civil war, ended invasion, restored order and prosperity, but stayed on the throne for 20 years was nothing short of miraculous given the political history of the last 50 years.

Furthermore, Diocletian was a pragmatist, and contrary to opinions of scholars writing perhaps three generations ago, he was also very much a conservative Roman to the core. He made this arrangement known as the Tetrarchy, or the rule of a college of four emperors, a virtue out of, essentially, a weakness. He had no sons; he had one daughter; and he used marriage alliances and adoption to create, in effect, a new imperial family. Diocletian also recognized that no single emperor could meet all the threats on the frontiers and civil war as well as administer the Roman Empire, given the number of demands now made on the imperial office. Therefore, in 285, he elevated as his co-emperor or senior Augustus—and "Augustus" became a term to mean a senior emperor who was ruling in his own right—a man named Maximianus. Maximianus, too, was from a Balkan military family; he was very similar in outlook to Diocletian; and they'd been colleagues in the Eastern army for years.

In 293 A.D., they extended the college. They created two junior emperors, or Caesars. Caesars were emperors in training; and Diocletian picked out two men, again of similar background; that is, men from the Balkans from military families, very typical of the emperors since 268. The man in the East was a man named Galerius, and he was married to Diocletian's only child, a daughter, Galeria Valeria. The other man was named Constantius, Constantius Chlorus, or often indicated as Constantius I; and Chlorus means someone of a rather pale, greenish complexion. Constantius happened to be the father of Constantine the Great, and he was married to a woman named Helena, the later saint, the mom of Constantine. He had to divorce her and marry a stepdaughter of Maximianus. The two Caesars were linked by marriage to the senior emperors, and it was assumed that the senior emperors would retire at one point and the two Caesars would step up and take over the position.

Diocletian ruled in the East with Galerius as his Caesar in the East; Maximianus ruled in the West with Constantius as his Caesar in the West. The Emperors had their capitals on the frontiers: Constantius at Trier (Treveri), the great imperial city on the Mosel near the Rhine frontier. Maximianus resided at Milan in Northern Italy, which was the major base and nexus of all military routes for the defense of the upper Danube. Diocletian took his residence up at Nicomedia, which is on the Asian side of Turkey, today on the Sea of Marmara; it's the modern city of Izmit. Then Galerius resided at Antioch in Syria. The arrangement of this college of four emperors was intended to provide an imperial presence at each of the four key frontiers: the Northwest; the Danube frontiers, where there were the two senior emperors; and the Eastern frontier on the Euphrates.

It worked; it worked incredibly well. Imperial armies scored major victories under the Tetrarchs, beating back the Persians in 298 and imposing a treaty on the Shah that resulted in the annexation of crucial provinces across the Tigris. Constantius put down a rebellion in the island of Britain. In Egypt, there was a major rebellion in 296; again, rapidly put down. We didn't have the kind of chaotic disorder we had in the 3rd century. In part, the system operated so effectively because Diocletian had the superior influence, *auctoritas*; that Roman term that's so difficult to translate that means that Diocletian was recognized as senior among the three partners. This imperial college not only gave victory and unity to the Roman Empire, but it also allowed Diocletian and his colleagues to carry out a series of sweeping reforms that made sense out of the rationalizations and makeshifts in government and army over the past 50 years. That 20 years—the so-called period of the Tetrarchy—proves to be a crucial turning point in Roman history.

As I said, the arrangement worked until May 1, 305, when Diocletian, who was at that point ailing—and he would die about three years later; he died late in 308—decided to retire, and he prevailed upon his reluctant colleague, Maximianus, who was Augustus in the West and really didn't want to retire, that the two should step down and make way for the Caesars, Galerius and Constantius. Two junior emperors, Caesars, had to be appointed now that Galerius and Constantius were senior emperors; Galerius in the East, Constantius in the West. Here, Galerius took charge. He was married to the daughter of Diocletian; he was Caesar of the East; he had undue influence over an ailing Diocletian—and the Christians claim that the influence is what caused Diocletian to persecute Christians, which we'll get to later on in this lecture—and the result was that two men were appointed who were essentially appointees of Galerius: a man called Severus (Severus II) in the West; and a man called Maximinus Daza, known affectionately by the Christians as "the beast of the East" because he was a virulent persecutor of Christians, who happened to be Galerius's nephew. The college was renewed—this was the so-called Second Tetrarchy—and it only lasted a little over a year.

It had two flaws in it: First, it set aside the succession principles that were so near and dear to the Imperial Army. Maximianus had a son, Maxentius, then at Rome, and Constantius had a brilliant son, Constantine. Both of those young men were cut out of the imperial college deliberately by Galerius; and the army, of course, was very impatient with this. Second, Constantius Chlorus, who was essentially odd man out of the four, waged a war in Britain, won a significant victory over the Picts of Scotland, and then died at the city of York on July 24, 306 A.D. The Western Army immediately declared his son, Constantine, Augustus of the West in violation of the arrangements of Galerius and much to the dismay of the other three ruling emperors. Later in the year, in October, the Praetorian Guard—that is, the guard of the city of Rome—declared Maxentius emperor; and Galerius, who at first would recognize neither of these men, elevated his comrade Severus II to Augustus of the West and immediately, within 18 months of the abdication of Diocletian, the Roman Empire experienced a new wave of civil wars.

The details of these wars need not detain us. What's important about them is these civil wars were significantly different from those waged in the earlier 3rd century. Emperors carved out regional states and waged wars for years; and, in effect, the Empire broke up at one point into six competing states. Eventually, in 324, Constantine, the son of Constantius, reunited the Empire. As we'll find out in the upcoming lecture, he also converted to Christianity in 312 during one of the decisive battles in which he removed one of his first rivals—that is, Maxentius, the emperor declared at Rome—and that would be the second turning point in the late Roman world; that is, Constantine's conversion and the state he built upon the Tetrarchic reforms.

In one way, the Tetrarchy can be looked upon as a failure, that it didn't achieve the political stability that Diocletian had hoped for; but nonetheless, for those 20 years, it did give Diocletian and his colleagues the opportunity to carry out some very significant reforms. Among these reforms was the building of a new Imperial Army and bureaucracy dependent upon the emperor. Diocletian and his colleagues dropped the fiction of ruling as a first magistrate, the image that was so dear to the emperors of the 2nd century, where any citizen could approach the emperor with a petition. The famous story of Marcus Aurelius of the Italian peasant woman on the road to Italy who says, "Emperor, Emperor, I have a petition," and Marcus Aurelius says, "I have no time"; he stopped being emperor, and the emperor got off his horse and listens to the petition. "You are a citizen, good lady, what is your complaint?" This would never happen in Diocletian's time. The emperors were now elevated to a ceremonial position where they were virtually divine. Diocletian was the favorite of Jupiter. Maximianus was the favorite of Hercules. Constantius Chlorus, the father of Constantine, stressed Mars. Galerius also was a favorite of Jupiter. In many ways, these emperors now put themselves on the level of autocrats.

Beneath them was a new army; legions and cavalry that bore dynastic names stressing the connection with Jupiter and Hercules. Furthermore, the army was reorganized on a new scale in which the cavalry was elevated to the level of a premier military force. Above all, in this new world of the late Roman military and the late Roman civil bureaucracy, there were certain significant changes. The old senatorial elite—that is, the educated supreme aristocracy of the Roman world that had come to encompass the most wealthy and educated of the property classes of the Roman world—were now cut out of military commands; that goes back to a reform under Gallienus. They were henceforth barred from military commands. They could, however, go into civil administration. The army was reorganized in such a way that commands went to men who moved through the ranks; that is, they were from humble origin, they were soldiers just like the emperors themselves. Some scholars would argue the army was greatly increased; that doesn't seem to be the case. There would be further military changes under Constantine, but Diocletian and his colleagues took a first step in transforming the Roman army from the imperial professional army of the High Empire increasingly into the personal army of emperors, which ultimately ends up being a mercenary army of German barbarians and other federates hired to fight for the Roman emperor.

In addition, the civil administration was vastly increased. By our best count, the number of senior officials by Diocletian's time was 35,000. Before Diocletian—say, at the start of the crisis in 235—it may have been 3,000. Civilian and military administration was split. There was a complicated division of the provincial administration to three different levels, a level that is reflected in the later organization of the Christian church. These changes were carried out for two reasons: One, to prevent civil wars—that is, usurpation and rebellion by powerful governors by dividing up the provinces and dividing the administration of civil and military—and also to increase taxation.

However, these reforms—expanding the army and the bureaucracy—had certain advantages, particularly for the emperors. For one, the emperor no longer depended on the traditional elites of Rome; he was not challenged by the senators. This was an important point to remember in the religious history of the Roman world because Roman emperors, as a result of the 3rd century crisis, became increasingly associated with the gods. They were the favorite of the Gods; they were expected to have miracles on the battlefield. I've mentioned in passing several of those miracles. One by Marcus Aurelius, the so-called Battle of the Rain miracle, when he's fighting the Germanic tribes, the Quadi and the Marcomanni, and they pray to Mercury, Hermes, and a great hail storm comes up and blows the wind and the hail into the eyes of the Germans and they win. This is depicted on his column in Piazza Cologne in Rome today. Or in 272, when Aurelian defeated the Palmyrene Army because the Sun God intervened on Aurelian's side, sent rays into the eyes of the Palmyrene cavalry, and won the battle for Rome. As a result, Sol Invictus ("the Unconquerable Sun") became a very prominent god for the soldier-emperors—with Aurelian, Diocletian, later Constantius, and Constantine; all of these emperors—because Sol Invictus delivered victory.

The emperors now had an administration and army that would follow them unquestionably, so long as they were paid. To play to their new servants, as well as to their subjects, the emperors created a whole new ceremonial, and this is to elevate them to the status of autocrats who have some kind of divine aura, divine legitimacy. This was reassuring to these emperors in certain ways. Ceremony focused power. The Roman emperors, starting with Diocletian, ruling as the favorite of gods—or later, as Christian emperors, as the favorite of God—didn't have to deal with senators and aristocrats as equals anymore. It was all handled by ceremony, and therefore the traditional elites had to pay homage to the emperor. Furthermore, it created a barrier between the emperor and the traditional elite so they couldn't challenge these emperors; and this was very reassuring.

Diocletian and his colleagues were from very humble backgrounds. They spoke—or in the opinion of Roman senators, grunted—a rather crude Latin. They came up through the ranks. Whenever you see the portraits of the Tetrarchs—whether on coins or sculptures—they have this closely cropped beard; it looks like they're too busy killing barbarians to shave properly, the way emperors had done earlier in the time of Augustus. Furthermore, it meant that the emperors could dispense with consent by the senatorial families; they didn't have to mix with them as equals. This was reassuring because in social settings, these emperors would very quickly come to realize they didn't have the education, they didn't have the ethos, they didn't have the polish of the traditional elite classes; so what they did is they created their own civil bureaucrats, drawing very heavily on the decurions of the cities, and they created a new officer corps, drawing very heavily on the provincial soldiers and eventually on the barbarians who were recruited on the frontiers. This gave the Tetrarchs a new position of power with which they could issue the various reforms.

Such a government was premised, as I mentioned in a previous lecture, on honor coming from the emperor, and the whole tradition of honor changed. It's been noted by Peter Brown and other scholars working in social history: The route to advancement was now to serve one's emperor, not to serve one's city, not to serve one's traditional Gods, not to show patriotism and piety the way we explained in the earlier part of this course, which was so fundamental to pagan worship, but instead to stage events in arenas, or in hippodromes, or in stadiums; races, chariot races, some kind of event that would bring you to the attention of the emperor and therefore allow your promotion into the civil administration or into the army. This administration and army proved extremely expensive to fund. There were tax increases; but to the credit of Diocletian and his colleagues, they made a serious effort to roll back prices, to carry out currency reforms, to impose, at one point they imposed prices and wages, they had to pull it back and allow market values to dictate the money. But contrary to what is usually thought, prosperity did return.

A keystone to this reform was, of course, winning the favor of the gods. Here, the Tetrarchs, in many ways, took their cue from Augustus and the earlier emperors. The proper worship of the gods was all-important, and the emperors had now forged a new ideology centering on imperial ceremonial in which the emperors were the favorites of the gods. This could take the form of panegyrics—that is, not orations, but orations of praise, so to speak—that would be delivered at imperial palaces. One of the most famous of those late imperial palaces is the retirement palace of the emperor Diocletian—the modern city of Split, on the Dalmatian shore, now in the Croatian Republic—and Split survives; it's actually part of the city of Split. You can imagine an oration being delivered before the emperor Diocletian seated on a great throne with the Adriatic in the background, with all of his various eunuchs and ministers and ceremonial figures around him, and the idea was to really impress upon anyone coming to the imperial palace the distance between the emperor and the subject. Similar types of ceremonies were staged at the Court of Milan, at Treveri, where Constantius held court and later his son Constantine; probably at the city of Antioch, although no imperial palace has been excavated because the Roman city is essentially underneath the new current Turkish city of Antakya.

Furthermore, the emperors were seen in the company of the gods; that is, the iconography of the 3rd century culminated in a new image of emperors and their association with the divine. Emperors were the equals or the comrades of gods. We see this with Diocletian and Jupiter, Maximianus and Hercules. One of the most spectacular depictions of this iconography comes from the Imperial Villa—I believe it's an Imperial Villa, it's questioned—at Piazza Armerina in Sicily where the mosaics and the frescoes stress the imagery of Hercules, and we believe this was the retirement villa of Maximianus and was later used by his son Maxentius, who was one of the emperors in the civil wars from 306–324. He's the emperor who got killed at the Battle of the Milvian Bridge where Constantine had his vision. Maxentius stressed Hercules but also the goddess Roma; and you can see in that imperial palace with its artwork and on their coins that new stress on the association of emperor and the gods.

These were not the gods of mystery cults; these were not the flight to some type of irrationality or non-Classical gods; these were the Gods of Rome, the traditional gods that had protected the armies: Sol Invictus, the Unconquerable Sun; Mars Propugnator, Mars the Conqueror; Jupiter Conservator, Jupiter the Preserver; Hercules, obviously a very important god because he was a mortal who became a God. Emperors always liked to associate themselves with Hercules; it looked neat. In Piazza Armerina, there's a mosaic that shows the apotheosis; that is, the receiving of Hercules on Mount Olympus. It's one of the reasons for associating the villa with the emperor Maximianus and his son Maxentius.

All of the Imperial success—the restoration of prosperity, the securing of the frontiers—was closely tied to what was, in effect, a religious revival. The Tetrarchs didn't just invoke the gods, they went out of their way to support and to give assistance to decurions and cities who had come through the hardships of civil war, invasion, and higher taxes so that the public worship could be funded and continued as it had been in the High Roman Empire.

Increasingly, archaeology is revealing that at the end of the 3rd and opening of the 4th centuries—that is, during the period of Diocletian and his successors—that there was a revival, a refurbishing, a restoring of many of the shrines and sanctuaries across the Roman world. This can be documented at very famous sites, especially in Turkey where I do a lot of my work. Two of the best examples of this are the Temple of Aphrodite at Aphrodisias, where there are apparently repairs and restoration of the temple, and also the city of Aezanis, which is in Western Turkey, where the great sanctuary of Zeus was; a sanctuary that gained a great deal of favor under the emperor Hadrian and then was refurbished in the Tetrarchic period. Perhaps more familiar to some members of the Teaching Company community would be the city of Ephesus, the great first city of Asia where St. Paul preached. That's the home of Artemis Ephesia, the great Mother Goddess of Asia Minor, who is mistakenly regarded as a fertility goddess with many breasts; I noted that that's incorrect, that's actually Christian invective. Her cult statue was recognized across the Roman world, and those breasts are more likely bull testicles. There's a very learned monograph, of course, in German on it that has conclusively proved it. But the Artemisium had been damaged in the 3rd century by Goths; it's restored. The Tetrarchs restored a number of temples in the city of Ephesus, including a temple to Hadrian; and if one goes by the temple to Hadrian in Ephesus, which is one on the main drag from the state agora (that is, the upper marketplace) down to the library of Celsus and then you hook a right to the theater—and this essentially follows the route of the cult of Artemis, which I discussed in an earlier lecture—the temple of Hadrian is on a very prominent point on that thoroughfare through the city, and it was rebuilt, it was restored, and there are four altar bases that carry the statue to each of the Tetrarchs and an inscription proclaiming their virtues, their unconquerable ability, and also their association with the city of Ephesus.

This type of rebuilding, restoration; giving tax breaks to cities; showering cities with patronage; making special trips to cities that were noted for their shrines; at great oracles such as Didyma, which is outside of Miletus, and Claros, which is on the shore of Western Asia Minor; all of this was part of a single policy to do homage to the traditional gods who had been the protectors of the Roman world. That meant that when the emperor Diocletian reformed the currency and issued a new fiduciary coin, the so-called nummus, in 293, the appeal on that coin was *Genio Populi Romani*, "To the spirit of the Roman people"; and that appeal embodied all of these traditional religious values. It was a general appeal that all Romans could agree; that the spirit of the Roman people—that is, the divine representation of the Roman people that, in effect, was all of its shrines, cults, and religious traditions— was now on the rise and was common to all Roman citizens, who now were ruled by emperors expected to defend the Empire with the help of the gods.

That very, very strong conservative appeal—which to me hardly represents a rearguard action by a dying paganism, but rather a much more sharpened and focused conservative revival—carried implications for Christians; and those implications were not particularly happy for the Christian community living under the Tetrarchs. I had noted that back in 260 the persecutions had been halted by the emperor Gallienus and there had been no persecutions for almost a generation. This is the so-called period of the peace of the church. In 303 A.D., in February, this abruptly changed when Diocletian issued the first of four edicts against the Christians. Ostensibly, the reason was he was sacrificing at the city of Nicomedia—that was his capital, which is on the Asian shores of the Sea of Marmara today, which the ancients would have called the Propontis—and he claimed that the Christians present at the public sacrifices had probably caused ill omens and that the gods were angry. That followed with additional edicts of persecution; these included confiscation of churches and Christian property, ordering the destruction of books, and prohibiting Christian services.

We have an inscription that comes from a city in Asia Minor, in southern Asia Minor, at the city of Arycanda, a rather beautiful site built in the mountains of Lycia, a region in Southwestern Turkey. This is an inscription that indicates while this was, again, an empire-wide persecution, it depended very heavily on the support of the local decurions; that is, the local elites. This is what the decurions of Arycanda said in the year 312 to the then-ruling emperors Maximinus and Lucinius, two of the successors of Diocletian. They call the emperors "saviors of every province and nation of mankind" and they give a request and supplication of volition and Pamphylian provinces:

> Your kinsmen the gods [they say this directly in this public petition; that is, the emperors are kinsmen of the gods] have rendered kindness to everyone who concerns himself with their cult on behalf of the eternal well-being of your all-conquering majesties. We have thus thought it right to apply to your eternal monarchy to request that the Christians, long raging mad to this day maintaining their mania unchanged, should at last be stopped and not trespass against the cult due to the gods with any sinister novelty of worship; ... and that the power of the atheist [that is, the Christians who deny the gods] to pursue their detestable devotions is forbidden and barred, while all men show their zeal, on behalf of your eternal and incorruptible emperorship, in the worship of your kinsmen the gods. For this, it is obvious, is of the greatest benefit to all of your subjects.

That petition, which has been recently discovered and published, gives you a better sense of what the ceremonial and religious values were of the Tetrarchy. The emperors had now come to marshal their subjects behind the gods of Rome, behind victory against the enemies both outside and inside the Roman Empire. The Christians, while they had not been persecuted for a generation, their legal position hadn't changed. They were still technically outlawed; and the emperors for about a generation had, in effect, extended an act of clemency to the Christians. The persecution that followed was not only legal in the eyes of the Roman legalist, but it also was in keeping with imperial policy of the Tetrarchy: that the spirit of the Roman people took precedence over all other religious values, and that any—Christians particularly, but also Mannichaeians—who didn't worship to the gods must be forced to conform; and therefore, a new wave of persecutions, the so-called Great Persecutions, were launched. These would go on down to 313; that is, for the next 10 years.

Again, the enforcement of these persecutions would depend on the effectiveness of the imperial government. Constantius, the father of Constantine, was credited with not paying attention to the edict; we're not sure if that's just Christian rewriting of history. But one point is significant: The Roman emperor had come to a position where he could legislate on the religious loyalties and worship of his subjects. He was close to the divine, and therefore he had a particular position as the Pontifex Maximus, the Chief Priest of the Roman Empire, to legislate on the favor of the gods. Loyalty now depended on the emperor, and the emperors provided the favor and patronage of the gods.

This arrangement was further reinforced by the new imperial bureaucracy and army that served these autocrats. Ironically, in the civil wars of 312, Constantine would emerge as the victor, and he had his battle miracle. Except it wasn't one of the pagan gods, it was the Christian god; and the irony is that the Tetrarchs had forged the institutions, the ceremonies, and the legal position for Constantine, now a Christian emperor, to not only just legislate on worship but to change the religion of the Roman world. That religion would be the new faith, Christianity.

The Conversion of Constantine
Lecture 16

The conversion of Emperor Constantine has been a topic of debate among scholars almost since the moment it happened. But an examination of the physical evidence, much of it in the form of Constantine's coinage, makes a few things clear: Constantine understood his experience at Milvian Bridge, whatever that experience was, but he also understood the perils of imposing his minority faith on his people and was careful to introduce change gradually in the empire. Whatever the details, Constantine's conversion was indisputably a major turning point in the history of Europe.

Constantine's Conversion—Facts and Surmises

- On October 28, 312, Emperor Constantine defeated Maxentius, at the Battle of Milvian Bridge. This victory was not just a miracle; it was the Christian God who was invoked; and this battle was seen by Constantine as a justification and vindication of the power of the Christian God. From that point on, he began to identify himself with the Christian faith and, in my opinion, he converted.

- The information we have on his conversion is not nearly as good as we would like. Our two main literary accounts are written by Christian authors: **Lactantius**, who was living at the time of the battle but in far-away Nicomedia, and Eusebius, who also was not present at the battle. The fullest account comes from Eusebius's second version in his *Life of Constantine*, written almost a half a generation later.

- The conversion of Constantine has been subject to all sorts of criticisms and interpretations by both scholars and popular writers since the 4th century, and particularly since the 19th century with the advent of modern scholarship. One source neglected by most scholars is Constantine's imperial iconography—that is, the images and inscriptions on his coins.

- Lactantius's work, *De mortibus persecutorum* (*On the Death of the Persecutors*), includes gleeful accounts of the horrible deaths of pagan emperors who persecuted Christians. He tells us that on the eve of the battle, Constantine ordered that a symbol like the Christogram be put on the banners and shields of his soldiers. He also describes Maxentius consulting magicians and practicing black magic. These are clearly overdrawn accounts.

- Eusebius reports in his *Ecclesiastical History*, written just a couple of years after the battle but revised some 10 years later, that Constantine prayed to the Christian god and won the battle. In the *Life of Constantine*, Constantine has a succession of visions, and ultimately the entire army has a vision of the Christogram and the motto *In hoc signo victor eris*, "In this sign you will conquer."

Objections to and Support of the Contemporary Accounts

- Scholars have doubted the accuracy of the later account on various grounds. However, this account is supported by the coin evidence. In 328–329, some coins issued at Constantinople show the labarum with the Christogram. We also know in 350, a loyalist general issued coins showing the labarum, Emperor Constantius II, and the inscription *hoc signo victor eris*).

- Most scholars now believe that Eusebius did write this account, and Eusebius claims that he wrote it with the advice of the Emperor Constantine, although almost 30 years after the battle, even Constantine's memory might be subject to embroidery and elaboration.

- In the 19th century, Swiss humanist Jacob Burkhardt was the first scholar to reject Eusebius's account and generated a line of inquiry that persists down to this day, suggesting that Constantine, either before or after the battle, used Christianity as a cynical device for legitimacy, co-opting the power of the growing church and its institutions.

- This view is still held by many. However, we know that Constantine effectively created the Christian church and that the organization and even the terms such as "vicar" and "diocese" all come out of the administrative reforms of Diocletian. Also, there is little evidence for large numbers of Christians in 312. They were not represented in the Senate, the army leadership, or the Roman elite, so there was no advantage in playing to the Christians in a civil war.

- Some scholars, such as Henri Gregoire, have argued that Constantine is better understood as a syncretist. In addition to the Christian god, he worshiped the sun god, Sol Invictus; he had a vision of Apollo in 312 near Aachen; and the Christogram as described by Lactantius could be interpreted as Celtic religious symbols.

- Serious scholars still argue that perhaps Constantine fought under a variety of symbols, some of which were ambiguous and later interpreted or explained as Christian. According to legend, Bishop **Hosius of Cordoba**, whom Constantine summoned to tutor his sons in 315, had to explain to Constantine the meaning of the symbol he saw at Milvian Bridge. Perhaps Constantine crossed a bridge of solar cults from paganism to Christianity.

- That said, there is very little evidence that Constantine or his family were solar monotheists. His coinage early in his reign associates him far more with Mars; images of the sun god only occur after the conversion and after Constantine conquered the Balkan provinces, where Sol was popular among the soldiers of the Danube army.

- It seems most likely that at Milvian, Constantine knew he was fighting under a Christian symbol. He may well have had pagan symbols there, too, invoking all the gods. But there is no reason to believe that he did not know that the Christogram was the symbol of Christ. The victory likely made Constantine realize that the

Christian god was a true god, perhaps the only god, and within a few years, he came to identify himself as a Christian and monotheist.

Evidence from Coinage

- The coin evidence is significant for other reasons. Coins were disseminated in vast numbers, and repeated coinage reforms meant old money was called in and new money was issued. Iconography could change rapidly.

- There are few Christian symbols on Constantine's coins. Far more common were those continuing to invoke the pagan gods, even eight or nine years after the Battle of Milvian Bridge. Some of that is just the routine of mint masters; however, the vast majority of Constantine's subjects were pagans, and putting overt symbols of Christianity on the coins was too dangerous.

- Instead, Constantine steadily, between 313 and 324 when he reunited the Roman Empire, emptied the coinage of religious content, making himself the leading figure on the coins. He created a new portrait in which he appeared looking up to heaven. He wore the diadem, the symbol of royalty that went back to Alexander the Great. No emperor had ever worn that.

- On the reverse of the coins, where you had images of the gods traditionally, were images that celebrated the imperial family. A few divinities remained: personifications of the city of Rome or Constantinople; several personifications of the virtues. To Christians, these were classical symbols and not goddesses. Constantine was cleverly using the few religious symbols remaining on his coinage to convey ideas rather than divinities.

- By his death in 337, the coinage had been emptied of religious content and the celebration was centered on the emperor and his family—an inspired emperor who has the favor not only of the Christian god, but the pagan gods. It really was in the eye of the beholder exactly which divine power was favorable to Constantine.

- The sons of Constantine were more direct. They put the labarum on their art and coins. Emperor Magnentius, who was a rebel emperor in Gaul, actually put the Christogram on his coins. The irony is that Magnentius might have been a pagan and the symbols were being used to appeal to the army.

Constantine's Legacy

- The conversion of Constantine is significant for several reasons. One is that Constantine's conversion is the only well-documented conversion we have between Saint Paul and Saint Augustine.

- Both Paul and Augustine were intellectuals, and their conversions were based on intellectual and spiritual considerations that would appeal to the elite classes of the Roman world. Constantine was a soldier-emperor. As a pragmatic man, his conversion was much closer to the conversion experience of most of the Roman world.

- What convinced him was not the kind of subtle arguments that Augustine would make. What convinced Constantine that this god was worth invoking was that this god delivered on promises of victory.

- Eusebius plays this up in the *Life of Constantine*: Constantine's victories are cast in the traditions of the righteous kings of the Old Testament, and this is an image that will persist through the history of medieval Europe and down almost to the modern age.

- Why Constantine turned to the Christian god, we really do not know. But his conversion will be paralleled by many conversions of pagan monarchs in medieval Europe, particularly among the Scandinavian kings and the Merovingian kings of Gaul.

- On a more mundane level, the peasants and citizens of towns did not need a battle miracle from the Christian god, but there were other miracles that could be performed. One was exorcism. Other times, monks and ascetics simply defied the pagan gods, casting down their statues. When there were no consequences, that was dramatic proof to many pagans that these holy men were protected by the true god.

- Not only did Constantine convert to Christianity, but in 313 he issued the **Edict of Milan**. This not only halted the persecutions; it gave legal legitimacy to Christianity. With that decisive change, the Christians had captured the Roman monarchy.

- As the 19th-century scholar J. B. Bury put it, the conversion of Constantine is probably one of the most audacious acts carried out by an autocrat in violation of the religious opinions of the majority of his subjects. While Saint Paul gave Christianity the potential to be a world faith, Constantine, by his conversion and the institutions he forged, would make Christianity the religion of not only the Roman world, but ultimately of Europe.

Important Term

Edict of Milan: The imperial rescript issued jointly by Constantine I and Licinius I in 313 that ended the Great Persecutions and recognized Christianity as a religion.

Names to Know

Hosius (257–359): Bishop of Corduba (modern Cordova) before 300, he suffered exile during the Great Persecution of 303–305. In 313, he was invited to Treveri, where he advised the emperor Constantine on doctrinal matters. After the death of Constantine, Hosius staunchly opposed the Arian policies of Constantius II.

Lactantius (a.k.a. **Lucius Caecilius Firmianus Lactantius**; c. 240–320): Roman rhetor and tutor to Crispus, eldest son of Constantine I. Born in Roman Africa, he taught rhetoric at Nicomedia. In about 315, he composed *On the Deaths of the Persecutors* (*De mortibus persecutorum*), the prime source for and the earliest report of the conversion of Constantine in 312.

Suggested Reading

Burckhadt, *The Age of Constantine the Great.*

Drake, *Constantine and the Bishops.*

Eadie, ed. *The Conversion of Constantine.*

Eusebius, *The History of the Church from Christ to Constantine.*

————, *Life of Constantine.*

Harl, "Make Haste Slowly."

Lactantius, *On the Manner in Which the Persecutors Died.*

MacMullen, *Constantine.*

Odhal, *Constantine and the Christian Empire.*

Van Dam, *The Roman Revolution of Constantine.*

Questions to Consider

1. How trustworthy are the accounts of Lactantius and Eusebius on the conversion of Constantine? What has accounted for the debate over the conversion of Constantine?

2. Why are coins and medallions vital sources on the conversion?

3. How did Constantine view the Christian god on the eve of the Battle of Milvian Bridge? How did Constantine come to understand his new faith?

4. How did Constantine's conversion decisively change the course of the conflict between pagans and Christians?

The Conversion of Constantine
Lecture 16—Transcript

In this lecture, we are going to deal with what I believe is one of the most decisive turning points, not only in Roman history but the whole of Western civilization.

On October 28, 312, the emperor Constantine defeated one of his rivals, a man named Maxentius, at the Battle of the Milvian Bridge. This bridge is just north of Rome today and crosses the Tiber. The Milvian Bridge was associated with many important events in Roman history. The most famous was in 49 BC when the councils of the Republic entrusted Pompey with a sword to defend the Republic against Julius Caesar, and the result was a civil war that ended the Republic and brought the reign of emperors. At that same decisive point, Constantine defeated a rival, Maxentius, went on to reunite the Western Roman Empire, and some 12 years later was master of the entire Roman world. The difference of this battle was that it was not just a miracle—that is, divine intervention—that gave an emperor one more victory and yet another civil war, it was the Christian God who was invoked; and this battle was seen by Constantine as a justification and vindication of the power of the Christian God. From that point on, he began to identify himself with the Christian faith and, in my opinion, he converted.

The information we have on this conversion is not nearly as good as we would like, and that is a significant point that must be stressed; that is, our two main literary accounts are written by Christian authors. One is a man named Lactantius, who was living at the time of the Battle of Milvian Bridge, but it was in the city of Nicomedia—that is, the capital of the emperor Diocletian and later the capital of Galerius—and so he was not at all present at the battle; he was not even in Italy at the time. He was a teacher of rhetoric. He later became tutor to the eldest son of Constantine, Crispus. The other account comes from Eusebius—actually, Eusebius penned two accounts in Greek—and again, he was not present at the battle. The longest account, the fullest account, we have from Eusebius comes from the *Life of Constantine*, and that was written almost a half a generation later. What we have are two Christian reports of a battle in a civil war in which they argued, and they claimed, that the emperor won the battle and believed that he won the battle with the help of the Christian God.

It is therefore necessary to take a little time and slow down the pace of this course to concentrate on the conversion of Constantine for several reasons. First, it is the decisive point. Second, it allows us to look at these various sources. Third, the conversion of Constantine has been subject to all sorts of criticisms and interpretations by both scholars and popular writers, really since the start of the whole issue back in the 4th century A.D., and particularly since the 19th century with the advent of modern scholarship. First, let us take a look at what these authors tell us about the conversion; and then I want to turn to some of the interpretations of the sources, and bring in a source that has been neglected by most scholars: the iconography—that is, the images and inscriptions on coins—that help elucidate the conversion.

First, what did Lactantius and Eusebius tell us? Lactantius wrote a work known as *On the Death of the Persecutors*, *De Mortibus Persecutorum*— that is, on the deaths of those emperors like Maximinus II Daza, the nephew of Galerius, that so-called beast of the East; Galerius himself—and he takes delight in pagan emperors who persecuted dying horrible deaths with worms and all sorts of stuff like that; it is really good stuff. In this account, he tells that on the eve of the Battle of the Milvian Bridge, Constantine ordered that a Christian symbol be put on the banners and shields of his soldiers. This symbol is described as a version of what later became known as the Chi-Rho, the Christogram, which is the Greek letters chi (X) and rho (P); Khristos, the first two letters in Greek of Christ's name; Khristos, "the anointed one," which is the Greek equivalent of Messiah. The description is rather awkward, and actually it is difficult to make sense of it; and Lactantius does not quite have it correct. In addition to telling us about Constantine on the eve of the battle invoking the Christian symbol, we are told that his rival Maxentius was an evil guy consulting magicians and black magic, consulting oracles, and doing everything but sacrificing children to the powers of the underworld. The whole account is drawn in quite stark terms. Constantine, the Christian emperor; Maxentius the evil devil worshiper; and it is clear that these are overdrawn accounts. Nonetheless, he does report this Christian symbol; a version of the Chi-Rho.

Eusebius reports the event in two accounts. The first is in his *Ecclesiastical History*, written just a couple of years after the battle but revised some 10 years later; and there he only says that Constantine prayed to the Christian God and won the battle. The fullest account comes from the so-called *Vita Constantani*, the *Life of Constantine*; a biography—or better described as an imperial hagiography; that is, a holy writing—in which Constantine has a succession of visions, first in the form of a dream but ultimately there is a vision that is experienced by the entire army (that is, they see it in the failing light of the day), and in that vision in the sky is the Latin *hoc signo victor eris*, "In this sign you will conquer"; Eusebius, writing in Greek, says *En touto nikesis*. The Chi-Rho is clearly described. We are told that Constantine puts this on his banner; that later there is a dream in which the symbol is explained to him by Christ; and he goes into battle with not just the symbol, but the symbol carried on a banner known as the labarum, which essentially is a flag stuck up on a pole with the Chi-Rho, and it is carried into battle by his soldiers. In this fuller account, many scholars have doubted whether Eusebius is really accurate, and if he has not attributed a symbol that might have been used by Constantine—or actually one of Constantine's colleagues and rivals, Licinius—in a later battle and then projected back to the famous Battle of the Milvian Bridge. But there is also an argument that Eusebius did not write this life; that it was written two or three generations later, and we are dealing with an entire legend.

That opinion about it being a legend and manufactured several generations after Eusebius—that is, someone is writing this under the assumed name of Eusebius—is vitiated by the coin evidence. In 328–329, there were some coins issued at Constantinople that show the labarum with the Chi-Rho. We also know in 350 AD, a loyalist General Vetranio, loyal to the family of Constantine's sons, issued coins showing the labarum, showing the Emperor Constantius II, and with the inscription *hoc signo victor eris*; so at least a generation after the battle it was well known that the battle had been won under this Christian symbol and with this slogan, "In this sign, you will conquer" (the usual English translation). Most scholars now believe that Eusebius did write this account, and Eusebius claims that he wrote it with the advice of the Emperor Constantine; Constantine told him what happened, and he is simply reporting what the Emperor said. This is almost 30 years after the battle, so even Constantine's memory is subject to a lot of embroidery and elaboration. Nonetheless, these are the accounts we have; essentially three reports from two Christian writers.

You can see that it is very easy for scholars to doubt the veracity and accuracy of these reports. It was first raised by a brilliant scholar of the 19th century, a Swiss humanist, Jacob Burkhardt, who wrote both on the ancient world and the Renaissance; he was a prodigious and really prolific scholar. He was the first to reject Eusebius's account and suggest that the account may well have been embroidered and really may be a case of just blatant propaganda. He questioned the genuineness of the biography of Eusebius; he questioned whether Lactantius reported the event accurately and truthfully—there were problems in Lactantius's account; the Latin is not quite clear—and he has generated a line of inquiry that persists down to this day that some scholars pursue and many popular writers pursue: that Constantine's conversion was not genuine; it was simply a case of political expediency. Constantine, either before the battle or more likely after the battle, used Christianity as a cynical device for legitimacy; that he realized he could co-op the Christian church and get bishops behind him. He saw the advantage of Christian organization. It is not clear what banners he fought under at this battle. He halted the persecutions of the Tetrarchs and won favor with his Christian subjects; and in many ways used the whole story about the miracle as a means to create an imperial church that he controlled and to co-op the Christian leadership to the benefit of his own personal power.

This view is still held by many. There are some very subtle and sophisticated variations on it today: a work by Hal Drake called *Constantine and the Bishops*, which is a much more modified version. It is not a crude case of just a power grab by Constantine, but he forged a consensus with bishops, with pagan monotheists and syncretists, as some would say (that is, people who believed in the sun god). So you have variations of this position still being argued by scholars, and some of them with quite sophisticated points.

I think, however, this method of approach is incorrect. We know that Constantine effectively created the Christian church—an imperial church, if you will—and that the organization and even the very terms such as "vicar" and "diocese" all come out of the administrative reforms of Diocletian; and that in many ways, the church was the creation of Constantine, not a device that Constantine found on hand that he could use for imperial purposes. Second, I do not believe there were large numbers of Christians. In the opening lectures, in the development of the whole question of Christian numbers, I have argued as one line of scholars do that Christians were very few. Furthermore, they were not represented in the senate, in the army offices, in the elites of the Roman world; so there was no great advantage in playing to the Christians in a civil war. That really raises a question whether Constantine had cynical motives with this conversion on the eve of October 28, 312, where he won his decisive battle.

Some scholars have argued, especially since the early 20th century, led by a brilliant Belgian scholar Henri Gregoire, who is really one of the preeminent Byzantinist of the 20th century, and he argued that maybe Constantine is better understood as a syncretist; that is, one who accepted various gods. I've talked about syncretism. He believed in the sun god, Sol Invictus. Constantine is reported to have had a vision from Apollo in 312 when he was visiting the shrine of the god outside of the modern city of Aachen; that would be in Latin Aquae Granni; those would be thermal waters. Emperors such as Caracalla visited the sanctuary. Gregoire also pointed out that the symbol as described by Lactantius could be interpreted as Celtic religious symbols.

An argument was developed—which is still said today by serious scholars—that perhaps Constantine fought under a variety of symbols, some of which were quite ambiguous and were later interpreted or explained as Christian, particularly by the Bishop Hosius. Hosius was the Bishop of Cordoba in Spain. He was very quickly, after the victory in 312, admitted to the court of Constantine at the city of the Treveri; that is, modern Trier. Lactantius was summoned to tutor the son of Constantine by 315; and it would be the Christians who were associated with the court of Constantine who would then explain to Constantine that the symbols under which he fought at the Milvian Bridge were Christian. "It was the Christogram; you didn't quite understand it, but God was working through you. He was working through you the way he was with Moses and the Hebrews who were being pursued by the Pharaoh and the parting of the Red Sea." Eusebius loves to play up those images with Constantine. Therefore, there is a very serious body of scholarship that argues that Constantine, himself a syncretist—his father perhaps a solar syncretist or even a solar monotheist; that is, a pagan monotheist—crossed a bridge of these strange solar cults, mystery cults, from paganism to Christianity.

I do not believe in those mystery cults and bridges—I have made that quite clear in earlier lectures—and there is very little evidence that Constantine was strictly a solar monotheist. In fact, his coinage, in iconography early in his reign, associates him far more with Mars. There is no evidence his family, especially his father, venerated Sol any more than other gods; and the coinage of Constantine that comes to have many images of the sun god only occurs after the conversion and after Constantine has conquered the Balkan Provinces where Sol is very popular among the soldiers of the Danube Army. Furthermore, the vision that Constantine had on his way to Aachen (Aquae Granni) was not of Sol, but of Apollo. Some scholars have said, "Apollo, Sol; the same god. Apollo has solar attributes." Ancients knew their gods. Imperial iconography, religious iconography of the Greek world carefully distinguished Apollo from Sol or his Greek equivalent Helios, and this idea that the two gods were confused into some kind of composite solar god or monotheistic solar cult is really a modern creation and has very little to do with the ancients.

My opinion: When Constantine fought that battle, he fought under Christian symbols. He may well have had pagan symbols, too; I suspect he did. He was invoking all the gods on his side; after all, this was the battle that was going to make him or break him at the start of the civil war. But there is no reason to believe that he did not know that the Christogram was the symbol of Christ, and I find it very implausible that he fought the battle, won under the symbol, and then a year or two later Hosius shows up at the court of Treveri and says, "Constantine, let me explain to you what that symbol was. You were fighting under the Chi-Rho" and Constantine says, "Hosius, I'm glad you told me that. This has been bothering me for a year; I didn't know what that dream was all about. Thank you very much." I do not believe it happened that way. When he chose that symbol, he knew it was a Christian symbol, and the victory in battle made Constantine realize that the Christian God was the only god. Was he a monotheist at this point? Probably not. But within a couple of years, he comes to identify himself with the Christian community and he learns his monotheism. He finds out that the Christian God is not only a comrade like other gods, but is the only god. But that is a change that comes as he learns more about his faith. In my opinion, the argument that there is some kind of syncretism, solar cult, leading the Christianity is really vitiated just by looking at the evidence on some of the coins.

Furthermore, the coin evidence is significant for other reasons. Coins were disseminated in vast numbers in the late Roman world. There were repeated coinage reforms where the old money was called in and new money was issued. One could change the iconography very rapidly. There are very few Christian symbols on Constantine's coins. There are a couple of rare medallions and coins that show the Chi-Rho on the helmet of Constantine, and Eusebius tells us that the Chi-Rho was put on the symbol of his ceremonial helmet. Yes, we have a few coins that show that; the vast majority do not. There are few instances of the labarum on imperial coins. But these are just a fraction of the literally hundreds of millions of coins that were issued by Constantine, let alone by his pagan rivals, and there are very, very few; they are a fraction of one percent out of the vast majority of coins in circulation.

Far more common on the coins of Constantine were those continuing to invoke the pagan gods. This includes Mars, who was apparently the most favorite god of Constantine early in his reign, up until 310. There are also coins of Sol Invictus; and these images carrying the pagan gods continued at least eight or nine years after the Battle of the Milvian Bridge. Some of that is just the routine of mint masters; that is, they simply put on the coins images that they have always put on. Some of it is just routine bureaucratic traditions. But you cannot dismiss all of it in that regard. The simple fact is, the vast majority of Constantine's subjects were pagans, and putting overt symbols of Christianity on the coins was too dangerous, and denying the gods immediately was too dangerous. What most scholars have failed to realize, it is not that there are gods that continue on the coins of Constantine and there are very few, if any, Christian symbols, it is that Constantine steadily, from 313 down to 324 when he reunited the Roman Empire, emptied the coinage of religious content. That is the significant change that has usually been missed. The emperor is now projected as the leading figure on the coins.

Constantine created a new portrait, quite different from that of the Tetrarchs, in which he appears looking up to heaven, inspired; whether by the pagan gods or the Christian god, no one can tell from the coins. He wears the diadem, the symbol of royalty that goes back to Alexander the Great. No emperor had ever worn that. He created a portrait that harkens back to Augustus, and ultimately to the golden boy and conqueror of all Western traditions, Alexander the Great; and Constantine saw himself in a tradition of an Alexander and of Augustus.

On the reverse of the coins—that is, the back of the coins, where you had images of the gods traditionally—the gods exited the coinage, and in place came all sorts of iconography that celebrated the imperial family. There were a few divinities that remained: the city of Roma, the city of Constantinopolis (that is, goddesses representing the city—several personifications—goddesses of virtue, such as Victory, Felicitas, which is felicity, that is, blessedness). But to Christians, these were Classical personifications and symbols and not goddesses. Pagans would see them as goddesses; and Saint Augustine had to remind his flock in the 5th century A.D.: Felicitas is just a virtue of God, not a goddess. But what Constantine was very cleverly doing was turning the few religious symbols, the few goddesses or virtues remaining on his coinage and on his public art, into personifications—or representations as we understand them today—as conventions to convey ideas and virtues rather than divinities. The result was, by his death in 337, the coinage, the medallions (those are special medals handed out to high members of state), the relief work, the sculpture (if one looks at the Arch of Constantine in Rome today), all of the art now had been emptied of religious content. It is very vague; it is very indirect; and the celebration is centered on the emperor, the imperial family— an inspired emperor who has the favor not only of the Christian God, but the pagan gods—and it really was in the eye of the beholder of that iconography exactly what divine power was favorable to Constantine.

The sons of Constantine were more direct. They put on their art and on their coins the labarum. There are symbols of the labarum used by rebel emperors; the emperor Magnentius, who was a rebel emperor in Gaul, actually put the Chi-Rho on his coins in the alpha and the omega, the beginning and the end. The irony is we believe that Magnentius might have been a pagan general and that the symbols were being used to appeal to the army and to legitimacy of Constantine's family because he was, in effect, a usurper. There are the coins issued with *hoc signo victor eris* by a general-turned-emperor who opposed Magnentius and was loyal to the surviving son of Constantine, Constantius II.

As you go through the course of the 4th and 5th centuries, imperial art becomes increasingly Christian in its iconography; and by the opening of the 5th century, you have angels and crosses; by the early 5th century, emperors will proclaim their Christianity much more overtly, especially after the laws of 391–392 that outlaw the pagan cults. But in Constantine's day, he could not do this. Most of his subjects were still pagan; all of his rivals were pagans, rival emperors, most of the soldiers; and therefore, what the coinage shows is a steady shift away from religious symbols to symbols that everyone could agree upon. That is a significant shift in and of itself; and the way I always put the issue is: What the coins do is render a Scottish verdict. They do not prove it guilty. In Scotland, the decision can be innocent, guilty, or not proven, which is, "We know you did it, but we cannot improve it"; and in a way, the currency essentially is a Scottish verdict, in my opinion. It is consistent with what the literary sources tell us.

That conversion of Constantine is significant for several reasons. One is that Constantine's conversion is the only really documented conversion we have between Saint Paul and Saint Augustine. Saint Paul's conversion is from his own letters as well as from the account in Acts of the Apostles. Saint Augustine gives us an incredible intellectual journey as Augustine goes from Christianity to Manichaeism to Platonism, and eventually back to Christianity. In both instances with Saint Paul and Saint Augustine, we are dealing with powerful intellects; certainly in the case of Saint Paul a mystic; two of the great thinkers of the Christian tradition. Their conversion was based on intellectual and spiritual considerations that would be understood by the elite classes of the Roman world.

On the other hand, Constantine was an emperor. He came from a Balkan military family. His mother, Helena—later a saint—was hardly a figure of any great nobility; in fact, her early career was a lot more like Mary Magdalene rather than the Virgin Mary (we do not need to go into that). His father Constantius was a tough general and was originally an associate of Diocletian. Therefore, Constantine as a general, as an emperor, as a soldier, as a pragmatic man, his conversion was much closer, I think, to what the conversions of most of the Roman world would be like. What convinced him was not the kind of subtle arguments that Saint Augustine could make. You have to remember, Saint Augustine was born a Christian, and his mother

Monica never gave up hope that her son would come back to the true faith. Saint Paul was a Pharisee Jew who understood his Torah, understood his Plato. Both of them were monotheists at birth. Constantine was clearly a pagan at birth, a polytheist; and what would bring him around to accept the Christian God; a god whose worshipers had been banned since 64 AD?

What convinced Constantine that this god was worth invoking was that this god delivered on victory; the victory at the Battle of the Milvian Bridge was a dramatic demonstration of the power of the Christian God. This was the Christian God of the Old Testament, the lord of hosts; and Eusebius plays this up in the *Life of Constantine*. He compares Constantine to King David; to Moses, leading the Hebrews to the Promised Land; to the parting of the Red Sea. Constantine's victories are cast in the traditions of the righteous kings of the Old Testament; and this is an image that will persist through medieval Europe and down almost to the modern age among the monarchs of Europe.

Why Constantine shows the Christian God, how he learned about him, we really do not know; and I am content to say there is really no evidence why Constantine turned to the Christian God. His mother was not a Christian; she actually embraced Christianity after her son converted. There are later legends that some scholars have tried to use to argue the opposite; but whatever caused Constantine to turn to the Christian God, it was a genuine invocation of that god in battle. When Constantine went into battle, I assume that his soldiers carried the banners of Mars and Sol Invictus. They had always carried these banners; but they now carried the banner of the Christian God, and that Christian God was seen as the giver of victory. As I mentioned, pagans would consider a divinity legitimate if that divinity could perform a miracle or some act of power; and for an emperor, that was victory in battle. Constantine's conversion will be paralleled by many conversions of pagan monarchs in medieval Europe, particularly among Scandinavian kings and Merovingian kings of Gaul.

In addition, on the more mundane level, peasants and citizens of towns did not need a battle miracle from the Christian God, but there were other miracles that could be performed. One was exorcism; and while exorcism is sometimes largely neglected in the whole question of the emergence of Christianity, Christian holy men were credited with very good powers in casting out demons, particularly my favorite figure, Gregory the Wonderworker, a contemporary and actually fellow student of Origen who was Bishop of Neocaesarea (Niksar, in Eastern Turkey today), and he was remembered in the 240s and 250s as carrying out exorcisms that led to conversions. There is another story of Saint Porphry that is set in the year 402 AD at the city of Gaza. Gaza was a pagan city; it has always been a pagan city, and at that particular city there had been a drought for a long time. The saint came in. He told the citizens of Gaza, "The reason you have a drought is you're praying to an idol, the false god Marnas. If you cast down that god in the tradition of the Old Testament, like a prophet, Elisha, you will get rain." Whether the story is true or not, apparently the idol was cast down; the cult statue was destroyed; rain came down; and there was a conversion on the spot. When we get to the conversions of the later 4th and 5th centuries A.D. when there was a new set of what I like to call the "shock troops" of Christianity—that is, the hermits, the monks, the ascetics—who will attack the statues in the tradition of Old Testament prophets, when they attacked those statues and cast them down and there were no consequences, that was a dramatic proof to many pagans who thought, "Maybe our gods are false and the god protecting these holy men is the true god." In many ways, Constantine's conversion was very much in line with the way many pagans would be converted once you had Christian emperors on the throne.

Therefore, spending a lecture on the conversion of Constantine is all-important because not only did he covert to Christianity, in 313, in the year after the battle, he issued the so-called Edict of Milan. This not only halted persecutions, but it gave legal legitimacy to Christianity and their faith; and we are going to discuss that in the coming lectures and its implications. With that change, with that decisive change, the Christians had captured the Roman monarchy; and it should be remembered, in the words of a scholar of the end of the 19th century, a man named J. B. Bury, that the conversion of Constantine is probably one of the most audacious acts carried out by an autocrat in violation of the religious opinions of the majority of his subjects. While Saint Paul was the genius who made Christianity potentially a world faith, it was Constantine who, by his conversion and the institutions he forged, would make Christianity eventually the religion of not only the Roman world, but ultimately of Europe. The conversion of Constantine was the first and decisive step in the conversion of Europe.

Constantine and the Bishops

Lecture 17

onstantine's church was an imperial institution built on the bureaucracy of the tetrarchs, a dramatic change from the apostolic church that had been in existence from the time of Saint Paul. The bishops were elevated to the legal status of *honestiores*—"honorable ones"— and took on many of the duties formerly assigned to the decurions. Two events that best defined the relationship between the emperor and the church in the public's eye were the building of the Christian capital Constantinople and the First Ecumenical Council at Nicaea.

The Church and the Law

- The churches in existence at the time of Constantine's conversion were largely the apostolic churches that went back to Saint Paul and the disciples of Christ. What Constantine did, in effect, was co-opt the bishops of those churches and create a new hierarchy within the Roman imperial system.

- In early 313, Constantine and co-emperor and brother-in-law, **Licinius**, issued an imperial rescript called the Edict of Milan. It differs significantly from earlier Christian reprieves, which were acts of clemencies, or criminal pardons. This edict not only halted all persecutions but defined Christianity as a legal religion.

- The edict made all members of the Roman world free to practice the faith they wished; it halted all persecutions and declared that property of the Christians should be returned to them, that church institutions likewise should be returned to bishops, and that henceforth Christian churches and their clergy were under the legal protection of the imperial government.

- Constantine also declared that Christian bishops, under Roman law, were constituted as an **ordo** (pl. **ordines**), or legal class, with specific rights and privileges. The highest ordo in the Roman world was the senatorial order, followed by the equestrians and then the decurions. In the late empire, imperial soldiers and officials became legal classes as well. Ordos were not economic and social classes as we understand them today; class went far beyond that.

- Sometime between the 2nd and 3rd century, the traditional Roman distinction between citizen (*civis*) and noncitizen (*peregrinus*) had been replaced by **honestiores**, "those who are honored," and **humiliores**, "the humble ones." Members of the honorable ordines had many economic and legal privileges not accorded to the humble. The bishops were in one of the honored ordines, on par with imperial officials and soldiers.

Episcopal Administration in Everyday Life

- Constantine invested many powers in the bishops, so that they increasingly displaced the pagan decurion leaders in provincial cities. Over a period of 30 years, Constantine expanded the powers of the episcopal courts to include issues beyond the immediate Christian community, such as marriages, contracts, and inheritance. It was now often to the advantage of even pagan litigants to bring their cases before bishops.

- Some scholars have seen this as a loss of imperial power and the church becoming a deathless corporation, but this is really an overstatement. There was little doubt as to who was the senior partner in this arrangement. The emperor was the fount of patronage. He was turning over to the bishops the powers he did not have sufficient administrators to handle.

- The emperor used the law to convert the empire in other ways. He could legislate in favor of Christian subjects. Roman soldiers and officers who embraced the new faith were given Sundays off. Towns that converted to Christianity were given city status.

- The precise role of the emperor within the imperial church is a matter of debate. But remember that Constantine was a true Roman; he created the Christian Roman Empire the way Augustus had created the original Roman Empire. He thus had such influence, authority, charisma, and patronage that the bishops were in no position to challenge him on legal or religious matters.

Constantine as a Source of Christian Doctrine

- Shortly after Constantine's conversion, there was a schism in the North African over the status of *lapsi*—those who had lapsed into paganism and sacrificed during the persecutions of 303–312. The Donatists, followers of Donatus, felt *lapsi* must be rebaptized before being readmitted to the church. Followers of Caecilian felt that confession was sufficient.

- Representatives of each side presented letters and petitions to Constantine, and in 315 Constantine ruled in favor of the Caecilianists. Constantine exercised his legal powers as emperor to make rulings regarding Christian institutions and Christian discipline—arguably even defining dogma.

- Bishops and authors like Eusebius hailed Constantine as the equal of the apostles, comparing him to King David and Moses, a great lawgiver. Some historians have gone so far as to argue that Constantine thus understood the politics of consensus. It would be more accurate to say that Constantine was an autocratic emperor with a vast army behind him; consensus meant, "Do what I tell you, or else."

- Compare Constantine's ability to make rulings with regard to the Christian church versus the Sāsānid shah's position in relation to Zoroastrianism. The creed depended heavily on Iranian traditions, and the shah's power rested on the traditional elite. As a result of Diocletian's reforms, the Roman emperor was no longer in that position; he had his own bureaucracy and army and the means to enforce his religious decisions.

Constantinople—The New Rome

- Two other important acts of Constantine ensured the advancement of Christianity. The first of these was the creation of a new Christian capital at Constantinople. This was far more effective than any legislation he passed against the pagan cults—of which he passed little.

- The city of Rome was no longer a strategic capital; Constantinople, on the site of the former colony of Byzantium, was on an important land and sea crossroads between the Black Sea and the Aegean. Also, shifting the capital eastward reflected the shifting makeup of the senatorial class, which increasingly came from Asia Minor and Syria.

- Constantinople was founded as a Christian city. Pagan Byzantium disappeared into the new capital, which grew in less than a century from a city of 35,000 to more than 350,000 people. Constantine constructed a whole new Christian center of imperial palaces, churches, and government offices. There were villas for the senators and a hippodrome for the masses.

- Meanwhile, the senators back in Rome were delighted because these old, distinguished pagan families could ignore the Christian capital and run Rome as a pagan city well into the 5th century.

- Constantinople's churches—particularly the original Hagia Sophia (the current building is the third of that name)—became the models for Christian churches all over the empire. The standard domed basilica church represents what we believe the churches in Constantinople looked like in the early 4th century.

The Council of Nicaea

- While building a Christian capital was a significant statement, Constantine could not outlaw the pagan cults nor make Christianity the official religion of the Roman Empire—that would happen in

391–392 under Emperor Theodosius. However, in 325, Constantine presided over the Council of Nicaea, which had several profound effects on the growing church.

- The council addressed both theological and practical matters. Among the most important theological issues addressed was the nature of the Trinity. Was Christ the same substance as the father (**homoousia**) or just similar (**homoiousia**)?

- **Athanasius**, the future patriarch of Alexandria, argued for homoousia. **Arius** argued the contrary position and apparently understood it as a hierarchy, perhaps in the vein of Origen; his position was condemned. Constantine ruled in favor of the majority position on this issue. He also offered the language of similar and same substance.

- The council also determined the reckoning of the date of Easter as the first Sunday after the new moon following the spring equinox, ensuring that Easter and Passover never coincided so that Christianity and Judaism were distinct.

- The side of the Council of Nicaea that is often not noted is the impact it had on onlookers, pagans and Christians alike. A mere 12 or 13 years since the end of the persecutions, some 330 bishops from all over the Roman world, with their great retinues, were traveling to the city of Nicaea to discuss religion with the emperor. Many of these bishops had been arrested and tortured under Diocletian; now they were in Constantine's favor. It must have seemed a true miracle.

- Constantine inverted the relationship between the emperor and the gods. The pagan emperor had visited the sanctuaries; the Christian emperor summoned the bishops instead. Together, bishops and emperor ruled over the new faith and rewarded its adherents. There was now a new, fundamentally different relationship between the imperial government and its subjects. What counted in the world of Constantine was not Roman citizenship, but Christian faith.

homoiousia: From Greek for "similar substance"; the term used by Arians to define the Christ logos as inferior to the father in the Trinity.

homoousia: From Greek for "same substance"; the term used by Nicene Christians to define the Christ logos as identical in essence to the father in the Trinity.

honestiores: Latin for "more honorable ones"; an order of society in later Roman law accorded privileges and exemptions from torture in criminal proceedings.

humiliores: Latin for "more humble ones"; an order of society in later Roman law subject to direct taxation and, in criminal proceedings, to torture and corporal punishment.

ordo (pl. **ordines**): A legal class of citizens according to Roman law, or the town council of a Roman colony or municipality.

Arius (c. 250–336): Presbyter in the church of Alexandria, he argued that Christ was generated as an inferior creature from God the father. His theology, Arianism, was condemned at the First Ecumenical Council (325), but his followers converted the East Germans to the Arian confession.

Athanasius (c. 293–373): Theologian and clergyman who opposed Arius at the First Ecumenical Council of Nicaea in 325, arguing the Orthodox positions. As patriarch of Alexandria (329–373), he opposed Emperor Constantius II, a devoted Arian, and later the pagan emperor Julian II. His writings are regarded the touchstone of Orthodoxy. In about 360, he wrote the hagiography of Saint Antony of Egypt.

Licinius I (a.k.a. **Gaius Valerius Licianus Licinius**; c. 263–325; r. 308–324): A veteran officer, Licinius was elevated as Augustus of the West by Galerius after Severus II had been defeated and executed by Maxentius. In

311, Licinius succeeded to the Balkan provinces. In 313, he contracted an alliance with Constantine and married Constantine's half-sister Constantia. That same year, he defeated Maximinus II Daza and took over the eastern provinces. Twice—in 314 and 323–324—Licinius clashed with Constantine. Licinius was defeated and deposed by Constantine in 324; he was executed in 325. Licinius issued jointly with Constantine the Edict of Milan in 313. Initially tolerant of Christians, Licinius was criticized for persecution of Christians during his final war with Constantine.

Suggested Reading

Barnes, *Constantine and Eusebius.*

Drake, *Constantine and the Bishops.*

Eusebius, *The History of the Church from Christ to Constantine.*

———, *Life of Constantine.*

Garnsey, *Social Status and Legal Privilege in the Roman Empire.*

Krautheimer, *Three Christian Capitals.*

MacCormack, *Art and Ceremony in Late Antiquity.*

Odhal, *Constantine and the Christian Empire.*

Rapp, *Holy Bishops in Late Antiquity.*

Van Dam, *The Roman Revolution of Constantine.*

Questions to Consider

1. Why was the Edict of Milan such a turning point for Christianity and the Roman Empire? Why was legal status so important for the success of Christianity?

2. What was the impact of the dedication of Constantinople as a Christian capital? How did pagans react to this change? What was the opinion of the pagan senators at Rome?

3. Why would Christians and pagans alike see the Council of Nicaea as a veritable miracle? What did Constantine hope to achieve by summoning the council? What were the consequences of the council?

Constantine and the Bishops

Lecture 17—Transcript

In this lecture, I plan to deal with Constantine and the construction of the imperial church, as I would like to call it. This imperial church was built on imperial institutions—that is, the bureaucratic institutions—of the emperor Diocletian and his associates, the Tetrarchs; but the churches themselves that were in existence at the time of Constantine's conversion were largely apostolic churches that went back to Saint Paul, Saint Peter, and to the early apostles and disciples of Christ.

What Constantine did, in effect, was co-op the bishops of those churches and made them a new hierarchy within a Roman imperial system. When I speak of the imperial church, it's not as if Constantine simply invented it out of whole cloth; there were these apostolic churches with a tradition of a powerful bishop, as well as all sorts of Roman legal and administrative institutions that Constantine could invest into the hands of the bishops. What we're looking at is the emperor Constantine, his relationship to the bishops, and how emperor and bishops together constructed a new imperial Roman church after the conversion of Constantine in 312.

That will also require us to look at two major events that helped define the relationship between emperors and bishops: the building of the Christian capital Constantinople and the First Ecumenical Council at Nicaea; and those will be coming up later in the lecture.

First, let's turn to Constantine's relationship with different bishops. In early 313 at Milan, Constantine and his erstwhile ally, an emperor named Licinius—who was married actually to a half-sister of Constantine and was temporarily in alliance with Constantine—issued an imperial *rescript*, which is essentially an answer to a petition. It's usually called the Edict of Milan; it's recorded in the Christian sources. It differs significantly from earlier reprieves that emperors had issued when they halted persecutions. In earlier instances, pagan emperors, in effect, carried out an act of clemency (*clementia*)—that is, they spared the Christians future persecutions—and this was done in the same light as when you give reprieves to criminals, to all sorts of outcasts when an emperor is on his death bed or an emperor feels that he should reconsider; it's essentially a pardon.

In 313, however, Constantine and Licinius together issued not only a halt to the persecution, but defined Christianity now as a legal religion. It was couched in language in which the emperor and his ally Licinius said that all members of the Roman world were free to practice the faith they wished; that persecutions were to be halted, that property of the Christians should be returned to them, that church institutions likewise should be returned to bishops, and that henceforth, Christian churches and their clergy were under the legal protection of the imperial government. These legal rulings by Constantine were all-important because this was a significant change in the whole relationship of Christianity vis-à-vis the imperial government, as well as the relationship between the emperor Constantine and the leadership of the Christian church; that is, the bishops, particularly, the bishops of those apostolic churches that claimed to go back to the earliest missions. Henceforth, bishops, according to Constantine, using Roman law were constituted as an ordo, a legal class. I have mentioned the ordo (or its plural ordines) in earlier parts of this course; and an ordo is clearly a legal class. It's defined with having rights and privileges; they're Roman citizens. The highest ordo in the early Roman world and the Roman Republic was the senatorial order, and then you have the equestrian order. The decurions were an ordo. Roman imperial soldiers and officials of the late Empire became legal classes; and these were not strictly economic and social as we would understand it today, which is primarily a question of income or wealth. It went beyond that. The Christian clergy now constituted an ordo, and it was in the ordines—that is, it was in the categories—of those who were classified as *honestiores*.

In Roman law, there was an important distinction that evolved in the 2nd and 3rd century AD. The distinction between citizen (*civis*), and non-citizen (*peregrini*)—that is, between Roman and provincial—had been replaced by a new distinction of *honestiores*, which means "those who are honored," and the *humiliores*, those who look down at the earth (the *humus*, the humble ones). What happened was that those classes that were in the honorable ranks, the honorable ordines, they got elevated and had all sorts of privileges—that might be tax exemptions, no corporal punishment, special favors from the emperor—and the humble ones, those fellows were not so lucky. They perhaps could be subject to corporal punishment, even though they're Roman citizens. From the 2nd century on, Roman jurists came to evolve a system that has often been called the law of dual penalties, especially in criminal proceedings, in which the *honestiores* are favored; and this begins to approach something of the class distinctions, as we understand.

The result of Constantine's conversion to Christianity was that bishops were now put in one of those honored ordines. They're very high up; they're on par with imperial officials and imperial soldiers. Furthermore, Constantine invested in the bishops all sorts of powers that made the Christian bishops increasingly potential leaders in provincial cities who could displace the pagan decurion class; those families that ran the town councils and administered the cults of the cities that were so important to pagan worship. These were a series of rulings over a period of 30 years in which Constantine expanded the competence of Episcopal courts; that is, the courts that were held by bishops. Originally, bishops had to adjudicate disputes within their congregations; but with Constantine, bishops began to acquire a competence over litigation and issues that went beyond the immediate Christian community.

What were some examples of this? One would be any kind of issue that involved oaths; taking an oath before God or to the divine. That would include various types of law dealing with marriages, with even contracts, with inheritance. Bishops could rule on these cases, especially if both litigants were Christian. In many instances, if one litigant was Christian and one was pagan, under certain circumstances the Christian litigant could argue or could appeal to have a decision or a case transferred from the imperial to the Episcopal court; that is, to get a bishop to rule on it. There were a number of issues of customary or local law in the cities of the Roman world, and these varied from city to city. It was now often to the advantage of litigants, pagan and Christian alike, to bring their cases before bishops who were, in effect, administering a version of imperial law.

Some scholars have often seen this as a way of the emperor losing power, creating an institution within the Roman Empire—that is, the church becomes a deathless corporation, it gains legal powers— but this is really an overstatement. Constantine invested certain powers in the bishops that were very similar in many ways to powers once executed and administered by pagan decurions, and also there was very, very little doubt who was the senior partner in this arrangement. The emperor was the fount of patronage. He had a vast army and bureaucracy behind him. He had the power of Roman law. Therefore, the bishops understood very clearly that the emperor was the senior partner in this relationship, and the emperor wasn't giving away anything that was really vital to him; in fact, in many ways he was turning over to the bishops powers that he just didn't have sufficient imperial administrators or offices to do. The way the Roman world had always been run was by co-opting local elites; and what Constantine, in effect, was doing was creating a Christian local elite and co-opting them to imperial service.

There were other ways that the emperor could change the religious makeup of the Roman Empire. Constantine, for instance, could legislate in favor of those subjects who were Christians. Roman soldiers and officers who embraced the new faith were given Sundays off; there's a law in 326 that allows that. Towns that converted to Christianity would be given the status of a city. We have an inscription from a town in Asia Minor. It was a satellite town of the city of Amorium, which is a city being excavated by Chris Lightfoot, which is the late Roman Byzantine city; and this little community, Orcistus, really was probably just nothing more than a glorified village. But they petitioned the emperor and said, "Everyone has turned Christian, could you grant us civic status?" which meant, "Free us from Amorium so that we can run our own events; we are now a city," and Constantine says "Yes, you now have a bishop. You have municipal institutions; you have your own taxes." This was incentive for a number of cities to convert.

Over the course of the 4th and 5th centuries, you have a number of these cases embracing Christianity, or least openly professing through their bishop that the majority are Christians or they're all Christians (probably a bit sanguine in their claims), and then getting a favorable ruling from the emperor. We even get cases—the most famous case from Roman Mesopotamia—of the city of Edessa (today Urfa in Turkey) goes Christian and gets favors, and its rival city, Carrhae Harran stays pagan (actually, it's still pagan when the Arabs arrive in the 7th and 8th centuries). What happens is by the power of Roman law, Constantine can promote, augment, the various attractions of embracing the new faith, and this comes in various ways.

What was the precise role of the emperor within this new imperial church? There are a lot of debates on this, but you have to again remember: Constantine was a Roman; he was a Roman Emperor. I always like to think of Constantine as essentially the second founder of the Roman world; that is, he plays the role of the Christian emperor who creates the Christian Roman Empire the way the emperor Augustus had created the original Roman Empire, the pagan Roman Empire. Just like Augustus, Constantine understood a very important principal in government, which was expressed by the imperial biographer Suetonius talking about Augustus, but applies just as well to Constantine: Make haste slowly. Constantine essentially had superior *auctoritas*. He had the influence, the authority; that charisma; the patronage that meant that he had a special position vis-à-vis the bishops. That authority was inherited by his sons and by Christian emperors well into the 5th century; so it really is anachronistic to think that the bishops were in any way going to challenge the emperor or represented some sort of alternate power. Far from it; the bishops wanted the emperor's input and innovation. This is seen at the very start of Constantine's career as a Christian emperor. I believe he converted in 312, and by that I mean he accepted the Christian god as a legitimate power and by, I think, 315—within two years, maybe three years after that conversion—he also understood that that meant monotheist.

There was a split in the North African church. It had come about as a result of the Tetrarchic persecutions from 303 down until they were halted by Constantine in 312. The African Church was very important; I mentioned that it was the first significant set of Latin-speaking churches. It boasted of brilliant bishops of Carthage; one thinks of Saint Cyprian one of the earliest writers in Latin, and Tertullian, the apologist. This church had been really split over the persecution because many Christians had lapsed and had offered sacrifices during the persecution; they were *lapsi*. Then there were other Christians who refused to buckle under; who went into the arena or in many instances were arrested and would have been executed, and then Constantine won the Battle of the Milvian Bridge and they were released. There was a reprieve; it was a miracle. Those guys who were released came to be associated with the leader of the movement in the North African church known as Donatus—they became known as Donatists, the followers of Donatus—and their argument was if you had sacrificed during the persecution, you had lapsed; you were no longer a Christian. You had to be re-baptized. This was a very powerful and rigorist argument. The other side, which followed a man named Caecilian—and what you're in effect dealing with were rival bishops, Caecilian versus Donatist for bishop of Carthage—they argued, especially looking at the example of Peter in the gospel accounts that, "No, we are the church of all sinners; that all you have to do is make confession. You never really lost your Christianity, you had only temporarily lapsed." This issue split the African Church.

What happened is representatives of both sides presented letters and petitions to the emperor Constantine, and in 315 Constantine ruled in favor of the Caecilianists; that is, the broader position that only a confession was necessary. That split the African church into a schism—that is, that Donatists refused to accept the emperors ruling; they maintained their own churches really down into the 5th century when the Vandals showed up—but nonetheless, what's important is Constantine was exercising his legal powers as emperor to order Christian institutions and Christian discipline and even was probably to the point of almost defining dogma in a sense, because this deals with the whole question of what does baptism mean and what is salvation.

That was a vast expansion of the earlier precedence of the few Roman emperors who had ruled on legal issues about Christian property. Therefore, there's a good reason why bishops and authors like Eusebius hailed Constantine as the equal of the apostles (*isoapostolicus* in Greek); compared him to King David; often compared him to Moses, as the Roman equivalent of Moses, a great lawgiver; a man who could win over the bishops and create a unity within the leadership of the Christian church. Some historians have gone so far as to argue that Constantine was an emperor who understood the politics of consensus, which I think is essentially anachronistic. Constantine's an autocratic emperor with a vast army behind him; consensus means "Do what I tell you, or else," which is true of most Roman emperors.

In any event, these changes were very, very important. Constantine had the power to back up these rulings with regard to the Christian church because of two reasons: He had an imperial army, an imperial bureaucracy, beholden to him. If we can step back for a moment and look at the other rival empire of Rome; that is, the Sassanid Empire of Persia and Central Asia. The Sassanid Shahs were Zoroastrians, and that is a monotheistic creed. It depended very heavily on Iranian traditions. The Shah of Persia really can't change his religion—he can't become a Manichaean, although several of them toyed with the idea; they can't become Christians—because the power of the Iranian Shah rested on its traditional elites. The traditional elites also provided the Magi—that is, the religious elites, the clergy of the Zoroastrian faith—which is quintessentially Iranian. The Roman emperor didn't have that problem. When the Christians converted the Roman emperor, they converted him at the best time. As a result of Diocletian's reforms and Constantine's building on those reforms, the Roman emperor had his own bureaucracy and army that would do what he told them to do; and therefore, he had an awesome magistery, and when he decided Christianity was the faith, he had the means to enforce it.

This is significant because the pagan emperor that follows Constantine, his nephew Julian—who only rules for a brief time, from 360–363—was a very, very odd pagan ruler. He was actually reared as a Christian and then was an apostate; he went over to the pagan beliefs. Julian, what he did was, in the words of one scholar, Peter Brown, he tried to out-Constantine Constantine by essentially taking that Christian imperial church of Constantine and turning it into a pagan church in order to counteract all the activities of Constantine and Constantine's sons. What Constantine built was an imperial church in which emperor and bishops together cooperated and attempted to carry out the greater mission of converting the Roman world and winning the favor of God. That's a much better way of understanding the relationship between emperor and bishops than these notions that there was some kind of conflict or that there were opposing oppositions.

The logical conclusion of Constantine's relationship with the bishops and the Christian church is, in some ways, the caliphate of medieval Islam, where secular and religious power essentially became embodied in one. Not as close to it would be the Byzantine situation of the Byzantine emperor and the patriarch in Constantinople. But what developed in the medieval West of a pope and independent secular rulers; that's the farthest from what Constantine and the bishops of his day thought the relationship of secular and divine should be.

Constantine had two other very, very important acts that really ensured the advancement of Christianity. One was the creation of the city of Constantinople as the new Christian capital; the new Rome. This was far more effective than any legislation he passed against the pagan cults; and he passed very limited legislation against the pagan cults. Most of the efforts to ban cults that were seen as offensive were really taken by his sons. What, in effect, he did was create a new Christian capital that would replace the old Rome of Italy.

There were several reasons for doing this. For one, Rome was no longer a strategic capital. In the course of the fighting of the 3rd century and the civil wars of the early 4th century, Rome was really out of position. Soldier-emperors had made their capitals at far more important strategic cities. Trier or Treveri on the Mosul near the Rhineland, the city of Milan, Nicomedia in Asia Minor, Antioch, all of these functioned as imperial capitals. Constantine choosing the ancient city of Byzantium, a Greek colony on the European side of the Bosporus, was just within that tradition; and Byzantium had a very important strategic role: It was on important crossroads, both land routes and sea routes, going from the Black Sea into the Aegean. In that sense, what Constantine was doing was simply following what a lot of his pagan predecessors had followed.

In addition, Constantine moved the locus of imperial power from the Western part of the Roman world to the East. This, too, was the culmination of a long process. That is, ever since the mid-2nd century A.D., increasingly the senatorial aristocracy, the ruling elites of Rome, came from the eastern cities, particularly from Asia Minor and Syria; and those elites had come ever more to define the role of the Roman emperor. I like to see Constantine, in effect, as the Eastern senatorial elites brought the emperor home, close to where their cities were.

But even taking into account these two historical factors that were influencing Constantine's decision, it was still a very momentous and dramatic change. The reason is Constantinople, the city of Constantine—or, as it was often called, the new Rome—was, from the start, a Christian city. When it was dedicated in 330 A.D., pagan Byzantium had essentially disappeared into imperial Christian Constantinople. Those of you who perhaps have visited the city of Istanbul today—that is, Constantinople—have noted remarkable churches, particularly Hagia Sophia. You're looking at the third version of that church; the first version goes back into the 4th century, it was burned during the rioting of the deposition of John Chrysostom in 404. There are elements of that earlier church actually in the garden of Hagia Sophia today, particularly the pulpit. But, in any case, from the start, all of the pagan temples were dismantled; the columns were used for building Christian churches. Many of those columns got recycled into the cisterns, particularly if you see the cistern of Justinian today where, I think, there's an opening sequence from James Bond *From Russia with Love* with him flying around in a speedboat; which is a really rather strange episode, but it's all in good fun.

In any event, what happened is Byzantium, city of 35,000, was replaced by a Christian capital that in less than a century grew from 35,000 to over 350,000. There was a new downtown, the hippodrome; that is, a vast stadium where games could be staged for the population of Constantinople. An imperial palace, which essentially occupies the grounds today of the Blue Mosque the Sultan Ahmet Camii built in the early 17th century. Then across the way was the Hagia Sophia, the Hagia Irene; and this was to replace the new Rome.

There was an imperial senate comprised of officials and officers of the imperial government who were now elevated to senators and, of course, they would give them pensions, villas, and were expected to be Christians. In addition, Rome had seven hills. Constantinople has seven hills; they actually had to fake one of them, but there were the seven hills. The city of Rome had a mob, which essentially acted as the proxy of the Roman people; so Constantinople had its own Christian mob, which was entertained by chariot races in the hippodrome just opposite from the imperial palace. I often wondered, what were the advertisements like in order to try out for "Mob of Christian Constantinople, capable of rioting at the right time"? You can get into some rather silly and amusing would-be or possible advertisements. But in any case, seriously, the city of Constantine was to replace the new Rome; and the senators in Rome were delighted because the senators in Rome of the old distinguished families, they just ignored the Christian capital and ran Rome well into the 5th century as a pagan city. The political and religious center of the Roman Empire had now come to rest at Constantinople, and that was a Christian city.

Furthermore, Constantinople, with its churches—and we'll be discussing this in greater detail—was the model for building churches in provincial cities, particularly the Hagia Sophia, and we'll see that particularly in the 6th century A.D.; but even in Constantine's day and the reign of his sons, especially Constantius II who ruled from 337–361, the churches in Constantinople were taken as models for building cathedral churches in provincial cities. You can see that at Ephesus: The church of the Virgin Mary, the Mary Theotokos, mother of God, which is being reconstructed today; that vast double church of the early 5th century, which was actually built, in part, in the old temple of Zeus Olympus, is in many ways a basilican church modeled after what we think the churches in Constantinople looked like in the early 4th century; that is, the original Hagia Sophia. Visiting Ephesus today and seeing that church—and at least you can see the foundations of a very, very impressive church with a huge nave and apse, with a courtyard that is paved with all sorts of classical *spolia* (recycled inscriptions from the 2nd and 3rd centuries), with a baptistery—that church really approximates pretty well what churches must have looked like in Constantinople in Constantine's day. The reconstruction and restoration of that church is a very, very important element in understanding the Christianizing of the Roman East. Constantinople played this major role as acting as a beacon for Christians in the Roman East and also providing a model of how to build churches and Christianize your city.

The importance of Constantinople cannot be exaggerated. By the end of the 4th century A.D. or the opening of the 5th century A.D., it had probably surpassed all cities in the Roman world except for Rome and Alexandria in population. Within a century, by the year 400, it eclipsed Rome and Alexandria. It had grown to a city that some would think by the time of Justinian may well have been as much as a million; certainly it was 750,000 strong. Therefore, Constantinople became the queen of cities; the dominant Christian center in the Roman Eastern Empire.

Building the capital at Constantinople, creating a Christian capital, was a significant statement by the emperor Constantine. As I said, he couldn't outlaw the cults; there were just too many pagans. But he could build a Christian capital and therefore inspire cities to follow that example. Many popular works say that Constantine made Christianity the official religion of the Roman Empire, and he couldn't; he didn't do that. That's not going to be done until 391–392 by the emperor Theodosius. But the building of Constantinople was a significant step in that direction.

The other crucial step in that direction was the Council of Nicaea, held in 325 A.D. The Council of Nicaea can be studies in several ways. One is on theological arguments. There was a major debate on the nature of the Trinity. What was the relationship of Jesus, the Christ logos, to the Father; and ultimately what was the relationship of the Holy Spirit? I mentioned earlier in the lecture on Origen that this whole issue, in effect, came out of Origen's terminology that the Son is internally generated from the Father; and fundamentally the issue was: Was Christ the same substance as the Father or similar? Was he *homoiousia*, similar substance, or *homoousia*, the same substance? The difference was that little iota in the word, that extra iota for "similar"; and that's where we get the phrase "an iota of difference," which really determined whether you were on the winning or losing side of the Council of Nicaea. Athanasius, the future patriarch of Alexandria, argued for the same substance; that Father and Son were coequal and coeternal, so was the Holy Spirit, and that leads to the definition of Trinity. Athanasius's position won; it was voted by the majority of bishops. Arius, who argued the contrary position and apparently understood it as a hierarchy perhaps in the vein of Origen, his position was condemned. Constantine presided over this council as if he was a Roman judge and jurist, and he ruled in favor of the majority position. He actually offered the language, similar and same substance; and he also enforced the decrees of the majority of bishops, some 330 bishops, who attended.

That's the theological side; they also determined the reckoning of Easter, when it should be done. That would be the Roman reckoning; that is, Easter is the first Sunday after the new moon that brings in the Equinox, and that made sure that Easter and Passover never coincided so that Christianity and Judaism were distinct. You can understand Constantine's position here. As a pagan emperor, he now was a Christian; he wanted to know, "How do I pray to my God [and that is the Nicene Creed, which recites the Trinity, which is, in effect, effect a prayer] and when do I worship this God [the most important festival being Easter] and how do I reckon it?" These two issues were determined and Constantine enforced them.

On the other hand, there's another side of the Council of Nicaea that's often not noted, and that's the impact it had on onlookers, pagans and Christians at the same time. Here it had the same impact as building the city of Constantinople. Think of it: In 325, maybe 12 or 13 years since the ending of the persecutions, bishops from all over the Roman world—the vast majority from the Eastern part of the Roman Empire, some 330 of them—with great retinues, were traveling to the city of Nicaea to see the Roman Emperor Constantine on religious matters. These included men like Patriarch Alexander of Alexandria, who had been arrested during the Tetrarchic persecutions. Many of these bishops had suffered tortures or arrests under Diocletian. They were now summoned to the presence of the emperor in order to converse about this new faith.

If that wasn't a miracle to pagans, I don't know what was. We have a contemporary report from a Christian writer, Gregory Nazianzus, who reports while bishop of Caesarea (Kayseri today in Turkey), and Gregory Nazianzus says that his father, who was also named Gregory, saw the bishops going to Nicaea for the great council. He was so impressed that this pagan Decurion within four years not only had converted to Christianity but had been consecrated the bishop of Caesarea, and he represents an example of a number of decurions and imperial officials who, seeing the Council of Nicaea and Constantine's petition, embraced the new faith.

What Constantine did was invert the role between emperor and the gods. Now the emperor summoned the bishops, whereas pagan emperors used to visit the sanctuaries. But those bishops and emperor together ruled and legislated over the new faith, and was clear that Constantine would enforce those decisions and that he could reward the subjects of his who were followers of the new faith. There was now a new, fundamentally different relationship between the imperial government and its subjects. What counted in the world of Constantine was not Roman citizenship, but Christian faith.

Christianizing the Roman World
Lecture 18

Architecture was an enormous part of how the new Christian elite asserted the new religious identity of the Roman world. Churches were sometimes newly built structures created on the basilica plan; other times, they were co-opted pagan shrines; whenever possible, they were situated for maximum effect. Bishops took over the decurions' former role in distributions, now predicated on need rather than citizenship. New centers of worship, particularly in the Holy Land, became new pilgrimage sites, and Christian identity began creating political bonds between Rome and the world beyond its borders.

The First Imperial Church Buildings

- Constantine and the bishops claimed Roman public and religious spaces for the new faith, turning the urban landscape from a pagan one into a Christian one between the 4th and 6th centuries. During this time, the **basilica** was adapted as the premier type of church building.

- There were subtle transformations of public religious spaces that varied from city to city and province to province. One example took place in Ephesus, where the Church of Mary Theotokos was built inside the temenos wall of the sanctuary to Zeus and the temple to Zeus and other public buildings were dismantled for building materials.

- Many of these very early churches only survive as foundations. Some of them can be dated based on the coin finds in or under these foundations.

- The basilica churches were constructed in prominent places: Ephesus's Church of Mary Theotokos was near the port; Hierapolis had a series of churches on the axial road running from the city gate to the cemetery. This was part of what might be called an intercept policy, diverting the crowds from the famous pagan sanctuaries in these cities.

- Another method, dictated in part by costs but also quite effective, was to convert a temple into a church. Aphrodisias, a city devoted to the worship of Aphrodite, defied the emperors and continued in pagan worship well into the 5th century. When Emperor Zeno finally brought them to heel, the Christian architects added an apse at the temple's east end and extended the rest to create a basilica layout.

- Several exceptional sanctuaries were not turned into churches, either because they were too famous and important as pagan centers or because of structural problems. The Temple of Artemis Ephesia at Ephesus is a case of both. Eventually, the sanctuary was leveled, with a single column of the original 128 left standing as a memorial to show the victory of the new faith over the old.

As the empire was converted, pagan temples were converted, too.

Episcopal Patronage

- This changing of public and religious space was paralleled by changes in social and economic life in the cities. Bishops had the patronage of the emperor; they had money, and they employed hundreds or thousands of people in constructing and decorating the new churches. This made the bishops the fount of patronage in provincial cities.

- We have a monumental inscription from Bishop Marcus Julius Eugenius of Laodicea Combusta, who boasted of turning his city Christian by architecture. The inscription is similar to those of decurions of the 1st and 2nd centuries putting up pagan and public buildings.

- Some Christians deplored these men as having lithomania—putting up buildings at random. Others saw these bishops as nourishers of the city. That meant that in addition to all this public construction, they took on the social obligations that once characterized the pagan elites.

- Pagan decurions had always given out distributions to citizens at the festivals; the higher your rank, the more you received. The Christian bishops turned this into almsgiving and reversed the precedence: The more you needed, the more you received. Its purpose was not to demonstrate the donor's honor but as an act of piety. Well-off Christian families often donated anonymously.

Christian Pilgrimage

- Pilgrimage routes changed in the Roman world from the time of Constantine on. Before Constantine, people traveled great distances to visit the oracles and the major shrines and festivals. Now, new Christian centers with little or no relationship to the old sanctuaries were emerging.

- The most obvious was the Holy Land. Saint **Helena**, Constantine's mother, made many efforts to find places associated with the early Christian traditions in the region between 326 and 328.

- Church fathers were divided on the issue. Some were avid about finding relics; others saw too much potential for fraud. But by the year 400, there was an extremely well-developed pilgrimage and trade route from the western half of the Roman Empire into the Holy Land. The region that the Romans called Palestine experienced an enormous economic boom as a result that would continue well into the early Middle Ages.

- Other sites developed along the pilgrimage routes in Italy, the Balkans, and in Asia Minor. The development of these pilgrimage routes was important in redirecting the focus of religious life in the Roman world to new locations, locations associated with the mission and crucifixion of Jesus and the early apostles.

The Revival of Missionary Activity

- Constantine initiated missionary activity outside the Roman world. This changed the diplomatic and political dimensions of Roman foreign policy on many levels.

- According to tradition, King **Tiridates III** of Armenia embraced Christianity several years before Constantine's conversion. Some historians think it is more likely the Armenians embraced Christianity because of Rome's conversion. Either way, it created a new political bond.

- The king of Axum, in northern Ethiopia, also embraced Christianity late in the reign of Constantine, as did various Arabian tribes along the frontiers between Rome and the Sāsānid Empire.

- Missions were sent to the northern peoples. The most famous of these was commissioned by Emperor Constantius II, led by **Ulfilas**. He translated the Bible into Gothic and converted the East Germanic peoples to Arian Christianity. These tribes, previously classified as barbarians, were now part of the *oikoumene*, the Christian community.

- As a result of these missions, the barriers between Rome and the outside world crossed by religious bonds. For example, Roman Emperors began intervening on Armenia's behalf against the

Persian shahs. Armenia—which in the classical age had culturally and religiously leaned toward the Iranian world—now reoriented itself toward Rome.

- Henceforth, the identity that determined one's citizenship or position in the Roman world was not "Are you a Roman citizen?" but "Are you a Christian?"

Important Terms

basilica: A Roman public building with apses at each end and a central hall, or narthex. The design was applied to a Christian church in the 4th century. The longitudinal axis of the basilica was distinct from the centrally planned church in the form of square with a dome at the intersection—the design favored in the middle and late Byzantine ages.

oikoumene: Greek for "inhabited"; the universal Christian world.

Names to Know

Helena (a.k.a. **Flavia Julia Helena**; c. 246–330): Saint, first wife of Constantius I, and mother of Constantine I. In about 289, Constantius divorced Helena so that he could marry Theodora, daughter of Maximianus, Augustus of the West. In 326–328, Helena traveled to Jerusalem and Bethlehem, where she reportedly found the True Cross.

Tiridates III (250–339; r. 285–339): Arsacid king of Armenia who was a loyal ally of Rome in the wars against the Persians. In 301, he reportedly converted to Christianity and was baptized by Gregory the Illuminator. There is reason to believe that Tiridates might have converted after the conversion of Emperor Constantine I.

Ulfilas (a.k.a. **Wulfila**; 311–381): Arian bishop of the Goths consecrated at the synod of Antioch in 341. As missionary to the Goths, Ulfilas adapted the Greek alphabet to Gothic and translated the Bible into Gothic in 341–343.

Suggested Reading

Atkins and Osborne, eds., *Poverty in the Roman World*.

Brown, *Poverty and Leadership in the Later Roman Empire*.

————. *Power and Persuasion in Late Antiquity*.

Dietz, *Wandering Monks, Virgins and Pilgrims*.

Drijvers, *Helena Augusta*.

Finn, *Almsgiving in the Later Roman Empire.*

Fowden, *From Empire to Commonwealth*.

Harl, "From Pagan to Christian in the Cities of Asia Minor.

Holman, *The Hungry are Dying*.

Holum, *Theodosian Empresses*.

Hunt, *Holy Land Pilgrimage in the Later Roman Empire*.

MacMullen, *The Second Church*.

van Dam, *Families and Friends in Late Roman Cappadocia*.

Questions to Consider

1. What advantages did the bishops enjoy over pagan decurions in gaining control of cities? Why were building activities so crucial for Christianizing cities?

2. How important were charity and Christian festivals in winning over city populations? How did these activities differ from earlier pagan ones?

3. What was the impact of pilgrimage in creating a wider Christian world? How did Christians view pilgrimage as an expression of faith?

4. How did Christian emperors promote missions to the peoples beyond the imperial frontiers? How did a sense of Christian commonwealth come into being? What was the historical significance of this new perception?

Christianizing the Roman World
Lecture 18—Transcript

In this lecture, I wish to deal with some of the implications of Constantine's activities from the previous two lectures: his conversion, construction of a Christian capital, and summoning the Council of Nicaea. We should think of this lecture as essentially dealing with the Christianizing of the Roman world and those regions immediately beyond the Roman world, because Constantine's efforts to promote Christianity were not only within the empire, but among various allied and associated powers beyond the imperial *limes*, or frontier, which came to mark the political and cultural barriers of the Roman world vis-à-vis the rest of the world. That cultural political barrier begins to lose its significance in the increasingly Christian world created by Constantine and his successors.

What we want to look at in this particular lecture are several related issues. First, we want to see how Constantine and the bishops claimed public and religious space for the new faith, particularly in the Classical cities. That represents a whole issue of turning the urban landscape increasingly from a pagan one into a Christian one, and this is a long process between the 4th century and 6th centuries A.D., and it's not really completed until the time of Justinian, who rules between 527 and 565. Another related issue that we'll deal with is the whole social change and economic change in the cities where the bishops and the Christian emperor came to play a new role. Then we can turn and look at the issue of Christian pilgrimage and Christian missionary activity, which are two very important related issues that tie in with the first subject: changing the Classical city into a Christian city. With these three issues in mind, let's take a look at what Constantine initiated by becoming a Christian emperor.

First, Constantine—and some historians would go so far as if it was Constantine himself and not members of his court—is somehow behind the adaptation of the basilica, a Roman public building, as the premier building for the construction of a church. In an earlier lecture, I mentioned at the city of Sardis there is a synagogue that is essentially a remodeled public building, a basilica—which is a Roman public building in the city of Sardis—that had been turned over to the Jewish community around 280 A.D.

and in some ways acted as a model for the Christian basilican church. But whatever the precedents were for this, Constantine was clearly behind the creation of a building that is distinctly Christian and religious, and Roman at the same time. The Roman basilica is a quintessentially Roman building. It is a brick and concrete building with vaults, with various types of arches; it is a vast enclosure of space, and this comes to mark the typical premier Christian church.

At the same time, besides creating this new ecclesiastical religious architecture, there is a subtle transformation of the public and religious space of many cities in the Roman world, and this is the benefit of the new faith. The way this was done varied from city to city; it varied from province to province. Archeologists who work in different parts of the Roman world can each provide their own story of how it is done. There is now increasingly very good work being done in Spain; there has been a lot of work done in Tunisia, in Italy, and in Greece. I have spent the last 25 years of my career working in Asia Minor, so I will draw on examples from Asia Minor, today Turkey; and you have to keep in mind that these examples are pretty much similar to, at least in broad terms, changes going on across the Roman Empire. There are some exceptions in the northwestern provinces—that is, along the Rhine and Danube frontier—where Christians were still pretty much a minority, or certainly they did not have the same impact as they did in the core lands around the Mediterranean. But overall, these examples should serve pretty much for the Roman world.

One of the most obvious examples is the city of Ephesus. I spoke about Ephesus on several occasions. It is the center of the goddess Artemis Ephesia. It is where Paul tried to make some of his most important conversions. The city of Ephesus, which was the first city of Asia, had a cult of Artemis Ephesia that was recognized across the Roman world. Ephesus was granted Christian churches perhaps as early as the 4th century, certainly by the early 5th century. The church that we have today, which is associated with the Third Ecumenical Council, the church of Mary Theotokos, was actually built in a *temenos* wall colonnade of a larger sanctuary to Zeus. When you see this church today, which is being reconstructed, and you stand at the apse and look down at the nave towards the courtyard, what you are seeing is part of a pagan sanctuary that has been taken over and remodeled as a basilican church. It essentially is on the floor plan a part of a much larger pagan sanctuary, and the temple of Zeus was essentially dismantled and the sanctuary was turned into a Christian church that is very close to the port.

It is a long nave church. It has an impressive courtyard that is paved with various *spolia*. *Spolia* is a term we use to indicate recycled material from earlier times; and so the pavement includes inscriptions and elements from various public buildings that have been laid down as a marble flooring to a large courtyard. Just to the north of that courtyard is a baptistery. The baptisteries are usually built as circular buildings. They are very, very important in churches of the 4th and 5th centuries because there are an enormous number of adult conversions; and there is another one on the church of Saint John at Ephesus, which we will talk about later in the reign of Justinian.

The church of Mary Theotokos in Ephesus is a good example of the type of basilican churches that were constructed by Constantine and his sons throughout the empire. Many of these very early churches only survive in foundation. This is particularly true with the city of Sardis, where we have that synagogue that is the model for a Christian church. There is an early 4th century church, but it's only in a floor plan; and unless you know what you are looking at, you can easily pass it by. That church has been dated; I was asked to help date that church. Under the floor are coins of the 4th century A.D., which date the church very securely to either 348 or 354 A.D. based on the coin finds. There are a number of these examples of churches; I know of examples in Spain.

These basilican churches were constructed in prominent places; the church of Mary Theotokos at Ephesus at the port. In the city of Hierapolis, today modern Pamukkale, we have a series of basilican churches on the axial road that runs north to south that connects the northern cemetery, where the pagan cemeteries are, to the south end, and those churches are on the main road you would take as you go through the city gate, and they, in effect, replace the Temple of Apollo and the so-called Plutonium. The Plutonium is next to the Temple of Apollo. It apparently had various noxious gases and animals, particularly birds, were sacrificed to Apollo by tossing them down in that subterranean chamber. It was regarded as one of the openings into the underworld. What you get is the subtle placement of churches along highways in what I like to call an intercept policy; that is, as someone is coming into what was originally a pagan city, they are immediately hit with Christian churches at strategic points on the main streets or coming in at the port, and these divert the crowds away from the famous pagan sanctuary. This is very well seen at Hierapolis. That is one way you claim the public space: putting in these monumental basilican Roman-style churches at key points in cities so you attract crowds; you're drawn to the building.

There was another way, and this was one dictated in part by practicality of money but also very, very effective, and that was to convert a temple into a church. We have, again, examples across the Roman world, but I would like to dwell on the city of Aphrodisias. This is an extremely well-excavated site. I have mentioned it earlier as a city that had a special relationship to Rome, and it was a city that was devoted to the worship of Aphrodite; and really, this Aphrodite is nothing more than a Greek version of the mother goddess cult. Aphrodisias defied the laws of the emperors and continued to worship the goddess Aphrodite well into the 5th century A.D. We know they were doing this in violation of the laws, and we believe that the Emperor Zeno finally cracked down on the city when it blundered into backing a rebel emperor, a man named Illis, at the end of the 5th century.

What was done at Aphrodisias is again indicative of how the Christians claimed public and religious space in cities. The temple is a typical Greek temple except it faces west rather than east. It's an Ionic-style temple that is from the late 1st century B.C. What the Christians did was essentially build an apse at the east end. At the west end, they moved the columns out to join the long colonnade on the north and south. They built a narthex or entryway hall and then a courtyard, so when you are looking at the temple you see a courtyard, you see a narthex, and you have these columns. They then built an outside wall and essentially turned the temple into sort of a basilican church, often with a dome, and what happens was the church swallowed up the temple. The colonnades, which were on the exterior of the temple of Aphrodite, now became the colonnades of the interior partition between the nave and the aisles. The columns on the short end have been moved to either lengthen the nave or to provide columns for the courtyard in the front; and the east end, you have built and apse with a synthronon where the clergies are seated, and what, in effect, you have done is claim the sacred space.

Think of it for a moment: At Aphrodisias, for centuries, the pagans—particularly the people in the countryside—came to the temple to worship at high holidays. That temple had been built over a spring, we know that from coin evidence from the reign of Tiberius; it was oriented facing a sacred mountain west to the mother goddess named Ninowy, later named Aphrodite; so when pagans came now to the Christian version of that building, they came to the same space. However, the temple was now within a larger building to the new faith and the goddess was no longer there, but instead there was this new building to the new faith; and that meant that the public and religious space of the city was now in the hands of the Christians, so that instinctively many would think, "Well, maybe we should find out about this. We've always worshiped here; what is this version of worship compared to what our forefathers had? As a result of this, you had a number of these temple conversions across the Roman world. We have a number of very good examples from Asia Minor, and many leading temples were turned into essentially Christian churches this way.

There were, however, several exceptional sanctuaries that were not turned into churches; and that is because they were too famous and they were too important as pagan centers. One of them is the temple of Artemis Ephesia at Ephesus, the Artemisium. That temple had always had problems. It was on the shore; it was in a marshy area; it was constantly be shored up with pilings. It had been damaged by the Goths; it was rebuilt by the Tetrarchic age and repaired. The temple was too important. It was enormous. It was one of the great Seven Wonders of the Ancient World. We believe it was the patriarch of Constantinople, John Chrysostom, who was in the area around 400–401 A.D. for a very important council at Sardis, who gave the orders to dismantle the temple and to turn it into ruins. What happened is that great sanctuary was leveled; there is only 1 column standing—it was re-erected in the late 19th century—and that column is 1 of 128 original columns in a massive temple; and that temple was essentially left as a war memorial to show the victory of the new faith over the old faith.

Across the Roman world, in the course of the 5th, 6th, and 7th centuries, temples gradually gave way to basilican churches. Basilican churches in time acquired bell towers; they had domes at their construction; and between the time of Constantine and the time of Justinian, cities of the Roman world increasingly acquired a Christian skyline, and that was a very, very significant move in converting the Roman world.

This changing of public and religious space was also paralleled by changes in social and economic life in the cities. In the previous lecture on Constantine and the bishops, I discussed how Constantine gave various powers to the bishops so they could emerge as leaders in provincial cities; and in many ways, they replaced the old pagan decurions. There are a number of reasons why bishops emerged so quickly in the 4th and 5th centuries as such major figures. Think of it for a moment. One is they had great patronage. They had access to the emperor. They had money. They were involved in constructing new churches or converting temples into churches, and therefore they employed hundreds of people, if not thousands of people, as laborers as well as architects. They had to hire people to do the mosaics and frescoes; we will be talking more specifically about the types of arches that the Christians favored in the 4th and 5th centuries. But from a financial viewpoint, just think of it: The Christian emperors made the bishops the fount of patronage in provincial cities. That alone meant that many pagan artists, artisans, architects, and laborers were accepting money from the bishop.

We have a monumental inscription from one of them, a man named Marcus Julius Eugenius, who was bishop of the city of Laodicea Combusta from 315–340 A.D. He set up a monument in which he boasted how he turned his city into essentially a Christian city by architecture, by buildings. The inscription is very much similar to the types of praise that you would get from decurions of the 1st and 2nd centuries A.D. who were putting up pagan and public buildings in the time of the High Empire. Activites by men such as bishop Julius Eugenius—who actually had suffered under the persecutions and was elected bishop because of his piety—activities by these men were very, very important in the social transformation of cities as well as the architectural. However, some Christians deplored these guys as being involved in what is called "lithomania"; they were just putting up buildings at random. But others would see these bishops as more than just putting up buildings, but as what is a term that is used in Greek inscriptions, they are either *tropheus* or *syntropheus*; they are nourishers to the city. That meant that in addition to doing all of these building activities, they took on the social obligations that once characterized the pagan elites.

There were some subtle changes here. Pagan decurions always gave out distributions at the festivals—that is, in honor of the god or the goddess—and those distributions were handed out by hierarchy. The higher members of societies got gold coins and lots of goodies; the lower members of society got less money and less goodies based on their rank. The Christian bishops also carried out what you would call distributions; you can call it charity, or better yet almsgiving (and there is an old tradition going back in the Hebrew tradition of doing this). But there was a significant difference here: This charity was not directed towards citizens. It was not directed to honor the donor so much as to get charity as an act of piety to the poor and destitute who needed it. A whole new terminology emerges in Greek; and there are now, I think, three major studies that are dealing with this whole question of how almsgiving and charity of the 4th and 5th centuries represented a major social change from the types of public distributions at festivals in the pagan cities of the Roman Empire. Terms such as *penetes* (the poor), the *ptochoi* (the destitute, the really down on their luck, the 10 percent of the city that really were living on the edge); these groups now became attached to the bishops and to the churches of the city, and they lived on that charity. That charity was an expression of piety by the bishops and those Christian families who often donated anonymously.

This is a big difference from the kind of public distributions we had in the pagan period and where we know that receiving a sum of money—we have that from an oration by Dio Chrysostom—was, in effect, an indication that you got that money because you were a citizen and not a non-citizen. What has happened was the social hierarchy had now been adjusted to reflect the piety of the Christian leadership, and charity and almsgiving was a sign of piety and it went to those who really needed it, who were destitute. The poor, by virtue of their piety, were deserving; they were members of that wider Christian community. This was a significant change in the social life of the cities of the Roman Empire.

There were other important changes I mentioned at the start of this lecture that plug into the social and architectural changes of cities, and one was pilgrimage. Pilgrimage roots, in effect, changed in the Roman world from the time of Constantine on. In the time of the pagan Roman Empire, before Constantine, there were great oracles; there were great international shrines like Ephesus; great festivals put in that attracted spectators and visitors to the cities. At the very least, a local or regional festival brought in the people from the countryside. Now, certain sanctuaries, certain places important to the Christian faith, emerged as pilgrimage centers; and these had very little relationship in many cases to the previous pagan sanctuaries.

The most obvious is the Holy Land. Saint Helena, the mother of Constantine, after a lot of troubled problems in the family of Constantine between 326 and 327, made a pilgrimage to the Holy Land; she went to Jerusalem. She reputedly found the True Cross. She carried out operations of what we might call Christian archeology where she made efforts to find places that were associated with the early Christian traditions. She stayed in the Holy Land from 326–328, and she is responsible, almost singlehandedly, for initiating a process whereby Jerusalem and Bethlehem, Mount Sinai—which became the center of Saint Catherine's, one of the most important monasteries even today in the orthodox world with some of the earliest icons that have come down from early Christianity—for turning these locations into pilgrimage centers where Christians all over the Roman world would trek out to see the place where Christ was born, to see where the crucifixion took place, to see the resurrection, to see the Holy True Cross, which was still intact up until the early 7th century when it was smuggled out during the Arab attacks and then split up into the splinters in the Middle Ages. We have very, very good reports on the development of pilgrimage sites and the Holy Land; the finding of relics.

Church fathers were divided on the issue. Some of them, such as Saint Jerome or the empresses of the imperial family in the 5th century A.D., were avid about findings these different relics; for instance, where was the burning bush of Moses or the well of Abraham? All of these became attractions. Others were far more skeptical and thought a lot of this had to do with fraud. But even if some of these sites were hypocrisy or hypocritical, hypocrisy always pays homage to true faith by imitation. By the year 400, there was an extremely well-developed pilgrimage trade going from particularly the western half of the Roman Empire into the Holy Land.

The region of what the Romans called Palestine—today that would be essentially Israel and the West Bank and parts of Lebanon; and I am not trying to make any kind of political statement, I am using it as the Roman province, as I said before—that whole region, which was the cradle of Christianity, the cradle of Judaism; that whole area experienced an enormous economic boom because of the pilgrimage trade, and that would continue well into the early Middle Ages. There were other sites that were developed along the pilgrimage routes; some of them in Italy, some in the Balkans, particularly in Asia Minor. One of the most famous that I have looked at is the site to Saint Thecla—she was first reported in the Gospel of Saint Paul and Saint Thecla, a 2nd-century work—and her tomb is near the modern city of Silifke (the ancient city of Seleucia ad Calycadnum) and it was regarded as a pilgrimage route almost on par with those in the Holy Land. We have a marvelous account by a Spanish nun who goes by several different names—Egeria is one of them, Aetheria is another; she comes on a number of names, we have several versions of the manuscript—and she has a sort of wide-eyed excitement of seeing the church and the sanctuary, which still exists today in Turkey and still can be visited. The development of these pilgrimage routes were very important in redirecting the whole focus of the religious life of the Roman world to new locations; locations associated with the mission and crucifixion of Jesus and the early apostles.

Besides pilgrimage within the Roman Empire, there was also missionary activity outside the Roman world. Constantine was the first emperor to initiate this on a grand scale. This had major consequences in several different ways. First, the sending of missions beyond the imperial frontiers to convert lands that were either allied or important to the Roman world changed the whole diplomatic and political dimensions of Roman foreign policy or frontier policy, whatever you want to call it. The earliest such kingdom is the kingdom of Armenia. There is an Armenian tradition that King Tiridates III embraced Christianity several years before Constantine's conversion, and this was carried by Saint Gregory the Illuminator; it is a very famous story told in Armenian literature and, in fact, Saint Gregory is depicted on that marvelous 10th-century church Aght'amar on the island in Lake Van, which is a medieval church of the 9th century. In any case, these missions that were sent out; it is more likely in my mind that the Armenians—and especially the Armenian king—embraced Christianity not before Constantine but because Constantine had already become a Christian; that is, they were following the lead of the Roman emperor. That is an issue that is still being worked out by scholars. But the Armenians were the first as an ethnic group to follow the Roman world into adopting Christianity as the religion, at least of the monarchy.

We have other examples from the 4th century: The king of Axum, Ethiopia; he, too, embraced Christianity sometime late in the reign of Constantine. What develops in Ethiopia is a very, very distinct version of Christianity still closely linked to the orthodox, especially the Greek Orthodox, tradition down to this day. Various Arabian tribes along the frontiers between Rome and the Sassanid Empire; they, too, embraced versions of Christianity, usually sectarian versions of it.

Above all, missions were sent to the northern peoples. The most famous of these was a mission commission by the emperor Constantius II, the son of Constantine, and he finds a bishop, a man who knows the Gothic language, who is sent out as the apostle of the northern peoples. This fellow—who went by several different versions of his name—Ulfilas was responsible for creating a Gothic script. He adapted the Greek script in order to translate the bible into Gothic, and his efforts in the 4th century led to the conversion of the East Germanic peoples to Christianity. This is the Arian version of Christianity; the version that was defeated at the Council of Nicaea. But nonetheless, it was a significant change; and that is tribes across the imperial frontier that were previously classified as barbarians were now, by virtue of embracing Christianity, part of that wider community; part of what is called in Classical text the *oikoumene*, the inhabited world of the Christian communities. The Western Germanic tribes, too, in time, would come to embrace Christianity, but that was more of a case of the 5th and 6th centuries after the breakup of Roman power.

The results of these missions were significant in several ways. First, the barriers between Rome and the outside world were now crossed by these religious ties. Roman Emperors, for instance, would intervene in Armenia as coreligionists against the Persian Shahs. Armenia—which in the Classical

Age, in the time of the high Roman Empire, leaned culturally and religiously far more toward the Iranian world—now reoriented itself towards Rome, and the bond was Christianity.

In addition, emperors such as Constantine himself, as well as his successors, now waged wars in the interest of Christians living beyond the imperial frontier. One of the finest examples of this is a brief war in 421–422 when the armies of the emperor (really worthless emperor) Theodosius II—it was really his sister, Aelia Pulcheria, who was directing it—but those armies fought under the cross and on behalf of the Armenians against the Persian Shah and won a significant victory. While the war was very brief and it ended in a Roman victory, what is important about it: It was fought under Christian symbols and it was fought on behalf of Armenian coreligionists who were living outside the boundaries of the Roman world.

This meant that, henceforth, the identity that determined one's citizenship or position in the Roman world was not a legal identity ("Are you a Roman citizen?") but "Are you a Christian?" The supreme irony in all of this is the Christianizing cities of the Roman world, particularly in the Roman West; the creation of a bishop, a clergy, which in many ways was a new Romanized Christian elite; the conversion of the various Germanic and barbarian peoples of Western Europe meant that when the Roman Empire in the West breaks up in the 5th century, the potential catastrophe of it is greatly lessened because the newcomers are either Christians themselves or they respect Christianity. They come to terms with the bishops; and those Romanized bishops in the provincial cities of the Roman West and the newcomers, the Germanic peoples, come to an accommodation and they create, based on those Roman traditions, a new civilization: medieval Christendom.

The Birth of Christian Aesthetics and Letters
Lecture 19

Christians took over the cultural heritage of the pagan past and made it distinctly Christian, preserving their pagan as well as their Jewish heritage. The so-called classics became a fundamental part of the education of a Christian gentleman, particularly the high language of Platonic Greek and Ciceronian Latin. In the visual arts, Roman architectural forms were decorated with art in the classical mode—mosaics, frescoes, and relief sculpture—to deliver the Christian message through the visual language developed by paganism.

Christianizing the Basilica

- Once churches were built to claim public spaces for Christianity, the visual and decorative arts were employed to raise a sense of awe, as well as to instruct the Roman Christians in their new faith. The arts were also used to inspire and awe pagans, who might then consider converting.

- The original Roman basilicas were created in the 2nd century B.C. as administrative and law courts. When adapted for worship, a few significant changes were made. Basilica churches were always entered from one of the short ends, which faced west. The apse and altar would be on the east, where the clergy sat on a synthronon, partitioned off from the congregation.

- Sometimes a transept (a perpendicular hall) was added, as were subsidiary buildings. Light entered from windows in the upper levels. Sometimes, a dome was added where the nave and transept crossed.

- There was no mistaking that the basilica was a Roman building. However, it differed significantly from pagan temples in that it was an architecture of the interior. It was ideally suited as a place to hold worship inside.

- Another building from the Roman tradition adapted for use as a church was the dome on a square, best epitomized by the Pantheon. This type of building might be used as a mortuary church or a church to a martyr saint and was a convenient way of Christianizing a pagan sanctuary.

The 4th-Century Decorative Art Style

- To convert already existing buildings, they had to be decorated to inspire and instruct. One common technique was through typology—paired scenes from the Old and New Testament.

- In terms of style, Christians followed the aesthetic changes that characterized all arts of the later Roman world. After 235, the stress in art was on hierarchy, symmetrical presentations, and inspiring awe rather than realistic imagery. Imperial portraits, for instance, became increasingly stylized.

- In the classical period, mosaic work tended to be limited to floors, and the style was influenced by representational art. Christians, however, put mosaics on ceilings and floors, and they emphasized not realism but the message, which was highlighted by stylized artistic conventions: elongated figures with enlarged eyes that loomed impressively over the congregation.

- Most of the mosaic work was done in rough-cut stone on a gold leaf background. This was not because they could not make flatter mosaics but because these surfaces scattered light throughout the church, to impressive effect.

- Frescoes, too, were used for decoration, sometimes for financial reasons, but more often because the surface lent itself better to painting rather than mosaic. Christian artists avoided freestanding sculptures because they resembled pagan cult statues, using relief carvings instead.

- Classical art forms did not disappear. In private villas, Christian families decorated their homes with three-dimensional sculptures, floor mosaics, and decorative furniture.

The New Christian Literature

- Until Constantine's conversion, Christians had by and large been writing for other Christians. Now their writing had a much wider audience and cultural implications because increasingly the Christians were taking over the cultural leadership of the Roman world.

- Starting with Saint Paul, the Christians had perfected the epistle, or letter. Letter-writing had been the hallmark of a gentleman in both Latin and Greek; men like **Cicero** and Pliny the Younger were masters of this form.

Cicero's letters had been the model of Latin rhetoric for pagan gentlemen, and they became the model for Christian writers, too.

- Soon after, Christian writers came to excel at the Platonic dialogue. This form, a debate between two (but sometimes more) characters, was used by many philosophers writing both in Latin and Greek. The apologists were really the first Christians to master this form.

- Tertullian, who perfected the apology, also became skilled in the philippics (condemnation) and was one of the first Christians to attempt exegesis—that is, explaining biblical text.

- Christian letters really came of age with Saint Clement and Origen in the 4th century. They described Christian theology in a philosophical language (Atticizing Greek) that had to be read seriously by pagan critics. Latin literature did not come of age until the time of Saint Augustine, about a century later.

- New genres sprang into use by the Christians. One was the sermon, the particular genre of **John Chrysostom**, patriarch of Constantinople. Christian biography and history were both pioneered by Eusebius, who is one of our principle sources for this course. Saint Athanasius, also a patriarch of Alexandria, wrote a biography of Saint Antony that made hagiography one of the most popular genres in the Christian medieval world.

- By the opening of the 5th century, Christians had evolved a literature that was serious in intent, was written in sophisticated language (whether Latin or Greek), and could not simply be dismissed by their pagan contemporaries as ramblings of a vulgar superstition. This literature was a profound coming of age for Christian culture.

Christian Literature Looks to the Past

- In creating this literature, Christian authors drew very heavily on the classical past. If they wrote in Greek, they were trained in Homer and Plato; in the Greek historians; in Demosthenes, the famous Athenian orator of the 4th century B.C. If they wrote in Latin, they were trained in Vergil; they were trained in the writings of Cicero.

Saint Augustine was an impeccable Ciceronian, and the same was true of Saint Jerome, who translated the Bible into Latin.

- All of these Christian authors had fine classical educations; which had two long-term implications for the Roman world: First of all, it meant that the classics, these pagan literary traditions, would be preserved and transmitted to later generations. They would not be denounced, renounced, and rejected. Therefore, there was enormous cultural continuity, literary and visual, between the pagan Roman world and the Christian Roman world.

- The second important point is in preserving the visual and literary culture of the pagan world, these Christian authors, writers, and thinkers gave the Western tradition a peculiar dynamic. Thereafter, the canonical texts of the Western tradition were not only Christian, nor even a combination of Christian texts and Jewish texts translated into Greek. It also included a large body of pagan literature that had nothing to do with the Christian message.

- It is this dual tradition—the Greek and Roman pagan on the one hand and the Christian on the other—that became the basis of Western literary tradition and accounts for some of the dynamic and unusual aspects of the Western literary tradition down to this day.

Names to Know

Cicero (a.k.a. **Marcus Tullius Cicero**; 106–43 B.C.): Roman lawyer, orator, statesman, and consul of 63 B.C., Cicero was a prolific writer and master of Latin prose. He left a number of works dealing with philosophy and Roman religious practices in addition to his letters and political speeches.

John Chrysostom (349–407): Patriarch of Constantinople (398–405). A brilliant orator, he asserted the primacy of Constantinople over the Eastern churches and clashed with the emperor Arcadius.

Suggested Reading

Beckwith, *Early Christian and Byzantine Art.*

Bregman, *Synesius of Cyrene.*

Brown, *Augustine of Hippo.*

————, *The World of Late Antiquity.*

Elsner, *Imperial Rome and Christian Triumph.*

Hanfmann, *Sardis from Prehistoric to Roman Times.*

Kitzinger, *Byzantine Art in the Making.*

Krautheimer, *Early Christian Architecture.*

————, *Three Christian Capitals.*

MacCormack, *Art and Ceremony in Late Antiquity.*

Perkins, *Art of Dura-Europos.*

Rousseau, *Basil of Caesarea.*

Weitzmann, ed., *The Age of Spirituality.*

Weitzmann and Kessler, *The Frescoes of the Dura Synagogue and Christian Art.*

Questions to Consider

1. How did the Christians evolve church forms out of Roman architecture? How important were Jewish synagogues (such as the one at Sardis) as prototypes? How did Christian emperors from Constantine on contribute to this process? What were the visual and religious purposes of the basilica and centrally planned churches?

2. What were the visual and iconographic elements in Christian art in 300–450? How did Christian artists reshape classical forms to express the new faith? Did Christian art break with or transform the Greco-Roman arts? What were the elements of continuity with classical art?

3. How did Christian thinkers and writers create a distinct literature from the Greek and Latin pagan texts? What authors and genres were favored? How did this literary development ensure Christians of cultural leadership in the Roman world?

The Birth of Christian Aesthetics and Letters
Lecture 19—Transcript

In this lecture, I plan to deal with Christian visual arts and literary developments. This is a lecture that is going to handle the issue of how the Christians took over the cultural heritage of their pagan past and made it distinctly Christian, and at the same time preserved a good deal of that pagan past, which has come down to us in the form of the Classics—that is, capital "C"; the visual arts and the literary arts of pagan Greece and Rome—which were seen as fundamental for training Christian gentleman. Christian emperors played an important role in this; but so did the prelates, the thinkers, and the artists themselves. These three groups interacted to create a new set of visual arts and also changes in literature.

What I want to concentrate on first are the visual arts. This is to build upon a previous lecture in which I talked about how churches were used as a way of claiming public space and a way of plugging into social and economic changes in the cities of the Roman world, which made those cities fundamentally Christian by the 6th century. I want to look more closely at what those churches were; what type of visual arts, what type of decorative arts, were necessary to carry out the worship of the new imperial church; as well as to instruct the many converts that were coming into Christianity with the conversion of Constantine; and finally—something that we should always stress—that these great churches were also a way to inspire and awe pagans, who in turn might consider Christianity and might convert.

First, I mentioned earlier the basilican church. The basilica was a Roman public building. The term is Greek, actually, and it originally designated, in effect, a palace. But the Romans in the 2nd century B.C. created a type of public hall, a basilica, which could be used for law courts and administrative courts. It was based on the fact that the Romans had mastered concrete and brick construction. It was an architecture of the interiors is what historians of architecture would like to call it; that is, with barrel vaults, with various arches and domes. You could enclose a vast space. We have a number of basilicas that come down to us. One could wonder in the Roman Forum and see the foundations of several from the Republic, notably the Basilica Aemilia, the so-called Basilica Maxentius, which was later completed by Constantine, so sometimes it is called the Basilica of Constantine. All of these monuments were clearly available as prototypes for the Christian church. Furthermore, there is the synagogue; and I should mention that there are some scholars who think that the synagogue at Sardis is much later than late 3rd and 4th centuries A.D., that is a question that is still being debated. That, too, is an example of how you can take a Roman public building and adapt it to worship.

There were a couple of important innovations to turn a Roman public building, a basilica, into a church. First was the orientation of the building. Churches in the Roman period, especially from the 4th century on and well into the Reformation, were always oriented west. You faced west in order to really be ready for the End of Days, because the early Christians were really convinced that the apocalypse would come from the west, the final day; so you wanted your church in that direction. The east end is where you traditionally have the apse and the altar. In a Roman public building, such as the Basilica of Constantine or the Basilica of Maxentius—whatever name you wish to use—you usually came in on the long side. There would be several doors; various entryways. The basilica was a vast open space and you had these various alcoves and areas where magistrates would have courts; they would be administering justice; or you would go in there to present petitions. The church, however, was in a very different arrangement. You came in on the west side, the short side, and you walked into this vast hall—which is usually called the nave in a church—and at the other end, the Christians have an apse where the altar is, so the worshiper is immediately drawn down that nave and the attention is on the altar and the whole mystery of the Christian faith.

Furthermore, Christian churches from a very early date on also had aisles flanking that nave, and then from the aisles you would add eventually transepts; you would have subsidiary buildings, particularly baptisteries; I mentioned that in tandem with the Church of Mary Theotokos at Ephesus in a previous lecture. The church, while a Roman building, was a very, very different building in its feel. You came in at the west end; your eye was directed to the mystery of the faith; and furthermore, at the end of the church was this apse and there was a set of seats known as a synthronon. That is where the clergy sat. There was a partition that usually cut them off from view at the nave. The altar was often behind that partition—it is later called an iconostasis in the Byzantine period—and it would only open up and reveal the altar during the time of a major service.

In addition, the church was illuminated by windows in the upper levels; usually basilican churches were at least two stories or three stories high. Furthermore, at various points in the church, particularly over what became essentially the transepts—that is, the intersection of these side wings down towards the east apse so that the church would assume the form of a cross in its plan—there would be a great dome, which came to be regarded as the Dome of Heaven.

The evolution of this basilican church in the 4th century was an extremely important turning point in Christian art and Christian architecture. For one, it provided the Christians with a building that was quintessentially Roman. There was no mistaking the fact that where the Christians now worshipped was a Roman building. Some scholars of architecture have gone so far as to say that Constantine was somehow behind pushing the adaptation of the basilica into a church. It is a reasonable surmise; we really cannot prove it, but it is a reasonable surmise. Certainly Ward Perkins, one of the great architectural historians of Rome, would argue that position.

In addition to the fact that the basilica is a Roman building, it also is an architecture of the interior. It accommodates a very different worship from what we had in pagan temples. Pagan temples, I stressed earlier, were essentially places where the god's statue resided, and the cult statue would be taken out at the procession—we talked about that with the processions that were well known at Ephesus, for instance—and worship was in the public and generally ended up in the theater where there was a great festival. Christian services were conducted inside, within a church. That meant that Christian cities needed large numbers of churches and chapels to accommodate worship, even if you had multiple services during the course of a Sunday; and therefore, there was a great surge in building basilican-style churches once a city moved over to the new faith. The basilica was ideally suited, both as a place to hold worship inside—whereas a Roman temple was not; it was never intended to accommodate and interior service—and second, it was a Roman building.

There was another important building from the Roman tradition that was essentially a planned building, which is essentially a dome on a square or a circle on a square, best epitomized by the Pantheon, the temple that was rebuilt by Hadrian in the 120s and is really one of the most beautiful buildings, certainly in the city of Rome if not in the world; and the Pantheon was eventually converted into a church. That type of circular building, in effect—that is, the plan was fundamentally a circle, or sometimes it was a hexagonal or octagonal grid to accommodate a dome so that the altar could be in the middle of the church—that type of church was used for some very specific purposes. It was very good for mortuary churches—in effect, churches that acted as mausoleums, especially to members of the imperial family. One of the earliest is Santa Constanza in Rome; this is for one of the daughters of Constantine. She died in 354; Constantia is her name in Latin, Constanza is her name in modern Italian.

One of the favorite ones I always love to see is the Church of Saint Philip the Evangelist at Hierapolis, the modern city of Pamukkale in Turkey. This church is built to a martyr saint; and very often churches to martyr saints, or martyria, were built in the form of some kind of centrally-planned church. In the case of the one at Hierapolis, it is a hexagonal plan that had a very impressive dome with flanking chapels. You, in effect, circle around the altar; when you enter it, you have several different directions from which you can enter the church. The church is actually positioned at a point overlooking the city of Hierapolis, and in my opinion it sits on top of, or essentially right next, to an ancient spring that probably had been a pagan sanctuary; and this particular church was regarded as a way of Christianizing a former pagan sanctuary, and this circular type of church was thought as particularly appropriate for martyr saints. We believe that Saint Philip may have been constructed somewhere in the late 5th century, in the 470s, 480s, and it really does epitomize a whole class of churches, lesser churches, which were also constructed in the course of the 4th and 5th centuries.

That form of circular church, it is amazing how that became popular. It is rather technically difficult to do; and we find it, for instance, reproduced in the art of the Georgian kingdoms. There is one at Bana, a very early one, probably early medieval—the Georgian city of Bana, now in Turkey—that follows very closely the Santa Constanza in Rome and the types of martyr churches we have in Asia Minor. Basilican or centrally-planned churches together were really a major achievement in which Christians adapted the architectural principles of Roman architecture to their own service, and in so doing created a religious architecture that was absolutely, definitively Roman. I keep stressing: The way for the Christians to make their faith acceptable was to make it Roman, and the architecture certainly achieved that.

Once you had the buildings, you also had to decorate them, for various reasons. One, it was appropriate; it was a way of inspiring and awing the worshipers. Another was to instruct the believers. I mentioned in passing in previous lectures the whole approach known as typology; that is, the Old Testament prefiguring of the fulfillment of the Christian message. This is worked out in text by Origen; but in the 4th and 5th centuries, it essentially applied to the visual arts, and so you will have decorations in churches in which will, in effect, show Old Testament scenes matched against New Testament scenes. Something like the story of Jonah and the Whale is often juxtaposed to an image of some aspect of the salvation in the New Testament because the story of Jonah and the Whale is often seen as a story of redemption. You take this Old Testament story and you match it against the New Testament story in the church; you juxtapose these images.

The Christians used several different important media to convey these messages for worship. One was sculpture—particularly relief sculpture—and a very limited amount of freestanding sculpture, which was so characteristic of Classical cities. In part, the Christians were reacting to aesthetic changes that characterized all arts of the later Roman world. Even among pagan artists and Roman emperors after 235 A.D., the stress in art was on hierarchy; was on symmetrical presentations; on presenting figures so that they conveyed a message or they inspired a sense of awe or some sort of respect rather than realistic imagery. Imperial portraits, for instance, became increasingly stylized; the hair style; the eyes were enlarged. There were abstract and symmetrical depictions of imperial images, and in the 4th century of the images of the elite classes that served the emperor. For instance, there is a whole array of sculptures of imperial officials of the 4th and early 5th centuries from the city of Aphrodisias, which really characterizes a general trend in late antique arts, whether it be public or religious, whether it be Christian or pagan, and gives you some sense of where the aesthetics of Classical art were moving. The Christians—now recognized as the favored religion under Constantine and then eventually to become the official religion of the Roman world—utilized these aesthetic traditions to decorate their churches.

One such way of doing this was to essentially adapt mosaics and frescoes to the decorations of the ceilings and the walls of Christian churches. This was a major innovation in arts. In the Classical period, mosaic work tended to be floor mosaics. Anyone who has visited Classical mosaics—you can see them on many Roman sites, they have survived from particularly sites in North Africa; there are a number of them that have been excavated at the ancient city of Antioch, today, the modern city of Antakya—all of these sites with mosaics are really based on representational art. Some of them were clearly inspired after painting; a type of painting that would stress realism and perspective, which we know did exist in the Classical world. What those floor mosaics were, were a way of displaying one's opulence as well as one's good taste. They would have mythological scenes; they would have hunting scenes; scenes from daily life. Therefore, mosaics laid down on floors were done with various types of stones and tesserae—that is, tiles—and the idea was to recreate some type of brilliant visual image.

Christians, however, took the mosaics and put them on ceilings and floors. Their intention was not to stress the realism, but the message; and that message was highlighted by certain conventions that were now applied to mosaics and frescoes. One was elongating the figures; enlarging the eyes; stylizing those figures so they would be seen from above and they would loom impressively, larger and grander, than if you were looking at them at eye level. In addition, for the mosaic work, the mosaic work was done in roughly-cut stone; there was often a background in gold (gold leaf background). All of this was intentional. It was not because they had lost the ability to do realistic mosaics, but it was done because those types of surfaces will scatter light throughout the church, and as the light comes through the windows in the upper levels of the church, or often through windows of the dome—those who have been to Hagia Sophia, which is the great 6th century masterpiece of Justinian, can see it in full play—that means the light is bounced off, scattered, and refracted and it gives very, very dramatic effects within the interior of the church where services are held. Not only were the mosaics put to use depicting messages from the Christian tradition, juxtaposing Old and New Testament, working out in iconography that would instruct the illiterate, but they were also part of the whole drama of the building and of the worship within the building. This led to beautiful services being evolved over the course of the 4th century, and one can still get some sense of what those services were like, particularly in the orthodox churches, Greek orthodox churches, conducted in traditional churches decorated in that style.

Frescoes, too, were used for decoration, and very often frescoes were used either out of monetary concerns, or more often the surface lent itself to painting rather than mosaics, and many churches show a combination of frescoes and mosaic; but the intent is the same and it was part of an overall program to instruct and impress the worshiper.

As I mentioned, the changes in sculpture and relief sculpture, which you see in pagan and public arts, were only partially adapted. From the start, the Christians were a little nervous about using too much freestanding sculpture because it looked like a pagan cult statue. There was a tendency to go for two-dimensional decoration. This is an issue that will later be debated in the 8th and 9th centuries A.D. in the so-called iconoclastic controversy. In terms of Christian arts, by the opening of the 5th century, both architecture and visual arts had been put into the service of the new faith very, very successfully.

That does not mean Classical arts disappeared. Far from it; in the private villas of individuals we know were Christians but were clearly of high rank, such as the Slope Houses at Ephesus and probably the mosaics of the so-called Great Palace of Constantinople—the Slope Houses of Ephesus are now quite well-known and have been opened to the public—they show that well into the 6th and probably the 7th century A.D. that many Christian families in private art still would prefer Classicizing art; there would still be sculptures, statues, and decorative furniture and the like, the furnishings, which would resemble very much the decorative arts, the furnishings, and even the wall paintings and floor mosaics of a Classical villa of the 2nd century A.D. I have to stress that that tradition continued.

In addition to the visual arts, there were some very important changes that went on in literary arts at the same time; and again, this was brought about by the fact that the Christians were now being put in charge of the civilization. They had the emperor Constantine and his sons who were backing the bishops; Christianity is no longer an illegal sect, writing literature largely by Christians for Christians, but was writing a literature now that had much wider applications, much wider cultural implications, because increasingly the Christians were coming to take over the cultural leadership of the Roman world. That requires us look a little bit at before and after, and put some of those authors I talked about from the 2nd and 3rd centuries A.D. in context with what happens after the conversion of Constantine; that is, in the 4th century, in the 300s A.D.

Let us back up for a moment. Starting with Saint Paul, Christians perfected one literary form very well: the epistle, the letter. Letters were a common way of communicating; writing a very fine letter was certainly the hallmark of a gentleman. Those who studied Latin, for instance, know Cicero was a master of the epistle. Pliny the Younger; one his letters I read to the Emperor Trajan. Starting with Saint Paul, with Saint Ignatius—the first bishop of Antioch who penned seven very important letters around 107 A.D.—the Christians really evolved a very successful way of communicating with other leaders and congregations over questions of church discipline, theology, and the like. The letters of Saint Paul were actually the prototype for a whole tradition of Christian letters.

Another area that they excelled in was the Platonic dialogue; that is, the setting up of a debate over theological issues. This was a genre that is very well-represented in the Classical tradition. The master, of course, was Plato; but it was used by many philosophers writing both in Latin and Greek. Cicero was one of the masters in Latin; there were all the successors of Plato, the so-called Middle Platonists; and these dialogues, usually a debate between two individuals, or sometimes a group discussion where you have different interlocutors—one thinks of the *Timaeus* of Plato or even the *Republic* of Plato—this type of form was adapted by the first Christian authors, notably the apologists. Theophilus of Antioch made use of this technique. His apology is an odd combination of both letter and Platonic dialogue. The same is true of the *First Apology* of Justin, which is in the form of a very long letter to the emperor Antoninus Pius. Christian apologists writing in the 2nd and early 3rd century A.D. in Greek really pioneered the use of the dialogue as a way of investigating theological issues.

In Africa—that is, the Roman province of Africa; essentially the country of Tunisia today—the earliest Christian Latin writers in the end of the 2nd and the opening of the 3rd centuries really did some marvelous pieces; the most famous is by Minucius Felix, probably writing in the middle of the 2nd century A.D. and the earliest of the apologists. I discussed him in context with the whole issue of answering pagan criticisms. His *Octavius* is called an apology, but it is really a dialogue. In fact, in some ways it resembles the *Dialogues*—that is, the *Dialogue* of Tacitus—which is a debate set in a villa by a very prominent Roman over the issue of oratory. What Minucius Felix does is take that conceit—which is very common; Cicero uses it—and he essentially invents a debate between a Christian, Octavius, and a pagan, Caecilius Natalis, over the virtues of the Christian faith and how it fits into philosophy, and, of course, the Christian wins. It is a very clever work and a work that shows some very impressive polished Latin style. It is the first significant Christian work in the Latin language. Tertullian, who perfected the apology, tended to go along the lines of using Cicero's *Philippics* (that is, condemning). He was a polemical, but he also was one of the first to do the so-called technique of exegesis; that is, explaining biblical text, writing commentaries on biblical text. By the time of the early 3rd century A.D., the Christians had made the letter, the epistle (the dialogue), the philosophical debate (whatever you want to call it), and exegesis (the analysis or commentary of text) genres of their own.

Unfortunately for the Christians in terms of propagating the message, they really did not have much interest of pagans. Christian letters really came of age with Saint Clement and Origen, and I discussed that in some detail with their theology; and the only point I wish to stress at this moment is that both Clement and Origen made philosophy and describing Christian theology in philosophical terms a very serious genre that, by the time of the 4th century A.D., had to be read seriously by pagan critics. Already Porphyry, the pagan critic at the end of the 3rd century, was answering point-by-point arguments made by Origen. With Saint Clement and Origen, at least Greek Christian literature leaped to a new plateau. Henceforth, Christians writing in Greek were trained in the Atticizing style, the polished language of the Second

Sophistic; they were turning out works that the pagans could no longer dismiss as bad Greek—"Oh, it's the vernacular of the New Testament," the so-called koine Greek—they had to take it seriously just on its literary style alone. Latin literature was a bit later on that score—it really doesn't come of age until the time of Saint Augustine; that is, about a century later—but the 4th century sees the flourishing of a new Christian Greek literature that can be read by pagans who have been trained in the Classics, and they have to appreciate it.

That meant there were new genres that spring into use by the Christians. One was the sermon. There were several writers, particularly John Chrysostom, the patriarch of Constantinople who made Constantinople the great center of the Greek East, the Roman East. He wrote a series of sermons, which were essentially orations—so they're almost orations out of Demosthenes—in which he presents a very, very powerful presentation to the *ekklesia*; that is, to the assembly of worshipers. *Ekklesia* originally meant "assembly" in Greek; it now meant "the congregation" in a Christian context. A whole new genre of sermon was created.

There was the development of Christian biography and history. Eusebius, who is one of our principle sources for this course, pioneered both. I have discussed how Eusebius created the narrative Christian history, which becomes the basis for the medieval chronicles. He wrote a life of Constantine, which becomes a model for a Christian monarch in the Middle Ages; and he also wrote a very important work known as the *Tricennial Oration*, which is a Christian panegyric that praises a Christian ruler, and at the same time in a very clever way forces Christian rulers to think that they are following, or they have to follow, in the path of the righteous kings of Israel; one thinks of Hezekiah in particular, or Josiah. These were very, very common parallels that would be drawn, starting with Constantine's reign right up through the Reformation and beyond. Finally, Saint Athanasius, the brilliant theologian—the patriarch of Alexandria from 329 to his death in 373—wrote the biography of Saint Antony, the great ascetic, which made hagiography (sacred biography of saints) one of the most popular genres in the Christian medieval world.

In the course of the 4th century, we add to the literary arts of the 3rd century works with much wider appeal: the Christian oration, the sermon, the hagiography, the biography, the writing of more letters and of theological tracts in serious terms; one thinks of the Cappadocian fathers, of Athanasius's work. So by the opening of the 5th century, the Christians had evolved a literature for their purposes that was both serious and intent, had a high sophisticated language in both Latin and Greek, and could not simply be dismissed by their pagan competitors and contemporaries as the language of a vulgar movement, a superstition. It was a very, very important mark of the coming of age of Christian culture traditions.

Finally, there is one other point I want to stress. In creating this literature, just as in creating the visual arts, the Christian authors drew very heavily on that Classical past. They were trained in Homer and Plato; in the Greek historians; in Demosthenes, the famous Athenian orator of the 4th century B.C. Or if they were in Latin, they were trained in Vergil; they were trained in the writings of Cicero. Saint Augustine was an impeccable Ciceronian, and the same was true of Saint Jerome, who translated the Bible into Latin, the so-called Vulgate text.

All of these Christian authors had a very, very fine classical education; and that had two long-term implications for the Roman world: It meant that the Classics (capital "C"), the pagan literary traditions, would be preserved and transmitted to later generations by the Christian successors to that pagan world. They would not be denounced and renounced and rejected. Therefore, there was an enormous cultural continuity, literary and visual, which goes from the pagan into the Christian Roman world. The second important point is in doing this, unintentionally, these Christian authors and writers and thinkers gave the Western tradition a very, very peculiar dynamic, because thereafter the canonical texts of the Western tradition were not only just Christian, or even the Jewish tradition translated into Greek—the so-called *Septuagint* and other texts—but it also included a large body of pagan literature that really had nothing to do with the Christian message. It is this dual tradition—the Greek and Roman pagan on the one hand and the Christian on the other—that became the basis of Western literary tradition and accounts, in my opinion, for some of the dynamic and unusual aspects of the Western literary tradition down to this day.

The Emperor Julian and the Pagan Reaction
Lecture 20

J ulian the Apostate was the last pagan emperor of Rome. Raised a Christian but isolated from the imperial family and educated in the classics, he turned to paganism in his 20s and, on ascending the throne, attempted to re-convert the empire by turning Constantine's Christian, bureaucratic, and military institutions to his own purposes. His reign was cut short by a disastrous military expedition in Persia, but had he lived, might he have succeeded in restoring the pagan faith, or some henotheistic version of it? And how far would he have gone to accomplish his goals?

Julian's Anti-Revolution

- Emperor **Julian II** is sometimes known as Julian the Apostate or Julian the Philosopher. He is without a doubt one of the best-known figures from late antiquity. On December 11, 361, he entered Constantinople at the head of a victorious army that was supposed to fight a civil war and did not and ordered that the pagan temples immediately be reopened and the sacrifices resumed.

- This incident is a reminder that the success and triumph of Christianity was by no means inevitable after the work of Constantine and his Christian sons, who ruled between 337 and 361. Julian proved that it was by no means certain what the religious loyalties of the Roman world would be.

Who Was Julian?

- Julian was born into the imperial family. He was a nephew of the emperor Constantine. An intellectual, his native language was Greek, and from birth he was to be trained to be a theologian and bishop, probably the bishop of Constantinople.

- Julian has engendered interest from both detractors and admirers, both past and present. His foremost admirer was the historian **Ammianus Marcellinus**, who lived in the 4th century and is often called the last great imperial historian of Rome. He wrote a narrative history in Latin in which Julian's career was the centerpiece.

- Julian wrote an enormous amount in his two and a half years as emperor. He composed nine major philosophical works, plus hymns, letters, and administrative documents. One of his most important works is a critique of Christianity called *Against the Galileans*, which was so incisive that Christian students used it for centuries to hone their debate and analysis skills.

- Julian is a perplexing figure. Some see him as a hero of a lost cause; others dismiss him as an eccentric or a zealot. Still others see him as a man of great vision who could have out-Constantined Constantine had he only lived to enact his reforms.

- In September 337, Constantine died, and all potential rivals to his sons were purged from the imperial family. Constantine's youngest son, **Constantius II**, would eventually reunite the empire and rule from 337–361. He was a devout Arian Christian.

- The only males of the imperial family to survive the purge were Julian, then 6, and his half-brother Constantius Gallus, who was 12. They grew up essentially under house arrest and then, in 341, were banished to Cappadocia, in Asia Minor.

- Julian spent his formative years reading Homer and the classics, looking up at Mount Argaeus—home to the mother goddess Ma— and unsurprising by age 20, he tells us, he went back to worshiping the old gods.

Julian and the Imperial Succession

- Constantius Gallus was made Caesar and heir to Constantius II in 351 while Constantius was waging a war in the West. The

Western army was rebelling because it was mostly pagan and wanted to continue the sacrifices. However, Constantius Gallus was so incompetent and tyrannical that he was arrested and executed in 354.

- Meanwhile, Julian was allowed to return from exile to study at Constantinople, Nicomedia, Pergamon, and Ephesus. Constantius's intent was likely to make him patriarch of Constantinople—the religious counterpart to his stepbrother the emperor.

- Julian came under the influence of two middle Platonist philosophers at this time: Maximus of Ephesus and Aedistus. At this point, he secretly converted to the worship of the gods and was initiated into the Eleusinian Mysteries, keeping his true beliefs secret from the emperor.

- In 355, Julian was summoned to the imperial court. Constantius had no choice but to make Julian his heir and Caesar. Julian was sent to Gaul to command the Western army; Gaul was being overrun by German barbarians.

- Julian read up on his Julius Caesar, won brilliant victories, and re-established the frontier. The Western army came to adore their strange, bookish, Greek-speaking prince. Then the news came from Constantius of war against Persia. The emperor wanted soldiers to be transferred from the West to the East.

- This sparked a revolt in December 360. The Western army saluted Julian as emperor, and a civil war was on. Julian now publicly revealed what some of his officers already knew: He was a worshiper of the old gods.

- The Western army began to march eastward to encounter the army of Constantius II. But before the war could be fought, Constantius succumbed to illness and died in November 361. He also did something that was a blessing to the empire: He recognized Julian as his heir.

Julian the Pagan Emperor

- As recounted at the start of the lecture, Julian entered Constantinople in December 361 and immediately ordered the restoration of the gods. Between December 361 and March 363—a period of about 16 months—Julian issued sweeping legislation and administrative reforms across the Roman Empire.

- Julian attacked corruption abuses with the imperial administration, cracked down on taxes, and carried out important religious reforms. But he was not slow or cautious like his uncle, Constantine. He did not persecute the Christians, but he abruptly and completely cut off their funding. He proclaimed religious toleration and then allowed the Arians and the Nicenes, who were divided over the issue of the Trinity, sue each over who had control of which bishopric.

- Julian also began to organize a pagan counterchurch. They were to take over all the charitable actions of the Christian bishops and therefore win over the poor in the cities. At the same time, he remitted taxes to cities. He passed legislation in favor of the pagan decurions. He understood that the restoration of the pagan cults depended on promoting this new imperial religious hierarchy and the decurion pagan families in the provincial cities.

- Julian's paganism was not the traditional restoration of the cults, but a new faith he called Hellenism. It involved study of philosophy as well as the worship and veneration of the cults, all subsidized by the imperial state and supported by the bureaucracy that Constantine had built up for the Christian church. This was perplexing to pagans, who never in their traditions had anything like this type of state organization.

- This leads to debates about what Julian really intended in the long run. Some scholars even argue that, once the Persian threat had been put down, Julian would have begun persecuting the Christians.

- The idea of a Julian persecution is borne out by several of his writings, the most peculiar one called the ***Misopogon*** (*Beard Hater*), a strange piece of satire in which he indulges in a fair amount of self-criticism, then turns the criticism back on his Christian critics. It suggests a nervous, zealous, and impatient personality that might have turned to violence, given the chance. Other scholars argue that Julian had a much more tolerant nature.

- Several important reforms went in tandem with restoring the pagan gods and switching patronage from the Christian church to the pagan cults. One regarded with the greatest bitterness by his Christian opponents was a law requiring that teachers only teach what they believe in and that students read texts that they believed in. This prevented Christian scholars from teaching the classics and Christian students from reading them, relegating them to second-class status in intellectual circles.

- Julian also supported the Jews and attempted to rebuild Jerusalem; that is, Julian upheld the validity of the Old Israel against the New Israel. In *Against the Galileans*, he wrote some incisive biblical criticism, particularly on the apocalyptic literature of the Old Testament.

The Death of Julian

- The war against Persia and Shah Shāpūr II had a religious dimension for Julian. As he left Constantinople and made his way east, he visited the various cult centers to win the favor of the traditional gods. This was in the tradition of pagan emperors who had battled the Iranian foe for centuries.

- The attack on the Persian capital city of Ctesiphon went badly awry, whether due to Julian's mistakes or the quality of the Roman army is debated by many scholars. The army arrived in Mesopotamia at the height of the blazing summer. Provisions were not delivered on time, and Julian had to order a retreat.

- On retreat, Julian was mortally wounded in a skirmish. In the Middle Ages, the story would be elaborated to say he was killed by a Christian in the employ of a Persian shah.

- That evening, as Julian lay dying, the senior officers met in the imperial tent. They turned to the pagan Praetorian Prefect, Salutius, and asked him to become emperor. He refused. Then they turned to the second in command, a Nicene Christian named Jovian, and offered him the throne.

- Jovian was nervous. He reminded them that he was a Christian. The officers replied, "Tonight in this tent, we are all Christians. Get us out of Persia." Jovian accepted the emperorship. He signed an ignominious peace where he gave up strategic provinces, but got the army back to the Roman Empire.

- The campaign was disastrous for the pagan cause. To the Christians, it was a vindication of their faith. The death of Julian meant the end of his reforms, and the Christians would assume their cultural and political dominance in the Roman world.

Important Term

Misopogon: "Beard Hater"; the satirical tract written by the pagan emperor Julian to refute his Christian detractors at Antioch in 362. Julian was jeered at for sporting the long beard of a pagan philosopher.

Names to Know

Ammianus Marcellinus (330–395): Soldier and last great pagan historian of Rome. Born in Antioch, Ammianus served under emperors from Constantius II (r. 337–361) to Theodosius I (r. 379–395). He composed a history in 31 books (of which books 1–12 are lost) covering Roman history from A.D. 96 to 378. Ammianus displays exceptional objectivity in discussing the pagan revival by Emperor Julian (r. 360–363), so that his account is fundamental to the religious history of the 4th century.

Constantius II (a.k.a. **Flavius Julius Constantius**; 317–361; r. 337–361): Son of Constantine I and Fausta, Constantius II was proclaimed Caesar in 324 and succeeded jointly as Augustus with his brothers Constantine II and Constans in 337. Constantius ruled in the East, waging a war against the Persians. He crushed the rebellion by Magnentius and the Western army in 350–353. In 361, Constantius died of illness while en route to face his cousin Julian, who had been declared emperor by the Western army. An Arian Christian, Constantius sponsored Ulfilas, the so-called apostle to the Goths.

Julian II (a.k.a. **Julian the Apostate** or **Flavius Claudius Julianus**; 332–363; r. 360–363): Nephew of the first Christian emperor, Constantine I, he survived the purge of 337 and was raised and educated in the wastes of Cappadocia. Devoted to the classics, Julian secretly renounced his Christianity in 351. Promoted to Caesar in 355, Julian brilliantly cleared Gaul of Germanic invaders, and he was proclaimed emperor by the Western army. His brief reign saw the restoration of paganism to civic life; his reforms were cut short by his untimely death while on campaign in Persia. His works include orations, philosophical tracts, hymns to Helios and Magna Mater, and critiques on Christian dogma.

Suggested Reading

Ammianus Marcellinus, *The Later Roman Empire*.

———, *Roman History*.

Athanassadi-Fowden, *Julian and Hellenism*.

Barnes, *Athanasius and Constantius*.

Bowersock, *Julian the Apostate*.

Browing, *The Emperor Julian*.

Chuvin, *A Chronicle of the Last Pagans*.

Dill, *Roman Society in the Last Century of the Western Empire*.

Julian, *Works*.

Tougher, trans. and ed., *Julian the Apostate*.

Trombley, *Hellenic Religion and Christianization.*

Vidal, *Julian.*

Zosimus, *New History.*

Questions to Consider

1. What led Julian to return to the worship of the gods? How was Julian both intellectual and mystic? How important were the pagan classics, notably Homer and Plato, in leading Julian back to paganism?

2. Was Julian's Hellenism a plausible counter to the Christian church created by Constantine? Why would many pagans not understand Julian's Hellenism? What were the long-term prospects of Julian's laws if he had won in Persia and ruled for 30 years? Was Julian the hero of a lost cause?

3. How was Julian's mystical henotheism typical of many pagan intellectuals? What was the role of theurgy?

4. Why did pagan officers elect Jovian as Julian's successor? What were the consequences of the pagans' failure to find a pagan successor to Julian?

The Emperor Julian and the Pagan Reaction
Lecture 20—Transcript

In this lecture, I'm going to deal with the career and the policies of the emperor Julian II, who's sometimes known as Julian the Apostate; a man who'd been born a Christian and stood away, became an apostate; that is, renounced his Christianity and returned to the worship of the old gods. He's also often called Julian the Philosopher. He is without a doubt one of the best-known figures from late antiquity. Before we look at this figure Julian, who's really invited debate and controversy ever since his death on June 26, 363 A.D., I'd like to start with a snapshot from the middle of this lecture, in effect.

On December 11, 361 A.D., the emperor Julian, at the head of a victorious army that was supposed to fight a civil war and didn't, entered the city of Constantinople. He ordered immediately that the temples be opened and the sacrifices proceed. The population in Constantinople was aghast. This was the Christian population of the new Rome, the city that had been founded by Constantine, and here's Constantine's nephew, less than a generation later, ordering the reversal of all the policies I'd talked about in the last four lectures. This incident is a reminder that the success and triumph of Christianity was by no means inevitable as a result of the so-called revolution wrought by Constantine, or even by the efforts of his sons that followed him between 337 and 361. Julian suddenly and abruptly turned the entire direction of the religious and cultural history of the Roman Empire back to the world of paganism.

It's a point that's important to stress, not only the importance of individuals in history, but how easy it is for us with a sense of perspective to say that with Constantine it's inevitable that Christianity is on the rise, and all of the developments that I've discussed in the last several lectures on Christian arts, aesthetics, the claiming of public and religious space makes the success of Christianity inevitable, and we should just simply follow out the story and be done with it. Julian proved that it's by no means certain what the religious loyalties of the Roman world would be. He died 18 months later on a distant frontier and his reforms died with him; but in December, 361, the Christian population of Constantinople didn't know that.

What makes Julian so controversial? He was born into the imperial family. He was a nephew of the emperor Constantine; his father was a half-brother of the emperor Constantine. Furthermore, he's a figure that's quite unusual among the emperors of Rome. One, he was an intellectual. Second, his native language was Greek. It was clear from birth he was to be trained to be a theologian bishop, probably the Bishop of Constantinople itself. In addition, he has engendered all sorts of interest, both by his detractors—that would be Christian authors writing in his lifetime—as well as his admirers, both past and present.

Foremost is the historian Ammianus Marcellinus, who lived in the 4th century A.D. He was probably born either in the city of Beirut or Antioch. He was of a Roman colonial family. He is often called the last great imperial historian of Rome. He wrote a narrative history in Latin in which Julian's career was the centerpiece. Ammianus Marcellinus is one of our major sources on the emperor Julian. He does have a remarkably balanced view of Julian and Julian's policies, even though Julian was a fellow pagan. Other authors include famous novelist Gore Vidal, who in 1962 published a novel on Julian. Vidal's novel is largely anachronistic; he's more interested in dealing with the literary criticism and also advancing positions against religious intolerance. Nonetheless, it's a significant and interesting read, and it goes to show how controversial and how important Julian still is to us; that he lives in novels, he lives in philosophical works, in historical accounts, and he is still a popular figure. Anyone familiar with the world of late Rome knows who Julian is. Julian comes in probably second after Constantine.

Julian also wrote an enormous amount of works in a very short time as emperor. Essentially an emperor for two-and-a-half years, he wrote nine major philosophical works, hymns, letters, and administrative documents. His writings alone fill three volumes of the Loeb Classical Library. One of his most important works is a critique, *Against the Galileans*—that's his word for the Christians—which survives in part because it's such an incisive criticism of Christian theology that Christians preserved it and would hone the debating skills of promising Christian students who would refute the analysis of Julian against the Christian doctrine and against the Christian text.

Julian is a perplexing figure. Some see him as a hero of a lost cause; some of that in a positive light, some of that in a negative light. Those who think that Julian was just an anachronism, he had no chance of reversing Constantine's revolution, often will dismiss Julian as a rather eccentric and zealous pagan ruler. Others will see him as a man who had great visions, who could've out-Constantine'd Constantine; that is, he would've used the patronage and the power of the imperial administration and army to restore the worship of the old gods the way his uncle had upheld the new faith of Christianity.

Let's take a look at Julian himself, and what I wish to do in this lecture is talk about his career, his reforms, and then his unfortunate death on the Persian expedition in June, 363, which marks in my mind a very, very important turning point in the religious history of the Roman world in the 4th century A.D. First, Julian's early career: In September, 337, the emperor Constantine died, and there was a purge of all the male members of the imperial family; anyone who was a potential rival to the three surviving sons of Constantine, and those sons were named Constantine II, Constans, and Constantius II. It was the youngest, Constantius II, who would eventually reunite the empire; and he would rule for quite a long time, from 337–361. He was a devout Christian; however, he was a Christian of the Arian confession, not of the Nicene Creed.

Julian and his half-brother, a man named Constantius Gallus, were the only two male members of the imperial family who were spared from that purge. Julian was perhaps 6 years old at the time, his half-brother was about 12; and it was probably their young age that resulted in their lives being spared. There are some scholars who go so far as to argue that in later life Julian actually blamed his cousin Constantius, who himself was quite young, for the murder of his father and his various male members of his family. That's going a bit too far; doing too much psychoanalysis without the kind of information we'd like to have.

From the start, Julian and his older half-brother, Constantius Gallus, were reared as Christians. They were entrusted to a Eusebius—not the Eusebius who wrote the history; a man who was Bishop of Nicomedia and later Bishop of Constantinople—and he saw to the instruction and the baptism of the brothers. Eusebius died in 341 A.D.—that is, early in the reign of the sons of Constantine—and Julian and Constantius Gallus were something of a problem. They were potential threats to the family of Constantine, to the sons of Constantine. So the two brothers grew up under the understanding that they were essentially under house arrest, and they really had to act on their good behavior.

In 341, the brothers were, in effect, banished to Cappadocia. Cappadocia today is well known to tourists of Turkey as one of the most wild and dramatic landscapes that you would ever want, and it's clearly a geologist's dream to go out there. They were dumped in an imperial ranch at a place called Marcellum, which we think is near the modern city of Kasyeri, ancient Caesarea Mazaka; and therefore, Julian grew up in his formative years, between the ages of 8 and 18, reading Homer and the traditional Classics, looking up at Mount Argaeus—which was the home to the mother goddess Ma, sometimes identified with Cybele—and in that landscape, reading Homer, there isn't much surprise to me that by age 20 he tells us in his writings he went back to the old gods. If you're in Cappadocia, every other mountain and rock look sacred; it's an amazing landscape to this day. He was clearly instructed by individuals who were well-versed in the Classics and whose religious affiliation to this day is still uncertain.

The brothers had different career trajectories. Constantius Gallus was eventually dragged out of this exile in 351 and made Caesar an heir to Constantius while Constantius was waging a war in the Western provinces against the Rhine army that had put on the throne, a man named Magnentius, a general; and the Western army was angry, as it was through the entire 4th century, that the sacrifices had been suspended. Most of the Western army was provincial Romans and Germans from across the frontier. They had about 30 basic Latin attack words, and they're overwhelmingly pagan. Constantius Gallus was told, "You run the East as Caesar, as heir," to his cousin Constantius II, and he turned out to be so incompetent and tyrannical that he was eventually arrested and executed in 354.

Meanwhile, Julian was allowed to come back and study at Constantinople, Nicomedia; he eventually ended up at Pergamon and also at the city of Ephesus in the early 350s. Julian was designated for a theological career. He was going to probably become Bishop of Constantinople; so the older half-brother would be a potential emperor, and Julian would effectively be the patriarch of Constantinople, so the two half-brothers would succeed as Christian rulers to Constantius II. It didn't work out that way. Julian came under the powerful influence of two philosophers at the time: a man called Maximus of Ephesus, who was a theurgist—that is, he was trained in the solartheurgy of Iamblichus of Chalcis—and another fellow named Aedesius. Both of them were very much Middle Platonists, they understood the whole tradition of Plotinus, and Julian was enraptured by their lectures. He secretly converted to the worship of the gods, probably when he turned age 20. He had to however, learn to dissemble; not to let his cousin know that he, in effect, had renounced his Christianity (he had been baptized as a Christian).

Julian's position was always very chancy at best. At one point, he's summoned to the court at Milan and he thinks, "That's it, I'm going to get my head chopped off." Constantius, however, who was one of the most suspicious emperors in the 4th century, relented, largely because his wife Helena interceded for the young prince Julian. Julian was sent back to complete his studies. He does a visit to Athens. He secretly was initiated within the Eleusinian mysteries; he claimed he had a vision from the mother goddess; and it's clear, by the mid 350s Julian is a convinced pagan, a convinced theurgist, a Platonist in his theology, and yet he has to keep it quiet.

In 355, this secret or crypto-pagan prince, who had been essentially set aside by the entire imperial family—he was bookish; he wasn't serious; he was rather short, not particularly impressive in stature; and he spoke Greek as his first language, not Latin, which was an indication that no one took him seriously. (The last emperor who was disregarded like this was the emperor Claudius back in the 1st century A.D.) Julian was brought back to the imperial court. Constantius had no choice but to make Julian his heir and Caesar because there's no one else left in the family. Constantius had done a pretty good job in eliminating most of the imperial family that had escaped that purge back in 337. Julian was sent packing to Gaul; he was to go command the Western army because the provinces in Gaul were being overrun by German barbarians. Julian, ever the bookish prince, read up on his Julius Caesar, which actually is not bad for learning how to command, and he got all geared up and this nephew of Constantine, probably standing about 5'3", showed up on the Rhine commanding all these Germans and Celts who were like six inches taller, and what it shows is that a man of ability could actually learn generalship on the spot.

Julian won brilliant victories, threw the barbarians back over the Rhine, reestablished the frontier; and the Western army came to adore this rather strange, bookish, Greek-speaking prince who grew up in the wilds of Cappadocia. Then the news comes from Constantius: We've got a war against the Persians yet again; they've sacked an important city in Mesopotamia. The emperor wanted soldiers to be transferred from the West to the East. This sparked a revolt, a mutiny, in December of 360. The Western army saluted Julian as emperor, and that meant a civil war was on.

The Western army, which was very, very much pagan in its loyalties—it revolted back in 350 under Magnentius in 350–353; it would revolt again in the 4th century over religious issues—they now rallied around Julian, and Julian came out and publicly revealed what some of his officers already knew: He was a worshiper of the old gods. Soldiers claimed that the eagle of Jupiter appeared; it was a propitious sign that the gods would be restored; and the Western army began to march eastward to encounter the army of Constantius II. Before the civil war could be fought, Constantius succumbed to illness and died in November, 361; and he did something that really was a blessing to the empire: He recognized Julian as his heir. Julian, in effect, became Roman emperor without the need of a civil war.

Back to that incident I started this lecture with: In December, 361, he entered the Christian capital as the heir of his uncle Constantine and his cousin Constantius II and orders immediately the restoration of the gods. Between December, 361 and March, 363—a period of about 16 months—Julian issued sweeping legislation and administrative reforms across the Roman Empire. There had not been so many reforms since the time of Diocletian. Julian, in many ways, attacked corruption abuses with the imperial administration; cracked down on taxes; projected himself in many ways as a prince, a princeps, of the old order. At the same time, he carried out important religious reforms.

In this case, Julian had to be cautious just like his uncle; only he didn't quite learn Constantine's lesson: Make haste slowly. He moved quickly. He didn't persecute the Christians, but he abruptly and completely cut off their funding. He proclaimed religious toleration and then allowed the Christians, who were divided over the issue of the Trinity—that is the Nycenes and the Arians—to sue each other in courts over who had control of what bishopric, and Julian encouraged divisions within the Christian church. He ordered the temples to be reopened and the sacrifices to proceed. He began to organize a pagan counter-church, and this is what led Peter Brown to say that Julian's attitude or his policy was he'd out-Constantine Constantine; that is, he'd create a pagan religious hierarchy modeled very closely after the Christian hierarchy and these pagan priests would conduct the same kind of activities that the bishops did, which I described in the previous lecture. They were to take over all the charitable actions that were done by bishops and therefore win over the poor in the cities. The priests were to be funded and maintained by the imperial government. Julian himself wrote a letter to a pagan priest, which is a theoretical piece, but it's a letter in which he describes that he's creating a pagan religious ordo, which is equivalent to the Christian ordo created by Constantine. Priests were supposed to conduct them in very moral lives; they were supposed to carry out activities in buildings and public events that would be very similar to the bishops. At the same time, he remitted taxes to cities. He passed legislation in favor of the pagan decurions. He understood that the restoration of the pagan cults depended on promoting this new imperial religious hierarchy and the decurion pagan families in the provincial cities.

There are a number of stories told about Julian in pressing this goal. One is the famous story of his barber. Julian, who wore a philosopher's beard—he didn't cut the image of the clean-shaven Alexander look that Constantine and his sons had made popular—had his barber come in, he was supposed to cut his hair, and he found out that this imperial barber, who was on the payroll, received an enormous salary far greater than many of the civic elites in the provincial cities, and he was outraged. Furthermore, he learned that this barber had gone into imperial service to escape civic obligations, so he immediately dismissed him, demoted him, and sent him back to his native city and told him, "Behave like a proper decurion. Carry out your civic offices; worship the gods." The story was circulated as a way of promoting Julian's pose that he was going to be a new Marcus Aurelius. He was going to be accessible; he was going to be a philosopher. He was going to be a ruler who recreated in some ways that accessible emperor of the 2nd century A.D., not the supreme autocrat created by Diocletian and then by Constantine, whether it be in the pagan or the Christian gods.

This was a pose; and there's good reason in reading Julian's own works and some of his actions, particularly during the Persian campaign, to realize that Julian was impatient; that this emperor, when he came to the throne, he'd just about turned 30; that he was a zealot in his religious beliefs; that he'd been born a Christian, went over to paganism, and as a convert to paganism was extremely zealous in promoting his religious beliefs; had very, very little patience with those who disagreed with him; and, above all, that impatience translated into some serious military blunders that ended up getting Julian killed in the retreat from Ctesiphon in June, 363. While he posed like an emperor of the 2nd century A.D., that's more for effect and, in some ways, was contrary to his nature.

However, pagans and Christians alike were kind of confused by them; they didn't quite know what to make of Julian. Even the historian Ammianus Marcellinus, the pagan author who thought of Julian as a fellow pagan and really approved of the worship of the gods, even he made comments that the way Julian behaved was not proper to an emperor. Ever since the mid-3rd century, Romans of all religious faiths believed that the emperor should have divine power, he should have the favor of the gods or the Christian God. He had to behave in a certain ceremonial way, and Julian didn't behave that way; and that was seen somehow as inappropriate, or distasteful, and in some ways a bit confusing to the ruling classes of the Roman world.

Julian also saw his paganism not as the traditional restoration of the cults, but a new pagan counter-church. Julian himself used a term to describe this counter-church: He called it Hellenism. That was the study of philosophy, the worship and veneration of the cults; all of this to be subsidized by the imperial state. That bureaucracy and army created by Diocletian and Constantine that had been supporting Christianity for over 30 years was now going to be immediately and abruptly shifted to support this new pagan Hellenism. That, too, was perplexing, especially to pagans, who never in their traditions had anything like this type of state organization. The reason was that Julian was reared as a Christian. His religious views were colored by the fact that his at least initial goal, or what he was trained for, was to be the Bishop of Constantinople; so he thought in terms of that Christian hierarchy. He also understood the power of that Christian hierarchy that had been created by Constantine, and he thought that the only way to counter it was to essentially imitate it and take it over.

This gets to certain debates about what Julian really intended in the long run; that is, if he hadn't been killed in Persia, if he hadn't ruled for 3 years and instead for 30 years, would he have persecuted, or was he a clever man who would've incited the Christians to dispute among themselves and not persecute? I think that Julian's inclination in the long run was that he might've persecuted once he had his victory in Persia; and that's borne out by several of his writings, the most peculiar one called the *Misopogon* (the *Beard Hater*), which he penned in the city of Antioch before he went on his Persian war.

In that work, he answers the criticisms of the Christian population of Antioch who criticize Julian's beard, a philosopher's beard, which was obviously a pagan conceit; the coin types, which were regarded as pagan; the policies of the emperor restoring the gods and all those traditions; all of that was mocked by the Christians of Antioch, and what Julian did was write a rebuttal, which is a very strange piece of satire in which he actually indulges in a fair amount of self-criticism about himself and then he had this pamphlet nailed to the city gate of Antioch. If you read that work today, it's a very learned and rather interesting work to us; but I'm sure the majority of the public in Antioch, it went right over their heads, and then to guys like Ammianus Marcellinus and all the pagans supporting Julian, this was not what an emperor's supposed to do—involve themselves in some sort of self-deprecating humor in order to answer a bunch of Christian detractors—and it suggests very much a nervous, zealous, and impatient personality. Given the right chances and circumstances, Julian may well have issued his own edicts of persecution if he'd stayed on the throne long enough and was followed by a pagan successor. I come down on that side of the arguments; others would argue that Julian had a much more tolerant nature.

There were several important reforms that went in tandem with restoring the gods and switching patronage from the Christian church to the pagan cults.

One of the most important pieces of legislation, and one that was regarded with the greatest bitterness by his Christian opponents, was a law that required that teachers teach what they believe in and that students read texts that they believed in. Julian himself was a Platonist, and he articulated a version of the Platinian great chain of being; his god was seen as a solar divinity manifested in many ways. He therefore argued as a devoted Platonist and a theurgist that you must believe in these traditions to teach them—to teach Homer; to teach Plato—and therefore Christians, both teachers and students, were to be denied the Classics. This was a law that had long-term implications. It was bitterly resented, because in doing this, what Julian would do was deny the Christian leadership—which for the last 30 years since Constantine had been appropriating the classics, evolving their own arts, evolving their own literary genres—and it would demote them to second rate status culturally and reverse the Constantinian revolution and allow pagans once more to look down smugly at the Christian intellectual elites as a bunch of second-raters and people who spoke vernacular Greek and really couldn't hold an argument in proper Platonic terms. Even Ammianus Marcellinus admits that this was a harsh law. That law would be rescinded after his death, but it was one of the long-term reforms that Julian had in mind in advancing the cause of the restoration of the old gods.

He also supported the Jews and attempted to rebuild Jerusalem; that is, to uphold the validity of the Old Israel against the New Israel. In his work against the Galileans, he wrote some incisive criticisms, particularly on the apocalyptic literature of the Old Testament, the later books, which he saw were works written in the time of Maccabees; his critique on the Book of Daniel still stands up as a very good piece of scholarship. Overall, Julian tried to attack the organization of Christianity and the patronage of Christianity on all sorts of fronts.

He died in a war against Persia, and all too often that campaign—and I'm included in this—is usually studied by scholars from a military and diplomatic angle. But the war against Persia had a very important religious dimension, and it was part of this overall policy of Julian to restore the worship of the gods. In 362 A.D., Julian left the city of Constantinople and traveled east, visiting the various cult centers to win the favor of the traditional gods as he was to fight the Shah of the Persians, a man named

Shapur II. This war had been going on since 359; he'd inherited it from his cousin Constantius. En route, Julian took time to visit shrines such as the cult of Cybele at Pessinus; the cult of Asclepius at Ankara; various important cults like Apollo of Daphne outside of Antioch; and in many ways, he trekked east in the tradition of pagan emperors who had battled the Iranian foe for centuries.

He then invaded Mesopotamia, attacking the Persian capital city of Ctesiphon to force the Persian Shah to a decisive battle, and he botched it. In his impatience, he made some important strategic and logistical mistakes. In part, the army of the East was really not up to the capabilities of Julian's strategy, whether it was Julian's mistakes or the quality of the Roman army; and this is debated by many scholars. The army arrived in Mesopotamia at the height of the blazing summer. Provisions weren't delivered on time, and Julian had to order a retreat. On that retreat, he's killed in a skirmish as the Roman army was trying to get back to Roman territory; and the word was put out that he was actually killed by a Christian in the employ of a Persian shah—that is, an auxiliary Arab soldier who happened to be a Christian—and it's a legend that's embroidered in the Middle Ages.

The death of Julian on June 26, 363, was a fateful event. That evening, the senior officers met in the imperial tent. The emperor was dying, and initially the officers turned to the Praetorian Prefect, a man name Salutius, a senior pagan respected by all members of the army, he'd been with Julian from the start, and asked, "Would you become emperor?" Salutius turned down on grounds of age; also, he didn't want the job of taking a Roman army out of Persia into Rome. It's a rather chancy job description. They next turned to a Christian, a Nicene Christian, Jovian—who was second in command—and asked Jovian, "Would you take the emperorship?" Jovian was nervous and said, "You know I'm a Christian, and the emperor was a pagan," and the other officers said to Jovian, "Tonight in this tent, we're all Christians; get us out of Persia." Jovian accepted the emperorship. He signed an ignominious peace where he gave up strategic provinces, but he did get the army back to the Roman Empire.

The result of this campaign was disastrous for the pagan cause. The pagans had lost their emperor, despite all of his piety to restore the worship of the gods. He was the first emperor since Valerian back in 260 who suffered an ignominious defeat. To the Christians, it was a vindication of their faith and it was a way for the Christians to draw a parallel between Julian fighting under the old gods, being defeated by the Persian foe, and then Constantine and Constantius who won brilliant victories under the labarum, the Christian symbols. The death of Julian meant the end of his reforms. But it was more than that: The pagans were disorganized; they were demoralized; they didn't have a leadership. With the death of Julian, a very important turning point had been made; and the Christians would assume their cultural and political dominance in the Roman world. Within the next generation, the second turning point would come with the emperor Theodosius I.

Struggle over Faith and Culture
Lecture 21

A fter the death of Emperor Julian II, the pagan elite, particularly in Rome, Athens, and Alexandria, were not so certain Christianity had won the battle for Roman culture. A new pagan literature developed to defend the old faith, some of it in imitation of Christian literary forms. But lacking a leader like Julian and with an essentially conservative outlook, they were unable to mount an effective counter-revolution to restore their faith, and by the middle of the 5th century, the intellectual and cultural leadership of the Roman world was decisively Christian.

Julian's Successors

- In the generation or so after the death of Julian the Apostate, the question was reopened: Which religion was going to take charge of the Roman world? It quickly became clear that the pagans were in no position to re-establish the leadership. Even if they had a pagan emperor, they had no one with Julian's vision.

- On the other hand, Emperor Jovian, although a Christian, turned out to be a feckless ruler. He was found dead under mysterious circumstances in February 364; two senior army officers, the brothers **Valentinian I** and **Valens**, were proclaimed the next emperors. Neither was a man of first-rate ability, although they were respected by the army at the time.

- Valentinian and Valens were provincials of barbarian origin. Both Arian Christians at their accession, Valentinian converted to Nicene Christianity when he took over the western half of the Roman world, while Valens remained an Arian and ruled in the eastern half, reflecting the religious sentiments of each region.

- Because they were not connected to the imperial family of Constantine, they had to establish the second Christian dynasty of Rome. At first, they tried to cloak themselves in the symbols of Constantine: Coins, medallions, and public arts all featured the labarum with the Christogram.

- The brothers did get rid of some of Julian's laws—the law on education and imperial funding of the cults, for example—they did not outlaw the sacrifices or ban the traditional rites; they had to take a moderate position because the pagans had regained ground under Julian. Many army officers and soldiers were still pagans, and many of the provincial cities were in the hands of a pagan elite.

Hypatia of Alexandria was murdered by Christian monks.

- Until 391–392, the pagans found themselves in a position somewhat analogous to the early years of Constantine: Christianity was the favored faith; yet the old gods had not been outlawed. This ambiguous situation meant the pagans were caught off guard when Emperor Theodosius I eventually outlawed the cults.

- Furthermore, Valens and Valentinian did not inherit a united imperial church; Christianity was still divided between the Arians and Nicenes over the Trinitarian issue. That, too, would change with Theodosius, who would come down decisively on the side of the Nicene Creed.

The State of Pagan Culture after Julian

- Archaeologists have documented that the shrines and temples continued to operate throughout the 4th century and into the

5th century, some of them even after Theodosius I outlawed the sacrifices.

- There was a resurgence in Neoplatonic thought in Athens; one outstanding figure in the movement was **Proclus**, who wrote in the 5th century. At Alexandria, the great school continued to flourish. One of its most controversial figures was the mathematician **Hypatia**; she was hacked to death by a crowd of Christian monks in 414, as dramatized in the film *Agora*, but little of her work survives and her exact positions are unknown.

- Philosophers writing in Athens and Alexandria continued to articulate the Great Chain of Being of Plotinus and fostered the traditions of theurgy. These philosophers also evolved the doctrine sometimes proxy sacrifice: the learned philosopher can offer up sacrifices, knowing the intellectual meaning of these rites, on behalf of the entire community and can win the favor of the gods for the entire Roman world.

- There was enormous literary output by pagan authors. This included histories, such as that of Ammianus Marcellinus. Most literary production came from Rome in the West or Athens, Alexandria, and Antioch in the East.

The City of Rome in the Late Empire

- The administration of the city of Rome fell to the great senatorial families, who had never abandoned the goddess Roma or the traditional gods of Rome. They had enough wealth, power, and distance to ignore the upstart Christian emperors in Constantinople, and they essentially did as they wished. That included holding old offices of the city of Rome, conducting pagan ceremonies and sacrifices, and engaging in literary production.

- A number of individuals from this late senatorial aristocracy were great patrons of the gods and also edited the works of Vergil and of Cicero. One was Vettius Agorius Praetextatus; he and his wife epitomized pagan patronage, putting on festivals that lasted weeks. By one calculation, two-thirds of the calendar year in the city of Rome was engaged in pagan holidays.

- Another illustrious Roman was **Symmachus**, the leading pagan of the 4th century. Christian emperors had to pay attention to him; he was urban prefect of the city and governor of Africa. He alone could fund a remarkable circle of literati who edited text and carried out pagan festivals.

- The letters of Symmachus are not only in Ciceronian Latin; they contain no references to Christianity or Constantine and his successors whatsoever. They contain no references to the pope, who happened to be right on the other side of the Tiber River at the Ianiculum, which will eventually become Vatican City. This illustrates how difficult it sometimes is to date religious change in the Roman world.

- Only during the pontificate of Pope Leo I, in the mid-5th century, did the Roman aristocracy finally come over to Christianity.

The Great Eastern Cities in the Late Empire

- In the East, the picture was much the same as in Rome. Athens remained a pagan city into the 5th century. Alexandria was divided between pagans and Christians, and when the laws of 391–392 outlawed the cults, there were riots and demonstrations. The **Serapeum** and the Mouseion (the Library of Alexandria) were destroyed, as also dramatized in the film *Agora*.

- In the late 4th and early 5th centuries, a significant amount of pagan literature was composed in Greek, which became the final blossoming of pagan literature. Most classicists do not bother reading it. It is generally written in a high-blown style, particularly the epic poetry.

- **Quintus of Smyrna** wrote what is probably the longest written work in all antiquity; at more than 20,000 verses, it is longer than the *Iliad* and the *Odyssey* combined. The poem is interesting only to specialists today, but it demonstrates that it was by no means assured, at least in the minds of these pagans, that they had lost the struggle for Roman cultural dominance.

- A new brand of pagan history was produced. Most of these works have only survived in fragments. One that has come down to us intact is **Zosimus**'s *New History*. It is a continuous, linear narrative in the Greek and Roman tradition. But it is also a new kind of pagan apologetic literature: Zosimus argues that the reason the Roman Empire was suffering military reverses on the frontier was because the Christian emperors had abandoned the worship of the traditional gods.

- Orators operated in the same light. **Themistius of Constantinople** and **Libanius of Antioch**, who both knew Julian, continued to write into the reign of Theodosius I. They composed traditional panegyrics to the emperor and trained students in letters and the classics. They devised with new forms of oratory to appeal to Christian emperors for toleration of pagans, modeled on arguments the Christians had made in the 2nd century: We are loyal Roman citizens following Roman traditions. You Christian emperors should tolerate us.

- A similar type of literature was penned by Symmachus. He wrote a series of letters to the Christian emperors Gratian and Valentinian II arguing that the Altar of Victory in the Roman senate house, which was removed as offensive on orders of Valentinian I—should be restored.

The Ultimate Failure of the Pagan Resurgence

- This literature is indicative of the mixed religious situation after Julian and of one other point: The pagans never understood that there was a religious conflict. They did not understand that what was at stake was which religious system would control the destinies of the Roman world and eventually the cultural future of the Western tradition.

- The pagans never had a coherent thought of proselytizing. Part of this was in the nature of the pagan religious outlook; but also, this was because the pagan leaders of the Roman world were essentially a Mandarin elite. They were social conservatives, wary of defying the emperor openly. To defy the emperor would invite civil war. Civil war would invite revolution and social change, something that none of the pagan literati wanted.

- The pagans never had a coherent sense of how to win the emperor back to the old gods. They lacked the leadership and vision to mount a coherent effort. As a result, many pagans, particularly of the upper classes, eventually crossed over to Christianity, particularly via the philosophical and aesthetic bridge of Neoplatonism.

Important Term

Serapeum (a.k.a. **Serapeion**): A temple of Serapis, the Hellenized Osiris who was the tutelary god of Alexandria, Egypt. The destruction of the Serapeum of Alexandria by Christians in 391 marked a major defeat for paganism.

Names to Know

Hypatia (c. 360–415): Daughter of the mathematician Theon (c. 335–405) who taught mathematics and astronomy at Alexandria. She succeeded to the head of the pagan philosophical school at Alexandria in 400 and so was perceived as a threat by Patriarch Cyril. In 415, she was assaulted and hacked to pieces by a crowd of monks. Her works do not survive, but she apparently wrote commentaries on philosophy and astronomy.

Libanius of Antioch (314–394): Pagan rhetorician and sophist of Antioch who trained talented young men, pagan and Christian, destined for imperial service. He was a friend to the emperor Julian II, and yet he was allowed to present an oration protesting the desecration of temples in 383–388 to Theodosius I. Sixty-four orations of Libanius—along with commentaries, rhetorical exercises, and over 1,500 letters—have survived.

Proclus (c. 410–485): Brilliant Neoplatonic thinker and theurgist who was born of a wealthy family in Lycia but studied in Athens under Syrianus and succeeded the latter as head of the Academy in Athens. His *Elements of Theology, Platonic Theology*, and *Elements of Physics* are the climax of Greek philosophical thinking. He composed commentaries on Plato's *Timaeus* and *Alcibiades I*, as well as religious hymns.

Quintus of Smyrna (fl. 4th century A.D.): Pagan poet who composed the epic *Posthomerica*, a work of more than 20,000 lines (twice the length of the *Iliad* and the *Odyssey* combined), which told of events at Troy after Homer's epic leaves off.

Symmachus (a.k.a. **Quintus Aurelius Symmachus**; c. 340–402): The most distinguished Roman pagan senator of the 4th century and an accomplished man of letters. He served as proconsul of Africa (373), urban prefect (384–385), and consul (391). He presided over the pagan cultural and literary revival of Rome. In a series of orations (*relationes*), he pleaded for the restoration of the Altar of Victory to the Senate house (*Curia*) in 382–390. He supported Magnus Maximus in 387–388, but Theodosius pardoned him, and he retired from public life after 391.

Themistius of Constantinople (317–391): Pagan rhetorician and philosopher born of a noble family in Asia Minor, he was a loyal servant at Constantinople to successive emperors between Constantius II (r. 337–361) and Theodosius I (r. 379–395). Constantius II elected Themisitius, although a pagan, into the Christian senate of Constantinople (355). Themistius served as proconsul (358) and urban prefect (359–360). He favored Julian II, but he was respected as the senior pagan senator by Julian's Christian successors. Thirty-six orations of Themistius have survived, but his philosophical works and commentaries survive only in fragments.

Valens (a.k.a. **Flavius Valens**; c. 328–378; r. 364–378): Born of a military family in Pannonia, he served under Julian and Jovian. In 364, his brother Valentinian I created Valens emperor of the East. A devoted Arian Christian, Valens faced opposition from the Nicene bishops. His Persian war was inconclusive. In 378, he was decisively defeated and slain by the Goths at Adrianople.

Valentinian I (a.k.a. **Flavius Valentinianus**; 321–375; r. 364–375): Born to a Pannonian military family, he was a senior officer acclaimed emperor by the Eastern army after the death of Jovian. Valentinian appointed his brother Valens emperor of the East and campaigned against the Germans on the Rhine and Upper Danube, where he strengthened fortifications. He was succeeded by his two sons, Gratian (r. 367–383) and Valentinian II (r. 375–392).

Zosimus (c. 480–515): Greek historian who wrote *New History*, in which he attributes the decline of Roman power to the rejection of the gods in favor of Christianity.

Suggested Reading

Alföldi, *A Conflict of Ideas in the Late Roman Empire.*

Ammianus Marcellinus, *The Later Roman Empire.*

———, *Roman History.*

Bregman, *Synesius of Cyrene.*

Brown, *Augustine of Hippo.*

Barnes, *Athanasius and Constantius.*

Barrow, Prefect and Emperor.

Chauvin, *A Chronicle of the Last Pagans.*

Dill, *Roman Society in the Last Century of the Western Empire.*

Green, *The City of the Moon.*

Harl, "Sacrifice and Pagan Belief in Fifth- and Sixth-Century Byzantium."

Lenski, *Failure of Empire.*

Matthews, *Western Aristocracies and the Imperial Court.*

Saltzman, *The Making of a Christian Aristocracy.*

Segal, *Edessa, the Blessed City.*

Trombley, *Hellenic Religion and Christianization.*

Zosimus, *New History.*

Questions to Consider

1. How did pagans and Christians view the failure of Julian? How could pagans maintain their roles as cultural leaders and the validity of the gods in the later 4th and 5th centuries?

2. How conscious were pagan writers of representing an older order being replaced by a Christian one? How could the senators at Rome ignore the Christian world into the 5th century? How was the flowering of Greek pagan literature after Julian II the Indian summer of the classical world?

3. How did Christian prelates and writers accommodate the pagan literary heritage as a means to win converts? How typical was the conversion of Synesius of Cyrene? Why did Roman senators convert in the early 5th century?

Struggle over Faith and Culture
Lecture 21—Transcript

In this lecture, I plan to look at some of the implications in the generation or so after the death of the emperor Julian the Apostate. For lack of a better term, it's really a question of the struggle over faith and culture. That is, with the end of this pagan emperor and his program to bring back the gods, the question then was reopened: Exactly what faith, what religion, was going to take charge of the Roman world? Would the Christians be able to reestablish their position, or would the pagans find a new leadership?

It very quickly became clear that the pagans were in no position to reestablish the leadership; they had no one to act as an alternate to Julian, and even if they did have a pagan emperor, they had no man who would've had the kind of vision Julian did of what it would take to reverse the Constantinian revolution. The death of Julian, the death of that particular individual, was a serious blow to paganism in the Roman world.

On the other hand, the Christians didn't get the best of emperors with the death of Julian. Jovian, the man who'd been elected by the officers of the Eastern army, turned out to be a rather feckless ruler. He did get the army out of Persia, back to Roman territory, at a very high price. He was found mysteriously dead in February of 364, and two senior officers of the army, brothers Valentinian and Valens, were proclaimed emperors. Valens and Valentinian were emperors of a whole different quality of the family of Constantine. Neither one of those emperors was really a man of first-rate ability, although they were respected by their officers and the army at the time.

They had several problems. First, they were from Pannonia, which is essentially the region of Hungary today. They were provincials; they were of barbarian origin. In some circles, it was circulated that their ancestors had only been Romans for a generation or two. They were both Arian Christians at the time of their accession, but Valentinian very astutely and adroitly converted to Nicene Christianity because he took over the Western half of the Roman world, and that was part of the Roman world where the Nicene position was stronger. The brother, Valens, remained an Arian. He was the younger brother and a lesser figure. The brothers also lacked legitimacy.

They weren't connected to the Imperial family of Constantine; and what, in effect, they had to do was establish the second Christian dynasty of Rome. It was really a question of exactly what they could achieve. First, they tried to cloak themselves in the symbols of Constantine. Coins, medallions, public arts from this period show very much a return to the images of Constantine; the labarum, the Chi-Rho, are all projected.

On the other hand, Valentinian and Valens, while they did get rid of some of the offending literature of Julian—the law on education, for instance, was rescinded; the imperial funding of the cults and the temples—otherwise, they didn't move to outlaw the sacrifices to ban the traditional rites; they had to take a moderate ground. The pagans had regained ground under Julian's reign, even though it was a short time. Many officers and soldiers were still pagans; and it's clear that many of the provincial cities of the Roman world continued to be in the hands of the pagan elite. Even in major cities, such as Caesarea (today, the modern city of Kayseri in Turkey), or in cities of the second rank in the Roman provinces of North Africa or certain cities in Spain, it's clear that the pagan decurions were still powerful figures and that bishops had not yet asserted themselves against those pagan families, and it was still a very tentative situation religiously. Valens and Valentinian, out of pragmatism, had to tolerate the existence of these cults; and for the next generation, down to 391–392 after Julian's death, the pagans found themselves in a position that was somewhat analogous to the early years of Constantine; that is, a position their parents or grandparents were in. Christianity was the favored faith; the old gods had not been declared outlawed. There were still many indications in certain parts of the Roman world that the traditional faith and religious rites went on, but it was also clear that the gods were not favored at the imperial court and that the city of Constantinople was very much a Christian capital.

This led to a rather peculiar religious situation at the end of the 4th century, and in some ways, I think this ambiguous situation meant that the pagans were really caught off guard when, in 391–392, the emperor Theodosius I dramatically outlawed the cults and really moved against them, and that would spark a really halfhearted revolt in Italy by the pagan senators. The second was that the pagans weren't really ready to face the new Christian shock troops—that is, the ascetics and monks—who increasingly came to play an important role in the conversion of the Roman Empire at the end of the 4th and particularly in the 5th and 6th centuries. In the aftermath of Julian's death, that first generation after Julian, the situation was still quite ambiguous.

Furthermore, the two brothers, Valens and Valentinian, also didn't inherit a united imperial church, and Christianity was still divided over the Trinitarian issue between Arians and Nicenes; so the Christians themselves, within the imperial-sponsored church let alone the so-called heresies, were still not a united front. That, too, would change with Theodosius, who would come down decisively on the side of the Nicene Creed and would impose a certain unity in the imperial church, and then he would move to outlaw the cults.

In what ways was the situation rather favorable to the pagans still in the aftermath of Julian's death? This could be measured in several ways. One would be just looking at the cities in the Roman world. When Julian issued his edicts and allowed the sacrifices to continue, many of the pagan elites, in the cities of the Roman East particularly but also in Africa, in Italy, in Spain, hailed the return of the worship of the old gods. Archaeology is able to document that these shrines and temples continued to operate well through the 4th century and into the 5th century, some of them even after those laws I mentioned of Theodosius that outlawed the sacrifices and therefore outlawed the worship and belief in the gods.

In these cases, we know, for instance, that the city of Aphrodisias—a city I've mentioned several times before; a very important excavation that's been conducted by NYU and Berkeley—there's a villa that's been excavated from the 4th and early 5th centuries, we call it the Villa of the Philosophers; and that villa was a major Neoplatonic school, a pagan Neoplatonic school, that flourished well into the 5th century A.D. In excavations in this house, a set of *tondos* were found, which are on display in the museum, showing Alcibiades and Socrates, Alexander the Great and Aristotle, stressing the men of action, the men of philosophy and disputation, and it's one of the indices of the rich pagan philosophical tradition that continued after Julian.

At Athens, there's a whole resurgence in Neoplatonic thought, particularly with Proclus, one of the great platonic thinkers of the 5th century A.D. At Alexandria, the great school continued to flourish. One of the most controversial figures known to the popular mind is a mathematician called Hypatia. She was hacked to death by a crowd of monks in 414 A.D., which has been dramatized in an early movie. She was also popularized by the series of Carl Sagan; and really she was a mathematician, and her exact position within the pagan intellectual tradition is really questionable, we really have nothing about her except some later comments about her works.

Far more significant were the philosophers who were writing in Athens and Alexandria who continued to articulate the Great Chain of Being of Plotinus, who fostered the traditions of theurgy that go back into the 3rd century A.D.; that is the philosophical justification for the rites. In some instances, these philosophers even evolved a doctrine, which I often call proxy sacrifice; that is, the learned philosopher can offer up sacrifices, knowing the intellectual meaning of these rites, on behalf of the entire community. It's a way of the pagans of the 4th and 5th centuries intellectually coming to terms that emperors and the imperial government are no longer sponsoring the sacrifices; but nonetheless, the learned, true pagan philosophers—whether they be in Alexandria, whether they be in Athens—can do so, and by revering the gods they can win favor for the gods for the entire Roman world. This is a thesis that is transmitted through the literature of the late 4th, 5th, and even into the 6th century A.D.; and it's an indication of how pagans are coming to terms with the fact that, "Yes, we may've lost the cultural leadership with Julian's death; but nonetheless, we still represent very important numbers," where there were still probably, in my opinion, a majority of members of the Roman Empire. Inhabitants of the Roman Empire were still pagans until well into the 5th century A.D., and it's only in the 5th century A.D. that the balance begins to really shift in favor of the Christians. You have all of this philosophical activity.

You also have an enormous amount of literary output by pagan authors. This includes histories, such as Ammianus Marcellinus, who is without a doubt one of the most remarkable figures of late antiquity. His historical account actually starts in the reign of Trajan and ends at the Battle of Adrianople of 378; the death of Valens, one of those two fraternal emperors who followed shortly after Julian's death. We only have the later account of his history. Would that we had the earlier account and then the 3rd century wouldn't have been as dark as it is to us in the nature of sources. The literary production is characterized by two different centers producing important outpourings of pagan literature that shows that the pagan elites still saw themselves as the guardians of culture and the guardians of the traditional gods despite this upstart Christian capital called Constantinople. The first was the city of Rome, and then the second were the major intellectual centers in the East: Athens, Alexandria, and Antioch, which I'll be talking about afterwards. Let's take a look at Rome in the West first.

I mentioned in passing with the lecture on Constantine that once Constantine established Constantinople as the new Rome, the emperors checked out of Rome. No one went back to the original city of Rome on the Tiber; it wasn't worth it. Strategically, it had been out of the picture since the mid-3rd century, and the between 357 and probably 392, no Roman emperor visited the city of Rome. They'd be at Constantinople; they would be in the strategic capitals; but Rome was simply ignored. As a result, the administering of the city of Rome fell into the hands of the great senatorial families. These were the families that could trace some of their descent back to the old aristocracy of the 3rd century by bloodlines and connections, and culturally, intellectually, religiously claim to be the descendents of that Roman aristocracy that went back in the mists of time to the early Republic back in 509 B.C. They postured as the guardians of Roman tradition. They'd never abandoned the goddess Roma or the traditional gods of Rome, and they could just ignore those upstart emperors in Constantinople because they were left free to run Rome. Furthermore, they'd been barred from imperial service, particularly army commands; and as a result, the senatorial families—which amassed vast amounts of wealth, particularly landed wealth in Italy and Gaul—were essentially left on their own to do what they wished. That included holding the priesthoods, the old offices of the city of Rome, and conducting pagan ceremonies and sacrifices, and engaging in literary production.

We have a number of individuals we know from this late senatorial aristocracy who were great patrons of the gods; who carried out the editing of the works of Vergil and of Cicero in particular. One of them was a fellow called Vettius Agorius Praetextatus who, in the 4th century, he and his wife epitomized the types of patronage that was expected of these senators. They would put on vast festivals, issuing special medallions with pagan symbols. In fact, by one reckoning, by the middle of the 4th century A.D.—that is, at the time of Valentinian and Valens; or let's say the third quarter of the 4ᵗʰ century A.D., the 370s—this family alone could put on festivals stretching for weeks. By one calculation, two-thirds of the calendar year, the city of Rome was engaged in pagan holidays.

By far, one of the illustrious was a man name Symmachus, who was one of the great leading senators; he died in 402. He claimed descent from a number of important imperial families; and he was essentially the leading pagan senator in Rome for the 4ᵗʰ century. Christian emperors had to pay attention to him. He was made Urban Prefect to administer the city of Rome; he was governor of Africa; he held a titular consulship. He alone could fund a remarkable circle of literati who edited text, who carried out pagan festivals, who continued to venerate the gods, all of this in defiance of the Roman emperor in Constantinople; and actually, they didn't even pay attention to the Roman emperor. If you read the letters of Symmachus, not only are they in Ciceronian Latin, there's no reference to Christianity, no reference to that damnable Emperor Constantine or any of his successors, and there's no reference to the Pope, who happens to be on the other side of the Tiber at the Ianiculum, which eventually becomes the Vatican, outside the traditional city of Rome. It's as if the Roman senators could literally escape in the late 4ᵗʰ century, early 5ᵗʰ centuries into an eternal literary religious world where everything since 312 never happened. It's a remarkable warning in studying the careers of these senators how difficult it is sometimes to date religious change in the Roman world. So much depended on the effectiveness of Christian emperors; on the role of bishops in particular cities. If a powerful family took control of a city—that's documented in the city of Caesarea where Saint Basil was bishop for a long time; he wrote the rule for ascetics—they could turn the situation around.

The inscription I referred to the Bishop of Laodicea Combusta in Turkey, a man named Marcus Julius Eugenius in the early 4ᵗʰ century; he could tip the balance in that city. But if you're in a great city such as Rome, with a powerful Roman aristocracy who controlled half of the real estate of the Western Empire and who took the reading and writing of the Latin Classics as an act of piety and spent two-thirds of the year entertaining 250,000 citizens on the scale of festivals that even the emperor in Constantinople, that Christian emperor, would love to be able to do, you could see that the city of Rome remained essentially a pagan city well into the 5th century A.D.; and it's only in the time of the pontificate of Leo I, who was the first really successful and great Roman pope, that the Roman aristocracy in the middle of the 5th century finally came over to Christianity. Through the course of the second half of the 4th and the 5th centuries, Rome remained largely a pagan center. There's a secession of popes; they're in the Ianiculum, the Vatican; but the senators simply ignored them, and the real running of Rome and Italy fell to the hands of the great senatorial families.

If you turned to various cities in the Roman East, you'd come with the same picture. I mentioned the importance of the philosophical schools at Athens and Alexandria. Athens remained a pagan city probably into the 5th century A.D. Alexandria, on the other hand, was a city that was divided between pagans and Christians, and when the laws came out in 391–392 ending the cults, there were riots; there were demonstrations; there was the destruction of the Serapeum and the Musaeum, the library of Alexandria—this was dramatized in that recent movie *Agora* that was released in 2009—and there, the situation was far more evenly split, and by 392, the Christians had taken control of Alexandria. But Athens continued to be a pagan city; and many of the lesser cities of the Roman East, the same thing.

We have not only archeology I mentioned for the city of Aphrodisias, we also have, in the late 4th and very early 5th centuries—that is, the generation and a half after Julian's death—the outpouring of a significant amount of pagan literature in the Greek East, which is essentially the final blossoming, the final blooming, of that pagan literature. As literature goes, most Classicists don't bother reading it. It's pretty tough stuff, and pretty tough going. For one, it's generally written in a rather high-blown style, particularly the epic poetry. We have a number of epics that were written by Greek speakers in the Roman East. There's a famous epic to Dionysus, the *Dionysiaca*, written by Nonnus, who's an author writing in Egypt, which tries to put all the traditions of Dionysus into an epic form using the hexameter meter.

One of my favorite figures that sort of sums up the whole literary tradition of the late 4th and early 5th centuries is a fellow called Quintus of Smyrna. Quintus of Smyrna has the distinction of probably writing the longest—it isn't probably, I think it is—epic poem in Greek and I think also in Latin coming from antiquity; I think he beats Flavius, I think he beat Silius Italicus on this. It's well over 20,000 verses; it's longer than the *Iliad* and the *Odyssey* combined. What it is, it's a learned retelling of all the events that Homer didn't tell you about; that is, after the death of Hector. Many of the stories we know of the later *Iliad* are embodied in this poem. The poem is composed as an act of piety in the Homeric tradition; it's composed in the generation after Julian's death. Quintus was writing in the city of Smyrna, today the modern city of Izmir; a very important city in Asia in which there was a bishop, but there's still a very large pagan population in there. The epic is the epitome of the kind of learned style of late pagan authors, and at the same time, this almost pious reverence for the epics and the traditions that go back to Homer and Hesiod. The poem itself is interesting only to specialists today, but it epitomizes the type of literary production that you got in the late 4th and early 5th centuries. It was by no means assured, at least in the minds of these pagans, that they had lost, even with the death of the emperor Julian. One could go on and number various poems and epics written by different Greek authors from the late 4th and 5th centuries.

There was also a production of a new brand of pagan history. There were a number of writers that have come down to us, usually in fragments, but the one that has survived intact was written by a man named Zosimus, who wrote a work that's often called the *New History*. Zosimus's history is rather peculiar in a number of ways. It's a continuous narrative in the Greek and Roman tradition; that is, it's a linear view of time. It talks of emperors; it talks of battles. But Zosimus epitomizes a new kind of apologetic literature that the pagans now have to write. He argues in his account the *New History* that the reason the Roman Empire was suffering military reverses on the frontier was because the emperors had abandoned the worship of the gods. This led to the collapse of the Western Empire in 476, and Zosimus went out of his way to criticize not only Christianity, but the policies of Christian emperors, and above all Constantine; Constantine's criticized for his military policies as much as for his abandonment of the gods of Rome. He wrote in a vein of history that characterized a number of these Greek authors of the late 4th and 5th centuries who were trying to use history as a way to appeal to the emperors and the Christian elites that return to the old gods will assure success; that they've always assured success. The reason Rome came to rule the world was the fact that they'd given their trust to the ancient gods of Rome.

Orators operated in the same light. We have two significant orators—I would call them both orators—one is Themistius, who was at Constantinople; the other is a man, Libanius, of Antioch. They both knew the emperor Julian. They continued to operate under the emperors Valens and Valentinian, and even into the reign of the emperor Theodosius I. These orators, who composed traditional panegyrics to the emperor and also trained students in letters and the Classics, came up with new forms of oratory to appeal to Christian emperors' for toleration. This was the first time the pagans ever mad this argument, in the late 4th century after the death of Julian, because up until that point they never had to make that argument. These were significant works in which the pagan authors tried to make the kind of argument that Christians were forced to make in the 2nd century A.D.: "We are loyal Roman citizens. We are worshipping the traditions of the gods. You Christian emperors should really tolerate us. If you're not going to worship the gods, we'll handle worshiping the gods." It's a whole inversion of the situation that we had in the period before the emperor Constantine; and so we have a number of these orations.

We also get a similar type of literature penned by Symmachus. He wrote a series of letters to the Christian emperors Gratian and Valentinian II that the altar of victory—the pagan altar in the Roman senate house, which was removed as offensive on orders of Valentinian I—should be restored; and, again, because it's for the proper worship of the gods. What he did was write a series of learned letters, they're all rejected; but again, it's within the same light: The pagans were now forced to be put on the defensive. They either had to make arguments to prove their case from history; they had to make appeals and letters and orations that the traditional worship should continue.

This literature is indicative of the mixed religious situation after Julian—it's by no means certain the Christians necessarily will win—and it's also indicative of one other point: The pagans really never understood that there was a religious conflict. Julian did, but Julian was an apostate. These pagan authors still didn't understand that what was at stake was what religious system would control the destinies of the Roman world and eventually the cultural future of the Western tradition. This was far beyond that. Even under the persecutions I discussed earlier, when you had pagan emperors, the idea was to get Christians to conform and sacrifice to the gods. The pagans themselves never had a coherent thought of proselytizing, of opposing the Roman emperors the way martyrs did—Christian Roman emperors—and most of their resistance came in the form of orations and letters, and almost a passive resistance in what was becoming an increasingly Christian world. After 391, that often took the form of offering sacrifices and defiance of the law, or secretly.

This is something that's very curious to many of us studying the religious change in the late Roman world. You have all of this pagan literary production. You have clear archeological evidence that many cults and oracles continued to function in the 4th and even into the 5th century; that at select cities, such as Athens and Rome, the traditional elites continued to control the public institutions, put on festivals; that Christian Roman emperors were very hesitant to move against those cities until quite late in the 5th century. The question is: Why didn't the pagans mount a far more effective resistance in that generation of Julian? Why did they lose that battle over who would control the culture and faith of the Roman world?

Part of it is in the nature of the pagan religious outlook; but also, there's even a stronger and more important reason. The pagan leadership, the literary classes of the Roman world, was essentially a Mandarin elite. They were social conservatives. When a Roman emperor ruled against a pagan sanctuary at a particular place in a particular time, it would generate an oration; it would generate a letter; but most of these pagan elites were very wary of defying the Christian Roman emperor openly. That would invite civil war. Civil war would invite revolution and social change; and that's something that none of the pagan literati—that is, literate, learned classes—wanted. They were willing to put up with a certain amount of legal disabilities; they were willing to put up with the fact that they no longer were in charge of the imperial government; so as long as they were allowed to practice their rites, to continue their traditions, with minimal interference from the imperial government. They never had any kind of coherent sense of how they could win the emperor back to the old gods, or even how they could challenge that Christian emperor; and so from the start with Julian's death, the pagans really lacked both the leadership and vision to mount another effort to bring back the old gods. They had, in effect, in the words of Ramsay MacMullen, been taught to be passive and quiet; and that's perhaps the most significant development culturally and intellectually for the pagans after the death of Julian.

The result is that this peculiar situation resulted in many pagans, particularly of the upper classes, eventually crossing over to Christianity. Arguments that Platonism was a bridge to Christianity; that the appropriation of Classical letters and of Classical visual arts were a way of moving pagans from their ancestral faith over to Christianity; those arguments really gain force when you look at the situation in the 4th century A.D. One of the best examples of that is a fellow called Synesius of Cyrene. He was a Neoplatonist from the city of Cyrene, today in Libya. He was born in 373, died in 414. There's very good evidence to believe—and there's a definitive biography on him by a dear colleague and friend of mine, Jay Bregman, who really is one of the few people who can understand this Neoplatonic literature—that Synesius was in many ways a classic Neoplatonic philosopher. But he ended his career being ordained bishop of his home city; as representing his city vis-à-vis the imperial government, even advising the government of Arcadias— that worthless prince who followed Theodosius I—and what Synesius represents is a pagan philosopher who was able to reconcile in his mind that Christianity, and especially institutional Christianity of the imperial church, in its language, in its visual arts, in its literature, had appropriated so much of the Classics that he could buy the argument going back to Clement that the true philosopher was a Christian and he could cross that bridge. He could move from pagan philosopher to Christian bishop with complete ease.

The same crossing was achieved by many of the senatorial families in the Roman West. Their Stoic philosophy was more their taste than Platonic; but they, too, in the course of the 5th century, crossed that bridge over to Christianity, so that by the middle of the 5th century A.D., the intellectual and cultural leadership of the Roman world had decisively become Christian. With that, Christianity was now the faith of the elite classes who would dictate the subsequent course of Western history.

New Christian Warriors—Ascetics and Monks
Lecture 22

W hile the emperor and the bishops presided over Christian life in the cities, a separate and parallel source of Christian authority was developing in the countryside: the ascetics. They did not arise out of the classical or Jewish intellectual traditions but were a unique development that arose from an attempt to live like Christ. These hermits and monks became the Christian warriors of the post-persecution world: performing miracles, attacking pagan shrines, and affecting mass conversions through inspiration and, occasionally, fear.

The Ascetic Precedent

- What we know about the first Christian ascetics, often collectively known as the friends of God, comes from the literature of the 4th, 5th, and 6th centuries. These are hagiographies, the lives of particular ascetics who were later declared saints, rather than examinations of how these figures fit into the wider picture of religious change in the Roman world.

- Many of Julian's reforms addressed the institutional church created by Constantine, but the ascetics were a popular tradition that stood in many ways outside the control of both the emperor and the bishops. Had Julian lived to push through his reforms, they might have presented a real challenge to him and might have significantly limited his success.

- Asceticism was not new to the Mediterranean world, but among the pagans, particularly followers of the various Greek philosophical traditions, asceticism was an individual choice usually associated with an intellectual effort to focus on a problem.

- Perhaps the only exceptions to this rule were the Cynic philosophers, who rejected the traditional Greco-Roman world, often with a great deal of panache and ostentatious display. But they were essentially perceived as a fringe group of troublemakers, and the number of cynics who took this stance were very few, as far as we know.

- Some Egyptian cults had ascetic traditions, usually associated with ritual purity. Priests who undertook ascetic discipline were often called the *katochoi*, a term used by later Christian authors, meaning someone who is possessed with the gods.

- There were some Jewish ascetics; we have references to them in the writings of Philo of Alexandria and Flavius Josephus. In Egypt, they were known as the Therapeutae. The Essenes lived in Roman Palestine; scholars traditionally connected them with the Dead Sea Scrolls, although that view has now been called into question.

- These Jewish sects were seen later by Christian authors, particularly Eusebius, as prototypes for the Christian monk and the Christian hermit, but these communities were not on the scale of the Christian communities in the 4th century.

Christian Asceticism

- From Christianity's earliest days, all the way back to the New Testament text, sexual renunciation and withdrawal from the world were the hallmarks of holiness. In the early 2nd century, Christians agreed that, to paraphrase Saint **Cyprian**, those who had chosen the path of virginity were the most pious and holy of the Christian flock.

- This was quite different from pagan philosophy terms, or even the early Christian philosophy of Origen or Saint Clement, who would argue that the true Christian is the true intellectual. Asceticism was the popular vision of Christianity: Those who gave up the material world, who left their own people and registered themselves in the citizenship in heaven, those were the true Christians.

- Two events crystallized the emergence of an organized ascetic movement, first among hermits and then in communal organizations. The first was the end of the persecutions, which meant the end of martyrdom. Martyrs had been regarded as Christian heroes. Ascetics succeeded to that role. In some ways, they were seen as greater heroes because their sacrifice was a perpetual one.

- The second development, less well studied, was the challenge presented by Manichaeism. The Manichaeans had an organized elect, called the Hearers, organized along the lines of ascetic cells. Some have seen comparisons between the Hearers and the Jewish ascetic traditions; others see them as a version of Buddhist monastic traditions. Either way, Christian monasticism, consciously or unconsciously, was also a response to this Manichean threat.

Antony and Pachomius—Defining Christian Monasticism

- Saint **Antony of Egypt** was born to a Greco-Egyptian family of some wealth and distinction in the city of Alexandria sometime in the mid-3rd century. Around the age of 20, he decided to imitate the life of Christ. He gave away his possessions, put his sister in a proto-convent, and went to study asceticism with Christian hermits living in the Libyan Desert, the Wadi el-Natrun.

- Antony had to learn discipline very quickly: how to live on very little food and water and concentrate on the oneness of God. Above all, he had to learn to resist temptation and madness. Several times, he went alone into the desert and had to be rescued from his own excesses.

- Eventually, he developed a serenity and a union with God that awed all who saw him. He had achieved detachment—which to pagan philosophers would be the apathy of the Stoics or the union with the One of Plotinus. It was hailed a triumph.

- Saint Augustine claims in his *Confessions* that reading the life of Antony is what finally brought him back to Christianity. The role

Antony played in inspiring others to embrace the ascetic tradition cannot be underestimated.

- Saint **Pachomius** was a near contemporary of Antony. A Roman Egyptian, he had been forcefully drafted into a Roman civil war, possibly by Maximinus of Gaza. Each night, his commanders locked him and his fellow soldiers up to prevent desertion, and he was impressed by the Christians who fed these imprisoned recruits. He thus converted to Christianity.

- In 323, shortly before Constantine reunited the Roman world, Pachomius established the first monastic community at Tabennisi in Upper Egypt that became the prototype for the medieval monastery. It was the first community devoted to what Antony did on his own.

- Pachomius established what is called in Greek a cenobium, or a common living. It was walled off from the outside world. Each member was assigned tasks, and they were supervised by an abbot—"father" in the Coptic language. Activities were therefore divided between religious devotions and duties necessary to support the self-sustaining community.

Monasticism in the Wider Roman World

- Pachomius's monastic community was an instant success. By the time Julian was proclaimed emperor in December 360, by one count there were more than 7,000 monasteries in the Nile Valley alone. At the start of the 6th century, the city of Constantinople proper had something like 60–70 known monasteries; there were 40 or 50 more in the surrounding cities.

- Monastic communities became the characteristic form of late antique Christianity and the touchstone of medieval Christianity. They emerged outside the control of the imperial government and largely outside of the control of the bishops.

- Monasticism was a popular movement, with its own institutions and its own traditions in which the celibate life and the pious life were fused as the supreme expression of Christianity. Ascetics may have constituted a tiny minority of the Roman world, but to the Christians, they were the most important and notably pious members of the Christian community.

- Given this position, they had a number of important roles to play in popular Christianity. They acted as arbiters for Christian peasants and as a link between the bishops of the city and the peasants of the countryside.

- Ascetics were Christian warriors who promoted conversion. This happened in several ways. Often they simply built monasteries in desolate areas and acted as an example of the Christian way of life to the pagan locals.

- The ascetics also succeeded to the role of the prophets of the Old Testament. The hagiographies repeatedly compare them to Elijah and Elisha. They cast down pagan idols and cult statues. They performed exorcisms and miracles.

- Several monks epitomized the image of the Christian warriors; one was **Barsuma**, an Aramaic-speaking peasant. He had a beard down to his toes, wore an old Roman breastplate, ran around barefoot, and carried a cudgel. He and his similarly clad followers went from village to village in Syria, challenging the cult statues and throwing priests in the fire. There are reports that when Barsuma showed up, whole villages would convert on the spot.

- Among so-called pillar saints of Syria and in southeastern Turkey, the most famous was Saint **Symeon Stylites**. He performed remarkable feats, usually standing in the form of a cross on top of his pillar. Every morning he touched his toes 1,244 times as an act of devotion.

- When Emperor Theodosius II wanted to rescind some of the legislation of his grandfather, Theodosius I, who had outlawed paganism, Symeon Stylites thundered Theodosius II, calling down the wrath of God. The emperor withdrew his acts of toleration.

- The power of these saints and ascetics was well beyond any kind of definable organization. They were the revered holy ones of popular Christianity.

Names to Know

Antony of Egypt (c. 260–357): Early Christian monastic and saint. Born of a wealthy Greco-Egyptian family, Antony embraced an ascetic life in the Libyan desert from c. 280. His example inspired many Christians to embrace the ascetic life. In about 360, Patriarch Athanasius of Alexandria wrote a life of Antony, which served as the model for all later hagiographies.

Barsuma (fl. c. 380–440): Fierce Syrian ascetic who converted pagan villages in the style of the prophets of Israel.

Cyprian of Carthage (a.k.a. **Thasciius Caecilius Cyprianus**; d. 258): Saint and bishop (250–257) who composed in Latin numerous tracts on issues of baptism of *lapsi*, readmission of heretics into the church, and episcopal authority. He was martyred during the persecution of Valerian.

Pachomius (c. 290–346): Saint and pagan convert to Christianity who undertook an ascetic life, founding the first monastery at Tabennesi in Upper Egypt in 323.

Symeon Stylites (c. 390–459): Christian ascetic who followed the example of Saint Antony. During his last 37 years, he spent his life atop a pillar east of Antioch as a symbol of his withdrawal from the world. He was hailed as the most pious saint of the Roman East, respected by the emperors Theodosius II and Marcian.

Suggested Reading

Athanasius, *The Life of Saint Antony and the Letter to Marcellinus.*

Brown, *The Cult of Saints.*

———, "The Rise and Function of the Holy Man in Late Antiquity."

Chitty, *The Desert, A City.*

Dawes and Baynes, trans., *Three Byzantine Saints.*

Hirschfeld, *The Judaean Desert Monasteries in the Judaean Period.*

MacMullen, *The Second Church.*

Rousseau, *Pachomius.*

Waddell, *The Desert Fathers.*

Questions to Consider

1. What were the sources for Christian asceticism? In what ways did Christian ascetics differ from those of paganism and Judaism? What led to the spread of ascetic ideals from the late 3rd century on?

2. Why did the example of Saint Antony inspire imitation or pilgrimage by so many Christians? Why was hagiography so popular?

3. What was the impact of Saint Pachomius on Christian asceticism? Why did monasticism come to define medieval Christianity? What were the cultural and economic impacts of monasteries?

4. How did monks see themselves as the heirs to the prophets of Israel? Why were they the most effective warriors against paganism?

New Christian Warriors—Ascetics and Monks
Lecture 22—Transcript

In this lecture, I plan to talk about what I like to call the new Christian warriors. These are the aesthetics, usually solitary hermits or monks who are living in communities, who came to form essentially what I would call the new Christian warriors.

There's a considerable body of modern scholarship dealing with these ascetics who're often collectively known as the friends of God. Much of that literature deals with them as succeeding to the roles of martyrs, to the roles that aesthetics play to the Christian community, and there's a good deal of literature coming down from the 4th, 5th, and 6th centuries—these are hagiographies in the forms of the lives of particular ascetics who were then later declared saints—and much of the attention on the ascetics and monks has been focused on that role. What I want to do in this particular lecture is see how the ascetics and monks fit into this wider picture of religious change in the Roman world. That requires us to look at some of their antecedents; how they were so distinct from both Jewish and pagan predecessors. Also, we want to look at the careers of several individuals who made asceticism such a fundamental part of late antique Christianity—that'll be Saint Antony and Saint Pachomius in particular—but what their role was in also directing these new Christian warriors along the lines of becoming the missionaries, one could even almost say the shock troops, who carried out the proselytizing and conversion of the Roman world, especially in the generations after the death of Julian.

It does raise a question in my mind, and it's always been a question in my mind, about the potential success of Julian's reforms: So much of what Julian addressed was against the bishops, the institutional church created by his uncle Constantine; these were all institutions he understood. But the ascetics and monks were a whole tradition of popular Christianity that in many ways was outside the control of both the emperor and the bishops, and it would've represented a force to Julian if he had ruled for 30 years, or especially if Julian left pagan successors, it would've been a force for the pagan successors of Julian to deal with, and it does qualify how much success Julian might've had in bringing back the gods in the face of the rising role of monks and ascetics in the Christian world.

First, let's look at why they were so distinct from Jewish and pagan predecessors. Asceticism was not new to the Mediterranean world, and it certainly went back very early in the documentary history of the ancient Near East. But in the case of the pagans, particularly Platonists, Pythagoreans, followers of various Greek philosophical traditions, there was a tradition of asceticism—that is, abstaining from certain types of foods, particularly meat (vegetarian diets); sexual abstinence was also sometimes practiced—but these represented individual choices; and such ascetic practices among pagans were usually to be associated with an intellectual effort to focus on a problem. Plotinus characterized this. There were several comments made in the biography of Plotinus written by his student Porphyry that at times you got the feeling that Plotinus really found the body rather inconvenient. He practiced a very abstemious lifestyle, and almost at times you felt, Porphyry said, that he was almost in communion with the One.

Perhaps the one exception to all of this was the cynic philosophers, who rejected the traditional Greco-Roman world, and often did it with a great deal of panache and even ostentatious display in some instances. But they were essentially perceived as troublemakers in a fringe group among pagan philosophers, and the number of cynics who took this stance were really very few, at least from the records that survive, and those have been very well studied by social historians looking at the cynics as one of the rare cases of elements outside the traditional Classical order that were tolerated.

There were traditions of asceticism in Egyptian cults. These were usually associated with ritual purity, especially with the cult of Serapis; that is, the Hellenic or Hellenized cult of the god Osiris, which came to be a very dominant and important cult in Rome and Egypt and then was exported to the Mediterranean world. Such priests who undertook an ascetic discipline were often called the *katochoi*, a term that's later used by Christian authors, and it essentially means someone who's possessed or enthusiastic with the gods. When all of this was added up on the pagan side, there really wasn't much of a precedent for the kind of institutional asceticism that we associate with Christian monasticism that emerges in the 4th century or with the definition of asceticism as the highest expression of piety. As I said, for most pagan priests it would've been a sort of ritual purity, and for pagan philosophers it's a way of focusing one's intellect on understanding the greater mysteries of whatever particular doctrines you happen to be studying.

There were some Jewish ascetics; we have references to them in Philo of Alexandria, also in Flavius Josephus writing in the 1st century A.D. These descriptions, these reports, suggest to us that in Egypt the Jewish ascetics were known as the Therapeutae. They were individuals who were devoted to Torah. Josephus talks about this rather poorly-understood group known as the Essenes, who have sometimes been connected with the Dead Sea Scrolls, and that's an identification that is really quite questionable now. In any event, there were certain Jewish ascetic communities that were in existence in the 1st century B.C, 1st century A.D., and they were seen later by Christian authors, particularly Eusebius, as somehow prototypes for the Christian monk and the Christian hermit.

But there was nothing really on the scale of what would develop in the 4th century A.D. in the Roman world with monasticism and the ascetic tradition that's embodied by the figure of Saint Antony. From the start, Christian asceticism, Christian monasticism, was a new turn in the religious history of the Mediterranean world, and it represented a very distinct aspect of Christianity that marked Christianity off just as much as the organizations of bishops, the development of canon, and the unique theology that was forged by the Christian thinkers in the 3rd and 4th centuries that reconciled a Hebrew tradition with the Platonic traditions first expressed in the *Timaeus*.

Since earliest times in Christianity, going back into the New Testament text, sexual renunciation, withdrawal from the world, were the hallmarks of holiness. This could be found in Jesus's testing in the desert against Satan. It could be found in the career of John the Baptist. It's repeated time and time again in early Christian writers. Some of them are rigorous sectarians like the Montanists, who apparently were really devoted to the notion of asceticism. It's often thought that Saint Thecla, whose tomb in southeastern Turkey was a major pilgrimage shrine in the 4th century, that Saint Thecla was to be associated with this type of rigorous Christianity. She refused a marriage to her fiancé; she followed Saint Paul, according to the gospel of

Paul and Thecla, took up an ascetic life in order to achieve holiness, and she actually acts as the model of the female ascetic in the late antique world. This is probably a document of the 2nd century A.D., but already, in the early 2nd century A.D., Christians agreed on the fact, in the words of Saint Cyprian, to paraphrase it, "Those who had chosen the path of virginity were the most pious and holy of the Christian flock"; that is, chastity and withdrawal from the material world was seen as the mark of a true Christian.

This is very, very different from what you have from pagan philosophical terms, or even what someone like Origen or Saint Clement would say; which is, "The true Christian is the true intellectual"; the one who really understood the faith by studying all the texts of Plato and doctrines. What asceticism was, was the popular vision of Christians; that those who really gave up the material world, and renounced it in all of its aspects, could, in the words of Athanasius, the patriarch of Alexandria—and never was there a more intellectual in the 4th century than Athanasius—would say that those who had left their own people and registered themselves in the citizenship in heaven, those were the ascetics and monks; those were the true Christians; those were the greatest epitome of what the Christian should be. This is a very different religious view than paganism offered; and any of the so-called precedents to the asceticism of Christianity.

There were two immediate events, in my opinion, that crystallized the emergence of an organized ascetic movement; first among solitary hermits— "hermit" comes from the Greek word meaning "a desert"—men and women who renounced the world and separately went out to recreate the life of Christ meeting the temptations in the desert, and then in the communal organizations that eventually were called monasteries. One of those was the end of the persecutions. The end of the persecutions meant that martyrs no longer played the same role in Christian society they had done up to the time of Constantine. Martyrs had been regarded as the true Christian heroes, the Christian athletes; those individuals, men and women, who were willing to offer up their witness to their faith—the term "martyr" was a legal term; it meant a witness to their faith—and die horrible deaths in the arena, sometimes in mock charades imitating very, very lugubriously different types of myths, like being dressed up like Icarus and thrown off a ladder and shown that you can't fly. They're really, really hideous ways of death; and martyrs were remembered and revered by the Christians, but after the Edict of Milan there were no more martyrs.

What happened was ascetics, in effect, succeeded to that role. In some ways, they're seen by church fathers as actually being greater than the martyrs because their sacrifice, their renunciation of the world, was a perpetual sacrifice through their entire life. They gave up the concerns of the world; they imitated the holiness of Christ; and as a result, they're often said in the literature to have one foot already in heaven. That is, they'd detached themselves so much from this physical world that they were already halfway to heaven, because the mundane concerns of humanity had fallen away and their simple piety and holiness had moved them closer to God.

There's another development that still needs to be studied by scholarship, and that is the challenge of Manichaeism, which I'd mentioned in an earlier lecture, as part of the spiritual change of the 3rd century. That independent religion that in some way straddles the paganism of the Roman Empire, Christianity on the one side, on the Western side, and Zoroastrian and Buddhism on the other. The Manichees, as you may recall, had an organized "Elect" or "Hearers," as they're sometimes called; those who have heard the call to the true nature of the godhead and would ascend and join the godhead. They were organized along the lines of ascetic cells. Some have seen comparisons to some of the Jewish ascetic traditions; others see it as a version of the type of Buddhist monastic traditions in northern India. We really at this point don't have enough evidence to come to this conclusion. What the Christians did encounter by the time of the Tetarchic persecutions— that is, between 303 and 313—a world religion, universal in appeal, which could cross political boundaries; that had an ascetic tradition and a monastic tradition of its own, a developed proselytizing faith and doctrine; and in part, Christian monasticism, whether consciously or unconsciously, was also a response to counter this Manichean threat.

This, then, gets us to the two individuals I mentioned at the start of this lecture: Saint Antony and Saint Pachomius. These two men in Egypt were really responsible for defining what Christian monasticism and asceticism was all about. It's necessary to take a bit of time to discuss their contributions and how they came to define the role of what I would collectively call the friends of God.

Saint Antony was born from a Greco-Egyptian family of some wealth and distinction in the city of Alexandria; that is, he was probably a Greek speaker. His date of birth is still debated. He is reported to have died in the year 357, and according to several accounts he was something like 107 or 106 years old. We don't know if that's true. He may have been really 70; he just looked 107. But whatever his precise date is really not so significant; by the standards of the ancient world, he'd lived an extremely long time. Anyone who got beyond the age of 40 was beating the odds in a number of ways. Saint Antony, probably around the age of 20, reading the gospels, took quite literally the admonishments of Christ to "follow me and imitate me," particularly out of the gospel of Matthew. He gave away his possessions. He had a sister—his parents were deceased—and he dumped his sister in something like a proto-nunnery and he went out to become a devoted one, a *spoudaios* in Greek or *hermeus*, one who lives in a desolate area, or an ascetic, which comes from the Greek word "to exercise."

There are already men attempting to achieve this unity with God through asceticism; Saint Antony was not the first. They were out in this alkaline desert in the Libyan Desert, some of the worst desert territory on the planet; Wadi El Natrun as it's called today, the Nitrian Desert. He went out there and put himself under the tutorship of one of these holy men. Saint Antony learned very quickly the need for discipline; the need to be able to live on very little food and water to concentrate on the oneness of God; and above all, to resist temptations and also madness. Several times he went out to the desert in solitary retreat, and he literally had to be rescued from his own excesses. In one instance, he'd essentially barricaded himself in a small building and the peasants in the area who knew he was there had to literally pull him out. He was unconscious; it took him time to recover.

Somewhere close to the year 280 or 300 A.D.—it depends on what year you think he was born—he immured himself in an abandoned Roman fort in the western Libyan Desert and there he stayed for 20 years, communicating through a crevice to the pilgrims who came and fed him. Then when he emerged from that place, they broke down the door and he came out, he was whole; he was not mad. He had a serenity and a union with God that awed all who saw him. He'd achieved that detachment—which to pagan philosophers would be the *apatheia* of the Stoics, or the union of the one to Plotinus— and he had a sense and feeling for God that few would ever have. He had already—as the authors, someone like Athanasius, would say—registered himself in the kingdom of heaven. It was hailed a triumph. Antony was seen as having imitated Christ successfully, and Athanasius wrote a biography on Antony. It was translated into Latin. It's an instant success. Saint Augustine himself claims in his *Confessions* that reading the life of Saint Antony in Latin is what finally brought him back to Christianity. The role that Saint Antony played in inspiring others to embrace the ascetic tradition and elevating the ascetic tradition to the premier Christian by the time of the accession of the emperor Julian in 360 cannot be underestimated.

But those that would choose to follow Saint Antony, few had the same stuff as Saint Antony to do it on their own. That brings us to the second individual I wanted to talk about for a moment: Saint Pachomius. Saint Pachomius was probably a half a generation younger than Saint Antony, maybe born somewhere around 280 A.D. He claims that he was called up in a levy in a Roman civil war. He was actually a reluctant recruit; they used to lock him in at night. He was from Roman Egypt, and during the day and during the evening he was crying with the other recruits, locked up; "I want to go home to mom, I don't want to fight" (I think he's called up for the war of Maximinus Daza, the beast of the east). He was impressed by those Christians who came and fed these reluctant recruits and he converted to Christianity.

In 323, shortly before the emperor Constantine reunited the Roman world, he established the first monastic community at Tabennisi in Upper Egypt. This is the prototype of the medieval monastery. Pachomius is the first to organize an ascetic community devoted to achieving what Saint Antony could do on his own. That's a very important consideration, because many who went out and performed these ascetic acts, there's always the danger of doing it for the wrong reason; that is, trying to imitate Christ and boasting of what you achieved and then falling to the sin of pride. What Pachomius did was establish what is called in Greek a *cenobium*, or a common living; it's their term for what later becomes a monastery. That's a system whereby the various members can live together under a series of rules as a community of saints. That monastery or *cenobium* is walled off from the outside world, and you assign tasks to the various brothers, supervised by an abbot—which means in Coptic, the language of Egypt, "a father"—so that you divide your activities between religious activities and the activities necessary to support these communities, because from the start, Pachomius conceived of these communities as being self-sustaining.

The monastic community established by Pachomius was an instant success. We know of the monastic tradition, especially from the later Middle Ages, because one of the occupations later taken over by monks was the recording of texts, including Classical texts. But initially this wasn't its goal; initially, the goal was to provide a walled off community whereby Christians could achieve the ascetic success that Saint Antony did; and first and foremost, this way of living was the supreme expression of piety.

The monastic organization was an immense success. By the time the emperor Julian had been proclaimed emperor by the Western army on the Rhine in December, 360, by one count there were over 7,000 monasteries in the Nile Valley alone. At the time of the opening of the 6th century A.D., in the city of Constantinople proper—the capital of the Roman East, the queen of cities—there were at least something like 60–70 known monasteries in Constantinople, another 40 or 50 in the surrounding cities such as Nicomedia and Chalcedon. Monastic communities became the characteristic of late antique Christianity and the touchstone of medieval Christianity. The organization of monasteries was really something that emerged outside the control of the imperial government—that is, the Christian emperors—and largely outside of the control of the bishops, although bishops, particularly in the eastern cities, often tried to bring those monastic communities under their control. But what had emerged by the mid-4th century is a whole popular pious movement, ascetic movement, with its own institutions and its own traditions in which the celibate life and the pious life were fused as the supreme expression of Christianity. They may have constituted a very small minority of the Roman world—and the numbers game is very difficult to play; were they 5 percent, were they 10 percent, were they 3 percent?— but what mattered is, to the Christians, they were the most important, most notably pious of all the Christian community.

Given this position, they had a number of important roles to play in popular Christianity. This included acting as arbiters for Christian peasants. They acted as a link between the bishops of the city and the peasants of the countryside. But they also were the Christian warriors who promoted conversion. This came in several ways. One would be just simply the building of a monastery in a desolate area in which the monks acted as an example to the peasants. One of my favorite sites in Turkey is the Alahan, which is in the Taurus Mountains; it's a monastery literally on the top of the mountains. It dates probably from the 5th century A.D. We know the name of the abbot who established it, Tarasius, who was followed by a namesake. They're actually buried there. What these two churches and small monastic community represented was settling of monks who essentially Christianized the spring in the area and all of the pastoral and transhumanist peoples in the area, the peasants, would come to that spring and what would they find? They would find these Christian ascetics living a pious life. The establishment of these monastic communities in the mountains of Asia Minor, on the desert rim of Syria, in the villages of Asia Minor in Egypt, what they acted as were agents for disseminating Christianity into the countryside, something that the bishops in the cities couldn't really do.

But an even more important role was that monks and ascetics succeeded to the role of the prophets of the Old Testament. They were the New Hebrew prophets. Repeatedly in the hagiographies of the holy men, particularly those that came from Egypt in the 5th and 6th centuries A.D., they're compared to Elijah and Elisha. They cast down pagan idols and cult statues. They took on the ancient cults, starting in the late 4th and the 5th and the 6th centuries. They became, in effect, the Christian warriors. This was performed in different ways. One was the performance of exorcisms, casting out of demons; and in this they're often compared to the Hebrew prophets who would challenge the priests of Baal who were supported by King Ahab and Queen Jezebel. They're often compared to the earlier martyrs, and people like Gregory the Wonderworker who could cast out demons. In the 4th and 5th centuries, exorcisms and healing miracles became intimately associated with ascetics and monks. They could call down miracles and prove the power of God, such as the monk Saint Porphyry did at Gaza in 402. But above all, they could attack those cult statues and destroy them, and in so doing prove that these were false gods; that those were not cult statues, they were idols.

There are several monks—monks, because they did have followers—who really epitomized what these new Christian warriors were all about from the late 4th century on. One of my favorite is a fellow called Barsauma. He was from East Syria. He didn't speak Greek, he spoke Aramaic; he was from peasant background. This guy had a beard that went down to his toes, wore an old Roman breastplate, ran around barefoot, carried this cudgel; and he must've roasted in the summer, he froze in the winter. But he marched around the villages of Syria followed by devoted monks equally armed with cudgels and equally ferocious in their appearance, and he would go into villages in Syria and Phoenicia, challenge the cult statues, and throw priests in the fire. There are reports that when Barsauma showed up, whole villages would just convert on the spot; "We're not going to take this guy on." He really epitomized a tradition of the Old Testament prophets of challenging idols and casting them down.

Another was the famous pillar saints that were very well known in Syria and in southeastern Turkey, in the region of Silesia. Pillar is a little bit deceptive; they had these areas on top of an old Roman column and, again, one of the most famous was Saint Simeon Stylites living at the opening of the 5th century A.D. Saint Simeon Stylites performed remarkable feats, usually standing in the form of a cross on top of his pillar. He was an inspiration in the imitation of the life of Christ, and we have a number of stories told about him, how his activities had extremely important impact on converting various pagans. For one, besides standing in the form of the cross, every morning he essentially touched his toes 1,244 times as an act of devotion. As Peter Brown once said, the horror of this whole demonstration of piety, which is being quantified, isn't in the exertions of the saint, but rather the laymen who stood there and counted each morning as the saint touched his toes. He also stood in the form of a cross for hours on end. Bedouins Arabs would show up; they were inspired, "Who is this holy man?" They were impressed. Many of them said, "We're going to go back and convert," which means, "We're not going to kill our neighbors in blood feuds and we're not going to eat camel meat anymore, but otherwise we're going to act pretty much the same." But, "This holy man obviously is able to perform great feats in the blazing Syrian sun, he must be somehow inspired."

Pillar saints like Saint Simeon were appealed to for healing cults, for healing during plague; and when the Emperor Theodosius II, in a rare mood and act of toleration—really out of pragmatism—wanted to rescind some of the legislation of his grandfather Theodosius I, who had outlawed paganism, Saint Simeon Stylites on his pillar in Syria thundered against the law of Theodosius II that we should tolerate pagans and Jews and heretics and called down the wrath of God. Guess what happened? The emperor withdrew the law. The power of these saints and ascetics is really well beyond any kind of definable organization, administrative position. They were the revered holy ones of popular Christianity. As a result, most Christians had a lot more contact with monks and ascetics than they did with imperial officials or the bishops and their minions operating in the cities.

It was monks who stormed and destroyed the Alexandrian library and the Serapeum in 392. It was monks and saints who, over the course of the 5th century, destroyed the various cult centers in Egypt. I end with one anecdote that sums up their attitude to what these pagan cult statues were. An aged monk, recalling back in his early days when he was a very young boy around eight years old, why he embraced that monastic tradition said his father had worshiped a cult statue, he had a little idol, and he would go into the tent (the shekinah). This holy one peered into the tent one time at about age eight or nine and what he found was his father standing before that idol, and before his father were Satan and all the hosts and demons of Hell. One of those demons came forth and saluted his father. That scared this Egyptian boy into becoming a holy man working for the power of the true God and making sure that the Roman world would make that transition from paganism and the worship of demons to Christianity. Without these holy men and holy saints, one wonders how long it would've taken to create that Christian world by the 6th century.

Turning Point—Theodosius I
Lecture 23

The reign of Emperor Theodosius I was the final crucial turning point for the development of Christianity in the Roman world. He enacted legislation—backed up with force—that ended once and for all the open practice of traditional pagan worship in the Roman world. Nicene Christianity was established as the empire's official faith, and religion, not legal class, became the ultimate token of citizenship. In many ways, Theodosius's reign marks the birth of medieval Europe.

The End of Pagan Alexandria

- In 391, shortly after Emperor Theodosius passed the laws that outlawed sacrifice, and therefore pagan worship, the patriarch of Alexandria released his monks to attack the pagans who occupied the Serapeum and Mouseion. The excuse was that the pagans were secretly worshiping in underground sanctuaries.

- The pagans objected; they occupied both the Serapeum and Mouseion to protect them, and the monks and a large Christian crowd—really a rabble—stormed the buildings, smashed the statues, and destroyed papyrus scrolls. The fighting spread across Alexandria. The imperial army did nothing. Classical Alexandria was destroyed, and Christian Alexandria emerged.

- Scholars and popular writers have viewed this destruction as a turning point—for good reason. The pagans who witnessed this destruction were absolutely intimidated. There are reports of conversions on the spot. In addition, the entire action, while not ordered by the imperial government, was certainly approved of by the emperor, the logical result of his legislation.

Christianity Divided

- In 363, when Emperor Julian died, there was a strong chance of another civil war between the largely Christian Eastern army and the largely pagan Western army. Valentinian and Valens, as Christian emperors, were in a very uncertain position.

- Valentinian and Valens were very suspicious of the ruling classes, Christian and pagan both. They held a series of treason trials in which officials and officers were removed, in part to get rid of Julian's appointees, but also because they did not trust the polished elite.

- In addition, they lacked legitimacy. Valentinian had two sons by different marriages, an older son, **Gratian**, and a younger son, **Valentinian II**, who later married the surviving granddaughter of Constantine in an attempt to make a dynastic connection.

Valentinian II came to the throne as a child in a dangerous time.

- Under Julian, all the Christian confessions were recognized because Julian's official policy was toleration. As a result, the Nicene bishops had brought many suits against the Arians, declaring their version of the Trinity as official imperial church policy. The Arian position had gained favor in the later days of Constantine's reign; in fact, Constantine was formally baptized by an Arian bishop, and his sons were devoted Arians.

- Valentinian I, as western emperor, was astute enough to realize that he had to court the Nicene bishops in the Western provinces.

Valens, reigning in the East, remained an ardent Arian. He faced opposition in Egypt and division in the Balkans and Asia Minor. As a result, there was no united Christian policy, and by default the pagans were tolerated.

- In the big cities with a lot of imperial patronage, Christianity reigned, and powerful intellects came up with theology to counter the Arians. Rome, on the other hand, was largely in the hands of the pagans, as was Athens and the lesser cities of Gaul, northern Italy, Britain, and Spain.

Valentinian's Sons and Civil War in the West

- Valentinian proved to be an extremely able emperor, but he died suddenly in 375 and left his two young sons in control of the Western Empire. Gratian, the older, ruled over the Rhine frontier, Gaul, and Britain. Valentinian II, the younger, with his mother Empress Justina, ruled from Milan. Bishop **Ambrose of Milan** exercised a powerful control over this young emperor.

- The brothers did not get along, but they did agree that they should rule as Nicene Christians. They passed tentative legislation to cut back on pagan toleration. Gratian, for instance imposed some liabilities on pagan priests. They also removed the Altar of Victory—removed by their father but restored in the interim—from the Roman senate house again.

- The Western army did not take well to this legislation. In the 350s and 360s, the emperors had begun building their armies mostly from barbarian tribal regiments known as federates. These were usually Germanic peoples; if they were Christian, they were only Christian in name. Between the legislation and Gratian's fecklessness—he spent most of his time drinking and never led an army into battle— the Western army was sparked into rebellion.

- In 383, the army in Britain declared their commander, **Magnus Maximus**, emperor of the West. That army invaded Gaul and was received by the army in the Rhine. Gratian was deserted, captured, and executed.

- Magnus Maximus was willing, at this point, to cut a deal with Valentinian II, but Valentinian refused. Magnus Maximus invaded Italy and drove Valentinian II and his mother east to Constantinople.

Theodosius Outlaws Paganism

- At that point, **Theodosius I** was emperor in the East, having been elevated in 379. Theodosius had been married into the imperial family and been commissioned to take charge of the Roman East after the disaster of the Battle of Adrianople, where Emperor Valens was killed by the Goths.

- Theodosius was a devoted Nicene Christian. He was also a tough general who commanded the respect of the various German federate regiments. When the imperial family fled from Milan to Constantinople, Theodosius immediately mounted an attack against Magnus Maximus; and in 388, somewhere on the Sava River, defeated the Western army and killed Magnus Maximus.

- It looked as if the toleration of pagans was going to end. Theodosius outlawed Manichaeism and initiated a wave of persecution. He did not immediately move against the pagan cults, but he turned a blind eye to his administrators, particularly **Maternus Cynegius**, who was the prefect of the Roman East, when he and a cadre of monks attacked the pagan shrines.

- Learned pagans reacted as you would expect: with prose. Libanius wrote *On the Temples*—an oration arguing that it was unseemly to attack the great temples that were part of the classical tradition. Theodosius, of course, ignored these arguments.

- Theodosius was able to move against the gods in a way that the emperor Constantine had never dared to do for several reasons. One was his success as a general. But he also summoned, in 381, the Second Ecumenical Council at Constantinople, which enacted several important changes that unified the church and solidified his position. Theodosius presided over this council just as Constantine had presided over the first.

- The council reinstated all of the canons at the Council of Nicaea and declared Constantinople a **Petrine See**—that is, a see equivalent to that of Rome. It also proscribed Arianism and made the imperial church officially Nicene.

- In 391–392, Theodosius issued a series of three laws banning public sacrifice throughout the Roman world and declared that the only religion in the Roman Empire with any legitimacy was Nicene Christianity.

- Think about how dramatically the situation has changed in the 350 years covered in this course. Henceforth, the definition of a Roman would be based on religious affiliation. This would not only affect the pagans; it would eventually affect the Jews and so-called heretics as well.

- Inevitably, there were reactions, particularly in Alexandria and in the West. At the time of the promulgation of these laws, there was a Frankish general named **Arbogast**, who held the position of *magister militum*, or master of the soldiers, in the Western field army. Arbogast seems to have been behind the murder of Valentinian II in 392.

The Last Rebellion

- After Valentinian's murder, a grammarian named **Eugenius** was proclaimed emperor by the Western army of the Rhine. Eugenius, while technically a Christian, openly tolerated the sacrifices to the gods. Theodosius now faced yet another Western army—

the fourth in that century—of pagan soldiers rebelling against pro-Christian policies.

- For the first time, the Roman senators reacted and they proclaimed their loyalty to the Western usurper. Theodosius marched west, and a major battle was fought on September 5–6, 394—the **Battle of the Frigidus**.

- Eugenius was captured and executed; Arbogast committed suicide. The Roman senators—who had not fought, of course, but had written letters of support—were embarrassed and surrendered unconditionally. The result was a second miraculous victory for a Christian emperor, another Milvian Bridge.

- Fortunately for the pagans, Theodosius died suddenly on January 17, 395, before he could pass any more legislation. He was succeeded by his incompetent sons, Arcadius and Honorius, and so began the rapid collapse of the Western Empire, which disintegrated by 476.

- Christian monarchy was never again in question in the empire. The pagans were barred from all public worship. Increasingly, the word "pagan" came to denote a barbarian; the educated pagans began to disappear. By the early 5th century, many had converted to Christianity.

- Above all, Theodosius had defined Roman citizenship and Roman identity, by religion, not by legal rights; and those who did not follow were subject to the full punishment of Roman law. Theodosius had taken the first step to creating the persecuting society of medieval Europe.

Important Terms

Frigidus, **Battle of**: The victory of Theodosius I over the rebel Western army of Eugenius and the magister militum Arbogast on September 5–6, 394. It was hailed as a victory of Christianity over paganism.

Petrine Sees: The five great apostolic sees founded by Peter or his disciples. The order was fixed at the Fourth Ecumenical Council as Rome, Constantinople, Alexandria, Antioch, and Jerusalem. Rome claims primacy and Constantinople claims equality with Rome.

Names to Know

Ambrose of Milan (a.k.a. **Aurelius Ambrosius**; 337–397): Saint and staunch opponent of Arianism who was elected bishop of Milan in 374. He was mentor to the young Emperor Valentinian II (r. 375–392) and advocated measures against pagan worship. In 390, he compelled Emperor Theodosius I to seek penance for permitting the massacre of citizens of Thessalonica by Gothic soldiers. Ambrose was also patron to Augustine of Hippo.

Arbogast (c. 360–394): A Frankish officer under Gratian (r. 367–383) who rose to *magister militum* of the West in 388. In 392, he advanced as Emperor Eugenius (r. 392–394) in a pagan revolt against Theodosius I. The Western army was defeated at the Battle of Frigidus (394), and Arbogast committed suicide.

Eugenius (a.k.a. **Flavius Eugenius**; r. 392–394): Grammarian elevated as Western emperor by Arbogast, *magister militum* of the Western army, and backed by the Senate. He was defeated, captured, and executed after his defeat at the Battle of Frigidus on September 6, 394.

Gratian (a.k.a. **Flavius Gratianus**; 359–383; r. 367–383): The elder son of Valentinian I, he made his court at Treveri. Gratian pursed antipagan measures and promoted Nicene Christianity. In 383, he was betrayed and murdered near Lugdunum (Lyon) by supporters of Magnus Maximus, who had been proclaimed emperor by the army of Britain.

Magnus Maximus (a.k.a. **Flavius Magnus Maximus**; c. 335–388; r. 383–388): Soldier who rose in the service of Count Theodosius and then Emperor Gratian. In 380, he succeeded to the command of the army of Britain. In response to the antipagan laws, in 383, Magnus Maximus rebelled and invaded Gaul. Gratian was deserted and murdered. In 387, Magnus Maximus invaded the Italian Peninsula so that Valentinian II fled to Constantinople. In

388, Theodosius I defeated Magnus Maximus at the Battle on the Save. He fled to Aquileia, surrendered, and was executed.

Maternus Cynegius (d. 388): Christian from Spain who rose in the service of Theodosius I. As prefect of the East (384–388), he initiated riots by monks against pagan temples and synagogues. In protest, the pagan rhetorician Libanius wrote his *Pro templis* (*On the Temples*), an oration delivered to Theodosius I.

Theodosius I (a.k.a. **Theodosius the Great**; c. 346–395; r. 379–395): The son of Count Theodosius, a leading general of Valentinian I, Theodosius rose to high command under Gratian. In 379, as Augustus of the East, Theodosius restored order in the Roman East. In 387, he married Galla, sister of Valentinian II (r. 375–392). In return, Theodosius defeated the usurper Magnus Maximus (r. 383–388), who had overthrown the Western emperor Gratian. A devout Nicene Christian, Theodosius summoned the Second Ecumenical Council in 381 and outlawed pagan sacrifices in 391–392. He faced a revolt of the Western army in 392–394. By the victory at Frigidus (394), Theodoius crushed the rebels and reunited the Roman Empire.

Valentinian II (a.k.a. **Flavius Valentinianus**; 371–392; r. 375–392): The son of Valentinian and Justinia and half-brother of Gratian. In 375, he was declared joint emperor and resided at Mediolaunum (Milan) under the influence of his mother and Bishop Ambrose of Milan. Reared as a staunch Nicene, Valentinian supported antipagan measures that precipitated the revolt of Magnus Maximus. In 387, he fled to Constantinople and allied with Theodosius I against Magnus Maximus. In 388–392, Valentinian was restored as emperor of the West, and he was murdered on the orders of Arbogast.

Suggested Reading

Alföldi, *A Conflict of Ideas in the Late Roman Empire.*

Ammianus Marcellinus, *The Later Roman Empire.*

———, *Roman History.*

Barnes, *Athanasius and Constantius*.

Barrow, *Prefect and Emperor*.

Brown, *Power and Persuasion in Late Antiquity*.

Dill, *Roman Society in the Last Century of the Western Empire*.

Holum, *Theodosian Empresses*.

Kaegi, *Byzantium and the Decline of Rome*.

King, *The Emperor Theodosius and the Establishment of Christianity*.

Lenski, *The Crisis of the Roman Empire*.

MacMullen, *Christianizing the Roman Empire*.

Matthews, *Western Aristocracies and the Imperial Court*.

Trombley, *Hellenic Religion and Christianization*.

Zosimus, *New History*.

Questions to Consider

1. Why were Christian emperors cautious in their religious policy in 363–379? What were the limits of imperial power in enforcing religious conformity?

2. How powerful were bishops in their cities by 395? How did the failure of Julian and his institutional paganism (Hellenism) contribute to the rise of bishops? What factors were necessary for cities to remain faithful to the ancestral gods after 363?

3. How could Theodosius I mount such effective attacks against pagan cults? What accounted for the failure of pagans to rally against imperial coercion? Did the pagan senators who backed Eugenius and Arbogast have a coherent policy to restore the gods?

4. Why did pagans, given their numbers, fail to take action after 395? How does the reign of Theodosius I represent a turning point?

Turning Point—Theodosius I
Lecture 23—Transcript

In this lecture, I'm going to be dealing with really what I think is the crucial turning point of the entire development of Christianity in the Roman world: the career of the emperor Theodosius I, usually known as Theodosius the Great.

I'd like to start with an anecdote. In 391 A.D., shortly after the emperor had passed laws that outlawed sacrifice, and therefore pagan worship, the patriarch of Alexandria, Theophilus, released his monks to attack pagans who'd occupied the Serapeum and Museion. If you recall, the Serapeum was a temple to Serapis in Alexandria; it was also the center of an important library and lecture halls. The Museion, or Museum, was really more of an academy of arts and sciences that had been founded in the 3rd century B.C. by King Ptolemy I. Those monks attacked the pagans, and the argument was that the pagans were secretly worshiping in underground sanctuaries and this was in violation of the laws that had recently been passed by the emperor Theodosius. The pagans objected; they occupied both the Serapeum and Museion to protect them; and the monks and a large Christian crowd, really a rabble—it would be the equivalent of the old mob in the early Roman Empire—stormed into these buildings, smashed the statues, destroyed papyrus scrolls, and the fighting then spread across the city of Alexandria.

Of course, the imperial army did nothing. The population was maddened over the issue. They broke in and the cult statues were carted off and melted down; they were turned into cookery or they were turned into liturgical objects for the use by Christians. Cult statues such as the great phallus of Priapus, one of the famous fertility gods, were paraded around and cast in the streets as absolutely disgusting idols that the Christians would have nothing to do with. The result of this attack on both the Serapeum and the Museion was that Classical Alexandria essentially was destroyed and Christian Alexandria emerged. As I've mentioned before, the movie *Agora* depicts this event as one of the central incidents in the movie; and I've mentioned this movie several times before, maybe too many times before, but nonetheless it gives a sense of what that iconoclasm represented.

Scholars and popular writers have viewed this destruction as a turning point, and there's a good reason to do so. For one, the pagans who witnessed this destruction were absolutely intimidated. There are reports of conversions on the spot. The Christian mob led by the monks had destroyed these cult statues; nothing had happened. In addition, the entire action, while it wasn't ordered by the imperial government, certainly the emperor Theodosius I approved, and it's the climax to a series of legislation issued by Theodosius, who came to the throne in 379, who would forever ban the pagan sacrifices and also impose unity within that imperial church.

It's very important to keep this in mind, because remember that, in two lectures back, I discussed how in 363, when the emperor Julian died, the Christians regained the control of the emperorship; but the situation was by no means clear. It could be argued that in 363, the Christians could still blow it. The emperor Jovian turned out to be a feckless ruler; he was probably assassinated by his own officers on his return towards Constantinople. He never made it there; he was found mysteriously dead. The Eastern army essentially settled the succession issue and declared two brothers, Valentinian and Valens, as emperors. These were tough Balkan soldiers who apparently were Arian in confession, but were popular in the army. Above all, there was an Eastern army that still included a number of Christian officers and men, an army devoted to the House of Constantine, and not particularly favorable to Julian. It was really a question of whether there would be another civil war between an Eastern army and a Western army, which was still largely pagan; which included many recruits from the German barbarians from across the Rhine; and was very much committed to the memory of the emperor Julian, who had won their favor back in the mid-350s.

As a result, the two brother emperors, Valentinian and Valens, who established essentially the second Christian dynasty of the Roman world, were in a very uncertain position. I mentioned in a previous lecture that this allowed the pagans to continue their worship. There's lots of evidence from archeology that many shrines that were reopened under Julian continued to function in the later 4th century; and again, some of them would continue, particularly the more remote ones, or sanctuaries and oracles that were in secondary cities. My favorite example of that is Aezanis, a city in Western Turkey, which is a temple to Zeus—I mentioned it earlier—and had acquired membership in the Panhellenian; that magnificent Hadriatic temple was still operating into the 5th century, and apparently it was toppled by an earthquake and was never converted into a church. You have instances of temples operating well into the 5th century and even into the 6th century. Furthermore, I noted that there was an outpouring of pagan literature at the end of the 4th and very opening of the 5th century.

From the start, these two Christian emperors, Valens and Valentinian, were the real successors to Julian. Jovian was more like a hiccup than anything else; he really did nothing except evacuate the army from Persia and give up strategic provinces to the Shah Shapur II. Ammianus Marcellinus, the pagan author who was devoted to Julian and Julian's policy, continued to write his history under these Christian rulers, and he makes some very important comments about them. Both of these emperors were very suspicious of the ruling classes, Christian and pagan both. There's a series of dreary treason trials in which officials and officers were removed; part of this was to get rid of Julian's appointees, but also both of these emperors were very much like many late Roman emperors: They came from a rough and ready provincial background; they didn't trust the polished elite. Ammianus Marcellinus could be classified as such an individual. He spoke excellent Latin; he came from an old Roman colonial family; obviously attended schooling at either the city of Beirut or Antioch; and he himself was very, very suspect in the eyes of these emperors.

In addition, they lacked legitimacy. They tried to get it by fighting under the labarum; they tried to cut the image of a Constantine. Valentinian had two sons by different marriages, an older son Gratian, a younger son Valentinian II; and Valentinian II was married into the surviving relative of Constantine, a granddaughter, the only daughter of Constantius II. There's an effort by these Christian emperors to link themselves to the House of Constantine.

Another important aspect—and we need not get into all the sectarian issues because this is a course far more dealing with the whole religious sweep and the change from paganism to Christianity—but it's important to consider that under Julian, all the different Christian confessions were recognized because Julian's official policy was toleration. I believe that might've changed when he won a victory in Persia, and he could well have had in mind an edict of persecution; but that never took place. As a result, there was a series of litigations, usually suits initiated by the Nicene bishops—that is, those bishops who would subscribe to the council in 325 A.D., which declared the Trinity and that the three persons in the Trinity were coequal and eternal—against the Arian position that had lost. As I noted, the Arian position had gained favor in the later days of Constantine's reign; in fact, Constantine was formally baptized by an Arian bishop and his sons, particularly Constantius II, were devoted Arians. Those are members of the doctrines preached by Arian back at the Council of Nicaea in 325. The result was the imperial church was divided.

The two brothers were clearly aware of this. Valentinian, who got the Western Empire—that is, the Western half of the empire, which was the much more difficult frontier; he was the senior man; he had two sons, Valens did not have any children, and Valens, the younger brother, was a rather colorless figure—Valentinian I was certainly astute enough to realize that he had to court the Nicene bishops in the Western provinces, particularly the Pope of Rome, and above all Athanasius, patriarch of Alexandria, who spent more of his time in exile being run out of Alexandria for his position on the Trinity rather than actually in Alexandria. But Athanasius was one of the great doctors of the church—he's still regarded in that light by orthodox Christians, especially in the Greek Orthodox Church—and he was immediately aligned with Valentinian I, and that gave great legitimacy to Valentinian, at least for the Western church. Whereas Valens remained an ardent Arian; he faced opposition in Egypt; the communities of the Balkans and Asia Minor were divided; and as a result, there was no united Christian policy, and by default the pagans were tolerated. In large part, that accounts for why the pagans could carry out the kind of cultural activities that I mentioned in a previous lecture, especially the senatorial aristocracy in Rome; why so many of the lesser cities across the Roman Empire still presented very much a pagan face in worship and in public images; that is, there would be cult statues, there would be all sorts of inscriptions that reminded one of the Classical city of the 2nd century A.D.

The Christianization at this point was still very uneven. The big cities, the cities with imperial patronage: Caesarea and Cappadocia, home to a very important Christian family, the so-called Cappadocian fathers who were so important in Christian theology. Basil the Great and his brother Gregory of Nyssa, and their good friend Gregory Nazianzus, I mentioned him earlier, talking about how his father had been converted at the time of the Council of Nicaea. They were powerful intellects who came up with a theology to counter the Arians. Caesarea really went Christian. Constantinople; it was the new Christian capital. Antioch; essentially the same. Rome, on the other hand, was largely in the hands of the pagans, even though there was a pope across the way in what became the Vatican, but the pope was really a rather restricted figure until the mid-5th century. Athens was pagan. Alexandria was pretty much evenly split until that incident I started this lecture off where the Christians finally destroyed the pagan sanctuaries, and essentially between 391 and 414 wiped out that elite class that provided the Neoplatonic philosophers. The court at Milan, at Treveri; they would be Christian. But the lesser cities of Gaul, northern Italy, Britain, many of the cities of Spain were still largely pagan.

This second Christian dynasty was a very, very tentative operation. They knew from the start that their position rested on the loyalty of the army, and part of that army, especially in the West was very, very pagan. They had only the most tenuous of links to the family of Constantine, which is essentially they were Christians and one of Valentinian's sons had married a granddaughter of Constantine; that's about it.

Valentinian proved to be an extremely able emperor. He won victories on the northern frontier; but he died suddenly in 375 and left his two rather young sons in control of the Western Empire. That meant Gratian, the older of the two, ruled over essentially the Rhine frontier, Gaul and Britain; that is, the more difficult frontiers. The younger son by the second marriage of Valentinian, with his mother, they ruled from Milan. There, Bishop Ambrose of Milan, who was later to become the patron of Saint Augustine, exercised a very powerful control over this young emperor.

The two brothers didn't get along; they didn't play well together; but they did agree on one point: They should at least make an effort to appear like Christian rulers; after all, they're Nicene emperors, they're heirs to the Constantinian tradition. They tentatively began to pass legislation—particularly Gratian seems to have been behind this—to cut back on some of the toleration, which really was more a question of just pragmatism, which had existed since 363. Gratian, for instance, passed certain laws that imposed liabilities on pagan priests. There's a particularly unpopular law that put liabilities on the Vestal Virgins, which was a very, very sacred college in the city of Rome.

The two brothers also agreed—and again, I mention this in connection with the senatorial aristocracy in Rome, particularly that famous figure Marcus Aurelius Symmachus—that the altar of Victory, which used to be in the Curia or the Senate house at Rome, and when you went into the Senate house you saw the altar of Victory, that the altar of Victory had to be removed because it's such an obviously pagan symbol. This was ordered in an imperial edict in 382; the altar was dutifully carried out, it's locked away. It wasn't destroyed or smashed, but it's an important symbolic message by both Gratian and Valentinian II—who never went to the city of Rome, by the way; in fact, no emperor was in the city of Rome between 357 and essentially 394—that the city of Rome was now going to have to get with the program and start becoming more and more a Christian city.

It was a particularly offensive action to the Roman senators. It resulted in a series of letters—they're known as the *Relationes*—that were penned by Symmachus, the leading pagan senator of Rome, requesting that the altar be restored. He wrote a series of these letters in 382, again in 383; his final one was in 391 to the emperor Theodosius I and that went nowhere. But in these letters, he made the argument that it's inappropriate, not decorous, not proper to *mos maiorum*, ancestral custom—that word I've talked about before; that phrase—that this monument, which goes back to the republic, which was conceived as celebrating Trajan's campaign, that his should be removed. As a result, he wrote a series of such letters trying to stress that this was a monument closely linked to the entire history of Rome, and it really should be seen that way even by Christian rulers.

The Western army, however, didn't take so well to this. As I mentioned, the Western Roman army—that is, the army in Britain, the army in the Rhine— many of the soldiers in there were not Roman citizens but were what is known as federates. In the 350s and 360s, increasingly the emperors had shifted over to recruiting barbarian tribal regiments known as federates.

These were usually Germanic people, sometimes they were Iranian people such as the Alans or Sarmatians, but these people, if they were Christian, they were only Christian in name. Many of them were still pagan, and large numbers of the Western army were still pagan and the laws that were imposing civil liabilities on pagan priests and seen as interfering with the sacrifices, this sparked another rebellion in the Western army, it was one of several reasons. Another reason was Gratian was so feckless. He spent most of his time hunting and drinking in Treveri and he never led an army.

In 383, the army in Britain rose in rebellion and they declared their commander Magnus Maximus—which is a great name in Latin for those of you who know Latin, it means great, greatest; he's obviously coming up through the ranks from humble origins—that army invaded Gaul; they were received by the army in the Rhine. Gratian was deserted; he was caught, executed; and at that point, Magnus Maximus thought, "Well, let's cut a deal with Valentinian II, the surviving brother of Gratian." "No deal; we're not going to deal with this guy, the rebellious governor, he's too dangerous," and the result was Magnus Maximus invaded Italy and drove Valentinian II and his mom east to Constantinople.

At that point in Constantinople there was an emperor, Theodosius. He'd been elevated to the throne in 379. He was the son of a famous count and namesake—Count Theodosius, one of the great generals of Spanish origin who'd fought in the earlier 4th century—and Theodosius had been married into the imperial family and been commissioned to take charge of the Roman East after the disaster of the Battle of Adrianople. The Battle of Adrianople is well known to those of you who are familiar with Roman frontier history, barbarian invasions; that is, the famous battle where the Goths for a second time killed an emperor, Valens, the Arian emperor, which went a long way to discrediting the Arian position and nailed most of the Eastern army, which included a lot of Arian officers. That defeat in 378 had posed a crisis. There's no imperial figure in the East, no one to represent the imperial family; the Goths were running all over the Balkans. Theodosius was brought in to take charge of the East by Gratian and Valentinian II, and he did an excellent job by recruiting Goths into the army and establishing his position in Constantinople.

Another important point is Theodosius was a devoted Nicene Christian. He was a tough general. He commanded the respect of the various German federate regiments, which is extremely important, and there was no question of his religious loyalties. When the imperial family fled from Milan to Constantinople, Theodosius immediately mounted an attack against Magnus Maximus; and in 388, somewhere on the Save River, that tributary to the Danube, that strategic frontier in the Roman world, Theodosius and his army nailed the Western army and killed Magnus Maximus, and restored order in the Roman West. It looked as if everything was hunky dory at this point. We now have Nicene rulers in both Milan and Constantinople. Rome had, again, more requests to restore the altar; they just turned them down. It looked as if this uneasy alliance, or this uneasy toleration, between Christian and pagans was going to soon come to an end.

Theodosius gave good indications of this. He outlawed Manichees and initiated a new wave of persecution of the Manichaeans; the last persecution had been by a pagan emperor, the Manichaeans were condemned as heretics. Again, Theodosius in the 380s didn't move directly against the cults in law, but he turned a blind eye to his administrators, particularly a certain fellow known as Maternus, who was the Prefect of the Roman East; that would be Asia Minor, Syria, and Egypt. The Prefect was the senior civil administration in the late Roman government. There were four of them in the East, in the Balkans, in Italy, and in the West. Maternus, backed by various monks in the 380s, attacked different pagan shrines. The monks had a field day playing the role of Old Testament prophets, and a number of famous sanctuaries were damaged.

Learned pagans reacted as I mentioned earlier, as you would expect. Libanius, the great teacher of rhetoric at Antioch and a man who was very much impressed by Julian the Apostate, trained both pagans and Christians of high rank so they would have a good command of the Classics and occupy or obtain positions in the imperial government. He wrote a work—*On the Temples*, as it's called; *De Templis* is the Latin term—again, pleading with a lot of the same arguments that you'd read in Symmachus's letter in Latin to the Western emperors; Libanius wrote in Greek essentially an oration pleading with Theodosius that this is unseemly; it's not *eudoxos*, as they would say in Greek. It's not proper to carry out the sort of iconoclasm against great temples that, of course, they're the ancestral gods, but they're also great cultural centers; they're part of this whole tradition. It isn't proper that crazy monks led by a rogue Prefect should do this. Of course, Theodosius didn't pay any attention to this, and he was steadily moving towards a position that once he had secured Constantinople, had secured the loyalty and the army of the East, he was going to move against the gods in a way that the emperor Constantine had never dared to do.

Theodosius could do this for several reasons. One, his success as a general. Two, in 381, he summoned the Second Ecumenical Council, held at Constantinople, the imperial capital. He presided over it just as Constantine had presided over the first, and it reinstated all of the canons at the Council of Nicaea as well as declared Constantinople for the first time a Petrine see; that is, a see equivalent to that of Rome. The language in Canon II, which is the second chapter of the proceedings of the Second Ecumenical Council—it's a little vague on this—the Roman pope always said, "It means Constantinople is number two out of the five," which eventually came to be Rome, Constantinople, Alexandria, Antioch, and Jerusalem. The patriarch in Constantinople said, "No, we are equal; we are of the same rank." Therein is a long history that which properly belongs to a course in Byzantine history and church-state relations.

Nonetheless, what the Second Ecumenical Council did was it ended Arianism as an issue. Some of the Germanic peoples, the East Germanic peoples converted by Constantius II, they remained Arian Christians; notably Goths, Vandals, and the Goths were later split into Ostrogoths and Visigoths. But it meant that the disunity that had disrupted the imperial church, that was gone. Constantinople was now definitely the orthodox capital of the Roman East, and that meant Theodosius was in a position first to allow monks and his administrators to attack pagan sanctuaries, second to turn down appeals by pagans that this was not proper, and then in 391, he issued a series of three laws; actually, the last law was issued early in 392. These laws banned public sacrifice throughout the Roman world and declared that officially from now on the only religion in the Roman Empire with any legitimacy was Nicene Christianity. This is a turning point.

Think about how the situation has changed so dramatically in 350 years from when we started this course; that is, henceforth the definition of what is a Roman is going to be based on your religious affiliation. This is going to affect all the pagans; it's eventually going to affect the Jews as well because they aren't within the Christian community, whereas under pagan emperors, Jews could have Roman citizenship. It was a matter of legal definition, not religious. Of course, it also affected "heretics," those Christians who didn't buy the Council of Nicaea. These laws carried major implications, and everyone knew it as soon as they were promulgated and publicly announced in the cities of the Roman world.

There was inevitably a reaction. One of those reactions was in Alexandria, I had mentioned it earlier, where the Serapeum was stormed and the pagans were essentially discredited. There was also a reaction in the West, and obviously where's it going to happen? It's going to happen in the Western army. At the time of the promulgation of these laws there was a Frankish general named Arbogast. He held a position known as magister militum, which is best translated, it means "master of the soldiers," but it's really a position of generalissimo. Arbogast was the first of a series of barbarian or provincial generals who held the supreme military command, especially of the Western field armies, because emperors increasingly were absorbed in ceremonial roles in their capitals. Arbogast seems to have been behind the murder of Valentinian II, the second and youngest son of the emperor Valentinian I. Valentinian was murdered under mysterious circumstances in 392, and a grammarian named Eugenius—where we get the name Eugene— was proclaimed emperor by the Western army of the Rhine.

There are several issues involved in this rebellion; it isn't all strictly religious. But Eugenius, while technically a Christian, openly tolerated the sacrifices to the gods. Arbogast was a Frankish general; if he was a Christian, it was of the most nominal sort. Many of his German soldiers, who were Franks and Alemanni, the two principle tribes recruited in the Western army, definitely were pagan. Theodosius I now faced a second Western army, the fourth in the 4th century, which has been propelled by pagan soldiers objecting to the Christian policies; the first being Magnentius, the second being Julian, the third Magnus Maximus, now you've got Arbogast and his puppet emperor.

For the first time, the Roman senators finally react. They're outraged over the laws of 391 and 392, and they proclaim their loyalty to the Western usurper. Theodosius marches from the east to the west again and confronts this mixed army of rebels, and a major battle is fought on September 5–6, 394, at the Frigidus. That's a river just north of the city of Aquileia, which is essentially the Roman predecessor to Venice; it's in the Julian Alps; it's been a strategic city ever since the 2nd century B.C. On the first day, Theodosius's army gets a rough showing of it; and it's mostly Goths who get killed, and so that's not too bad. On the second day, a hail storm emerges and blows the hail into the eyes of the rebels and Theodosius wins an immense victory. Eugenius is captured and executed; Arbogast commits suicide. The Roman senators are totally embarrassed. The Roman senators didn't fight; no, they wrote letters of support, of course. They're not expected to fight. But they were now embarrassed, and they surrendered unconditionally. The result was a second miracle victory for a Christian emperor. This battle at the Frigidus was hailed by Christians as essentially the second Milvian Bridge. Once again, God gave his favor to a Christian emperor and the pagans were cast down. Theodosius entered in triumph and ordered the removal of the altar of Victory, and everyone knew that it was going to be a rough day for the pagans.

Fortunately for the pagans, Theodosius suddenly died in January—January 17, 395—before he could pass anymore legislation, and he was succeeded by his two worthless sons, Arcadius and Honorius; and so begins the rapid collapse of the Western empire, which disintegrates by 476, and the near loss of the Eastern empire. Nonetheless, Theodosius's reign was a turning point. From this point on, the Christian monarchy was never again in question; there's no way the pagans will ever get it. Henceforth, the pagans have been barred from all public worship and therefore their faith has now been made illegal.

Increasingly, the word "pagan" comes to denote a barbarian, a peasant; the educated pagans that we'd had for so long began to disappear. By the early 5th century, many convert to Christianity; particularly the Roman senators by the mid-5th century. Above all, Theodosius now defined Roman citizenship, Roman identity, by proper religion, not by legal rights; and those who didn't follow were subject to the full punishment of Roman law. The result was Theodosius had taken the first step to creating the persecuting society of medieval Europe.

Justinian and the Demise of Paganism
Lecture 24

O ver a century passed between the reigns of Theodosius I and Justinian, but the latter emperor completed the logic of the former's laws, ensuring that Theodosius's world became the world of medieval Europe. Justinian extended the persecution and suppression of pagans to Jews and heretics. He called ecumenical councils to condemn not only contemporary non-mainstream thinking but unconventional writings of long-dead theologians. His building programs created a Christian skyline that circled the Mediterranean. To some, he is a hero of the faith; to others, he is the father of medieval persecution.

Justinian against the Apostates

- Theodosius outlawed the pagan cults, and he redefined Roman identity along religious lines. But the majority of the Roman population was still by no means Christian. Most scholars agree that, during his reign, the pagan population of the empire was certainly over 50 percent.

- **Justinian I**, in effect, completed the logic of Theodosius's laws of 391–392. He conducted a number of important changes, reforms, and measures that insured that, by the time he died in 565, the Roman world was essentially Christian both in numbers and outlook.

- Justinian operated within a framework of legal precedents to crack down on the crypto-pagans. These were individuals who were outwardly Christians but privately sacrificing to the pagan gods. These included many high-ranking Roman officials, including a powerful prefect named Phocas.

- In 529, Justinian ordered a crackdown in his administration. The crypto-pagan officials were given the opportunity to renounce what Justinian regarded as black magic and to reaffirm their faith as Christians.

- In 546, after a plague and some unsuccessful attempts to recapture the Roman West, Justinian conducted another crackdown and many of the same officials were caught again, including Phocas. Phocas was executed, and his body was mutilated as a warning to others.

- To Justinian, the crypto-pagan problem was more than simple apostasy. Many Christians saw the old gods as demons. The crypto-pagans were not expressing innocent, private belief; they were in league with the devil himself, which could account for the empire's various setbacks.

- It should be noted that these pagans' faith was as genuine as Justinian's. They continued to sacrifice in defiance of the laws because they believed. Some of them were theurgists; others believed in proxy sacrifice for the good of the empire.

Justinian's Christian Army

- The imperial army was now definitively Christian, fighting under the banners of the cross or the crucifix, not the Christogram, which could be misinterpreted as the talisman of the family of Constantine. Military saints emerged as important figures as well.

- All battles were preceded with sermons by priests, who accompanied the armies. The victories won by Justinian's commanders took place where the imperial army had not won battles since the Battle of Adrianople almost 150 years earlier. All of that confirmed that God was favorable to a Roman Christian army.

Converting the Countryside

- Justinian made a concerted effort to spread the faith to the lesser cities and the countryside of the Roman Empire. He appointed very able bishops in the cities of the Roman East to carry out aggressive proselytizing, especially in the villages, towns, and satellite communities their cities administered.

- **John of Amida** was consecrated as bishop of Ephesus around 535. He spent a generation proselytizing in the countryside around Ephesus, and most scholars believe that this was one of the most Christianized areas of the Roman world in the time of Justinian.

- John's biographer claims John was personally responsible for converting 80,000 pagans. John razed temples and ordered the construction of 12 monasteries and 96 churches. He also brought in tough monks from Syria, like Barsuma, to aid in these efforts.

Justinian Architecture

- Justinian was responsible for a whole new wave of building, particularly the construction of impressive cathedral churches. The most famous of these by far is the current church of Hagia Sophia, but many similar structures are being uncovered by archaeologists, especially in cities in Asia Minor.

- These domed basilican cathedral churches came to dominate the skyline of the cities of the Roman world under Justinian. That included the eastern half of the Empire and a good deal of the western: the provinces in Africa, the provinces in Italy, parts of Spain, and the western provinces lost in the 5th century to the Germanic peoples and reconquered by Justinian's armies.

The Other Non-Christians

- The word "Hellene" had come to designate a pagan, a nonbeliever; "pagan" came to designate, by Justinian's time, someone one step away from the barbarians—the equivalent of the English word "heathen."

- By the end of Justinian's reign, there were no longer any pagan intellectuals. The Academy at Athens came to an end. The patriarchs of Alexandria were essentially Christian pharaohs; there was no intellectual life in Alexandria that was not Christian. This became increasingly the case across the Roman world, whether under the direct rule of the Roman emperor or under the various Germanic kings who ruled the West in the 5th century.

- Less palatable in any number of ways were Justinian's efforts to achieve religious unity through converting the Jews and the Samaritans. Justinian ordered the first forced baptisms of Jews on record, beginning a dreary record of anti-Semitism that continued throughout the Middle Ages and into the modern age.

- Justinian's less brutal methods of conversion included forbidding the Jews to read the Torah in Hebrew; they had to use the Septuagint, the logic being that if they read Greek, maybe they would eventually convert to Christianity.

- The image of Jews as living in ghettos—that is, in distinct communities—in the Middle Ages and into the modern age had now come about in the 6th century, thanks to Justinian's attempts at conversion.

- Justinian also made a concerted effort to convert peoples beyond the imperial frontier. Various Roman allies, particularly along the eastern frontiers, were now classified as Christians and members of the Roman community. These included the Armenians; the various Georgian peoples of Transcaucasia; some Arabian tribes; a few cities on the western shores of India; Axum; Yemen; Nubia; parts of Persia; and several Germanic tribes.

- Justinian often moved against cult centers that were perceived as particularly important on these frontiers. Even strategic locations where emperors had previously turned a blind eye were Christianized.

- Justinian made a concerted effort to remove cult statues not only from these frontier areas but also from the great sanctuaries such as Olympia, Delphi, and Athens bring them to Constantinople, where they were turned into park elements. In doing so, he announced the victory of Christianity, emptied the statues of their religious content, and deprived the pagans of their focus of worship.

Justinian's Ecumenical Council

- The Council of Ephesus in 431 and the Council of Chalcedon in 451 had built upon the rulings of Nicaea and defined the nature of Christ as it is now accepted by most Christians: the nature of Christ is human and divine, comingled, and distinct.

- One of the most important losing positions at Chalcedon was the Monophysite (from Greek *monophysis*) position that argued that Christ was essentially divine—that is, he has a single nature. This issue was a sharp divisor of Justinian's empire.

- To heal the divide and persuade all Christians to accept the ruling of Chalcedon, Justinian targeted a common enemy by persecuting Jews, pagans, and heretics. In addition, Justinian tried to target the writings of Origen and three **Nestorian** heretic writers from the 5th century.

- In 553, Justinian summoned the Fifth Ecumenical Council to condemn these writings. With this act, he effectively created medieval censorship: In all previous councils, the losing side was given the chance to present its case. Here, the writings of men long deceased and who had died in communion with the then-Christian church were posthumously condemned and sent into the flames.

The World Justinian Made

- Justinian's empire would disintegrate within two generations of his death. Europe became the heir to classical Rome. The classical arts and writing survived, but in a Christian world, a world that reckoned time by the birth of Christ and saw Jerusalem as the center of the Earth.

- This world was rather parochial in its views: The pagan gods were demons and utterly intolerable. There was an immense gap between the divine and the mundane that could only be crossed by the holy ones. As Iamblichus of Chalcis once said, "You Christians have emptied the world of gods, and you have made it a lonely place."

- For the next 12 centuries, a civilized individual in the West was one who was a Christian, who was an heir to the imperial church of Constantine, Theodosius, and Justinian. For the next 12 centuries, the notions of the divine and of ethics came out of the age of Justinian. His world was the basis for the religious and ethical values of the West down to this day.

Important Terms

monophysis: Greek for "single nature"; The doctrine stressing the single, divine nature of Christ from which the Monophysites got their name. This became the doctrine of the Egyptian, Armenian, Syriac, and Ethiopian churches.

Nestorianism: The followers of Nestorius, patriarch of Constantinople from 429 to 431, who argued that Mary was the mother of Christ the human (Christotokos), rather than mother of Christ the God (Theotokos). Nestorius's views were rejected at the Third Ecumenical Council at Ephesus in 431. *See* **Theotokos**.

Names to Know

John of Amida (c. 507–585): A Monophysite ascetic trained in the Syrian tradition. As bishop of Ephesus (535–575), he carried out aggressive efforts to convert pagans in Western Asia Minor.

Justinian I (a.k.a. **Justinian the Great**; 483–565; r. 527–565): Byzantine (Eastern Roman) emperor. Justinian succeeded his uncle and adoptive father Justin I as a mature, experienced ruler of 46. The greatest emperor since Constantine, he restored imperial rule in the Italian Peninsula and Africa. His most enduring achievements are Hagia Sophia and the *Corpus Iuris Civilis*.

Suggested Reading

Brown, *The Body and Society*.

Browning, *Justinian and Theodora*.

Cameron, *The Mediterranean World in Late Antiquity*.

Dawes and Baynes, *Three Byzantine Saints*.

Fowden, *Empire to Commonwealth*.

Kitzinger, *Byzantine Art in the Making*.

Harl, "Sacrifice and Pagan Belief in Fifth- and Sixth-Century Byzantium."

Frend, *The Rise of the Monophysite Movement*.

Mainestone, *Hagia Sophia*.

Meyendorff, *Imperial Unity, Christian Divisions*.

Moorhead, *Justinian*.

Procopius, The Secret History.

———, *Works*.

Rosen, *Justinian's Flea*.

Trombley, *Hellenic Religion and Christianization*.

von Simson, *Sacred Fortress*.

1. How ruthless was Justinian in imposing religious uniformity on his subjects? Why did he remove pagans from imperial administration? Why did he move to close temples and remove cult statues? How important was Justinian in the demise of paganism?

2. What were the respective roles of bishops and monks in converting cities and the countryside in the era of Justinian? Why did these later pagans fail to oppose Justinian? How did the nature of pagan worship contribute to the demise of paganism?

3. How important was Justinian in promoting the spread of Christianity beyond the empire? What was the impact of the theological debates within the imperial church in defining doctrine and spreading Christianity? How did Justinian use architecture and arts to uphold and spread the Christian message?

4. In what ways was Christianity, by the death of Justinian, medieval and quite different from that of the high Roman Empire?

Justinian and the Demise of Paganism
Lecture 24—Transcript

In this final lecture to the course, I wish to deal with the emperor Justinian and the demise of paganism; and it may be a question as to why we have to deal with Justinian after I talked about how Theodosius had essentially created the institutions and the legal basis for what I call medieval Christianity.

Theodosius certainly outlawed the pagan cults, and he also redefined Roman identity along religious lines. But the Roman world was by no means a majority of Christians. I had mentioned in earlier lectures that what has happened by the time of Theodosius's death in 395, the pagans had been taught to be quiet. They certainly were not going to mount a revival the way Julian did, and even that abortive a rather pathetic rebellion in 392–394, there was no chance of that happening again. But still, the vast majority of the Roman world was pagan, certainly over 50 percent, and most scholars now agree on that.

The Christians; however, had captured the cultural, political, military institutions of the Roman world. Justinian, in effect, completed the logic of the laws of 391–392. He conducted a number of important changes, reforms, and measures that insured that by the time he died in 565—and Justinian was on the throne for a very long time; he came to the throne in 527, but he was really ruling with his uncle and adoptive father from 519, so he spanned well over a half century, he dominated the 6th century—by the time he dies in his 80s, the Roman world, the Mediterranean world, is essentially a Christian world, both in numbers and outlook; I mentioned that the cities will have a Christian skyline. It is important for us to look at exactly what Justinian did to contribute to the final process of taking that Mediterranean world in the time of the emperor Augustus—that is, in, say, the year 1—and turning it into a truly Christian world by the time that Justinian died in 565.

For one, Justinian used the power of Roman law, and that is not something we should take lightly. Justinian's great legalist, Tribonian, undertook the great summation of Roman law, the Corpus Juris Civilis, which everyone knows. Emperors before Justinian had legislated in the spirit of Theodosius, imposing civil liabilities on teachers and officials who were pagans;

outlawing pagans—there was a famous law of 415—in the imperial schools; that is, schools that were supported by the imperial government. In 423, the emperor Theodosius II—the rather worthless grandson of Theodosius I—expressed his sanguine belief that there were no longer any pagans in the empire; and we know that is not true. Justinian, therefore, was operating within the framework of a whole number of legal precedents, and he took severe measures, especially in his capital—the Christian capital of Constantinople—to crack down on what are known as crypto-pagans. These are individuals who were sacrificing to the gods, although outwardly they passed as Christians. They would attend services. In fact, they claimed to be Christians of the Chalcedonian creed, which we will be talking about briefly later in the lecture; that is, what was the orthodox creed based on the Council of Nicaea, and then later the Fourth Ecumenical Council of Chalcedon.

In 529, Justinian ordered a crackdown in his administration. It was embarrassing who showed up as a crypto-pagan. It included a quaestor, who is a major treasury official, a notorious and rather unctuous character known as Phocas, who happened to be a Prefect. These were men of extremely high rank—there were a number of lesser officials who were not named—and in 529, they were all sacrificing in violation of the laws of Theodosius and a lot of subsequent legislation since. These officials were given the opportunity to renounce what Justinian regarded as black magic—that is exactly what pagan worship was to him—and to reembrace, reaffirm their faith as Christians. That was done by many of these officials; therefore, they escaped execution, confiscation of property. But in 546, after the impact of the plague and increasing anxiety on the unsuccessful wars in the Roman West, Justinian conducted another crackdown and a lot of the same officials were caught again sacrificing, including Phocas who was executed and his body was mutilated and desecrated as a warning not to slide back into paganism. There was a subsequent investigation in 562, and later ones in the 6th century by Tiberius II, Maurice Tiberius, in which a number of crypto-pagans were caught.

One would wonder, why bother? Especially for those of us in the modern world; these guys were practicing their paganism in private, probably in secret at night, very much the way Christians had been practicing their faith in the time of the 2nd century A.D. when Pliny the Younger noted that the Christians met at night. Are we cracking down on the Christians because of what they believe (nomen Christianum), or because of the way they behaved? They met at night, they were secretive, they may be subversive; some of the same concerns involved with those early Christians were now applied to the pagans.

But it was more significant than that. First, these pagans were outwardly Christians; they were apostates; they were denying their faith, they had moved against it. Second, as I have tried to drive home especially in the lecture on the monks and the ascetics, that starting in the later 4th century, while intellectuals and some of the educated could appreciate Classical arts and letters, the monks, the ascetics, and many of the simple Christians saw the old gods as demons; they were in league with Satan. What these crypto-pagans were doing was not expressing some kind of innocent, private belief that we could ignore, they were in league with the devil himself. That could account for various setbacks, the disfavor of God. Particularly in the 540s, there was a major plague that swept the Roman world in 542–543. It was the first of a series of pandemics that drastically reduced the population and is often compared to the impact of the Black Death. Justinian, who had an ambitious policy of reconquering the Western provinces in Italy and the Western provinces that had fallen to German invaders, there were major military setbacks. Even his brilliant General Belisarius was having difficulty in Italy. All of this could be attributed to the disfavor of God, and one of the main reasons was these pagans continued to practice what was black magic. There were also various heretics, there were Jews, there were all sorts of individuals and groups who were not with the program; they were not good orthodox Christians, and hence the urgency of carrying out these measures. As I said, Justinian completed the logic of the Theodosian laws, and those Theodosian laws are premised on persecuting society. Either you are in the imperial church, you're in the orthodox church, or you are not; and in that case, you are in league with the devil.

These measures, therefore, were seen as extremely important. Again, I have written on this subject in learned articles; and the pagans continued to sacrifice in defiance of the laws because they believed in the faith of the old gods. Some of them were theurgists; that is, they believed that the rites had a higher significance. Some of them believed in what I have called proxy sacrifice, as I mentioned in an earlier lecture, especially starting in the late 4th century; that those who still remained true to the old gods could sacrifice on behalf of the entire community and therefore avert disaster for what was becoming increasingly a Christian world. No one denies the faith of these pagans who continued to sacrifice in violation of the imperial laws, except their numbers were being thinned and they were seen by Christian emperors—not only seen, they were targeted by Christian emperors—as essentially enemies of god and enemies of the state at the same time.

This dovetails with what else we know about Justinian's legislation and Justinian's religious policies. For one, the imperial army was now definitively Christian. By the time of Justinian's reign, the imperial army was now fighting under the banners of the actual cross of the crucifixion, not the Chi-Rho, which could be misinterpreted as nothing more than a talisman of the family of Constantine. At least since the war of 421–422, all Roman armies went into battle under the sign of the cross. There were military saints that now emerged as important figures. The saints Sergius and Bacchus, they have a church built to them in Constantinople. It is today called Küçük Ayasofya; it is now a mosque. It has been beautifully restored. It was Justinian's first domed church before the great Hagia Sophia. It is to two supposed martyr saints of Byzantium when it was still a pagan city, and they were supposed to be Christian soldiers who refused to sacrifice in the reign of Diocletian and were beheaded. It is probably a legend, but the legend emerged in the late 5th century; it is certainly regarded as true by the time of Justinian, hence the church; and it is an indication how so much of the imperial army was being reconfigured around Christian symbols. By the opening of the 6th century, the armies of Justinian fight as Christian armies under the symbols of the cross, invoking martyrs, eventually invoking icons; all battles were preceded with great sermons by the priests who were accompanying the armies; and the victories won by Justinian's commanders—notably Belisarius, one of the great Roman commanders of all time—these were victories that the imperial army had won for the first time since the Battle of Adrianople almost 150 years earlier. All of that confirmed that God was favorable to a Roman Christian army, whether they were fighting Persians in the East or the German barbarians who had occupied the Western provinces.

This was a very, very important turning point. The imperial armies now functioned as we think medieval armies did—that is, fighting in the name of

God—and there was now a Christian dimension to all these battles that you really did not have in the 4th and early 5th centuries, where the armies were far more mixed in their religious affiliations and composition.

In the lesser cities and the countryside of the Roman Empire, Justinian really did try to make those policies that go back to the 4th century of turning cities and countryside into Christian centers a reality. For one, he appointed very able bishops in the cities of the Roman East to carry out aggressive proselytizing in cities, and especially in the villages, towns, and satellite communities that cities administered. We have a particularly good record of this of a figure known as John of Amida. Amida is today the modern city of Diyarbakir in southeastern Turkey; it is an early Christian center in what the Romans called Mesopotamia. John of Amida was consecrated as Bishop of Ephesus around 535. He is the bishop who presided over the construction of the church that one now sees on the hill—the original citadel of Ephesus, which is probably the center of the Bronze Age site; the so-called Apasas in the Hittite text—and that church of Saint John is a magnificent domed structure, a naved church, a basilican church, commissioned by Justinian with columns carrying the monogram of Justinian and his rather notorious wife Theodora (who was, shall we say, a practitioner of the oldest profession who made it as empress; and that is a story in itself that is probably better reserved for a different lecture at a different time in a different course).

In any case, John of Amida, who became Bishop of Ephesus, spent a generation proselytizing in the countryside around Ephesus, and it's significant. Ephesus is in western Asia Minor. Most scholars believe that this was one of the most Christianized areas of the Roman world in the time of Justinian, and it probably was. Yet, John's biographer claims that this bishop personally was responsible for converting 80,000 pagans around Ephesus, raising temples, cutting down oak groves, ordering the construction of 12 monasteries and 96 churches. Many of these churches clearly had baptisteries attached to them—I mentioned the importance of baptisteries in an earlier lecture in Christianizing the downtowns of Roman cities—and baptisteries were particularly important because you had so many adult conversions, and you find baptisteries everywhere as prominent additions to the churches. Furthermore, John brought in tough monks from Syria, the kind of guys in the tradition of Barsauma, who would absolutely brook no opposition from pagan priests in the countryside—they would throw them in the fire; they would throw the idols in the fire—again, those fearsome holy men who sometimes could simply intimidate villagers to convert on the spot.

This is a particularly well-documented case from around Ephesus, but throughout the Roman East—in Asia Minor, in Syria, in Egypt; that is in the eastern half of the empire that Justinian ruled at his accession, the part of the empire that did not fall in the 5th century A.D.—there was a concerted effort to bring Christianity to the countryside. Many of the stories of the saints of the Egyptian holy fathers, an anecdote I read earlier, from the late 5th century or from the 6th century, those again were part of this concerted effort to turn the Roman world into a truly Christian world.

Justinian himself was responsible for a whole new wave of buildings, particularly impressive cathedral churches. The Church of Saint John at Ephesus, which I mentioned a moment ago, is probably very close to what the Hagia Sophia looked like in Constantinople before it was torched in the Nike Revolt in 532, and then was later rebuilt and rededicated by Justinian; and that is the current church, the domed church that you see today in Istanbul; the Hagia Sophia. But you had similar such cathedral churches, and they're being uncovered by archeologists especially in cities in Asia Minor. There is one at Hierapolis, modern Pamukkale, at Myra, which is a site on the shores of Turkey today, which is regarded as the home of Saint Nicholas; and there is a rather peculiar tourist bureau with images of Saint Nicholas dressed up in his Dutch costume, with his reindeer and everything as he is understood in the United States, on tourist maps at Myra, and Saint Nicholas has a long evolution well after his initial proclamation as a saint in Roman Asia Minor. Nonetheless, there is a major church, it was restored by the Russians in the 19th century rather imaginatively; but again, it is typical of the types of cathedral churches, cathedral domed basilican churches, which come to dominate the landscape of the cities of the Roman world in Justinian. That is the eastern half of the Empire, and a good deal of the west: the provinces in Africa, the provinces in Italy, parts of Spain; all of these Western provinces lost in the 5th century to the Germanic peoples and then reincorporated by Justinian's armies in his wars of reconquest, so that the Mediterranean world, at least the shores of the Mediterranean world, were once again Roman and Justinian was going to make sure that this restored Roman Empire would not only just look like, it would be, a Christian empire.

There was another significant development, and I mentioned it in passing with Theodosius: the change of what the term "pagan" and "Hellene" meant (Hellene, Greek; pagan). Hellene came to designate a pagan, a nonbeliever; pagan came to designate, by Justinian's, time a people who were one step away from being barbarians, probably it is the equivalent of the English word "heathen." With Justinian's death, there were no longer pagan intellectuals. The school at Athens came to an end. We know that the philosophers at Athens, at the academy, for a time they migrated to Persia, probably in 529. They eventually returned to the Roman world, but essentially Athens in the time of Justinian became a Christian city. The Temple of Athena on the Acropolis, the Temple to Athena Promachos, to Athena of the city, was turned into a church. The intellectual center of Alexandria suffered major blows in 391 and 414 when Hypatia was killed. By Justinian's time, it was the seat of the patriarch, particularly at the time of Cyril of Alexandria, who was the successor to Theophilus, the man who ordered the destruction of the Serapeum. The patriarchs who were in Alexandria were essentially Christian pharaohs. They dominated the city; there was no longer any intellectual life in Alexandria that was not Christian. This became increasingly the case across the Roman world, whether it was under the direct rule of the Roman emperor or under the control of the various Germanic kings who were succeeded to the Roman emperors of the West in the 5th century. That had come to an end; and really the last significant pagan author was that fellow Zosimus writing his new history I mentioned in an earlier lecture, and after that the pagan intellectual tradition was over.

Pagan intellectual tradition essentially survived in the curriculum designed to train Christian gentlemen. With the reign of Justinian, the Christians had not only claimed, they were the sole owners of the Classical tradition; and this was the case henceforth. Another change, and one that was less palatable in a number of ways, were Justinian's efforts to achieve religious unity through a conversion of the Jews and the Samaritans. As I mentioned earlier in lectures on Judaism, Judaism was an extremely important religious force in the Roman world in the early Roman Empire. Jews constituted a very important component of the early Roman Empire, many Jews were Roman citizens; certainly Saint Paul was. With Justinian, the marginalization of the Jews was completed. This already started with the laws of Theodosius, but Justinian orders the first forced baptisms of Jews that we have on record; and this begins a dreary record of anti-Semitism that goes through the Middle Ages and into the modern age.

In addition, Justinian tried more subtle—or maybe less brutal—ways of trying to convert the Jews. One was that he forbade the Jews to read the Torah in Hebrew. They had to use the Septuagint, and the thought there was if they do not know Hebrew and they read Greek maybe they will get the message and eventually convert to Christianity. The position of Jews changed significantly; and the image we have of Jews as living in ghettos—that is, in distinct communities in the Middle Ages and into the modern age, really in Europe until the 19th century—that world had now come about in the 6th century in the age of Justinian. There really was not any room for the old Israel anymore. From now on, they were going to worship at the sufferance of Christian Roman emperors who, after the 7th century A.D., we started to call Byzantine emperors.

Justinian also made a concerted effort to convert those peoples beyond the imperial frontier. I mentioned this in discussing some of the cultural changes of the late Roman world; and that is, Christianity now became the mark of education, of culture, as well as faith. This became very true, not only in the Roman world but outside the Roman world. That is, if peoples beyond the imperial borders, or in strategic frontier cities and centers that were vital to the imperial government where imperial law really did not run, if they became members of the Christian community they were, in effect, members of a wider world; an *oikoumene*, where we get the word "ecumenical," it means the inhabited world. That means religious royalty trumped even the fact that you were not directly within the Roman Empire. Therefore, various allied peoples, particularly in the eastern portions of the Roman Empire or along the eastern frontiers, were now classified as Christians and therefore as members of this Roman community. These included the Armenians; the various Georgian peoples of Transcaucasia. The Armenians essentially opted for a so-called Monophysite, which was regarded as heretical version of Christianity. There were conversions of various Arabian tribes in the Fertile Crescent. There were Christian missions in the cities on the western shores of India going back to the 2nd century. There was the Christian kingdom of Axum; that is Ethiopia. Christian kings ruled in Yemen, in Nubia; that is, in the northern portions of the Sudan. These were all part of that wider *oikoumene*. There were Christians in Persia. The Germanic peoples beyond the frontier who would otherwise be barbarians in the 1st and 2nd centuries A.D., if they had embraced Christianity they too were part of this community.

As a way of ensuring this, Justinian often moved against cult centers that were perceived as very important pagan cult centers on the frontiers that had been allowed to operate. These included, for instance, the cult center to the god of the moon, Sin in the Mesopotamian tradition, at Harran, ancient Carrhae; or at the cult of Isis at Philae in Upper Egypt, which was very important for the Nubian—that is, the Sudanese—people who were allies. The cult of Zeus Ammon at the oasis where Alexander consulted the oracle; that was allowed to operate because it was Libyan allies who used to go there. Justinian shut them all down. Even in strategic frontiers where emperors had previously turned a blind eye, these areas must be Christianized, too.

Justinian made a concerted effort of removing the cult statues, not only from these frontier areas where there were famous shrines, but also from great sanctuaries such as Olympia, Delphi, or Athens to Constantinople and turning them into park elements. There were two reasons for doing this: First, by removing cult statues to Constantinople, you announced the victory of Christianity, and you turned those cult statues into park elements, into art as we understand them, emptied of their religious content. Second, you have removed the cult statue that allowed pagans to worship and invoke these gods, and therefore the pagans, without the cult statues, cannot sacrifice, and if they do you can crack down on them as magicians and practicing black magic the way Justinian did with those crackdowns against the crypto-pagans in his administration. Justinian carried out a very concerted effort there.

Finally, Justinian made a major bid to reunite the imperial church. I have not gotten into all of the details about Christian theology, the divisions within the imperial church; that is handled in other courses and a number of courses I have dealt with, and actually in the course I do on the Byzantine world. It is important to keep two important points in mind: One is that by the time of Justinian's reign, the great patriarchates, or popes, at Rome, Constantinople,

Alexandria, and Antioch had emerged as powerful figures as we understand in the Middle Ages. These great prelates—that is, they controlled a Petrine see, a see that claimed descent from Saint Peter, succession from Peter—they controlled churches, monks, the whole apparatus. They could now dominate and influence the Ecumenical Councils in a way they could not in the 4th century.

There were two important Ecumenical Councils in the 5th century: one was the Council of Ephesus in 431, the other the Council of Chalcedon in 451. Both of those councils built upon the rulings of Nicaea and defined the nature of Christ as it is now accepted by most Christians: the nature of Christ is human and divine, comingled, and distinct. One of the most important losing positions was at Chalcedon, and that was the Monophysite position that argued that Christ was essentially defined as divine; that is, had a single nature. *Monophysis* in Greek means "single nature."

That division in 451 really divided Justinian's Christian empire, because perhaps as much as a majority—or close to it, particularly in Syria and Egypt—were Monophysites. In an effort to promote Christian unity within his imperial church, Justinian targeted Jews, pagans, and other heretic groups like Arians as a way of finding common enemies for those who accepted Chalcedon, who eventually became the orthodox Christians, and those who accept the Monophysite church. In addition, he tried to target common enemies, such as the writings of Origen, or three authors who were reputedly Nestorian heretics from the 5th century; and those three authors wrote works. They had died in communion with the then-orthodox church; their names are not so important, but they are Theodore of Mopsuestia, Theodoret of Cyrrhus, and Ibas of Edessa; they had written works that were found to be offensive in their theology to later Monophysites in Chalcedonians. What Justinian did in 553 was summon the Fifth Ecumenical Council to condemn these writings.

This was act two to creating the persecuting society. What Justinian, in effect, did was create medieval censorship. In all previous Ecumenical Councils, the losing side at least was given the chance to present their case. In this case, the writings of men long deceased and who had, it was assumed, died in communion with the then-Christian church were now hauled up and condemned and their works were sent into the flames, particularly those of Origen; and I mentioned that in the discussion of Origen that a lot of his text comes in the passages sites at the Fifth Ecumenical Council. I never quite forgave Justinian for that one; Origen didn't deserve this. The council itself was a fiasco. It never ended up in unity; the pope refused to accept it, he was arrested and eventually had to be released. The Monophysites just ignored it. But what it represented was a turning point in the creating of that medieval persecuting society.

It is a good point to wrap up at this moment with the Fifth Ecumenical Council and the consequences of all of Justinian's legislation and efforts. The Byzantine or Eastern Roman or the restored empire of Justinian, however we wish to call it—that is, this last Mediterranean empire essentially ruled by over Justinian that would disintegrate within two generations of his death—this empire was Christian in a majority of its population, in its art and architecture, epitomized by Hagia Sophia at the city of Constantinople. There were some very significant changes in this new world that emerged as heir to Classical Rome. To be sure, Classical arts and writing survived; but it was now a Christian world, a world that reckoned time by the birth of Christ or the creation of the world according to the Bible; that was worked out by a fellow called Dionysus the Little. A world that saw Jerusalem at the center of the Earth; a view that would persist through the Middle Ages. That came out of the works of a man called Cosmas Indicopleustes, who created a map of the world where he reconciled Greek geography to Christian scripture, and Jerusalem is in the middle of the three continents.

Henceforth, this world was in some ways rather parochial in its Christian view. Above all, the pagan gods were demons; the gods had to be exorcised. They cannot in any way be tolerated, hence the crackdown; hence the saints who carry out exorcisms, who cast down demons. My favorite one is Saint Theodore of Sykeon. This was a result of a major crossing in religious perception in which henceforth the divine and the mundane, there was an immense gap between them and they could only be crossed by the holy ones. Henceforth, the world was now Christian in its view; and this view of the divine and the mundane would dictate the Western tradition's ethical and religious outlook down to this day.

But what the pagans would say in the time of Justinian would be the words echoing what Iamblichus of Chalcis noted in the 4th century. Iamblichus's comment was, "The trouble with you Christians is you empty the world of gods and you make it a lonely place." The human and divine no longer interact, henceforth the divine is transcended. It is a great magistry of the universal god, but that god can only be approached by the holy ones and through the imperial Church. This was a change of fundamental consequence for the next 12 centuries, because henceforth the identity of what was a civilized individual in the West was one who was a Christian, who was an heir to this imperial church of Constantine, Theodosius, and Justinian. For the next 12 centuries, the notions of what the divine is, what the ethical system is, how one approaches the divine is that which has come out of the age of Justinian. That is the basis for the religious and ethical values of the West down to this day.

Timeline

40... Parthian invasion; flight of Herod
the Great to Rome; Rome recognizes
Herod as king of the Jews.

37... Herod the Great captures
Jerusalem; Mark Antony confirms
Herod as king of the Jews.

37–4.. Reign of Herod the Great.

31... Battle of Actium; Octavian (Augustus)
reorganizes the Roman East;
Herod's kingship is reconfirmed;
first abandonment of Qumran by
the Essenes due to earthquake.

27... Octavian is acclaimed as
Augustus, Emperor of Rome.

27 B.C.–14 A.D............................... Reign of Augustus.

20... Construction of the Second
Temple commenced by Herod.

c. 10.. Birth of Marcus Julius Agrippa, later
King Herod Agrippa I of Judaea.

c. 6?.. Birth of Jesus Christ
(Joshua bar Joseph).

4.. Death of Herod the Great; division
of the Herodian kingdom.

4 B.C. –6 A.D.................................. Archelaus serves as ethnarch of Judaea.

4 B.C. –34 A.D................................ Philip serves as tetrarch of Iturea.

37–41.. Reign of Emperor Caligula (Gaius);
anti-Jewish policy of Caligula provokes
unrest in Jerusalem and Judaea.

38.. Anti-Jewish riot in Alexandria, Egypt.

c. 40–45.. Heretic Simon Magus *flourit* in Samaria.

41.. Jewish embassy to Claudius in
Rome; accession of Herod Agrippa I
as king of Judaea and Samaria; end
of direct Roman rule in Judaea.

41–54.. Reign of Emperor Claudius.

42.. Martyrdom of James.

44.. Death of Herod Agrippa I;
Rome annexes Judaea again.

46–48.. First Missionary Journey of Paul
and Barnabas; churches founded
in Cyprus, Galatia, and Pisidia.

48.. Council of Jerusalem accepts the
mission to preach to gentiles.

c. 48–62.. Composition of the Pauline
Epistles (Romans, Philippians,
Galatians, 1 and 2 Corinthians, 1
Thessalonians, and Philemon).

49.. Expulsion of the Jews from Rome.

64... Great Fire in Rome; Neronian persecution of Christians.

c. 65–80... Composition of the pastoral Epistles.

66–74... First Jewish Revolt.

68.. Suicide of Nero; civil war in the Roman Empire; Qumran destroyed.

68–69... Year of the Four Emperors.

69–79... Reign of Emperor Vespasian.

70.. Fall of Jerusalem to Titus; end of serious Jewish resistance in Palestine.

73.. Fall of Masada.

c. 75.. Flavius Josephus writes *History of the Jewish War*.

79–81... Reign of Emperor Titus.

c. 80–100....................................... Synoptic Gospels (Mark, Luke, and Matthew) take on their final form.

81–96... Reign of Emperor Domitian.

c. 95–100....................................... Composition of the book of Revelation, the Letter to the Hebrews, and the Catholic Epistles.

c. 93.. Flavius Josephus writes *The Antiquities of the Jews*.

96–98... Reign of Emperor Nerva.

Timeline

c. 125.. Quadratus composes the first work
of Christian apologetics; Hadrian
creates the Panhellenion, the league of
Greek cities with great sanctuaries and
games throughout the Roman world.

c. 130.. Conversion of Justin the Martyr;
composition of the *Letter of Barnabas*;
date of the oldest known papyri
fragments of the Gospels and the
works of Papias; beginning of the
Gnostic schools of Alexandria and
Rome; Basilides *flourit*; first Gnostic
Gospel composed in Egypt.

132–135.. Second Jewish Revolt
(Bar Kochba War).

135.. Destruction of the Temple of Jerusalem;
Jerusalem is turned into the Roman
colony of Aelia Capitolina.

138–161.. Reign of Emperor Antoninus Pius.

c. 140–160.. Marcion of Pontus edits the Gospel of
Luke and the Pauline letters, founding
his own church at Rome; Valentinus is
active at Rome, applying Gnostic-style
interpretation to scripture; school of
Valentinus emerges; imperial rescripts
are issued concerning treatment of
Christians in Macedonia and Achaea.

c. 143.. Marcion writes *Contradictions*.

172...................................... Montanus proclaims his mission and the New Prophecy in Phrygia; rise of the Montanist heresy in Asia Minor.

175...................................... Gnostic Heracleon *flourit*; Hegesippus (anti-Gnostic historian and source of Eusebius) active; writer Tatian *flourit*.

177...................................... Persecution of Christians at Lugdunum (Lyon); Athenagoras writes his apology *Supplication for the Christians*.

178...................................... Celsus writes *True Reason*, a critique of Christianity; Irenaeus becomes Bishop of Lyon.

c. 180................................... Scillian Martyrs at Carthage; Theophilus of Antioch writes his apology *Against Autolycus*; Apollinaris and Miltiades write anti-Montanist tracts; Bishop Avircus Marcellus of Hierapolis takes measures against the Montanists; Catechetical School established at Alexandria; Clement of Alexandria active.

180–192................................. Reign of Emperor Commodus.

185...................................... Birth of Origen; Irenaeus writes *Against Heresies*.

189–199................................. Pope Victor becomes the first Latin-speaking pope.

190–200................................. The first catacombs are constructed in Rome.

193–211 .... Reign of Emperor Septimius Severus.

193–197 .... Roman civil war over succession to Commodus.

c. 195 .... Conversion of Tertullian to Christianity.

195–197 .... First Parthian War of Septimius Severus.

197 .... Tertullian writes *Apology*; local persecutions in Africa.

199–200 .... Second Parthian War of Septimius Severus.

c. 202–206 .... Persecutions in North Africa; Tertullian writes tracts against Gnostics and Marcionites.

203 .... Origen succeeds Clement at the Catechetical School at Alexandria.

205 .... Birth of Plotinus, the Neoplatonic philosopher.

c. 207 .... Tertullian converts to Montanism (a.k.a. the Cataphrygian heresy).

208–211 .... British campaign of Septimius Severus.

211–217 .... Reign of Emperor Caracalla.

212 .... *Constitutio Antoniniana* extends Roman citizenship to all free residents of the empire.

213.. Tertullian writes *Against Praxeas* criticizing the Monarchians.

c. 215... Philostratus writes *Life of Apollonius of Tyana*.

215–217... Parthian War of Caracalla.

215–219... Origen withdraws from Alexandria.

216.. Birth of Mani.

217–218... Reign of Emperor Macrinus.

218–222... Reign of Emperor Elagabalus; introduction of Baal of Emesa (sun god) at Rome.

c. 220–230...................................... Apologist Marcus Minucius Felix *flourit*; Lucius Cassius Dio writes *Roman History*.

222–235... Reign of Emperor Severus Alexander.

c. 229–230...................................... Origen composes *On First Principles*.

230–233... Persian War of Severus Alexander.

c. 230.. Origen departs from Alexandria for Caesarea in Palestine; the heretic Artemon *flourit*.

c. 230–240...................................... Synods of Iconium and Synnada on rebaptism of heretics and schismatics.

232.. Birth of Porphyry of Tyre, disciple of Plotinus and critic of Christians.

Timeline

243–260...Missionary activities of Gregory Thaumaturgus (the Wonderworker) in Pontus and Cappadocia.

244–249...Reign of Emperor Philip I "the Arab"; toleration of Christianity in the empire begins.

248...Millennian Games of Rome celebrated; Origen writes *Against Celsus*; anti-Christian pogroms in Alexandria; first major Gothic incursions in the Balkans.

248–300.."Christians for Christians" funerary monuments in northwest Phrygia.

249–251...Reign of Emperor Decius.

250–251...Decian persecution begins as general orders for sacrifice are circulated throughout the empire and Christian leaders are arrested; Cyprian flees Carthage; Dionysius flees Alexandria; Pope Fabian is arrested and executed.

251...Cyprian reasserts his authority over the African church by council and writes *On the Unity of the Catholic Church*, the first defense of papal leadership; Novatian Schism; defeat and death of Decius at the hands of the Goths ends the persecution; Cornelius is elected pope.

251–253...Reign of emperors Trebonianus Gallus and Volusian.

261–272 .... Paul of Samosata serves as bishop of Antioch.

262–272 .... Eastern Roman provinces fall under the sway of Odenathus and then Zenobia of Palmyra.

262 .... Goths invade the Aegean world and Asia Minor, burning the Artemision of Ephesus.

c. 263 .... Porphyry visits Rome.

264–268 .... Council of Antioch issues three condemnations of Paul of Samosata.

268–270 .... Reign of Claudius II Gothicus; beginning of imperial recovery.

269 .... Claudius defeats the Goths at Naissus (Nish).

270 .... Outbreak of plague; death of Plotinus in Rome; Saint Antony of Egypt withdraws into the desert; Felix I becomes pope.

270–275 .... Reign of Emperor Aurelian.

272 .... Aurelian recovers the eastern provinces from Zenobia; church of Antioch appeals to Aurelian against Paul of Samosata; first imperial intervention in church affairs.

273.. Aurelian recovers the western provinces; restoration of the Roman Empire; Aurelian promotes the cult of Sol Invictus as his comrade (*comes*).

c. 275... Porphyry writes *Against the Christians*.

276–282.. Reign of Emperor Probus.

276.. Mani is executed by King Bahram II of Persia; Manichaean missions spread across the Persian and Roman empires.

c. 280.. Commodian and Anatolius *flourit*.

282–283 .... Reign of Emperor Carus.

283–284.. Reign of Emperor Carinus.

284–305.. Reign of Emperor Diocletian; restoration of imperial order.

285.. Maximian is elevated to Augustus of the West by Diocletian.

293.. Galerius and Constantius I Chlorus elevated as Caesars of East and West, respectively; formation of the first Roman tetrarchy is complete.

296–299.. Persian War of Galerius.

296–304.. Marcellinus serves as pope.

297.. Diocletian issues an edict of persecution of Manicheans.

298–302.. Christians are forced to resign from the Roman army and administration.

c. 300... Reputed conversion of the royal family of Armenia by Gregory the Illuminator.

c. 300–318...................................... Lactantius *flourit*

301... Diocletian issues the Edict of Maximum Prices.

303... Diocletian issues three edicts of persecution of Christians, initiating the Great Persecution.

304... Diocletian's fourth edict of persecution is issued, ordering general sacrifice; apostasy of Pope Marcellinus.

305... Abdications of Diocletian and Maximianus; accession of Galerius and Constantius I as Augusti; accession of Severus II as Caesar in the West and Maximinus II Daza as Caesar in the East.

306... Fifth edict of persecution is issued in the East; Maximinus II reorganizes pagan cults in the East; Constantius I orders toleration for Christians in Rome and Africa; death of Constantius I; Western army proclaims Constantine I "the Great" emperor while Maxentius is proclaimed emperor at Rome; civil war breaks out.

306–312.. Reign of Emperor Maxentius.

316.. Constantine acquits Caecilian; Donatist opposition forms in North Africa.

c. 318... Outbreak of Arian Controversy.

321–324.. Persecution of Christians by Licinius in the East.

323... Pachomius organizes the first ascetic community at Tabennisi in Upper Egypt; growth of cenobitism.

324... Battle of Chrysopolis marks the final victory of Constantine in the East; Eusebius revises his *Historia ecclesiastica*.

325... Council of Nicaea condemns Arius.

329–373.. Athanasius becomes patriarch of Alexandria.

330... Dedication of Constantinople, the "New Rome," as the Christian capital; Athanasius moves against the Meletians.

330–337.. Constantine issues edicts against certain pagan practices.

335... Council of Tyre condemns Athanasius; exile of Athanasius to Treveri (Trier); Constantine accepts Arian views; Constantine celebrates *tricennalia* in Jerusalem.

342	Imperial prohibition of pagan sacrifices; at the Arian Council of Sardica, Arian missionaries are promoted within and beyond the Roman Empire; Ulfilas translates the Bible into Gothic; conversion of the Goths, Gepidae, and Vandals to Arian Christianity.
344–46	Julian studies at Marcellum.
346	Return of Athanasius to Alexandria; death of Pachomius and spread of the monastic movement; Julian commences study at Nicomedia.
348	Council of Carthage; "Catholic" ascendency in North Africa.
350	Usurpation of Magnentius in the West; death of Constans.
351	Constantius II defeats Magnentius at the Battle of Mursa and reoccupies the Italian Peninsula; Constantius Gallus becomes Caesar in the East; Julian studies with Maximus at Ephesus; final conversion of Julian to paganism.
353	Final defeat and death of Magnentius; reunification of the Roman Empire under Constantius II.
354	Birth of Augustine.
354–358	Germanic invasions of Gaul.

Timeline

363.. Publication of *Misopogon*; failure of
                                                     the Roman offensive against Ctesiphon;
                                                     retreat and death of Julian II; peace
                                                     with Persia; Romans surrender Nisibis.

363–364.. Reign of Emperor Jovian,
                                                     a Nicene Christian.

364–366.. Return and fifth exile of Athanasius.

364–375.. Reign of Emperor Valentinian
                                                     I, a Nicene, in the West.

364–378.. Reign of Emperor Valens,
                                                     an Arian, in the East.

366–367.. Usurpation of the imperial
                                                     throne by Procopius.

366–384.. Pontificate of Damasus.

367.. Elevation of Gratian as Augustus;
                                                     Ausonius becomes tutor of Gratian.

c. 370–79.. Basil of Caesarea *flourit*.

373.. Consecration of Ambrose as bishop
                                                     of Milan; death of Athanasius;
                                                     consecration of Gregory of
                                                     Nazianzus as bishop of Sasima.

374.. Jerome retires to the desert
                                                     of Chalcis; consecration of
                                                     Gregory as bishop of Nyssa.

384.. Conflict between Valentinian
II and Ambrose.

384–387.. Augustine at Milan.

385.. Condemnation and execution of
Priscillian; Jerome arrives in Bethlehem.

386.. Augustine returns to
Catholic Christianity.

388.. Defeat and death of Magnus
Maximus; restoration of legitimate
imperial rule in the West.

390.. Massacre at Thessalonica; Ambrose
forces the penance of Theodosius I

391.. Edict of Theodosius I closes
the pagan temples and outlaws
sacrifices; Christian riots destroy
the Serapeum in Alexandria.

392.. Revolt of Eugenius in the West begins,
backed by the Western army and
pagan Roman senators; renewed anti-
pagan and anti-heretical legislation
is issued by Theodosius I; Theodore
is made bishop of Mopsuestia.

394.. Battle of the Frigidus ends the
revolt in the West; Theodosius
I reunites the Roman Empire;
Donatist Council at Bagai.

395.. Death of Theodosius I; division
of Roman Empire.

412.. Consecration of Cyril as patriarch of
                                                    Alexandria; emergence of Alexandria
                                                    as the leading see of the East.

413.. Beginning of construction of the
                                                    land walls of Constantinople.

415.. Constantius, *magister militum*
                                                    of the West, campaigns in Gaul;
                                                    murder of Hypatia in Alexandria;
                                                    imperial edict bars pagans from
                                                    military and civil positions.

415–421.. Stabilization of the Western Empire.

416–418.. Visigoths invade Spain

c. 420–440?..................................... Anglo-Saxon migrations
                                                    into Britain begin.

423.. Death of Honorius; accession
                                                    of Usurper John; political
                                                    crisis in the West.

425.. Valentinian III is placed on the Western
                                                    throne by the Eastern Roman army.

428.. Consecration of Nestorius as
                                                    patriarch of Constantinople.

429.. Germanus visits Britain; Gaiseric and
                                                    the Vandals conquer North Africa;
                                                    Nestorius and Cyril's debate over
                                                    Christology leads to the outbreak
                                                    of the Nestorian Controversy.

449.. Dioscurus proclaims the Monophysite Christology during the Latrocinium ("Robber Council") of Ephesus; deposition of Flavian; Pope Leo I writes his *Tome* in support of Flavian.

450.. Death of Theodosius II; accession of Marcian as emperor in the East; Attila delivers ultimatum to Court of Ravenna.

451.. Aetius checks Attila's invasion of Gaul at the Battle of Chalons; Orthodox Christology of Two Natures is proclaimed at the Fourth Ecumenical Council at Chalcedon; deposition of Dioscorus; Jerusalem is raised to Patriarchical status; Constantinople is recognized as the "New Rome"; anti-Chalcedonian riots in Syria and Egypt.

452.. Attila and the Huns invade the Italian Peninsula; embassy of Pope Leo I to Attila; withdrawal of the Hun army from the peninsula; Leo rejects Canon 28 of Chalcedon; Death of Attila and the collapse of Hun Empire.

455.. Death of Valentinian III leads to dynastic and political confusion in the Western Empire; Vandals sack Rome; Avitus becomes emperor in the West; Ricimer, *magister militum*, manipulates the imperial throne.

457–461.. Reign of Emperor Majorian in the West.

457–473.. Reign of Emperor Leo I in the East.

476	Odoacer deposes Romulus Augustus and recognizes Zeno as the sole emperor; end of the Western Roman Empire.
482	Zeno proclaims the Henoticon; Monophysite Peter Mongo becomes patriarch of Alexandria.
483	Consecration of Pope Felix III; Vandals persecute Orthodox Christians.
484	Felix condemns the Henoticon and excommunicates Acacius; Acacius excommunicates Felix III; Zeno moves toward reconciliation with the Monophysites.
484–488	Revolt of Leontius and Illus in Asia Minor.
484–519	Acacian Schism.
489–491	Theodoric and the Ostrogoths conquer the Italian Peninsula.
491–518	Reign of Emperor Anastasius I.
496–498	Failure of Anastasius to end the Acacian Schism.
c. 498	Conversion of Clovis and the Franks to Catholic Christianity.
502	Mission of the nine saints to Ethiopia.

Timeline

530... Belisarius defeats the Persians
at the Battle of Daras.

532... Nika Revolt and the destruction of
Hagia Sophia; "Perpetual Peace" is
concluded with Shah Chosroes I;
abortive conference with Monophysite
leaders at Constantinople.

533... Belisarius retakes North Africa from
the Vandals; publication of *Digest*.

534... Publication of the revised
Codex Justinianus.

535... Belisarius invades Sicily; imperial
laws against are declared against
heretics in North Africa.

536... Belisarius invades the Italian
Peninsula and reoccupies Rome;
outbreak of the Great Mutiny
in North Africa; Goths depose
Theodahad and elect Wittigis king.

537... Deposition of Pope Silverius
by Belisarius; election of Pope
Vigilius; dedication of Hagia
Sophia; Gothic siege of Rome.

538–540.. Renewed imperial offensive
in the Italian Peninsula.

540... Belisarius captures Ravenna;
outbreak of the Second Persian
War; Persians sack Antioch.

553.. Fifth Ecumenical Council at
Constantinople; condemnation
of the Three Chapters; arrest and
imprisonment of Vigilius; imperial
forces recover southern Spain.

554.. Narses issues the Pragmatic
Sanction; reorganization of the Italian
Peninsula; Vigilius's *Constitutum*
and exile; alienation of Western
and Monophysite churches.

555–561... Pontificate of Pelagius I.

558.. Replacement of the Great
Dome of Hagia Sophia; raids
of Kotrigurs in the Balkans.

562.. Justinian and Chosroes I conclude the
Fifty-Year Peace; third purge of pagans
from Justinian's administration.

565.. Initiation of new discussions
with Monophysites; Justinian
proposes the Apthartodocetist
doctrine; death of Justinian.

565–578... Reign of Emperor Justin II.

Glossary

acropolis: A Greek city's citadel and location of its main temples.

adventus: "Arrival"; the ceremony of official welcome extended by a provincial city to the Roman emperor between the 2nd and 4th centuries A.D. The cult statues of the leading civic gods were often presented on the emperor's arrival.

aei gennetos: "Eternally generated"; term used by Origen in *On First Principles* to explain the relationship between God the father and the Christ-*logos* in the Trinity.

agora: The market and public center of a Greek city, equivalent to a Roman forum.

amphitheater: A freestanding Roman structure built for spectacles, notably gladiatorial and animal combats. It is the largest building in any Roman city. The Colosseum (Flavian Amphitheater) at Rome, dedicated in 80 A.D., is the largest example.

aniconic: An outlook rejecting the representation of the divine by images.

apatheia: Apathy; detachment from emotions, the highest state of enlightenment for a Stoic. *See* **Stoicism**.

apocalypse: "Revealing what is hidden"; in Jewish and Christian literature and thought, the final reckoning of God. The book of Revelation is a prophecy of the apocalypse.

apologist: Defender; a Christian writer who penned defenses against pagan criticism. The most important of the early apologists were Justin the Martyr (103–165), who wrote in Greek, and Tertullian (160–220), who wrote in Latin.

apostate: "One standing apart"; one who has renounced his or her original faith. The emperor Julian (360–363), for example, was born and baptized a Christian but is called the Apostate because he renounced Christianity and embraced the pagan gods.

apostle: From Greek *apostolos*, *stello* meaning "sending away" in the diplomatic or military sense. Christians used the term to denote the original followers of Jesus who established the first churches.

archbishop: The highest bishop of the metropolis of a Roman (and therefore ecclesiastical) province with authority over bishops in the dioceses of his province. Called a metropolitan in Orthodox Christianity.

Arianism: The doctrine of Arius (c. 250–336) that maintains Christ is lesser in substance to God the father. The doctrine was rejected at the First Ecumenical Council in 325 and again at the Second Ecumenical Council in 381.

Artemision: A temple of Artemis, more specifically the one near Ephesus considered one of the Seven Wonders of the Ancient World.

Asclepieion: A sanctuary to Asclepius, god of healing; the most celebrated ones were at Epidaurus, on the island of Cos, and outside of Pergamon.

atheism: "Denying gods"; term applied by pagans to Christians who denied the ancestral gods.

Avesta: The liturgical texts of Zoroastrianism that survive in later, redacted versions from between the 3rd and 9th centuries A.D. The oldest hymns of the Avesta, the Gathas, are believed to have been composed by Zoroaster in the 6th century B.C.

Baal: "Lord"; the pious title of respect accorded to a city's leading god in the Semitic-speaking provinces of the Roman Empire.

baetyl: An aniconic representation of a god (*baal*) in the Semitic-speaking provinces of the Roman Empire.

basilica: A Roman public building with apses at each end and a central hall, or narthex. The design was applied to a Christian church in the 4th century. The longitudinal axis of the basilica was distinct from the centrally planned church in the form of square with a dome at the intersection—the design favored in the middle and late Byzantine ages.

bishop: The ordained leader of the church of a diocese. The first known bishop is Ignatius of Antioch (d. A.D. 107). The bishops of Rome, Alexandria, and Antioch claimed an apostolic succession to Saint Peter, and so their dioceses were recognized as Petrine Sees at the Second Ecumenical Council of Constantinople in 381.

boule (pl. *boulai*): Council, either elected or chosen by lot, that summoned the assembly of citizens and supervised officials.

bouleuterion: A council hall.

Byzantine: Of the Eastern Roman Empire.

Byzantium: The name of the Greek colony founded on the site of modern Istanbul in 668 B.C. In A.D. 330, Emperor Constantine the Great refounded the city as Constantinople, or New Rome. Byzantium is applied to the Eastern Roman civilization of the 4th through 15th centuries to distinguish it from the parent state of Rome.

canon: From Greek *kanon*, "a rod," hence a measuring stick; those Christian books of supreme authority in which dogma is revealed.

Catechetical School: Founded at Alexandria, Egypt, c. 190, the first Christian school to train theologians and clergy.

Catholic: "Universal"; term used to designate the Western medieval Latin-speaking church that accepted the doctrines of the Fourth Ecumenical Council (451) and the primacy of the pope at Rome. *See also* **Orthodox**.

Cenobium: "Living together"; the first communal centers of ascetics organized by Saint Pachomius (280–346) in Egypt.

Chaldaean Oracles: An allegorical poem in Greek hexameter, this inspired revelation was attributed to Julianus the Chaldaean, who was reputed to have lived in the time of Marcus Aurelius (r. 161–180). Neoplatonists from Porphyry on considered a sacred book of theurgy. The poem was apparently penned by Neoplatonists influenced by Syrian solar cults, middle Platonic theurgy, and even contemporary Jewish ideas.

Christogram: The combined Greek letters chi and rho, the first two letters of *Christos*. Before the Battle of Milvian Bridge, Constantine applied this symbol to his military standard (vexillum) and so created a Christian banner, or labarum.

Christology: The theology of the two natures (human and divine) of Christ.

collegium (pl. **collegia**): A Roman burial society to which members contribute and celebrate rites with ritual meals.

commune: From Greek *koinon*, a league of cities with a province devoted to the worship of the Roman imperial family.

consecratio: Consecration; the rite of deifying a deceased emperor.

Constitutio Antoniniana de Civitate: Edict of A.D. 212 issued by Emperor Caracalla extending Roman citizenship to all free residents of the empire.

consul: One of two annually elected senior officials of the Roman Republic with the right to command an army (imperium). A consul became a proconsul whenever his term of office was prorogued or extended. *See also* **proconsul**.

Corinthian order: The most ornate classical architectural order favored by the Romans.

cosmology: From Greek *kosmos*, "ordering"; the study or theology of the creation and operation of the universe.

council: A meeting of prelates and theologians to determine dogma. *See* **ecumenical council**.

Cybele (a.k.a. **Kubaba**): The great mother goddess of Anatolia, whose principal shrine was at Pessinus. She was known to the Romans as the Great Mother (Magna Mater).

cynicism: From *cynos*, "dog"; the Greek philosophy of Diogenes of Sinope (c. 412–323 B.C.) that rejected the material world.

deacon: From Greek *diakonos*; an assistant, lay or ordained, to the clergy in the Roman world.

decurions: The landed civic elites defined as capable of holding municipal office with wealth assessed in excess of 25,000 denarii or one-tenth the property qualification of a Roman senator.

Demiurge: "Craftsman"; the term used by Plato in his dialogue *Timaeus* (c. 360 B.C.) to describe the creator God.

Deutero-Pauline letters: Letters attributed to Saint Paul that were likely written by his disciples. These are Colossians, Ephesians, 2 Thessalonians, Hebrews, 1 and 2 Timothy, and Titus.

Diaspora: "Scattering"; the settlements of Jews living outside the homeland in the Hellenistic and Roman ages.

Diatessaron: The Syriac translation of the four canonical Gospels into a single, reconciled narrative by Tatian (c. 120–180).

Didachē: From Greek, "instruction"; a treatise of the early 2nd century, probably written in Syria, dealing with ritual and discipline within the early church.

dike: "Justice"; first expressed in the poems of Hesiod (c. 700 B.C.). It is the rule of law in a *polis*, and the virtue was personified as a goddess.

divus/diva (m. pl. *divi*; fem. pl. *divae*): Latin for "defied one"; the spirit (*genius*) of an emperor or member of the imperial family that was, on his funeral pyre, taken to join the gods. This deification was confirmed by a decree of the Senate.

Docetists: From Greek *dokein*, "to seem"; Christian heretics who maintained that the physical body of Jesus only appeared to have been crucified. This view is often regarded as Gnostic because it is premised on a material view of evil. *See* **dualism**.

dogma: Greek for "that which is surmised"; a religion's established beliefs.

Dominate: The late Roman Empire (284–476), in which the emperor ruled as an autocrat or lord (dominus). The designation is used in contrast to the Principate (27 B.C.–A.D. 284), when emperors ruled like magistrates of a Roman Republic. *See* **Principate**.

Donatists: Followers of Donatus, the bishop of Carthage in Roman North Africa, who maintained that Christians who lapsed and sacrificed to pagan gods during the persecution of 303–313 must be re-baptized.

Doric order: The austere architectural order used for Greek temples and favored in the Peloponnese.

dualist: One who believes in a stark division between a good spiritual world and an evil physical or material world. Gnostic teachers were apparently dualists in their cosmology. Zoroastrianism is premised on a dualist view of an eternal conflict between the creator god of good, Ahura Mazdā, and the evil destructive spirit Ahriman.

ecumenical council: A world council summoned by the Roman emperor to determine Christian dogma. The First Ecumenical Council at Nicaea (325) and the Second at Constantinople (381) proclaimed the Trinity and rejected Arianism. The Third Ecumenical Council at Ephesus (431) proclaimed the Virgin Mary as the mother of God (Theotokos) and rejected Nestorianism. The Fourth Ecumenical Council at Chalcedon (451) defined the two natures of Christ and rejected Monophysitism.

Edict of Milan: The imperial rescript issued jointly by Constantine I and Licinius I in 313 that ended the Great Persecutions and recognized Christianity as a religion.

ekkesia: An assembly of all citizens of a *polis* with the right to vote for laws and elect magistrates. Christians adapted the word to designate a church or congregation.

emanation: One generation of the descending levels of reality from the One in the great chain of being posited by Plotinus (205–270).

Enneads: The writings of Plotinus (205–270) as collected and edited by Porphyry of Tyre.

epibatereion: Greek for "the boarding"; the spring ceremony to Isis at the start of the sailing season.

epigraphy: The scholarly study of inscriptions.

epiphany: From Greek *epiphanein*, "to appear"; the appearance of a divinity within its cult statue when sacrifices and prayers were offered.

Episcopal: Matters concerning a bishop.

episkopos (pl. *episkopoi*): Greek for "overseer"; a bishop.

equestrian: The landed property class of Roman citizens (assessed at 100,000 denarii) who stood below the senatorial order in the Principate. They provided the jurists, officials, and army officers of the imperial government.

eschaton: Greek for "last"; the ultimate reckoning by God.

Essenes: Members of an ascetic Jewish sect, called a "philosophy" by Josephus, from the 2nd century B.C. to 1st century A.D. Some scholars have attributed the composition of the Dead Sea Scrolls to the Essenes.

evangelist: From Greek *eu anglein*, "well-bringer," or bringer of good news; bringer of the faith of Christ.

evocatio: Latin for "calling out"; the Roman ceremony of winning over the gods of a foe with promises of temples and votive offerings. The ceremony was performed by a magistrate with imperium—the right to command an army.

Frigidus, Battle of: The victory of Theodosius I over the rebel Western army of Eugenius and the magister militum Arbogast on September 5–6, 394. It was hailed as a victory of Christianity over paganism.

genius: Latin for "spirit"; The spirit of each man. The genius of the emperor may be defied upon his death and consecration. Juno is the spirit of each woman. *See* **divus**.

Gnostics: From Greek *gnostikos*, "knowledgeable"; mystics and teachers with a deeper esoteric knowledge of religious texts and therefore of the path to salvation. Many Gnostics premised their cosmology on dualist beliefs. *See* **dualism**.

Great Persecution: The empire-wide persecutions of Christians ordered by Emperor Decius in 250–251, Valerian in 258–260, and the tetrarchs in 303–313.

gymnosophist: Greek for "naked wise men"; the classical name for the holy men of India, particularly Buddhist ascetics.

Hasmonaean: The royal dynasty of Judaea, founded by Simon Maccabaeus in 165 B.C. and ruling until 37 B.C. when Herod the Great seized power in the Jewish homeland.

Hellene, Hellenic: The name Greeks apply to themselves.

Hellenistic: Greek-like; the period between the death of Alexander the Great and the Battle of Actium (i.e., 323–31 B.C.). It also denotes the civilization of this period, which was fusion of Hellenic and Near Eastern traditions.

Glossary

henotheism: The religious outlook regarding traditional pagan gods as aspects of a single transcendent godhead. This was the religious vision of the Neoplatonic philosopher Plotinus and the emperor Julian II.

heresiarch: The leader of a heretical sect of Christians.

heresiologist: A Christian author who writes about and refutes heresies.

heresy: From Greek *hairere*, "to choose"; a doctrine condemned by formal council as outside accepted Christian theology and teachings.

Hexapla: Greek for "sixfold"; a set of texts complied by Origen (185–254) to establish the canonical text of the Old Testament. It comprised the Hebrew text, the Hebrew transliterated into Greek letters, and the translations in Greek of Aquila of Sinope, Symmachus the Ebionite, the Septuagint, and Theodotian.

hippodrome: A stadium for chariot races.

hodēgētria: Any icon of Mary Theotokos (Mary, mother of God), but it referred to the icon reputedly painted by Saint Luke that was the palladium of Constantinople from 626 on.

homoiousia: From Greek for "similar substance"; the term used by Arians to define the Christ logos as inferior to the father in the Trinity.

homoousia: From Greek for "same substance"; the term used by Nicene Christians to define the Christ logos as identical in essence to the father in the Trinity.

honestiores: Latin for "more honorable ones"; an order of society in later Roman law accorded privileges and exemptions from torture in criminal proceedings.

humiliores: Latin for "more humble ones" an order of society in later Roman law subject to direct taxation and, in criminal proceedings, to torture and corporal punishment.

icon: The depiction of Christ, Mary Theotokos, or a saint on perishable material to which believer prays for intercession before God.

iconoclast: "Destroyer of icons"; those who argued that icons were idols and should be removed from Christian worship, particularly in the years 726–843.

iconodule: "Servant of icons"; those favoring the use of icons as means of intercession.

interpretatio Graeca: The identification of a local god with a Greek equivalent.

interpertatio Romana: The assimilation of a local god into the Roman equivalent.

Ionic order: Architectural order favored by Greek cities of Asia Minor.

kairos: To the pagan Greeks, an opportune moment, believed to be the gift of the gods. For Christian writers, the period of the ministry and crucifixion of Jesus that transcends strict linear time (*chronos*).

Koine: From Greek *koinē*, "common"; the vernacular, simplified Greek spoken in the Hellenistic world and the Roman Empire. The books of the New Testament are written in Koine Greek rather than the archaizing literary Greek of the upper classes.

labarum: The Roman military banner (vexillum) carrying the Christogram. Constantine ordered its creation before the Battle of Milvian Bridge in 312.

lapsus (pl. *lapsi*): Latin for "lapsed"; Christians who sacrificed to pagan gods during the persecutions.

Lares: The guardian spirits of Roman homes, settlements, and roads. *See also* **penates.**

legion: The main formation of the army of the Roman Republic and Principate. Each legion (of 5,400 men) comprised professional swordsmen and specialists, all Roman citizens. The auxiliaries (*auxilia*) were provincial units providing cavalry, archers, and light armed infantry.

liturgy: From Greek *leitourgia* (in Latin, *munera*), "service for the people"; a civic or religious obligation assumed by citizens out of patriotism. For Christians, denotes the pattern of worship. *See **philotimia** and **philopatris**.*

Logos: Greek for "word"; in Stoic philosophy, the divine active intelligence of the universe. Christians (based on John 1:1) applied the term to Christ as the second person of the Trinity.

Manichaean: A follower of the dualist faith of the prophet Mani (216–276) who taught a universal monotheism often dismissed by Christian writers as a heresy.

martyr: Greek for "witness"; a Christian who refused to sacrifice to the gods and renounce Christianity in a Roman legal proceeding. The martyr was consigned to the arena.

Messiah: Hebrew for "anointed one"; in Jewish Apocalyptic literature, the Messiah is a descendant of King David who will restore Israel. The Greek equivalent is *Christos*.

metropolitan: The equivalent of an archbishop in the Orthodox Church.

Milvian Bridge, **Battle of**: The victory of Constantine the Great over his rival Maxentius north of Rome on October 28, 312. Constantine credited his victory to the Christian God.

Misopogon: "Beard Hater"; the satirical tract written by the pagan emperor Julian to refute his Christian detractors at Antioch in 362. Julian was jeered at for sporting the long beard of a pagan philosopher.

mission: From Latin *mittere*, "one having been sent," especially in a diplomatic or military sense; the term was adapted by Christians to denote preaching the faith.

Mithraism: The Roman cult of the god Mithras, originally a Persian god of oaths. The cult was popular among Roman soldiers and customs officials in the 1st–4th centuries A.D.

monophysis: Greek for "single nature"; The doctrine stressing the single, divine nature of Christ from which the Monophysites got their name. This became the doctrine of the Egyptian, Armenian, Syriac, and Ethiopian churches.

Mos maiorum: Latin for "custom of the ancestors"; the Roman expression for the superior authority of traditional religious and social practices.

Montanism: The Christian heresy of Montanus, who in 157 or 172, proclaimed direct inspiration from the Holy Spirit. Also called the New Prophecy.

mystery cults: In older scholarship, this name was given to certain pagan sects seen as ecstatic, irrational cults that displaced traditional worship in anticipation of Christianity. Mystery cults had initiation rites and conformed to general pagan expectations of piety.

necropolis: Greek for "city of the dead"; cemeteries outside the walls of a Greek or Roman city. This was intended to prevent ritual pollution of the living.

neokoros: Greek for "temple-warden"; A Greek city possessed of a temple dedicated to the Roman emperor.

Neoplatonism: The Platonic philosophical doctrines as interpreted by Plotinus (205–270) and later philosophers.

Nestorianism: The followers of Nestorius, patriarch of Constantinople from 429 to 431, who argued that Mary was the mother of Christ the human (Christotokos), rather than mother of Christ the God (Theotokos). Nestorius's views were rejected at the Third Ecumenical Council at Ephesus in 431. *See* **Theotokos**.

New Prophecy: *See* **Montanism**.

nous: Greek for "mind"; The second level of reality—rational intelligence—in middle Platonic and Neoplatonic philosophy.

numismatics: The scholarly study of coins.

oikoumene: Greek for "inhabited"; the universal Christian world.

One, the: In Greek, "*to hen*"; term used by Plotinus (205–270) to define the ultimate, infinite divine reality that is the source of all creation by emanation.

ordo (pl. **ordines**): A legal class of citizens according to Roman law, or the town council of a Roman colony or municipality.

Orthodox: Greek for "correct"; the term used to designate the primarily Greek-speaking church of the Byzantine Empire that accepted the doctrines of the Council of Chalcedon (451). It was extended to include those Slavic and other churches that acknowledged the spiritual authority of the patriarch of Constantinople.

pagan: From Latin *pagus* (pl. *pagi*), "a rural district"; a worshiper of the ancestral gods.

Panhellenion: The religious league of Greek sanctuaries founded by Emperor Hadrian (r. 117–138).

patriarch: Greek for "paternal ruler"; the Greek equivalent of the Latin pope (from *papa*, "father"). The patriarch of Constantinople is the head of the Orthodox Church.

Pauline letters: The seven letters of the New Testament written by Saint Paul in about A.D. 48–65: Romans, 1 and 2 Corinthians, Galatians, Philippians, 1 Thessalonians, and Philemon. *See also* **Deutero-Pauline letters**.

Peace of the Church: The period between the persecution of Valerian and that of the tetrarchs (260–303). It is regarded as the golden age by Christian writers.

penates: Roman guardian spirits of the hearth. *See also* **Lares**.

Petrine Sees: The five great apostolic sees founded by Peter or his disciples. The order was fixed at the Fourth Ecumenical Council as Rome, Constantinople, Alexandria, Antioch, and Jerusalem. Rome claims primacy, and Constantinople claims equality with Rome.

Pharisees: Jewish teachers and moral leaders who interpreted the Torah more broadly and dominated the synagogues of the Diaspora from the 2nd century B.C. onward. Pharisee Judaism became the basis for Rabbinical Judaism after A.D. 70.

philotimia and *philopatris*: The prized public virtues of a *polis*—love of honor and love of country that motivated public gift giving and service.

polis (pl. *poleis*): City-state; the Greek political community that permitted citizens to live according to the rule of law and so distinguished Greeks from other peoples.

presbyter: From Greek *presbyteros*, "elder"; often used in classical Greek for an ambassador. It was a term used in synagogues and early churches to denote a senior minister.

Principate: The Early Roman Empire (27 B.C.–A.D. 284), when the emperor, styled as the princeps ("prince"), ruled as the first citizen of a republic. *See* **Dominate**.

psyche: Greek for "soul"; the Greek philosophical term for the eternal soul. In middle Platonic and Neoplatonic cosmology, the world soul is the third reality below the divine mind (nous).

rescript: The response of a Roman emperor to a petition that had the force of law.

rigorist: A Jewish or Christian sectarian who argues for strict adherence to doctrine as the only path to salvation or enlightenment.

sacramentum: Latin for "oath," particularly the annual oath sworn by Roman army to the emperor.

Sadducees: Members of the Jewish upper classes from the mid-2nd century B.C. through the late 1st century A.D. who practiced strict ritual purity, maintenance of the sacrifices at the temple, and adherence to the Torah.

Sanhedrin: The governing religious council at Jerusalem first reported in the reign of the Hasmonaean king Alexander Jannaeus (103–76 B.C.).

Sāsānid: The dynasty of shahs who ruled the New Persian Empire (227–642).

schism: From Greek for "cutting"; a dispute resulting in mutual excommunication that arose over matters of church discipline or organization rather than theology. *See* **heresy**.

Second Sophistic movement: Late 1st century A.D. cultural movement among the Greek elite classes of the Roman Empire to revive Attic Greek and classical arts and aesthetics.

senator: A member of the aristocratic families of Rome of the highest property qualification (250,000 denarii) who sat in the Senate and served in the high offices of state.

Senatus consultum: Decree of the Senate; a resolution by the Roman Senate that gave its backing to a proposed law.

Septuagint: Greek for 70; the earliest translation of the Hebrew Bible into Koine Greek, created during the 3rd century B.C. It was produced at Alexandria and by 70 interpreters—hence the name.

Serapeum (a.k.a. **Serapeion**): A temple of Serapis, the Hellenized Osiris who was the tutelary god of Alexandria, Egypt. The destruction of the Serapeum of Alexandria by Christians in 391 marked a major defeat for paganism.

Shepherd of Hermas: A Christian tract written in Greek in the early 2nd century A.D. that reports the visions of Hermas, a freedman and brother of Bishop Pius of Rome.

sophist: Greek for "wise one"; a learned writer and thinker of the Greek elite classes in the Roman Eastern provinces. Sophists promoted the Second Sophistic movement.

sortition: The selection of officials by lot, characteristic of Greek constitutions.

Stoicism: The philosophical doctrines of Zeno of Citium (334–262 B.C.). Zeno could not afford a school, so he taught under the public stoas—hence the name of the philosophy.

strategos (pl. **strategoi**): Greek for "general"; the leading magistrate of a Greek city, annually elected.

synagogue: From Greek *synagoge*, "gathering together"; a consecrated prayer space in Judaism. The synagogue did not replace the Temple of Jerusalem.

syncretism: From Greek for "mixing with"; the identification of one's national gods with their counterparts of other peoples, so that Roman Jupiter was equated with Greek Zeus, Syrian Baal, and Egyptian Amon, for example. Such an outlook encouraged diversity in pagan worship rather than an incipient monotheism.

synnaos: Greek for "temple sharing"; the placement of a cult statue of the Roman emperor within a temple of a city god.

synod: From Greek *synodos*, "sitting around"); a regional council of bishops.

synoecism: A union of villages and towns to form a single *polis*.

Synoptic Gospels: The Gospels of Mark, Luke, and Matthew, composed between A.D. 75 and 85, which offer a synopsis of the ministry and crucifixion of Jesus.

taurobolium: A votive sacrifice of a bull or pig to the goddess Cybele; it was misrepresented by the Christian critic Prudentius, writing around A.D. 400, as distorted blood baptism.

tetrarchy: Rule of four; the collective imperial rule established by Diocletian in 285, with two senior Augusti and two junior Caesars.

theophobeis: Greek for "God-fearers"; pagans who accepted Jewish monotheism without converting to Judaism.

theos (pl. ***theoi***) Greek for "god"; used as hyperbole to describe the Roman emperor. It is often used to designate Zeus or the principal god of a city without implying monotheism.

Theotokos: Greek for "mother of God"; title designating Mary as the mother of the human and divine natures of Christ, accepted at the Third Ecumenical Council (431).

theurgy: The esoteric practices of the enlightened Neoplatonist who understands how traditional rites have a deeper meaning to achieve mystical union with the One.

Three Chapters: Select passages from the works of Theodore of Mopsuestia, Theodoret of Cyrrhus, and Ibas of Edessa that were condemned as Nestorian at the Fifth Ecumenical Council in 553. Emperor Justinian (527–565) had hoped to use this issue as a means to win over the Monophysites to the imperial church.

Torah: The five books of the Bible that constitute the Law of Moses (Genesis, Exodus, Leviticus, Numbers, and Deuteronomy). Known in Greek as the Pentateuch.

votive offerings: Gifts promised to the gods in return for the granting of a favor expressed in a prayer.

Vulgate: The Latin translation of the Bible by Saint Jerome (347–420) that was used in the medieval West.

Yahweh: The Hebrew name for God, often written as four consonants (the Tetragrammaton) and not pronounced aloud when reading the Torah.

Zealot: From Greek *zelotes*, "emulator"; a member of a Jewish sect promoting rebellion against Rome to bring about the restoration of Israel under a messiah.

Zoroastrianism: The universal monotheism of Iran attributed to the teacher Zoroaster, who lived in the 6th century B.C. and reformed as the state religion of the Sāsānid Empire (227–642). *See also* **Avesta**.

Biographical Notes

Aelia Pulcheria (399–453): Sister of Emperor Theodosius II (r. 408–450) and wife of Emperor Marcian (r. 450–457); she defined the role of a Christian empress. Created Augusta in 414, she directed policy for her weak-willed brother and upheld Orthodox positions at Ephesus (431) and Chalcedon (451).

Aelius Aristides (117–180): Greek rhetorician, orator, and stylist of the Second Sophistic movement. Born at Hadriani, Mysia, in northwestern Asia Minor. After traveling widely, including a visit to Rome, he settled at Smyrna. His poor health turned him into a hypochondriac so that he was devoted to Serapis and the healing god Asclepius. His surviving works include speeches on religious and political life, his *Sacred Tales*, and poems. Foremost of his orations are *Panatheneia* and *To Rome*.

Alexander of Abonouteichos (c. 105–c. 170): Charlatan philosopher who founded the cult of the serpent god Glycon in northern Asia Minor. He gained the patronage of Emperor Marcus Aurelius and the contempt of Lucian, who wrote a satirical critique of Alexander and the cult of Glycon.

Alexander the Great (356–323 B.C.; r. 336–323 B.C.): King of Macedon and captain general of the Hellenic League; conquered the Persian Empire in 334–324 B.C. and so founded the Hellenistic world. In about 324 B.C., Greek cities offered divine honors to Alexander and so created the ruler cults of the Hellenistic world.

Ambrose of Milan (a.k.a. **Aurelius Ambrosius**; 337–397): Saint and staunch opponent of Arianism who was elected bishop of Milan in 374. He was mentor to the young Emperor Valentinian II (r. 375–392) and advocated measures against pagan worship. In 390, he compelled Emperor Theodosius I to seek penance for permitting the massacre of citizens of Thessalonica by Gothic soldiers. Ambrose was also patron to Augustine of Hippo.

Ammianus Marcellinus (330–395): Soldier and last great pagan historian of Rome. Born in Antioch, Ammianus served under emperors from Constantius II (r. 337-361) to Theodosius I (r. 379–395). He composed a history in 31 books (of which books 1–12 are lost) covering Roman history from A.D. 96 to 378. Ammianus displays exceptional objectivity in discussing the pagan revival by Emperor Julian (r. 360–363), so that his account is fundamental to the religious history of the 4th century.

Anicetus (fl. 2nd century A.D.): Pope (r. 150–167) who summoned the first reported synod of the Roman church to condemn Marcion and Montanists.

Antony of Egypt (c. 260–357): Early Christian monastic and saint. Born of a wealthy Greco-Egyptian family, Antony embraced an ascetic life in the Libyan desert from c. 280. His example inspired many Christians to embrace the ascetic life. In about 360, Patriarch Athanasius of Alexandria wrote a life of Antony, which served as the model for all later hagiographies.

Apollonius of Rhodes (c. 300–250 B.C.): Composer of a learned epic about Jason and the Argonauts (*Argonautica*) typical of the Hellenistic age.

Apollonius of Tyana (c. 15–100): Sophist and Neopythagorean philosopher whose legendary travels and exploits were recorded in a biography written by Philostratus. Apollonius was hailed as archetypical pagan sage.

Apuleius (a.k.a. **Lucius Apuleius**; fl. 2nd century A.D.): Latin rhetorician and priest. Born at Madaura in North Africa, he was educated at Carthage and Rome. Apuleius composed *Metamorphoses* (*Golden Ass*)—a romantic novel of the amazing adventures of Lucius, who is turned into an ass and is eventually restored by the Egyptian goddess Isis.

Arbogast (c. 360–394): A Frankish officer under Gratian (r. 367–383) who rose to *magister militum* of the West in 388. In 392, he advanced as Emperor Eugenius (r. 392–394) in a pagan revolt against Theodosius I. The Western army was defeated at the Battle of Frigidus (394), and Arbogast committed suicide.

Arcadius (377–408; r. 395–408): The weak-willed elder son of Theodosius I and Aelia Flaccilla. He was proclaimed Augustus in 383 and in 395 succeeded to the Eastern Roman throne. He was dominated by his ministers, who averted the crisis posed by Alaric and the Visigoths.

Archelaus (23 B.C.–A.D. 18; r. 4 B.C.–A.D. 6): Son of Herod the Great and Malthace who succeeded his father as ethnarch of Judaea and Samaria. He was deposed for tyrannical rule and replaced by Roman procurators.

Ardashīr I (fl. 3rd century A.D.): Shah of Persia (224–240 who verthrew the Arsacid dynasty of Parthia and founded the Neo-Persian or Sāsānid Empire. Ardashīr waged war against Rome, proclaiming his aim to conquer the Roman East.

Aristotle (384–322 B.C.): Greek philosopher who studied at Plato's Academy in Athens from 366 to 347 B.C. and then became tutor to Alexander the Great between 343 and 341 B.C. In 335 B.C., Aristotle settled once more in Athens, establishing his school, the Lyceum. He wrote on a vast array of subjects (philosophy, natural sciences, mathematics, morality, logic, and politics). His critique on Plato's cosmology and conception of a rational creator god influenced middle Platonic and Neoplatonic writers.

Arius (c. 250–336): Presbyter in the church of Alexandria, he argued that Christ was generated as an inferior creature from God the father. His theology, Arianism, was condemned at the First Ecumenical Council (325), but his followers converted the East Germans to the Arian confession.

Athanasius (c. 293–373): Theologian and clergyman who opposed Arius at the First Ecumenical Council of Nicaea in 325, arguing the Orthodox positions. As patriarch of Alexandria (329–373), he opposed Emperor Constantius II, a devoted Arian, and later the pagan emperor Julian II. His writings are regarded the touchstone of Orthodoxy. In about 360, he wrote the hagiography of Saint Antony of Egypt.

Augustine (354–430): Saint and bishop of Hippo Regius (395–430). Born at Thagaste, Africa, Augustine mastered rhetoric and philosophy, gaining powerful patrons at Rome and Milan. In his beliefs, he progressed from a pagan Platonist to Platonized Christian. His voluminous writings, notably *City of God* and *Confessions*, defined Western Christianity in the Middle Ages.

Augustus (a.k.a. **Gaius Julius Caesar Octavianus**; 63 B.C.–A.D. 14; r. 27 B.C.–A.D. 14): First Roman emperor, or princeps, and grand-nephew and adopted son of the dictator Gaius Julius Caesar. Called by convention Octavian, 43 B.C., he allied with Mark Antony and Marcus Aemilius Lepidus in the Second Triumvirate to defeat the Liberators. Octavian secured the Italian Peninsula, while Antony ordered the Roman East. In 31 B.C., Octavian defeated Antony and his unpopular consort Cleopatra VII, queen of Ptolemaic Egypt, at Actium. The suicides of Antony and Cleopatra left Octavian master of the Roman world. In 27 B.C., Octavian relinquished his extraordinary powers as triumvir. The Senate voted Octavian tribunician power, proconsular imperium, and the name Augustus. Henceforth, Octavian ruled as emperor. As emperor, he restored peace and prosperity for 45 years, doubled the size of the Roman Empire, and founded the institutions of the Principate.

Aurelian (a.k.a. **Lucius Domitius Aurelianus**; c. 207–275; r. 270–275): "Restorer of the Roman world." Born of a military family in Dalmatia, Aurelian distinguished himself as a cavalry commander under Gallienus and Claudius II. In 270, the Danube army saluted Aurelian emperor, and he secured Rome after a brief civil war. Aurelian restored the political unity of the Roman Empire, defeating Zenobia of Palmyra in 272 and the Gallo-Roman emperor Tetricus in 274.

Barnabas (fl. early 1st century A.D.): An early Levite convert and Christian teacher of Antioch who accompanied Saint Paul on his first trip to Asia Minor (Acts 13:14) in about 45–47. He attended the council of Jerusalem in about 48.

Barsuma (fl. c. 380–440): Fierce Syrian ascetic who converted pagan villages in the style of the prophets of Israel.

Basil of Caesarea (a.k.a. **Basil the Great**; 330–379): Christian saint, theologian, and bishop of Caesarea (370–379) who wrote refutations of Arian theology and the monastic rule *Ascetica*, which still governs Orthodox monasteries. He was brother to Gregory of Nyssa.

Basilides (fl. c. 117–138): Gnostic thinker and teacher at Alexandria who founded a distinct school of Gnosticism based on his (now lost) commentaries on the Gospels.

Benedict of Nursia (480–547): Saint and monastic who founded the monastery of Monte Cassino in 529 and composed *Opus Dei*, the rule for Benedictine monks.

Caligula (a.k.a. **Gaius Julius Caesar**; 12–41; r. 37–41): Roman emperor, son of Germanicus and Agrippina the Elder nicknamed Caligula ("little boots") by the Rhine legions. He succeeded his uncle Tiberius as a popular ruler of Julian descent, but his arbitrary and savage rule, aggravated by madness and divine pretensions, led to his assassination by officers of the Praetorian Guard.

Caracalla (a.k.a. **Marcus Aurelius Severus Antoninus**; 188–217; r. 198–217): The savage son of Septimius Severus and Julia Domna nicknamed Caracalla after his favorite Gallic cloak. He was created co-emperor by his father in 198 and succeeded as joint ruler with his brother Geta in 211. In 212, he ordered the murder of Geta and issued the *Constitutio Antoniniana*. He was murdered by his Praetorian prefect Macrinus during the Parthian expedition (214–217). Carcalla patronized the sanctuaries of Asia Minor, notably the Asclepieion of Pergamon.

Carus (a.k.a. **Marcus Aurelius Carus**; r. 282–283): Praetorian Prefect of Probus who was declared emperor by the Eastern legions. He elevated his sons Carinus (r. 283–285) and Numerian (r. 283–284) as co-emperors. He invaded Mesopotamia, defeating the Persian army, but was killed by lightning near Ctesiphon.

Cato the Elder (a.k.a. **Marcus Porcius Cato Maior**; 234–149 B.C.): Roman conservative statesman and spokesmen for ancestral custom (*mos maiorum*). Elected consul in 195 B.C., Cato waged a campaign in Nearer Spain and gained a triumph. He is known for his practical writings and stern measures when censor in 184–183 B.C.

Catullus (a.k.a. **Gaius Valerius Catulus**; c. 84–54 B.C.): Born at Verona, he is the brilliant lyric poet of the late Roman Republic. Over 100 of his poems survive, including 63 which deal with the cult of Cybele and Attis, the Phrygian fertility divinities of Asia Minor.

Celsus (fl. 2nd century A.D.): Pagan critic of Chrsitianity who wrote *On the True Doctrine* in 177. His work is largely known from quotations by Origen.

Chrysippus (c. 280–207 B.C.): Native of Soli in Cilicia and a leading Stoic philosopher who taught at Athens, perfecting Stoic physics and logic.

Cicero (a.k.a. **Marcus Tullius Cicero**; 106–43 B.C.): Roman lawyer, orator, statesman, and consul of 63 B.C., Cicero was a prolific writer and master of Latin prose. He left a number of works dealing with philosophy and Roman religious practices in addition to his letters and political speeches.

Claudius (a.k.a. **Tiberius Claudius Drusus**; 10 B.C.–A.D. 54; r. A.D. 41–54): The second son of Drusus and Antonia Minor. Claudius received no political training because he was assumed to be weak minded due to his grotesque appearance—a result of infantile paralysis and a stutter. In A.D. 41, after the assassination of Caligula, the Praetorian Guard declared Claudius emperor. He proved an able administrator, and in 43, led the invasion of Britain. He is believed to have been murdered by his fourth wife and niece, Agrippina the Younger, in the interests of her son, Nero.

Claudius II Gothicus (c. 215–270; r. 268–270): An Illyrian provincial, Claudius rose through the ranks to become a senior officer of Gallienus. He participated in the murder of Gallienus and ascended the throne as the first soldier-emperor. In 269, he defeated a major Gothic force at Naissus in Upper Moesia (modern Niš, Serbia), and was hailed Gothicus. He died of plague early in 270.

Clement (c. 150–215): Saint and theologian who refounded the Catechetical School at Alexandria in about 202 and composed the *Stromata*, in which he elucidates his doctrine of salvation that influenced his most brilliant student, Origen.

Cleopatra VII (r. 51–30 B.C.): Ptolemaic queen of Egypt who established liaisons with Julius Caesar and then Marc Antony to secure the independence of her kingdom.

Commodus (a.k.a. **Marcus Aelius Aurelius Commodus**; 161–192; r. 177–192): The only surviving son of Marcus Aurelius and Faustinia II. In 177, Commodus was made co-emperor by his father, and in 180, on the death of Marcus Aurelius, he abruptly ended the German campaign to return to Rome. Lazy and savage by nature, Commodus devoted his genius to the arena, fighting as a gladiator to the outrage of the ruling classes. In 189, after a mental collapse, he believed he was Hercules reincarnated, so that his increasingly arbitrary rule resulted in his assassination.

Constantine I (a.k.a. **Constantine the Great**; after 280–337; r. 306–337): Emperor who first legalized Christianity in the Roman Empire. Declared emperor by the Western army, Constantine reunited the empire in 324. In 312, after the Battle of Milvian Bridge, he was convinced his victory was the gift of the Christian God and converted to Christianity. The first Christian emperor, he created the imperial church. In 325, he summoned and presided over the First Ecumenical Council at Nicaea that declared heretical the views of Arius. In his later years, Constantine was won over by the Arians, so that on his deathbed he was baptized by an Arian bishop. He built a new Christian capital at Constantinople on the site of Byzantium in 330.

Constantius I Chlorus (a.k.a. **Flavius Valerius Constantius**; c. 250–306; r. 305–306): Born to an Illyrian military family, Constantius served under Probus and Diocletian. In 293, Maximianus adopted Constantius as his heir and appointed him Caesar. Constantius divorced his wife Helena, mother of Constantine I, and married Theodora, the stepdaughter of Maximianus. In 305, Constantius I succeeded as Augustus of the West. He died in 306, after conducting an expedition against the Picts.

Constantius II (a.k.a. **Flavius Julius Constantius**; 317–361; r. 337–361): Son of Constantine I and Fausta, Constantius II was proclaimed Caesar in 324 and succeeded jointly as Augustus with his brothers Constantine II and Constans in 337. Constantius ruled in the East, waging a war against the Persians. He crushed the rebellion by Magnentius and the Western army in 350–353. In 361, Constantius died of illness while en route to face his cousin Julian, who had been declared emperor by the Western army. An Arian Christian, Constantius sponsored Ulfilas, the so-called apostle to the Goths.

Cosmas Indicopleustes (fl. c. 525–550): Greek merchant of Alexandria who visited India in about 550 and composed *Christian Topography*, in which he reconciled Greek geography with Christian doctrine. He proposed a single landmass of three equal continents in the form of a box, with Jerusalem in the center—a worldview passed on to medieval Christendom.

Cyprian of Carthage (a.k.a. **Thasciius Caecilius Cyprianus**; d. 258): Saint and bishop (250–257) who composed in Latin numerous tracts on issues of baptism of *lapsi*, readmission of heretics into the church, and Episcopal authority. He was martyred during the persecution of Valerian.

Cyril (c. 376–444): Patriarch of Alexandria (412–444) who elevated Alexandria to the leading see of the Eastern Roman world. He condemned the doctrines of Nestorius in his *Twelve Anathemas* and defined the tenets of the Trinity and Mary Theotokos, so that his writings were accepted at the Third and Fourth Ecumenical Councils.

Demetrius of Alexandria (d. 231): Bishop of Alexandria (189–231) who appointed Origen to succeed Clement as the head of the Catechetical School. In 230, Demetrius protested the ordination of Origen by Theoctistus of Caesarea in 230 so that Origen retired to Caesarea Maritima.

Dio Chrysostom (a.k.a. **Dio the Golden Mouthed**; c. 40–120): Greek sophist and philosopher born at Prusa, Bithynia, in northwestern Asia Minor. Dio taught at Rome until he was banished by Emperor Domitian. A convert to Stoicisim, Dio left some 80 orations on a host of subjects.

Diocletian (245–316; r. 284–305): Roman emperor. A humble Dalmatian soldier declared emperor by the Eastern army, Diocletian ended the crisis of the 3rd century and retired from the throne 305. His administrative, monetary, and fiscal reforms established the Dominate, or late Roman state. He created collegial rule, the so-called tetrarchy, whereby imperial power was shared by two senior emperors called Augusti and two junior emperors called Caesars. In 305, Diocletian retired from public life to his fortress palace of Spalato (modern Split, Croatia).

Dionysius Exiguus (c. 470–544): A monk of the Scythian community at Tomi, on the shores of the Black Sea. He calculated the reckoning of Easter and devised the system of dating by A.D. (*Anno Domini*).

Domitian (a.k.a. **Titus Flavius Domitianus**; 51–96; r. 81–96): The younger son of Vespasian who succeeded his popular brother Titus as emperor. Domitian warred against the Chatti in 82–85, but he faced criticism for setbacks in Dacia and for his treaty with their king, Decebalus, in 92. Suspicious by nature, Domitian terrorized the Senate after 93, so that he was murdered by a palace plot.

Dioscorus (d. 454): Patriarch of Alexandria (444–451) and successor to Cyril. He failed to impose the Monophysite doctrine as the Orthodox faith. He was condemned and deposed at the Fourth Ecumenical Council (451).

Epictetus of Hierapolis (55–136): Stoic philosopher who arrived at Rome as the slave of Epaphroditus, freedman secretary of Emperor Nero, studied Stoic philosophy with Gaius Musonius Rufus, and acquired his freedom. In 93, Epictetus, along with several other philosophers, were banished from Rome on the orders of Domitian. His writings on moral conduct gained him admirers among the senatorial class and from Emperor Hadrian.

Epicurus (341–270 B.C.): Athenian philosopher who taught the goal of avoiding pain and finding pleasure by a balanced moral life. He established a school known as the Garden, and his doctrines, dubbed Epicureanism, were popular among the ruling classes of the Hellenistic world and Roman Empire. Epicurus based his cosmology on the early atomists, and so he concluded the gods took no note of human affairs.

Epiphanius of Salamis (c. 320–403): Native of Roman Palestine and monk who consecrated bishop of Salamis, Cyprus, in 367. He compiled a compendium *Against Heresies* (*Panarion*) in 374–377 that is a major source for early sectarian Christianity.

Eugenius (a.k.a. **Flavius Eugenius**; r. 392–394): Grammarian elevated as Western emperor by Arbogast, *magister militum* of the Western army, and backed by the Senate. He was defeated, captured, and executed after his defeat at the Battle of Frigidus on September 6, 394.

Eusebius (260–340): Bishop of Caesarea (314–340) and friend of Emperor Constantine. He composed important pastoral theological works, the most important of which was his *Ecclesiastical History*, the prime source for early Christianity. Eusebius set the standard for later Christian historians. He also composed a life of Constantine, the main source for the emperor's conversion in 312, and the *Tricennial Oration* (336), praising Constantine as the ideal Christian ruler.

Ezana (c. 325–360): King of Axum who received missionaries from Alexandria and converted to Christianity, thereby founding the Ethiopian church.

Fabian (r. 236–250): Pope respected by African and Italian bishops and credited with missions to cities in Gaul. He was martyred during the persecution of Trajan Decius on January 20, 250.

Galen of Pergamon (a.k.a. Aelius Galenus; 129–205): Physician and philosopher born of a prominent family with Roman citizenship. A product of the Second Sophistic movement, Galen wrote extensively on human physiology and biology. He studied at the Asclepieion and was physician to gladiatorial schools at Pergamon and Rome. He was also physician to the young Emperor Commodus. In his writings, Galen makes a number of references to Christians and martyrdoms.

Galerius (a.k.a. **Gaius Galerius Valerius Maximianus**; c. 250–311; r. 305–311): Balkan officer created Caesar of the East in 293. He married Diocletian's daughter Galeria Valeria. In 305, Galerius succeeded Diocletian as Augustus of the East, but his political arrangements denied the succession to both Constantine and Maxentius (each the son of an emperor), so that civil war erupted after 306. Galerius was credited with the initiative for the Great Persecution in 303–313.

Gallienus (a.k.a. **Publius Licinius Egantius Gallienus**; 218–268; r. 253–268): Son of Valerian I, Gallienus was proclaimed joint ruler with his father by the army of the Rhine. Gallienus failed to contain the Germanic invaders; thus the West seceded under the Gallo-Roman emperor Postumus (260–269), and the East fell under the control of Odenathus, the merchant prince of Palmyra. Christians fondly remembered Gallienus, however, because he halted the persecutions.

Gordian III (a.k.a. **Marcus Antonius Gordianus**; 225–244; r. 238–244): Grandson of Gordian I, the young Gordian III was proclaimed emperor by the Praetorian Guard and Senate at Rome in opposition to Maximinus I. His father-in-law and Praetorian prefect Gaius Furius Timisitheus directed policy after 240. In 242–244, Gordian took the field against the Persian Shah Shāpūr I. The young emperor was slain in a mutiny, staged by his prefect, Philip the Arab (who had succeeded Timistheus in 243).

Gratian (a.k.a. **Flavius Gratianus**; 359–383; r. 367–383): The elder son of Valentinian I, he made his court at Treveri. Gratian pursed anti-pagan measures and promoted Nicene Christianity. In 383, he was betrayed and murdered near Lugdunum (Lyon) by supporters of Magnus Maximus, who had been proclaimed emperor by the army of Britain.

Gregory Nazianzus (329–390): Born near Nazianzus in Cappadocia, he entered a religious life in 361 and was staunch opponent to the pagan emperor Julian II. He was ordained Bishop of Sasima in Cappadocia in 372 and then patriarch of Constantinople in 380. Classically educated, Gregory penned important refutations of Arianism and treatises on the nature of the Holy Spirit, views accepted at the Second Ecumenical Council in 381.

Gregory of Nyssa (335–394): Saint and bishop of Nyssa (372–394). Born at Caesarea in Cappadocia, he was the younger brother to Saint Basil of Caesarea. Gregory penned important tracts on the Trinity and the omnipotence of God, thereby rejecting the views of Origen and the pagan Neoplatonists.

Gregory Thaumaturgus (a.k.a. **Gregory the Wonderworker**; 213–270): Bishop of Neocaesarea in Asia Minor (240–270) who studied with Origen at Caesarea Maritima in 231–239. He was credited with aggressive proselytizing among pagans in eastern Asia Minor, but these exploits now appear to be anachronistic creations by his hagiographer, Gregory of Nyssa.

Gregory the Illuminator (c. 257–313): Apostle to the Armenians. Educated as a Christian and studied at Caesarea in Cappadocia, in about 301 Gregory baptized King Tiridates III, although there is reason to believe that Tirdiates embraced Christianity later, following the example of Constantine.

Hadrian (a.k.a. **Publius Aelius Hadrianus**; 76–138; r. 117–138): Fatherless child reared as the ward of his second cousin and future emperor Trajan and his wife, Plotina. In 100, Hadrian married the emperor's grand-niece Sabina. He later succeeded his adoptive father Trajan. Hadrian relinquished Trajan's eastern conquests. By inclination an architect and philhellene, Hadrian was unpopular with the Senate, but he proved a brilliant emperor. Hadrian was also a tireless traveler who patronized the cities of the Roman East.

Hegesippus (c. 110–180): Reportedly a convert from Judaism and the earliest known Christian chronicler. His work was a major source for Eusebius's *Ecclesiastical History*, but it does not survive.

Helena (a.k.a. **Flavia Julia Helena**; c. 246–330): Saint, first wife of Constantius I, and mother of Constantine I. In about 289, Constantius divorced Helena so that he could marry Theodora, daughter of Maximianus, Augustus of the West. In 326–328, Helena traveled to Jerusalem and Bethlehem, where she reportedly found the True Cross.

Herod Agrippa I (10 B.C.–A.D. 44; r. A.D. 41–44): Grandson of Herod the Great, Herod Agrippa was educated at Rome, where he became a boyhood friend of the future Roman emperor Claudius. In 41, Claudius appointed Herod Agrippa king of Jews. He initiated building programs and won the affection of his Jewish and Samaritan subjects. In 44, he died before he could raise a rebellion against Rome.

Herod Antipas (c. 20 B.C.–A.D. 39; r. 4 B.C. –A.D. 39): Son of Herod the Great and Malthace of Samaria who succeeded to the throne of Galilee and Peraea (east of the Jordan) after his father's death. He is remembered in the New Testament for ordering the execution of John the Baptist. In 39, he was deposed and exiled to Lugdunum on the orders of Caligula.

Herod the Great (74–4 B.C.; r. 37–4 B.C.): Second son of Antipater of Idumaea who rose in Hasmonaean service and was appointed governor of Galilee in 49 B.C. From 43 B.C., Herod adroitly exploited his friendship with leading Romans, first Marc Antony and then Octavian, so that he ousted the Hasmonaean dynasty and ruled the Jewish lands from 37 B.C. in the interests of Rome. Herod built on a grand scale, notably Caesarea Maritima and the fortress of Masada. He was despised by his Jewish subjects as a tyrant and a slack adherent to Judaism. In the Gospel of Matthew, he is charged with the Slaughter of the Innocents.

Herodotus (c. 490–425 B.C.): Called the father of history, Herodotus was born at Halicarnassus on the shores of Asia Minor and traveled widely in the Persian Empire and Greece. His *History*, about the wars between the Greeks and Persians, contains invaluable observations on religious practices and Greek attitudes, notably books 2 (Egypt), 3 (Persia and Babylon), and 4 (Scythia).

Hesiod (c. 750–700 B.C.): Boeotian poet inspired by the Muses under Mount Helicon who composed in epic verse *Works and Days* and *Theogony*. Hesiod was regarded as second only to Homer; his *Theogony* gives the first literary definition of the gods and myths of Greece.

Homer (fl. c. 750 B.C.): Reputedly a native of Smyrna, this blind poet was credited with the composition of the epic poems the *Iliad* and the *Odyssey*, which were regarded as the foundation of Hellenic religious beliefs.

Honorius (a.k.a. **Flavius Honorius**; 384–421; r. 395–421): Second son of Theodosius I and Aelia Flaccillia; created Augustus in 393 and succeeded as Western emperor in 395. Real power was in the hands of Stilicho down to 408. Honorius, at his capital at Ravenna from 402 on, witnessed the loss of northwestern and Spanish provinces.

Horace (a.k.a. **Quintus Horatius Flaccus**; 65–8 B.C.): Poet and soldier. Born at Venusia and son of a freedman, Horace fought for the Republican cause at Philippi (42 B.C.), but he was pardoned and promoted at the court of Augustusthrough the efforts of Maecenas. His works include *Carmen Saeculare* (chorus for the Saecular Games of 17 B.C.), *Odes*, Epodes, Epistles, Satires, and *Ars Poetica*. He is considered the master of the Roman lyric and poet laureate of the Golden Age.

Hosius of Cordoba (257–359): Bishop before 300, he suffered exile during the Great Persecution of 303–305. In 313, he was invited to Treveri, where he advised the emperor Constantine on doctrinal matters. After the death of Constantine, Hosius staunchly opposed the Arian policies of Constantius II.

Hypatia (c. 360–415): Daughter of the mathematician Theon (c. 335–405) who taught mathematics and astronomy at Alexandria. She succeeded to the head of the pagan philosophical school at Alexandria in 400 and so was perceived as a threat by Patriarch Cyril. In 415, she was assaulted and hacked to pieces by a crowd of monks. Her works do not survive, but she apparently wrote commentaries on philosophy and astronomy.

Iamblichus of Chalcis (c. 250–325 A.D.): Neoplatonist theurgist from Syria who studied with Porphyry at Rome. Iamblichus composed *De mysteriis* (*On the Mysteries*), an exposition of theurgy and the efficacy of sacrifice that influenced Julian and Proclus. He also composed three treatises on mathematics and a tract on the Pythagorean life.

Ignatius of Antioch (d. c 107): Saint and bishop. He wrote seven letters that offer the first insight into the authority and role of bishops in apostolic churches.

Irenaeus (d. c. 202): Native of Smyrna, saint, bishop of Lugdunum (Lyon), and Christian apologist and theologian. He wrote an eyewitness account of the persecution at Lugdunum in 177 and an important refutation of the Gnostics, *Against Heresies*.

James the Righteous (d. 62) Called the brother of Jesus by Saint Paul (Galatians 1:19). He succeeded to the authority of the Jerusalem church after the crucifixion.

Jerome (a.k.a. **Sophronius Eusebius Hieronymus**; c. 347–420): Saint and philosopher. A native Latin speaker of Dalmatia who mastered rhetoric and philosophy, he assumed an ascetic life and was ordained a priest in about 378 or 379. He translated the Bible from Greek into Latin, a version called the Vulgate. He enjoyed the patronage of leading aristocratic ladies of Rome. From 388, he settled as an ascetic near Bethlehem.

John Chrysostom (349–407): Patriarch of Constantinople (398–405). A brilliant orator, he asserted the primacy of Constantinople over the Eastern churches and clashed with the emperor Arcadius.

John of Amida (c. 507–585): A Monophysite ascetic trained in the Syrian tradition. As bishop of Ephesus (535–575), he carried out aggressive efforts to convert pagans in Western Asia Minor.

John the Baptist (c. 6 B.C.–A.D. 36): A prophet and hailed forerunner of Jesus (*prodromos*) in the Synoptic Gospels. He baptized Jesus at Bethany beyond the Jordan River. He was arrested and beheaded on orders of Herod Antipas to please the seductive Salome, daughter of Herodias (c. 14–71). His followers included the founders of Mandaeism, a faith that accepted John the Baptist as prophet, but not Jesus. There is no direct evidence that the Essenes influenced John the Baptist.

Josephus (a.k.a. **Flavius Josephus**, b. c. 37): A prominent Pharisee and historian of the first rank who composed an eyewitness account of the Jewish War of 66–73 A.D. His *Antiquities of the Jews* is invaluable for Jewish religious attitudes and custom. He also composed an apology for Judaism in two books, *Contra Apionem*.

Jovian (a.k.a. **Flavianus Jovianus**; 337–364; r. 363–364): a Nicene Christian commanding the imperial guard who was elected as emperor after the death Julian during the retreat from Ctesiphon in 363. Jovian surrendered provinces in Mesopotamia to Shah Shāpūr II in exchange for the safe return of the Roman army. In February 364, Jovian was found dead in his tent during the march to Constantinople.

Judas Maccabaeus (a.k.a. **Judah Maccabee**; d. 160 B.C.): Jewish priest and son of Mattathias of the Hasmonaean house who led the revolt against Seleucid king Antiochus IV Epiphanes (175–164 B.C.), who sought to Hellenize the cult of Yahweh at Jerusalem. In 167–163 B.C., Judas won spectacular victories, acquiring the nickname Maccabaeus ("hammer" in Aramaic), and he reoccupied and rededicated the Temple at Jerusalem.

Julia Domna (170–217): Daughter of Gaius Julius Bassianus, equestrian and high priest of the cult of Baal at Emesa (identified with Helios and Sol). The beautiful and intelligent wife of Septimius Severus (193–211), she presided over a court of savants and artists. She was mother to the emperors Caracalla and Geta.

Julia Mamaea (180–235): The second daughter of Julia Maesa, sister of Julia Domna, and the equestrian Julius Avitus. She was mother of the emperor Severus Alexander and guided imperial policy. She was murdered, along with her son, by mutinous soldiers of the Rhine army.

Julian II (a.k.a. **Julian the Apostate** or **Flavius Claudius Julianus**; 332–363; r. 360–363): Nephew of the first Christian emperor, Constantine I, he survived the purge of 337 and was raised and educated in the wastes of Cappadocia. Devoted to the classics, Julian secretly renounced his Christianity in 351. Promoted to Caesar in 355, Julian brilliantly cleared Gaul of Germanic invaders, and he was proclaimed emperor by the Western army. His brief reign saw the restoration of paganism to civic life; his reforms were cut short by his untimely death while on campaign in Persia. His works include orations, philosophical tracts, hymns to Helios and Magna Mater, and critiques on Christian dogma.

Julius Caesar (a.k.a. **Gaius Julius Caesar**; c. 100–44 B.C.): Statesman, general, and author who championed the popular cause in the late Roman Republic. As proconsul of Gaul, he forged an invincible army and overthrew the Republic in a civil war (49–45 B.C.). His dictatorship marked the birth of a Roman monarchy, but his disregard for Republican conventions led to his assassination.

Justin the Martyr (103–165): Christian apologist who wrote (in Greek) two Apologies and *Dialogue with Typhro*.

Justinian I (a.k.a. **Justinian the Great**; 483–565; r. 527–565): Byzantine (Eastern Roman) emperor. Justinian succeeded his uncle and adoptive father Justin I as a mature, experienced ruler of 46. The greatest emperor since Constantine, he restored imperial rule in the Italian Peninsula and Africa. His most enduring achievements are Hagia Sophia and the *Corpus Iuris Civilis*.

Juvenal (a.k.a. **Decimus Junius Juvenalis**; c. 60–140): Roman lawyer and satirist whose surviving 16 satires represent a fraction of his poems in five books.

Kartir Hangirpe, (c. 240–280): Religious advisor to Shahs Shāpūr I, Hormizd I, and Bahrām I. He reorganized Iranian religious practices and stressed the universal, aniconic worship of Ahura Mazdā, claiming to have restored the pure teachings of Zoroaster. He also opposed Mani and likely instigated the arrest and crucifixion of Mani in 276. *See* **Zoroaster**.

Lactantius (a.k.a. **Lucius Caecilius Firmianus Lactantius**; c. 240–320): Roman rhetor and tutor to Crispus, eldest son of Constantine I. Born in Roman Africa, he taught rhetoric at Nicomedia. In about 315, he composed *On the Deaths of the Persecutors* (*De mortibus persecutorum*), the prime source for and the earliest report of the conversion of Constantine in 312.

Leo I (a.k.a. **Leo the Great**; c. 400–461): Pope (440–461), politician, and theologian. Born in Tuscany, he laid the foundations of the medieval papacy. He composed the *Tome* in 449, the first major Latin work on the nature of Christ; it was accepted as canonical at the Council of Chalcedon (451). He persuaded Attila the Hun to withdraw from Italy in 452, thereby making the papacy the moral authority of the Roman West.

Libanius of Antioch (314–394): Pagan rhetorician and sophist of Antioch who trained talented young men, pagan and Christian, destined for imperial service. He was friend to the emperor Julian II, and yet he was allowed to present an oration protesting the desecration of temples in 383–388 to Theodosius I. Sixty-four orations of Libanius—along with commentaries, rhetorical exercises, and over 1,500 letters—have survived.

Licinius I (a.k.a. **Gaius Valerius Licianus Licinius**; c. 263–325; r. 308–324): A veteran officer, Licinius was elevated as Augustus of the West by Galerius after Severus II had been defeated and executed by Maxentius. In 311, Licinius succeeded to the Balkan provinces. In 313, he contracted an alliance with Constantine and married Constantine's half-sister Constantia. That same year, he defeated Maximinus II Daza and took over the eastern provinces. Twice—in 314 and 323–324—Licinius clashed with Constantine. Licinius was defeated and deposed by Constantine in 324; he was executed in 325. Licinius issued jointly with Constantine the Edict of Milan in 313. Initially tolerant of Christians, Licinius was criticized for persecution of Christians during his final war with Constantine.

Lucian of Samosata (c. 125–180): Greek satirist and brilliant prose stylist, he composed works on religious themes, including *Dialogues of the Gods*, *Banquet of Philosophers*, and a life of the false prophet Alexander of Abonouteichos.

Loukas of Cyrene (d. 116): Messianic leader of the Jewish rebellion in Cyrene in 115–116.

Macarius (c. 300–390) Saint and Egyptian ascetic who established *lavrae* ("cells") whereby holy men could live in support of each other—an innovation that led to the establishment of monastic houses.

Macrobius (a.k.a. **Ambrosius Theodosius Macrobius**; 395–423): Pagan grammarian and Neoplatonic philosopher. He wrote *Saturnalia*, a learned discussion on literary and religious topics set in the house of his patron Vettius Agorius Praetextatus. He also wrote a commentary on the "Dream of Scipio" in Cicero's *De re publica*.

Magnentius (a.k.a. **Flavius Magnus Magnentius**; c. 303–353; r. 350–353): Born of a German family settled in Gaul, Magnentius commanded the cavalry under Constans. In 350, the Western army revolted, declaring Magnentius emperor and slaying Constans. In the ensuing civil war, Constantius II defeated Magnentius, who committed suicide. The fighting weakened defenses on the Rhine so that in 355–357, Franks and Alemanni overran Gaul.

Magnus Maximus (a.k.a. **Flavius Magnus Maximus**; c. 335–388; r. 383-388): Soldier who rose in the service of Count Theodosius and then Emperor Gratian. In 380, he succeeded to the command of the army of Britain. In response to the antipagan laws, in 383, Magnus Maximus rebelled and invaded Gaul. Gratian was deserted and murdered. In 387, Magnus Maximus invaded the Italian Peninsula so that Valentinian II fled to Constantinople. In 388, Theodosius I defeated Magnus Maximus at the Battle on the Save. He fled to Aquileia, surrendered, and was executed.

Mani (216–276): Prophet and founder of the dualist monotheistic religion Manichaeism. Born into a community of Elcesaites, an ascetic sect of Judaizing Christians, near Ctesiphon in Babylonia, between 218 and 228 Mani experienced mystical visions, and in 240–242 he traveled to India, where he might have conversed with Buddhist monks. He returned to Persia and gained favor at the court of Shāpūr I. His teaching, however, offended Kartir and the strict Zoroastrians, who likely contrived his arrest and crucifixion by Shah Bahrām I in 276. Mani's writings, originally written in Syriac, have survived in translations.

Marc Antony (a.k.a. **Marcus Antonius**; c. 83–30 B.C.): Lieutenant of Julius Caesar and triumvir in 44–31 B.C., he ruled the Roman East after 44 B.C.; his defeat at Actium and subsequent suicide marked the end of the Roman civil wars.

Marcian (a.k.a. **Flavius Valerius Marcianus**; c. 390–457; r. 450–457): An officer of Illyrian origin, Marcian was elected to the Senate of Constantinople. In 450, the empress Aelia Pulcheria married Marcian, who was hailed Eastern Roman emperor. Marcian refused payment of tribute to Attila the Hun, reformed the Eastern army, and presided over the Fourth Ecumenical Council (451).

Marcion of Sinope (c. 85–160): Christian theologian and editor of the New Testament. In 143–144 he emigrated to Rome. He produced his own edited version of the New Testament based on the letters of Paul and the Gospel of Luke. His teachings were rejected and condemned at the first reported synod at Rome, presided over by Pope Anicetus. Marcion then founded his own church that flourished into the 5th century.

Marcus Aurelius (a.k.a. **Marcus Annius Verus** or **Marcus Aurelius Antoninus**; 121–180; r. 161–180): Son of Annius Verus and nephew of Emperor Antoninus Pius (r. 138–161). He was adopted by Antoninus Pius in 138 and was promoted to Caesar (heir apparent) in 139. A brilliant general, modest ruler, and conscientious administrator, Marcus Aurelius is regarded as the best of the Five Good Emperors. His *Meditations* are letters on the oral precepts of Stoic philosophy.

Maternus Cynegius (d. 388): Christian from Spain who rose in the service of Theodosius I. As prefect of the East (384–388), he initiated riots by monks against pagan temples and synagogues. In protest, the pagan rhetorician Libanius wrote his *Pro templis* (*On the Temples*), an oration delivered to Theodosius I.

Maxentius (a.k.a. **Marcus Valerius Maxentius**; c. 278–312; r. 306–312 A.D.): Son of Maximianus, Maxentius revolted at Rome and declared himself emperor after he had been denied the succession by Galerius. Maxentius controlled Italy and Africa. In 312, he was defeated and slain by Constantine at the Battle of Milvian Bridge.

Maximianus (a.k.a. **Marcus Aurelius Valerius Maximianus**; c. 250–310; r. 286–305): A Pannonian comrade of Diocletian, Maximianus was promoted as Augustus in the West. He abdicated in 305 but reentered politics, first as co-emperor with his son Maxentius and then with his son-in-law Constantine. He committed suicide at Massilia in 310 after he failed to raise a revolt against Constantine.

Maximinus II Daza (a.k.a. **Galerius Valerius Maximinus Daia**; c. 270–313; r. 309–313): Nephew of Galerius, he was named Caesar of the East in 305. Devoted to the old gods, Maximinus persecuted Christians. In 309, he proclaimed himself Augustus and warred against Galerius and later Licinius. In 313, defeated by Licinius, he died a refugee at Tarsus.

Maximinus I Thrax (a.k.a. **Gaius Julius Verus Maximinus**; 173–238; r. 235–238) A Thracian peasant who rose through the ranks to the equestrian order. In 235, he was proclaimed emperor after the murder of Severus Alexander. His reign marked the inception of 50 years of civil wars. The first soldier-emperor of low social origins, Maximinus was detested by the landed classes despite his success in waging frontier wars. In 238, a revolt that began in Africa and spread to Rome precipitated his downfall.

Maximus of Ephesus (d. 372): Neoplatonist philosopher and student of Porphyry. He instructed the future emperor Julian in philosophy and theurgy at Pergamon in 351–352.

Melito of Sardis (d. c. 180): Perhaps bishop of Sardis, he wrote an apology in Greek addressed to Emperor Marcus Aurelius. He also expressed his anxiety over Judaism and so reflected the fact that Jews occupied a favored position at Sardis.

Minucius Felix (c. 150–270): This otherwise anonymous figure wrote the earliest surviving Latin apology, *Octavius*, set as a debate between Christian Octavius and pagan Caecilius Natalis.

Montanus (c. 150–200): Credited with apocalyptic revelations from the Holy Spirit either in 157 or 172, Montanus and his associates, Maximilla and Priscilla, offered a so-called New Prophecy that promised redemption only to the elect. Montanus challenged the authority of bishops in apostolic churches, who condemned Montanus as a heretic and convert from paganism. Montanist churches, however, survived in Asia Minor into the 7th century.

Nero (a.k.a. **Lucius Domitius Ahenobarbus**; 37–68; r. 54–68): The last Julio-Claudian emperor. Nero was the son of Gnaeus Domitius Ahenobarbus and Agrippina the Younger (the great-granddaughter of Augustus). In 49, his mother married Claudius and secured Nero's adoption as Claudius's heir. Nero took the name Nero Claudius Caesar. In 54, Nero succeeded as emperor, but he craved popularity as an artist and therefore entrusted the affairs of state to his ministers down to 62, when he assumed direct control. By his amoral and outrageous conduct, he alienated the ruling classes and legions and thus precipitated his downfall and suicide in 68. In 64, Nero ordered the first persecution of Christians at Rome.

Nestorius (b. c. 386): Brilliant theologian at Antioch who, on the recommendation of Theodosisus II, was elevated to patriarch of Constantinople (429–431). He taught that Mary was Christokos, or mother of the human nature of Christ. His views were condemned at the Third Ecumenical Council (431); he was deposed and exiled. His followers established a Nestorian church in Persian Mesopotamia or rejoined the imperial church under the Formula of Reunion (433).

Nonnus of Panopolis (c. 375–425): Pagan poet of a prominent Greco-Egyptian family who composed the epic *Dionysiaca,* the myths and traditions of the god Dionysus.

Octavian: *See* **Augustus**.

Odenathus (a.k.a. **Septimius Odenathus**; r. 262–267): Merchant prince of the caravan city Palmyra, Roman senator, and Roman general (*dux*). He imposed his authority over the Roman eastern frontier after the capture of Valerian I in 260. In 262, he imposed a treaty on Shah Shāpūr I. He was murdered at Emesa.

Opamonas (fl. 2nd century A.D.): Leading citizen of Rhodiapolis who listed on his funerary monument gifts totaling nearly 500,000 denarii to the cities and sanctuaries of Lycia between 114 and 153. Opromoas epitomizes the values of *philopatris* and *philotimia* in the Roman age.

Origen (185–254): Brilliant Christian theologian. Born at Alexandria of a Christian family and studied under Saint Clement, whom he succeeded as head of the Catechetical School. He was sent a number of diplomatic missions by Bishop Demetrius of Alexandria. In 230, Origen removed himself to Caesarea Maritima because Demetrius protested Origen's ordination. Origen wrote numerous commentaries on books of the Bible and pastoral works, establishing the discipline of exegesis and typology. In 215–217, Origen composed *On First Principles*, the first serious theological work that reconciled Christian faith and Platonic philosophy. He also produced the *Hexapla*, a study of the Hebrew and Greek texts of the Old Testament. His views on cosmology and salvation were later condemned at the Fifth Ecumenical Council in 553.

Ovid (a.k.a. **Pubius Ovidius Naso**; 43 B.C.–17 A.D.): Poet and lawyer who initiated the silver age of Latin literature. Born at Sulmona, he was in A.D. 8 banished by Emperor Augustus to the city of Tomi (Constantia) on the Black Sea. A prolific writer, he composed *Metamorphoses*, an epic poem on Greek and Roman mythology, and *Fasi*, on the holidays of the Roman sacred calendar.

Pachomius (c. 290–346): Saint and pagan convert to Christianity who undertook an ascetic life, founding the first monastery at Tabennesi in Upper Egypt in 323.

Patrick (c. 387–460): Saint and son of a Roman decurion who was enslaved by Irish pirates at age 16; he escaped to Gaul and entered the monastery of Lerins. Commissioned apostle to the Irish, Patrick sailed to Ireland in around 432 or 433 and preached in Ulster, establishing a church at Armagh.

Paul (a.k.a. **Paul of Tarsus**; c. 5–67): Saint and early Christian writer and missionary. Born to wealthy Pharisee family with Roman citizenship, after his conversion on the road to Damascus in about 35, Paul defined the universal message of Jesus as the conversion of the wider pagan world. He conducted three missions establishing churches in the Greek cities of Asia Minor and Greece in 46–48, 49–52, and 53–57. At the council of Jerusalem (c. 48), Peter and James the Righteous accepted Pauline converts in a compromise. Paul was arrested and imprisoned at Caesarea Maritima in 58–59. He was conveyed to Rome and martyred in the wake of the Great Fire. His seven Epistles (Romans, 1 and 2 Corinthians, Galatians, 1 Thessalonians, Philippians, and Philemon) are fundamental to Christian theology.

Paulus Orosius (375–418): Christian apologist who studied under Saint Augustine of Hippo. Orosius wrote *History against the Pagans*, a work in seven books, to refute pagan critics who said that abandonment of the worship of the gods led to Rome's decline. Orosius's apology is a detailed narrative listing disasters suffered by pagans due to their ignorance of God and the true faith.

Pausanias (fl. late 2nd century A.D.): Greek author of the *Description of Greece*, a tour guide to the sites and shrines of Greece in the Roman age. It is filled with information about heroes, gods, and cult practices.

Peregrinus Proteus (c. 95–165): Cynic philosopher born at Parium, Mysia. According to Lucian, Peregrinus had contact with early Christians and adopted the ascetic life of an itinerant Cynic. His abusive and outrageous conduct earned him expulsion from Rome on the order of Emperor Antoninus Pius. At the Olympic Games in 165, he immolated himself just east of the sanctuary.

Peter (a.k.a. **Simon Cephas**; d. c. 67): Saint and one of the 12 original disciples of Jesus Christ. Born Bethsida in the Galilee, Peter figures as the leading apostle in the Synoptic Gospels, and he was the first to enter the empty tomb of Jesus. He actively proselytized in the Levant after the crucifixion and, according to the Acts of the Apostles, supported the admission of Pauline converts at the Council of Jerusalem in the year 48. He arrived at Rome in about 63 and was martyred, along with Saint Paul, in the persecutions after the Great Fire.

Philip I (a.k.a. **Philip the Arab** or **Marcus Julius Philippus**; r. 244–249): An equestrian of Arabian origin who succeeded Timisitheus as Praetorian prefect of Gordian III in 243. Philip instigated the murder of Gordian and so succeeded as emperor. He concluded a treaty with Shāpūr at the price of 500,000 aurei. Philip faced rebellions in Pannonia and the East in protest to his fiscal exactions. In 249, he was defeated and slain by Trajan Decius, who had been hailed emperor by the Danube legions.

Philip the Evangelist (fl. c. 35–80): Saint and one of the seven deacons of the Jerusalem church, who converted Simon Magus and the Ethiopian eunuch at Gaza. He preached in the cities of Samaria, and later traditions placed him and his four virgin daughters, who were prophetesses, at Hierapolis (Pamukkale) in Asia Minor.

Philo of Alexandria (c. 15 B.C.–45 A.D.): Jewish thinker and Platonist who headed the prosperous Jewish community of Alexandria and represented Jewish interests in the embassy to Emperor Caligula in protest of the laws requiring sacrifice in A.D. 39–40. A prolific writer, Philo used Platonic analysis and schemes in *On the Creation* to elucidate the Jewish faith and so set the model for Christian Platonic thinkers.

Philostratus (a.k.a. **Lucius Flavius Philostratus**; c. 170–247): Athenian sophist and stylist associated with the court of the empress Julia Domna, wife of Septimius Severus. His works include *Lives of the Sophists* and a biography of Apollonius of Tyana, the Neopythagorean magician and miracle worker of the 1st century. His *Life of Apollonius* is sometimes regarded as a response to the Gospels.

Plato (428–348 B.C.): Athenian philosopher and disciple of Socrates (470–399 B.C.) who founded the Academy and defined Western philosophy. He was from a noble family and despised the Athenian democracy. His dialogue *Timaeus*, composed around 360 B.C., defined all subsequent Greek and Roman speculation on cosmology and morality. His philosophical dialogues also set the standard of literary Attic Greek prose.

Pliny the Younger (a.k.a. **Gaius Plinius Caecilius Secundus**; 61–112): Roman senator from northern Italy and adopted son of a famous naturalist, Pliny penned letters to Emperor Trajan that reveal the workings of civic life in Asia Minor during the Roman peace.

Plotinus (205–270): Born at Lycopolis, Egypt. Plotinus gained the favor of Emperor Gallienus. He defined Neoplatonism, and his disciple Porphyry compiled Plotinus's teachings into the *Enneads*. Plotinus's vision of the Great Chain of Being and synthesis of Platonic thought provided the intellectual basis for the revival of the pagan cults by Emperor Julian (360–363).

Plutarch of Chaeronea (c. 45–120): Platonic philosopher, biographer, and scholar born at Chaeronea, Boeotia, in central Greece. He studied at both Athens and Rome and was a friend of Emperor Trajan. His works include the *Moralia*, 60 essays on a wide range of topics, and *Parallel Lives of Greeks and Romans*.

Polycarp of Smyrna (fl. 2nd century A.D.): Saint and bishop martyred at an uncertain date during a persecution in c. 150–155. He established the role of bishops in apostolic churches and was in the forefront of fixing the Christian canon by editing the books of the New Testament.

Pompey (a.k.a. **Gnaeus Pompeius Magnus**; 106–48 B.C.): The most talented of Sulla's lieutenants, Pompey rose to be the most celebrated general of the late Roman Republic by series of extraordinary commands. He sided with the Senate against Julius Caesar in 49 B.C., and he was defeated at Pharsalus (48 B.C.) and fled to Egypt, where he was treacherously murdered.

Pontius Pilate (r. 26–36): Roman procurator of Judaea and fifth equestrian governor of Roman Palestine (Judaea and Samaria, notorious for his inept and venal rule. In the Synoptic Gospels, Pilate is presented as reluctant to order the crucifixion of Jesus.

Porphyry of Tyre (c. 232–304): Greek Neoplatonic philosopher who wrote a life of his mentor, the philosopher Plotinus, a work *Against the Christians* (15 books), and a historical chronicle from the fall of Troy to about A.D. 270.

Posidonius of Apamea (135–51 B.C.): Stoic philosopher, historian, and astronomer who studied under Panaetius at Athens. Favorable to Rome, he traveled the lands of the western Mediterranean, writing on geography and ethnography. In his philosophical writings, he refined Plato's doctrine on the soul (*pysche*) and Stoic cosmology.

Praetextatus (a.k.a. **Vettius Agorius Praetextatus**; (315–384): An illustrious pagan senator who was urban prefect in 367 and Praetorian prefect in 384. He and his equally illustrious wife Aconia Fabia Paulina patronized the cults of Rome, protested the anti-pagan legislation of Gratian and Valentinian II, and sponsored traditional letters.

Priscilla and **Maximilla** (fl. mid-2nd century A.D.): Prophetesses and associates of Montanus, through whom the Paraclete (Holy Spirit) was believed to have spoken.

Proclus (c. 410–485): Brilliant Neoplatonic thinker and theurgist who was born of wealthy family in Lycia but studied in Athens under Syrianus and succeeded the latter as head of the Academy in Athens. His *Elements of Theology, Platonic Theology*, and *Elements of Physics* are the climax of Greek philosophical thinking. He composed commentaries on Plato's *Timaeus* and *Alcibiades I*, as well as religious hymns.

Quintus of Smyrna (fl. 4th century A.D.): Pagan poet who composed the epic *Posthomerica*, a work of more than 20,000 lines (twice the length of the *Iliad* and the *Odyssey* combined), which told of events at Troy after Homer's epic leaves off.

Rufinus of Aquileia (c. 350–410): Roman monk who translated Greek theological and historical writings into Latin. In 372, he traveled to Alexandria and then resettled at Jerusalem, where he disputed with Saint Jerome the doctrines of Origen. In 397, Rufinus returned to Rome and translated and adapted into Latin Origen's *On First Principles*.

Salutius (c. 340–370): Author of the Latin treatise *On the Gods and the Cosmos*, a pagan defense of theurgy. A friend to Emperor Julian II, Salutius is sometimes identified with Flavius Salutius, prefect of Gaul (361–363) and consul (363), or with Saturninius Secundus Salutius, Praetorian prefect of the East (361–367), who declined the emperorship after the death of Julian.

Seneca (a.k.a. **Lucius Annaeus Seneca**; 1 B.C.–A.D. 65): Stoic philosopher and tutor of Emperor Nero who was born of a noble Hispano-Roman family of Cordoba. He was exiled from Rome by Emperor Claudius in 41. Agrippina the Younger, fourth wife of Claudius, had Seneca recalled in 49 as a tutor to the future emperor Nero. In 54–62, Seneca and Lucius Afranius Burrus, the Praetorian prefect, acted as regent ministers for Nero. Seneca retired in 62 and was implicated in the Pisonian Conspiracy of 65. He was forced to commit suicide. Seneca wrote philosophical essays, moral letters, and tragedies. He epitomized the Stoic philosopher in public service during the Principate.

Septimius Severus (a.k.a. **Lucius Sepimius Severus**; 146–211; r. 193–211): A native of Lepcis Magna, Africa, who became legate of Upper Pannonia in 193. In 193–195, he defeated his rivals in the second civil war of imperial Rome and founded the Severan dynasty. Septimius Severus made harsh reprisals against his opponents in the Senate, but he secured the frontiers and forged links with the provincial elites, especially those in the East and Africa. He was succeeded by his sons Caracalla and Geta.

Severus Alexander (a.k.a. **Marcus Aurelius Severus Alexander**; 208–235; r. 222–235): Son of Julia Mamaea and the senator Gessius Marcianus, he was the last Severan emperor. In 221, he was promoted to Caesar by his cousin Emperor Elagabalus (r. 218–222), whose devotion to the orgiastic rites of the Syrian sun god of Emesa compromised the dynasty. In contrast, Severus Alexander ruled judiciously under the guidance of his mother, Julia Mamaea. His inconclusive wars against the Persians and Germans led to his assassination by mutinous soldiers of the Rhine army.

Severus II (a.k.a. **Flavius Valerius Severus**; c. 260–307; r. 306–307): An Illyrian officer who was created by Caesar of the West by Galerius in 305. In 306, after the death of Constantius I, Galerius elevated Severus II to Augustus of the West. In 307, Severus invaded the Italian Peninsula, but his soldiers defected, and he fell into the hands of Maxentius, who executed him.

Shāpūr I (r. 241–272): The second Sāsānid shah of Persia, who waged three successful campaigns against the Roman Empire (242–244, 253–255, and 258–260). In 260, he captured Emperor Valerian. He sacked Antioch, the third city of the Roman Empire, in either 253 or 260. Odenathus, prince of Palmyra, compelled Shāpūr to negotiate a peace.

Shāpūr II (r. 309–379): Sāsānid shah of Persia who pursued aggressive policies against Armenia and Rome. In 255–261, he waged a desultory frontier war over the Roman fortresses of Mesopotamia. In 363, he checked the invasion of Julian and compelled Jovian to surrender the strategic fortresses of Mesopotamia, thereby giving Persia the initiative in future wars against Rome.

Shimon bar Kokhba (a.k.a. **Simon ben Kosiba**; r. 132–135): Ruler of Judaea during the Second Jewish Revolt. He was accepted as Messiah by the rabbi Akbia, but in later rabbinical writings he was denounced as Simon bar Kozeba ("son of lies").

Simon Magus (fl. 1ˢᵗ century A.D.): Samaritan magician and convert to Christianity. Simon was accused by Saint Peter of sales of offices (that is, the sin of simony) in Acts 8:9–24). Christian authors condemned Simon as the founder of heresy. Gnostic apocryphal works were attributed to Simon and his reputed followers, the Simonians.

Symeon Stylites (c. 390–459): Christian ascetic who followed the example of Saint Antony. During his last 37 years, he spent his life atop a pillar east of Antioch as a symbol of his withdrawal from the world. He was hailed as the most pious saint of the Roman East, respected by the emperors Theodosius II and Marcian.

Symeon Stylites the Younger (521–597): Born at Antioch, he survived the great plague and so dedicated himself to an ascetic life in imitation of his namesake, living atop a pillar for 68 years.

Symmachus (a.k.a. **Quintus Aurelius Symmachus**; c. 340–402): The most distinguished Roman pagan senator of the 4ᵗʰ century and an accomplished man of letters. He served as proconsul of Africa (373), urban prefect (384–385), and consul (391). He presided over the pagan cultural and literary revival of Rome. In a series of orations (*relationes*), he pleaded for the restoration of the Altar of Victory to the Senate house (*Curia)* in 382–390. He supported Magnus Maximus in 387–388, but Theodosius pardoned him, and he retired from public life after 391.

Synesius of Cyrene (373–414): Philosopher and bishop of Ptolemais, Synesius studied philosophy at Alexandria under Hypatia and then at Athens in 395–399. He was drawn to embrace Christianity through philosophy, and in 410 he was ordained bishop. Besides his philosophical writings, Synesius urged the emperors Arcadius and Theodosius II to discontinue the use of Germanic tribal regiments in favor of native Roman soldiers.

Tacitus (a.k.a. **Publius Cornelius Tacitus**; 56–after 120): From a northern Italian or southern Gallic provincial family, Tacitus entered a senatorial career under Vespasian. In 77, he married Julia, daughter of Gnaeus Julius Agricola. In 97, he was consul, and in 112–113, he was proconsul of Asia. He is the greatest historian of imperial Rome. He wrote *Annals* and *Histories*, covering the periods 14–68 and 68–96, respectively. He also wrote *Germania*, *Agricola*, and *Dialogus de oratoribus.* In *Annals*, Tacitus reports the persecution of Christians by Nero in 64.

Tatian (c. 120–180) translated the Gospels from Greek into Syriac. His *Diatessaron* was a single narrative reconciling the four Gospels.

Tertullian (a.k.a **Quintus Septimius Florens Tertullianus**; c. 160–c. 220): Lawyer and Christian apologist at Carthage who wrote the first major Christian works in Latin. Of foremost importance was his *Apology*, defending Christianity.

Thecla (fl. mid 1st century A.D.): A legendary female apostle mentioned in the *Apocryphal Acts of Saints Paul and Thecla*, written in 2nd century A.D., perhaps by a Montanist. She was an early convert of Paul at Iconium, rejecting marriage and living an ascetic life. She miraculously escaped the arena at Pisidian Antioch and established ascetic communities at Iconium (modern Konya), Seleucia ad Calycadnum (Silifke), and Nicomedia (Izmit). Her tomb near Seleucia became a celebrated pilgrimage site in the 4th century.

Themistius of Constantinople (317–391): Pagan rhetorician and philosopher born of a noble family in Asia Minor, he was a loyal servant at Constantinople to successive emperors between Constantius II (r. 337–361) and Theodosius I (r. 379–395). Constantius II elected Themistius, although a pagan, into the Christian senate of Constantinople (355). Themistius served as proconsul (358) and urban prefect (359–360). He favored Julian II, but he was respected as the senior pagan senator by Julian's Christian successors. Thirty-six orations of Themistius have survived, but his philosophical works and commentaries survive only in fragments.

Theodore of Sykeon (d. 613): A healing saint of Galatia and bishop of Anastasiopolis, he was famous for his miracles and exorcisms that inspired pagan villagers to convert.

Theodosius I (a.k.a. **Theodosius the Great**; c. 346–395; r. 379–395): The son of Count Theodosius, a leading general of Valentinian I, Theodosius rose to high command under Gratian. In 379, as Augustus of the East, Theodosius restored order in the Roman East. In 387, he married Galla, sister of Valentinian II (r. 375–392). In return, Theodosius defeated the usurper Magnus Maximus (r. 383–388), who had overthrown the Western emperor Gratian. A devout Nicene Christian, Theodosius summoned the Second Ecumenical Council in 381 and outlawed pagan sacrifices in 391–392. He faced a revolt of the Western army in 392–394. By the victory at Frigidus (394), Theodoius crushed the rebels and reunited the Roman Empire.

Theodosius II (a.k.a. **Flavius Theodosius**; 401–450; r. 408–450): The son of Aracdius and Eudocia, Theodosius succeeded as a minor. He proved a weak emperor directed by his older sister, Aelia Pulcheria, and his ministers, who were responsible for the Theodosian Walls, the *Theodosian Code* (438), and the Third Ecumenical Council (431).

Theophilus of Antioch (d. c. 183): Bishop who wrote the apology *Ad autolycum*, in which he advanced the doctrine of creation *ex nihilo* and a doctrine of the Trinity.

Thrasea Paetus (a.k.a. **Publius Clodius Thrasea Paetus**; c. 20–66): Roman senator and leading Stoic critic of Nero. Born at Patavium, he was *consul suffectus* in 56 and in 59 retired from the Senate in criticism of Nero's murder of his mother Agrippina and other outrageous conduct. In 66, Thrasea Paetus, perceived as the inspiration behind the Pisonian Conspiracy of 65, was forced to commit suicide on the orders of Nero.

Tiberius (a.k.a. **Tiberius Claudius Nero**; 42 B.C.–A.D. 37; r. A.D. 14–37): The son of Livia Drusilla and her first husband Tiberius Claudius Nero (praetor in 42 B.C.), he was reared in the household of his stepfather Augustus. Tiberius was ill suited for the role of emperor; he withdrew to Capri and fell into depravity. During his reign, the crucifixion of Jesus occurred.

Tiberius Julius Alexander (fl. 1ˢᵗ century A.D.): Born in the reign of Tiberius, he renounced his Judaism and entered imperial service, serving as procurator of Judaea (46–48) and prefect of Egypt (68–69). He first declared for Vespasian as emperor in the civil war of 69 and served on the staff of Titus at the siege of Jerusalem.

Timothy (d. c. 80): The associate of Saint Paul during his second (49–52) and third (56–57) missions to the churches of Asia Minor and Greece. He is the recipient of Paul's Epistles 1 and 2 Timothy and possible author of many of the Deutero-Pauline letters in the New Testament. He was later reported to have been bishop of Ephesus (65–80), a tradition likely based on the chronicle of Hegesippus.

Tiridates III (250–339; r. 285–339): Arsacid king of Armenia who was a loyal ally of Rome in the wars against the Persians. In 301, he reportedly converted to Christianity and was baptized by Gregory the Illuminator. There is reason to believe that Tiridates might have converted after the conversion of Emperor Constantine I.

Thomas Didymus (fl. 1ˢᵗ century A.D.): Saint and one of Jesus Christ's 12 apostles, he was known as Doubting Thomas upon seeing Jesus after the resurrection (John 20:28). In the *Acts of Saint Thomas*, written in the early 2ⁿᵈ century A.D., Thomas was credited with missions to the cities of India and to the Parthian Empire. The reports are plausible, and Thomas would have traveled on ships crossing the Erythraean Sea (Indian Ocean). Thomas is thus the first apostle to have preached outside the Roman Empire.

Trajan (a.k.a. **Marcus Ulpius Traianus**; 52–117; r. 98–117): The son of the senator and namesake of a Hispano-Roman family of Italica. Trajan was adopted by Nerva (r. 96–98) and so succeeded as the first Roman emperor of provincial origin. Trajan conquered Dacia (101–102; 105–106), smashed Parthian power (113–117), and brought the Roman Empire to its territorial zenith. He initiated a spectacular building program at Rome. Hailed *optimus princeps*, Trajan founded the third dynasty of imperial Rome and was succeeded by his adopted son, Hadrian.

Trajan Decius (a.k.a. **Gaius Messius Quintus Traianus Decius**; 201–251; r. 249–251): A Pannonian provincial who attained senatorial rank under Severus Alexander and legate of Upper Pannonia, he was declared emperor by the Danube legions. He defeated and slew the emperor Philip at Verona in 249. Trajan Decius was defeated and slain by the Goths at Abrittus in Lower Moesia. He initiated the first empire-wide persecution of Christians in 250–251.

Trebonianus Gallus (a.k.a. **Gaius Vibius Trebonianus Gallus**; r. 251–253): A legate of Trajan Decius, he was declared emperor by the Roman army after Decius's death. Gallus faced attacks by northern barbarians and Persians. In 253, he was defeated and slain by Aemilian, governor of Moesia, whom the Danube legions had declared emperor.

Ulfilas (a.k.a. **Wulfila**; 311–381): Arian bishop of the Goths consecrated at the synod of Antioch in 341. As missionary to the Goths, Ulfilas adapted the Greek alphabet to Gothic and translated the Bible into Gothic in 341–343.

Valens (a.k.a. **Flavius Valens**; c. 328–378; r. 364-378): Born of a military family in Pannonia, he served under Julian and Jovian. In 364, his brother Valentinian I created Valens emperor of the East. A devoted Arian Christian, Valens faced opposition from the Nicene bishops. His Persian war was inconclusive. In 378, he was decisively defeated and slain by the Goths at Adrianople.

Valentinian I (a.k.a. **Flavius Valentinianus**; 321–375; r. 364–375): Born to a Pannonian military family, he was a senior officer acclaimed emperor by the Eastern army after the death of Jovian. Valentinian appointed his brother Valens emperor of the East and campaigned against the Germans on the Rhine and Upper Danube, where he strengthened fortifications. He was succeeded by his two sons, Gratian (r. 367–383) and Valentinian II (r. 375–392).

Valentinian II (a.k.a. **Flavius Valentinianus**; 371–392; r. 375–392): The son of Valentinian and Justina and half-brother of Gratian. In 375, he was declared joint emperor and resided at Mediolaunum (Milan) under the influence of his mother and Bishop Ambrose of Milan. Reared as a staunch Nicene, Valentinian supported anti-pagan measures that precipitated the revolt of Magnus Maximus. In 387, he fled to Constantinople and allied with Theodosius I against Magnus Maximus. In 388–392, Valentinian was restored as emperor of the West, and he was murdered on the orders of Arbogast.

Valentinus (c. 100–160): A noted Gnostic teacher and thinker born at Alexandria who founded school at Rome. His dualist cosmology, based on allegorical myths and middle Platonic principles, were rejected by Christians as heretical. The *Gospel of Truth*, among the texts found at Nag Hammadi, was penned by Valentinus.

Valerian I (a.k.a. **Publius Licinius Valerianus**; c. 195–260; r. 253–260): A senator of noble origins who became legate of Raetia in the civil war of 253. He was proclaimed emperor by the Rhine legions and defeated his rival Aemilian. Valerian issued the second empire-wide persecution of Christians in 258–260. Valerian faced barbarian assaults along the northern and eastern frontiers. He waged two Persian wars (253–256 and 258–260). He was treacherously captured by Shah Shāpūr in 260 and died in captivity.

Vetranio (d. c. 360; r. 350): Officer of the Illyrian army who was proclaimed emperor by his army in opposition to Magnentius. Vetranio checked Magnentius's advance, declared his loyalty to Constantius II, and abdicated and retired when Constantius II arrived. Vetranio minted the first coins carrying the labarum with the Latin inscription *In hoc signo victor eris*, the words Constantine was reported to have seen before the Battle of Milvian Bridge in 312.

Vergil (a.k.a. **Publius Vergilius Maro**; 70–19 B.C.): One of the most important poets of ancient Rome. Born at Mantua in Cisalpine Gaul (northern Italy), he was a friend of Horace. His patrons included Maecenas, Asinius Pollio, and Augustus. A poetic genius, Vergil composed the national Roman epic, the *Aeneid* and the pastoral poems *Eclogues* (or *Bucolics*) and *Georgics*. He shares with Horace the rank of poet laureate of the Augustan court.

Vigilius (r. 537–555): Pope elected with the support Empress Theodora so that he could work for religious unity with the Monophysites. An exile at Constantinople after the Gothic recapture of Rome in 546, he refused to compromise the papal position and so opposed Justinian at the Fifth Ecumenical Council (553). His arrest, exile, and premature death undermined Justinian's popularity in the Western church.

Xenophon of Ephesus (fl. early 2nd century A.D.): Novelist of the Second Sophistic movement who wrote the *Ephesian Tale*, a fanciful romance between Anthia and Habrocomes. The story provides details of cult practices and social mores in the Roman East.

Zeno (c. 425–491; r, 474-491): An Isaurian officer, he married Ariadne, daughter of Emperor Leo I, and so succeeded as Eastern Roman emperor. He sought reconciliation with the Monophysites by issuing the *Henotikon* (482), and he crushed serious rebellions of the provincial armies.

Zeno of Citium (335–263 B.C.): A merchant turned philosopher and founder of Stoicism. From 301 B.C., he taught in the Stoa Poikile at Athens because he could not afford a proper school. His ethnical and philosophical writings survive in fragments.

Zenobia (a.k.a. **Septimia Zenobia**; r. 267–272): The wife of Odenathus of Palmyra and mother of Vaballathus. In 267, she succeeded her husband's extraordinary position in the Roman East. Styling herself as Empress Augusta, she advanced her son Vaballathus as emperor in 270. In 270–271, Palmyrene forces occupied Asia Minor, Palestine, and Egypt. In 272, she was defeated by Aurelian and allowed to retire to a Campania villa.

Zoroaster (c. 625–550 B.C.): Prophet and reputed author of the oldest *gathas* in the Avesta, therefore claimed as the founder of Zoroastrian monotheism. He was believed to have originated from Eastern Iran. *See* **Kartir Hangirpe**.

Zosimus (c. 480–515): Greek historian who wrote *New History*, in which he attributes the decline of Roman power to the rejection of the gods in favor of Christianity.

Bibliography

Primary Sources

Ammainus Marcellinus. *The Later Roman Empire, A.D. 354–378.* Translated by Walter Hamilton. New York: Penguin/Viking, 1986. An abridged modern translation.

———. *Roman History.* 3 vols. Loeb Classical Library. Translated by C. Rolfe. Cambridge, MA: Harvard University Press, 1939—1950. The complete history of Ammianus with later chronicle *Excerpta Valensiana* included in volume 3.

The Ante-Nicene Fathers: Translations of the Writings of the Fathers down to A.D. 325. Vols. 1–10. Buffalo, NY, 1885–1896. Reprint, Peabody, MA: Henrickson Publishers, 1994. Indispensable translations of all Christian authors prior to the Council of Nicaea.

Apuleius. *The Golden Ass.* Translated by E. J. Kennedy. Baltimore: Penguin Classics, 1999.

Aristides, Aelius. *Aelius Aristides and the Sacred Tales.* Translated by C. A. Behr. Amsterdam, The Netherlands: Adolf M. Hakkert, 1968.

Athanasius. *The Life of Saint Antony and the Letter to Marcellinus.* Translated by R. C. Gregg. Mahwah, NJ: The Paulist Press, 1979.

Augustine. *The City of God against the Pagans.* Translated by R. W. Dyson. Cambridge: Cambridge University Press, 1998. Recommended translation.

———. *Confessions.* Translated by Henry Chadwick. Oxford: Oxford University Press, 2009. Excellent recommended translation and introduction.

Celsus. *On True Doctrine: A Discourse against the Christians.* Translated by R. J. Hoffman. Oxford: Oxford University Press, 1987. Text reconstructed from the quotations by Origen.

Cicero, M. Tullius. *De re publica, de legibus*. Vol. 16 of the Loeb Classical Library. Translated by C. W. Keyes. London: William Heinemann, 1928. "Dream of Scipio" in book 6 of *De re publica* is the most elegant Latin exposition of the Stoic cosmology.

Clement of Alexandria. *Works*. Loeb Classical Library. Translated by G. W. Butterworth. Cambridge, MA: Harvard University Press, 1919.

Copenhaven, Brian P. *Hermetica. The Greek Corpus Hermeticum and the Latin Asclepius in a New English Translation with Notes and Introduction*. Cambridge: Cambridge University Press, 1992. Late antique pagan mystical texts.

Dawes, Elizabeth A. S., and Norman H. Baynes, trans. *Three Byzantine Saints: Contemporary Biographies of Saint Daniel the Stylite, Saint Theodore of Sykeon, and Saint John the Almsgiver*. Yonkers, NY: Saint Vladimir's Seminary Press, 1977. The lives of these three saints of the 6th and 7th centuries are vital sources on the conversion of the countryside.

Doran, Robert, trans. *Stewards of the Poor: The Man of God, Babbula, and Hiba in Fifth-Century Edessa*. Kalamazoo, MI: Cistercian Publications, 2006. Important translation of the role of bishops at Edessa (modern Urfa) as patrons of the power.

Eusebius. *The History of the Church*. Rev. ed. Translated by G. W. Williamson. Baltimore: Penguin Classics, 1990. Recommended translation of this indispensable source.

———. *The Life of Constantine*. Translated by Averil Cameron and Stuart G. Hall. Oxford: Oxford University Press, 1999. Superb edition with excellent notes and introduction.

Gardmer, Iain, and Samuel N. Lieu. *Manichaean Texts from the Roman Empire*. Cambridge: Cambridge University Press, 2004. Definitive modern translations.

Hadot, Pierre. *Plotinus or the Simplicity of Vision*. Translated by Michael Chase. Chicago: University of Chicago Press, 1991. Best modern translation and discussion of Plotinus's mystical vision.

Hardy, Edward R., trans. and ed. *The Christology of the Later Fathers*. Philadelphia: The Westminster Press, 1964. Translations of the crucial texts for the First Four Ecumenical Councils.

Iamblichus of Chalcis. *De mysteriis*. Translated by Emma C. Clarke, John M. Dillon, and J. P. Hershbell. Leiden, The Netherlands: Brill, 2004.

Irenaeus. *Irenaeus of Lyons*. Translated by Robert M. Grant. New York: Routledge, 1996. Recommended modern translation.

————. *Saint Irenaeus of Lyons: Against Heresies*. Reprint ed. N.p.: CreateSpace (www.amazon.com), 2010. Reprint from Alexander Roberts, James Donaldson, and A. Cleveland Coxe, eds. Ante-Nicene Fathers volume.

Josephus. *Antiquities of the Jews*. Vols. 5–11. Loeb Classical Library. Translated by Henry St. John Thackeray and Ralph Marcus. Cambridge, MA: Harvard University Press, 1930–1965. Fundamental source for Jewish history.

Josephus, Flavius. *The Jewish Wars*. Translated by B. Radice. Rev. ed. Baltimore: Penguin Classics, 1984.

Justin Martyr. *Saint Justin Martyr: The First and Second Apologies*. Translated by L. W. Barnard. Mahwah, NJ: Paulist Press, 1996.

Julian. *Works*. 3 vols. Loeb Classical Library. Translated by W. C. Wright. Cambridge, MA: Harvard University Press, 1913–1923.

Lactantius. *On the Manner in Which the Persecutors Died*. Whitefish, MT: Kessinger Publishing, 2004; reprint of the translation from Ante-Nicene Christian Library, vol. 21, edited by Alexander Roberts and James Donaldson. Edinburgh: T and T. Clark, 1871.

Layton, Bentley, trans. and ed. *The Gnostic Scriptures: A New Translation with Annotations and Introductions*. Garden City, NY: Anchor Books. 1995. The indispensable modern translation of Gnostic texts with superb commentary.

Louth, Andrew, and M. Saniforth, ed. and trans. *Early Christian Writings: The Apostolic Fathers*. Baltimore: Penguin Classics, 1987.

Lucian. *On the Syrian Goddess*. Translated by J. J. Lightfoot. Oxford: Oxford University Press, 2005.

————. *Selected Dialogues*. Translated by Desmond Costa. Oxford: Oxford University Press, 2005. Excellent modern translations especially for the dialogues on Pergerinus and Alexander of Abonouteichos.

————. *Works*. 8 vols. Loeb Classical Library. Translated by A. M. Harmon. Cambridge, MA: Harvard University Press, 1968–1979. Volume 4 includes the life of Alexander of Abonouteichos.

MacMullen, Ramsay, and Eugene N. Lane, eds. *Paganism and Christianity*. Minneapolis: University of Minnesota Press, 1992. Important translations of many inscriptions, legal texts, and other documents not otherwise available.

Marcus Aurelius. *Meditations*. Translated by M. Hammond. Baltimore: Penguin Classics, 2006. The reflection of the emperor who was the quintessential Stoic.

Musurillo, Herbert, ed. and trans. *Acts of the Christian Martyrs*. Oxford: Clarendon Press, 1972. Recommended translations for the early acts of the Christian martyrs.

Nixon, C. E. V., and Barbara S. Rodgers. *In Praise of Later Roman Emperors: The Panegyrici Latini*. Berkeley: University of California Press, 1994. Translation and discussion of the late Roman panegyrics essential for imperial ideology.

Origen. *On First Principles.* Translated by G. W. Butterworth. New York: Peter Smith Publishers, 1973. Recommended translation.

Philo of Alexandria. *On Creation: Interpretation of Genesis.* Vol. 1. Loeb Classical Library. Translated by F. H. Colson and G. H. Whitaker. Cambridge, MA: Harvard University Press, 1929. Crucial Platonized cosmology of the most learned Jewish scholar of the Roman era.

Philostratus. *The Life of Apollonius of Tyana.* 2 vols. Loeb Classical Library. Translated by C. P. Jones. Cambridge, MA: Harvard University Press, 2005–2006.

Plato. *Timaeus and Critias.* Translated by D. Lee. Baltimore: Penguin Classics, 1972. The indispensable Platonic dialogues on cosmology.

Pliny the Younger. *The Letters of Pliny the Younger.* Translated by B. Radice. Baltimore: Penguin Classics, 1963. Letters, book X, 96–97 contain the exchange between Pliny and Trajan on Christians.

Plotinus. *The Enneads.* Translated by Stephen MacKenna. London: Faber, 1969. Older, literate translation.

Plutarch. *Moralia.* Vol. 5. Loeb Classical Library. Translated by Frank Cole Babbit. Cambridge, MA: Harvard University Press, 1968. Contains Plutarch's essay on the moral and philosophical meaning of the myth of Serapis and Isis.

Porphyry. *Against the Christians: The Literary Remains.* Translated by R. J. Hoffman. Amherst, NY: Prometheus Books, 1994. Reconstructed text of Porphyry's critique.

Procopius. *The Secret History.* Translated by Peter Sarris and G. A. Williamson. Baltimore: Penguin Classics, 2007.

———. *Works.* 7 vols. Loeb Classical Library. Translated by H. B. Dewing. Cambridge, MA: Harvard University Press, 1914–1940. Primary source on the reign of Justinian.

Rees, Roger, ed. and trans. *Diocletian and the Tetrarchy*. Edinburgh: University of Edinburgh Press, 2004. Modern translation of legal texts, inscriptions, and other sources vital for the Great Persecution.

Richardson, Cyril C., ed. *Early Christian Fathers*. New York: Collier Books, 1995. Recommended modern translation of the works of key church fathers before the Council of Nicaea. Excellent introduction and notes.

Tacitus, Cornelius P. *The Annals of Imperial Rome*. Translated by Michael Grant. Baltimore: Penguin Classics, 1956. Includes an eyewitness account of the persecution of 64.

Theophilus of Antioch. *Ad autocylum*. Translated by Robert M. Grant. Oxford: Clarendon Press, 1970.

Tertulllian. *Apologia and De spectaculis*. Minucius Felix. *Octavius*. Loeb Classical Library. Translated by T. R. Glover and Gerald H. Rendall. Cambridge, MA: Harvard University Press, 1931.

Vermes, Geza, trans. *The Complete Dead Sea Scrolls in English*. Rev. ed. Baltimore: Penguin Books, 2004. Excellent translation and introduction by leading scholar.

Wilkinson, John, trans. *Egeria's Travels*. 3rd ed. Warminster: Aris and Phillips, 1999. Translation of the first account of a pilgrimage to the tomb of Saint Thecla and the Holy Land.

Zosimus. *New History*. Translated by Ronald T. Ridley. Sydney: Australian Association for Byzantine Studies, 1982. Modern translation of this polemical pagan historian.

Secondary Literature

Alföldi, Andrew. *A Conflict of Ideas in the Late Roman Empire: The Clash between the Senate and Valentinian*. Translated by Harold Mattingly. Oxford: Clarendon Press, 1979.

————. *The Conversion of Constantine and Pagan Rome*. Translated by Harold Mattingly. Oxford: Oxford University Press, 1948.

Anderson, James C. Jr. *Roman Architecture and Society*. Baltimore: Johns Hopkins University Press, 1997.

Arnold, Edward Vernon. *Roman Stoicism, being Lectures on the History of Stoic Philosophy with Special Reference to its Development within the Roman Empire*. Cambridge: Cambridge University Press, 1911.

Athanassiadi-Fowden, Polymnia. *Julian and Hellenism: An Intellectual Biography*. Oxford: Oxford University Press, 1981. Arguing that Julian was a devotee of Mithras.

Atkins, Margaret, and Robin Osborne, eds. *Poverty in the Roman World*. Cambridge: Cambridge University Press, 2009.

Ayres, Lewis. *Nicaea and Its Legacy: An Approach to Fourth-Century Trinitarian Theology*. Oxford: Oxford University Press, 2004.

Barker, John. *Justinian and the Later Roman Empire*. Madison: University of Wisconsin Press, 1966. Mediocre narrative of the reign.

Barnes, Timothy D. *Athanasius and Constantius: Theology and Politics in the Constantinian Empire*. Cambridge, MA: Harvard University Press, 1993.

————. *Constantine and Eusebius*. Cambridge, MA: Harvard University Press, 1986. Arguing for an implausible rapid conversion of the Roman world.

————. *The New Empire of Diocletian and Constantine*. Cambridge, MA.: Harvard University Press, 1982. Controversial reconstruction of late Roman chronology.

————. *Tertullian: A Historical and Literary Study*. Oxford: Oxford University Press, 1985.

Barrow, Reginald H. *Prefect and Emperor: Relationes.* Oxford: Oxford University Press, 1973. Study with text and discussion on the dispute over the Altar of Victory in 382–390.

Beckwith, John. *Early Christian and Byzantine Art.* New Haven, CT: Yale University Press, 1986.

Bigg, Charles. *The Christian Platonists of Alexandria.* Oxford: Clarendon Press, 1888. Thoughtful essays on Saint Clement and Origen.

Bowersock, G. W. *Augustus and the Greek World.* Oxford: Oxford University Press, 1982.

———. *Greek Sophists in the Roman Empire.* Oxford: Oxford University Press, 2003. Concise introduction to the leading figures of the Second Sophistic movement.

———. *Hellenism in Late Antiquity.* Ann Arbor: University of Michigan Press, 1990.

———. *Julian the Apostate.* Cambridge, MA: Harvard University Press, 1978.

Brandon, S. G. F. *Jesus and the Zealots: A Study of the Political Factor in Primitive Christianity.* New York: Charles Scribner's Sons, 1967. Controversial study on the political aspects of Jesus's teachings; excellent on the turbulent politics of Roman Palestine in the 1st century A.D.

Bregman, Jay. *Synesius of Cyrene, Philosopher-Bishop.* Berkeley: University of California Press, 1982. Model study of the conversion of the pagan intellectual classes in late antiquity.

Brown, Peter. *Augustine of Hippo.* Berkeley: University of California Press, 1967. Brilliant biography evoking the world of the late antiquity; a masterpiece.

————. *The Body and Society: Men, Women, and Sexual Renunciation in Early Christianity.* Rev. ed. New York: Columbia University Press, 2008. Brilliant and recommended discussion of asceticism and spirituality.

————. *The Cult of Saints: Its Rise and Function in Latin Christianity.* Chicago, IL: Chicago University Press, 1981.

————. *The Making of Late Antiquity.* Cambridge, MA: Harvard University Press, 1977. Thoughtful essays on the social and spiritual changes; superb read.

————. *Poverty and Leadership in the Later Roman Empire.* Waltham, MA: Brandeis University Press, 2001. Excellent on the role of bishops in late antiquity.

————. *Power and Persuasion in Late Antiquity: Towards a Christian Empire.* Madison: University of Wisconsin Press, 1992. Concise and masterful analysis of the power of rhetoric.

————. "The Rise and Function of the Holy Man in Late Antiquity." *Journal of Roman Studies* 61 (1971): 80–101; reprinted in *Society and the Holy in Late Antiquity.* Berkeley: University of California Press, 1982. Seminal article.

————. *Society and the Holy in Late Antiquity.* Berkeley: University of California Press, 1982. Reprint of seminal articles.

————. *The World of Late Antiquity: A.D. 150–750.* New York: W. W. Norton and Company, 1989. Concise introduction.

Brown, Raymond E. *The Churches the Apostles Left Behind.* New York: Paulist Press, 1984

————. *An Introduction to New Testament Christology.* New York: Paulist Press, 1994.

Brown, Raymond E., and John P. Meier. *Antioch and Rome: New Testament Cradles of Catholic Christianity*. New York: Paulist Press, 1983. Important scholarly study on the early traditions about Saints Paul and Peter.

Browning, Robert. *Justinian and Theodora*. Piscataway, NJ: Gorgias Press, 2009.

Burckhadt, Jakob. *The Age of Constantine the Great*. Translated by Moses Hadas. Berkeley: University of California Press, 1983. Classic rationalist study by brilliant humanist and scholar of the 19th century.

Burkert, Walter. *Ancient Mystery Cults*. Cambridge, MA: Harvard University Press, 1987.

———. *Greek Religion*. Translated by John Raffan. Cambridge, MA: Harvard University Press, 1985.

———. *Homo Necans: The Anthropology of Ancient Greek Sacrificial Ritual and Myth*. Translated by Peter Bing. Berkeley: University of California Press, 1983. Recommended modern study.

Burrell, Barbara. *Neokoroi: Greek Cities and Roman Emperors*. Leiden, The Netherlands: Brill, 2004. Learned study on the role of the imperial cult in Greek cities.

Cameron, Alan. *The Last Pagans of Rome*. Oxford: Oxford University Press, 2011. Newest and indispensable study of the decline of paganism after the 391–392 laws.

Cameron, Averil. *The Mediterranean World in Late Antiquity: A.D. 395–600*. 2nd ed. New York: Routledge, 2011. Excellent introduction.

Chitty, D. J. *The Desert, A City: A Introduction to the Study of Egyptian and Palestinian Monasticism under the Christian Empire*. Yonkers, NY: St. Vladimir's Seminary Press, 1977.

Chuvin, Pierre. *A Chronicle of the Last Pagans*. Translated by B. A. Archer. Cambridge, MA: Harvard University Press, 1990.

Corcoran, Simon. *The Empire of Tetrarchs: Imperial Pronouncements and Government, A.D. 284–324*. Rev. ed. Oxford: Oxford University Press, 2000.

Cornford, Francis M. *Plato's Cosmology: The Timaeus of Plato*. London: Kegan Paul, Trench, Trubner and Co., 1937; Reprint, Indianopolis: Hackett Publishing, 1997. Outstanding analysis by a leading scholar of Plato.

Cumont, Franz. *The Mysteries of Mithra*. Translated by Thomas J. McCormack. Chicago: Open Press, 1903; Reprint, F.Q. Legacy Books, 2010. Seminal work on the cult of Mithras.

———. *Oriental Religions in Roman Paganism*. Translated by Grant Showerman. New York: Dover Books, 1956; Reprint, Charleston, SC: Biblo Bazaar, 2007. Seminal work on mystery cults.

Dietz Maribel. *Wandering Monks, Virgins and Pilgrims: Ascetic Travel in the Mediterranean World, A.D. 300–800*. State College: Pennsylvania State University Press, 2005.

Digeser, Elizabeth DePalma. *The Making of a Christian Empire: Lactantius and Rome*. Ithaca, NY: Cornell University Press, 2000.

Dill, Samuel. *Roman Society in the Last Century of the Western Empire*. 2nd ed. London: Macmillan, 1899. Still a superb evoking of the literary and cultural life of late pagan Rome and the Senate.

Dillon, John. *The Great Tradition: Further Studies on the Development of Platonism and Early Christianity*. Aldershot, UK: Ashgate Publishing, 1997.

———. *The Golden Chain: Studies in the Development of Platonism and Christianity*. Brookfield, VT: Variorum, 1990.

———. *The Middle Platonists: A Study of Platonism, 80 B.C. to A.D. 200*. Ithaca, NY: Cornell University Press, 1977. Indispensable study.

Dodds, Eric R. *The Greeks and the Irrational*. Berkeley: University of California Press, 1951. Provocative work on Greek religious values.

———. *Pagan and Christian in the Age of Anxiety: Some Aspects of the Religious Experience from Marcus Aurelius to Constantine*. Cambridge: Cambridge University Press, 1991. Classic study on the pagan spiritual crisis.

Drake, H. A. *Constantine and the Bishops: The Politics of Intolerance*. Baltimore: Johns Hopkins University Press, 2002. A controversial view of the politics of conversion based on modern analogies from political science.

Drijvers, Hendrik Jan Willem. *Helena Augusta: The Mother of Constantine the Great and the Legend of Her Finding of the True Cross*. Leiden. The Netherlands: Brill, 1992. Excellent scholarly work.

Eadie, John, ed. *The Conversion of Constantine*. Pittsburgh, PA: Krieger Publishing, 1977. Excellent introduction of sources and excerpts of the modern controversy.

Elsner, John. *Imperial Rome and Christian Triumph: The Art of the Roman Empire, A.D. 100–450*. Oxford: Oxford University Press, 1999. Recommended introduction to aesthetics and arts.

Finn, Richard. *Almsgiving in the Later Roman Empire: Christian Promotion and Practice (313–450)*. Oxford: Oxford University Press, 2006.

Fishwick, Duncan. *The Imperial Cult in the Latin West: Studies in the Ruler Cult in the Western Provinces of the Roman Empire*. Leiden, The Netherlands: Brill, 2005.

Fowden, Garth. *The Egyptian Hermes: A Historical Approach to the Late Pagan Mind*. Princeton, NJ: Princeton University Press, 1986. Study of late pagan mysticism.

————. *Empire to Commonwealth: Consequences of Monotheism in Late Antiquity*. Princeton, NJ: Princeton University Press, 1994. Insightful work on the role of monotheism across Eurasia between A.D. 300 and 700.

Fox, Robin Lane. *Pagans and Christians*. New York: HarperCollins, 1988. Popular and literate work on the conversion.

Frend, William Hugh Clifford. *The Donatist Church: A Movement of Protest in Roman North Africa*. 2nd ed. Oxford: Clarendon Press, 1985. Classic study.

————. *Martyrdom and Persecution in the Early Church: A Study of Conflict from Maccabees to Donatus*. Oxford: Blackwell, 1965; Reprint, Grand Rapids, MI, 1981. Seminal and magisterial work; indispensable.

————. *The Rise of Christianity*. Philadelphia: Fortress Press, 1984. Excellent reference work on Christianity; dated on scholarship about paganism.

————. *Rise of the Monophysite Movement: Chapters in the History of the Church in the Fifth and Sixth Centuries*. Cambridge: Cambridge University Press, 1972.

Garnsey, Peter. *Social Status and Legal Privilege in the Roman Empire*. Oxford: Oxford University Press, 1970.

Garnsey, Peter, and Richard Saller. *The Roman Empire: Economy, Society and Culture*. Berkeley: University of California Press, 1987. Recommended introduction.

Gibson, Elsa. *The "Christians for Christians" Inscriptions of Phrygia*. Missoula: The Scholars Press, 1978. Collection and translations of the pre-Nicene Christian funerary monuments of the Upper Tembris valley in Asia Minor.

Goodman, Martin. *The Ruling Classes of Judaea: The Origins of the Jewish Revolt against Rome, A.D. 66–70*. Cambridge: Cambridge University Press, 1966. Excellent on the social and political conditions for Jews under Roman rule.

————. *State and Society in Roman Galilee, A.D. 132–212*. Totowa, NJ: Rowman and Allanheld, 1983.

Grant, Robert M. *Augustus to Constantine: Thrust of the Christian Movement in to the Roman World*. New York: Collins Press, 1971. Recommended introduction.

————. *Formation of the New Testament*. London: Hutchinson Press, 1965. Superb discussion of the issue.

————. *Gnosticism and Early Christianity*. New York: Columbia University Press, 1954.

Green, Tamara. *The City of the Moon: The Religious Traditions of Harran*. Leiden, The Netherlands: Brill, 1992. Learned study for the survival of paganism at Carrhae (Harran) into the 10th century.

Gregory, Kent. *Vox Populi: Popular Opinion and Violence in the Religious Controversies of the Fifth Century A.D.* Columbus: Ohio State University Press, 1979. Fine on the urban riots and ecclesiastical politics of the Great Councils.

Guthrie, W.K.C. *The Greeks and Their Gods*. Boston: Beacon Press, 1955. Dated classic study on Greek religion.

Harl, Kenneth W. *Civic Coins and Civic Politics in the Roman East, 180–275 A.D.* Berkeley: University of California Press, 1987. Arguing against the spiritual decline of paganism.

————. *Coinage in the Roman Economy, 300 B.C.–A.D. 700*. Baltimore: Johns Hopkins University Press, 1996. Reassessment of the impact of debasement of the coinage.

————. "From Pagan to Christian in the Cities of Asia Minor." *Urban Centers and Rural Contexts in Late Antiquity*. Vol. 3 in Shifting Frontiers in Classical Antiquity. Edited by John Eadie and Thomas Burns. East Lansing: Michigan State University Press, 2001.

————. "Sacrifice and Pagan Belief in Fifth- and Sixth-Century Byzantium." *Past and Present* 128 (August 1990): 7–27.

Hatlie, Peter. *The Monks and Monasteries of Constantinople, c. 350–850.* Cambridge: Cambridge University Press, 2007.

Herrin, Judith. *The Formation of Christendom.* Princeton, NJ: Princeton University Press, 1987. Thoughtful synthesis of cultural and religious change between A.D. 300 and 800.

Harris, William V. *Ancient Literacy.* Cambridge, MA: Harvard University Press, 1989.

Hirschfeld, Yizhar. *The Judean Desert Monasteries in the Byzantine Period.* New Haven, CT: Yale University Press, 1992.

Holman, Susan R. *The Hungry Are Dying: Beggars and Bishops in Roman Cappadocia.* Oxford: Oxford University Press, 2001.

Holum, Kenneth G. *Theodosian Empresses: Women and Imperial Dominion in Late Antiquity.* Berkeley: University of California Press, 1989. Excellent on the role of Christian empresses as patrons of holy men and conversion.

Hopkins, Keith. "Murderous Games." *Death and Renewal.* Cambridge: Cambridge University Press, 1983. Seminal study on the role of gladiatorial combats and cult of blood in the Roman arena.

Hunt, Edward D. *Holy Land Pilgrimage in the Later Roman Empire, A.D. 312–460.* Oxford: Oxford University Press, 1982. Excellent.

Jones, Arnold H. M. *Constantine and the Conversion of Europe.* London: Macmillan, 1948. Available from the University of Toronto Press MART (Medieval Academy Reprints for Teaching), 1970.

————. *The Decline of the Ancient World.* London: The Longman Group, 1975. Strong on institutional and legal history.

————. *The Greek City from Alexander to Justinian*. Oxford: Clarendon Press, 1940. Fundamental study with excellent citation of sources.

Jones, C. P. *Culture and Society in Lucian*. Cambridge, MA: Harvard University Press, 1986.

————. *Kinship Diplomacy in the Ancient World*. Cambridge, MA: Harvard University Press, 1999.

————. *The New Heroes in Antiquity: Achilles to Antinoos*. Cambridge, MA: Harvard University Press, 2010.

————. *Plutarch and Rome*. Oxford: Clarendon Press, 1971.

————. *The Roman World of Dio Chyrsostom*. Cambridge, MA: Harvard University Press, 1979. Excellent view of the social and cultural world of the Second Sophistic movement.

Kaegi, Walter E., Jr. *Byzantium and the Decline of Rome*. Princeton, NJ: Princeton University Press, 1968. Important study on how the Christian elite of Constantinople theologically and ideologically redefined themselves in light of the decline of the Roman West.

Kaster, Robert A. *Guardians of Language: Grammarian and Society in Late Antiquity*. Berkeley: University of California Press, 1988.

King, Noel Q. *The Emperor Theodosius and the Establishment of Christianity*. London: Westminster Press, 1960.

Kitzinger, Ernst. *Byzantine Art in the Making: Main Lines of Stylistic Development in Mediterranean Art, 3rd–7th Century*. Cambridge, MA: Harvard University Press, 1980. Provocative and wide-ranging essays.

Koester, Helmut, ed. *Ephesos: Metropolis of Asia. An Interdisciplinary Approach to its Archaeology, Religion, and Culture*. Vol. 41 in Harvard Theological Studies. Valley Forge, PA: Trinity Press International, 1995.

————, ed. *Pergamon, Citadel of the Gods: Archaeological Record, Literary Description, and Archaeological Development*. Vol. 46 in Harvard Theological Studies. Valley Forge, PA: Trinity Press International, 1995.

Krautheimer, Richard. *Early Christian Architecture*. 4th ed. New Haven, CT: Yale University Press, 1984. Recommended.

————. *Three Christian Capitals: Topography and Politics*. Berkeley: University of California Press, 1987. Excellent study on role of Christian capitals (Milan, Rome, and Constantinople) in Christianization.

Lenski, Noel. *The Crisis of the Roman Empire: Valens and the Roman State in the Fourth Century A.D.* Berkeley: University of California Press, 2002. With excellent chapter on Arianism and paganism.

Liebeschuetz, J. H. W. G. *Continuity and Change in Roman Religion*. Oxford: Oxford University Press, 1975. Recommended for ritual and practice.

Lieu, Samuel. *Manichaeism in the Later Roman Empire and Medieval China: A Historical Study*. Manchester: Manchester University Press, 1985. The standard study based on source.

L'Orange, Hans Peter. *Art Forms and Civic Life in the Late Roman Empire*. Princeton, NJ: Princeton University Press, 1965. Provocative study on changes in society and religion reflected in art and architecture.

Luck, Georg, trans. *Arcana Mundi*. Baltimore: Johns Hopkins University Press, 1985. Translations and discussion of magical texts from the Roman world.

MacCormack, Sabine. *Art and Ceremony in Late Antiquity*. Berkeley: University of California Press, 1982. Learned study with an important discussion on the influence of Christainity in shaping late Roman ideology.

MacMullen, Ramsay. *Changes in the Roman Empire: Essays in the Ordinary*. Princeton, NJ: Princeton University Press, 1990. Seminal articles on social history republished.

————, *Christianizing the Roman Empire, A.D. 100–400*. New Haven, CT: Yale University Press, 1986. Social forces at work in conversion.

————. *Constantine*. New York: Routledge, 1987. Excellent on the social world of Constantine.

————. *Enemies of the Roman Order: Treason, Unrest, and Alienation in the Empire*. Cambridge, MA: Harvard University Press, 1966. Recommended.

————. *Roman Government's Response to Crisis, 235–337 A.D.* New Haven, CT: Yale University Press, 1972. Essays on transformation wrought by crisis.

————. *Paganism in the Roman Empire*. New Haven, CT: Yale University Press, 1982. Indispensable.

————. *The Second Church: Popular Christianity A.D. 200–400*. Atlanta: Society of Biblical Literature, 2010. Provocative study of popular Christianity.

Mainestone, Rowland J. *Hagia Sophia: Architecture, Structure, and Liturgy of Justinian's Great Church*. London: Thames and Hudson, 1997.

Matthews, John. *Western Aristocracies and the Imperial Court, A.D. 364–425*. Oxford: Oxford University Press, 1975.

Markus, Robert A. *Christianity in the Roman World*. London: Thames and Hudson, 1978.

Maxwell, Jaclyn L. *Christianization and Communication in Late Antiquity: John Chrysostom and His Congregation in Antioch*. Cambridge: Cambridge University Press, 2009. Sensitive study of the impact of sermons on ordinary Christians.

Meeks, Wayne R. *First Urban Christians. The Social World of Saint Paul*. New Haven, CT: Yale University Press, 2003. Seminal and recommended study.

Meyendorff, John. *Imperial Unity, Christian Divisions: The Church from 450 to 680 A.D.* Yonkers, NY: St. Vladimir's Seminary Press, 1989. Superb discussion.

Miller, Patricia Cox. *Biography in Late Antiquity: A Quest for the Holy Man.* Berkeley: University of California Press, 1983.

————. *Dreams in Late Antiquity: Studies in the Imagination of a Culture.* Princeton, NJ: Princeton University Press, 1984.

Momigliano, Arnaldo. *Conflict of Paganism and Christianity in the Fourth Century.* Cambridge: Cambridge University Press, 1970. Provocative study.

Moorhead, John. *Justinian.* London: Longman Group, 1994. Fine introduction.

Mylonas, George E. *Eleusis and the Eleusinian Mysteries.* Princeton, NJ: Princeton University Press, 1961.

Naiden, F. S. *Ancient Supplication.* Oxford: Oxford University Press, 2006. Indispensable study reinterpreting the nature of Greek and Roman cults and rituals.

Nickelsburg, George W. E. *Jewish Literature between the Bible and the Mishnah.* 2nd ed. Minneapolis: Fortress Press, 2005.

Nilsson, Martin P. *The Dionysiac Mysteries in the Hellenistic and Roman Age.* New York: Arno Press, 1975.

Nock, Arthur D. *Conversion: The Old and the New Religion from Alexander the Great to Augustus.* Oxford: Oxford University Press, 1933. Classic study.

Norris, Richard A. *God and World in Early Christian Theology: A Study in Justin Martyr, Irenaeus, Tertullian, and Origen.* London: Black, 1967. Useful introduction.

Odahl, Charles M. *Constantine and the Christian Empire.* New York: Routledge, 2004. Recommended biography.

Osborn, Eric. *Irenaeus of Lyons*. Cambridge: Cambridge University Press, 2005.

Parke, Herbert William, and Donald Ernest W. Wormell. *The Delphic Oracle*. Vols. 1–2. Oxford: Oxford University Press, 1956.

————. *The Oracles of Apollo in Asia Minor*. London: Croom Helm, 1985.

Parvis, Sara. *Justin Martyr and His World*. Minneapolis: Fortress Press, 2007.

Patterson, Lloyd G. *God and History in Early Christian Thought*. New York: Seabury Press, 1967.

Pelikan, Jaroslav. *The Emergence of the Catholic Tradition (100–600)*. Chicago: University of Chicago Press, 1975. Classic study by leading scholar on theology.

Perkins, Anne L. *Art of Dura-Europos*. Oxford: Oxford University Press, 1973. Important study on the Jewish and Christian arts.

Potter, David. *The Roman Empire at Bay, A.D. 180–395*. New York: Routledge, 2004. The best one-volume study on the late Roman world.

Price, Simon. *Rituals and Power: The Imperial Cult in Roman Asia Minor*. Cambridge: Cambridge University Press, 1986. Seminal study on ruler cults and nature of pagan worship.

Rapp, Claudia. *Holy Bishops in Late Antiquity: The Nature of Christian Leadership in the Age of Transition*. Berkeley: University of California Press, 2005.

Richardson, Cyril C. *The Christianity of Ignatius of Antioch*. New York: AMS Press, 1967.

Rist, John M. *Plotinus: The Road to Reality*. Cambridge: Cambridge University Press, 1977.

————. *Stoic Philosophy*. Cambridge: Cambridge University Press, 1969. Excellent study by a leading scholar.

————. *The Stoics*. Berkeley: University of California Press, 1978. Essays on the leading Roman senatorial Stoics and critics of the emperor.

Robinson, Thomas A. *Ignatius of Antioch and the Parting of the Ways: Early Jewish-Christian Relations*. Grand Rapids, MI: Baker Academic Press, 2009.

Rogers, Guy M. *The Sacred Identity of Ephesos: Foundation Myths of a Roman City*. New York: Routledge, 1991.

Rogers, Rick. *Theophilus of Antioch: The Life and Thought of a Second-Century Bishop*. Lexington, MA: Lexington Books, 2000.

Roller, Lynn E. *In Search of God the Mother: The Cult of Anatolian Cybele*. Berkeley: University of California Press, 1999. The indispensable study.

Rosen, William. *Justinian's Flea: The First Great Plague and the End of the Roman Empire*. Baltimore: Penguin Books, 2007. Excellent essays on the impact of the plague on religious and social life.

Rousseau, Philip. *Basil of Caesarea*. Berkeley: University of California Press, 1998. Model study of the role of bishops in cities.

————. *Pachomius: The Making of a Community in Fourth Century Egypt*. Berkeley, 1985. The major study.

Sainte Croix, G. E. M. de. "Why Were the Early Christians Persecuted?" *Past and Present* 26 (1963): 6–38. Seminal article on the legal proceedings at trials of Christians.

Saltzman, M. R. *The Making of a Christian Aristocracy: Social and Religious Change in the Western Roman Empire*. Cambridge, MA: Harvard University Press, 2002.

Sambursky, S. *The Physical World of Late Antiquity*. Princeton, NJ: Princeton University Press, 1987. Concise recommended work on pagan cosmology.

Sandwell, Isabella. *Religious Identity in Late Antiquity: Greeks, Jews, and Christians in Antioch*. Cambridge: Cambridge University Press, 2007. Model study of legal and social change wrought by Christianization.

Schott, Jeremy M. *Christianity, Empire, and the Making of Religion in Late Antiquity*. Philadelphia: University of Pennsylvania Press, 2008.

Schweitzer, Albert. *The Mysticism of Saint Paul*. Baltimore: Johns Hopkins University Press, 1998 Reprint.

————. *The Quest of the Historical Jesus*. New York: Dover Publications, 2005. Reprint of the 1906 edition.

Segal, Alan F. *Paul the Convert: The Apostolate and Apostasy of Saul the Pharisee*. New Haven, CT: Yale University Press, 1992. Excellent study.

————. *Rebecca's Children: Judaism and Christianity in the Roman World*. Cambridge, MA: Harvard University Press, 1986. Provocative, recommended study.

Segal, J. B. *Edessa, the Blessed City*. Piscataway, NJ: Gorgias Press, 2001. Model study of the Christianizing of a Roman city.

Shaw, Gregory. *Theurgy and the Soul: The Neoplatonism of Iamblichus of Chalcis*. Philadelphia: University of Pennsylvania Press, 1967.

Sherwin-White, Adrian N. *Racial Prejudice in Imperial Rome*. Cambridge: Cambridge University Press, 2010. Recommended.

Smallwood, E. Mary. *The Jews under the Roman Rule from Pompey to Diocletian*. Boston: Brill, 2001. The classic and recommended study.

Smith, Morton. *Jesus the Magician*. New York: Barnes and Noble, 1993. Controversial study, but excellent on popular Judaism of the 1st century A.D.

Swain, Simon. *Hellenism and Empire: Language, Classicism, and Power in the Greek World, A.D. 50–250.* Oxford: Oxford University Press, 1998. The scholarly study on the Second Sophistic movement.

Talbert, Richard J. A. *Rome's World: The Peutinger Map Reconsidered.* Cambridge: Cambridge University Press, 2010. Crucial for Roman worldviews.

Taylor, Lily R. *The Divinity of the Roman Emperor.* Middleton, CT: American Philological Association, monograph no. 1, 1931.

Tougher, Shau, trans. and ed. *Julian the Apostate.* Edinburgh: Edinburgh University Press, 2007.

Toynbee, Jocelyn M. C. *Death and Burial in the Roman World.* Baltimore: Johns Hopkins University Press, 1971.

Trebilco, Paul. *Jewish Communities in Asia Minor.* Cambridge: Cambridge University Press, 1981. Survey of the archaeological, literary, and epigraphic evidence.

Trevett, Christine. *Montanism: Gender, Authority, and New Prophecy.* Cambridge: Cambridge University Press, 2002. Controversial study on the social aspects of Montanism.

Trigg, Joseph W. *Origen.* New York: Routledge, 1998.

——. *Origen: The Bible and Philosophy in the Third-Century Church.* Atlanta: John Knox Press, 1983.

Trombley, Frank R. *Hellenic Religion and Christianization: c. 370–529.* 2 vols. Leiden, The Netherlands: Brill, 2001. Learned study with collection of the sources.

Tyson, Joseph B. *Marcion and Luke-Acts: A Defining Struggle.* Charleston: University of South Carolina Press, 2006.

Van Dam, Raymond. *Families and Friends in Late Roman Cappadocia*. Philadelphia: University of Pennsylvania Press, 2003. Excellent on the roles of bishops.

———. *The Roman Revolution of Constantine*. Cambridge: Cambridge University Press, 2009. Important study.

Veyne, Paul. *Bread and Circuses: Historical Sociology and Political Pluralism*. Translated by Brian Pearee. Introduction by Oswyn Murray. London: Penguin Press, 1976. Brilliant study of the ethos of pagan gift giving in the Hellenistic and Roman ages.

Vermes, Geza. *Jesus the Jew*. Minneapolis: Fortress Press, 1981. Recommended work by a leading scholar of Judaism.

Vermeule, Emily. *Aspects of Death in Early Greek Art and Poetry*. Berkeley: University of California Press, 1981. Still the best study on Greek notions of the afterlife.

von Harnack, Adolf. *Marcion: The Gospel of an Alien God*. Translated by J. E. Steely and L. D. Bierma. Eugene, OR: Wipf and Stock, 2007. The classic study on Marcion and a modern English translation.

———. *The Mission and Expansion of Christianity in the First Three Centuries*. Translated by James Moffat. 2nd ed. New York: G. P. Putman's Sons, 1924. The classic and indispensable.

von Simson, Otto Georg. *Sacred Fortress: Byzantine Art and Statecraft in Ravenna*. Princeton, NJ: Princeton University Press, 1987.

Waddell, Helen. *The Desert Fathers*. New York: Vintage, 1998.

Wallis, Richard T. *Neoplatonism*. London: Duckworth Publishers, 2008.

Watson, A. *Aurelian and the Third Century*. New York: Routledge, 1999. Model study on the changes wrought by the so-called crisis of the 3rd century.

Bibliography

Watts, Edward J. *Riot in Alexandria: Tradition and Group Dynamics in Late Antique Pagan and Christian Communities.* Berkeley: University of California Press, 2010.

Weinstock, Stefan. *Divus Julius.* Oxford: Oxford University Press, 1972. Scholarly study on the creation of the ruler cult at Rome.

Weitzmann, Kurt, ed. *The Age of Spirituality: A Symposium.* New York: The Metropolitan Museum of Art, 1980.

Weitzmann, Kurt, and Herbert Kessler. *The Frescoes of the Dura Synagogue and Christian Art.* Washington, DC: Dumbarton Oaks, 1990.

Wilken, Robert L. *The Christians as the Romans Saw Them.* 2nd ed. New Haven, CT: Yale University Press, 2003. Excellent study and recommended.

————. *John Chrysostom and the Jews: Rhetoric and Reality in the Late Fourth Century.* New Haven, CT: Yale University Press, 1983. Seminal study on the origins of medieval anti-Semitism.

Witt, Reginald E. *Isis in the Ancient World.* Baltimore: Johns Hopkins University Press, 1997.

Yadin, Yigael. *Bar-Kokhba: The Rediscovery of the Legendary Hero of the Second Jewish Revolt against Rome.* New York: Random House, 1971. Popular account strong on archaeology by a leading Israeli scholar.

Notes

Notes

Notes